DATE DUE			

Readings in Childhood Language Disorders

Wiley Series on Communication Disorders

Thomas J. Hixon, Advisory Editor

This collection of books has been developed by John Wiley & Sons to meet some of the needs in the field of communication disorders. The collection includes books on both normal and disordered speech, hearing, and language function. The authors of the collection have been selected because they are scientific and clinical leaders in their field and, we believe, are eminently qualified to make significant and scholarly contributions to the professional literature.

Language Development and Language Disorders
Lois Bloom and Margaret Lahey

Readings in Language Development
Lois Bloom

Readings in Childhood Language Disorders
Margaret Lahey

Elements of Hearing Science: A Programmed Text
Arnold M. Small

Readings in Childhood Language Disorders

Edited by
Margaret Lahey
Hunter College of the
City University of New York

JOHN WILEY & SONS
New York / Chichester / Brisbane / Toronto

Library of Congress Cataloging in Publication Data
Main entry under title:
Readings in child language disorders.

(Wiley series on communication disorders)
1. Children—Language—Addresses, essays, lectures.
2. Handicapped children—Education—Language arts—Addresses, essays, lectures.
I. Lahey, Margaret   II. Series.

LB1139.L3R38 1977   371.9'14   77-21408
ISBN 0-471-51167-6

Printed in the United States of America

10 9 8 7 6 5 4 3

CONTRIBUTORS

John P. Berberich, University of
California at Los Angeles

Judith P. Blott, Nisonger Center
Columbus, Ohio

Jacquelin G. Bolders, Children's
Hospital Memphis, Tennessee

John D. Bonvillian, Vassar College

John B. Brannon, Jr., University of
Missouri

Diane D. Bricker, Mailman Center for
Child Development Miami, Florida

Irene Chiarandini, St. Lukes Hospital
New York, New York

Don N. Churchill, Indiana University

Illene C. Courtright, Cleveland State
University

John A. Courtright Cleveland State
University

Morris A. Cunningham, Crichton Royal
Dumfries, Scotland

Susan Curtiss, Venice, California

Katrina deHirsch, Columbia
Presbyterian Medical Center
Columbia University

Jon Eisenson, California State
University at San Francisco

Barbara Fish, University of California at
Los Angeles

Uta Frith, Medical Research Council
Developmental Psychology Unit
London, England

Victoria Fromkin, University of
California at Los Angeles

Tanya M. Gallagher, University of
Michigan

Robert Goldstein, University of
Wisconsin

Kathleen Gordon, Nisonger Center
Columbus, Ohio

Donald D. Hammill, Austin, Texas

Marianna Hartmann, Nisonger Center
Columbus, Ohio

Beate Hermelin, Medical Research Council Developmental Psychology Unit London, England

Susan Inglis, University of Washington

David Ingram, University of British Columbia

Jean-Marc-Gaspard Itard, (Trans. by George Muriel Humphrey) France

Robert J. Jarvella, Rockefeller University

Leo Kanner, Baltimore, Maryland

Frank R. Kleffner, Beaumont-May Institute of Neurology, Washington University School of Medicine, St. Louis, Missouri

Robert Koegel, University of California at Santa Barbara

Stephen Krashen, University of Southern California

Elinor Kreigsmann, University of Washington

James R. Lackner, Brandeis University

William M. Landau, Beaumont-May Institute of Neurology Washington University School of Medicine St. Louis, Missouri

Stephen C. Larsen, University of Texas

Laura L. Lee, Northwestern University

Eric H. Lenneberg, Cornell University

Lawrence B. Leonard, Memphis State University

O. Ivar Lovaas, University of California at Los Angeles

Jay Lubinsky, Case Western Reserve University

James D. MacDonald, Nisonger Center Columbus, Ohio

James E. McClean, George Peabody College

Linda P. McCormick, University of Alabama

Arnold Miller, Language and Cognitive Development Center, Boston, Massachusetts

Eileen Ellen Miller, Language and Cognitive Development Center, Boston, Massachusetts

Judith A. Miller, Memphis State University

Barbara Mills, Sidney, British Columbia

Donald Morehead, Stanford University School of Medicine

Anthony Mulac, University of California at Santa Barbara

Keith Nelson, New School for Social Research

Bernard F. Perloff, University of California at Los Angeles

Malcolm Piercy, University of Cambridge, Cambridge, England

Carol A. Prutting, University of California at Santa Barbara

Richard Rehm, University of California at Los Angeles

David Rigler, Children's Hospital of Los Angeles

Marilyn Rigler, Pacific Oaks College

Benson Schaeffer, University of California at Los Angeles

Laura Schreibman, Claremont Men's College

Theodore Shapiro, Cornell Medical Center New York, New York

Bernard Spiegel, Ohio Department of Health

Paula Tallal, John F. Kennedy Institute, Johns Hopkins University

Margaret Wulbert, San Diego County Mental Health Services

PREFACE

This collection of readings was selected and organized for two purposes: first, to expand and complement the text *Language Development and Language Disorders*, co-authored by Lois Bloom and Margaret Lahey and published by John Wiley & Sons; and second, to provide a source of readings in language disorders for advanced undergraduate and graduate students in fields related to speech pathology, special education, psycholinguistics, early childhood and elementary education, and developmental psychology. Thus, the book is intended as a supplementary text for courses in any of the above fields (particularly courses in language disorders, learning disabilities, assessment of language skills, and education of the deaf, mentally retarded, or emotionally disturbed) or as a primary text in a seminar related to language disorders.

Both the selection and organization of readings in the field can be approached from a number of different perspectives. The perspective that dominates this collection is a focus on the language of the child with a language disorder. The majority of readings, therefore, either describe the language of children with deviant language development or discuss methods of teaching language to such children. In addition, many articles relate to the various clinical syndromes associated with childhood language disorders (such as childhood aphasia, deafness, emotional disturbance, and mental retardation) or to correlates of childhood language disorders (such as perceptual skills, mother-child interactions, hemispheric dominance, and physical maturation). Most articles are based on empirical data. They were selected to sample a variety of children, types of language disorders, means of obtaining, describing, and interpreting evidence, and issues relating to facilitating language learning. Authors were invited to add comments to their original articles. The comments that were received appear at the end of the relevant reading.

The book is divided into six parts which essentially follow the organization of the second half of *Language Development and Language Disorders*. Part I presents an historical overview of the methods used to study deviant language; Part II is concerned with the description of deviant language for clinical assessment; Part III focuses on the definition and use of clinical syndromes associated with childhood language disorders; Part IV presents information on some correlates of childhood language disorders; Part V includes articles on facilitating language learning; and Part VI deals with the use of alternative modalities in facilitating language learning.

Margaret Lahey

ACKNOWLEDGMENTS

A number of people were helpful in assembling this collection of readings in childhood language disorders. I thank, in particular, Lois Bloom for her assistance at all levels of preparation, Norma Rees and the editor's reviewers for their comments on an early draft, and Judy Levinson, Evelyn Pollack, Naomi Schiff, and Elaine Silliman for their comments and suggestions concerning the inclusion of one or another article. I am grateful to Teachers College, Columbia University, where I am a Research Associate, for their institutional support during the preparation of this collection. In addition, my thanks go to my daughters, Diane and Denise, who prepared the articles for the manuscript, and to Pam Maffei and Barbara Kennedy who took care of most of the correspondence regarding permissions for reprinting. The greatest debt, however, is to those authors who have allowed their works to be reprinted here.

M.L.

CONTENTS

Readings in Childhood Language Disorders

Part 1
DESCRIBING DEVIANT LANGUAGE

The articles included in this part present an overview of the methods used to study deviant language and an historical perspective of the changes that have occurred in both the focus and the methodology of such study.

Early descriptions of deviant language were generally of two types—case studies of a few children, or "count studies" which compared larger numbers of language disordered children in terms of their use of adult linguistic forms. The article by Kanner (1946) represents a case study approach. It was selected because it is a forerunner of the more recent emphasis on description of the regularities in deviant language. Kanner not only identified how the language of a small group of children was different from normal, but he also was among the first to recognize and describe how these differences were systematic and rule governed. By exploring the earlier histories of a few children, he was able to describe the consistency between form and context that existed in apparently "irrelevant" utterances.

The study by Brannon (1968) represents the count studies which compared larger numbers of children in terms of their use of adult forms of language. In this study three groups of children, matched according to age and intelligence, were compared on their use of various parts of speech.

Changes in linguistic theory, particularly the introduction of generative transformational grammar by Chomsky (1957 and 1965), began to influence the study of deviant language by mid-1960. The first attempts to apply generative trans-

formational grammar to the study of childhood language disorders used the comparative methodology similar to the earlier count studies as represented here by Brannon
(1968). (For example, see Menyuk, 1964, not reprinted here, who was the first to
apply the grammar of adult language that was proposed by Chomsky as a basis for
comparing the sentences of normal and language-disordered children.)

As a result of Chomsky's theory, a major change in methodology was effected: an
attempt was made to formalize regularities in deviant language with rules of grammar.
The first, and at this time the most complete, published grammars of deviant language
are reprinted here in the article by Lackner (1968). Lackner's study illustrates the
methodology used to obtain evidence for writing a grammar. His work is unique in
that comprehension and imitation tasks were used to refine the grammars that were
based on a larger sample (1,000 utterances) of spontaneous speech.

Morehead and Ingram (1973), also influenced by the generative transformational
theory of Chomsky (1957 and 1965), compared rules of grammar used by normal
and language-disordered children in order to determine whether there were qualitative differences between them. Their study was the first to intentionally match children on a measure of syntactic development (mean length of utterance). In contrast,
most prior studies had used age and intelligence rather than linguistic development
for matching comparative subject populations. This shift in criterion for matching has
influenced subsequent studies designed to compare normal and deviant language
development, for example, Leonard, Bolders, and Miller (1976).

The article by Leonard et al. is included here because it represents another major
shift in methodology—this time a shift in the aspect of deviant language that is
described. While some of the earlier descriptions of deviant language that were
based on case studies, as, for example, Kanner (1943, an excerpt of which is reprinted in Part III), discussed meaning, most other descriptions of deviant language
have focused only on the forms of children's language. Leonard et al. were the first
to publish a description of the meaning relations coded by language-disordered
children. This change in emphasis from form alone to form in relation to meaning was
influenced by semantic theory in linguistics (Fillmore, 1968, and Chafe, 1971) and
by studies of normal child language (e.g., Bloom, 1970, Brown, 1973, and Bowerman, 1973).

In the past, there have been descriptions of what some language-disordered children do with the linguistic forms they produce. These works have dealt particularly
with the effectiveness of "emotionally disturbed" children in communicating with
language (for example, see Cunningham, 1968, reprinted in this volume). The more
recent sophisticated descriptions of language use (as for, example, Garvey, 1975;
Halliday, 1974; and Warden, 1976) have not yet been applied, in published form,
to deviant language.

Each of the above articles describes deviant language as produced in a relatively
relaxed setting where no attempt was made to elicit particular forms or particular
meaning relations. An alternative methodology for obtaining evidence about a child's
knowledge of language is to elicit responses in a more formalized or structured
manner. The article by Jarvella and Lubinsky (1975) is an illustration of the more
formal procedure. It is included here because it describes experimental techniques
for obtaining evidence about the production of particular linguistic forms to encode
particular meanings; the comprehension of particular linguistic forms to decode

particular meaning relations; and the children's non-linguistic knowledge of the concept (or meaning relation) coded by the linguistic forms being studied.

Thus, two major strategies for obtaining evidence about deviant language are represented in the readings included in Part I: one strategy in which responses obtained by experimental elicitation were observed (as illustrated by Jarvella and Lubinsky, 1975); and another in which responses obtained in a more naturalistic, relaxed setting were observed (as illustrated by the remaining articles). In addition, the articles included here present an historical perspective of the methodologies used to describe deviant language. There have been changes in the descriptions themselves —from comparisons with adult parts of speech based on structural linguistics (as illustrated by Brannon, 1968) to a focus on rule systems (as illustrated by Lackner, 1968). There have been changes in the components of language that have been described—from descriptions of form (as illustrated by Lackner, 1968; Brannon, 1968; and Morehead and Ingram, 1973) to descriptions of meaning relations (as illustrated by Leonard et al., 1976), and, too, there have been changes in the criteria used to match normal and language-disordered children for purposes of comparing them: criteria based on age and intelligence (as illustrated by Brannon, 1968) have changed to linguistic criteria (as illustrated by Morehead and Ingram, 1973, and Leonard et al., 1976). While most of these articles describe deviant language in order to determine whether deviant language is qualitatively different from normal, some of these same techniques have been used to describe deviant language for clinical assessment—which is the topic of Part II.

REFERENCES

Bloom, Lois 1970 *Language development: Form and function in emerging grammars.* Cambridge, Mass.: The M.I.T. Press.

Bowerman, M. 1973 *Learning to talk: A cross-linguistic study of early syntactic development, with special reference to Finnish.* Cambridge, Eng.: Cambridge U. Press.

Brown, Roger 1973 *A first language, the early stages.* Cambridge, Mass.: Harvard University.

Chafe, W. 1971 *Meaning and the structure of language.* Chicago: University of Chicago Press.

Chomsky, N. 1957 *Syntactic structures.* The Hague: Mouton.

Chomsky, N. 1965 *Aspects of the theory of syntax.* Cambridge, Mass.: The M.I.T. Press.

Fillmore, Charles 1968 The case for case. In E. Bach and R. Harms (Eds.), *Universals in linguistic theory.* New York: Holt, Rinehart and Winston.

*Garvey, C. 1975 Requests and responses in children's speech. *Journal of Child Language, 2,* 41–63.

*Halliday, M.A.K. 1974 A sociosemiotic perspective on language development. *Bulletin of the School of Oriental and African Studies, 37,* 60–81.

Menyuk, Paula. 1964 Comparison of grammar of children with functionally deviant and normal speech. *Journal of Speech and Hearing Research, 7,* 109–123.

*Warden, David A. 1976 The influence of context on children's use of identifying expressions and references. *British Journal of Psychology, 67*(1), 103.

---

*Reprinted in L. Bloom (Ed.), *Readings in Language Development,* New York: John Wiley and Sons. 1978.

Irrelevant and Metaphorical Language in Early Infantile Autism[1]

Leo Kanner, M. D.

During the past few years, I have had occasion to observe 23 children whose extreme withdrawal and disability to form the usual relations to people were noticed from the beginning of life. I have designated this condition as "early infantile autism." Phenomenologically, excessive aloneness and an anxiously obsessive desire for the preservation of sameness are the outstanding characteristics. Memory is often astounding. Cognitive endowment, masked frequently by limited responsiveness, is at least average. Most patients stem from psychometrically superior, though literal-minded and obsessive, families.

This condition offers fascinating problems and opportunities for study from the points of view of genetics, of the psychodynamics of earliest parent-infant relationship, and of its resemblances to the schizophrenias. Among numerous other features, the peculiarities of language present an important and promising basis for investigation. I should like to mention briefly the "mutism" of 8 of the 23 children, which is on rare occasions interrupted by the utterance of a whole sentence in emergency situations; the use of simple verbal negation as magic protection against unpleasant occurrences; the literalness which cannot accept synonyms or different connotations of the same preposition; the self-absorbed inaccessibility which has caused most of the parents to suspect deafness; the echolalia-type repetition of whole phrases; and the typical, almost pathognomonic, pronominal reversals which consist of the child's reference to himself as "you" and to the person spoken to as "I."

Frequently these children say things which seem to have no meaningful connection with the situation in which they are voiced. The utterances impress the audience as "nonsensical," "silly," "incoherent," and "irrelevant." These are the terms used by the reporting parents, physicians and nursery school teachers.

We were fortunate in having opportunities to trace some of these "irrelevant" phrases to earlier sources and to learn that, whenever such tracing was possible, the utterances, though still peculiar and out of place in ordinary conversation, assume definite meaning. I should like to illustrate this with a few characteristic examples:

Paul G., while observed at our clinic at five years of age, was heard saying: "Don't throw the dog off the balcony." There was neither a dog nor a balcony around. The

From *American Journal of Psychiatry*, 242–245 (1946).

[1] Read at the 102d annual meeting of the American Psychiatric Association, Chicago, Ill., May 27–30, 1946.

remark therefore sounded irrelevant. It was learned that three years previously he had thrown a toy dog down from the balcony of a London hotel at which the family was staying. His mother, tired of retrieving the toy, had said to him, with some irritation: "Don't throw the dog off the balcony." Since that day, Paul, whenever tempted to throw anything, used these words to admonish and check himself.

"Peter eater" was another of Paul's "nonsensical," "irrelevant" expressions. It seemed to have no association with his experiences of the moment. His mother related that, when Paul was two years old, she once recited to him the nursery rhyme about "Peter, Peter, pumpkin eater," while she was busy in the kitchen; just then she dropped a saucepan. Ever since that day Paul chanted the words "Peter eater" whenever he saw anything resembling a saucepan. There was, indeed, in the play-room a toy stove on which sat a miniature pan. It was noted then that Paul, while saying these words, glanced in the direction of the stove and finally picked up the pan, running wildly around with it and chanting "Peter eater" over and over again.

John F., at five years of age, saw Webster's Unabridged Dictionary in the office. He turned to his father and said: "That's where you left the money." In this instance the connection was established by the fact that John's father was in the habit of leaving money for his wife in the dictionary which they had at home. Upon being shown a penny, John said: "That's where play ten pins," as a sort of definition of penny. His father was able to supply the clue. He and John played ten pins at home with a children's set. Every time that John knocked over one of the ten pins, his father gave him a penny.

Elaine C. had been surrounded in her infancy with toy animals of which she was very fond. When she cried, her mother used to point out to her that the toy dog or toy rabbit did not cry. When Elaine was seen at seven years of age, she still kept saying when she was fearful and on the verge of tears: "Rabbits don't cry." "Dogs don't cry." She added a large number of other animals. She went about, when in distress, reiterating the seemingly irrelevant words: "Seals don't cry." "Dinosaurs don't cry." "Crayfishes don't cry." She came to use the names of these and other animals in a great variety of connections.

Jay S., not quite four years old, referred to himself as "Blum" whenever his veracity was questioned by his parents. The mystery of this "irrelevance" was explained when Jay, who could read fluently, once pointed to the advertisement of a furniture firm in the newspapers, which said in large letters: "Blum tells the truth." Since Jay had told the truth, he *was* Blum. This analogy between himself as a teller of the truth and Blum does not differ essentially from the designation of a liar as Ananias, a lover as Romeo, or an attractive lad as Adonis. But while these designations are used with the expectation that the listener is familiar with the analogy, the autistic child has his own private, original, individualized references, the semantics of which are transferable only to the extent to which any listener can, through is own efforts, trace the source of the analogy.

The cited examples represent in the main metaphorical expressions which, instead of relying on accepted or acceptable substitutions as encountered in poetry and conversational phraseology, are rooted in *concrete, specific, personal* experiences of the child who uses them. So long as the listener has no access to the original source, the meaning of the metaphor must remain obscure to him, and the child's remark is not "relevant" to any sort of verbal or other situational interchange. Lack of access to the source shuts out any comprehension, and the baffled listener, to whom the remark means nothing, may too readily assume that it has no meaning at all. If the metaphorical reference to Ananias, Romeo or Adonis is not understood, dictionaries, encyclopedias or informed persons can supply the understanding. But the personal metaphors of the autistic children can convey "sense" only through acquaintance with the singular, unduplicated meaning which they have to the children themselves. The only clue can be supplied by the direct observation and recall of the episode which started off the use of each particular metaphorical expression.

Occasionally, though not very often, a chance gesture or remark of the child himself may lead to the understanding of a metaphor. This was the case when Jay S. happened to point to the Blum advertisement. This was also the case when five-year-old Anthony F. solved the puzzle of his frequently expressed fondness for "55." On one occasion, he spoke of his two grandmothers. We knew that one of them had shown little interest in him, while the other had reared him with much patience and affection. Anthony said: "One is 64 [years old], and one is 55. I like 55 best." The seemingly irrelevant preoccupation with a seemingly arbitrary number can now be recognized as being heavily endowed with meaning. It is Anthony's private way of expressing affection for his grandmother.

This phenomenon of metaphorical substitution is very common among our autistic children. Donald T., at seven years of age, was asked the Binet question: "If I were to buy 4 cents worth of candy and give the storekeeper 10 cents, how much money would I get back?" He obviously knew the answer. His reply, however, was not "6 cents" but: "I'll draw a hexagon." Two years previously, at 5 years of age, Donald had been scribbling with crayons; all the while he kept saying seriously and with conviction: "Annette and Cecile make purple." It was learned that Donald had at home five bottles of paint. He named each after one of the Dionne quintuplets. Blue became "Annette," and red became "Cecile." After that, Annette became his word for blue, and Cecile for red. Purple, not being one of the five colors, remained "purple."

It is mainly the private, original frame of reference which makes these substitutions seem peculiar. We witness similar processes in the introduction of trade names for perfumes, wines, cigarettes, cigars, paints and many other items. Etymology abounds with similar derivations. Common usage makes it unnecessary to know the original source in order to get the meaning. An ulster is a certain type of top coat whether or not you connect it with the county in Ireland from which it has its name. You need not know that a serpent is a "creeper" or that a dromedary is a "runner." It does not matter whether or not you know that filibuster is a corrupted form of "freebooter."

The autistic child does not depend upon such prearranged semantic transfers. He makes up his own as he goes along. In fact, he can keep transferring and retransferring to his heart's desire. Gary T., at five years, designated a bread basket as "home bakery." He did not stop there. After this, *every* basket to him became a "home bakery." This was his term for coal basket, waste basket or sewing basket. This procedure, too, has its etymological counterparts. The original meaning of "caput" is transferred from anatomy to anything which, literally or figuratively, is at the top or at the "head," whether this be "captain," the head of a group of people, "capitol," the top of a pillar, or "chapter," the inscription over a section of a book. The transfer does not even stop there, for a "chapter" then becomes not only the "heading" of the section but the whole section itself.

From these observations we may safely draw a number of significant conclusions:

1. The seemingly irrelevant and nonsensical utterances of our autistic children are metaphorical expressions in the sense that they represent "figures of speech by means of which one thing is put for another which it only resembles." The Greek word metapherein means "to transfer."

2. The transfer of meaning is accomplished in a variety of ways:

a. Through substitutive analogy: Bread basket becomes "home bakery"; Annette and Cecile become "red" and "blue"; penny becomes "that's where play ten pin."

b. Through generalization: *Totum pro parte.* "Home bakery" becomes the term for *every* basket; "Don't throw the dog off the balcony" assumes the meaning of self-admonition in *every* instance when the child feels the need for admonishing himself.

c. Through restriction: *Pars pro toto.* The 55-year-old grandmother becomes "55"; a teller of the truth becomes "Blum"; the number 6 is referred to as "hexagon."

3. The linguistic processes through which the transfers are achieved do not as such differ essentially from poetical and ordinary phraseological metaphors. Etymologically, much of our language is made up of similar transfers of meaning through substitutions, generalizations and restrictions.

4. The basic difference consists of the autistic privacy and original uniqueness of the transfers, derived from the children's situational and emotional experiences. Once the connection between experience and metaphorical utterance is established, and only then, does the child's language become meaningful. The goal of the transfer is intelligible only in terms of its source.

5. In contrast to poetry and etymology, the metaphorical language in early infantile autism is not directly communicable. It is not primarily intended as a means of inviting other people to understand and to share the child's symbols. Though it is undoubtedly creative, the creation is in the main self-sufficient and self-contained.

"The abnormality of the autistic person," say Whitehorn and Zipf, "lies only in ignoring the other fellow: that is, it lies in his disregard of the social obligation to make only those changes which are socially acceptable in the sense that they are both understandable and serviceable in the group. Naturally, once the autistic person pursues his own linguistic and semantic paths of least effort, the result may well appear to his perplexed auditor as a disorder of meanings, or even as a disorder of association. Yet the autistic speaker, in making his own language, without the nuisance of satisfying the auditor's needs, may employ the same principles of linguistic and semantic change as does the normal person, though not with the same care to insure community acceptance."

The above observations and conclusions gain additional importance because they give concrete evidence to the long-felt assumption that similar mechanisms prevail in the "irrelevant," "incoherent" and metaphorical language of adult schizophrenics. In the case of the latter, the earlier and earliest connections and pertinences have often been lost irretrievably, as they have been even for some of the expressions of our children at so early an age. But the examples cited (and the study by Whitehorn and Zipf) justify the conviction that schizophrenic "irrelevance" is not irrelevant to the patient himself and could become relevant to the audience to the extent to which it were possible to find the clues to his private and self-contained metaphorical transfers.

BIBLIOGRAPHY

Kanner, L. Autistic disturbances of affective contact. The Nervous Child, **2** : 217–250, 1943.
———. Early infantile autism. J. Pediat., **25:** 211–217, 1944.
Whitehorn, J. C., and Zipf, G. K. Schizophrenic language. Arch, Neur. Psychiat., **49:** 831–851, 1943.

Linguistic Word Classes in the Spoken Language of Normal, Hard-of-Hearing, and Deaf Children

John B. Brannon, Jr.

The spoken language of three groups of subjects—normal, hard-of-hearing, and deaf—was analyzed by means of a new classification system devised by Jones, Goodman, and Wepman. Each spoken word was sorted into one of 14 word classes. Group means for each word class were compared. It was concluded that significant hearing impairment reduces productivity of both tokens and types of words. A moderate impairment lowers the use of adverbs, pronouns, and auxiliaries; a profound impairment reduces nearly all classes. In proportion to total word output, the deaf overused nouns and articles, underused prepositions, quantifiers, and indefinites.

Recently, Jones, Goodman, and Wepman (1963) have proposed a system for classifying words into distinct grammatical classes to provide a better means of comparing the speech of various pathological groups (such as aphasics) with that of normals. Their system includes 14 word classes, unique among which are relatives, indefinites, auxiliaries, and quantifiers. One could use this system to compare the relative frequencies of usage within these word classes for certain groups of subjects. The outcomes of the comparisons would permit one to generalize as to the effects of certain disorders upon the acquisition or use of certain words. Also, by examining the unique features of a certain word class, it might be possible to explain why that class is more difficult for certain groups.

The classification of words and the meanings of words have been of interest to linguists, semanticists, psychologists, and educators. For example, de Groat (1957) discussed word classification for various languages. He stated that in English the number of main types is about 14 and that some of these can be subdivided according to parts of speech. By "types" he meant large classifications such as "coordinative groups," including a series of nouns, verbs, etc. He pointed out that there are many ways of classifying word groups depending upon purpose and listed features that might be criteria. This author included prosodic as well as syntactic features.

Whorf (1945) deplored the use of traditional grammatical categories such as using functional definitions as parts of speech. He developed some concepts by which categories may be classified, such as overt versus covert and selective versus modu-

From *Journal of Speech and Hearing Research, 11,* 279–287 (1968). Reprinted by permission of the American Speech and Hearing Association.

lus. For example, an overt category has an observable mark, such as the suffix s for the plural of nouns, whereas in a covert one the word must be applied in a certain context to define it.

Another large distinction often made between word groups is that of "content" as distinguished from "function" words. The first group includes words with concrete referents such as nouns, verbs, adjectives, and adverbs (major parts of speech), which carry the thought-content of the sentence; the second group contains the smaller words such as conjunctions and auxiliaries which form the skeletal framework of the sentence. It is known from work such as that of Miller, Newman, and Friedman (1958), who quantified the length-frequency relation for function and content words, that "function words are shorter than the content words." According to them the average length of a function word was 3.13 letters, of a content word, 6.47 letters. They concluded that these two sets of words have very different statistical properties. As Miller (1951) has commented, the function words account for over half of the word tokens (words including those repeated, or total words) we utter. Content words are repeated much less often in our speech. Verbal behavior follows lawful patterns.

Among those with a psychological orientation to language, Osgood and Brown are prominent. For some years, Osgood (Osgood, Suci, and Tennenbaum, 1957) has been concerned with the meaning of words and has developed a descriptive device, the semantic differential, to tease out all connotative and denotative aspects of a word. He points out that many "signs" are actually "assigns," that is, their meanings are derived by association with other signs rather than by direct association with objects. In attempting to apply these notions to word classification, one might conjecture that certain classes of words, such as nouns, are more loaded with associative possibilities, which may facilitate their learning.

Brown (1957) has pointed out that the naive person is apt to think of the parts of speech in semantic terms, such as the idea that nouns name substances, whereas in descriptive linguistics such a procedure is held to be erroneous. The linguistic scientist looks for attributes of exceptionless validity, which is an impossible task. Brown demonstrated that children are more likely than adults to understand nouns as names of things and verbs as names of actions.

Recently, educators have become interested in the application of linguistic techniques to a description of language problems of children. Deaf children show many unique features in their language productions, spoken or written, that some have termed "deafisms": stereotypy, syntactical errors, limited vocabulary, and wrong choice of words. Studies of the characteristics of the language of the deaf have been completed by Myklebust (1964), Simmons (1962), Goda (1964), and MacGinitie (1964). These studies are somewhat in agreement that the verbal output of the deaf is deficient in certain word classes. Their output seems to consist mainly of Fries' (1952) Class 1 (nouns) and Class 2 (verbs) words and to be deficient in Class 3 (adjectives), Class 4 (adverbs), and function words. The deaf seem to use only a small number of different expanding words such as auxiliaries and connectives.

The study reported here was undertaken to compare the spoken output of three groups of children by means of the system devised by Jones, Goodman, and Wepman. The outcomes would suggest to what extent hearing impairment impedes or distorts the acquisition of linguistic word classes. An impairment of the hearing sense is hypothesized to represent a filtering out of certain features of the language. Some features, such as those inherent in intonation, may be entirely precluded. For those individuals who can receive conversational speech only minimally at best (the profoundly deaf, usually defined audiometrically as those with an average hearing loss of 75 dB ASA or greater in the better ear), words are received mainly through the remaining distance sense, vision. This paper reports an attempt to show whether predominant use of vision is sufficient for learning certain classes of words.

METHOD

SUBJECTS.   Three groups of subjects were obtained from classes in the Columbus Public Schools: 30 normals from a junior high school, 15 hard-of-hearing children, and 15 deaf children in special classes. The normal group was composed of 15 girls and 15 boys with normal hearing whose mean age was 12.6 years. The hard-of-hearing group consisted of 8 boys and 7 girls with average hearing losses (500-2000 Hz) ranging from 27 to 66 dB in the better ear, the group mean being 52.1 dB. The deaf group included 7 boys and 8 girls; the group had a range of average hearing losses (three midfrequencies) from 75 to 100 dB and a mean of 82.0 dB in the better ear (all ASA values). The two hearing-impaired groups had a mean age of 12.6 years with a range from 8.7 to 18.5 years.

Intelligence quotients were available on each child, obtained by the Henmon-Nelson Test of Mental Ability for the normals and by the Leiter International Performance Scale or other nonverbal test for the hearing-impaired children. The IQ's ranged from 90 to 118, mean 102, for the normals; for the hearing-impaired the range was 86 to 127, with a mean of 100.

No normal child was selected with physical abnormalities, low IQ, or speech problem. No hearing-impaired child was used who had any of the following characteristics according to school records: age of onset of deafness after three years; brain damage; IQ below 85; or abnormally poor vision (not corrected to 20/40 in the eye with less acuity).

MATERIALS AND EQUIPMENT.   Fourteen colored pictures (size 8" × 10") depicting children and adults in daily activities, including indoor and outdoor scenes, were employed to elicit 50 spoken sentences from each child. The sentences were recorded on magnetic tape by means of a Wollensak Model T-1500 recorder. In addition, for each hearing-impaired child a response form was provided so that he could write down each sentence after speaking it, to assist in understanding poorly spoken words. A sample of 10 sentences from a hearing child is given in Table 1, as well as 10 sentences from a deaf child, in order to illustrate the method.

For hearing screening of the normal subjects and for threshold measurements of the hearing impaired, a Beltone portable audiometer was used.

MEASUREMENT OF RESPONSES.   Each sentence was typed based upon listening to the tapes and examining written words. Every intelligible word spoken was sorted into one of the 14 word classes of the Jones, Goodman, and Wepman system based upon the criteria set forth. The total number of words (tokens) sorted were: normals, 11,400; hard-of-hearing, 5149; and deaf, 4385. Among these were 84 unintelligible

Table 1   Samples of the Types of Sentences Obtained From Normal and Hearing-impaired Subjects

Stimulus Picture	Spoken Sentence
	Normal Subject
G	1. Two little girls are in a pet store.
(Pet Shop)	2. One little girl is looking at some mice.
	3. The storekeeper is watching the two little girls.
	4. There are four cages seen in the picture.
K	5. This is a picture of two little girls making caramel apples.
(Kitchen Scene)	6. They have a very nice stove in the kitchen.
	7. One little girl is wearing a light blue dress.
	8. The mother is wearing a green skirt with a light green blouse and an apron.
L	9. The children and parents in this picture are in a birthday party.
(Birthday Party)	10. The table has a lovely birthday cake on it.
	Deaf Subject
G	1. The girl look at some animal. (Written: The girls look some animals.)
	2. The man (unintelligible word) a cat. (Written: The man look a cat.)
	3. They are going to a pet shop. (Written: The girl went to pet shop.)
	4. The girl saw a mouse. (Written: The girl saw a mouse).
K	5. The girl cook a pie. (Written: The girl cook a pie.)
	6. The mother (unintelligible word) the girl. (Written: Mother look girl.)
	7. The mother cook (two unintelligible words). (Written: Mother cooking a salad.)
	8. The girl has book. (Written: The girl has book.)
L	9. The family has a birthday. (Written: The family has a birthday.)
	10. The family will eat a cake. (Written: The family will eat a cake.)

words for the hard-of-hearing and 665 such words for the deaf. The total number of different words (types) excluding unclassified and unintelligible were: normals, 828; hard-of-hearing, 569; and deaf, 298. Thus, the reduced vocabularies of the hard-of-hearing and the deaf are apparent.

A separate analysis was also made of the basic vocabularies of the three groups, defined as all words used six times or more. In this analysis the tokens were: normals, 10,974; hard-of-hearing, 4440; and deaf, 3256. Types included: normals, 243; hard-of-hearing, 144; and deaf, 87. The reduction of known words due to hearing impairment is again apparent.

STATISTICAL PROCESSING.   Group means and standard deviations for each word class for both tokens and types were compared by means of the *t* test for unequal *N*'s (Walker and Lev, 1953). The results are presented below.

RESULTS

TOTAL WORDS.   Table 2 shows the group means and standard deviations for each word class. This applies to tokens only. The results of the *t*-test comparisons of these

Table 2   **Mean Number of Tokens and Standard Deviations (SD) by Linguistic Word Class for Each Group**

| | Group | | | | | |
| | Normal | | Hard-of-Hearing | | Deaf | |
Word Class	Mean	SD	Mean	SD	Mean	SD
Noun	99.80	28.97	96.93	13.86	77.93	11.84
Verb	38.60	17.17	42.73	13.31	24.60	14.28
Adjective	11.80	5.14	14.40	6.89	5.60	3.86
Adverb	16.76	10.53	7.40	8.10	2.13	3.39
Pronoun	31.26	17.83	21.66	13.77	10.46	12.80
Relative	1.23	1.71	0.73	1.53	0.33	0.61
Article	59.26	22.50	65.06	16.64	76.06	20.13
Indefinite	0.46	0.77	0.53	1.35	0.00	0.00
Auxiliary	50.43	8.14	38.20	15.12	22.60	11.94
Quantifier	16.16	6.62	12.60	7.43	5.93	6.34
Preposition	38.86	16.69	29.00	15.73	15.93	9.58
Conjunction	10.20	7.24	6.73	7.41	6.33	5.65
Interjection	0.10	—	0.20	—	0.13	—
Unclassified	5.13	—	7.07	—	44.33	—
Mean number of words per subject	380.00		342.26		292.33	
Mean number omitting unclassified	374.87		336.20		248.00	

Table 3   Results of *t* Tests for the Comparison of Groups in Terms of
Mean Tokens by Word Class

Word Class	Normals vs. Hard-of-Hearing *t* Value	Comparison Normals vs. Deaf *t* Value	Hard-of-Hearing vs. Deaf *t* Value
Noun	0.44	3.58**	4.03**
Verb	0.88	2.89**	3.59**
Adjective	1.29	4.53**	4.31**
Adverb	3.30**	6.94**	2.32*
Pronoun	2.69*	6.27**	2.31*
Relative	0.99	2.57*	0.93
Article	0.97	2.54*	1.63
Indefinite	0.17	3.29**	1.52
Auxiliary	2.90**	8.14**	3.13**
Quantifier	1.57	5.02**	2.65*
Preposition	1.88	5.84**	2.64*
Conjunction	1.49	1.96	0.16

*Significant at the 0.05 level. The degrees of freedom are 43 for the first two columns and 28 for the last column.
**Significant at the 0.01 level.

means are shown in Table 3. These outcomes suggest that in general the hard-of-hearing group were not significantly different from the normals for most classes, whereas the deaf differed from the normals in all classes except conjunctions. Thus, the deaf were reduced in word productivity for all word classes. The hard-of-hearing were deviant only in the use of adverbs, pronouns, and auxiliaries. It also seems that the deaf children were the most deficient in these three word classes, since the *t* values are greater in these cases. For example, the average deaf child used adverbs only two times, usually the words *there* and *very;* used pronouns 10 times, the most common ones being *they* and *her;* and used auxiliaries 22 times, the most common being *is* and *are.* The deaf did not use indefinites at all.

Another way of analyzing the data seemed advisable: to convert the number of words used by each group in each class to a percentage, thus making the output in each class relative to total output. For example, the deaf spoke 1169 nouns; dividing this by all 3720 words produced (excluding unclassified), it was found that nouns constituted 31% of the total. These percentages for the three groups are displayed in Figure 1 (content words) and Figure 2 (function words). When compared in this manner, the hard-of-hearing and deaf alike seem mainly deficient in the output of adverbs, auxiliaries, and pronouns as before, and both groups have a tendency to overuse nouns and articles. The deaf, unlike the hard-of-hearing, also seem to underuse prepositions, quantifiers, and indefinites.

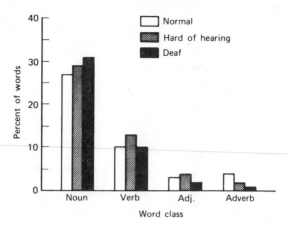

Figure 1.   Comparisons of groups as to percentages of all words used in terms of word
classes, restricted to content words.

DIFFERENT WORDS.   The groups were also compared as to mean number of different words (types) per word class. The average vocabularies omitting unclassified
words were: normals, 131.8 words; hard-of-hearing, 115.4 words; and deaf, 75.4
words. The graphical representations of the outcomes in terms of percentages are
in Figures 3 and 4. These show us the compositions of the vocabularies of the three
groups. Because of the greatly reduced vocabulary of the deaf, the relationships
mentioned concerning tokens are altered. The word classes are placed in rank order

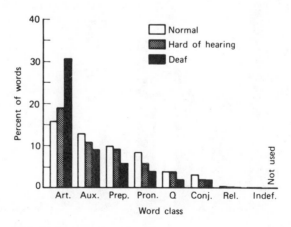

Figure 2.   Comparisons of groups as to percentages of all words used in terms of word
classes, restricted to function words. Interjections are omitted.

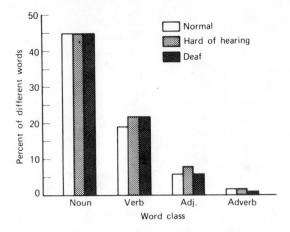

Figure 3. Comparisons of groups as to percentages of different words used in terms of word classes, restricted to content words.

in each figure based upon the percentages for normals. It is apparent that about 45% of the vocabularies of all groups were nouns, about 20% verbs, and so on. When the data are presented in this way, the groups seem more nearly alike than they did in Figures 1 and 2. From this it might be concluded that a hearing impairment interferes with the acquisition of all word classes, not certain ones. However, there are certain

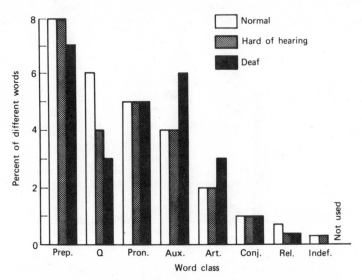

Figure 4. Comparisons of groups as to percentages of different words used in terms of word classes, restricted to function words. Interjections are not shown.

exceptions. The deaf seem to have more deficiencies in adverbs, prepositions, quantifiers, and indefinites (not used). Figure 4 illustrates that the vocabulary of the deaf contained 6% auxiliaries, although it was noted in Figure 2 that they failed to repeat them as often as the normals.

DISCUSSION

The outcomes of this investigation suggest that significant degrees of hearing impairment produce several effects upon the output of spoken words: (1) reduced productivity of tokens; (2) reduced productivity of types; and (3) a greater deficiency in certain classes of words. A moderate hearing deficit seems to cause much less reduction in these three areas than a profound hearing loss. The study confirms the finding of Goda (1964) that the oral language of deaf children tends to be more telegraphic as seen in less use of auxiliaries and other expanding words, and tends to contain many fewer different words than normal.

Concerning linguistic word classes, the findings would suggest that a moderate hearing loss does not significantly impede the acquisition of all of them, only adverbs, pronouns, and auxiliaries. On the other hand, profound impairment limits the output of word tokens in all classes, especially the mentioned ones. While hearing impairment seems to create underuse of some classes, it results in a tendency to overuse nouns and articles. This effect seems to be due to the limitations imposed by deafness upon the learning of abstract concepts, particularly those related to time. That is, adverbs relate to time concepts, which depend upon a fuller knowledge of language. An adverb is linked in meaning to another word and does not have a concrete referent such as many nouns do. The deaf learn nouns more easily, since they can be associated with tangible objects. It is surmised that the deaf overuse articles because they overgeneralize from what they are taught, that nouns are preceded by articles. Their language contains more naming words and fewer abstract words.

When the classes of words are divided into the two large categories of content and function types, an important generalization seems in order. Hearing impairment interferes with the learning of function words much more than with the learning of content words. Among the content group, adverbs are found to be an exception, since they seem more difficult for the hearing-impaired. Among the function group, articles are used frequently by them. This is confirmative of Goda's conclusion that his deaf group used fewer function words than the normals.

REFERENCES

Brown, R. W., Linguistic determinism and the part of speech. *J. Abnorm. Soc. Psychol.*, **55**, 1–5 (1957).

de Groat, A. W., Classification of word groups. *Lingua*, **6**, No. 2, 113–157 (1957).

Fries, C. C., *The Structure of English*. New York: Harcourt, Brace (1952).

Goda, S., Spoken syntax of normal, deaf, and retarded adolescents. *J. Verb. Learn. Verb. Behav.*, **3**, 401–405 (1964).

Jones, L. V., Goodman, M. F., and Wepman, J. M. The classificiation of parts of speech for the characterization of aphasia. *Lang. Speech*, **6**, 94–107 (1963).

MacGinitie, W. H., Ability of deaf children to use different word classes. *J. Speech Hearing Res.,* **7,** 141–150 (1964).

Miller, G. A., *Language and Communication.* New York: McGraw-Hill (1951).

Miller, G. A., Newman, E. B., and Friedman, C. A., Length-frequency statistics for written English. *Information and Control,* **7,** 370–389 (1958).

Myklebust, H. R., *The Psychology of Deafness.* New York: Grune & Stratton (1964).

Osgood, C. E., Suci, G. J., and Tennenbaum, P. H., *The Measurement of Meaning.* Urbana: Univ. of Illinois Press (1957).

Simmons, A. A., A comparison of the type-token ratio of spoken and written language of deaf and hearing children. *Volta Rev.,* **64,** 417–421 (1962).

Walker, H. M., and Lev. J., *Statistical Inference.* New York: Holt, Rinehart and Winston (1953).

Whorf, B. L., Grammatical categories. *Language,* **21,** No. 1, 1–11 (1945).

A Developmental Study of Language Behavior in Retarded Children*

James R. Lackner†

The purpose of this study was to achieve a slow motion perspective of normal language development by studying retarded children of different mental ages. Results from a variety of language tasks were used to develop transformational grammars which described the language behavior of each child as a self-contained system. Developmental trends were noted by comparing grammars of different complexity. The grammars of the retarded children are subsets of an adult grammar. They are very general, non-specific, and lack context sensitivity at the phrase-structure as well as the transformational level. The grammars of the retardates with higher mental ages begin to take on the specificity and wide range of applicability so characteristic of the adult grammar.

1. INTRODUCTION

Human languages are systems of tremendous complexity which until recently have defied adequate formal description [1, 2]. And yet, on the basis of unprompted fragmentary exposure to the language, the child learns to understand and create a virtually infinite number of sentences that he has never heard before [4]. It remains a complete mystery how he is able to do so.

It is now possible to characterize the language capability of adult speakers of English as a set of rules which generate all the sentences understandable or produceable within the language [1–4]. In the present study, an attempt was made to write "grammars" (sets of rules) for retarded children at different stages of language development. The assumption was made that retardation does not yield a different form of language behavior but simply a slowing of the normal developmental sequence

From *Neuropsychologia, 6,* 301–320 (1968). Reprinted by permission of Pergamon Press.

* This research was supported in part by grants from the National Aeronautics and Space Administration (Contract number NsG 496) and the National Institute of Mental Health (Contract number MH 05673) to Professor Hans-Lukas Tueber. The author also holds an NDEA fellowship.

† I should like to thank Dr. H.-L. Teuber for the enthusiasm, encouragement, and advice he gave me during this study. I am grateful to Drs. Suzanne Corkin, Jerry Fodor, Merrill Garrett, and Thomas Twitchell for helpful discussions of the procedures and implications of this study. Dr. Corkin administered the intelligence tests, and Dr. Twitchell performed the neurological examinations on the retarded children.

and a termination of development at a stage below that attained by normal children. There is independent evidence to support this hypothesis [5–7].

By comparing the grammars of children at different levels of language development, insight into the acquisition and ordering of language rules could be obtained. Thus, it could be determined whether an invariant ordering exists in the acquisition of syntax, for example, whether subject-verb number agreement precedes or follows correct use of pronouns, or whether a given child may learn either first. Such knowledge would provide insight into the actual dynamics of language acquisition and could be used in evaluating competing theories of language development. The latter is beyond the scope of the present discussion, but see Chomsky [4] and Fodor [8, 9].

Using the grammars developed to describe the speech of the retarded children, sentences were constructed for presentation to normal children. Knowing the age at which a normal child understood all the sentences generated from a particular retardate's grammar, it was possible to establish a rough correlation between a given grammar and a given chronological age in normal development.

2. METHODS

2.1. SUBJECTS
Five mentally retarded children, three female and two male (R.P. and W.C.), were selected for intensive study. The primary basis for selection was mental age. An

Table 1   Medical Data for the Five Retarded Children Whose Language Behavior was Intensively Studied

Subject	Diagnosis	Major findings	C.A.	M.A.
L.L.	Encephalopathy, congenital, secondary to prematurity	Infantile spastic diplegia, mental retardation	6-5	2-3
S.W.	Encephalopathy, probably congenital with arrested hydrocephalus	Mental retardation, kyphoscoliosis, multiple skeletal anomalies	13-1	2-11
R.P.	Encephalopathy, congenital, secondary to complicated prematurity	Spastic quadriparesis, mental retardation	7-10	3-3
M.F.	Encephalopathy, early acquired, secondary to influenzal meningitis age 6 months	Left hemiparesis, mental retardation	16-2	4-9
W.C.	Encephalopathy, early acquired, sagittal sinus thrombosis or meningo-encephalitis at 2 years 10 months	Right spastic hemiparesis, right attention hemianopia	14-4	8-10

ascending order from approximately 2 to 9 was desired. Children with aphasia or dysarthria were not considered. At the time of the investigation, four of the children were wards of the state and were living in state homes for the mentally retarded. W.C. lives at home and goes to a special ungraded school. The chronological ages (C.A.), mental ages (M.A.), and medical histories are summarized in Table 1.

Five normal control subjects, three boys and two girls, all from middle-class families, were selected on the basis of chronological age, normal physical and mental development, and average performance in school. These children were brought in by their mothers for a single test session which lasted approximately two hours.

2.2 TAPE RECORDINGS

Each retarded child was admitted to the M.I.T. Clinical Research Center for approximately eight weeks. L.L. and R.P. came together and shared a room, as did S.W. and M.F.; W.C. came alone. A microphone was suspended from the ceiling in the children's bedroom and tape recordings of their spontaneous speech were made when they got up in the morning, during their afternoon nap (during which they usually lay in bed and talked back and forth), and at bedtime.

In addition, recordings of each retarded child's speech were made while he performed naming tasks, sentence repetition and imitation tasks, and sentence comprehension tasks administered by the experimenter.

Tape recordings were made of the normal children's speech during the same naming, sentence repetition, and sentence comprehension tasks.

2.3. SENTENCE LENGTH

One thousand sentences were selected randomly from the tape recordings of each of the retarded children's spontaneous speech. The sampling was divided equally among the morning, afternoon and bedtime tapes. These sentences were analyzed according to sentence length, and average sentence length for each retardate was calculated.

2.4. SENTENCE TYPE

The one thousand sentences for each retardate were classified according to sentence type: declarative (D), question (Q), negative (N), passive (P), negative passive (NP), and negative passive question (NPQ). A tabulation was made for each retardate giving the number of each sentence type out of the total one thousand sentences.

2.5. PHRASE STRUCTURE GRAMMAR

The concept of phrase structure grammar has been developed within contemporary linguistic theory. Chomsky [1–4] has shown that the grammar of a language may be represented as a system of rules. These rules "generate" or account for all of the sentences in a given corpus or language. Such a set of rules is called a "generative grammar." It consists of three components: a syntactic component, a semantic and a phonologic one. Only the syntactic component is of concern in the present study. If it is a transformation syntax, it is divided into two subparts: a phrase structure grammar and a set of transformational rules. The phrase-structure subcomponent is a set of ordered rewriting rules that generates strings of formatives (minimal, syntactically functioning components). Each output string is a *phrase marker;* that is, a labeled bracketing indicating the syntactic category of each substring of formatives. The transformational subcomponent maps the phrase markers of terminal strings generated by the phrase structure subcomponent into *derived phrase markers* of *T terminal strings.* These complex mapping operations called transformations are partially ordered; some are obligatory such as tense and number, while others are optional. The structural description (specification of linguistic elements and their structural relationships) of a T terminal string consists of the underlying phrase markers, the derived phrase marker of the entire string, and a "transformational history."

The "output" of the phrase structure subcomponent is not a sentence but an abstract underlying form. Obligatory and optional transformations operate on this underlying form to derive the structure of actual sentences. An underlying phrase marker on which only obligatory transformations have been applied becomes the derived phrase marker of a declarative sentence. Different types of sentences (questions, passives, or negatives, and so on) are derived by the application of different sets of optional transformations.

A simplified version of a phrase structure grammar is shown in Table 2.

The derivation of the sentence "The boy had watched the sunrise" up to the phrase

Table 2   Representative Example of a Simplified Phrase Structure Grammar

$$\text{Sentence} \rightarrow \text{NP} + \text{VP}$$

$$\text{NP} \rightarrow \left\{ \begin{array}{l} \text{NP}_{\text{sing}} \\ \text{NP}_{\text{pl}} \end{array} \right\}$$

$$\text{VP} \rightarrow \text{aux.} + \text{VP}^1$$

$$\text{VP}^1 \rightarrow \text{V} + \text{NP}$$

$$\text{aux} \rightarrow \text{C(M) (have} + \text{en) (be} + \text{ing)}$$

$$\text{M} \rightarrow \text{can, will, may, shall, must}$$

$$\text{C} \rightarrow \text{past, present}$$

"→" means "rewritten as";
"NP" stands for noun phrase;
"VP" stands for verb phrase;
"aux" stands for auxiliary;
"M" stands for modal;
"C" stands for tense;
"{ }" means obligatory selection of one of the items within the brackets;
"( )" denotes optional selection.

marker level is shown in Fig. 1. The full derivation of the sentence is completed with application of the auxiliary transformation which maps the phrase marker in Fig. 1 according to the rule:

SD (Structural description): (X, AF, V, Y)
SC (Structural change) X_1-X_2-X_3-X_4 X_1-X_3+X_2-#-X_4
Where Af is en, ing, C. V is M, have, be, V.

Thus by   The boy—past+have—en watch the sunrise
T aux   The boy had watched the sunrise.

The one thousand sentences for each retardate were analyzed individually and a complete derivational history was written. Phrase structure grammars were then written for each corpus. Each phrase structure grammar could generate the phrase marker of any sentence in the corpus from which it was developed. Writing phrase structure grammars for each child permitted easy comparison of rule structures.

2.6. TRANSFORMATIONS

The derivational histories of the sentences in each retardate's corpus were analyzed and information was tabulated on the incidence of different grammatic transformations employed. For each transformation, it was noted whether it was used in full generality or in a restricted form. The set of transformations used by each child in conjunction with his phrase structure grammar is necessary and sufficient to generate "correctly" and in its entirety each sentence used by each child.

2.7. SENTENCE COMPREHENSION AND IMITATION TASK

Novel sentences were devised for each retardate from vocabulary items and transformations present in his grammatic repertoire. In addition, sentences were constructed

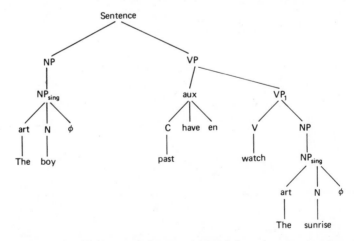

Figure 1. Phrase marker generated by phrase structure rules for the sentence "The boy had watched the sunrise."

that were syntactically more complex than any the child had spontaneously used. Such sentences involved grammatic transformations or combinations of transformations which had not been used by the child.

These sentences were presented to the child who had been instructed so that either a verbal response, a pointing or retrieval movement, or a pantomime would demonstrate his interpretation of the syntax of the sentence. Systematic care was taken to insure that the child could not give correct responses on the basis of key words or intonational patterns of the sentences.

The results of the sentence comprehension task were used to refine the phrase structure grammar and transformations for each retardate. If he understood a form which was not generable by his phrase structure grammar, then it was revised to include that form. Likewise, if he understood a transformation or particular combination of transformations that he did not use himself, this was noted also. The phrase structure grammars and lists of transformations in the results section represent the sets of rules after modification to include forms the child understood but did not use spontaneously.

The same sentences used in the comprehension task were used in a sentence imitation (repetition) task. The sentence was read aloud to the child who had been instructed to repeat the sentence as soon as he heard it. Errors in repetition were scored according to whether the child (a) maintained the same syntactic form but dropped out non-content words (articles, conjunctions, etc.): (b) changed the syntactic form and dropped out non-content words: (c) lost the syntactic form and was just able to repeat a few disconnected words.

The sentence comprehension and imitation tasks using the same sets of sentences developed for the retardates were administered to normal subjects. It was then established for each normal child which set of rules developed for a retardate best described his own level of language attainment. This simple control was used to indicate whether there is an invariance in the ordering of rule structures in normal language behavior.

3. RESULTS

3.1 SENTENCE LENGTH
The data on sentence length are presented in Table 3.

Sentence length, measured in words, increases with mental age. McCarthy[10] has

Table 3   Average Sentence Length for a One-thousand Sentence Sample for Each Retarded Child

	L.L.	S.W.	R.P.	M.F.	W.C.
Mental age (years, months)	(2-3)	(2-11)	(3-3)	(4-9)	(8-10)
Sentence length (words)	4.4	6.7	7.2	7.4	7.8

Table 4   Sentence Length as a Function of Age in a Group of Gifted
Children Studied by Fisher
(Information was Extracted from McCarthy [10])

	N	Chronological age							
		1 ½	2	2 ½	3	3 ½	4	4 ½	5
Boys	35	3.4	4.7	3.4	7.0	8.4	6.9	10.1	
Girls	37	3.9	4.8	5.3	6.3	5.6	7.6	8.3	
All	72	3.7	4.8	4.7	6.7	6.9	7.2	9.5	

Sentence length (words)

summarized data on sentence length in children's speech. Table 4 represents data extracted from her comprehensive presentation.

There are no striking differences in sentence length for a retardate of a given mental age and a gifted child of that chronological age. However, by the age of four-and-a-half the gifted children have surpassed the most advanced retardate. It must be noted that if normal children and retarded children of the same chronological age were compared, the normal children would have longer sentences at all ages [10].

3.2 SENTENCE TYPES
The data on sentence types are summarized in Table 5. A regularity is apparent in the order of appearance of sentential types as mental age increases. A given sentential type is found only if all sentential types of a lower order of complexity are also found. This regularity parallels the increasing complexity of the sentential types when complexity is defined in terms of the amount of structural change involved in the transformational histories of the sentence types. However, the number of transformations involved in the derivation of a sentence is not necessarily an index of its complexity. Syntactic complexity, for sentence recognition at least, seems to be a function of the degree to which surface structure cues are present to indicate the deep structure relations of the sentence [11]. The present result may be considered a "natural history" approach to syntactic complexity.

3.3 PHRASE STRUCTURE GRAMMARS
The phrase structure grammars presented in Appendix A are based on an analysis of the children's recorded utterances and their performance on the sentence imitation and comprehension tasks. The rules are presented in the form developed by Chomsky [1, 2]. An examination of these grammars reveals that, with increasing mental age, phrase structure rules become more differentiated and specific. Omissions and

redundancies of NP, VP, T, Prt, and Prep decrease as the grammars become more specific. The rules become increasingly context sensitive, and number agreement between subject and verb becomes firmly established. None of the structures generated by the rules is incompatible with adult usage; rather, each phrase-structure grammar seems a subset of the grammar at the next level of complexity.

These phrase-structure grammars must be considered grammars of the children's competence rather than of their performance. That is, these grammars generate the underlying phrase markers of any sentence the children were able to understand and not just of sentences they spoke.

3.4 TRANSFORMATIONS
Information is presented in Appendix B on sixteen grammatic transformations used by one or more of the retarded children. It is noteworthy that the number of transformations a child understood, as well as used, increased with mental age. Some transformations can apply to a number of different underlying phrase markers. A child may have one of these base structures, but not all of them, in his phrase structure rules. In that case he may use the transformation in a limited context only.

The combinations of transformations as well as the types of transformations understood increase as mental age increases. At earlier ages the understanding and usage of transformations singly does not imply comprehension of sentences involving multiple transformations. Only the child with a mental age of 8–10 showed full understanding and usage of all the transformations in all their possible combinations.

3.5 SENTENCE COMPREHENSION AND IMITATION TASK
It was systematically demonstrated that each retardate could understand any non-semantically anomalous sentence constructed from vocabulary items and syntactic transformations present in his speech sample of one thousand sentences.

Test sentences were then presented with the same vocabulary items as the previ-

Table 5   Frequency of Sentential Types in the One-thousand Sentence Samples for Each Retarded Child

| M.A. | Sentence type | | | | | | |
	D	N	Q	NQ	P	NP	NPQ
2-3	563	275	162				
2-11	517	293	171	19			
3-3	516	337	99	37	11		
4-9	430	393	127	41	9		
8-10	438	351	119	45	24	18	5

ous test sentences but of a more complex syntactic structure, thus involving transformations or combinations of transformations which had not been found in the child's spontaneous speech. The two children who had not used passive constructions could understand many passive constructions, though not all of them. Of the two children who used passive constructions but not negative passive constructions, the older (in mental age) was able to understand all negative passive constructions in his test, but the younger was able to understand only a few (3 out of 10). The two children who did not spontaneously use passive constructions, but who could still understand some of them, were unable to understand any of the negative passive constructions used in the test.

These results received substantiation from a sentence imitation test using the sentences constructed for the comprehension task. The children were able to repeat with few errors sentences constructed from vocabulary items and of the syntactic types found in their spontaneous repertoire. This was true despite the fact that the length, in words, of the sentence exceeded the child's immediate memory span for a list of random words. It implies that if the child is able to detect structure, namely, syntactic structure, he will "chunk" the input into larger segments, thus effectively increasing his his memory span [12].

The results obtained with sentences involving familiar vocabulary items but more complex syntactic structures are of interest. The children were unable to repeat correctly those sentences which they had been unable to understand. They would repeat two or three words from the sentence, usually function words as substantives. Often these words were not repeated in the same order as they appeared in the test sentence, and their order of recall bore no relationship to syntactic structure.

With more complex sentences which they had been able to understand, the children's behavior was strikingly different. Often the child would be able to repeat the sentence correctly except for the omission of one or two function words, which were irrelevant to the syntactic structure of the sentence. These latter cases are particularly interesting. A typical example is illustrated by two sentences that were presented:

(1) John hit Mary with the ball.
(2) Mary was hit by the ball.

Each sentence has six words, and these were common to the children's speech; however, it was much easier for them to repeat sentence (1). Mistakes are also made in repeating sentence (1), but they show that the child understands the sentence structure and meaning. Some examples are:

"John hit Mary"
"John's ball hit Mary"
"John ball hit Mary"

Whereas for sentence (2):

"Mary . . . the . . . hit"
"Mary . . . ah . . . ball"
"Mary . . . hit . . . ah . . . ball"
"The ball hit Mary"

The first three of these repetitions were produced by a child who did not understand the meaning of the sentence, while the fourth was by a child who did understand the meaning of the sentence. The differences in ease of repeatability of sentences (1) and (2) may be related to the differences in syntactic complexity of these sentences and the child's perception of the complexity. Sentence (1) is a simple declarative sentence with only obligatory transformations present in its derivation. Sentence (2), which is one of the most complicated types, is a passive construction. It is of interest to note that the last response to sentence (2), "the ball hit Mary," corresponds to the base form of (2) before the passive transformation has operated.

Many other examples of this "regression"* to a lower level of the grammar have been obtained. These "regressions" were made only on syntactic forms which were not part of the child's production constellation. They further illustrate the fact that production lags behind comprehension in the acquisition of language. They also constitute evidence for the psychological reality of abstract underlying structures and transformational operations.

Some preliminary results indicate that if a sentence with a transformational derivational history peculiar to the child's production capability is changed so that a particular grammatical transformation is incomplete (i.e., there is a structural element missing in the sentence), the child upon repeating the sentence may complete it. Thus, the oldest child (in mental age) would complete the sentence "Mary hit by the ball" as "Mary was hit by the ball." After this subject had successfully completed a number of passive transformations in this manner, sentences like the following were presented for repetition: "The ball was hit the boy." In this case many spontaneous corrections would be possible, the boy could be either the doer or the receiver of the action, i.e., it could be "The ball was hit by the boy" or "The ball was hit to (or near, past, etc.) the boy." The child always passivised this form to "The ball was hit by the boy," never noticing that this sentence is ambiguous—i.e., "by the boy" could mean "close to the boy" or the boy doing the hitting. The practice with a particular form, the passive transformation, temporarily limited the child's spontaneous corrections to passive corrections. If an ambiguous form similar to "the ball was hit the boy" was presented to the child for imitation prior to practice repetitions (which could only be spontaneously corrected as passive), then the child would respond seemingly indifferently with "The ball was hit to the boy" or "The ball was hit by the boy," i.e., he did not seem to have any bias.

Spontaneous corrections constitute further evidence for the psychological internalization of grammar. The nature of the child's spontaneous corrections should be investigated systematically since they yield valuable information about grammatic competence. If semantically deviant sentences were also "corrected" by the child, this technique might serve as a tool for investigating the nature of concept formation in young children.

The sentences used in the comprehension and imitation tasks with the retardates

---

* Lenneberg et al. [7] found similar grammatical "regressions" during sentence repetition tests administered to Mongoloid children.

were also presented to normal children of different chronological ages in similar test situations. All the effects found with the retardates were also found with the normal children. They were unable to repeat correctly any sentence which they were unable to understand; they, too, showed what have been referred to above as "grammatic regressions"; they showed completion effects in grammatically incomplete sentences which they had been asked to repeat; and, they showed perseveration in the types of grammatic completions after prior practice with a given form. No qualitative differences were apparent between the language behavior of the normal children and the retarded children in the sentence comprehension and imitation tasks.

The normal children were evaluated in comparison to each of the five grammars describing the language behavior of the retarded children. The results of this evaluation are presented in Table 6. An "x" indicates that the normal child understood all the sentences generated with that grammar.

These results are noteworthy in that an ordering is maintained between the complexity of the grammars and the mental ages of the retarded children, and the chronological ages of the normal children. This result should not be interpreted as meaning that the language behavior of a retarded child of a given mental age is equivalent to that of a normal child of a particular chronological age. Rather, these findings suggest that the language behaviors of normal and retarded children are not qualitatively different, that both groups follow similar developmental trends, but that the most severely retarded children become arrested in their development and remain at a lower level of normal language acquisition.

4. DISCUSSION

The primary concern of most studies of language acquisition has been to describe overt aspects of language behavior. Vocabulary size, sentence length, and sentence complexity (defined in terms of compound and coordinate sentence structures) have been shown to increase as the child grows older [10]. Unfortunately, such measures yield little insight into the dynamics of language acquisition. Some recent studies [13, 14] utilizing the concept of a transformational grammar have attempted to write "grammars" for normal children at different stages of language development. This is a difficult task; the child's acquisition of language progresses rapidly and his grammar changes continually, so that a stable perspective of a particular level of development is virtually impossible to attain.

It has been assumed by some writers [13] that the grammar of a young child learning his native language is more primitive than that of the adult. If this were so, writing "child grammars" would give insight into the framework of a fully ramified adult grammar. But this may not in fact be true. It is possible to write more than one grammar to account for a child's recorded utterances, and there is often no way of choosing one over another. In choosing the grammar for an adult, much more is required. The grammar has to assign degrees of grammaticality or well-formedness to linguistic sequences. It must also account for the creative aspect of linguistic capability—the ability to understand and produce sentences which have never been encountered before. Chomsky [4] has pointed out that most of what the child, as well as the adult, hears and produces is of such low likelihood of occurrence as to ap-

Table 6   Shows for Each Normal Child the Grammars Which He Was Able to Understand. The Grammars Were Written to Describe the Language Behavior of the Retarded Children Studied. Each Grammar Is Identified by the Initials of the Retarded Child and His Mental Age

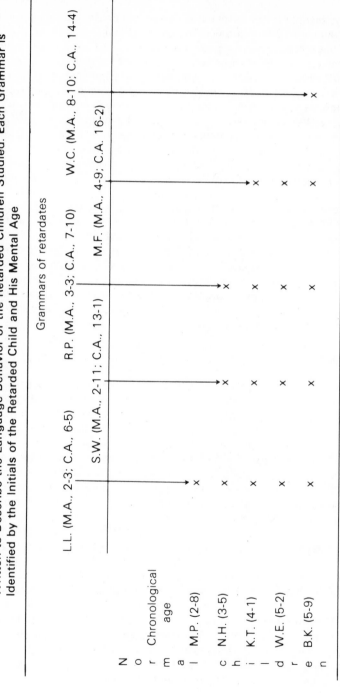

Grammars of retardates

Normal child Chronological age	L.L. (M.A., 2-3; C.A., 6-5)	S.W. (M.A., 2-11; C.A., 13-1)	R.P. (M.A., 3-3; C.A., 7-10)	M.F. (M.A., 4-9; C.A. 16-2)	W.C. (M.A., 8-10; C.A., 14-4)
M.P. (2-8)	x				
N.H. (3-5)	x	x	x		
K.T. (4-1)	x	x	x	x	
W.E. (5-2)	x	x	x	x	
B.K. (5-9)	x	x	x	x	x

proach zero probability. In effect this means that, except for a few stereotyped phrases and social greetings, most of what is said and heard is new. This, of course, only refers to the structuring and ordering of sentences, not their vocabulary.

Until the last decade, studies of language acquisition have been based largely upon analyses of tape-recordings of children's speech. These studies are assessments of the child's language *performance* rather than his language competence, where *performance* is taken to mean the child's actual linguistic productions, and *competence* the child's ability to understand more constructions than than he actually uses and his knowledge of grammatical relations [3]. It is true that language competence can be studied only through language performance, but other more subtle techniques are needed in addition to tape-recordings, as many non-linguistic factors such as mood and attention-span may influence speech. In order to assess the child's full linguistic capabilities, it is necessary to take the creative aspects of language usage into account and develop techniques for elucidating them. A variety of evidence must be brought to bear in exacting the child's full language competence.

The present study was based on the hypothesis that retarded children develop language functions in the same sequence as normal children but with increased spacing between major developmental landmarks. Retarded children were selected who had either already reached the apex of their linguistic development or who were progressing so slowly that a stable perspective of their language development was attained. With such a population of retarded children, it was possible to investigate systematically the child's use and comprehension of sentences, his ability to detect and correct grammatic deviance, and his application of grammatic rules in new situations.

Individual grammars were developed for each of the five retarded children. The grammar of each child could "generate" sentences that the child spontaneously used and, in addition, forms understood by the child. The basic structures generated by the grammars of these children were presented to normal children in comprehension and imitation tasks. An ordering between complexity of the grammar and chronological age of the normal child was found. The youngest normal child could understand all forms generated with the lowest level grammar, and the oldest normal child all forms generated by the most advanced grammar.

The grammars of the retarded children appear to be subsets of an adult grammar. The lower-level grammars are very general, non-specific, and lack context sensitivity. The same is true of their transformational levels. It is only in the grammars of the children with higher mental age that the specificity and wider range of applicability, so characteristic of the adult grammar, come to the fore.

REFERENCES

1. CHOMSKY, N. *Syntactic Structures.* Mouton, The Hague, 1957.
2. CHOMSKY, N. A transformational approach to syntax. In *The Structure of Language: Readings in the Philosophy of Language,* J. FODOR and J. KATZ (Editors). Prentice Hall, Englewood Cliffs, New Jersey, 1964.
3. CHOMSKY, N. *Aspects of the Theory of Syntax.* The MIT Press, Cambridge, 1965.
4. CHOMSKY, N. A review of B. F. Skinner's *Verbal Behavior.* In *Language* **35,** 26–58, 1959.
5. LENNEBERG, E. Understanding language without ability to speak: A case report. *J. Abnorm. Soc. Psychol.* **65,** 419–425, 1962.

6. LENNEBERG E. *New Directions in the Study of Language.* MIT Press, Cambridge, 1964.
7. LENNEBERG, E., NICHOLS, I. and ROSENBERGER, E. Primitive stages of language development in mongolism. *Proc. Assoc. Res. Nerv. Ment. Dis.* **42**, 119–137, 1964.
8. FODOR, J. A. Could meaning be an r$_m$? *J. Verb. Learn Verb. Behav.,* **4**, 73–81, 1965.
9. FODOR, J. A. How to learn to talk: Some simple ways. In *The Genesis of Language*, F. SMITH and G. MILLER (Editors). MIT Press, Cambridge. 1966.
10. McCARTHY, D. Language development in children. In *A Manual of Child Psychology*, L. CARMICHAEL (Editor), Second Edition. Wiley, New York, 1954.
11. FODOR, J. A. and GARRETT, M. Some determinants of sentential complexity. *Perception and Psychophysics,* **2**, 289–296, 1967.
12. MILLER, G. A. The magical number seven. *Psychol. Rev.* **63**, 81–97, 1956.
13. BROWN, R. and FRASER, C. The acquisition of syntax. In *Verbal Learning and Behavior,* N. COFER and B. S. MUSGRAVE (Editors). McGraw-Hill, New York, 1963.
14. FRASER, C., BELLUGI, U. and BROWN, R. Control of grammar in imitation, comprehension and production. *J. Verb. Learn. Verb. Behav.* **2**, 121–135, 1963.

Appendix A

PHRASE STRUCTURE GRAMMARS OF THE FIVE RETARDED CHILDREN

Case L.L.

C.A.$=6-5$ M.A.$=2-3$

1. $S \rightarrow (NP)+(VP)(adv.)$

2. $VP \rightarrow aux. \left\{ \begin{matrix} be \\ VP_1 \end{matrix} \left\{ \begin{matrix} adj. \\ adv. \end{matrix} \right\} \right\}$

3. $VP_1 \rightarrow \left\{ \begin{matrix} V(\left\{ \begin{matrix} (NP) \\ adj. \end{matrix} \right\}) \\ (V) \left\{ \begin{matrix} (NP) \\ adj. \end{matrix} \right\} \end{matrix} \right\}$

4. $V \rightarrow \left\{ \begin{matrix} V_s \text{ in env.}-(adj.) \\ V_t \text{ in env.}-(NP) \\ V_1 \text{ in env.}- \left\{ \begin{matrix} \# \\ adv. \end{matrix} \right\} \end{matrix} \right\}$

5. $Adv. \rightarrow \left\{ \begin{matrix} \text{Prep. phrase of time} \\ \text{Prep. phrase of place} \\ \text{Adv. of time} \\ \text{Adv. of place} \end{matrix} \right\}$

6. $NP \rightarrow \left\{ \begin{matrix} NP_{sing} \\ NP_{pl} \end{matrix} \right\} \text{ in env. } \left\{ \begin{matrix} NP_{sing} \\ NP_{pl} \end{matrix} \right\} +aux.+be-.$

7. $\left\{ \begin{matrix} NP_{sing} \rightarrow (T)+N+\emptyset \\ NP_{pl} \rightarrow (T)+N+S \end{matrix} \right\}$

8. $N \rightarrow \begin{Bmatrix} N_h \\ N_c \end{Bmatrix}$

9. $V_t \rightarrow \begin{Bmatrix} V_{t1} \text{ in env. } N_h \ldots - \\ V_{t2} \text{ in env. } \ldots - \ldots N_h \\ \begin{matrix} V_{t31} \\ V_{t32} \end{matrix} \text{ in env. } N_h \ldots - \ldots N_c \\ V_{tx} \text{ in env. } \ldots -Prt. \end{Bmatrix}$

10. $Prt. \rightarrow (prt.)(prt.)$
    $Prt. \rightarrow in, on, \ldots$

11. $T \rightarrow (T)(T)$
    $T \rightarrow a, the, \ldots$

12. $aux. \rightarrow C(M)(have+en)(be+ing)$

13. $C \rightarrow present, past$

14. $M \rightarrow can, will$

15. $\begin{Bmatrix} N_h \rightarrow I, me, girl \\ N_c \rightarrow it, doll, \ldots \end{Bmatrix}$

16. $V_i \rightarrow come, \ldots$

17. $V_s \rightarrow hurt, \ldots$

18. $V_{t1} \rightarrow hate, \ldots$
    $V_{t2} \rightarrow scare, \ldots$
    $V_{t31} \rightarrow find, lose, \ldots$
    $V_{t32} \rightarrow eat, \ldots$
    $V_{tx} \rightarrow take, \ldots$

19. $Adj. \rightarrow tiny, \ldots$

<u>Case S.W.</u>
C.A.$=13-1$ M.A.$=2-11$

1. $S \rightarrow (NP)(NP)+(VP)(VP)(adv.)$

2. $VP \rightarrow aux. \begin{Bmatrix} be \\ VP_1 \end{Bmatrix} \begin{Bmatrix} adj. \\ adv. \end{Bmatrix}$

3. $VP_1 \rightarrow V \begin{Bmatrix} (NP) \\ adj. \end{Bmatrix}$

4. $V \rightarrow \begin{Bmatrix} V_s \text{ in env. } \ldots (adj.) \\ V_t \text{ in env. } \ldots (NP) \\ V_i \text{ in env. } \ldots \begin{Bmatrix} \# \\ adv. \end{Bmatrix} \end{Bmatrix}$

5. Adv. → $\begin{cases} \text{Prep. phrase of time} \\ \text{Prep. phrase of place} \\ \text{Adv. of time} \\ \text{Adv. of place} \end{cases}$

6. NP → $\begin{Bmatrix} NP_{sing} \\ NP_{pl} \end{Bmatrix}$ in env. $\begin{Bmatrix} NP_{sing} \\ NP_{pl} \end{Bmatrix}$ + aux. + be—.

7. $\begin{cases} NP_{sing} \rightarrow (T)(T) + N + \phi \\ NP_{pl} \rightarrow (T)(T) + N + S \end{cases}$

8. N → $\begin{Bmatrix} N_h \\ N_c \end{Bmatrix}$

9. $V_t \rightarrow \begin{cases} V_{t1} \text{ in env. } N_h \ldots - \\ V_{t2} \text{ in env.} \ldots - \ldots N_h \\ \begin{Bmatrix} V_{t31} \\ V_{t32} \end{Bmatrix} \text{ in env. } N_h \ldots - \ldots N_e \\ \begin{cases} V_{ta} \text{ in env. } N_h \ldots -NP \\ V_{tx} \text{ in env.} \ldots -Prt. \end{cases} \end{cases}$

10. Prt. → (Prt.)(Prt.)
    Prt. → in, on

11. T → (T)(T)
    T → a, the

12. aux. → C(M)(have + en)(be + ing)

13. C → Present, Past

14. M → Can, will, may

15. $\begin{cases} N_h \rightarrow I, \text{ you, boy} \\ N_c \rightarrow \text{dog, doll, it,} \end{cases}$

16. $V_i \rightarrow$ come, . . .

17. $V_s \rightarrow$ hurt, burn, ...

18. $V_{t1} \rightarrow$ like, ...
    $V_{t2} \rightarrow$ scare, surprise. . . .
    $V_{t31} \rightarrow$ find, . . .
    $V_{t32} \rightarrow$ eat, drink, . . .
    $V_{ta} \rightarrow$ want, ...
    $V_{tx} \rightarrow$ take, put, ...

19. adj. → little, big, . . .

<u>Case R.P.</u>
C.A. = 7 − 10   M.A. = 3 − 3

1. $S \rightarrow (NP)(NP) + VP(adv.)$

2. $VP \rightarrow aux. \begin{Bmatrix} be & \begin{Bmatrix} adj. \\ adv. \end{Bmatrix} \\ VP_1 \end{Bmatrix}$

3. $VP_1 \rightarrow V \begin{Bmatrix} (NP)(NP) \\ adj. \end{Bmatrix}$

4. $V \rightarrow \begin{bmatrix} V_s \text{ in env.} \ldots \text{ adj.} \\ V_t \text{ in env.} \ldots NP(NP) \\ V_i \text{ in env.} \ldots \begin{Bmatrix} \# \\ adv. \end{Bmatrix} \end{bmatrix}$

5. $Adv. \rightarrow \begin{Bmatrix} \text{Prep. phrase of time} \\ \text{Prep. phrase of place} \\ \text{Adv. of time} \\ \text{Adv. of place} \end{Bmatrix}$

6. $Adv_1 \rightarrow \begin{Bmatrix} \text{Prep. phrase of place} \\ \text{Adv. of place} \end{Bmatrix}$

7. $NP \rightarrow \begin{Bmatrix} NP_{sing} \text{ in env. } NP_{sing} + aux. \text{ be.} - \\ NP_{pl} \text{ in env. } NP_{pl} + aux. \text{ be} - \end{Bmatrix}$

8. $\begin{Bmatrix} NP_{sing} \rightarrow (T)T + N + \phi \\ NP_{pl} \rightarrow (T)T + N + S \end{Bmatrix}$

9. $N \ldots \begin{bmatrix} N_h \\ N_e \\ N_{ab} \text{ in env. } \begin{Bmatrix} \cdot \# \\ V_t \end{Bmatrix} (T)T \ldots \phi \end{bmatrix}$

10. $V_t \rightarrow \begin{Bmatrix} V_{t1} \text{ in env. } N_h \ldots - \\ V_{t2} \text{ in env.} - \ldots N_h \\ \begin{Bmatrix} V_{t31} \\ V_{t32} \end{Bmatrix} \text{ in env. } N_h \ldots - \ldots N_h \\ \begin{Bmatrix} V_{ta} \text{ in env. } N_h \ldots -Comp. \\ V_{tx} \text{ in env.} \ldots -Prt. \end{Bmatrix} \end{Bmatrix}$

11. $Prt. \rightarrow Prt. (Prt.)$
    $Prt. \rightarrow in, on, \ldots$

12. $T \rightarrow T(T)$
    $T \rightarrow a, the. \ldots$

13. $aux. \rightarrow C(M)(have + en)(be + ing)$

14. $C \rightarrow Present, Past$

15. $M \rightarrow Can, will, must$

16.
$$\left\{ \begin{array}{l} N_h \rightarrow \text{boy, girl, me . . .} \\ N_c \rightarrow \text{it, truck, toy, . . .} \\ N_{ab} \rightarrow \text{love, . . .} \end{array} \right\}$$

17. $V_i \rightarrow$ come, . . .

18. $V_s \rightarrow$ tickle, hurt, . . .

19.
$$\begin{array}{l} V_{t1} \rightarrow \text{love, like, . . .} \\ V_{t2} \rightarrow \text{scare, . . .} \\ V_{t31} \rightarrow \text{find, . . .} \\ V_{t32} \rightarrow \text{smoke, eat, drink, . . .} \\ V_{ta} \rightarrow \text{want, believe, . . .} \\ V_{tx} \rightarrow \text{take, bring, put, . . .} \end{array}$$

20. adj. $\rightarrow$ happy, little, . . .

Case M.F.

C.A. $= 16-2$ M.A. $= 4-9$

1. S $\rightarrow$ NP(NP)+VP(adv.)

2. $VP \rightarrow$ aux. $\left\{ \begin{array}{l} \text{be} \left\{ \begin{array}{l} \text{adj.} \\ \text{adv.}_1 \end{array} \right\} \\ VP_1 \end{array} \right\}$

3. $VP_1 \rightarrow V(\left\{ \begin{array}{l} \text{NP(NP)} \\ \text{adj.} \end{array} \right\}$

4. $V \rightarrow \left\{ \begin{array}{l} V_s \text{ in env. . . . . adj.} \\ V_t \text{ in env. . . . . NP} \\ V_i \text{ in env. . . . } \left\{ \begin{array}{l} \text{\#} \\ \text{adv.} \end{array} \right\} \end{array} \right\}$

5. Adv. $\rightarrow \left\{ \begin{array}{l} \text{Prep. phrase of time} \\ \text{Prep. phrase of place} \\ \text{Adv. of time} \\ \text{Adv. of place} \end{array} \right\}$

6. Adv.$_1 \rightarrow \left\{ \begin{array}{l} \text{Prep. phrase of place} \\ \text{adv. of place} \end{array} \right\}$

7. NP $\rightarrow \left\{ \begin{array}{l} \text{NP}_{sing} \text{ in env. NP}_{sing} + \text{aux.} + \left\{ \begin{array}{l} \text{be} \\ \text{become} \end{array} \right\} - \\ \text{NP}_{pl} \text{ in env. NP}_{pl} + \text{aux.} + \left\{ \begin{array}{l} \text{be} \\ \text{become} \end{array} \right\} - \end{array} \right\}$

8. $\left\{ \begin{array}{l} \text{NP}_{sing} \rightarrow \text{T(T)} + \text{N} + \phi \\ \text{NP}_{pl} \rightarrow \text{T(T)} + \text{N} + \text{S} \end{array} \right\}$

9. $N \rightarrow \begin{Bmatrix} N_h \\ N_c \\ N_{ab} \text{ in env. } \begin{Bmatrix} \# \\ V_t \end{Bmatrix} \text{ T(T)} \text{—} \phi \end{Bmatrix}$

10. $\begin{Bmatrix} NP_{sing} \rightarrow T + N + \phi \\ NP_{pl} \rightarrow T + N + S \end{Bmatrix}$

11. $N \rightarrow \begin{Bmatrix} N_h \\ N_c \\ N_{ab} \text{ in env. } \begin{Bmatrix} \# \\ V_t \end{Bmatrix} \text{ T—}\phi \end{Bmatrix}$

12. $V_t \rightarrow \begin{Bmatrix} V_{t1} \text{ in env. } N_h \ldots \text{—} \\ V_{t2} \text{ in env.—} \ldots N_h \\ \begin{Bmatrix} V_{t31} \\ V_{t32} \end{Bmatrix} \text{ in env. } N_h \ldots \text{—} \ldots N_c \\ \begin{Bmatrix} V_{ta} \text{ in env. } N_h \ldots \text{—Comp.} \\ V_{tx} \text{ in env.—Prt.} \end{Bmatrix} \end{Bmatrix}$

13. Prt. $\rightarrow$ out, in, up . . .

14. T $\rightarrow$ a, an, the

15. aux. $\rightarrow$ C(M)(have + en)(be + ing)

16. C $\rightarrow$ Present, past

17. M $\rightarrow$ can, will, . . .

18. $\begin{Bmatrix} N_h \rightarrow \text{I, you, he, etc.} \\ N_c \rightarrow \text{it, table, book, etc.} \\ N_{ab} \rightarrow \text{it, truth, sincerity, etc.} \end{Bmatrix}$

19. $V_i \rightarrow$ arrive, depart, . . .

20. $V_s \rightarrow$ feel, hurt, . . .

21. $V_{t1} \rightarrow$ like, . . .
    $V_{t2} \rightarrow$ scare, . . .
    $V_{t31} \rightarrow$ find, . . .
    $V_{t32} \rightarrow$ eat, smoke, . . .
    $V_{ta} \rightarrow$ catch, want, keep, . . .
    $V_{tx} \rightarrow$ take, bring, . . .

22. adj. $\rightarrow$ little, old, . . .

$$\underline{\text{Case W.C.}}$$
$$\text{C.A.} = 14-4 \quad \text{M.A.} = 8-10$$

1. $S \rightarrow NP + VP \text{ (adv.)}$

2. $VP \rightarrow \text{aux.} \left\{ \begin{array}{l} be \\ VP_1 \end{array} \left\{ \begin{array}{l} \text{Pred.} \\ \text{adv.}_1 \end{array} \right\} \right\}$

3. $VP_1 \rightarrow V \left\{ \begin{array}{l} NP \\ \text{Pred.} \end{array} \right\}$

4. $V \rightarrow \left\{ \begin{array}{l} V_t \text{ in env.} - NP \\ V_s \text{ in env.} - \text{Pred.} \\ V_i \text{ in env.} - \left\{ \begin{array}{l} \# \\ \text{adv.} \end{array} \right\} \end{array} \right\}$

5. $\text{Adv.} \rightarrow \left\{ \begin{array}{l} \text{Prep. phrase of time} \\ \text{Prep. phrase of place} \\ \text{Adv. of time} \\ \text{adv. of place} \end{array} \right\}$

6. $\text{Adv.}_1 \rightarrow \left\{ \begin{array}{l} \text{Prep. phrase of place} \\ \text{Adv. of place} \end{array} \right\}$

7. $NP \rightarrow \left\{ \begin{array}{l} NP_{sing} \\ NP_{pl} \end{array} \right\}$

8. $\text{Pred.} \rightarrow \left\{ \begin{array}{l} NP_{sing} \text{ in env. } NP_{sing} + \text{aux.} \left\{ \begin{array}{l} be \\ become \end{array} \right\} - \\ NP_{pl} \text{ in env. } NP_{pl} + \text{aux.} \left\{ \begin{array}{l} be \\ become \end{array} \right\} - \\ \text{Adj.} \end{array} \right\}$

9. $\text{Adj.} \rightarrow \text{(very)} + \text{adj.}$

10. $V_t \rightarrow \left\{ \begin{array}{l} V_{t1} \text{ in env. } N_h \ldots - \\ V_{t2} \text{ in env.} - \ldots N_h \\ \left\{ \begin{array}{l} V_{t31} \\ V_{t32} \end{array} \right\} \text{ in env. } N_h \ldots - \ldots N_c \\ \left\{ \begin{array}{l} V_{ta} \text{ in env. } N_h \ldots - \text{comp.} \\ V_{tx} \text{ in env.} \ldots - \text{prt.} \end{array} \right. \end{array} \right\}$

11. $\text{Prt.} \rightarrow \text{in, on, down} \ldots$

12. $T \rightarrow \text{a, the} \ldots$

13. $\text{Aux.} \rightarrow C(M)(\text{have} + en)(be + ing)$

14. $C \rightarrow \text{present, past}$

15. $M \rightarrow \text{can, will,} \ldots$

16. $\begin{cases} N_h \to I, \text{ you, he} \ldots \\ N_c \to it, \text{ chair, bird, book} \ldots \\ N_{ab} \to it, \text{ truth} \end{cases}$

17. $V_i \to$ come, leave . . .

18. $V_s \to$ feel, hurt . . .

19. $\begin{aligned} & V_{t1} \to \text{hate, like} \ldots \\ & V_{t2} \to \text{scare}, \ldots \\ & V_{t31} \to \text{find}, \ldots \\ & V_{t32} \to \text{smoke, eat}, \ldots \\ & V_{ta} \to \text{catch, want} \ldots \\ & V_{tx} \to \text{take, put}, \ldots \end{aligned}$

20. adj. $\to$ tiny, mean . . .

Appendix B

SYNTACTIC TRANSFORMATIONS USED BY THE FIVE RETARDED CHILDREN

1. *Number*

    a. Structural Description: $(NP_{sing}, \text{ Present, } X)$

       Structural Change: $X_1 - X_2 - X_3 \to X_1 - S - X_3$

    b. S.D. $(NP_{p1}, \text{ Present, } X)$

       S.C. $X_1 - X_2 - X_3 \to X_1 - \phi - X_3$

Four of the children S.W. (C.A. $= 13 - 1$, M.A. $= 2 - 11$), R.P. (C.A. $= 7 - 10$, M.A. $= 3 - 3$), M.F. (C.A. $= 16 - 2$, M.A. $= 4 - 9$), and W.C. (C.A. $= 14 - 4$, M.A. $= 8 - 10$) understood and used both parts of the number transformation. L.L. (C.A. $= 6 - 5$, M.A. $= 2 - 3$) confused them; for example, in (a) and (b) "X_2" went to either "S" or "ϕ".

2. *Auxiliary*

    S.D. (X, Af, v, Y)

    S.C. $X_1 - X_2 - X_3 - X_4 \to X_1 - X_3 + X_2 - \# - X_4$

    where Af is en, ing, or C. v is M, have, be, V.

L.L. and S.W. understood and used this transformation with Af $\to$ C, and v $\to$ V. R.P. understood the full form but did not always use it consistently. M.F. and W.C. understood and used the full form.

3. *Object*

    S.D. $(X, V_t \text{ or Prep, } T + \begin{Bmatrix} he \\ I \end{Bmatrix}, Y)$

    S.C. $X_1 - X_2 - X_3 - X_4 \to X_1 - X_2 - X_3 + M - X_4$

The application of this transformation yields "I hurt him" instead of "I hurt he." It applies to the second NP in the pretransformed stage of $NP+V_t+Comp$ he, thus resulting in "him" not "he" in these sentence.

L.L. and S.W. understood and used this transformation for S.D.:

$$X, V_t, T+ \begin{Bmatrix} he \\ I \end{Bmatrix}, Y$$

but not for the frame $NP+V_t+Comp$ he. The latter frame cannot be generated by their phrase structure grammars. R.P., M.F., and W.C. understood and used this transformation for both frames.

4. *Word boundary*

S.D.(X, Y), where $X=v$ or $Y=Af$

S.C. $X_1-X_2-\rightarrow X_1-\#-X_2$

All of the children understood and used this transformation correctly.

5. *Do*

S.D. $(X, \#, Af, Y)$

S.C. $X_1-X_2-X_3-X_4\rightarrow X_1-X_2-do+X_3-X_4$

All five children understood a restricted form of this transformation with $Af\rightarrow C$, but only R.P., M.F., and W.C. understood and used it in full generality with $Af\rightarrow en$, ing. C.

6. *Negation*

S.D. (a) NP, C, VP$_1$
(b) NP, C+M, X
(c) NP, C+have, X
(d) NP, C+be, X

S.C. $X_1-X_2-X_3\rightarrow X_1-X_2+n't-X_3$

L.L. and S.W. understood and used part (a), R.P. understood all four forms and used (a) often and (b), (c), and (d) infrequently. M.F. and W.C. understood and used all four forms.

7. *Interrogative*

S.D. (a) NP, C, VP$_1$
(b) NP, C+M, X
(c) NP, C+have, X
(d) NP, C+be, X

S.C. $X_1-X_2-X_3\rightarrow X_2-X_1-X_3$

L.L. and S.W. understood and used part (a), and they also understood part (b). R.P. understood all four forms though he had some trouble in using (b), (c), and (d) correctly. M.F. and W.C. understood and used all four forms correctly.

8. *Wh-*

S.D. $(X, T + \begin{bmatrix} he \\ it \end{bmatrix} (M) + \begin{bmatrix} \phi \\ S \end{bmatrix}, Y)$

S.C. $X_1 - X_2 - X_3 \rightarrow Wh - + X_2 - X_1 - X_3$

L.L., S.W., and R.F. used stereotyped questions of this form; however, they did not understand the generalized "Wh-" question transformation. M.F. and W.C. understood and used the form correctly.

9. *Affirmation*

S.D. (a) NP, C, VP$_1$
  (b) NP, C + M, X
  (c) NP, C + have, X
  (d) NP, C + be, X

S.C. $X_1 - X_2 - X_3 \rightarrow X_1 - X_2 + A - X_3$

L.L. and S.W. understood and used part (a), they also understood part (b). R.P. used forms (a) and (b) and understood all four forms. M.F. and W.C. understood and used all four forms.

10. *Contraction*

S.D. (a) NP, X, VP$_1$
  (b) NP, X + M, Y
  (c) NP, X + have, Y
  (d) NP, X + be, Y

S.C. $X_1 - X_2 - X_3 \rightarrow X_1 - X_2 + cntr. - X_3$

L.L. and S.W. understood and used part (a). R.P. understood all four forms but only used (a) and (b). M.F. and W.C. understood and used all four forms.

11. *Inversion*

S.D. $(S, C + V_t, Y)$

S.C. $X_1 - X_2 - X_3 \rightarrow X_3 - X_2 - (easily \ . \ . \ .)$

R.P., M.F., and W.C. understood this transformation, but only W.C. used it.

12. *Elliptic*

S.D. (a) NP, C, VP$_1$
  (b) NP, C + M, X
  (c) NP, C + have, X
  (d) NP, C + be, X

S.C. $X. - X_2 - X_3 \rightarrow X_1 - X_2$

L.L., S.W., and R.P. understood and used part (a). R.P. also used part (b). M.F. and W.C. understood and used all four forms.

13. *Separation*

(a) S.D. (X, V_t, Prt., NP)

S.C. $X_1 - X_2 - X_3 - X_4 \rightarrow X_1 - X_2 - X_4 - X_3$

(This transformation is obligatory if X_4 is a pronoun.)

(b) *S.D. (X, V_t, Comp., NP)

S.C. $X_1 - X_2 - X_3 - X_4 \rightarrow X_1 - X_2 - X_4 - X_3$

All five children understood and used both forms of the transformation, except L.L. and S.W. who did not use part (b).

14. *So*

S.D. (a) NP, C, VP

(b) NP, C+M, X

(c) NP, C+have, X

(d) NP, C+be, X

S.C. $X_1 - X_2 - X_3 \rightarrow so - X_2 - X_1$

Only W.C. understood and used this transformation. R.P. and M.F. understood it but did not use it.

15. *Deletion*

S.D. (X, V_{t32}, Y)

S.C. $X_1 - X_2 - X_3 \rightarrow X_1 - X_2$

All five children understood and used this transformation.

16. *Passive*

S.D. (NP, aux., V_t, NP $\left\{\frac{adv}{}\right\}$)

S.C. $X_1 - X_2 - X_3 - X_4 - X_5 \rightarrow X_4 - X_2 + be + en + X_3 - by + X_1 - X_5$

Only R.P., M.F., and W.C. understood and used passives. Occasionally L.L. and S.W. understood a passive but they appeared to have memorized that specific sentence rather than the generalized "frame."

The Development of Base Syntax in Normal and Linguistically Deviant Children

Donald M. Morehead and David Ingram

Language samples of 15 young normal children actively engaged in learning base syntax were compared with samples of 15 linguistically deviant children of a comparable linguistic level. Mean number of morphemes per utterance was used to determine linguistic level. The two groups were matched according to five linguistic levels previously established, and grammars were written for the language sample of each child. Five aspects of syntactic development were chosen as the basis of comparison between the two groups: phrase structure rules, transformations, construction (or sentence) types, inflectional morphology, and minor lexical categories. While few significant differences were found for the more general aspects of syntax, such as phrase structure rules, frequently occurring transformations, inflectional morphology, and the development of minor lexical categories, significant differences were found for the less general aspects of syntax. For example, significant differences were found between the two groups for infrequently occurring transformations and the number of major syntactic categories per construction type. In addition, the deviant group also showed a marked delay in the onset and acquisition time for learning base syntax. These results are discussed according to transformational and cognitive developmental theory.

Recent evidence suggests that early stages in first language acquisition are difficult to impede, save extensive brain dysfunction. Even with serious brain dysfunction, the prognosis for acquiring a base linguistic system is good due to the plasticity of the developing brain (Lenneberg, 1967). Despite this apparent strong biological component for language development, some children (including those without any detectable brain dysfunction) experience extreme difficulty in acquiring language. Children with language learning deficits are generally felt to demonstrate a linguistic system which is, in certain significant aspects, quite different from that of the normal child. Recently this "qualitative" difference has become the central focus for studying linguistically deviant children (Menyuk, 1964; Lee, 1966).

Menyuk's (1964) early work represents the first systematic attempt to compare normal and deviant children using descriptive techniques based on Chomsky's early transformational grammar. She matched both groups according to the criteria of age, IQ, and socioeconomic level and found that the utterances sampled from linguistically deviant children were qualitatively different from those of normal children. The

From *Journal of Speech and Hearing Research, 16,* 330–352 (1973). Reprinted by permission of the American Speech and Hearing Association.

deviant group used fewer transformations and produced more restricted or ungrammatical forms than did the normal group. More forms were also omitted by the deviant group in constructions representing the phrase structure, transformational, and morphological levels of the grammar. Since few statistically significant differences were found, these results were projected to indicate possible trends of differences between normal and deviant children. Menyuk (1964) did include a comparison between a normal two-year-old child and a deviant three-year-old child. The dissimilarities were again found to be more predominant than the similarities. Unfortunately, only two subjects were compared and they were not matched on any specific criteria.

Lee (1966) has designed four levels of developmental sentence types for comparing syntactic progress in normal and deviant children. In constructing the sentence types which postulate different linguistic levels, she followed closely the review of early work in syntactic development by McNeill (1966). As a pilot test of the utility of the sentence types and linguistic levels, a language sample of a normal three year old was compared with that of a deviant four and one-half year old. The normal child's utterances more closely approximated the sentence types at all four levels than did the utterances of the deviant child. The deviant child also omitted constructions that were not omitted by the normal child. From these findings, Lee concluded that there were qualitative differences between the two children.

The research involving rule-based behavior indicates that all level or stage changes appear to be qualitative (Piaget, 1970; Kohlberg, 1968). Therefore, unless subjects are matched according to criteria which reflect a specific level or stage of development, qualitative differences can be predicted on the basis that each level or stage of development is radically different from the preceding or following stage of development. Moreover, recent work in language acquisition suggests that finding qualitative differences may not be unique to deviant and normal subjects but may reflect linguistic level differences indicating individual differences in cognitive function and linguistic experience (Bloom, 1970; Brown, Cazden, and Bellugi, 1968).

During the past decade, research on language acquisition has focused primarily on the development of syntax. It appears that the most active period for learning base syntax is between 18 months and four years and that this period reflects distinct levels of linguistic development (McNeill, 1970; Brown, 1973). Thus, it is of considerable heuristic value to compare linguistically deviant children with normal children actively engaged in acquiring base syntax at a similar level of linguistic development.

In addition, recent methods for writing children's grammars vary considerably from the early notions of "pivot" grammars which do not include the important distinction between deep (semantic) and surface (phonetic) structure (Bloom, 1970; Brown, 1973). Moreover, if deep and surface structure relations are to be adequately described, it is necessary to collect contextual information for each utterance in a language sample. For example, noun + noun constructions, such as *Daddy bike*, may require two or more deep or semantic interpretations to separate the possessive form from such forms as the subject-object. Grammar writing for young children now includes analysis of both aspects of grammatical relations (Bloom, 1970; Brown, 1973).

This study compared language samples that included contextual information of young normal children (18-36 months of age) actively engaged in learning syntax with those of deviant children of a comparable level of linguistic development.

METHOD

SUBJECTS. The subjects were 15 normal and 15 linguistically deviant children, selected to represent as nearly as possible the five linguistic levels previously determined by Brown (1973), (Table 1). Mean morpheme per utterance was used as the criterion for establishing linguistic level and, thus, for matching the two groups. This measure appears to be a more reliable indicator of linguistic development than is chronological age up to three years of age (Menyuk, 1969; Bloom, 1970; Brown, 1973). The normal group, representing the age when children acquire a base syntactic system, was selected from the population of the Bing Nursery School at Stanford University and within the Stanford community. The deviant group was selected from the deviant population of children currently seen at the Institute for Childhood Aphasia, Stanford University School of Medicine.

Three children from each group were assigned to each of Brown's five linguistic levels of development on the basis of the mean number of morphemes per utterance. Level I utterances were slightly over two morphemes in length, while Level V utterances had slightly under six morphemes per utterance (Table 1). The age range for the normal group was one year, seven months to three years, one month, with a mean

Table 1   Description of Normal and Deviant Language-Development Groups in Terms of Mean Number of Morphemes per Utterance (MM/U), Mean Sample Size (Number of Relational Utterances), and Mean Age (Months). For Comparison, the Five Levels of Linguistic Development Defined by Brown (see Footnote 1) Are Presented. The Ranges on Which the Mean for Each Group Was Based Are Given Immediately Below the MM/U in Parentheses

Brown		Normal			Deviant		
Linguistic Level	MM/U	MM/U	Sample Size	Age	MM/U	Sample Size	Age
I	2.00	2.33	76.7	20.0	2.33	79.7	62.3
	(1.75-2.25)	(2.11-2.26)			(2.10-2.43)		
II	2.50	2.72	100.7	21.0	2.83	155.3	71.3
	(2.26-2.75)	(2.51-2.66)			(2.69-2.98)		
III	3.13	3.70	223.3	33.0	3.80	161.0	70.0
	(2.76-3.50)	(3.41-3.92)			3.31-4.05)		
IV	3.75	4.67	242.7	34.3	4.53	200.0	88.0
	(3.51-4.00)	(4.62-4.86)			(4.33-4.73)		
V	4.63	5.61	234.0	33.7	5.83	147.7	104.6
	(4.01-5.25)	(5.36-5.88)			(5.21-6.50)		

age of two years, four months. The deviant group had an age range of three years, six months to nine years, six months, with a mean age of six years, seven months (Table 1). The normal group was screened for speech and hearing pathologies. The linguistically deviant group was restricted to children who lacked sufficient intellectual or physiological impairment to account for their difficulties in acquiring language.

An adaptation of Chomsky's (1965) transformational grammar by Rosenbaum (1967) was modified (Ingram, 1970) and grammars were written for the language sample of each child. Rosenbaum's (1967) system was selected because it incorporates many of the recent advances on Chomsky's (1965) transformational grammar. The grammars accounted for all but 8 to 10% of the utterances in the samples of both groups. The two groups representing five linguistic levels of development were compared according to (1) phrase structure rules, (2) transformations, (3) construction types or surface realization of major syntactic categories and their relations, (4) inflectional morphology, and (5) select lexical items representing minor syntactic categories.

The five linguistic aspects were chosen because they reflect a broad assessment of base syntactic development. Phrase structure and transformational analysis presumably characterize some important aspects of the child's knowledge about sentence organization. From the characterization of the child's grammars, certain criterion measures were developed for comparing type and occurrence of phrase structures and transformations. In addition, construction types, inflectional morphology, and minor lexical items were selected to represent important aspects of the realization of the child's knowledge of sentences. However, the grammars were written from production data and therefore, in any strict sense, assess only language performance.

LANGUAGE SAMPLES.   The language samples were collected under three conditions: free play with the experimenter or parent, elicitation while playing with toys, and elicitation while viewing a standard children's book. It was generally possible to collect samples under all three conditions, except for the younger normal children and the lower-level deviant children. In cases where it was not possible to collect the samples under all three conditions, samples were collected only under the first two conditions. The utterances of each sample were divided into spontaneous and response utterances to determine whether the conditions under which the samples were collected had differential effects for the two groups. The proportion of spontaneous to response utterances was nearly identical in both groups. In addition, separate grammars were written for the two types of utterances in each sample to determine any differences which might be attributed to performance variables or to the conditions used in collecting the samples. Since few differences were found, the spontaneous and response utterances were pooled for group comparison.

A high-fidelity tape recorder was used to record the linguistic interaction between the adult and the child. In addition, an observer recorded the initial adult utterance, if any, the child's utterance, and the adult expansion of the child's utterance. The expansion of the child's utterance was determined by the contextual information collected when the language sample was taken. In this way, the child's intended grammatical and semantic relations were more closely approximated than by tape recordings or by observational records alone. The utterances were then transcribed, generally on the same day, and compared with the observer's records before a final decision was made.

The mean number of utterances for the normal group was 175.5, while the mean number of utterances for the deviant group was 148.7. One-word utterances were not included in the samples of either group so that each utterance would involve base syntactic relations. In addition, each linguistic structure had to occur two or more times in order to be considered part of the child's productive system.

Established criteria do not exist for determining what is an adequate sample size for linguistic analysis. The number of utterances used in analysis varies considerably from less than 100 (Menyuk, 1964) to over 1500 utterances (Bloom, 1970). Brown (1973) collected nearly 700 utterances, including one-word utterances, for each time sample. We attempted to collect 100 relational utterances for the two lower levels of linguistic development and 200 relational utterances for the three upper levels of linguistic development (Table 1).

RESULTS

The phrase structure grammars necessary to account for the utterances of the normal and deviant groups were nearly identical for each of the five levels. Minor differences did appear in the grammars for the two groups at each of the five levels, but these differences were no greater than the differences between subjects within the same group at a given linguistic level. Two examples of the phrase structure grammars taken from one normal and one deviant child are presented in the list below. (A detailed description of the grammars is available in Ingram [in press].) In the list, S = sentence, NP = noun phrase, VP = verb phrase, N = noun, VB = verb, ( ) = optional element, # = sentence boundary, and → = "is rewritten as."

Normal—MM/U-2.66	*Deviant—MM/U-2.69*
S → (NP) (VP)	S → (NP) (VP)
VP → VB (NP)	VP → VB (NP)
NP → N (S)	NP → N (S)
Conditions:	Conditions:
1. (S) is either an	1. (S) is a possessive
adjective or possessive	
2. (S) only occurs	2. (S) only occurs
when S → NP	when S → NP

The two grammars are equally capable of generating or accounting for the utterances of either the deviant or the normal child, with the single restriction that the deviant child does not include adjective modifiers in constructions taking the form N (S).

The two groups also did not differ significantly in the proportion of utterances reflecting only phrase structure relations across the five linguistic levels. The proportion of phrase structure utterances, however, decreased with linguistic level for both the normal and the deviant groups. Nearly half the utterances at Level II were without transformations, while fewer than 10% of the utterances were without transformations at Level III. This rather dramatic change in phrase-structure-transformations ratio between Levels II and III held for both groups. Despite these similarites, when chronological age rather than linguistic level was considered, the deviant group showed a marked delay as compared to normals in both onset and acquisition time. The age disparity between the two groups, although the data are cross-sectional, suggests that the onset time for base syntax or two-word utterances may be delayed as much as three and one-half years in the deviant child. Moreover, acquisition time, or the time required to go from Level I to V, is nearly two and one-half years longer for the deviant children. This delay in onset and acquisition time also holds for transformations, construction types, inflections, and minor lexical categories. Given that normal children initiate and acquire base syntax between approximately 18 and 40 months, it appears that deviant children take on the average three times as long to initiate and to acquire base syntax.

Forty different transformations were identified in the language samples of both groups. The transformations of each group were assigned absolute ranks based on their frequency of occurrence. Listed in Appendix A are the transformations in order of their frequency of occurrence and examples of each. The examples provide the base form and its corresponding transformation. A Spearman rank order correlation was significant ($r = 0.96, t = 21.30, p < 0.01$), indicating a high degree of similarity

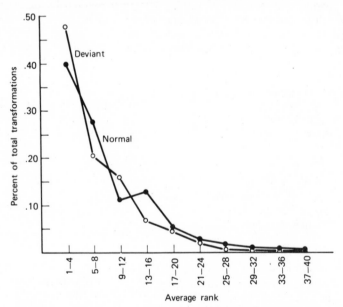

Figure 1.   The average rank of the 40 transformations and their frequency of occurrence for the normal and deviant groups.

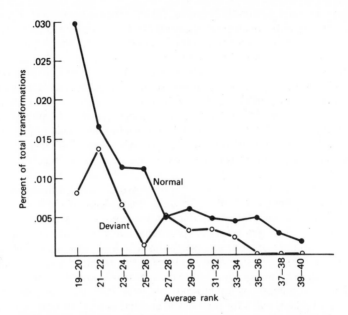

Figure 2.   The average rank of the infrequently occurring transformations and their frequency of occurrence for the normal and deviant groups.

between the two groups (Figure 1). In addition, the 40 transformations were compared individually for the two groups using the Mann-Whitney U Test (Siegel, 1956). Four of the 40 transformations showed significantly greater occurrence for the normal group (question *do* segment, locative segment, demonstrative segment, and noun deletion), while two showed significantly greater occurrence for the deviant group (progressive affix segment and plural affix segment).

To determine any differences between the two groups on infrequently occurring transformations, the 40 transformations were divided into frequently occurring and infrequently occurring transformations. Figure 1 shows that a convenient boundary exists between the frequent and infrequent transformations near the twentieth transformation for both groups. In order that an equal number of transformations could be compared, they were divided between the 20 most frequent and the 20 least frequent transformations. A sign test (Siegel, 1956) revealed no significant difference for the frequent transformations, while the infrequent transformations revealed a significant difference ($p < 0.06$). This finding suggests that while no overall significance exists between the two groups on the frequency of transformation types, the least frequent transformations, and those presumably more difficult as a group, were used significantly less by the deviant group. The infrequent transformations occurred 5% or less of the time (Figure 2).

An additional check was made to determine if more specific differential use of the transformations could be found between the two groups. The 40 transformations were divided into four general categories: (1) sentence transformations, (2) noun transformations, (3) verb transformations, and (4) question transformations. Significant linguistic level effects were found for sentence transformations ($F = 8.70$; $df = 4,20$; $p < 0.01$), noun transformations ($F = 48.62$; $df = 4,20$; $p < 0.01$), verb transformations ($F = 10.90$; $df = 4,20$; $P < 0.01$), and question transformations ($F = 9.32$; $df = 4,20$; $p < 0.01$). However, significant group differences were only found for question transformations ($F = 27.17$; $df = 1,20$; $p < 0.01$). In addition, a significant interaction was found between linguistic level and the two groups ($F = 5.53$; $df = 4,20$; $p < 0.01$) as a result of one deviant child having more questions marked at Level I, namely, marking questions by wh forms. The normal group had significantly more question transformations at the four remaining linguistic levels (Figure 3).

As noted previously, significant level differences were found for the transformation types across the five linguistic levels of development. Appendixes B and C present the transformations showing their frequency of occurrence at each of the five linguistic levels for the normal and deviant groups, respectively. The lists indicate that both the number and type of transformations change with each advancing level of development, and that there is considerable similarity in the transformational development of both groups across the five levels of linguistic development.

Finally, the mean number of transformations used per utterance was compared across the five linguistic levels for the normal and the deviant groups. No significant group differences were found; however, a significant level effect was found ($F = 66.12$; $df = 4,20$; $p < 0.001$), and the differences were significant for both groups across all five levels (Figure 4). When the mean number of transformations per utter-

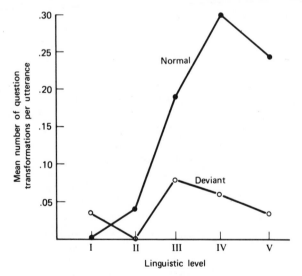

Figure 3.   The mean number of question transformations per utterance plotted across five linguistic levels for the normal and deviant groups.

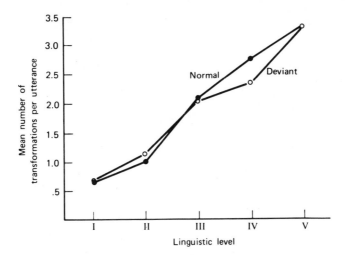

Figure 4. The mean number of transformations per utterance plotted across five linguistic levels for the normal and deviant groups.

ance was correlated with age, the normal group had high positive correlation ($r = 0.905; p < 0.01$), while the deviant group did not ($r = 0.161$). Again, a major finding is the marked delay in onset time and acquisition period for acquiring transformations.

The construction types depict major lexical categories (that is, noun, verb, and noun_object) and their syntactic frames or possible relations (noun-verb and noun-verb-noun). Appendix D provides a list of the construction types and their corresponding examples. Two measures were derived from the construction types and compared for the two groups. The mean number of major lexical categories per construction type was used to determine the occurrence of major categories in a variety of contexts for the language samples of both groups. Significant differences were obtained between the two groups ($F = 5.51; df = 1,20; p < 0.05$) and across the five linguistic levels ($F = 23.81; df = 4,20; p < 0.01$) (Figure 5). In addition, each syntactic relation or construction type was compared for the two groups on the basis of their frequency of occurrence. A low positive correlation was found when the construction types of the two groups were compared ($r = 0.435$). When age was correlated with mean number of lexical categories per construction type, the normals showed a high correlation with age ($r = 0.762; p < 0.01$), while the deviant group showed a low correlation with age ($r = 0.136$). The deviant group again manifested the marked delay in onset and acquisition time.

Linguistic level was found to be significant for both groups on the number of lexical categories per construction type. Appendixes E and F provide a list of the construction types in order of their frequency of occurrence for both groups at each of the five linguistic levels. The tables show that the type and number of constructions change for both groups with advancing levels of linguistic development. However,

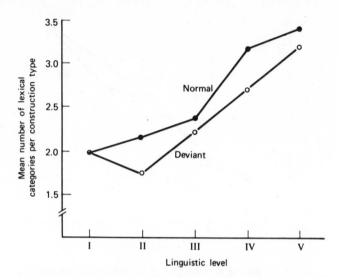

Figure 5.   The mean number of lexical categories per
construction type plotted across five linguistic levels
for the normal and deviant groups.

as the tables clearly indicate, the deviant group did not use major linguistic categories
in as many different contexts or syntactic frames as did the normal group.

To determine the relative increase in the occurrence of inflections such as plurals,
past tense, and possessives across the five linguistic levels, word-morpheme ratios
were computed for the two groups. Utterances had either no inflections (that is,

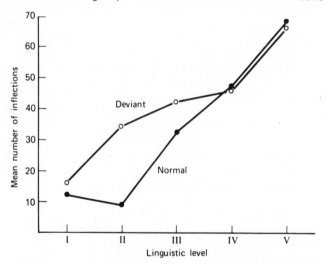

Figure 6.   The mean number of inflections plotted
across five linguistic levels for normal and deviant
groups.

two words, two morphemes) or two inflections (that is, five words, seven morphemes). The findings were not significant for the two groups, although a significant level effect was again found ($F = 71.81$; $df = 4,20$, $p < 0.01$). The deviant group did, however, have more inflections at the first three linguistic levels than did the normal group (Figure 6).

Select lexical items that represent minor lexical categories were also compared for the two groups. The lexical items used for comparison were pronouns, demonstratives, wh forms, prepositions, and modals. The primary concern in this comparison

Table 2   Linguistic Level and Order of Appearance of Minor Lexical Categories for the Normal Group

Linguistic Category Level	Normal				
	I	II	III	IV	V
Pronouns	I	my it it me	you your she them	we he they us you him his	her its her our
Demonstratives	that	this	these	those	
Wh forms		where	what	why	when
Prepositions		in on	to with	up at for	down of off like through over by under near
Modals	want		gonna hafta	can will could shall	won't don't can't gotta would may might should better

Table 3   Linguistic Level and Order of Appearance of Minor Lexical
Categories for the Deviant Group

Linguistic Category Level	Deviant				
	I	II	III	IV	V
Pronouns	it I my	him	you it he them they she we you us your his	her their	its our her
Demonstratives	that	these	this	those	
Wh forms		what		where why	how when who
Prepositions	in		on at to down	with like	up of off out of for over by after into about except
Modals			gonna	can't can want	don't won't gotta would hadda will could didn't hafta

was to determine at what level and in what order the various items appeared for the two groups. Thus, two or more children at each linguistic level had to use a given lexical category two or more times in order for that category to be included. With the exception of pronouns, only minor variance was found in the level or order of appearance of the lexical items. The deviant group by Level III had 16 pronouns, while the normal group had nine pronouns (Tables 2 and 3).

DISCUSSION

Clearly, the major differences between normal and linguistically deviant children of comparable linguistic level were not in the organization or occurrence of specific subcomponents of their base syntactic systems. Rather, the significant differences were found in the onset and acquisition time necessary for learning base syntax and the use of aspects of that system, once acquired, for producing major lexical items in a variety of utterances.

Phrase structure development showed similar rule systems as well as similar occurrences of phrase structure utterances for both groups across five distinct levels of linguistic development. No overall differences were found in the frequency or type of transformational rules produced in the language samples of the two groups. Of the 40 transformations compared, only six were significantly different in their frequency of occurrence. Four occurred more frequently in the normal group (question *do* segment, locative, demonstrative, and noun deletion), while two occurred more frequently in the deviant group (progressive affix and plural affix). Moreover, the mean number of transformations per utterance used by the two groups across the five levels was not significantly different, indicating no severe limitation in the deviant group in the number of transformations used in a particular utterance.

The two groups were also compared on frequently occurring and infrequently occurring transformations and four general categories of transformations. Significant differences were found between the two groups on infrequently occurring transformations and the general category of questions. The findings for differences in infrequently occurring transformations are similar to those of Menyuk (1964). Of the 28 transformations compared according to the number of subjects using a given transformation, she found that 16 were used less often by the deviant group. However, only one of the 16 transformations was used significantly less often by the deviant group. The relative absence of questions in the language samples of our deviant group could reflect either a general sampling problem inherent to children with productive liabilities or a general sociolinguistic posture which is antithetical to seeking information by linguistic code. It would be difficult to assume that question transformations are psychologically more difficult than many of the transformations acquired by the deviant group.

The development of inflections and minor lexical items (pronouns, demonstratives, wh forms, prepositions, and modals) was also compared in the two groups. In the case of minor lexical items, only minor variance was found in the level or the order of appearance of these items, save pronouns. The deviant group at Level III had 16 pronouns as compared to nine for the normal group at the same level. The amount of time the deviant group spent between Levels II and III seemed to allow them to make more distinctions between self and others and for those distinctions to be linguistically marked.

There were no significant differences in the development of inflections as determined by word-morpheme ratio. The deviant group, however, did have more inflections at the first three levels of linguistic development than did the normal group. This difference was also reflected in the comparison of transformation types where both the progressive and plural affix were used significantly more often by the deviant group. These differences may reflect both the increased time the deviant group spends at each linguistic level and the fact that since inflections are not introduced by major transformations, they are easily detected in the surface structure. Where cognitive distinctions such as number are easily marked linguistically, as in the case of plural forms, deviant children appear to be somewhat less delayed in acquiring these forms.

Though few differences were found in phrase structure or transformational development, save infrequently occurring transformations and questions and including the mean number of transformations used per utterance, significant differences were found in the number of major lexical categories per construction type. Since the two groups were matched on essentially mean number of major lexical categories per utterance, the finding suggests a specific restriction in the variety of construction types produced by the deviant group. This finding is further supported by the low correlation found when types of constructions were compared between the two groups. Transformations also affect the variety of construction types produced, and a significant difference was found between the two groups on the infrequently occurring transformations.

These results suggest that deviant children, when studied at their particular level of linguistic development, are not seriously deficient in the organization of phrase structure rules, types of transformations, number of transformations used in a given utterance, minor lexical items, or inflectional morphology. However, deviant children appear to be significantly restricted in their ability to develop and select grammatical and semantic features which allow existent and new major lexical categories to be assigned to larger sets of syntactic frames. To clarify the specific deficit these results indicate, it is useful to discuss the findings in terms of Chomsky's transformational grammar.

In Chomsky's (1965) linguistic system, the base component of transformational grammar is composed of a categorical component and a lexicon. The categorical component handles general properties of the deep structure, such as defining grammatical relations and determining base syntactic order. The lexicon handles less general properties, including (1) properties relevant to the function of transformational rules, (2) information regarding the varied placement of lexical items in a sentence, and (3) properties relevant to semantic interpretation. Thus, grammatical relations and order are determined by the categorical component, while contextual restrictions are determined by the lexicon.

The utterances produced by the deviant group manifested grammatical relations and base syntactic order not unlike that of the normal group. The finding of similar phrase structure rules indicates that the two groups were not different in their base organization for the categorical component. However, the members of the deviant group were restricted in their ability to handle less general properties specified by the lexicon as indicated by the finding of differences on infrequently occurring transformations and major lexical categories per construction type. When compared with normals, they also showed a low correlation on types of constructions. Specifically, these restrictions would involve the function of transformational rules and information regarding varied placement of lexical items in a sentence. In addition, the delay in both onset and acquisition time for base syntax is, no doubt, closely related to the deviant group's ability to assign an adequate semantic interpretation to an utterance in comprehension as well as production. The properties of the lexicon are also closely related to how well formed an utterance is. Our observations of the language samples and those of Menyuk (1969) suggest that the utterances produced by deviant children are on the whole less well formed than those of normal children.

Other research has also found that linguistically deviant children have a specific deficit that is quantitatively different from normal children rather than a general qualitative deficit. Studies in both language and cognitive development have reported similar findings on the nature of the difference between normal and deviant children. Lackner (1968) reported that retarded children of different mental ages do not develop language behavior differently from normal children, but rather reflect a delayed developmental sequence with lower terminal development.

Inhelder (1966) and de Ajuriaguerra (1966) have studied the cognitive development of linguistically deviant children. Using Piagetian-type tasks, they found that children with a slow rate of linguistic development frequently had normal operative or base intellectual development. However, the deviant children did show a specific deficit in the figurative or representational aspect of cognition. According to Piaget's (1970) cognitive developmental theory, the child develops a general capacity for representation which includes aspects of perception, deferred imitation, imagery, symbolic play, drawing, and dreaming, as well as language.

The importance of these findings is that they suggest a possible relationship between delayed language acquisition and an underlying aspect of cognitive development. For example, perceptual deficiencies, which in Piaget's theory are related to general representational development, have long been suspect in children who fail to develop language at a normal rate. Such deficits have been demonstrated in both vision and audition (Mackworth, Grandstaff, and Pribram, in press; Rosenthal and Eisenson[1]). Moreover, Grandstaff et al.[2] have shown that the performance of linguistically deviant children on a simple match to sample task is not different from that of normal children in terms of the number of matching errors. However, the deviant children take nearly twice as long, once the correct symbol is located, to indicate their choice. These findings are consistent with those of Inhelder (1966) and de Ajuriaguerra (1966), who also found that deviant children are deficient in their ability to evoke reproductive images necessary for solving simple matching tasks. Lovell, Hoyle, and Siddal (1968) report a significant correlation between mean morpheme per utterance length and the amount of time spent in symbolic play by linguistically

---

[1] W. Rosenthal and J. Eisenson, unpublished study on auditory temporal order in aphasic children as a function of selected stimulus features, personal communication.

[2] N. Grandstaff, N. Mackworth, A de la Pena, and K. Pribram, unpublished study on model formation and use by aphasic and normal children during visual matching to sample, personal communication.

deviant children, that is, the fewer the number of morphemes per utterance, the less time spent in symbolic play.

In summary, linguistically deviant children do not develop bizarre linguistic systems that are qualitatively different from normal children. Rather, they develop quite similar linguistic systems with a marked delay in the onset and acquisition time. Moreover, once the linguistic systems are developed, deviant children do not use them as creatively as normal children for producing highly varied utterances. Other research suggests that these children may have a specific cognitive deficit in all aspects of representational behavior which, according to Piaget, includes language.

ACKNOWLEDGMENT

This research was supported by the National Institute of Neurological Diseases and Stroke Research Grant NS-07514 to the Institute for Childhood Aphasia, Stanford University School of Medicine. We want to express our appreciation to Jon Eisenson, project director, and to Dorothy Tyack, Judith Johnston, and Geoffrey Loftus for their assistance in the collection and analysis of the data. The authors also wish to extend special gratitude to Mark Solomon whose general competencies were invaluable to the study.

REFERENCES

AJURIAGUERRA, J. DE., Speech disorders in childhood. In C. Carterette (Ed.), *Brain Function: Speech, Language, and Communication.* (Vol. III) Los Angeles, Cal.: Univ. of California Press (1966).

BLOOM, L., *Language Development: Form and Function in Emerging Grammars.* Cambridge, Mass.: The MIT Press (1970).

BROWN, R., *A First Language.* Cambridge, Mass.: Harvard Univ. Press (1973).

BROWN, R., CAZDEN, C., and BELLUGI, U., The child's grammar from I to III. In S. P. Hill (Ed.), *The 1967 Minnesota Symposium on Child Psychology.* Minneapolis: Univ. of Minnesota Press (1968).

CHOMSKY, N., *Aspects of the Theory of Syntax.* Cambridge, Mass.: The MIT Press (1965).

INGRAM, D., IBM Grammar II: An adaptation for child language. In *Papers and Reports on Child Language Development.* Stanford University, December (1970).

INGRAM, D., The development of phrase structure rules. *Lang. Learn., 22,* 23–33 (1972).

INHELDER, B., Cognitive development and its contribution to the diagnosis of some phenomena of mental deficiency. *Merrill-Palmer Quart., 12,* 299–319 (1966).

KOHLBERG, L., Early education: A cognitive developmental view. *Child Devel., 39,* 1013–1062 (1968).

LACKNER, J., A developmental study of language behavior in retarded children. *Neuropsychol., 6,* 301–320 (1968).

LEE, L., Developmental sentence types: A method for comparing normal and deviant syntactic development. *J. Speech Hearing Dis., 31,* 311–330 (1966).

LENNEBERG, E. H., *Biological Foundations of Language.* New York: John Wiley (1967).

LOVELL, K., HOYLE, H., and SIDDALL, M., A study of some aspects of the play and language of young children with delayed speech. *J. Child Psychol. Psychiat., 9,* 41–50 (1968).

MACKWORTH, N., GRANDSTAFF, N., and PRIBRAM, K., Prolonged orientation to pictorial novelty in severely speech-disordered children. *Neuropsychol.* (in press).

McNEILL, D., Developmental psycholinguistics. In F. Smith and G. A. Miller (Eds.), *The Genesis of Language: A Psycholinguistic Approach.* Cambridge, Mass.: MIT Press (1966).

McNeill, D., *The Acquisition of Language: The Study of Developmental Psycholinguistics*. New York: Harper and Row (1970).

Menyuk, P., Comparison of grammar of children with functionally deviant and normal speech. *J. Speech Hearing Res.*, **7**, 109–121 (1964).

Menyuk, P., *Sentences Children Use*. Cambridge, Mass.: The MIT Press (1969).

Piaget, J., Piaget's theory. In P. H. Mussen (Ed.), *Carmichael's Manual of Child Psychology*. (Vol. I) New York: John Wiley (1970).

Rosenbaum, P., *IBM Grammar II, IBM Research Report*. (1967).

Siegel, S., *Non-parametric Statistics*. New York: McGraw-Hill (1956).

Appendix A

Forty transformations listed in order of their combined frequency of occurrence for the normal and deviant groups. The examples provide the base form and its corresponding transformation.

Frequent Types	*Examples*
Pronoun segment	Ball . . . it
Article segment	Ball . . . a ball
Demonstrative segment	Ball . . . that ball
Preposition segment	Table . . . on table
Adjective genitive placement	Ball red . . . red ball
Verb particle segment	I go . . . I go up
Type placement	Not I go . . . I not go
Locative segment	Table . . . there
Plural affix segment	Ball . . . balls
Progressive affix segment	He go . . . he going
Copula contraction	It is red . . . it's red
Number segment	Ball . . . two ball
Wh question	That ball . . . what ball
Noun deletion	That ball . . . that
	John's ball . . . John's
Progressive auxiliary segment	He running . . . he is running
Present affix segment	He run . . . he runs
Conjunction segment	Boy girl . . . boy and girl
Question tone	Ball . . . ball?
Infinitive segment	I want go . . . I want to go
Question *do* segment	I go . . . do I go?

Infrequent Types	*Examples*
Copula segment	It red . . . I make it red
Negative *do* segment	I not go . . . I do not go
Tag question	I go . . . don't I?
Past affix segment	I bat . . . I batted
Question copula shift	He is going . . . is he going?
Pronoun number segment	Them . . . two of them
Complete all segment	It gone . . . it all gone
Genitive affix segment	John ball . . . John's ball
Vocative segment	I go home . . . Daddy, I go home

Verb deletion	I pick up ball . . . I up ball
Verb qualifier statement	I run . . . I (really) run
	(just)
Inchoative segment	It red . . . it got red
Particle intensive segment	I go up . . . I go (way) up
	(back)
	(right)
Verb particle shift	I pick ball up . . . I pick up ball
Question modal shift	He will go . . . will he go?
Noun object shift	Hit ball . . . ball hit
Stative verb particle shift	Ball up . . . up ball
Object noun retention	Hit ball . . . hit it ball
Repetition segment	I go . . . I go again
Demonstrative copula	That there . . . that's there

Appendix B

Transformation types pooled in order of their frequency of occurrence across five linguistic levels of development for the normal group.

Linguistic Level I
Locative segment
Pronoun number segment
Adjective genitive placement
Complete all segment
Pronoun segment
Vocative segment
Preposition segment
Stative verb particle shift
Demonstrative segment
Verb qualifier segment
Plural affix segment

Linguistic Level II
Adjective genitive placement
Article segment
Verb particle segment
Plural affix segment
Demonstrative segment
Pronoun segment
Locative segment
Noun object shift
Question tone
Noun deletion
Wh question
Pronoun number segment
Verb deletion
Object noun retention
Noun retention

Linguistic Level III
Demonstrative segment
Verb particle segment
Pronoun segment
Preposition segment
Article segment
Locative segment
Noun deletion
Pronoun number segment
Adjective genitive placement
Wh question
Type placement
Present affix segment
Question tone
Progressive affix segment
Plural affix segment
Infinitive segment
Copula contraction
Progressive auxiliary segment
Conjunction segment
Question *do* segment
Inchoative segment
Tag question
Question copula shift
Copula segment
Past affix segment
Verb particle shift
Verb deletion

Linguistic Level IV
Pronoun segment
Demonstrative segment
Type placement
Preposition segment
Adjective genitive placement
Article segment
Wh question
Verb particle segment
Copula contraction
Pronoun number segment
Locative segment
Noun deletion
Progressive affix segment
Plural affix segment
Question *do* segment
Progressive auxiliary segment
Present affix segment
Question tone
Conjunction segment
Tag question
Copula segment
Infinitive segment
Genitive affix segment
Question copula shift
Negative *do* segment
Question modal shift
Verb particle shift
Past affix segment

Linguistic Level V
Demonstrative segment
Pronoun segment
Article segment
Preposition segment
Type placement
Adjective genitive placement
Verb particle segment
Locative segment
Present affix segment
Copula contraction
Wh question
Noun deletion
Pronoun number segment
Plural affix segment
Question *do* segment
Infinitive segment
Conjunction segment
Negative *do* segment
Copula segment
Past affix segment
Question copula shift
Pronoun number segment
Progressive affix segment
Question tone
Tag question
Progressive auxiliary segment
Question modal shift
Verb qualifier segment
Repetition segment
Genitive affix segment

Appendix C

Transformation types pooled in order of their frequency of occurrence across five linguistic levels of development for the deviant group.

Linguistic Level I
Adjective genitive placement
Plural affix segment
Number segment
Locative segment
Wh question
Verb particle segment
Pronoun segment
Progressive affix segment

Linguistic Level I
Demonstrative segment
Preposition segment
Copula contraction
Noun object shift

Linguistic Level II
Article segment
Preposition segment

Linguistic Level II
Progressive affix segment
Adjective genitive placement
Verb particle segment
Pronoun segment
Demonstrative segment
Plural affix segment
Verb deletion
Genitive affix segment
Locative segment
Number segment
Noun deletion
Demonstrative copula

Linguistic Level III
Article segment
Pronoun segment
Preposition segment
Demonstrative segment
Progressive affix segment
Plural affix segment
Adjective genitive placement
Locative segment
Verb particle segment
Type placement
Wh question
Noun deletion
Conjunction segment
Copula contraction
Number segment
Question tone
Progressive auxiliary segment
Copula segment
Demonstrative copula
Pronoun number segment
Past affix segment
Verb particle shift
Present affix segment

Linguistic Level IV
Article segment
Pronoun segment
Preposition segment
Adjective genitive placement
Verb particle segment
Demonstrative segment
Plural affix segment

Linguistic Level IV
Progressive affix segment
Progressive auxiliary segment
Type placement
Question tone
Locative segment
Wh question
Conjunction segment
Number segment
Noun deletion
Infinitive segment
Copula contraction
Negative *do* segment
Past affix segment
Copula segment
Inchoative segment
Present affix segment
Demonstrative copula

Linguistic Level V
Pronoun segment
Article segment
Preposition segment
Adjective genitive placement
Type placement
Progressive auxiliary segment
Progressive affix segment
Copula contraction
Plural affix segment
Demonstrative segment
Verb particle segment
Conjunction segment
Number segment
Present affix segment
Infinitive segment
Past affix segment
Negative *do* segment
Locative segment
Wh question
Genitive affix segment
Verb qualifier segment
Copula segment
Question *do* segment
Question tone
Complete all segment

Appendix D

Construction types listed in order of their combined frequency of occurrence for the normal and deviant groups. Key: N = noun, VB = verb, V = copula, T = type, N_o = object noun (used only with copula), N_{loc} = locative noun, Q = question, S = sentence, and Tag_Q = tag question.

Construction Types	Examples
N-VB-N	Me find a hotdog
VB-N	Open the gate
N-VB	Ducks are quacking
N	Another hamburger
$N-V-N_o$	That's a ladder
N-T-VB-N	We will take this out
$N-V-N_{loc}$	Here's an owl
VB	Go up
N-S	Pretty shoe
Q-N-VB-N	Do you got a hurt?
N-T-VB	I hafta go
$Q-N-V-N_{loc}$	Where the dolls?
$Q-N-V-N_o$	Is this a hot dog?
N-VB-N-N	We have the bear for dinner
$N-V-N_o-S$	Here's my knee
Q-N-VB	Are you going?
VB-N-N	Put truck in garage
N-VB-N-S	I have blue box
Q-N-T-VB-N	Would you do this?
N-T-VB-N-N	I'm gonna put playdough on it
T-VB-N	Gonna take this
Q-N-T-VB	Why doesn't this stay up?
VB-N-VB-N	Let's take this off
VB-N-S	Fix Jim's car
N-VB-VB-N	He went to fix the baby
T-VB	Gonna go
N-T	It isn't
$N-S-V-N_{loc}$	Round balls in there
Q-N-T-VB-N-N	Where the people gon drive on it?
$Q-N-S-V-N_{loc}$	Where's his dinner?
VB-N-VB	Make this one stand up
Q-VB-N	Go here?
$Q-N-S-V-N_o$	What is the name of this color?
VB-N-VB-N-N	Let's put these back in here
N-T-VB-N-S	I can't ride a big bike
$N-VB-N-Tag_Q$	You put these back, okay?
Greeting N	Hi daddy

N-S-VB-N	My mommy put them on
N-S-VB	Poor snail cry
Q-N	Right here?
N-T-VB-N-Tag$_Q$	I have to put this away, okay?
Q-N-VB-N-N	What do you put in there?
N-T-V-N$_o$	There's no water
N-VB-S	I think it is
Q-N-T	It can?
Q-N-V-N$_o$-N$_{loc}$	What's that in there?
Q-N-V-N$_o$-S	That mommy's bear?
Adverb-S-S	When you have your mask on, it scares you
N-V-N$_{loc}$-Tag$_Q$	It was in here, wasn't it?
S-what-S	Look what he taked from you
VB-VB	Want go
N-S-S	A big big bear
VB-VB-N	Gonna put these away
VB-N-VB	Make this one stand up
N-V-N$_o$-Tag$_Q$	There a train, right?
Q-N-VB-N-S	When do we had the marble game?
Q-N-VB-VB	Who mommy want hit?
N-VB-N-VB	You make it stand up
N-VB-N-VB-N	I want you stay there
N-VB-VB	I want talk
S-because-S	This doesn't open because it's too little
N-VB-N-N-S	I have this in my program
N-V-N$_o$-N	There's more in it
N-N	Elephants and giraffes
T-VB-N-N	Gonna take this one home
N-say-S	My mom said I can't go
N-VB-VB-N-S	I want to go to the marble game
N-S-V-N$_o$	Dog name's Jippy
N-VB-N-S-N	It's got my thumb in this
N-T-VB-N-N-S	He will throw ball in his eyes

Appendix E

Construction types pooled in order of their frequency of occurrence across five linguistic levels of development for the normal group.

Linguistic Level I	*Linguistic Level I*	*Linguistic Level I*
N-VB	N-V-N$_{loc}$	N-VB-N
VB-N	N-V-N$_o$	N-T
N	N-S	Greeting-N
VB	T-VB	N-S-V-N$_{loc}$

Linguistic Level I
VB-N-S
Q-N-V-N$_o$

Linguistic Level II
VB-N
N-VB-N
N-S
N-VB
VB
N
N-V-N$_{loc}$
VB-N-S
VB-N-N
Q-N-VB
N-S-VB
N-VB-N-S
Greeting-N
VB-VB
N-S-S

Linguistic Level III
VB-N
N-VB-N
N-VB
VB
N
N-V-N$_o$
N-V-N$_{loc}$
Q-N-V-N$_{loc}$
VB-N-N
N-S
N-T-VB-N
N-VB-N-N
Q-N-VB-N
T-VB-N
N-T-VB
Q-N-VB
Q-N-V-N$_o$
N-V-N$_o$-S
N-VB-VB-N
N-VB-VB
N-S-VB-N
N-VB-S
Q-N-T-VB-N
VB-N-S
VB-VB-N
T-VB
VB-N-VB

Linguistic Level III
N-T
N-VB-N-S-N

Linguistic Level IV
N-VB-N
N-VB
N-T-VB-N
Q-N-VB-N
N-V-N$_o$
VB-N
N
Q-N-V-N$_o$
N-T-VB
N-V-N$_{loc}$
Q-N-T-VB
N-S
Q-N-V-N
Q-N-VB
N-V-N$_o$-S
VB-N-N
T-VB-N
Q-N-T-VB-N
VB-N-VB-N
VB
Q-VB-N
N-VB-N-S
N-V-N-N
N-VB-VB-N
N-T-VB-N-N
Q-N-S-V-N$_{loc}$
Q-N-V-N$_{loc}$
Q-N
VB-N-VB
Q-N-S-V-N$_o$
Q-N-T
N-T
Q-N-VB-N$_o$-N$_{loc}$
Q-N-VB-N$_o$-S
VB-N-S
Q-N-T-VB-N-N
N-S-VB
VB-N-VB-N-N
N-T-VB-N-Tag Q
N-V-N$_o$-Tag Q
Q-N-VB-N-S
Q-N-VB-N-N
Q-N-VB-VB

Linguistic Level IV
N-VB-N-Tag Q

Linguistic Level V
N-VB-N
N-T-VB-N
N-VB
N-T-VB
N-V-N$_{loc}$
VB-N
Q-N-VB-N
N-VB-N-N
N-V-N$_o$-S
N-V-N$_o$
Q-N-V-N$_o$
N
N-T-VB-N-N
N-VB-N-S
Adverb+S+S
Q-N-V-N
VB-N-VB-N
N-T-VB-N-S
N-S-V-N$_{loc}$
Q-N-T-VB-N
Q-N-T-VB-N-N
N-T-V-N$_o$
VB-N-VB-N-N
Q-N-VB
N-V-N$_{loc}$-Tag Q
N-VB-N-Tag Q
S-what-S
Q-N-S-V-N$_{loc}$
Q-N-T-VB
T-VB-N
VB-N-S
N-says S
N-S-VB-N
N-VB-VB
S-because-S
N-VB-S
N-VB-N-N-S
N-VB-VB-N
VB-N-VB
Q-N-S-V-N$_o$
Q-N-VB-N-N
N-T-VB-N-Tag Q
N-VB-N-VB-N

Appendix F

Construction types pooled in order of their frequency of occurrence across five linguistic levels of development for the deviant group.

Linguistic Level I
VB-N
N-S
N-VB
N
VB
N-V-N$_{loc}$
Q-N-V-N$_{loc}$
N-VB-N
N-V-N$_o$-S
VB-N-S
T-VB
T-VB-N
N-S-V-N$_{loc}$

Linguistic Level II
VB-N
N
VB
N-S
N-VB
N-VB-N
N-V-N$_{loc}$
VB-N-S
N-V-N$_o$
N-VB-N-S
N-S-VB-N
N-N
VB-N-N
N-T-VB
N-S-VB

Linguistic Level III
N
VB-N
N-VB-N
N-VB
VB
N-V-N$_o$
N-V-N$_{loc}$
N-S
Q-N-V-N$_o$
Q-N
N-VB-N$_o$-S

Linguistic Level III
N-VB-N-N
N-T-VB-N
N-S-V-N$_{loc}$
Q-N-V-N$_o$
Q-N-T-VB-N
Q-N-VB-N
T-V-N-N
T-VB-N
VB-N-N
N-T-VB-N-N
VB-N-S
N-T-VB-N-S
Q-N-T-VB-N-N
Q-N-V-N$_{loc}$
N-T-VB

Linguistic Level IV
N-VB-N
N-VB
N
VB-N
N-VB-N-S
N-T-VB-N
N-S
VB
N-VB-N-N
N-T-VB-N-S
Q-N-VB-N
N-T-VB
N-S-VB
T-VB-N
Q-N
N-V-N$_o$
N-VB-VB-N
N-S-VB-N
N-T-VB-N-N
N-V-N$_{loc}$
VB-N-S
N-say-S
N-VB-S
N-T
S-because-S

Linguistic Level IV
Q-N-VB
VB-VB-N
N-N
N-VB-VB-N-S
Adverb-S-S
N-VB-N-N-S
N-VB-S

Linguistic Level V
N-VB-N
N-T-VB-N
N-VB
N-VB-N-N
N-VB-N-S
N-T-VB
N
N-T-VB-N-N
VB-N
N-V-N$_o$
N-S
N-V-N$_o$-N$_{loc}$
N-VB-N-N-S
N-T-VB-N-S
N-VB-N-S-N
N-V-N$_{loc}$
VB
N-VB-N-VB
N-VB-VB-N-S
Q-N-VB-N
N-S-VB-N
N-V-N$_o$-S
N-say-S
VB-N-S
N-S-V-N$_o$
N-T
Q-N-V-N$_{loc}$
N-VB-N-S
N-T-VB-N-N-S
N-say-N
Adverb-S-S

An Examination of The Semantic Relations Reflected in The Language Usage of Normal and Language-Disordered Children

Laurence B. Leonard, Jacqueline G. Bolders, and Judith A. Miller

Language samples were obtained from 40 children in order to examine semantic relations reflected in language usage as a function of chronological age (three and five years) and linguistic status (normal and language disordered). Normal-disordered comparisons were made under both matched utterance length and matched age conditions. Results are interpreted as supporting the notion that the disordered-language usage reflected semantic relations consistent with an earlier level of development.

During the past 15 years, a number of investigations have compared the syntactic structures evidenced in the language usage of normal and language-disordered children (Menyuk, 1964; Lee, 1966; Leonard, 1972; Morehead and Ingram, 1973). Despite the valuable information gained regarding the syntax of language-disordered children, little has been said about the meanings underlying these syntactic structures. This situation must be remedied, particularly in light of the recent position taken by many developmental psycholinguists that underlying meanings play a crucial role in the child's language development (Bloom, 1970; Bowerman, 1973a; Brown, 1973). One aspect of meaning of recent interest to developmental psycholinguistics deals with the semantic relations underlying the child's language usage.

Semantic relations represent something beyond referential meaning by assuming responsibility for meanings expressed by the relations between words. The meaning of *mommy wash*, for example, is not totally contained in the single words *mommy* and *wash*, since no means would be available to distinguish *mommy wash* from *wash mommy*. Such relations do not simply play a syntactic role; the same semantic relation can be expressed in a number of different syntactic forms. The instrumental relation (represented when an inanimate is perceived as the cause of an activity), for example, can be expressed in an utterance such as *a hammer broke the glass* as well as in one such as *someone broke the glass with a hammer*.

From *Journal of Speech and Hearing Research,* **19**, 371–392 (1976). Reprinted by permission of the American Speech and Hearing Association.

While the specific role that semantic relations play in language is not yet conclusive, some proposals suggest that their importance may be considerable. Fillmore (1968), for example, suggested that some semantic relations may reflect certain innate judgments which humans are capable of making about events going on around them. Schlesinger (1971) noted that semantic relations appear to represent those cognitively based relations which make a difference linguistically. In light of the unknown etiologies and less than complete descriptions of disordered language, such proposals provide a strong justification for examining the semantic relations reflected in the language usage of the language-disordered child. The purpose of this study was to perform such an examination.

The means by which these semantic relations might be analyzed is a topic of some importance. Methods of analysis have varied in the psycholinguistic literature, and thus far the analysis of underlying semantic relations has been limited almost entirely to the two- and three-word utterance stages of language development.

Bloom (1970) was one of the first investigators to systematically attend to the semantic roles played by a child's utterances. Her method was that of "rich interpretation," in which the function of an utterance was determined by utilizing both the structural characteristics of the utterance and the non-linguistic context in which it occurred. The actual model of analysis adopted by Bloom (1970), however, was Chomsky's (1965) transformational grammar. In this model, the underlying structures are partially generated by phrase structure rules which specify the hierarchical organization of elements in a sentence, in addition to such structural information as the underlying order of these elements. Such familiar notations as S → NP + VP represent phrase structure rules. Thus, a good deal of information of a syntactic nature is presumed to be contained in the underlying structure.

The semantic interpretation is presumed to be derived by rules operating on the syntactically based underlying structure. Bowerman (1973b), among others, has discussed some of the problems this poses for the analysis of the semantic notions underlying child language. When Chomsky's (1965) transformational grammar is adopted as a model of analysis, along with it comes the implicit acceptance of underlying syntactic relations such as subject and predicate which may not only be unjustified according to the child's usage, but whose very postulation may obscure the underlying relations which are operative for the child. More recent work suggests that many of the underlying relations that are operative seem to be semantic in nature (Schlesinger, 1971; Bowerman, 1973b).

Another method of analyzing semantic relations was advanced by Schlesinger (1971). Of interest to Schlesinger (1971) were only those aspects of underlying structure that represent what the child intends to express in the linguistic output. The term *input marker* was used for the formalized representation of these intentions. Unlike the underlying structure of transformational grammar, input markers specify semantic notions. Input markers contain no information about syntactic categories or word order. "Realization rules" are postulated which convert the input markers into utterances, bypassing any underlying structure of a syntactic nature.

Unfortunately, Schlesinger's (1971) account seems suitable only for the early stages of child language. Semantic relations are defined in terms of relations holding between pairs of words, such as action + object and modifier + head. The generation of utterances involving a number of semantic relations requires the rather burdensome application of a number of different realization rules (Brown, 1973). Related difficulties seem to exist within this method of analysis as well. For example, modifier in this method refers to both attributes like *green* and possessors like *my*. The means by which a child at a three-word level of language development might produce an utterance like *my green ball* but never *green my ball* is unaccounted for, since in this method attributes and possessors seem to be semantically indistinguishable.

Antinucci and Parisi (1973) have presented a method of portraying underlying representations in child language that seems to have borrowed certain characteristics from generative semantics. In their method, underlying semantic notions are coded as n-place predicates. The predication is usually in the form of a verb which determines the number of noun phrases, serving as arguments, which are the complements of the predication. For example, *open* is a two-place verb serving as the predication whose meaning is represented by the argument *X causes Y to become accessible* where two noun phrases will be substituted for X and Y, corresponding presumably to an agent and an object, respectively.

Thus far, application of this method of analysis to children's language usage has been limited to one- and two-word utterances. Even at this level of language development, the Antinucci and Parisi (1973) method is not without its problems. Both Schlesinger (1974) and Bowerman (1974) have raised objections to the large number of elements contained in the semantic structures proposed by Antinucci and Parisi (1973). Their criticisms centered on the issue that the underlying notions adopted seem more appropriate for an adult model of linguistic capacity than for a description of the underlying semantic relations operative in a young child's linguistic system.

Another method used to analyze semantic relations underlying children's language usage is the case grammar approach proposed by Fillmore (1968). Case grammar was developed as a model of adult linguistic capacity and as such possesses the mechanisms to handle a broader range of language development than the methods of Schlesinger (1971) and Antinucci and Parisi (1973). Certain features of this approach have been sufficiently appealing to developmental psycholinguists to warrant its application to the analysis of young children's language usage (Bowerman, 1973b; Brown, 1973; Greenfield and Smith, in press).

In some ways, case grammar is similar to Chomsky's (1965) transformational grammar. Utterances are given both an underlying as well as surface representation linked by transformations. Like Chomsky, Fillmore (1968) also accepted the position that semantic rules would operate on the underlying structure to derive a semantic interpretation. Fillmore (1968) regards syntactic relations like subject and predicate as surface structure characteristics which may not be universal and therefore should be accounted for transformationally when necessary. Instead, the basic elements of the underlying structure in case grammar are case relations which are semantic concepts of syntactic significance.

In the underlying structure of case grammar, a sentence is composed of a modality and a proposition. The modality contains markers for that which acts on the sentence as a whole, such as negation, tense, and interrogation. The proposition consists of a verb and one or more nouns associated with the verb in a particular semantic relationship. All of the nouns have equal status with respect to the verb. Two or more nouns can be conjoined to represent a case relation, although each relation can occur only once. One rather important feature of case grammar is that the case relations and the verb with which they are associated are considered unordered. This feature permits a given relation to appear in different sentence positions. The instrumental relation, for example, can be seen in the initial and final sentence positions in the utterances *the hammer broke the glass* and *the glass was broken by the hammer,* respectively. Case grammar also includes provisions for deriving syntactic features such as noun phrases and morphological markers from these underlying semantic relations.

After applying case grammar in the analysis of one child's language usage, Brown (1973) noted that this method met the criterion of completeness as well as other methods of analysis (specifically, those of Bloom, 1970 and Schlesinger, 1971) and, at points, seemed more clearly and explicitly developed. After examining the usefulness of the case grammar approach in the analysis of language samples from young children speaking English, Finnish, Luo, and Samoan, Bowerman (1973b) suggested that the major value of this approach for the study of language development may be its insistence on the significance of semantic concepts rather than more abstract features like subject and predicate.

There are, however, certain weaknesses in the case grammar account. These include certain case relations which are too broad for categories proposed as semantic in nature (Bowerman, 1973b) and insufficient linguistic mechanisms to handle some of the more complex structures of the adult linguistic system (Brown, 1973). Despite these deficiencies, case grammar seems to represent a system of analysis that not only deals formally with semantic (rather than abstract syntactic) relations but does so in a system sufficiently detailed for application to different stages of language development. For these reasons, it is this approach, coupled with certain modifications to correct deficiencies, that was adopted as the method of analysis in the present study.

It should be pointed out that in a later paper, Fillmore (1971) has made attempts to correct some of the problems in the original account. However, since Fillmore's (1968) original formulations have been applied to child language and suggestions for modifications in this application have been made by other investigators, it is a modification of the original account that is employed in the present study.

The means by which semantic relations reflected in normal and disordered children's language usage are compared represented a further consideration. The lack of comparative studies dealing with semantic relations complicated this matter; however, the manner in which syntactic structures in normal and disordered children's language had been compared in earlier studies suggested two possibilities: (1) comparisons of normal and disordered children matched for chronological age, and (2) comparisons with the normal and disordered children matched for mean utterance length. Both types of comparisons have assets. Comparisons with matched age provide information concerning how a language-disordered child compares with a normal peer, while comparisons with matched utterance length suggest how a language-disordered child might compare with a normal child at the same general stage of linguistic development.

Unfortunately, the two different types of comparisons may be prone to yield two different types of normal–disordered differences. For example, the finding that the syntax of the language-disordered child differs qualitatively from the syntax of the normal child (Menyuk, 1964) and the conflicting finding that the language-disordered child's syntax is delayed in onset and acquisition time relative to normals (Morehead and Ingram, 1973) may well be related to the fact that the language-disordered and normal children were matched for chronological age (Menyuk, 1964) on the one hand, and mean length of utterance (Morehead and Ingram, 1973) on the other. It appears that adequate descriptions can only be obtained by the implementation of both matching tactics with the same body of data. In the present study, both types of comparisons were utilized.

Specifically, the purpose of this study was to compare the semantic relations reflected in the language usage of normal and language-disordered children employing a modification of Fillmore's (1968) case grammar as a method of analysis. To derive meaningful conclusions from the study, comparisons were made among (1) language-disordered children and normal children of the same age, (2) disordered children and younger, normal children, (3) younger and older disordered children, (4) younger or older normal children, and, to further clarify the nature of any normal–disordered differences, (5) language-disordered children and normal children with equal utterance length.

METHOD

SUBJECTS

Forty children served as subjects in this investigation. Twenty subjects were evaluated by a speech pathologist as displaying "defective" language usage and at the time of this study were enrolled in management designed to increase their linguistic skills. The test instruments used in the evaluation varied from subject to subject and included tests such as the Northwestern Syntax Screening Test (NSST) (Lee, 1969), certain subtests of the Illinois Test of Psycholinguistic Abilities (1961), and, less frequently, the Houston Test for Language Development (Crabtree, 1963) and the Utah Test of Language Development (Mecham, Jex, and Jones, 1967). No subject was considered to be mentally retarded, neurologically impaired, hearing impaired, or to possess any other condition that seemed related to organic factors. No subject revealed a history suggesting emotional difficulties. Rather, the language difficulties displayed by these subjects were generally of unknown etiology. All of the subjects were late in both first-word acquisition and the acquisition of two-word utterances. Other developmental milestones, while sometimes slow, did not appear to be as depressed as language development. The remaining 20 subjects were screened by a speech pathologist and were judged "normal" in linguistic functioning.

Ten of the language-disordered subjects and 10 of the normal subjects ranged in age from two years, 11 months to four years, two months. The mean chronological age for both groups was three years, seven months. The language-disordered and normal subjects in this age range will hereafter be termed the three-year-old disordered and three-year-old normal subjects respectively. The remaining 10 language-disordered and 10 normal subjects ranged in age from four years, eight months to five years, eight months. The mean chronological age for both of these groups was five years, two months. The language-disordered and normal subjects in this age range will hereafter be termed the five-year-old normal and five-year-old disordered subjects.

TESTING PROCEDURE

A 50-utterance sample obtained from each subject constituted the data analyzed in this study. The sample was obtained in the following manner. After a brief conversation with the subject, the experimenter gave the instructions: "I'd like you to tell me some stories. I'm going to show you some pictures and I'd like you to make up a story for each picture." The 10 test plates of the Children's Apperception Test (1954) were then presented. To insure consistency in the method of obtaining the language sample, as well as to insure that each subject produced 50 utterances, five "questions" were directed at each subject for each of the test plates. If a subject emitted a response such as "I don't know," a second question was given. The questions are presented below.

1. What do you think is happening in this picture? (Second—Just tell me anything.)
2. Look real hard all over the picture and tell me something else about it. (Second —Tell me anything else.)
3. What do you think was happening just before this picture was taken? (Second —How do you think he/they got there?)
4. Make up a story about what's going to happen next. (Second—What do you think will happen in just a little while?)
5. If this were you, what do you think you'd say? (Second—If this were you and this was your friend, what would you say?)

To insure that the samples were comparable, only the first utterance in response to each question was included in the analysis. All subject utterances were tape recorded and transcribed on the same day. Notations were also made at the time of recording in order to aid the accuracy of the transcriptions.

METHOD OF ANALYSIS

The method employed to analyze the semantic relations reflected in the subjects' language samples represented a modification of Fillmore's (1968) within-proposition case relations, incorporating the suggestions offered by Bowerman (1973b) and Brown (1973) for making this approach more suitable for analyzing children's language usage. Since the purpose of this study was to examine the semantic relations reflected in normal and disordered children's language usage and not features relating more directly to syntax, only the analysis of the case relations, contained within the proposition, were of interest to us. Fillmore's (1968) major case relations are presented below.

Agentive (A)   The animate perceived as instigator of the action identified by the verb.
"The *boy* is running."
"The ball was hit by the *boy*."

Instrumental (I)   The inanimate force or object causally involved in the action or state named by the verb.
"A *hammer* broke the glass."
"He was cut by the *knife*."

Dative (D)	The animate being affected by the action or state identified by the verb.
	"The *man* died."
	"The car belonged to the *woman*."
Locative (L)	The location or spatial orientation of the state or action identified by the verb.
	"The cup is on the *table*."
	"*Memphis* is quite humid."
Objective (O)	Anything representable by a noun whose role in the state or action identified by the verb depends on the meaning of the verb itself.
	"The *door* opened."
	"Mother closed the *window*."
Essive (E)	Anything whose role is that of being named.
	"This animal is a *cow*."
	"*Marston* is his name."

Bowerman (1973b) and Brown (1973) have outlined some weaknesses in the approach proposed by Fillmore (1968). The modifications in the case relations that were employed in this study seemed to remedy these weaknesses. In Fillmore's (1968) account, the objective relation represented a semantic category too general for practical use; this relation could include an object named, an object located, an object described, as well as an object acted upon. In the present method of analysis, the former three functions were included in a relation termed designated, with the relation termed objective reserved only for objects acted upon.

Fillmore (1968) treated adjectives as verbs in his account. Although this treatment was not new to linguistics, it seemed more motivated by syntactic than semantic considerations. To distinguish descriptions of objects from actions, then, the former were assigned to a relation termed attributive.

Finally, some modification proved necessary to properly portray the underlying semantic relations in utterances involving the copula as in *the ball is in the box*. Fillmore's (1968) underlying representation of such an utterance would contain no copula. To fill the empty verb node, he suggested making use of *have*, resulting in an underlying representation like *the box has a ball in it*. To avoid a representation not evidenced in the subjects' usage, we have not adopted this suggestion. Following Bowerman's (1973b) suggestion, we have allowed the verb to be an optional element in our method of analysis. Since this study deals only with underlying semantic relations, contained within the proposition, these modifications appeared sufficient to render a suitable analysis of the semantic relations represented in the subjects' language usage.

Each of the subjects' utterances in the language samples was analyzed according to the above method. The data were treated in two ways. To determine what differences may have existed in the semantic relations representative of each subject group, collective within-proposition rewrite rules were derived for each group from those individual rules written for each subject in the group. For convenience, these will hereafter be termed the representative proposition rules. The representative proposition rules were based on those within-proposition rules seen in the samples of at least half of the subjects in the group. Since only 50 utterances were obtained from each subject, it was important to insure that the utterances accounted for in the rules written for each subject were representative of his usage. Therefore, only those semantic relation utterance types that were seen at least twice in a subject's language sample were included in the proposition rules written for his sample.

The data were also analyzed in terms of the frequency with which each semantic relation utterance type accounted for by the representative proposition rules was used. Since differences have been observed between normal children of different ages as well as between normal and language-disordered children (Leonard, 1972) in the frequency with which certain linguistic structures are realized in usage, it seemed that useful information regarding the semantic relation utterance types represented in the subjects' usage might be obtained through the use of frequency data. The rationale for utilizing frequency data was that, with increasing frequency, a greater number of lexical items might be involved in the surface realization of each semantic relation utterance type. This assumption seemed warranted since, with five different questions probing for information pertaining to 10 different test plates employed as the testing materials in this study, a wide variation of lexical items should be expected. Thus, the assumption was made that with increasing frequency of usage, greater command of a particular semantic relation utterance type in terms of diversity of lexicon was being demonstrated.

An attempt was also made to provide for comparisons between normal and language-disordered subjects matched for general linguistic development since, often times, general linguistic development is a better predictor of the specific features of language used by the child than chronological age (de Villiers and de Villiers, 1973). Mean length of utterance seemed to serve as a useful measure of general linguistic development (Morehead and Ingram, 1973) and was therefore employed in this study. The normal and language-disordered subject samples utilized in this comparison were selected from the obtained samples of the three- and five-year-old normal and language-disordered subjects. Mean length of utterance was computed according to the procedure adopted by Brown (1973, p. 54).

A close match was obtained by employing the samples from seven normals with comparatively short utterance lengths and seven disordered subjects with comparatively long utterance lengths. The mean utterance length in morphemes was 5.03 and 4.97 for the two groups, respectively. The two groups were compared using both representative proposition rules and frequency of semantic relation utterance types accounted for by the representative proposition rules as data.

For each measure, the percentage of examiner agreement between the senior author and a speech pathologist trained in the method of analysis was computed. These percentages represented the ratio of agreed observations to total observations, using each utterance as an observation (total = 2000 observations). The percentage of examiner agreement was 91.95.

RESULTS

COMPARISONS AMONG THREE- AND FIVE-YEAR-OLD NORMAL AND LANGUAGE-DISORDERED SUBJECTS

Presented in Appendix A are the representative proposition rules for each subject group. The proposition rules are presented in the order of those reflected in the samples of shortest to longest mean utterance length.

As can be seen from Appendix A, a great deal of similarity exists among the representative proposition rules. The only subject group difference that is apparent is the appearance of the dative relation in the proposition rules of both normal subject groups, a relation not evidenced in the proposition rules for either handicapped subject group. The rule that includes this relation is one which permits utterances such as *I fed the baby* (verb + agentive + dative).

Subjects were compared according to the frequency with which each of the semantic relation utterance types in the representative proposition rules were reflected by utilizing a mixed design analysis of variance with one between subjects (subject group) and one within subjects (semantic relation utterance type) variables (Myers, 1966, p. 181). Since these utterance types represented the entire composition of the representative proposition rules and were mutually exclusive, this analysis appeared appropriate. In the representative proposition rules, locative, dative, and objective were optional when involved in utterance types that included verb + agentive. Verb + agentive + locative, verb + agentive + objective, and verb + agentive + dative were included as categories for analysis, and any utterance reflecting one of these semantic relation utterance types was not entered into the verb + agentive category. The latter category included utterances reflecting verb + agentive with no additional semantic relations.

Results indicated a significant main effect for subject group ($F = 5.83, df = 3,36$ $p < 0.005$). Posthoc comparisons utilizing a least significant difference test (Guilford, 1965, p. 277) indicated that overall, the semantic relation utterance types accounted for in the representative proposition rules were reflected in usage more frequently ($p < 0.05$) by the three- and five-year-old disordered subjects than the three- and five-year-old normals. A significant main effect for semantic relation utterance type was also observed ($F = 14.22, df = 6,216, p < 0.001$). A least significant difference test indicated that overall, utterances reflecting essive + designated, verb + agentive, and verb + agentive + locative were used more frequently ($p < 0.05$) than the other semantic relation utterance types.

The most important comparison of this analysis dealt with the interaction between the subject group and the semantic relation utterance type, since the results of such a comparison provided some indication regarding the specific differences among the subject groups. This interaction proved significant ($F = 3.03, df = 18,216, p < 0.001$). The mean frequency with which each semantic relation utterance type was reflected in usage according to subject group can be seen in Table 1. The results of the least significant difference test applied to this data also appear in this table.

As can be noted in Table 1, the three- and five-year-old disordered subjects used utterances reflecting essive + designated more frequently than the three- and five-year-old normals. In addition, the three- and five-year-old disordered subjects used

Table 1   Summary of the Frequency of Semantic Relation Utterance Types
Accounted for in the Representative Proposition Rules. N = Normal, LD
= Language Disordered, LSD = Least Significant Difference

Semantic Relation Utterance Type	Means				LSD Results (p < 0.05)	
	3-Year LD	5-Year LD	3-Year N	5-Year N		
Essive + Designated	10.00	11.20	3.90	2.20	3 Year LD,	3 Year N,
					5 Year LD,	5 Year N
Locative + Designated	3.70	2.10	3.00	1.80		
Attributive + Designated	1.50	1.50	3.00	2.30		
Verb + Agentive	10.40	10.40	3.70	7.70	3 Year LD	3 Year N
					5 Year LD	
Verb + Agentive + Locative	7.20	6.30	6.50	9.60		
Verb + Agentive + Objective	4.10	3.60	3.60	6.40		
Verb + Agentive + Dative	2.60	2.00	1.70	3.00		

utterances reflecting verb + agentive more frequently than the three-year-old normals. No other differences were observed.

Initially, we were somewhat surprised at the finding that some semantic relation utterance types in the representative proposition rules were reflected in usage more frequently by the two disordered subject groups. In fact, however, further inspection provided a possible explanation. Although they were not reflected in usage with sufficient frequency within and across subjects in the group to warrant the inclusion of representative proposition rules to account for them, a number of utterances reflecting other semantic relation utterance types with high complexity may have been used by the normal subjects. Given a sample of 50 utterances, these semantic relation utterance types may have resulted in a decrease in the frequency with which those semantic relation utterance types accounted for in the representative proposition rules were evidenced. The disordered subjects, on the other hand, may have been restricted primarily to utterances whose underlying semantic relation types were accounted for in their representative proposition rules.

This possible explanation prompted us to compare the subject groups according to the number of utterances used that reflected semantic relation utterance types exceeding those in the representative proposition rules in terms of complexity. The frequency of utterances reflecting at least three relations constituted the data for this comparison, since the representative proposition rules accounted for utterances reflecting a maximum of two relations.

A single factor analysis of variance (Myers, 1966, p. 70) yielded a significant difference among subject groups ($F = 8.56, df = 3,36 p < 0.001$). Least significant difference test results indicated that the three- (mean = 10.40) and five- (mean = 9.30) year-old normal subjects produced utterances that reflected semantic relation utterance types exceeding the representative proposition rules in complexity more frequently than the three- (mean = 2.10) and five- (mean = 1.50) year-old disordered subjects. It appears, then, that the normal subjects' language usage reflected a number of complex semantic relation utterance types not accounted for in their representative proposition rules.

COMPARISONS BETWEEN THE NORMAL AND LANGUAGE-DISORDERED SUBJECTS MATCHED FOR UTTERANCE LENGTH

The representative proposition rules for the normal and disordered subjects matched for mean utterance length are presented in Appendix B.

As can be seen from Appendix B, the two sets of representative proposition rules are identical. Thus, when employing this method of analysis, the semantic relation utterance types reflected in the language of normal and language-disordered subjects with mean utterance length at approximately five morphemes seem to be the same.

The comparison of the frequency with which each of the semantic relation utterance types in the representative proposition rules was reflected in the language usage of these two groups was handled through a mixed design analysis of variance with subject group and semantic relation utterance type serving as variables. No differences were seen between the subject groups ($F = 0.36$, $df = 1,12$, $p > 0.05$), nor the semantic relation utterance types ($F = 0.83$, $df = 5,30$, $p > 0.05$). In addition, no interaction was seen between the subject group and the semantic relation utterance type ($F = 0.41$, df E 5,30, $p > 0.05$). The failure to observe an interaction was most informative; when matched for mean utterance length, the normal and language-disordered subjects did not differ in the frequency with which their language usage reflected the different semantic relation utterance types. The mean frequency with which each semantic relation utterance type was reflected in the usage of the normal and disordered-subject groups can be seen in Table 2.

It should be noted that earlier comparisons revealed that three- and five-year-old disordered subjects used utterances reflecting essive + designated as well as verb + agentive more frequently than normal subjects. The finding that no differences

Table 2   Summary of the Frequency of Usage of Semantic Relation Utterance Types Accounted for in the Representative Proposition Rules of the Normal and Disordered Subjects Matched for Utterance Length. N = Normal and LD = Language Disordered

| Semantic Relation | Means | |
Utterance Type	LD	N
Essive + Designated	5.14	4.43
Locative + Designated	3.57	3.86
Attributive + Designated	3.14	4.29
Verb + Agentive	9.86	5.00
Verb + Agentive + Locative	7.43	6.86
Verb + Agentive + Objective	5.43	3.00

existed in the present comparison suggests that the frequency of particular semantic relation utterance types may be more related to general linguistic development, as measured by mean utterance length, than to any inherent differences in the semantic relation utterance types operative in the usage of language-disordered as opposed to normal children.

This assumption seemed borne out by the results of the matched mean utterance length subject comparisons according to the number of utterances used which exceeded the rules contained in the representative proposition rules in terms of complexity. No difference was observed between the normal and disordered subjects ($F = 1.32$, $df = 1,12$, $p > 0.05$).

Since these normal and disordered subjects appeared to be at the same general stage of linguistic development and, in addition, seemed to be using utterances reflecting the same semantic relation utterance types, it seemed useful to gain information concerning the factors that may differentiate them as normal versus disordered. One likely factor seemed to be chronological age. To examine age difference between the normal and handicapped subjects matched for mean utterance length, a single factor analysis of variance was utilized. Results indicated that the disordered subjects (mean = 57.43 months) were significantly older than the normal subjects (mean = 41.29 months) ($F = 12.54$, $df = 1,12$, $p < 0.005$).

The finding that normal and disordered subjects, when matched for utterance length, seemed to differ in chronological age but not in the semantic relation utterance types reflected in their language usage lends some support to the proposal that the disordered subjects may have possessed a semantic relation system suggestive of that of the younger, normal child.

Before this proposal is pursued further, a number of qualifications regarding the study itself must be stated. Following these qualifications, the topics of discussion will proceed in the order of their mention in the introduction: (1) the nature of the differences between the semantic relations reflected in the usage of normal and language-disordered children, (2) the usefulness of the adopted method of analysis in capturing underlying semantic relations, and (3) the value of matching normal and disordered children for both mean utterance length as well as chronological age.

DISCUSSION

SOME QUALIFICATIONS

The sampling procedure employed in this study was utilized as a means of insuring that the subjects' utterances would be directly comparable. Since this study examined semantic relations reflected in language usage, it was critical that utterances in response to the same stimuli be obtained from each subject. On the other hand, it is recognized that a complete set of proposition rules could not be written with a 50-utterance corpus. The proposition rules written merely represented some of the child's semantic relation system. The small sample size no doubt made the acquired data more likely to be altered by moods or other transitory factors affecting a child's linguistic performance. The questions asked of the child were quite open ended, however, and judging from the Morehead and Ingram (1973) finding that children's spontaneous and "response" utterances did not differ, we believed that the use of such questions would have benefits over comparisons of language samples in a setting with no controls. It appears that unless one can acquire utterances numbering in the several hundreds as seen in normative studies (Bloom, 1970; Brown, 1973) such "purely" naturalistic samples might be risky for comparative purposes. Nevertheless, the use of specific questions does leave the possibility that the child's language usage was influenced by his ability to comprehend the questions. It would also be difficult to dismiss the possibility that the experimenter's questions affected to some extent the form and content of the child's sampled language.

Though the language-disordered children in this study represented a random sample of children requiring language intervention, the number of disordered children employed (20) was not sufficiently extensive to rule out the exclusion of disordered children demonstrating language usage quite dissimilar to the usage described in this investigation. Caution should therefore be taken in interpreting the present data as representative of all language-disordered children's usage.

INTERPRETATION OF THE RESULTS OF THE NORMAL— LANGUAGE-DISORDERED COMPARISONS

An examination of the representative proposition rules written for the three- and five-year-old normal and three- and five-year-old disordered subject groups gives the impression of only a minor difference among the groups. This impression seems due in part to the requirements for inclusion into the representative proposition rules. The comparisons according to the number of utterances reflecting complexity exceeding that seen in the representative proposition rules suggested that a number of utterances reflecting complex semantic relation utterance types were used by the normal subject groups, but their infrequent use by a given subject, or across different subjects in a particular subject group prevented their inclusion in the representative proposition rules.

The particular difference between the representative proposition rules for the two normal- and disordered-subject groups was in the form of the presence versus absence of the optional semantic relation utterance type verb + agentive + dative. In this semantic relation utterance type, dative is not reflected in the subject of the sentence as in *he fainted,* but rather by the direct object, as in utterances like *he bit the monkey.* The dative relation represents the case where the animate is being affected by the state or action named by the verb. In this particular semantic relation utterance type, the animate is being affected by the action (named by the verb) performed by some agent.

Without benefit of the comparison between normal and disordered subjects matched for mean utterance length, the appearance of dative only in the representative proposition rules of the two normal groups could be construed as some sort of qualitative difference between the normal and language-disordered subjects. When the proposition rules of the normal and disordered subjects matched for mean utterance length were compared, however, identical representation of the dative relation was observed. This seems to suggest that the earlier difference was not qualitative but perhaps a reflection of differences in linguistic development, to the extent that such development can be estimated by utterance length.

An additional source of support for the interpretation that the normal-disordered differences may reflect differences in development can be provided by a look at the verb + agentive + dative semantic relation utterance type itself. In other semantic approaches to analysis, this dative is often contained within a category termed object. In Brown's (1973) account, for example, object represents someone or something either suffering a change of state or receiving the force of an action. Yet Brown (1973) himself noted that early in child language, object typically is reflected by inanimates rather than animates. Since the first objects acted upon that are expressed in child language seem to be those where the child himself is agent (Sinclair-deZwart, 1973), this finding should not be surprising; the child would seem to have much less occasion to act upon the relatively few animates with whom he is in contact (the caretaker, the pet dog) than the numerous inanimate objects in his environment (shoes, spoons, toy cars).

Since the semantic relation utterance type verb + agentive + dative reflects animates acted upon, a later appearing notion in children's language usage, the normal—disordered differences might be attributed to developmental factors. In short, since the expression of animates being acted upon is a later achievement, one would expect such expression in children with greater linguistic development. It should be noted, however, that the disordered subjects in this study were more advanced in linguistic development, judging from mean utterance length, than the young children studied by Brown (1973). It remains to be seen just how soon after the early stages of language animates as entities acted upon typically appear in the usage of normal children. Since the verb + agentive + dative semantic relation utterance type was not reflected in the representative proposition rules for the normals in the matched utterance length comparison, however, it might be concluded that this appearance is not a very early one in normal child language.

When the semantic relation utterance types in the representative proposition rules were examined according to the frequency with which they were reflected in usage, no differences among the subject groups in the frequency of verb + agentive + dative were observed. Even though this semantic relation utterance type was reflected in at least two utterances in the language samples of the majority of children in each of the two normal subject groups, these groups showed evidence of this semantic relation utterance type no more frequently than the two disordered subject groups.

This discrepancy raises an important issue concerning which types of data are to be regarded as best estimating a child's level of language functioning. Provided that they are based on semantic relations representative of a given subject group, it appears that frequency data are more useful than a listing of what is representative for a particular group. In the latter case, a single utterance from one subject could dictate whether or not some semantic relation utterance type is deemed representative of a given subject group. As a case in point, the individual proposition rules of four of the 10 five-year-old disordered subjects included verb + agentive (dative), indicating this semantic relation utterance type was reflected at least twice in their individual language samples. Another five of these subjects used one utterance reflecting this semantic relation utterance type. If any one of these five subjects had produced one more such utterance, the criterion for including verb + agentive (dative) as a representative proposition rule for this subject group would have been met; half of the members of the group would have showed evidence of this semantic relation utterance type at least twice in their language samples, resulting in a set of representative proposition rules identical to those of the two normal groups. Frequency data seem less susceptible to minor differences in usage. Another consideration, however, is whether frequency data provide valid information concerning the nature of normal—disordered differences. An examination of the results of the subject group comparisons according to the frequency with which the semantic relation utterance types were reflected in usage seems to suggest an affirmative answer to this question.

The semantic relation utterance types essive + designated and verb + agentive were reflected more frequently in the language usage of the two disordered subject groups. If frequency data provided information relevant to the purpose of this study, these findings should fit into some logical hypothesis concerning the nature of the difference between the semantic relations reflected in normal and language-disordered children's usage. This appears to be the case. These two semantic relation utterance types are attained extremely early in the language acquisition process. At this early stage, they are typically represented by the semantic categories nomination and agent + action (Brown, 1973). They are seen sufficiently early and with enough consistency across different children to qualify them as potential universal features of language (Bowerman, 1975). If such semantic relation utterance types are frequently reflected in a child's language usage, this usage would appear to resemble that seen at an early level of linguistic development.

This position is seemingly supported by the results of the comparisons of the normal and disordered subjects matched for utterance length. The two groups were identical in the frequency of the specific semantic relation utterance types reflected in their usage. The only difference between the normal and disordered subjects matched for utterance length was chronological age. Even this finding that the disordered subjects were older than the normal subjects of equivalent utterance length is consistent with the position that the disordered subjects were operating at an earlier level of development.

If the differences between the normal and disordered subjects were developmental in nature, it might be asked why differences were observed only between the disordered subjects and their normal counterparts and not between the five- and three-year-old normals or the five- and three-year-old disordered subjects. This can be attributed to two factors, both related to sampling. First, the language usage of the three-year-old normals and five-year-old normals was highly similar in terms of mean length of utterance (see Appendix A), suggesting that the three year olds were somewhat advanced in general linguistic development, the five year olds somewhat depressed, or a combination of the two. Second, even the three-year-old normals appeared to be functioning at a higher level of linguistic development than both the five- and three-year-old disordered subjects, judging from the subjects' utterance lengths.

Subject group differences were observed for the following variables: (1) the presence or absence of verb + agentive (dative) in the representative proposition rules, (2) the frequency with which essive + designated and verb + agentive were reflected in usage, and (3) the frequency of usage of utterances reflecting semantic relation utterance types exceeding in complexity those accounted for in the representative proposition rules. Each of the differences occurred between the normal- and disordered-subject groups and not between either of the two normal groups or either of the two disordered groups. Such differences, then, coincided with the greatest dissimilarities in mean utterance length between subject groups. When normal and disordered subjects were matched for mean utterance length, these differences were not observed. This implies a closer relationship between utterance length and underlying semantic relations than we had originally expected. Apparently, the presence versus absence of features such as auxiliaries, articles, and the like could not have been the sole contributors to the differences in mean utterance length between the normal- and disordered-subject groups. Such features have no bearing on underlying semantic relations. It seems that the specific role played by the development of underlying semantic relations in the child's increasing utterance length might be a useful topic for further research.

EVALUATION OF THE METHOD OF ANALYSIS

It seems possible at this point to assess the relative merits of the method of analysis adopted in this study. One conclusion that we feel can safely be drawn is that the employed method of analysis provided sufficient detail to permit an interpretation regarding the nature of the differences observed between the normal and disordered subjects. For example, the greater frequency with which verb + agentive was reflected in the usage of the disordered subjects could be interpreted as resembling an earlier level of linguistic development since the sentence subjects seen in early stages of language development tend to be agents (Bowerman, 1973b). If a more general category such as subject had been employed, it would not have been possible to determine how the normal—disordered subject difference should be interpreted. Similarly, the finding that verb + agentive (dative) was included in the representative proposition rules of only the normal subjects permitted the interpretation that such a semantic relation utterance type reflected a developmental level more advanced than that of the disordered subjects. The early objects of action observed in young children's usage are usually inanimates (Brown, 1973) which in the present method would be represented in verb + agentive (objective). The finding that animates also served as entities acted upon in the utterances of the normal subjects would be obscured if a category such as direct object was utilized.

Since our interest in this study focused on the semantic relations reflected in the language usage of normal and disordered subjects, we could safely confine ourselves to the semantic information contained within Fillmore's (1968) proposition. Even here, though, some modifications in the categorization of certain semantic relations were necessary. Fillmore (1971), too, has seen the need to modify some of the relations he initially proposed, although his motivation for doing so stemmed from linguistic rather than developmental psycholinguistic considerations.

Confining ourselves to proposition rules seemed to have one notable drawback, however. Bloom (1970) noted that the semantic notions underlying young children's utterances containing negatives were acquired in the order nonexistence, rejection, and denial. The use of such information was unavailable to us, because Fillmore (1968) assigned negation to the modality element of his case grammar, since in the adult system negation is said to operate on the sentence as a whole. Since negation is not subcategorized according to the different semantic relations which might underlie it, even the inclusion of Fillmore's (1968) modality element in the present method of analysis would not have been of much help. It can be seen, therefore, that although the present method of analysis seemed suitable as a whole in capturing semantic relations reflected in language usage, additional modifications should be made in order to provide for a complete account of the semantic relation systems of normal and language-disordered children.

MATCHING FOR MEAN UTTERANCE LENGTH AND CHRONOLOGICAL AGE

It seems clear that the strategy of making normal—disordered comparisons under both matched age and matched utterance length conditions added useful information for interpreting the results of this study. The only differences in the semantic relations underlying the subjects' language usage were observed between the three- and five-year-old disordered versus three- and five-year-old normal subject groups. Although the semantic relation utterance types most characteristic of the disordered groups were those identified with an earlier level of development, the fact that no differences were seen among the three and five year olds within each diagnostic category still left open the possibility that the observed differences were qualitative in nature. The virtually identical data for the normal and disordered groups matched for mean utterance length seemed to eliminate this possibility. One must wonder whether the employment of both matching tactics in comparative studies of children's syntax might be useful in placing the "delayed syntax versus different syntax" controversy in better perspective.

IMPLICATIONS FOR FURTHER STUDY

Thus far, we have noted several directions for future investigation in our discussion of issues central to the present study. These include further refinement of a semantically based method of analysis, an examination of the relationship between utterance length and underlying semantic relations, and the application of the subject-matching tactics employed in this study to investigations dealing with normal and language-disordered children's syntax. The specific findings of this study suggest other, important avenues for further research.

The evidence provided that the differences among subject groups were entirely consistent with expectations based on developmental considerations should be interpreted as support that the language-disordered subjects in this study were using language reflecting semantic relation utterance types consistent with those expected from that of the younger, normal child. It would seem, then, that further investigation of the semantic relations reflected in the usage of language-disordered children of different, known etiological categories and different stages of linguistic development is warranted. The results of such an investigation may provide a greater indication of whether a consideration of underlying semantic relations should be included in the notion of language disorder.

To the extent that underlying semantic relations are a function of the child's cognitive structures (Brown, 1973), these results may even suggest an alteration of our views concerning what constitutes such a disorder. Perhaps the recent studies signalling the important role that cognition plays in the meanings expressed by the normal child acquiring language should be viewed more carefully as they may relate to our view of the nature of the language-disordered child's difficulty.

ACKNOWLEDGMENT

The authors are grateful for the assistance of Joanne Kahane, Jeanette Leonard, Jacqueline Liebergott, and Polly Young during various phases of this study.

REFERENCES

Antinucci, F., and Parisi, D., Early language acquisition: A model and some data. In C. Ferguson and D. Slobin (Eds.), *Studies in Child Language Development.* New York: Holt, Rinehart, and Winston (1973).

Bloom, L., *Language Development: Form and Function in Emerging Grammars.* Cambridge, Mass.: The MIT Press (1970).

Bowerman, M., Structural relationships in children's utterances: Syntactic or semantic? In T. Moore (Ed.), *Cognitive Development and the Acquisition of Language.* New York: Academic (1973a).

Bowerman, M., *Early Syntactic Development: A Cross-Linguistic Study with Special Reference to Finnish.* Cambridge, Eng.: Cambridge Univ. Press (1973b).

Bowerman, M., Learning the structure of causative verbs: A study in the relationship of cognitive, semantic, and syntactic development. In *Papers and Repts. on Child Lang. Dev.,* **8,** 142–178 (1974).

Bowerman, M., Cross-linguistic similarities at two stages of syntactic development. In E. Lenneberg and E. Lenneberg (Eds.), *Foundations of Language Development: A Multi-disciplinary Approach.* New York: Academic (1975).

Brown, R., *A First Language: The Early Stages.* Cambridge, Mass.: Harvard Univ. Press (1973).

Children's Apperception Test. Larchmont, N.Y.: C.P.S., Inc. (1954).

Chomsky, N., *Aspects of the Theory of Syntax.* Cambridge, Mass.: The MIT Press (1965).

Crabtree, M., *The Houston Test for Language Development.* Houston: Houston Test Co. (1963).

deVilliers, J., and deVilliers, P., A cross-sectional study of the acquisition of grammatical morphemes in child speech. *J. Psycholing. Res.,* **2,** 267–278 (1973).

Fillmore, C., The case for case. In E. Bach and R. Harms (Eds.), *Universals in Linguistic Theory.* New York: Holt, Rinehart, and Winston (1968).

Fillmore, C., Some problems for case grammar. In R. O'Brien (Ed.), *Report of the Twenty-Second Annual Round Table Meeting on Linguistics and Language Studies.* Washington, D.C.: Georgetown Univ. Press (1971).

Greenfield, P., and Smith, J., *The Structure of Communication in Early Language Development.* New York: Academic (in press).

Guilford, J., *Fundamental Statistics in Psychology and Education.* New York: McGraw-Hill (1965).

Illinois Test of Psycholinguistic Abilities. Urbana, Ill.: Univ. Illinois Press (1961).

Lee, L., Developmental sentence types: A method for comparing normal and deviant syntactic development. *J. Speech Hearing Dis.,* **31,** 311–330 (1966).

Lee, L., *Northwestern Syntax Screening Test.* Evanston, Ill.: Northwestern Univ. Press (1969).

Leonard, L., What is deviant language? *J. Speech Hearing Dis.,* **37,** 427–446 (1972).

Mecham, M., Jex, J., and Jones, J., *Utah Test of Language Development.* Salt Lake City: Communication Research Associates (1967).

Menyuk, P., Comparison of grammar of children with functionally deviant and normal speech. *J. Speech Hearing Res.,* **7,** 109–121 (1964).

MOREHEAD, D., and INGRAM, D., The development of base syntax in normal and linguistically deviant children. *J. Speech Hearing Res.,* **16,** 330–352 (1973).

MYERS, J., *Fundamentals of Experimental Design.* Boston: Allyn and Bacon (1966).

SCHLESINGER, I., Production of utterances and language acquisition. In D. Slobin (Ed.), *The Ontogenesis of Grammar.* New York: Academic (1971).

SCHLESINGER, I., Relational concepts underlying language. In R. Schiefelbusch and L. Lloyd (Eds.), *Language Perspectives: Acquisition, Retardation, and Intervention.* Baltimore: University Park Press (1974).

SINCLAIR-DEZWART, H., Language acquisition and cognitive development. In T. Moore (Ed.), *Cognitive Development and the Acquisition of Language.* New York: Academic (1973).

Appendix A

Representative proposition rules for the language samples of the three-year-old disordered, five-year-old disordered, three-year-old normal, and five-year-old normal subjects. MLU = mean utterance length, → = is rewritten as, and ( ) = optional.

Three-Year-Old Disordered Subjects
(MLU = 3.48 Morphemes)

Proposition →
$$\left[\begin{array}{l} \left\{ \begin{array}{l} \text{Essive} \\ \text{Locative} \\ \text{Attributive} \end{array} \right\} \quad \text{Designated} \\[2em] \text{Verb + Agentive} \quad \left\{ \begin{array}{l} \text{(Locative)} \\ \text{(Objective)} \end{array} \right\} \end{array} \right]$$

Five-Year-Old Disordered Subjects
(MLU = 3.79 Morphemes)

Proposition →
$$\left[\begin{array}{l} \left\{ \begin{array}{l} \text{Essive} \\ \text{Locative} \\ \text{Attributive} \end{array} \right\} \quad \text{Designated} \\[2em] \text{Verb + Agentive} \quad \left\{ \begin{array}{l} \text{(Locative)} \\ \text{(Objective)} \end{array} \right\} \end{array} \right]$$

Three-Year-Old Normal Subjects
(MLU = 6.83 Morphemes)

Proposition →
$$\left[\begin{array}{l} \left\{ \begin{array}{l} \text{Essive} \\ \text{Locative} \\ \text{Attributive} \end{array} \right\} \quad \text{Designated} \\[2em] \text{Verb + Agentive} \quad \left\{ \begin{array}{l} \text{(Locative)} \\ \text{(Objective)} \\ \text{(Dative)} \end{array} \right\} \end{array} \right]$$

Five-Year-Old Normal Subjects
(MLU = 7.22 Morphemes)

Proposition →
$$\left[\begin{array}{l} \left\{ \begin{array}{l} \text{Essive} \\ \text{Locative} \\ \text{Attributive} \end{array} \right\} \quad \text{Designated} \\[2em] \text{Verb + Agentive} \quad \left\{ \begin{array}{l} \text{(Locative)} \\ \text{(Objective)} \\ \text{(Dative)} \end{array} \right\} \end{array} \right]$$

Appendix B

Representative proposition rules for the language samples for the normal & disordered subjects matched according to utterance length. MLU = mean utterance length, → = is rewritten as, and ( ) = optional.

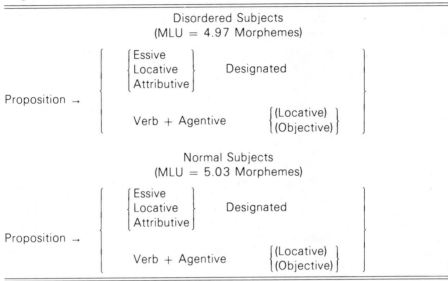

Disordered Subjects
(MLU = 4.97 Morphemes)

Proposition →

$$\left\{ \begin{array}{l} \left\{ \begin{array}{l} \text{Essive} \\ \text{Locative} \\ \text{Attributive} \end{array} \right\} \quad \text{Designated} \\ \\ \text{Verb + Agentive} \quad \left\{ \begin{array}{l} \text{(Locative)} \\ \text{(Objective)} \end{array} \right\} \end{array} \right\}$$

Normal Subjects
(MLU = 5.03 Morphemes)

Proposition →

$$\left\{ \begin{array}{l} \left\{ \begin{array}{l} \text{Essive} \\ \text{Locative} \\ \text{Attributive} \end{array} \right\} \quad \text{Designated} \\ \\ \text{Verb + Agentive} \quad \left\{ \begin{array}{l} \text{(Locative)} \\ \text{(Objective)} \end{array} \right\} \end{array} \right\}$$

Deaf and Hearing Children's Use of Language Describing Temporal Order Among Events

Robert J. Jarvella

Jay Lubinsky

Six experiments are described in which deaf and hearing subjects decided the temporal order of events in picture series and in sentences. The deaf subjects, eight and 11 years old, performed as well as hearing children on a nonverbal picture seriation task. Both deaf and hearing subjects also described most picture series in the natural left-to-right order in which they were shown, and identified the left-hand picture in most series as happening first and the right-hand picture as happening last. In most respects, the deaf children's linguistic performance resembled that of much younger hearing children. Two major results were that deaf children generally used a sequence of simple sentences to describe the events shown in a picture series, and responded to most multiple-clause sentences presented as though the events being described had occurred in the order they were mentioned.

The child's conception of time has often been considered an important aspect of his general cognitive development (Piaget, 1946; Fraisse, 1963; H. Clark, 1973; Miller and Johnson-Laird, 1975). A number of recent studies of the development of language in children have also focused on temporal concepts. These have included studies of both time reference in children's speech (Cromer, 1968; E. Clark, 1970, 1971; Ferreiro, 1971; Bronckart and Sinclair, 1973) and of children's understanding of sentences describing two temporally ordered events (Bever, 1970a; Weil, 1970; E. Clark, 1971; Ferreiro, 1971; Amidon and Carey, 1972; Barrie-Blackley, 1973). In the present research, we investigated deaf children's use of certain aspects of the "language of time" against this background of information on children with normal hearing.

A series of two events can generally be described either in the order in which the events occur in time, or in the opposite order. The range of forms for expressing the temporal order of two events, however, is quite wide, and use of a number of these forms has been investigated in previous studies of child language. An example where the events are described in the order of their occurrence is the sentence "He ate, and

From *Journal of Speech and Hearing Research, 18,* 58–73 (1975). Reprinted by permission of the American Speech and Hearing Association.

then he napped." In contrast, the sentence "He napped, but first he ate" mentions the later event before it mentions the earlier one. Similarly, the conjunctions "before" and "after" can be used to form both sentences that retain temporal order in order of mention ("He ate before he napped"; "After he ate, he napped") and that do not ("Before he napped, he ate"; "He napped after he ate"). We will abbreviate these general forms in the following by letting *1* stand for the earlier and *2* for the later of two events in time. Then, sentences of these kinds will be described as *1, and then 2, Before 2, 1,* and so forth.

LANGUAGE PERFORMANCE IN HEARING CHILDREN

The young child acquiring language can be viewed as developing and testing strategies for producing and understanding sentences (McNeill, 1966; Bever, 1970b: Slobin, 1973). Studies of young children's spontaneous and elicited speech (Cromer, 1968; E. Clark, 1970, 1971; Ferreiro, 1971) have found that events are most often described in the actual order of their occurrence. Thus, the earliest event in a series is usually mentioned first, then the next event is described, and so on. The most primitive form used by young children to represent a succession of events is generally a sequence of simple sentences. Somewhat later, children also form sentences using temporal *and* as a conjunction, often followed by *then, so,* and the like. The first sentences to appear in children's speech where *before* and *after* are used to relate two events in time also preserve temporal order in their sequence of clauses. Ferreiro (1971), for example, found that young French-speaking children used *et après* to indicate temporal order much more often than they used *et avant*.

The lexical items *before* and *after* themselves, however, are often not produced by children until relatively later on, and then they are usually used grammatically as adverbs or prepositions rather than conjunctions. While E. Clark (1970) reported that the children she observed tended to use *before* in their speech earlier than they used *after*, Cromer (1968) found just the opposite; in the longitudinal study directed by Roger Brown in the 1960s, the child referred to as Adam used *after* earlier, more frequently, and more flexibly than he used *before*.

The development of comprehension for sentences that describe temporal order among several events appears similar in several ways to that of production. Simple commands calling for a single action to be performed are usually responded to by two year olds (Buhler and Hetzer, 1935; Terman and Merrill, 1960; Shipley, Smith, and Gleitman, 1969), and children's comprehension of sentences describing two temporally ordered events has been studied from this age up. In most recent experiments, children have been asked to act out the events described in a sentence using toys, and the order in which they have done so has been taken to reflect the temporal order they understood.

The sentence types most widely used in studies of this kind have been *1 before 2; After 1, 2; Before 2, 1; and 2 after 1*. Interestingly, most children under four years of age seem to respond to such sentences on the basis of linguistic features other than the conjunctions themselves (Bever, 1970a, 1971; Weil, 1970; E. Clark, 1971; Ferreiro, 1971). Thus, two year olds usually act out the event mentioned in the main clause first, and sometimes act out only this event. Three year olds and some four year olds, on the other hand, tend to ignore syntax and simply act out the events in the order they are mentioned. And finally, when the constructions reversing temporal order are eventually mastered, it is usually *Before 2, 1* that is acquired first, and *2 after 1* second.

LANGUAGE PERFORMANCE IN DEAF CHILDREN

The prelingually deaf child probably also develops language-using strategies as he acquires the rudiments of English, but normally must acquire these linguistic skills in rather different circumstances than the hearing child. Thus, the language instruction that the deaf are typically given (Uden, 1970) is likely to diverge markedly from patterns of verbal communication commonly found in the home (Nelson, 1973). And even with preschool intervention, the deaf child's introduction to language is usually delayed and the period when it is most acquirable foreshortened (Lenneberg, 1967). Factors like these can be expected to have fairly long-term consequences for linguistic development. Previous observation of use of verb tense and aspect by deaf and hearing children, for example, suggests that the deaf do not usually acquire productive use of either (Myklebust, 1964; Neyhus and Myklebust, 1967; Pressnell, 1973). Thus, the deaf child's language system, or its cognitive basis, may not flexibly permit him to draw some of the temporal distinctions and perspectives commonly found in English.

The main question raised in the present research was to what extent deaf children's use of English describing temporal order among events would resemble that of young hearing children. In a series of six experiments, the performance of eight- and 11-year-old deaf pupils was compared with that of an age-matched control group of hearing children, and with the results of the studies of children with normal hearing, which are summarized above. In the present tasks, subjects were asked to arrange pictures into natural sequences, to describe series of pictures and arrange pictures in series to show meaning of sentences, and to answer questions by pointing to pictures from series and parts from sentences. Insofar as sequences of pictures were used to represent successions of events, the present studies were methodologically distinct from most previous ones described. However, a series of pictures is a widely used convention for representing spatio-temporal succession and one that is probably familiar to most young children in our culture. Several of the present studies were concerned with evaluating subjects' use of this convention as well as their use of language.

GENERAL METHOD

Forty children were each tested on two separate occasions several weeks apart. During the first test session, each child carried out four tasks involving sets of sequence pictures (Experiments I-IV).[1] These included a nonverbal picture arrangement task, a task in which written descriptions of picture series were elicited, and two

---

[1] The pictures used in Experiments II through V came from *Sequence Pictures for Pegboard*, Oak Lawn, Illinois: Ideal School Supply Company, and from *What Comes First, Next, and Last?* Paoli, Pennsylvania: The Instructo Corporation.

comprehension tasks concerned with the child's understanding of sentences formed with *before* and *after.* The four tasks were presented in several balanced orders over subjects. During the second test session, each child carried out two additional comprehension tasks (Experiments V-VI) concerned with his understanding of first and last events in picture series and in sentences. Again, task order was counterbalanced over subjects. All testing was conducted in a quiet room with a single subject seated at a table with the experimenter. Instructions and all other linguistic input to subjects were presented both orally and and in writing.

The hearing subjects were 10 male and 10 female second-grade pupils attending an elementary school in a Cleveland, Ohio, suburb. Their mean chronological age was 8-9 (eight years, nine months), with a range from 7-9 to 9-6.

The deaf subjects were 20 pupils attending a day school in a Cleveland suburb where instruction is given by an oral method. Deafness was in every instance prelingual, with two cases probably hereditary and five related to maternal rubella. All the children were equipped with auditory training units with individual earmolds while at school and wore their own hearing aids at home. None had learned to sign or to fingerspell.

Two subgroups of the deaf subjects were defined by age. The 10 youngest children had a mean age of 8-6 (range = 8-1 to 9-6) and the 10 oldest a mean of 11-11 (range = 10-3 to 12-11). In each age range, half the children were female and half male. Mean pure-tone hearing loss for 500-2000 Hz was 85.1 dB HTL (ANSI, 1969) in the better ear for the younger group of subjects, and 90.7 dB HTL for the older group. The children in the younger group had been fitted with hearing aids and received special instruction beginning 3-5 years on the average, as compared to 3-10 for the older group. Mean Merrill-Palmer Performance IQs were 110 and 105 for the younger and older groups, respectively, and mean reading levels, based on last available results for the American School Achievement Test, were 2.4 and 3.0.

EXPERIMENT I: ARRANGING PICTURES INTO NATURAL SEQUENCES

METHOD

The task used was the picture arrangement subtest for subjects eight years and older of the Wechsler Intelligence Scale for Children (1949). In this task, the child is shown one practice and seven test series of picture cards (for example, boy playing with matches, accidentally starting fire, firemen rushing to scene, fighting fire). The test series range from four to six cards in length, and each is presented in a single order. The subject's task is to rearrange the cards in each series into a sequence showing a likely order of occurrence. The test was administered to subjects according to guidelines in the WISC manual, except that instructions were shortened to read "I will show you some pictures. The pictures do not make a good story now. Move the pictures around to make a good story."

RESULTS

Both groups of deaf subjects performed the task somewhat more accurately than the hearing controls. The older deaf children arranged 100% of the four-picture series and 50% of the longer ones correctly, versus 92% and 37% correct for the younger deaf children. On the other hand, the hearing children placed only 81% of the four-picture series and 15% of the longer ones in orders defined as correct. The subjects' raw scores were also weighted using their ages and latencies to correct responses to obtain values on the standard 20-point WISC scale (mean = 10, *SD* = 3). The eight-year-old deaf subjects had a mean score of 14.1 on this scale, versus 12.4 for both the older deaf subjects and the hearing children. The mean difference between the eight-year-old deaf and hearing children on this measure failed to reach statistical significance at the 0.05 level ($t = 1.98$; $df = 28$).

EXPERIMENT II: DESCRIBING PICTURE SERIES

METHOD
Each subject was shown four series of pictures. There were three pictures in each series, glued in a left-to-right order on a sheet of construction paper. The pictures showed three events in their probable order of occurrence (for example, boy waking up, getting dressed, playing with bicycle). The subject's task was to write a description of the pictures in each series. The instructions given were "I will show you some pictures that tell a story. I want you to write down for me what happens in the pictures."

RESULTS
The children's descriptions of the picture series were scored for (1) the order in which the events shown were mentioned, (2) the use of words making explicit temporal reference, and (3) the number of sentences, clauses, and words that were produced. Some of the main results obtained are summarized in Table 1.

In both the deaf and hearing groups, subjects usually mentioned all three events shown in their left-to-right order. Of the 40 subjects tested, only one (from the

Table 1   Written Descriptions of Picture Series from Experiment II

Measure	Hearing-8	Deaf-8	Deaf-11
Left-middle-right order of mention	92%	80%	92%
Temporal conjunctions and			
adverbs (per story)	1.79	0.36	0.40
Verb forms used			
Fully unmarked	0%	44%	30%
Fully present tense	23%	8%	8%
Fully past tense	49%	20%	8%
Grammatical complexity			
Three short sentences	14%	73%	70%
One long sentence	48%	11%	10%
Length of description			
Clauses (per story)	4.1	3.2	3.2
Words (per story)	19.9	13.9	14.6

eight-year-old deaf group) described two pictures from a series from right to left. However in about 12% of descriptions, one or more of the events shown were not mentioned explicitly.

Second, the hearing subjects used substantially more words making explicit temporal reference than did the deaf subjects. This was true of both temporal conjunctions and adverbs and of verb tense inflections. Although the hearing subjects rarely used *before* or *after* (only five occurrences in 80 descriptions), they regularly used *and, and then, then, and so, now,* and so forth. The deaf subjects, on the other hand, never used *before* or *after* and used these other forms only occasionally. Similarly, the hearing subjects almost always marked verb tense when it was called for, and tended to use a single tense consistently within their descriptions. But the deaf subjects, and particularly the younger ones, often used no verb inflections in their descriptions.

Third, the descriptions that the hearing subjects produced of the picture series were also more elaborate in other respects than the deaf subjects' descriptions. While the dominant form used by the deaf subjects was a sequence of three simple sentences, for the hearing subjects it was one long sentence conjoining several clauses. The hearing children also referred to contextual events not directly observable in the picture series about five times as often as the deaf children; they correspondingly used both more clauses and more words per story.

EXPERIMENT III: ARRANGING PICTURES TO SHOW SENTENCE MEANING

METHOD

Each subject was shown four new series of pictures showing successions of three events (for example, boy dressing, leaving house, arriving at school). Over the course of the experiment, the pictures in each series were presented in a random order four times, each time paired with a different sentence. The sentence forms used were *1 before 2; After 1, 2; Before 2, 1;* and *2 after 1,* where *1* and *2* refer to descriptions of any pair of pictures from a series. A Greco-Latin square was used to vary picture series and sentence types over trials.

The subject's task was to arrange the two pictures described in each sentence to show its meaning. A sheet of paper containing two horizontally placed squares labeled *First* and *Second* was provided for the child to do so. The instructions given were "I will show you some pictures. The pictures do not make a good story now. I will tell you how to move two of the pictures to make a good story. Move the pictures the way I tell you." Each stimulus sentence was printed in large block letters.

RESULTS

In this experiment, and in Experiments IV and VI, the data obtained for the hearing and deaf subjects were submitted to separate parametric analyses of variance. In these analyses, orders of mention and conjunctions used in the stimulus sentences were treated as within-subjects factors (that is, repeated measures) and, for the deaf, age was treated as a between-subjects factor (Winer, 1962). In the present case, a response was scored correct whenever the pictures referred to in a sentence were placed in a left-to-right order corresponding to the temporal order described. A summary of the results obtained using this criterion is presented in Table 2.

Table 2   Percent Correct Arrangements of Pictures from Experiment III

Sentence Type	Hearing-8	Deaf-8	Deaf-11
Temporal order preserved			
1 before 2	92	80	92
After 1, 2	95	88	98
Temporal order reversed			
Before 2, 1	95	48	58
2 after 1	86	58	62

As can be seen, the hearing subjects who were tested arranged the pictures correctly over 90% of the time. As predicted by most previous results, however, they performed least satisfactorily (86% correct) on *2 after 1* items. For the deaf subjects, the pattern of results obtained was quite different. When the spoken order of the events coincided with the temporal order being described, these children also arranged the pictures correctly over 90% of the time. But when clause sequence reversed temporal order, they were correct only about half of the time. This difference was significant statistically at the 0.01 level ($F = 22.96$; $df = 1, 18$). Moreover, only about one-third of errors made by the deaf on sentence items retaining temporal order were picture reversals (the others being choices of a wrong picture), but three-fourths of errors on items not retaining temporal order were such reversals. However, it should also be noted that the deaf did make about one-third more correct responses than reversal-type errors on the latter, reverse-order items. Finally, there was also a consistent though nonsignificant tendency for the deaf children to perform better on items formed with *after* than with *before* (see Table 2).

EXPERIMENT IV: ANSWERING QUESTIONS ABOUT PICTURE SERIES, PART I

METHOD

Each subject was shown four new sets of sequence pictures showing successions of three events (for example, girl opening present, putting on skates, skating). Each series was presented in its conventional order four times during the experiment, each time paired with a different question. The question forms used were "What happened before 2?," "After 2, what happened?," "Before 2, what happened?," and "What happened after 2?," where 2 refers to a description of the middle picture in a series. A Greco-Latin square was again used to vary picture series and sentence types over trials. The subject's task was to point to one picture in answer to each question. The instructions given were "I will show you some pictures that tell a story. Look at the story. Now I will ask you something about the story. Point to the picture that answers the question." Each question was printed in large block letters.

RESULTS

Responses to questions formed with *before* were scored correct when the left-most picture in a series was identified, and those to questions formed with *after* when the right-most picture was chosen. The results obtained using this criterion are summarized in Table 3. As can be seen, the hearing subjects again responded appropriately over 90% of the time. However, questions formed with *before* were nevertheless answered more correctly than those formed with *after* ($F = 5.29$; $df = 1$, 18; $p < 0.05$). As in Experiment III and consistent with most previous results, the greatest number of errors were made on *after* items that failed to retain temporal order.

The deaf subjects' responses also followed a pattern roughly similar to that in Experiment III, except that they were now correct less than half of the time. In this instance, however, the deaf performed significantly better on sentences formed with *after* than on those formed with *before* ($F = 19.69$; $df = 1$, 18; $p < 0.01$), and only slightly (and nonsignificantly) better on sentences retaining temporal order than on those reversing it. Further analysis of the data revealed that about half the deaf subjects' errors involved choosing the middle picture in series—the one whose action was described explicitly in the questions. Among the remaining errors, there was a strong tendency for the righthand picture to be incorrectly identified.

EXPERIMENT V: ANSWERING QUESTIONS ABOUT PICTURE SERIES, PART II

METHOD

Each subject was shown four new sets of sequence pictures showing successions of three events (for example, girl packing suitcase, leaving home, arriving at grandmother's). During the experiment, each picture series was presented in its conventional order twice, each time with a single pair of questions. The pairs of questions were "What happened first?" followed by "What happened just after that?," and "What happened last?" followed by "What happened just before that?" A balanced order varying picture sequences and question pairs over trials was constructed, and the printed format for questions and instructions used was the same as in Experiment IV.

Table 3   Percentage of Correct Identifications of Pictures from Experiment IV

Sentence Type	Hearing-8	Deaf-8	Deaf-11
Temporal order preserved			
What happened before 2?	93	35	30
After 2, what happened?	89	65	55
Temporal order reversed			
Before 2, what happened?	94	20	25
What happened after 2?	85	52	62

RESULTS

Responses identifying left-most pictures in series as happening first, right-most pictures as happening last, and middle pictures as happening just after or before these others were scored as being correct. By this criterion, the hearing subjects answered all questions correctly. The deaf subjects also identified almost all left-most and right-most pictures in the series correctly, with slightly higher scores on "first" (98% correct at each age) than on "last" (88% and 95% correct for the eight and 11 year-olds, respectively). Subsequently, the deaf failed to pick the middle picture in the series about one-third of the time, however. Of these error responses, most involved not reidentifying the same picture, but picking the one at the other end of the series.

EXPERIMENT VI: ANSWERING QUESTIONS ABOUT SENTENCES

METHOD

Subjects were shown six types of sentences, each describing a pair of actions performed by a single agent (a man, woman, boy, girl, or dog). The sentence types were *1, and then 2; 2, but first 1,* and four used in Experiment III that can be formed with *before* or *after.* Four examples of each sentence type were presented twice each in a fully randomized order, once with the question "What did the (agent noun) do first?" and once with the question "What did the (agent noun) do last?" The subject's task on each trial was to point to one part of the sentence shown. To encourage unambiguous responses, the sentence's two clauses, not including the temporal conjunction, were underlined in different colors. The instructions given were "I will show you a sentence. Read the sentence. It has two parts. Now I will ask you a question about the sentence. Show me the part of the sentence that answers the question." Both questions and sentences were printed in large block letters.

RESULTS

Responses to "first" questions were scored correct when the clause describing the leading event in time was identified, and responses to "last" questions when the clause describing the following event was chosen. By this criterion, just as many

Table 4   Percentage of Correct Identifications of Clauses from Experiment VI

Sentence Type	Hearing-8	Deaf-8	Deaf-11
Temporal order preserved			
1, and then 2	97	72	62
1 before 2	89	68	44
After 1, 2	91	65	68
Temporal order reversed			
2, but first 1	97	48	60
Before 2, 1	86	50	42
2 after 1	79	44	38

"first" and "last" questions were answered correctly within each group of subjects. Table 4 presents a summary of the results obtained for the six sentence types pooled over the two kinds of questions.

As can be seen in Table 4, the hearing subjects correctly identified the clauses referred to about 90% of the time. As in Experiments III and IV, they were again most prone to make errors on sentences of the form *2 after 1*. In addition, however, the hearing subjects generally performed less accurately on sentences formed with *before* or *after* than on ones formed with *and then*, or *but first* ($F = 7.00$; $df = 2$, 36; $p < 0.01$ in main analysis of variance and in post hoc tests).

The deaf children, on the other hand, answered the questions appropriately only slightly over half the time. Their responses, however, also tended to replicate the results of the previous experiments reported. First, subjects tended to answer most "first" and "last" questions by pointing to the left-hand and right-hand clauses of the sentences, respectively. Thus, their answers were more correct on sentences retaining temporal order in their clause sequence than on sentences reversing it ($F = 4.45$; $df = 1$, 18; $p < 0.05$). Second, a *before/after* asymmetry was again obtained in the opposite direction as for the hearing subjects. This effect was quite marginal, however, being limited to the 11 year-olds' responses on sentences retaining temporal order. On sentences reversing temporal order, the 11 year-olds performed more accurately on items formed with *but first* than with either *before* or *after*. And finally, there was a trend for the deaf subjects to identify the left-hand clause from sentences. When temporal order was preserved, they answered about 10% more "first" questions correctly, but when it was reversed, they answered about 10% more "last" questions correctly.

DISCUSSION

The present findings can be grouped for discussion into four categories:

1. Evidence suggesting that the children serving as subjects interpreted the sequence pictures used in the conventional spatio-temporal sense intended;
2 and 3. Evidence suggesting which linguistic factors influenced the hearing subjects' performance on the one hand, and the deaf subjects' performance on the other; and
4. Differences in performance of the various tasks between the hearing and deaf subjects, and within the deaf, differences related to age.

Each of these topics will be taken up in turn.

PICTORIAL REPRESENTATION OF TIME

A portion of the results seems to confirm that the children tested did understand that picture sequences were being used to represent temporal order. First, the children were quite successful in arranging series appropriately. In Experiment I, both hearing and deaf subjects performed the WISC picture arrangement subtest at well above the fiftieth percentile for the standardization sample and correctly arranged about 90% of the picture series closest in length to those used in the remaining tasks. Similarly, in Experiment III, they arranged about 80% of series correctly when asked to illustrate the meaning of sentences describing pairs of events. In both tasks, chance performance would have fallen below 20% correct.

Secondly, the children appeared to interpret picture series already placed in their probable left-to-right order in a conventional way as well. In Experiment II, all subjects but one preserved this apparent temporal order in written descriptions made of the series. And in Experiment IV, they correctly answered well over 90% of questions about first and last events in series by pointing to the left-hand and right-hand pictures, respectively.

Taken together, these findings indicate that the children were generally interpreting the sequence pictures being used in the intended fashion. The results do not appear to have been seriously confounded by confusion at a pictorial level. Thus, it is likely that systematic differences in performance within tasks were primarily a function of linguistic features of the sentences being produced and comprehended. We can infer that the subjects recognized the spatio-temporal relations between events depicted in series, had a simple concept of order or succession, and knew conventions for using pictures both to demonstrate and abstract temporal order.

THE HEARING SUBJECTS' PERFORMANCE

The children with normal hearing performed the linguistic tasks used here very accurately, suggesting that they had also largely mastered the sentence structures being tested. Despite a general ceiling effect, however, two major results emerged, both tending to reconfirm findings of previous studies. First, in Experiment II, the children produced many more sentences conjoined with temporal *and* than with *before* or *after,* and in Experiment VI, also interpreted relatively more *and then* sentences correctly. This outcome seems predictable on the basis of younger subjects' habitual use of temporal *and* in their spontaneous speech (E. Clark, 1970). However, the hearing subjects also performed better in Experiment VI on sentences formed with *but first* than with *before* or *after.* Thus, a general effect was apparently obtained that could be due either to a difference between the two kinds of conjunctions used, or the form of adverb present.

Secondly, *2 after 1* was consistently the most difficult sentence type (as measured by response accuracy) for the hearing subjects to interpret. If, as suggested in the introduction, children frequently pass through stages of comprehending first on the basis of clause function and, later, clause order, then this third level of performance so commonly found (Weil, 1970; E. Clark, 1971; Ferreiro, 1971) might reflect only a renewed influence of clause function. *2 after 1* is the only one of the four sentence types formed with *before* or *after* that cannot be correctly interpreted using either the clause function or clause order strategy. A second plausible interpretation of this finding is that the earlier location of the temporal conjunction in *Before 2, 1* than *2 after 1* might have served as a more effective cue to the order of the events being described (Weil, 1970). Finally, poor performance on *2 after 1* might be explained in terms of order of acquisition of the two conjunctions. As indicated above, evidence from speech production does not strongly favor this hypothesis. However, relatively many differences in the linguistic properties of *before* and *after* have been described

(Anscombe, 1964; Heinamaki, 1974), and *before* has sometimes been taken to be a simpler semantic and referential term than *after* (E. Clark, 1971, 1973; H. Clark, 1973).

THE DEAF SUBJECTS' PERFORMANCE

Almost all the present findings for the deaf resembled previous results for younger children without hearing disorders. Perhaps most significantly, an effect of clause order was obtained in all sentence comprehension tasks in which it was manipulated, and a similar effect was obtained for sentence production. Thus, in Experiment III, practically all picture reversal errors occurred when linguistic and temporal order diverged; in Experiment IV, *Wh-* questions were more often answered correctly if they retained temporal order; in Experiment VI, most sentence-initial and sentence-final clauses were identified as happening first and last, respectively. Similarly, in Experiment II, the deaf subjects usually used nothing but linguistic order to represent temporal succession. This general influence of clause order on performance clearly suggests a language-using strategy similar to one previously identified for preschool hearing children. The deaf, moreover, may generally interpret verbally described events as occurring in the order they are mentioned. Uden (1970), for example, refers to separate Dutch studies by Calon and Puyenbrock in which deaf children were found to have trouble understanding discourse in which temporal order was not represented directly.

Clause order, however, was here by no means the only determinant of comprehension of temporal order by the deaf. Quite a few other similarities were obtained between these subjects' responses and present or previous results for hearing children. Several have to do with use of "first" and "last," or both. Thus, like Amidon and Carey's (1972) subjects, the deaf children responded more accurately when asked simple questions about "first" and "last" events than when presented with complex sentences containing *before* or *after* (Experiment V versus IV). Like E. Clark's (1971) subjects, they correctly answered more questions asking "What happened first?" than "What happened last?" (Experiment V). However, when asked similar questions in Experiment VI, the children performed better on "first" only when temporal order in the sentences being queried was preserved. There was thus a slight bias for them to identify the beginning (left side) of both kinds of stimulus sequences. Finally, like the present hearing subjects, the older deaf children tested answered more questions about *2, but first 1* sentences correctly than about reverse order sentences formed with *before* or *after* (Experiment VI).

When the deaf children were asked to locate one picture in relation to another in Experiment IV, they most frequently erred by choosing the one mentioned overtly (for example, *2* in "What happened after 2?"). A similar finding has been obtained for younger hearing children in various Piagetian tasks (Sinclair-de-Zwart, 1969) and by Cromer (1968) in another picture sequence experiment. On the other hand, subjects seldom chose the same picture twice in succession in Experiment V, where they were asked to identify first one picture and then locate the second by deixis (as *just after/before that*). Most of their errors in this case overreached the adjacent picture, suggesting that they did not yet fully control this linguistic form for distinguishing between closely and more distantly ordered events.

Two results obtained bear somewhat less resemblance to findings for hearing subjects. First, multiple-clause sentences formed with *after* were interpreted more correctly than similar sentences formed with *before* (Experiments III, IV, and VI). Only Barrie-Blackley (1973) has previously reported a systematic difference in this direction for comprehension of *before* and *after* sentences. As suggested earlier, both syntactic and lexical explanations of this type of finding are possible. One way of examining if subjects (deaf or hearing) simply tend to interpret main (subordinate) clauses as describing earlier (later) events would be to see whether the response pattern obtained on sentences formed with *before* or *after* also occurs when the conjunction used is meaningless. On the other hand, the present subjects may have been more familiar with *after* than with *before*. For example, the clearest opposition to *after* in their lexicon might have been not *before* but *first*. Finally, still another explanation seems plausible in the context of Experiment IV, where the conjunction effect was both strongest and most divergent from the hearing subjects' responses; namely, the overtly described middle pictures in series might have served as starting points from which the questions were taken as asking what happened subsequently or as a result (Piaget, 1946; Bronckart and Sinclair, 1973).

Secondly, verb affixes were used with different frequency by the present deaf and hearing subjects in their written descriptions of picture series (Experiment II). In almost 40% of these stories, none of the verb forms used by the deaf was inflected for tense or aspect. This result further confirms that the deaf frequently omit verb inflections in their speech and writing (Neyhus and Myklebust, 1967; Pressnell, 1973), but numerous such errors also occur in the speech of young hearing children. Moreover, a large proportion of the verbs actually used with some inflectional marking were past tense forms of English strong verbs, which are often the earliest marked verb forms used by hearing children. Thus, it may be worthwhile to compare the order of appearance of verb inflections in larger samples of deaf language with that in the speech of hearing children (Cazden, 1968; Brown, 1973).

INTERGROUP COMPARISIONS

Like their performance IQs in general, the deaf subjects' scores on the WISC picture arrangement subtest were slightly higher than obtained by previous investigators on the same type of task (K. Murphy, 1957; L. Murphy, 1957; Myklebust, 1964). They were not so high, however, to fall significantly above the scores obtained for the present control group. Since the deaf often do score above the normal median on nonverbal tests of cognitive abilities (Myklebust, 1964; Furth, 1966), the present subjects' performance on the WISC should probably not be considered unusual.

Secondly, the deaf subjects performed less consistently and less accurately than the hearing subjects on all the linguistic tasks used. These differences in performance were generally statistically significant. Most generally, they may further confirm that deaf children acquire English at a slower rate than children with both normal hearing and a rich early linguistic environment. However, the present results do not suggest many qualitative differences in language between the present deaf and younger hearing children.

Finally, it is not really feasible to draw any firm conclusions here about language development in the deaf as a function of age. The sample size used in the present studies was quite limited, and there were some differences between subjects in the two age ranges tested that might obscure significant developmental trends. Nevertheless, the older deaf children tested did tend to perform the various linguistic tasks used slightly more accurately than the younger subjects. In light of these results and many previous findings, it seems likely that deaf performance in this area would further improve with added age and experience with language.

ACKNOWLEDGMENT

This research was supported in part by the Grant Foundation and by the National Institute of Mental Health. An earlier version of some of the material discussed here was presented at the 1973 Annual Convention of the American Speech and Hearing Association, Detroit, Michigan. The authors wish to express their thanks to Joy Goldman Collas for her help in conducting the experiments reported, and to George A. Miller and Joyce Weil for commenting on many of the ideas that are expressed. The kind cooperation of the Lakewood, Ohio, Schools is also gratefully acknowledged.

REFERENCES

American National Standards Institute, *Standard Specification for Audiometers.* ANSI-1969, New York (1969).

Amidon, A., and Carey, P., Why five-year-olds cannot understand before and after. *J. Verb. Learn. Verb. Behav.,* **11,** 417–423 (1972).

Anscombe, G., Before and after. *Phil. Rev.,* **74,** 3–24 (1964).

Barrie-Blackley, S., Six-year-old children's understanding of sentences adjoined with time adverbs. *J. Psycholinguist. Res.,* **2,** 153–166 (1973).

Bever, T., The comprehension and memory of sentences with temporal relations. In G. Flores d'Arcais and W. Levelt (Eds.), *Advances in Psycholinguistics.* Amsterdam: North Holland (1970a).

Bever, T., The cognitive basis for linguistic structures. In J. Hayes (Ed.), *Cognition and the Development of Language.* New York: Wiley (1970b).

Bever, T., The integrated study of language behavior. In J. Morton (Ed.), *Biological and Social Factors in Psycholinguistics.* London: Logos (1971).

Bronckart, J., and Sinclair, H., Time, tense, and aspect. *Cognition: Int. J. Cognitive Psychol.,* **2,** 107–131 (1973).

Brown, R., A *First Language.* New York: Harper and Row (1973).

Buhler, C., and Hetzer, H., *Testing Children's Development from Birth to School Age.* New York: Farrar and Rinehart (1935).

Cazden, C., The acquisition of noun and verb inflections. *Child Develpm.,* **39,** 433–438 (1968).

Clark, E., How young children describe events in time. In G. Flores d'Arcais and W. Levelt (Eds.), *Advances in Psycholinguistics.* Amsterdam: North Holland (1970).

Clark, E., On the acquisition of the meaning of before and after. *J. Verb. Learn. Verb. Behav.,* **10,** 266–275 (1971).

Clark, E., What's in a word? On the child's acquisition of semantics in his first language. In T. Moore (Ed.), *Cognitive Development and the Acquisition of Language.* New York: Academic (1973).

Clark, H., Space, time, semantics, and the child. In T. Moore (Ed.), *Cognitive Development and the Acquisition of Language.* New York: Academic (1973).

Cromer, R., The development of temporal reference during the acquisition of language. Doctoral dissertation, Harvard Univ. (1968).

Ferreiro, E., *Les Relations Temporelles dans le Langage de L'enfant.* Geneva: Librairie Droz (1971).

Fraisse, P., *The Psychology of Time.* New York: Harper and Row (1963).

Furth, H., *Thinking Without Language.* New York: Free Press (1966).

Heinamaki, O., Semantics of English temporal connectives. Doctoral dissertation, Univ. of Texas (1974).

Lenneberg, E., *Biological Foundations of Language.* New York: Wiley (1967).

McNeill, D., The capacity for language acquisition. *Volta Rev., 68,* 17–32 (1966).

Miller G., and Johnson-Laird, P., *Language and Perception* Cambridge, Mass.: Harvard Univ. Press (1975).

Murphy, K., Survey of abilities of children aged twelve years in schools for the deaf. In A. Ewing (Ed.), *Educational Guidance and the Deaf Child.* Manchester: Manchester Univ. Press (1957).

Murphy, L., Tests of abilities and attainments: Pupils in schools for the deaf aged six to ten. In A. Ewing (Ed.), *Educational Guidance and the Deaf Child.* Manchester: Manchester Univ. Press (1957).

Myklebust, H., *The Psychology of Deafness.* (2nd ed.) New York: Grune and Stratton (1964).

Nelson, K., Structure and strategy in learning to talk. *Monogr. Soc. Res. Child Develpm.,* Serial No. 149, No. 1–2 (1973).

Neyhus, A., and Myklebust, H., Early-life deafness and mental development. In F. McConnell and P. Ward (Eds.), *Deafness in Childhood.* Nashville: Vanderbilt Univ. Press (1967).

Piaget, J. *Le Developpement de la Notion de Temps Chez L'enfant.* Paris: Presses Universitaires de France (1946).

Pressnell, L., Hearing-impaired children's comprehension and production of syntax in oral language. *J. Speech Hearing Res., 16,* 12–21 (1973).

Shipley, E., Smith C., and Gleitman, L., A study of the acquisition of language. *Language, 45,* 322–342 (1969).

Sinclair-de-Zwart, H., Developmental psycholinguistics. In D. Elkind and J. Flavell (Eds.), *Studies in Cognitive Development: Essays in Honor of Jean Piaget.* New York: Oxford Univ. Press (1969).

Slobin, D., Cognitive prerequisites for the development of grammar. In C. Ferguson and D. Slobin (Eds.), *Studies of Child Language Development.* New York: Holt (1973).

Terman, L., and Merrill, M., *Stanford-Binet Intelligence Scale.* Boston: Houghton Mifflin (1960).

Uden, A., *A World of Language for Deaf Children. Part I. Basic Principles.* Rotterdam: Rotterdam Univ. Press (1970).

Wechsler, D., *Wechsler Intelligence Scale for Children.* New York: The Psychological Corporation (1949).

Weil, J., The relationship between time conceptualization and time language in young children. Doctoral dissertation, City Univ. of New York (1970).

Winer, B., *Statistical Principles in Experimental Design.* New York: McGraw-Hill (1962).

Part 2
CLINICAL ASSESSMENT OF LANGUAGE SKILLS

Most of the methodologies illustrated in Part 1 have been applied to the clinical assessment of children with a language disorder. The usefulness of a particular methodology for the purpose of clinical assessment depends on whether the objective of assessment is: to identify children with a language disorder; to plan the goals of an intervention program; or to estimate the outcomes of intervention. The articles included in Part 2 illustrate or discuss methodologies relevant to each of these objectives.

Identification of children with a language disorder typically involves comparison of a child's language behavior with that of other children of the same age who were observed under similar conditions. In order to control the conditions of observation and to save time, responses are usually elicited in a standardized manner. The article by Lee (1970) presents an instrument designed to elicit, in a standardized manner, both the comprehension and the production of linguistic stimuli. Lee has pointed out, both in the article and in the comments appended to the article, that the information obtained from this type of norm-referenced observation is for the purpose of identifying children who may be having difficulty learning the syntax of English, not describing what they know about syntax. (To accomplish the purpose of identification, however, reliability and validity data are needed and are not reported for this instrument—see Arndt, 1977.)

The important distinction, between identifying children with a language disorder and describing what a child knows about language, is relevant to the choice of methodology in assessment. The problem of inferring *what* a child knows about language from procedures designed to identify children with a language disorder is discussed here by Prutting, Gallagher, and Mulac (1975) and has been discussed elsewhere by Dever (1972). The article by Prutting et al. concerns the use of a standardized norm-referenced instrument, the one described in the article by Lee (1970), for the purpose of description.

A more appropriate methodology for obtaining information about what a child knows about language, suggested by Prutting et al. and other researchers, is the analysis of free speech samples. See, for example, Chapter XVI in the accompanying text by Bloom and Lahey (1978) or Crystal, Fletcher, and Garman (1976), Lee (1974), and Tyack and Gottsleben (1974). None is reprinted here because most are too long for a collection of this nature. The few exceptions such as Lee and Canter (1971), are outdated or have been revised in a longer format.

A third possible purpose for describing deviant language during clinical assessment is to predict future language skills following some intervention procedures—that is, to make a prognosis. The article by Shapiro, Chiarandini, and Fish (1974) is included here as a rare example of a study designed for this purpose.

The articles in Part I and Part II focus on describing deviant language. Both clinicians and researchers, however, are interested in describing other aspects of language disorders and the language-disordered child. Such topics are taken up in the sections that follow.

REFERENCES

Arndt, W.B. 1977 A psychometric evaluation of the Northwestern Syntax Screening Test. *Journal of Speech and Hearing Research, 42,* 316–319.

Bloom, L. and Lahey, M. 1978 *Language development and language disorder.* N.Y: J. Wiley & Sons.

Crystal, D.,Fletcher, P., and Garman, M. 1976 *The grammatical analysis of language disability: A procedure for assessment and remediation.* London: Arnold.

Dever, R. 1972 A comparison of the results of a revised version of Berko's test of morphology with the free speech of mentally retarded children. *Journal of Speech and Hearing Research 15,* 169–178.

Lee, L. 1974 *Developmental sentence analysis.* Evanston, Ill. Northwestern University Press.

Lee, L., an Canter, S. 1971 Developmental sentence scoring: A clinical procedure for estimating syntactic development in children's spontaneous speech. *Journal of Speech and Hearing Disorders, 36,* 315–341.

Tyack, D., and Gottsleben, R. 1974 *Language sampling, analysis and training: A handbook for teachers and clinicians.* Palo Alto, Calif.: Consulting Psychological Press.

A Screening Test For Syntax Development

Laura L. Lee

The assessment of syntactic development in children with language problems has often been an imprecise judgment by the clinical diagnostician, based largely upon informal conversation with the child. Even when careful attention is given to individual syntactic features, such as pronouns, questions, negatives, and verb tenses, the comparison of the child's comprehension with his production of grammatical structures has often been made upon very dissimilar material. The child's receptive use of syntactic rules has often been judged by his ability to follow commands, identify pictures, or listen to a story. On the other hand, his expressive use of grammatical rules has often been judged by his responses to questions, stimulus pictures, or story-telling, although these procedures might elicit an entirely different level of syntactic complexity than did the receptive tasks. In this kind of conversational setting, the evaluator customarily has judged the child's use of grammatical rules without reference to specific linguistic tasks, developmental scales, or normative data.

Many clinical tests for syntactic and morphological development evaluate various aspects of grammatical skill without comparing the receptive and expressive uses of grammatical forms. Berko's (1958) method for investigating morphological development requires a child to add appropriate endings to nonsense words: "This is a man who knows how to spow. He is spowing. He did the same thing yesterday. What did he do yesterday? Yesterday he ———." The Grammatic Closure subtest of the Illinois Test of Psycholinguistic Abilities (Kirk, McCarthy, and Kirk, 1968) uses a procedure similar to Berko's except that the test items are in a developmental progression and real words are used rather than nonsense syllables: "Here is a bed. Here are two ———." The ITPA Grammatic Closure subtest, like Berko's method, measures expression only. Furthermore, both of these procedures present morphological tasks exclusively; no examples of word order, questions, negatives, passives, or subject-object identification are used. Carrow's (1968) investigation of auditory comprehension of language structure covers a great number of linguistic tasks in the areas of vocabulary, syntax, and morphology. Carrow's test, however, is entirely receptive, and no attempt is made to compare a child's performance on the test items with his spontaneous use of the same items in expressive language.

From *Journal of Speech and Hearing Disorders, 35,* 103–112 (1970). Reprinted by permission of the American Speech and Hearing Association.

The Michigan Picture Language Inventory, developed by Lerea (1958a, b), does make a comparison between comprehension and expression of vocabulary and certain language structures, including pronouns, possessives, comparative forms of adjectives, demonstratives, articles, adverbs, prepositions, and three verb tenses. Furthermore, the comprehension and expression measures are made on identical linguistic tasks; therefore, the derived norms present a meaningful comparison of receptive and expressive skills. Lerea's technique for eliciting expressive responses is to require the child to supply an omitted word, or words, from a sentence spoken by the examiner: "In this picture the girl sleeps in *her* bed. In this picture the rabbit sleeps in *its* bed. And in this picture the boy sleeps in ————." This missing word technique is the same method used by Berko and the ITPA Grammatic Closure subtest to elicit responses upon which a judgment of expressive grammatical skill can be based. However, this method puts limits on the kind of linguistic tasks which can be tested. It is highly effective in showing a child's ability to formulate a proper morphological form for a given lexical word or to select an appropriate function word, such as a pronoun or a preposition. But the missing word technique cannot incorporate syntactic tasks involving word order, i.e., questions, passives, negatives, noun phrases, subject-object distinction, or the more complicated auxiliary verb arrangements. Any test of language development which goes beyond morphology and function words to include the grammatical relationships underlying kernel sentence construction and transformational operations must use whole sentences, not single words.

The technique of sentence repetition has been used effectively in psycholinguistic research. Menyuk (1969) investigated the ability of preschool and kindergarten children to repeat sentences involving transformational structures, such as nominalization, question, conjunctions *so* and *because*, and verb forms, such as auxiliary *have* and *have got*. Analysis of the children's errors showed the grammatical rules under which they were operating. Thus, the child's underlying competence, his knowledge of grammatical rules, could be assessed from his expressive performance, his use of these rules in the speech he produced. But the psycholinguist's concern with the distinction between competence and performance is not the same as the speech pathologist's concern with the distinction between reception and expression. Psycholinguistic theory clearly puts both comprehension and production under the heading of performance, as something quite separate from the deeper level of competence (Cazden, in press). Speech clinicians need to consider a child's underlying competence with grammatical rules, but they also need to know whether this competence is more efficiently used in receptive than in expressive performance. The psycholinguist's method of assessing competence through the analysis of expressive performance is undoubtedly effective with normally developing children, but it cannot be used with assurance on a speech clinic population. Children with language problems often have good grammatical competence, which they have developed receptively and which they can demonstrate through receptive tasks, while handicapping conditions interfere with their expressive use of grammatical rules. Thus, sentence repetition, being largely an expressive task, is only of partial value in judging grammatical competence in a speech clinic population, and it certainly is not a technique which compares receptive with expressive performance.

If sentence repetition (as a measure of expressive performance) could be accompanied by a picture identification task, using the same sentences (as a measure of receptive performance), then both comprehension and production of whole sentences could be compared on identical syntactic material. But drawing pictures to be identified by the syntactic structure of a sentence rather than by its contentive words is not always an easy task. The test should employ decoy pictures so that chance selection of a correct picture is reduced. A set of test pictures for the identification of subject and object in "The car hits the train" would be easy to draw. It could include pictures of a car and a train running parallel, a train hitting a car, a car hitting a tree near the railroad track, as well as the test picture. But a set of test pictures for the identification of the possessive in "This is Mother's cat" presents some problems. Decoy pictures, from which the selection is made, could include Mother with a cat, Father with a cat, a cat alone, and so on. But the child would not need to know the possessive form to select the correct picture; he could do it from the contentives alone, simply by finding a picture that had *Mother* and *cat* in it. The examiner could not be sure that the syntactic task had been accomplished even though the correct picture had been selected. However, the technique of contrasting sentence-pairs allows a solution to this problem. If two sentences, using the same contentives and differing in only one syntactic feature, are presented together, and the child is asked to identify both sentences from a set of four pictures, then the grammatical task is clarified and can be pictured. Thus, the sentence "This is Mother's cat," paired with "This is a mother cat," can become a meaningful task in receptive syntactic performance. The technique of presenting sentences in contrasting syntactic pairs is a useful clinical device, similar to the minimal pairs commonly used in speech sound discrimination tests.

The Imitation, Comprehension, Production Test (ICP) of Fraser, Bellugi, and Brown (1963) was not designed for use by speech pathologists but was adaptable to clinical needs. It used the technique of contrasting sentence-pairs as a means of eliciting both receptive and expressive performance with whole sentences. Thus, the range of test items could include tasks involving word order as well as morphological forms and function words, and the reception-expression distinction could be made on tasks of identical complexity. In the ICP Test, ten contrasting sentence-pairs presented linguistic tasks such as subject-object identification, negative-affirmative distinction, noun phrase and prepositional phrase recognition, and direct and indirect object placement. The imitation portion of the test required only sentence repetition. The comprehension portion used stimulus pictures to be identified from the examiner's spoken sentence-pairs. The production portion used similar pictures to be named by sentence-pairs spoken first by the examiner, then repeated by the child. Thus, a comparison could be made between a child's ability to imitate, to comprehend, and to produce identical grammatical tasks involving whole sentences rather than single words. No attempt was made to establish a developmental order for the various items, and no reliable normative data could be derived from the small number of children included in the study. Fraser, Bellugi, and Brown were interested merely in showing the normal child's progression from imitation to comprehension to production, but their technique provided a means for precise assessment of receptive and expressive syntactic skill in a speech clinic population.

The Northwestern Syntax Screening Test (NSST) (Lee, 1969) has been developed along the lines of the Fraser, Bellugi, and Brown technique. The imitation aspect was

Figure 1.   Pictures for receptive distinction between "This is Mother's cat" and "This is a mother cat."

omitted to shorten the procedure, and the original test items were revised and expanded to include function words and morphological forms as well as word order. The NSST consists of 20 sentence-pairs to be identified receptively by picture selection and 20 similar sentence-pairs to be produced in response to stimulus pictures. Thus, the receptive and expressive tasks are of equal linguistic complexity. The receptive portion (Figure 1) presents a child with four pictures, two of them decoys and two of them identifiable by a grammatical contrast spoken by the examiner: "This is Mother's cat. This is a mother cat." The child is then asked to point to the pictures named, one at a time, as the examiner repeats the two sentences. The expressive portion of the test (Figure 2) superimposes the task of expression onto the task of reception, but the receptive task is simplified by the omission of the decoy pictures. Only two pictures are presented on the page, both of which are named by the examiner without pointing: "This is Baby's doll. This is a baby doll." If the examiner were to identify the two pictures first, then the task might be accomplished on the basis of auditory recall alone without real comprehension. This administration of the expressive portion of the test insures that the child is not just parroting a test sentence but is demonstrating expressive grammatical performance. After first saying the two sentences, the examiner points to each picture and asks, "What's this one? What's that one?" in order to elicit the sentences from the child. The child is asked to say the sentences exactly as the examiner said them. The 20 tasks cover such grammatical features as prepositions, personal pronouns, negatives, plurals, reflexive pronouns, verb tenses, subject-object identification, possessives, *wh*-questions, yes-no questions, passives, and indirect objects. The receptive items are as follows:

1. The cat is behind the chair. The cat is under the chair.
2. She goes upstairs. He goes upstairs.
3. The cat is on the cupboard. The cat is in the cupboard.
4. The boy is sitting. The boy is not sitting.
5. The deer is running. The deer are running.
6. The boy sees the cat. The boy sees the cats.
7. The boy sees himself. The boy sees the shelf.
8. The milk spilled. The milk spills.
9. The car hits the train. The train hits the car.
10. This is their dog. This is her dog.
11. This is a mother cat. This is Mother's cat.
12. The girl will drink. The girl is drinking.
13. Mother says, "Look who is here." Mother says, "Look what is here."
14. The dog is in the box. Is the dog in the box?
15. The boy writes. The boys write.
16. Mother says, "Where is that girl?" Mother says, "Who is that girl?"
17. Has Daddy finished dinner? Daddy has finished dinner.
18. The boy is pushed by the girl. The girl is pushed by the boy.
19. This is my hat. That is my hat.
20. The mother shows the kitty the baby. The mother shows the baby the kitty.

Figure 2. Pictures for expressive distinction between "This is Baby's doll" and "This is a baby doll."

The expressive portion of the test presents the same linguistic tasks but with different contentive vocabulary and pictures.

A score of 1 is given for each correct response. Thus, on each of the 20 sentence-pairs the child could receive a score of 0, 1, or 2, and a perfect score would be 40 on each of the two parts of the test, receptive and expressive. Failure on the receptive portion consists of a wrong picture identification in response to a spoken sentence. Failure on the expressive portion consists of any change of the examiner's spoken sentence which affects the test item. Thus, if the examiner said, "The girl will drink," and the child replied, "The girl is going to drink," this reply would be judged a failure on the test item, future tense marked by *will*, even though it is a semantically appropriate response to the picture. Similarly, if the child changed the passive, "The boy is pushed by the girl," to the active, "The girl is pushing the boy," this would be scored a failure, since the test item is the child's production of a passive sentence. Likewise, the response, "The mother shows the baby to the kitty," in place of the examiner's sentence, "The mother shows the kitty the baby," is a syntactic failure on indirect object placement, even though the two sentences are semantically interchangeable. A score of 0 is also given for a response which contains any grammatical error even if it is not the test item. Thus, "This Mother's cat" in response to "This is Mother's cat" would be judged a failure since the possessive, *'s,* may have introduced enough complexity to cause the *is* to be dropped. Similarly, a child might drop the verb inflection on *sees* in an effort to pluralize the noun *cats* and produce the sentence-pair "The boy sees the cat. The boy see the cats." However, any change of the examiner's spoken sentence which does not change the test item and which still produces a grammatical sentence is acceptable and scores 1. Thus, a change from the examiner's "The boy is not sitting" to "He is not sitting" or from the examiner's "Mother says, 'Look who is here' " to a simpler form, " 'Look who is here,' " is scored correct. A record form is used on which the sentence-pairs are printed, and as the child gives his responses, the examiner notes any alteration of the sentence which he may produce. Thus, the judgment of the correctness of the child's responses need not be immediate and does not interrupt the administration of the test. The whole test can be given in approximately 15 minutes.

Tentative norms have been established from data gathered from 242 children between the ages of 3-0 and 7-11. The lowest number in any of the 6-month age groups was 13, for ages 3-0 to 3-5; the highest number was 62, for ages 5-6 to 5-11. The children came from middle-income and upper middle-income communities and from homes where standard American dialect was spoken. One hundred eleven of the children were males and 131 were females, but no consistent difference was found between the boys' and the girls' performances at the various age levels. The sentence-pairs have been arranged in order of increasing difficulty according to the performances of these 242 children. This order was slightly different for receptive and expressive items. However, the test is too short to establish basal and ceiling scores, and the whole test should be administered to a single child.

In using these data for clinical purposes, an individual child's performance can be quickly evaluated by reference to two charts, one showing the receptive norms (Figure 3) and the other the expressive norms (Figure 4) for these 242 children. Both charts show the 90th, 75th, 50th, 25th, and 10th percentiles for each 6-month age group. Thus, a child in the 5-6 to 5-11 age group, who received a receptive score of 22, would fall below the 10th percentile for his age group and could be said to have performed as the average of the 3-6 to 3-11 age group. Similarly, a child in the 5-0 to 5-5 age group, who received an expressive score of 12, could be said to have performed as the average of the 3-0 to 3-5 age group. Furthermore, a child in the 4-0 to 4-5 age group, who received a receptive score of 23 but an expressive score

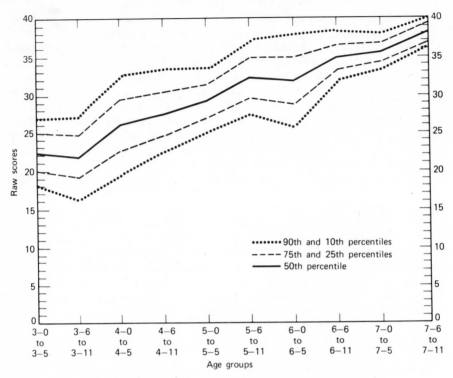

Figure 3.   Receptive scores of 242 children on the NSST.

of 12, could be said to have performed in the low-average range receptively but to have fallen considerably below the 10th percentile expressively.

Use of the NSST thus far has revealed that children already enrolled in speech and language development programs in clinics and in public schools regularly fall below the 10th percentile on either or both portions of the test, the receptive or the expressive. Thus, the NSST can be used as a quick method for identifying those children between 3 and 8 years of age who are sufficiently delayed in syntactic development to warrant further study and consideration for interventional language teaching. It is useful to speech clinicians who need a short test for screening large numbers of children, as in a public school setting, and to diagnosticians who need to make a quick estimate of syntactic development as part of a more elaborate speech and language evaluation. In the Northwestern University Speech Clinic, it has proved a valuable tool for the quick comparison of receptive and expressive syntactic development in diagnostic evaluations. The NSST is intended to be used as a screening instrument only. It is in no sense to be considered a measurement of a child's general language development nor even as a detailed study of syntax. It will be most useful when used in conjunction with other routinely administered tests in a speech and language evaluation.

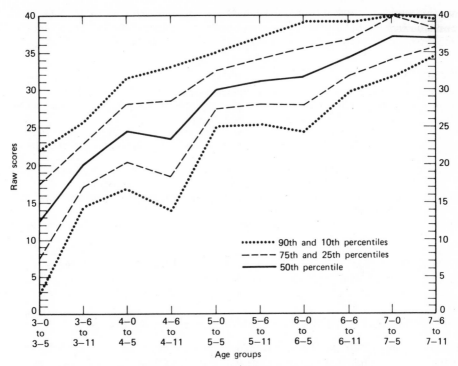

Figure 4.   Expressive scores of 242 children on the NSST.

SUMMARY

The Northwestern Syntax Screening Test (NSST) has been developed as an instrument which will quickly identify children between 3 and 8 years of age, sufficiently delayed in syntactic development to warrant consideration for interventional language teaching. It makes a comparison between receptive and expressive use of such grammatical features as prepositions, personal pronouns, negatives, plurals, reflexive pronouns, verb tenses, subject-object identification, possessives, *wh*-questions, yes-no questions, passives, and indirect objects. The procedure consists of picture selection in response to spoken sentences and sentence repetition in response to stimulus pictures, where the test sentences include grammatical contrasts of increasing difficulty. It can be administered in 15 minutes. It is useful to public school speech clinicians for screening large numbers of children and to clinical diagnosticians for quickly estimating syntactic development as part of a general speech and language evaluation.

ACKNOWLEDGMENT

Students who participated in the development of the NSST include Kyoko Ando, Mary Berger, Susan Canter, Joanne Colen, George Larsen, Susan Nathanson, and Sandra Ourth. The participating schools included the Evanston Day Care Nursery,

First Methodist Church of Evanston Nursery School, Convenant Methodist Church of Evanston Nursery School, First Unitarian Church of Chicago Sunday School, and the Public Schools of Wilmette, Illinois and Hamilton County, Ohio.

REFERENCES

Berko, J., The child's learning of English morphology. *Word,* **14,** 150–177 (1958).

Carrow, Sr. M. A., The development of auditory comprehension of language structure in children. *J. Speech Hearing Dis., 33,* 99–111 (1968).

Cazden, C., The psychology of language. In Lee E. Travis (Ed.), *Handbook of Speech, Hearing, and Language Disorders* (rev. ed.). New York: Appleton-Century-Crofts (in press).

Fraser, C., Bellugi, U., and Brown, R., Control of grammar in imitation, comprehension, and production. *J. Verb. Learn, Verb. Behav., 2,* 121–135 (1963).

Kirk, S., McCarthy, J., and Kirk, W., *The Illinois Test of Psycholinguistic Abilities* (rev. ed.). Urbana: Univ. Ill. Press (1968).

Lee, L., *The Northwestern Syntax Screening Test.* Evanston, Ill.: Northwestern Univ. Press (1969).

Lerea, L., Assessing language development. *J. Speech Hearing Res., 1,* 75–85 (1958a).

Lerea, L., *The Michigan Picture Language Inventory.* Ann Arbor: Univ. Mich. (1958b).

Menyuk, P., *Sentences Children Use.* Cambridge, Mass.: The M.I.T. Press (1969).

Author's Comment Written for *Readings in Childhood Language Disorders:*

Readers of this 1970 *JSHD* article should be aware that a revision of the NSST was made in 1971, a full year after the appearance of this article. The test itself was not altered, but more children (344) were included in the standardization group. The normative charts were redrawn to show one-year rather than six-month age groups. A new line, the second standard deviation below the mean, was added to the charts and was recommended as a more realistic cut-off point than the former tenth percentile line for identifying children in need of further examination. The instructions for the administration and interpretation of test results were considerably expanded. Therefore, the value of this 1970 article is not now in the normative data that it presents but in the discussion of problems that arise when evaluating something as elusive as grammatical development in young children.

It must be strongly emphasized that the NSST was never intended to be more than a clinical screening procedure. It is in no sense an in-depth assessment of grammatical ability. The use of the NSST, since its initial publication, has often gone beyond this intended purpose and has produced some misunderstanding of its values and limitations. Its chief value is in helping a clinician decide quickly whether grammatical development should be explored more fully in the diagnostic examination of a preschool child, whether it be in a clinic, kindergarten, or early childhood education program. When further investigation is indicated, the examination of a spontaneous language sample such as Developmental Sentence Analysis (Lee, 1974) is recommended. The information derived from such a detailed analysis provides guidelines for lesson planning, as illustrated in the Interactive Language Development Teaching approach (Lee, Koenigsknecht, and Mulhern, 1975).

The NSST alone does not examine a child's language development in sufficient depth to provide teaching goals. It contains too few items to reveal the full extent of a child's grammatical capabilities. It is useful only for children who are learning standard English. The norms might have to be modified for different socioeconomic levels and different geographical areas. Clinicians must bear in mind that all clinical tests have these kinds of limitations. They should guard against the overinterpretation of test scores and the over-reliance upon formal test results in determining which children will need clinical services.

REFERENCES

Lee, Laura L., *Developmental Sentence Analysis.* Evanston, Ill.: Northwestern University Press, 1974.

Lee, Laura L., Koenigsknecht, Roy A., and Mulhern, Susan T., *Interactive Language Development Teaching.* Evanston, Ill.: Northwestern University Press, 1975.

The Expressive Portion of the NSST Compared to a Spontaneous Language Sample

Carol A. Prutting

Tanya M. Gallagher

Anthony Mulac

This study was undertaken to determine the relationship between syntactic structures produced on the expressive portion of the NSST and those produced in a spontaneous language sample. The NSST was administered to 12 children previously diagnosed as delayed in language. In addition, spontaneous language samples were collected by a speech clinician and by the child's mother. The children ranged in age from four years one month to five years 11 months. We found that 30% of those syntactic structures incorrectly produced on the NSST were correctly produced spontaneously in the language sample. Furthermore, the sample obtained by the clinician was significantly richer in terms of number of structures produced correctly than the sample collected by the mother. Overall results indicate that an item analysis of the expressive portion of the NSST does not present an accurate representation of the child's language performance and therefore cannot be interpreted beyond its stated purpose, namely that of a screening instrument.

Speech pathologists attempting to diagnose the communicative abilities of language-delayed children must ultimately investigate their language skills in relation to the generation of specific language structures. Screening tests designed to differentiate populations do not perform this diagnostic function.

Unfortunately, while there are several reliable language screening tests available, such as Mean Length of Response (McCarthy, 1930) and Michigan Picture Language Inventory (Wolsi, 1958), there are relatively few diagnostic language instruments. Language screening tests provide information that separates populations delayed in language from normal language populations. On the other hand, diagnostic language tests yield information about specific errors that require remediation. Because of its construction, the expressive portion of a recent screening test, the Northwestern Syntax Screening Test (1969), might be able to fill this void by providing both screening and diagnostic information. The NSST consists of 20 grammatical distinctions and uses a variety of sentence frames; thus, it is a potentially valid diagnostic tool.

From *Journal of Speech and Hearing Disorders, 40,* 40–48 (1975). Reprinted by permission of the American Speech and Hearing Association.

Although it was not intended for use as a diagnostic test, the investigators' observations indicate that practicing clinicians are using the NSST to plan remediation programs.

The expressive portion of the NSST contains 20 sentence-pairs that sample a number of syntactic forms, each progressively more difficult. Two pictures are presented on each page of the test booklet and the examiner is instructed to identify both pictures, without pointing to them, using sentences provided in the manual. The examiner then points to each picture and elicits the test sentences by asking "What's this one?" and "What's that one?" The child must say the sentences exactly as the examiner said them to have the item scored correct. Any response containing a grammatical error is considered a failure, because even though the grammatical distinction being tested might be correct, it "may have introduced enough complexity to cause [other structures] to be dropped" (Lee, 1970). In other words, if the child misses any portion of the sentence, even though it is not the grammatical distinction being tested, it is scored incorrect because the distinction may have introduced complexity in processing other parts of the sentence. It is thus assumed by the test developer (Lee, 1970) that the grammatical distinction has not been acquired. Therefore, it is possible to compare a child's usage of structures on the NSST to his spontaneous language performance. The test was designed to sample such grammatical features as prepositions, personal pronouns, negatives, plurals, reflexive pronouns, verb tenses, subject-object identifications, possessives, *wh-* questions, yes-no questions, passive, and indirect objects (Lee, 1970). An item analysis, therefore, could conceivably provide information about a child's ability to generate specific linguistic forms.

It would be convenient and diagnostically important to be able to interpret the expressive portion of the NSST in terms of specific syntactic structures tested, but the validity of doing so has not been established. This study was designed to investigate the diagnostic potential of the expressive portion of the NSST. Specifically, the following questions were posted:

1. What is the relationship between grammatical distinctions produced by language-delayed children on the NSST and those generated within a spontaneous language sample?
2. Do the language profiles based on a spontaneous language sample vary according to stimulus situation?

METHOD

SUBJECTS

The subjects were eight boys and four girls enrolled in the University of California at Santa Barbara Speech and Hearing Clinic. All children had been diagnosed as language delayed by a standard diagnostic language test and had been referred for remediation. All were between four years one month and five years eleven months in age. All had normal hearing as indicated by an audiometric screening evaluation, and none had apparent physical defects as determined by case history reports. The mean age for the group was four years eight months, with a standard deviation of 5.8 months.

SAMPLING PROCEDURE

The NSST was administered in the standardized manner to each subject and two language samples were collected. One sample was collected by a speech clinician and the other by the child's mother. The clinician previously had been trained in techniques of collecting spontaneous language samples. Each sample was composed of 10 minutes of spontaneous dialogue and descriptions elicited by six pictures from the Peabody Language Development Kits (Dunn and Smith, 1966). These data were collected in two clinical sessions with the experimental conditions counterbalanced regarding order of task presentation. A sample of the procedure for the collection of the spontaneous dialogue elicited by the clinician using pictures is as follows:

Clinician: What does farmer John give to the chickens?
Child: Corn to the chickens.
Clinician: He gives corn to the chickens?
Child: Yes, in a bucket.
Clinician: I see a turkey in the picture.
Child: He's a turkey eating a bone.

Before collecting language samples, clinicians and mothers were instructed to engage in a spontaneous dialogue with the child. Both clinicians and mothers were requested not to model structures for the child. Inspection of the data revealed that modeling had not been employed in the language sample collection.

SCORING PROCEDURES

All samples were tape recorded using a Crown recorder (Model 702) and an Electro-Voice microphone (Model 666). Orthographic transcriptions of these samples were made by a graduate student in speech pathology. The spontaneous language samples of four of the 12 subjects were randomly selected and transcribed by a second speech pathology graduate student. Reliability of the transcripts, determined by computing intertranscriber point-by-point percentage of agreement, was 0.93. For the purpose of this study, a response was defined according to the criteria established by Johnson, Darley, and Spriestersbach (1963).

The expressive portion of the NSST was scored in the standard manner described in the test manual (NSST, 1969). In addition, the imitative responses made by the child were recorded, enabling the clinician to recheck the scoring of the test items.

Using the NSST criteria for judging grammatical distinctions, two of the investigators working independently analyzed the spontaneous language samples. The samples were examined for the 20 sentence-pair contrasts that comprise the expressive portion of the NSST. Any scoring differences between the investigators were resolved through discussion and consensus. Since the NSST manual does not indicate the grammatical distinctions sampled by each item, these distinctions were categorized by the investigators by examination of the sentence-pair contrasts. A description of the NSST test items indicating the grammatical features and sentence forms sampled is provided in the Appendix. The test items are numbered according to their appearance on the test.

For a child to receive credit for using these grammatical distinctions correctly in his spontaneous speech, the distinctions had to occur within a sentence form identical to that used in the NSST. For example, if a grammatical feature was presented on the NSST in a sample active declarative sentence, it would have to appear in a child's spontaneous speech sample within that sentence form to be scored correct. Each child's spontaneous language sample was examined for the grammatical features he had produced incorrectly on the NSST. The number of times a particular grammatical feature occurred and the number of times it was used correctly were calculated. If a structure was produced correctly 50% of the time or more, it was considered part of the child's language system. For the child to receive a correct score in the speech sample, the grammatical distinction and sentence frame had to be exactly the same as that found on the NSST. For example, to receive credit for Item 2a in the language sample, the child had to produce the preposition *on* in an affirmative declarative frame and all other parts of the sentence had to be grammatical. The lexical items could be different, but the grammatical distinction and sentence frame had to be identical to that represented on the NSST for Item 2a. An example of scored responses taken from the spontaneous language sample for this item is:

	Correct	*Incorrect*
2a A cat is on the car.	X	
2a A bird on the tree.		X

RESULTS

The subjects' scores on the expressive portion of the NSST indicated that they were all below the tenth percentile of the test's published norms. Of a possible score of 40, the mean score was 4.08, with a standard deviation of 3.60.

Data from the children's spontaneous speech were based on a sample of 2895 utterances. The interexaminer reliability for determining grammatical distinctions in the spontaneous language sample was 0.94, computed as the percentage of point-by-point agreement between the two. The relationship between grammatical distinctions produced on the NSST and those generated within the spontaneous language sample is shown in Table 1. It was found that 30% of those structures incorrectly produced on the NSST were correctly produced spontaneously in the language samples (range = 22 to 41%, standard deviation = 6.32%).

A comparison of the children's NSST performance and spontaneous production of grammatical features tested by NSST is shown in Figure 1. This comparison demonstrates that a child may fail to produce a grammatical distinction on the NSST, but correctly generate that distinction in spontaneous speech. On the average, 30% of the children who missed a particular item on the NSST correctly produced it spontaneously. The performance on Items a and b of the NSST often differed greatly. For instance, on Grammatical Distinction 7 (object noun singular-plural), 100% of the subjects examined produced Form a (singular) correctly in the spontaneous language sample, while only 40% of the subjects used b (the plural counterpart) correctly. This

Table 1   Summary of NSST Score (expressive) and Spontaneous Language Sample (SLS) for Language-delayed Children

Subject	Age (Year-Month)	Sex	NSST Score* (Expressive)	Number of Correct Structures†			SLS Correct and NSST Wrong (%)	Number of Responses		
				Clinician	Mother	Total‡		Clinician	Mother	Total
1	5-11	M	0	8	3	9	22	128	70	198
2	5-2	M	1	7	5	10	26	138	60	198
3	5-2	M	1	10	3	11	28	240	89	329
4	4-5	M	4	12	6	14	39	150	69	219
5	4-9	M	2	10	6	11	29	123	78	201
6	4-5	M	12	6	7	9	32	163	121	284
7	4-1	F	4	8	11	11	31	162	99	261
8	4-2	M	6	12	7	13	38	80	73	153
9	4-8	F	6	10	12	14	41	139	170	309
10	5-0	M	5	9	8	9	26	91	110	201
11	5-1	F	8	6	4	7	22	214	64	278
12	4-7	F	0	9	9	11	28	154	110	264
Mean	4-8	—	4.08	8.92	6.75	10.25	30.17	148.50	92.75	241.25
Standard deviation	4.78 mo.	—	3.60	2.02	2.90	2.45	6.32	45.08	3.63	53.63

*Highest NSST score possible for syntactic structures is 40.
†The number of structures the NSST indicated the child did not have, which he correctly displayed spontaneously ≥ 50% of the opportunities under the stimulus conditions.
‡Total number of different structures correctly displayed ≥ 50% of the opportunities.

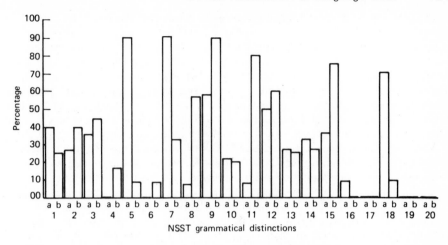

Figure 1. Percentage of subjects who failed each NSST item and correctly demonstrated that grammatical distinction on the spontaneous language sample.

demonstrates that while a grammatical distinction is held constant, the form in which it is enclosed may influence imitative performance.

The spontaneous language samples collected in each stimulus situation (clinician and mother) were then compared. As Table 1 demonstrates, these samples varied significantly in quantity and quality. The mean number of responses collected by the clinician was 148.50, while the mean number of responses collected by the mother was 92.75. A t test for paired observations revealed that this was a significant difference on mean number of responses ($t = 3.42$, $df = 11$, $p < 0.01$, two-tailed). Also, the language profiles found in each stimulus situation differed. The children demonstrated correct use of a greater number of grammatical distinctions within the language samples collected by the clinician. The mean number of NSST grammatical distinctions used correctly in samples collected by the clinician was 8.92; in samples collected by the mother it was 6.75. A t test showed that this difference in number of correct grammatical distinctions was statistically significant ($t = 2.29$, $df = 11$, $p < 0.05$, two-tailed). That is, the samples collected by the mothers underestimated the children's language performance as compared to those collected by the clinicians. However, even in the mothers' samples, the children demonstrated more correct grammatical distinctions than they did on the NSST.

DISCUSSION

The results indicate that an item analysis of the expressive portion of the NSST does not present an accurate picture of the spontaneous communicative skills of the language-delayed child and cannot therefore be interpreted beyond its stated purpose as a screening instrument. The discrepancies between the performance of children on the NSST and the spontaneous language samples might be caused by several factors.

Successful completion of the expressive portion of the NSST requires psychological operations that are not normally necessary for expressive language performance. A child must analyze the pictures presented to him, decode and store the sentences, match one of these sentences to each picture, and repeat the appropriate sentence when the examiner points to the picture. The psychological constraints of this task might be increased further if the sentence the child had to store and repeat were at variance with the sentence he would normally encode as a response to the picture.

A study by Fraser, Brown, and Bellugi (1963) provided the basis for the procedure of the expressive portion of the NSST. These investigators introduced a relatively unique sampling procedure: they elicited delayed imitative production of structures. While immediate imitation has been shown to provide useful information (Berry-Luterman and Bar, 1971), there are important differences among the psychological process of imitation, storage, and generation. The results of the present study support the recommendation of Slobin and Welsh (1971) that information obtained using imitative tasks should be supplemented by data from spontaneous speech. Our data and the results of Ervin (1964) indicate that an analysis of merely imitative production may underestimate the child's spontaneous communicative skills.

The language profiles obtained varied according to stimulus situation. As the work of Cowan et al. (1967) indicates, the experimenter and stimulus influence the language sample elicited. Further, the results of the present study reveal that the language profiles obtained by the clinician provided a richer corpus of more sophisticated language use than the corpus elicited by the mother. This result demonstrates the need for systematic training in sample collection to maximize the value of the information obtained.

The results of this investigation indicate that the expressive portion of the NSST can be used only as a screening instrument to differentiate clinical populations. Specific syntactic structures cannot reliably be evaluated by this imitative task. It is therefore recommended that a spontaneous language sample be used as a diagnostic tool to analyze specific syntactic structures.

ACKNOWLEDGMENT

This paper was presented at the Annual Convention of the American Speech and Hearing Association, Detroit, Michigan, October 1973. Research was supported by Grant 8-587517-19900-7 from the Academic Senate, University of California, Santa Barbara.

REFERENCES

Berry-Luterman, L. and Bar, A., The diagnostic significance of sentence repetition for language-impaired children. *J. Speech Hearing Dis.*, **36**, 29–39 (1971).

Cowan, P. A., Weber, J., Hoddinot, B. A., and Klein, J., Mean length of spoken response as a function of stimulus, experimenter, and subject. *Child Develpm.*, **38**, 191–203 (1967).

Dunn, L. M., and Smith, J. O., *Peabody Language Development Kits Level 2*. Circle Pines, Minn.: American Guidance Service (1966).

Ervin, S., Imitation and structural change in children's language. In. E. G. Lenneberg (Ed.), *New Directions in the Study of Language.* Cambridge, Mass.: MIT Press (1964).

Fraser, C., Brown, R., and Bellugi, U., Control of grammar in imitation, comprehension and production. *J. Verb. Learn. Verb. Behav.,* **2,** 121–135 (1963).

Johnson, W., Darley, F., and Spriesterbach, D., *Diagnostic Methods in Speech Pathology.* New York: Harper and Row (1963).

Lee, L., A screening test for syntax development. *J. Speech Hearing Dis.,* **35,** 103–112 (1970).

McCarthy, D., The language development of the preschool child. *Institute of Child Welfare Monograph Series No. 4.* Minneapolis, Minn.: Univ. of Minnesota Press (1930). *Northwestern Syntax Screening Test.* Evanston, Ill.: Northwestern Univ. Press (1969).

Slobin, D., and Welsh, C., Elicited imitation as a research tool in developmental psycholinguistics. In C. Lavatelli (Ed.), *Language Training in Early Childhood Education.* Urbana, Ill.: Univ. of Illinois Press (1971).

Wolsi, D., *Michigan Picture Language Inventory.* Ann Arbor, Mich.: Univ. of Michigan Press (1958).

Appendix A

Grammatical features (GF) and sentence forms (SF) sampled by the expressive portion of the Northwestern Syntax Screening Test, based on the investigators' structural description f NSST items.

1. a. GF: affirmative declarative
      SF: declarative sentence, present progressive verb tense
   b. GF: negative declarative
      SF: declarative sentence, present progressive verb tense
2. a. GF: preposition *on*
      SF: affirmative declarative sentence, present verb tense
   b. GF: preposition *in*
      SF: affirmative declarative sentence, present verb tense
3. a. GF: personal subjective pronoun *she*
      SF: affirmative declarative sentence, present verb tense
   b. GF: personal subjective pronoun *he*
      SF: affirmative declarative sentence, present verb tense
4. a. GF: preposition *behind*
      SF: affirmative declarative sentence, present verb tense
   b. GF: preposition *under*
      SF: affirmative declarative sentence, present verb tense
5. a. GF: subject-object identification
      SF: affirmative declarative sentence, present verb tense
   b. GF: subject-object identification
      SF: affirmative declarative sentence, present verb tense
6. a. GF: singular copula
      SF: affirmative declarative sentence, present progressive verb tense
   b. GF: plural copula
      SF: affirmative declarative sentence, present progressive verb tense

7. a. GF: object noun singular
      SF: affirmative declarative sentence, present verb tense
   b. GF: object noun plural
      SF: affirmative declarative sentence, present verb tense
8. a. GF: third person plural possessive pronoun *their*
      SF: affirmative declarative sentence, present verb tense
   b. GF: third person singular possessive pronoun masculine *his*
      SF: affirmative declarative sentence, present verb tense
9. a. GF: plural subject-verb agreement
      SF: affirmative declarative sentence, present verb tense
   b. GF: singular subject-verb agreement
      SF: affirmative declarative sentence, present verb tense
10. a. GF: *Wh* question, locative *where*
       SF: affirmative question, present verb tense
    b. GF: *Wh* question, nominative *who*
       SF: affirmative question, present verb tense
11. a. GF: singular masculine reflexive pronoun
       SF: affirmative declarative sentence, present verb tense
    b. GF: subject-object identification
       SF: affirmative declarative sentence, present verb tense
12. a. GF: locative determiner, near *this*
       SF: affirmative declarative sentence, present verb tense
    b. GF: locative determiner, far *that*
       SF: affirmative declarative sentence, present verb tense
13. a. GF: prepositional phrase, object position of verb phrase
       SF: affirmative declarative sentence, present verb tense
    b. GF: yes-no question form
       SF: affirmative question, present verb tense
14. a. GF: future verb tense
       SF: affirmative declarative sentence, future verb tense
    b. GF: present progressive tense verb
       SF: affirmative declarative sentence, present progressive verb tense
15. a. GF: regular past verb tense
       SF: affirmative declarative sentence, past verb tense
    b. GF: singular present verb tense
       SF: affirmative declarative sentence, singular present verb tense
16. a. GF: indefinite personal pronoun *who*
       SF: affirmative declarative sentence, singular present verb tense
    b. GF: indefinite general pronoun *what*
       SF: affirmative declarative sentence, singular present verb tense
17. a. GF: yes-no question form
       SF: affirmative question, present perfect verb tense
    b. GF: present perfect verb tense

      SF: affirmative declarative sentence, present perfect verb tense
18. a. GF: noun phrase containing one descriptive adjective and a noun
      SF: affirmative declarative sentence, present verb tense
  b. GF: noun phrase containing one regular possessive adjective and a noun
      SF: affirmative declarative sentence, present verb tense
19. a. GF: passive sentence form
      SF: affirmative passive sentence, present verb tense
  b. GF: passive sentence form
      SF: affirmative passive sentence, present verb tense
20. a. GF: indirect object
      SF: affirmative declarative sentence, present verb tense
  b. GF: indirect object
      SF: affirmative declarative sentence, present verb tense

Author's Comment Written for *Readings in Childhood Language Disorders:*

Numerous variables have been found to affect elicited imitation tasks such as sentence length (Menyuk, 1963; Osser, Wang, and Zaid, 1969; Slobin and Welsh, 1971; Miller, 1973), stress placed on a particular lexical item (Blasdell and Jensen, 1970; Risley and Reynolds, 1970; Freedle, Keeney, and Smith, 1970), grammaticality of the sentence (Menyuk, 1963; Freedle, Keeney, and Smith, 1970; Smith, 1970; Berry-Luterman and Bar, 1971), and communication context (Slobin and Welsh, 1971). Despite the unanswered questions this research raised regarding elicited imitation tasks, speech clinicians have employed these tasks as part of their language assessment procedure. One of the most widely used assessment instruments utilizing an elicited imitative format is the Expressive Portion of the Northwestern Syntax Screening Test (Lee, 1971). The reliability and internal consistency of the NSST have been examined (Ratusnik and Koenigsknecht, 1975); however, the more important question to speech clinicians has not been addressed. Was the procedure providing a valid representation of the child's spontaneous language? Our study attempted to determine whether we could validly predict a child's spontaneous language coding of particular grammatical features from this imitative coding of those features. The results indicated that we cannot assume a one-to-one relationship between imitative and spontaneous language performance.

REFERENCES

Berry-Luterman, L. and Bar, A. The diagnostic significance of sentence repetitions for language impaired children. *Journal of Speech and Hearing Disorders, 36,* 20–39 (1971).

Blasdell, R. and Jensen, P. Stress and word position determinants of imitation in first-language learners. *Journal of Speech and Hearing Research, 13,* 193–202 (1970).

Freedle, R. O., Keeney, T. J. and Smith, N. D. Effects of mean depth of grammaticality on children's imitations of sentences. *Journal of Verbal Learning and Verbal Behavior, 9,* 149–154 (1970).

Lee, L. *The Northwestern Syntax Screening Test.* Evanston, Illinois: Northwestern University Press (1971).

Menyuk, P. A. Preliminary evaluation of grammatical capacity in children. *Journal of Verbal Learning and Verbal Behavior, 2,* 429–439 (1963).

Miller, J. F. Sentence imitation in preschool children. *Language and Speech, 16,* 1–14 (1973).

Osser, H., Wang, M. and Zaid, F. The young child's ability to imitate and comprehend speech: a comparison of two sub-cultural groups. *Child Development, 40,* 1063–1075 (1969).

Ratusnik, D. L. and Koenigsknecht, R. A. Internal consistency of the Northwestern Syntax Screening Test. *Journal of Speech and Hearing Disorders, 40,* 59–68 (1975).

Risley T. R. and Reynolds N. J. Emphasis as a prompt for verbal imitation. *Journal of Applied Behavioral Analysis, 3,* 185–190 (1970).

Slobin, D. I. and Welsh, C. Elicited imitations and research tool in developmental psycholinguistics. In C. S. Lavatelli (Ed.), *Language Training in Early Childhood Education.* ERIC Clearinghouse: University of Illinois Press (1971).

Smith, C. S. An experimental approach to children's linguistic competence. In J. R. Hayes (Ed.), *Cognition and the Development of Language.* New York: John Wiley & Sons, (1970).

Thirty Severely Disturbed Children: Evaluation of Their Language Development for Classification and Prognosis

Theodore Shapiro, MD; Irene Chiarandini, MD; Barbara Fish, MD

Thirty psychotic children (mean age 4.5 years) with severe speech retardation and withdrawal from social relations were examined by a specific language scale we developed. This scale assesses developmental speech level (morphology) and communicativeness (function). Reliability and validity studies measured against more global clinical scales are presented.

The initial examination was compared to a short-term and long-term follow-up language examination. This molecular study of speech behavior shows that psychotic children may be subdivided with respect to retardation (using intelligibility norms) and then further divided into more and less communicative groups. These groupings have a relative stability after the second examination. Retrospective evaluation of factors that affect communicativeness suggests that this instrument can be used to make accurate prognoses at 3.6 years of age rather than at 5 years as formerly presented.

Communication by means of symbolic forms in grammatical arrangements is a uniquely human behavior. It is in the capacity for language that human beings can point to some discontinuity from lower phyletic levels.[1] Progress in this developmental line is central among the measure of human adaption, and information is available on the normal sequence of sound and word acquisition.[2-5]

When any global pathological state of the human condition occurs, as in childhood schizophrenia or early infantile autism, the disorder is apparent in those functions that converge on adequate language ability. The emergent distorted language provides the observer with a most accessible window to the defects and deviations of ego that have been detailed and inferred from more global clinical study. Furthermore, investigation of language acquisition of psychotic children is of practical importance be-

From *Archives of General Psychiatry,* **30,** 819–825 (1974). Copyright© 1974 by the American Medical Association. Reprinted by permission.

From the Child and Adolescent Services at the NYU-Bellevue Medical Center, New York. Dr. Chiarandini participated in this study as a third-year resident and Fellow in Child Psychiatry on research elective from the Harlem Hospital Center in New York and is currently in charge of Psychiatric Emergency Services at the St. Lukes Hospital in New York. Dr. Fish is currently at UCLA Medical School, Department of Psychiatry, Los Angeles.

cause children who do not develop communicative speech by the age of 5 have been found to have the poorest prognoses.[6,7]

The earliest descriptions of childhood schizophrenia and early infantile autism describe variations in language behavior.[8-10] More recent quantitative studies attempt to pinpoint the characteristics of schizophrenic speech.[11-17] Utilizing existing norms and some principles of Piagetian cognitive psychology, these latter authors have succeeded in describing the immaturities and variations from normality of the children whom they studied. A recent review by Rutter and Bartak[18] suggests that speech abnormalities and an aphasic-type disorder are probably central to the development of childhood psychosis. Churchill and Bryson[19] argue even further that psychotic children suffer from a central language disorder and that severity alone demarcates childhood psychosis from other aphasias.

Beginning in 1952, Fish[20-22] began to focus on the level of language development as a critical measure of initial severity and as a prognostic factor for improvement in young schizophrenic children. By 1966, Fish et al.[23] showed how behavioral rating scales weighted for language skills could be used in controlled studies of children under age 5, and by 1968, Fish et al.[24] reported on a classification of schizophrenic children under age 5 utilizing the language dimension as the critical measure in a behavioral rating scale that differentiated between subgroups with different prognoses as early as 3 years of age.

In 1968, Shapiro and Fish[25] presented their first study using a new method to classify speech events at a molecular level. The new scales included a measure of speech morphology (intelligibility) as did many prior scales, but also added a measure of communicativeness that had been estimated formerly only by clinical gestalt.

In an initial presentation of the new method, two children with communicative disorders were compared and the analyses distinguished between a child with a developmental speech lag and a child with schizophrenia. This initial clinical application was expanded to a cross-sectional study of imitation and echoing in psychotic children as compared to nonpsychotic children.[26] In that study, schizophrenic children at age 4 were significantly more likely to echo rigidly and use fewer creative constructions than even normally developing 2 year olds, thereby attesting to the fact that these children were developmentally deviant as well as immature.

In 1972, we reported a longitudinal study using the language data of 18 examinations of a single child between the ages of 2 and 6.[27] These language scales proved to be a sensitive measure of change as well as an indicator of cognitive skills, and pathological identification. Each study, whether cross-sectional or longitudinal, has illuminated the fact that the psychotic child's course is distinguishable from other language lags and retardation. Moreover, persistent attention to the microanalysis of a single function over time provides clues that are of practical clinical value.

In 1971 (*Infant Psychiatry*, in press),[28] we presented data on 11 of 30 children studied who were under 42 months of age at their first examination in order to show how our method aided in assessing prognosis. Data of our language examination three months after initial examination in children under 42 months provided an accurate indicator of subsequent school placement and language competence. Thus, our language measure enabled one to prognosticate, with reasonable accuracy, at 3½ years rather than having to await a child's fifth birthday.

We present here the data accumulated on 30 children studied using our language scales. In this investigation we attempted to uncover the structural and developmental precursors of poor prognosis reflected in speech and language development and, also, to arrive at functional subgroups based on language development that have prognostic importance. Such reproducible data, we believe, will provide a complement to and improvement on "good clinical judgment," and provide a more explicit index of a child's deviance and immaturity. A study of the reliability of our coding system and its relation to other methods of evaluation (validity) are also presented as well as theoretical comments that relate our results to broader clinical propositions regarding the structure and function underlying the behaviors that characterize childhood schizophrenia.

METHOD

POPULATION.   Thirty children under 7 years of age have been studied since 1965 by the method described by Shapiro and Fish.[25] All admissions to a special research nursery at the Bellevue Psychiatric Hospital were independently evaluated by two psychiatrists as severely withdrawn from social relationships and having gross retardation in speech function (most showed less than 70% of expected speech for their age according to Gesell norms). While in the nursery as inpatients or day-care patients, the children were provided with a variety of treatments including drug therapy, milieu and educational techniques, and psychotherapy.

The group consisted of 24 severely impaired schizophrenic and autistic children and four children with severe behavior disturbances of the withdrawing type with borderline psychotic features (patients 21, 10, 14, 25) and one behavior disorder and one OMS without psychotic features (patient 15) (Table 1). Children with specific central nervous system signs were excluded except for one child (patient 15) who had a known history of meningitis with residual gross motor incoordination and tendency toward febrile seizures. Two children developed convulsions during their hospitalization that were controlled, and one child was found to have a chromosomal picture consonant with Turner syndrome (patient 25). The 30 children (Table 2) ranged in age at initial examination from 27 months to 88 months, with a mean age of 45.3 months. Eleven of the initial 30 were under the age of 42 months. There were 13 who were between 43 and 60 months. Twenty of the children were followed for more than one year and 18 children, who were initially under 5, were followed past age 5 when the former literature suggests that prognoses are more accurately predicted. There were nine girls and 21 boys (Table 1). Their placement at the time of study (February 1971) ranges from special schools for psychotic children to normal public schools.

PROCEDURE.   Each child was seen at two- to four-month intervals by the examiner in a playroom for ten-minute recordings of his speech. When the child was reticent, there was a ten-minute warmup period when the examiner did not interfere; followed by a second ten-minute period in which the examiner attempted to elicit speech. The structure of the session was open, but the same materials were used at each examination, and the line of questioning was relatively constant for all children: The interviewer followed the child's lead or introduced material that included picture books, family figures, toy cars, and telephone as well as a doll and paper and pencil. As the

Table 1   Subjects, Age, and Diagnosis

Case	Exam 1, Age, mo	Exam 2, Age, mo	Exam 3, Age, mo	Length of Follow-Up	Diagnosis
6	27	31	74*	47	Childhood schizophrenia
29	32	35	39	7	Withdrawing reaction
8	34	34	40	6	Childhood schizophrenia severely retarded
17	35	39	66*	31	Childhood schizophrenia with aphasia
4	36	40	51	15	Developmental lag with withdrawing reaction†
15	38	40	55	17	OMS withdrawing reaction
16	38	40	66*	28	Childhood schizophrenia
14	39	41	81	42	Childhood schizophrenia
3	41	46	101*	60	Childhood schizophrenia
22	41	44	61*	20	Childhood schizophrenia
9	42	44	47	5	Childhood schizophrenia
18	44	47	78*	34	Childhood schizophrenia
23	46	53	64*	18	Childhood schizophrenia
27	46	49	58	12	Childhood schizophrenia

26	48	51	60*	12	Childhood schizophrenia
10	48	—	101*	53	Severe depression†
24	50	52	68*	18	Childhood schizophrenia
11	51	52	—	1	Childhood schizophrenia
13	51	—	114	63	Childhood schizophrenia
12	51	57	73*	22	Childhood schizophrenia
5	52	59	72*	20	Childhood schizophrenia
30	52	61	70	18	Childhood schizophrenia
28	54	57	60	6	Childhood schizophrenia
7	59	64	65*	6	Childhood schizophrenia
2	62	65	—	3	Childhood schizophrenia
25	62	66	77*	15	Withdrawing reaction†
21	62	65	71	9	Behav disorder†
20	64	66	87*	23	Childhood schizophrenia
1	76	78	—*	2	Childhood schizophrenia
19	88	90	—*	2	Childhood schizophrenia

Mean 45.3.
* > 5 yr at final examination.
† Borderline psychosis.

Table 2   Follow-Up by Age

Age at Exam 1	N	Follow-Up 12 mo	Follow-Up Past Age 5 yr
≤ 3.6	11	8	6
3.7-5.0	13	10	12
5.1-7.4	6	2	6
Total	30	20	24

child showed interest in a play thing, he was asked to name it, then to elaborate its qualities such as color and number, then its use and function were elicited, and finally general conversation or fantasy play.

The child's utterances were recorded using an audio tape recorder with a wide-range pickup while his activities and the context in which the utterances occurred were recorded by a second observer who was also in the room. (See Shapiro and Fish, 1969,[25] for details of method.) Each taped ten-minute period was transcribed after the session and each utterance was numbered and correlated with notes about the context of the interview. The utterances were coded in two dimensions of morphology and function.

Speech morphology is divided between *prespeech* and *speech* utterances. The prespeech sector includes a spectrum of vocalizations according to their clarity ranging from vowel sounds through babbling and jargon. The speech consists of intelligible single-word through five-word utterances. Poorly formed agrammatic phrases are also noted.

Morphology (intelligibility) offers an index of speech development that may be

Table 3   Relationship Between Earlier Clinical Classification and Language Classification

New Language Classification	Earlier Classification				
	ABC	D	E	Non-psychotic	Total
Most retarded,* 1	4		3		7
Less retarded 2		1	5		6
< 75% communicative 3	1		8	4	13
> 75% communicative Total	5	1	16	4	26

* Retardation refers to more or less than 50% intelligibility according to Sampson standards.

compared to existing norms[29] and could indicate whether or not a specific subject functioned at age level.

Speech function is divided into two major categories and separates noncommunicative from communicative utterances. Noncommunicative utterances include *isolated expressive* speech, *echoes,* and speech that is completely or partially *out of context.* Isolated expressive speech may range in morphology from simple vowel sounds through longer monologues that are not directed to any observer in the room and are part of the isolated play of the child. Echoing represents immediate repetitions without additions or alterations from the examiner's model. Out-of-context speech includes the inappropriate rigid remarks for which the examiner could find no current reference in the room or common experience between him and the child.

Communicative utterances, on the other hand, include *appeal utterances* that are simple social openers, wishes and commands, and *signal-symbol speech* that include the simple naming of objects or sharing of events or such complex behaviors as asking questions, answering questions, metaphor, and role play. The communicativeness measure derived from the functional scale may be used to indicate deviance, because it segregates utterances that are echoes, isolated and poorly contextualized from appeal and symbolic utterances. Language use weighted toward the noncommunicative sector is not like retarded functioning but represents a variant in the developmental pattern of language acquisition. While there are no published norms for this measure, our pilot investigation of ten normal children indicates that at 3 years old, more than 90% of the utterances of normal 3 year olds are communicative.

RELIABILITY.   The morphological scale depends on judgments of intelligibility of an utterance, decided at transcription by two examiners, and length of utterance is the total number of words per utterance. The functional scale requires judgments achieved by matching utterance to context notes and the examiners' prior communication.

The transcripts of 15 children were taken from the larger sample and scored for function by two independent raters (T.S. and I.C.). Each independent rater categorized each utterance into one of the five sectors of isolated speech and imitative speech, context disturbed speech, appeal-speech, or signal-symbol speech. The number of utterances in each group found by each examiner were analyzed by the Pearson correlation method: The raw score interobserver correlations were isolated speech .97, imitative speech .98, context disturbance .81, appeal speech .89, and signal-symbol speech .98. All are significant at $P < .001$.

RESULTS

METHOD OF DATA ANALYSIS.   This study reports on the analysis of 84 examinations. Of the 30 original children examined by the method described, 28 were examined from two to four months later for short-term followup, and six were evaluated at the final examination from 6 to 12 months later. Twenty of the original 30 were examined 12 to 63 months later (Table 1). The results of the initial examination are compared with examination two (short-term follow-up) and with the final examination done for each child by February 1971 (long-term follow-up). The three examinations provide an index of stability and short- and longer term outcome, according to the standards of this language coding procedure.

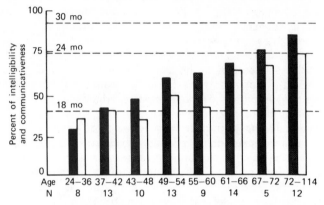

Figure 1.   Relation of intelligibility and communicativeness to age (entire sample).

The analyses of each speech sample include both an intelligibility and a communicativeness score. Each was used separately or in combination. When used together we have a more powerful classification that includes a *normative* as well as a *deviance* measure. We first segregated the less impaired from the more severely

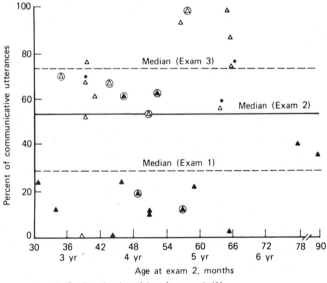

Figure 2.   Percent communicative utterances at second examination and placement.

speech-retarded children and then used the functional score to separate the better from the poorer communicators. Group 1 includes those children who were more than 50% retarded in their intelligibility according to Sampson's (1945) standards. The less retarded group, groups 2 and 3, were divided on the basis of their communicativeness. Group 2 has less than 75% communicative, and group 3 has more than 75% communicative utterances.

RELATIONSHIP TO OTHER MEASURES (VALIDITY)

CORRELATION WITH SYMPTOM SEVERITY SCALE (SSS).   During the period of observation in the nursery, the children of this study were also rated independently on a second scale (SSS) by another observer (B.F.). Observations were usually done in small-group interviews utilizing a symptom rating scale for 2 to 6 year olds developed by the NYU Children's Psychopharmacology Unit.[30] This scale is the only other objective measure that was used concurrently and available for comparison to our language rating.

The symptom severity scale (SSS) consists of four areas including (1) social symptoms with five items, (2) language symptoms with five items, (3) affective symptoms with two items, and, (4) motor symptoms with two items. Each symptom is scored on the basis of its severity from 0 to 6, 6 being very severe and 0 indicating that the symptom is absent. The total symptom score represents a global assessment of current disorders, the higher scores representing more symptoms of greater severity.

Examinations using the SSS done within two weeks of a language examination were compared to the percent of communicative utterances for examinations 1 and 2. There were insufficient numbers of final examinations using both scales to treat statistically. The Pearson correlation between total symptom score (SSS) and communicativeness (language scale) for the first examination was $r = .68$ and $r = .81$ for examination 2. (All are significant at $P < .001$ except $r = .51$ which is significant at $P < .01$ level.) Correlations using only the language subscore of the SSS and the communicativeness score were $r = .51$ for examination 1 and $r = .62$ for examination 2.

A number of factors may be considered to account for these correlations. (1) The children were not evaluated on the symptom rating scale at the same examination when the language study was done. The examinations were within one or two weeks of each other. The degree of correlation is surprising even at the level achieved, given the fact that the children may also have been on and off pharmacological agents during the examination period. (2) The increasing correlation from the first to the second examination may be due to the fact that observers had gained in experience using the symptom rating scale that had been newly introduced. (3) The global score of the SSS correlates with the communicativeness scale better than the language subscale of the SSS because each measures different functions. The language scale of the SSS includes five items: (1) comprehension, (2) amount of speech, (3) vocabulary range, (4) psychotic disorganization, and (5) initiation of speech. On the other hand, the percent communicativeness on our molecular language study implies social appropriateness, affect as well as linguistic production, possibly explaining the better correlation with the total symptom score.

CORRELATION WITH EARLIER CLASSIFICATION.   An earlier classification of our children was based on a global evaluation of language skills relative to norms for language DQ (Gesell) and clinical estimates of comprehension and adaptive skills.[24,30] The children were divided into psychotic and nonpsychotic groups on the basis of their severity of withdrawal and then rated from A-E according to whether the child lacked speech (A, B, C) or had speech (D & E). The subgroupings of D and E depended on whether their DQ was 33% of expected norms; group B consisted of children with minimal adaptive skills, and group C included children who in addition to adaptive skills showed some comprehension.

The final ratings using this earlier method were compared to our final speech· performance ratings, groups 1, 2, and 3. (See "Method" for language grouping procedure presented here) (Table 3). The 26 children evaluated in both classifications show only a rough correlation. Of the five children who were nonspeaking in the earlier classification, four were in our most retarded group 1. (The apparent anomaly of a mute child who later fell into group 3 is accounted for by the fact that the last examination of this child was a specific language study done on a revisit 27 months later when she had gained a substantial vocabulary of designative names. At discharge she was still mute, though comprehending, and was considered to have an expressive aphasia!)

Twelve of the 13 children in group 3 and all of the nonpsychotic group were in the best groups in the earlier classification including half of group E. The remaining children in class E, despite DQs above 33%, function on a lower level according to the current detailed language scale because of their poor communicativeness score. The comparison suggests that both scales pertain to similar clinical judgments, but the current scale adds additional important information regarding *effective* language functioning as measured in our functional scale.

COMBINED LANGUAGE CLASSIFICATION

Each of the categories, 1—most retarded, 2—less retarded but poor communicativeness, and 3—most communicative, were represented during the three examinations (Table 4). The initial 16 who were most retarded dwindled to seven by the third examination, and the initial seven children of group 3 who were most communicative increased to 13, indicating a trend toward better intelligibility with increasing age.

Table 4.   **Classification Based on Combined Morphology-Function Score**

| | Examination Number | | |
	1	2	3
Most retarded 1	16(7)*	14(4)	7(3)
Less retarded 2	7(4)	11(7)	6(3)
3	7(0)	3(0)	13(5)
Total	30	28	26

* Parentheses denotes those children under 42 months old at first examination.

While there is a general group trend toward improvement, each individual child's group (1, 2, and 3) tends to persist across examinations, suggesting persistent typologic differences in impairment. (Pearson correlation: group types 1, 2, and 3 for each child and his group on successive examinations: exam 1 vs 2, $r = .84$; exam 2 vs 3, $r = .72$; exam 1 vs 3, $r = .63$.) Thus, the grouping based on both retarded intelligibility and degree of communicativeness tends to withstand the developmental thrust associated with increasing chronological age.

Once a child achieves more intelligibility, the communicativeness of his speech is the factor that will mark his performance as deviant or not. The cutoff of 75% communicative used in our classification is only a rough dimension of social acceptability while *any* shift toward increasing communicativeness may be clinically noticeable. To avoid the restrictions of an arbitrary cutoff point and also to show the general maturation of our population, we compared the percent communicative utterances attained by each child among the three examinations regardless of their overall groupings. A one-way analysis of variance set up to determine whether the percent communicativeness scores were statistically different among the three exams was significant at $P < .01$ level ($F = 6.18$ df 2,81), and the dependent t-tests between examinations were also significant (exam 1 and 2, $t = 2.48$ $P < .01$; exam 2 and 3, $t = 3.35$ $P < .001$; exam 1 and 3, $t = 4.85$ $P < .001$). This increasing communicativeness is presented in Figure 2 by the shifting median from 28 at examination 1 to 52 at examination 2, to 73 at examination 3.

The clinical meaning of this numerical analysis can only be understood in relation to other dimensions of social recovery. We used school placement as a prognostic post hoc index. We divided our population according to current school placement (as of February 1971) and retrospectively examined the segregation of their communicative speech at the second examination after having been on the ward for two to four months (Figure 2). Children who are currently placed at either a state hospital, state school, and specialized school for schizophrenic children tend to cluster below the median communicativeness of the group. (Only three of this group are in classes offering special instruction for the retarded.) Those who were in normal public school classes or classes for the retarded cluster above the median. The median for the entire 28 children was 52.5. Paradoxically, the one child who fell exactly at the median at 40 months of age was retarded at the second examination, but then joined our best group at the final examination when he was 66 months old. His development accelerated at 42 months when at a mean sentence length of 1.7 he showed a burst of echoing and subsequent better communicativeness.

A median test was used to test the significance of the relationship between percent communicative utterances, and final placement and signifance was at the $P < .01$ level.

SUBGROUP UNDER 42 MONTHS.   A former and more detailed analysis was done on the 11 children who were under 42 months old at the initial examination (*Infant Psychiatry,* 1973) (Table 4, numbers in parentheses). The three children in that study in group 2 who remained noncommunicative during the third examination all showed more than 20% context-disturbed speech on their last examination. Whereas echoing accounted for the poor communicativeness of these children initially, by the third examination their context problems predominated. The shift to context problems occurred when each child achieved a mean sentence length of approximately 1.9. By contrast, the five children who advanced to the best communicative group 3 showed a decrease in echoing, with increasing sentence length without the context disturbance seen in group 2.

This suggestive finding was extended to the larger group of 26 children reported herein (Table 5). All of the six children who were in the poorly communicative group 2 had poor context scores ranging from 6% to 40%. (Patients 22 and 23 had 6% each and patients 7, 3, 14, and 6 ranged from 18%–40%.) Only three children of 13 in the best outcome group had more than 6% scores ranging from only 7% to 9% (patients 13, 28, and 20).

CONCLUSIONS

Ever since Kanner and Bender offered their unique descriptions of early infantile autism and childhood schizophrenia, clinicians have attempted to delineate relevant subcategories that are related to psychological structure, genetic-developmental hypotheses, and prognosis.[24,31,32,33-35] Such subcategorization is a frequent step in the historical process of clinical science. Recently, more molecular attempts to study specific behaviors of deviant children have begun to appear in the study of autism and schizophrenia of childhood. This current study represents such a molecular approach to one dimension, speech behavior, which can be quantified from seminaturalistic observations that do not require the cooperation needed for formal testing. Moreover, these studies are clinically relevant because they describe deviance as well as retardation and provide a quantitative means of measuring prognosis. At the same time, the study of language permits inferences about psychic structure by analysis of the communicative forms and strategies used by these disturbed children.

The current study defines a spectrum of deviant language patterns and their course. There are children at the most retarded level who never are able to come up to age standards of intelligibility (group 1). There are those who become more consistently verbal, but retain deviant communicative patterns (group 2) showing speech behaviors such as echoing and contextual inappropriateness, which imply different cognitive and social strategies from normal children. Finally, there are children who develop largely communicative speech (group 3) from very retarded and difficult beginnings. Careful study of linguistic development can help to distinguish the differ-

Table 5   Significant Context Disturbance in Relation to Language Groups

| | Examination 2 | | Examination 3 | |
	Total	≥ 6% Context Disturbed	Total	≥ 6% Context Disturbed
Most retarded 1	14	2	7	2
Less retarded 2	11	2	6	6
3	3	1	13	3

ences in course that may distinguish the latter group with best outcome from those who remain more deviant.

These small, as yet undeveloped, children are not simply retarded, they are also different. Our groupings persist and attest to the possibility that we are distinguishing among important clinical types. No normally developing child or simple retardate shows the kind of communicative disorder that our group 2 children present. The early, clear preference for echoing; the later high complement of poorly contextualized utterances; the overall poor communicativeness remain striking examples of difference. Moreover, the data seem to challenge those who would consider childhood schizophrenia a mere variety of severe aphasia. Some of the difficulties in language shown by these children are shared with aphasic children, but such a designation is not sufficient. Indeed, it ignores the clinical advances that we owe to Kanner, Bender, and their followers. Aphasia, as a name, is less enlightening than is childhood schizophrenia or infantile autism. The latter permits us to segregate a clinical group with rather specific linguistic behaviors in a unique pattern associated with other social behaviors. We would hesitate, at this point in our knowledge, to suggest that the language behaviors determine the remainder of the clinical picture. Rather, the language behavior is a part of a syndrome with some variability in its external form, which clearly involves a core cognitive and ego-disturbance that is distinguishable from retardation and aphasia. Geschwind's[36] enlightening review of the organization of language in relation to the brain offers a convincing argument for the anatomical bases of aphasic syndromes. Such specificity, as found in these defects, would demand that similar symptom complexes be found in children with schizophrenia. This does not seem to be the case.

The defects in coding complex relationships into grammatical forms and the difficulties using language for appropriate contexts came closer to recent cognitive[37-39] and linguistic models[1,40,41] than "simple" aphasias. By contrast, our data suggest that our children show defects in coding experience in flexible linguistic forms. They do not seem to be able to match environmental change with the appropriate verbal forms. They can make grammatical relationships of the simplest type *but* seem stuck in the here and now. They are remarkable imitators but poor creators of new sentences fitted for use in human contexts. These integrations of inner and outer world and of language with the substantial world are not in evidence.

Our experience using this method suggests that closer evaluation of language behavior alone will not only serve to illuminate the structure of childhood schizophrenia but point to more apt models for understanding the disorder and its varying prognosis.

REFERENCES

1. Chomsky N: *Aspects of the Theory of Syntax.* Cambridge, Mass: The MIT Press, 1965.
2. Irwin OC: Development of speech during infancy: Curve of phonemic frequencies. *J Exp Psychol* 37:187–193, 1947.
3. Lewis MM: *Infant Speech: A Study of the Beginnings of Language.* London, Routledge & Kegan Paul, 1951.
4. Nelson K: *Structure and Strategy in Learning to Talk.* Monographs of the Society for Research in Child Development 38 No. 1–2, Chicago, University of Chicago Press.

5. Lenneberg EH: *Biological Foundations of Language.* New York, John Wiley & Sons Inc, 1967.

6. Eisenberg L: The autistic child in adolescence. *Am J Psychiatry* 112:607–613, 1956.

7. Bender L: Schizophrenia in childhood: Its recognition description and treatment. *Am J Orthopsychiatry,* 26:499–506, 1956.

8. Bender L: Childhood schizophrenia, clinical study of 100 schizophrenic children. *Am J Orthopsychiatry* 17:40–56, 1947.

9. Kanner L: Autistic disturbances of affective contact. *Nerv Child* 2:217–250, 1943.

10. Kanner L: İrrelevant and metaphorical language in early infantile autism. *Am J Psychiatry* 103:242–246, 1946.

11. Goldfarb W, Braunstein P, Lorge I: A study of speech patterns in a group of schizophrenic children. *Am J Orthopsychiatry* 26:544–555, 1956.

12. Weiland H, Legg DR: Formal speech characteristics as a diagnostic aid in childhood psychosis. *Am J Orthopsychiatry* 34:91–94, 1964.

13. Wolff S, Chess S: An analysis of the language of 14 schizophrenic children. *J Child Psychol Psychiatry* 6:29–41, 1965.

14. Cunningham MA, Dixon C: A study of the language of an autistic child. *J Child Psychol Psychiatry* 2:193–202, 1961.

15. Cunningham MA: A five year study of the language of an autistic child. *J Child Psychol Psychiatry* 7:143–154, 1966.

16. Cunningham MA: A comparison of the language of psychotic and nonpsychotic children who are mentally retarded. *J Child Psychol Psychiatry* 9:229–244, 1969.

17. Ward TF, Hoddinutt BA: The development of speech in an autistic child. *Acta Paedopsychiatrica* 35:199–215, 1968.

18. Rutter M, Bartak L: Causes of infantile autism: Some considerations from recent research. *J Autism Childhood Schizo* 1:20–32, 1971.

19. Churchill DW, Bryson CQ: Looking and approach behavior of psychotic and normal children as a function of adult attention or preoccupation. *Compr Psychiatry* 13:171–177, 1972.

20. Fish B: Involvement of the central nervous system in infants with schizophrenia. *Arch Neurol* 2:115–121, 1960.

21. Fish B: The study of motor development in infancy and its relationship to psychological functioning. *Am J Psychiatry* 117:1113–1118, 1961.

22. Fish B: Evaluation of psychiatric therapies in children, in Hoch PB, Zubin J (eds): *The Evaluation of Psychiatric Treatment.* New York, Grune & Stratton Inc, 1964, pp 202–220.

23. Fish B, Shapiro T, Campbell M: Long-term prognosis and the response of schizophrenic children to drug therapy: A controlled study of trifluoperazine. *Am J Psychiatry* 123:32–39, 1966.

24. Fish B, et al: A classification of schizophrenic children under 5 years. *Am J Psychiatry* 124:109–117, 1968.

25. Shapiro T, Fish B: A method to study language deviation as an aspect of ego organization in young schizophrenic children. *J Acad Child Psychiatry* 8:36–56, 1969.

26. Shapiro T, Roberts A, Fish B: Imitation and echoing in young schizophrenic children. *J Acad Child Psychiatry* 9:548–567, 1970.

27. Shapiro T, Fish B, Ginsberg G: The speech of a schizophrenic child from 2 to 6. *Am J Psychiatry* 128:1408–1414, 1972.

28. Shapiro T: Language behavior as a prognostic indicator in schizophrenic children under 42 months. (Read before a panel on Primary Prevention, at the annual meeting of the American Academy of Child Psychiatry, 1971, Boston.)

29. Sampson OC: A study of speech development in children of 18–30 months. *Br J Educ Psychol* 20:144–201, 1945.

30. Fish B: Methodology in child psychopharmacology, in Efron DH, et al (eds): *Psychophar-*

macology: *Review of Progress, 1957–67,* Public Health Publication No. 1836, 1970.

31. Mahler MS: One child psychosis and schizophrenia: Autistic and symbiotic infantile psychoses. *Psychoanal Stud Child* 7:286–305, 1952.

32. Goldfarb W: *Childhood Schizophrenia.* Cambridge, Mass, Harvard University Press, 1961.

33. Rank B: Adaptation of psychoanalytic technique for the treatment of young children with atypical development. *Am J Orthopsychiatry* 19:130–139, 1949.

34. Rutter M: Concepts of autism: A review. *J Child Psychol Psychiatry* 9:1–25, 1968.

35. Creak M, et al: Schizophrenic syndrome in childhood. *Cerebral Palsy Bull* 3:501–504, 1961.

36. Geschwind N: The organization of language and the brain. *Science* 170:940–944, 1969.

37. Piaget J: *The Psychology of Intelligence.* London, Routledge & Kegan Paul, 1950.

38. Bloom L: *Language Development: Form and Function in Emerging Grammars.* Cambridge: The MIT, Press, 1970.

39. Brown R: Development of the first language in the human species. *Am Psychol* 28:97–106, 1973.

40. Miller W, Ervin S: The development of grammar in child language, in Bellugi U, Brown R (eds): *The Acquisition of Language.* Monographs of the Society for Research in Child Development, Chicago, University of Chicago Press, 1964, vol 24, No 1, pp 9–34.

41. McNeill D: The creation of language in children, in Lyons J, Wales RJ (eds): *Psycholinguistic Papers.* Edinburgh, Edinburgh University Press, 1966, pp 99–132.

Part 3
CLINICAL SYNDROMES ASSOCIATED WITH CHILDHOOD LANGUAGE DISORDERS

The behaviors that groups of children with a language disorder have in common, and that differentiate them from normal children, form clinical syndromes. Very often, individuals concerned with childhood language disorders have focused on such clinical syndromes for purposes of diagnosis and educational management. The clinical syndromes that are commonly identified with childhood language disorders include emotional disturbance, mental retardation, aphasia, and severe hearing impairment. The articles included in this section focus on two of these categories, aphasia and emotional disturbance, in order to illustrate how definitions of syndromes evolve, how they are used clinically, and how problems arise when they are presented as mutually exclusive explanations of a language disorder.

The first selection is the discussion section of the classic article by Kanner (1943) in which he first outlined the syndrome of infantile autism. It is included here both for its historical significance and for its illustration of how observations of deviant behaviors shared by a few children were recognized and used to form a syndrome— a syndrome that has since attracted considerable attention among clinicians and researchers. The article by Eisenson and Ingram (1972) provides an updated definition of the syndrome of childhood aphasia, based on a review of research in the literature. Both articles illustrate approaches to the definition of clinical syndromes.

In order to refine definitions of a syndrome, it is necessary to obtain extensive descriptions of individual children who fit one or another syndrome. A unique example of this type of research is the study by Landau, Goldstein, and Kleffner (1960) who presented postmortem descriptions of brain pathology found in a boy diagnosed as congenitally aphasic. The article is important because such tangible evidence of brain pathology is rarely available from language-disordered children and even more rarely obtained in conjunction with information about the child's premorbid language behaviors.

Another means of refining the definition of a clinical syndrome is to determine whether the language of children in one syndrome is different from that of other language-disordered children. In this case, comparisons need to be made between children who fit the description of one syndrome with children who fit the description of another syndrome (or no particular syndrome). Only a few studies have attempted such comparisons. The study by Cunningham (1968) included here is an example of such research; it is a rare example in which comparisons are made among children matched not only for age and intelligence, but also for level of linguistic knowledge (as estimated by mean sentence length).

Information about clinical syndromes is sometimes used for "differential diagnosis" in clinical assessment. A differential diagnosis is the result of observation and description of a child, with the purpose of determining which clinical syndrome best fits the behaviors and other information available about that child. The article by deHirsch (1967) is included here as an example of how the language behaviors of a child can be used to aid in such diagnosis and to point out some of the difficulties inherent in attempting to find a "best fit" between observed behaviors and definitions of clinical syndromes.

The relationship of a differential diagnosis to intervention depends on, among other things, whether particular clinical syndromes actually explain deviant behaviors. The study by Churchill (1972) represents some of the problems associated with the explanatory value of clinical syndromes. While many individuals consider the deviant language behavior of autistic children to be secondary to these children's inability to form affective relationships with others, Churchill argues an opposite point—that the language deficit may, in fact, be the cause of other behaviors and that the syndromes of aphasia and autism may not represent unique categories but, rather, a similar problem with differences related to degree of severity.

The readings presented in this section focus on two clinical syndromes in order to illustrate the definition, evolution, and use of clinical syndromes associated with childhood language disorders. Definitions of other syndromes and a discussion of the usefulness of such categories for intervention can be found in Chapter XVIII of Bloom and Lahey (1978).

REFERENCES

Bloom, L. and Lahey, M. 1978 Language development and Language disorders. N.Y.: J. Wiley & Sons.

Autistic Disturbances of Affective Contact

Leo Kanner

Since 1938, there have come to our attention a number of children whose condition differs so markedly and uniquely from anything reported so far, that each case merits —and, I hope, will eventually receive—a detailed consideration of its fascinating peculiarities. In this place, the limitations necessarily imposed by space call for a condensed presentation of the case material. For the same reason, photographs have also been omitted. Since none of the children of this group has as yet attained an age beyond 11 years, this must be considered a preliminary report, to be enlarged upon as the patients grow older and further observation of their development is made.

DISCUSSION

The eleven children (eight boys and three girls) whose histories have been briefly presented[a] offer, as is to be expected, individual differences in the degree of their disturbance, the manifestation of specific features, the family constellation, and the step-by-step development in the course of years. But even a quick review of the material makes the emergence of a number of essential common characteristics appear inevitable. These characteristics form a unique "syndrome," not heretofore reported, which seems to be rare enough, yet is probably more frequent than is indicated by the paucity of observed cases. It is quite possible that some such children have been viewed as feebleminded or schizophrenic. In fact, several children of our group were introduced to us as idiots or imbeciles, one still resides in a state school for the feebleminded, and two had been previously considered as schizophrenic.

The outstanding, "pathognomonic," fundamental disorder is the children's *inability*

From *Nervous Child*, **2**, 217, 242–250 (1943).
    [a] The descriptions have been deleted—only the introductory paragraph and discussion is reprinted here.

to relate themselves in the ordinary way to people and situations from the beginning of life. Their parents referred to them as having always been "self-sufficient"; "like in a shell"; "happiest when left alone"; "acting as if people weren't there"; "perfectly oblivious to everything about him"; "giving the impression of silent wisdom"; "failing to develop the usual amount of social awareness"; "acting almost as if hypnotized." This is not, as in schizophrenic children or adults, a departure from an initially present relationship; it is not a "withdrawal" from formerly existing participation. There is from the start an *extreme autistic aloneness* that, whenever possible, disregards, ignores, shuts out anything that comes to the child from the outside. Direct physical contact or such motion or noise as threatens to disrupt the aloneness is either treated "as if it weren't there" or, if this is no longer sufficient, resented painfully as distressing interference.

According to Gesell, the average child at 4 months of age makes an anticipatory motor adjustment by facial tension and shrugging attitude of the shoulders when lifted from a table or placed on a table. Gesell commented:

> It is possible that a less definite evidence of such adjustment may be found as low down as the neonatal period. Although a habit must be conditioned by experience, the opportunity for experience is almost universal and the response is sufficiently objective to merit further observation and record.

This universal experience is supplied by the frequency with which an infant is picked up by his mother and other persons. It is therefore highly significant that almost all mothers of our patients recalled their astonishment at the children's *failure to assume at any time an anticipatory posture* preparatory to being picked up. One father recalled that his daughter (Barbara) did not for years change her physiognomy or position in the least when the parents, upon coming home after a few hours' absence, approached her crib talking to her and making ready to pick her up.

The average infant learns during the first few months to adjust his body to the posture of the person who holds him. Our children were not able to do so for two or three years. We had an opportunity to observe 38-month-old Herbert in such a situation. His mother informed him in appropriate terms that she was going to lift him up, extending her arms in his direction. There was no response. She proceeded to take him up, and he allowed her to do so, remaining completely passive as if he were a sack of flour. It was the mother who had to do all the adjusting. Herbert was at that time capable of sitting, standing, and walking.

Eight of the eleven children acquired the *ability to speak* either at the usual age or after some delay. Three (Richard, Herbert, Virginia) have so far remained "mute." In none of the eight "speaking" children has language over a period of years served to convey meaning to others. They were, with the exception of John F., capable of clear articulation and phonation. Naming of objects presented no difficulty; even long and unusual words were learned and retained with remarkable facility. Almost all the parents reported, usually with much pride, that the children had learned at an early age to repeat an inordinate number of nursery rhymes, prayers, lists of animals, the roster of presidents, the alphabet forward and backward, even foreign-language (French) lullabies. Aside from the recital of sentences contained in the ready-made poems or other remembered pieces, it took a long time before they began to put words together. Other than that, "language" consisted mainly of "naming," of nouns identifying objects, adjectives indicating colors, and numbers indicating nothing specific.

Their *excellent rote memory,* coupled with the inability to use language in any other way, often led the parents to stuff them with more and more verses, zoologic and botanic names, titles and composers of victrola record pieces, and the like. Thus, from the start, language—which the children did not use for the purpose of communication —was deflected in a considerable measure to a self-sufficient, semantically and conversationally valueless or grossly distorted memory exercise. To a child 2 or 3 years old, all these words, numbers, and poems ("questions and answers of the Presbyterian Catechism"; "Mendelssohn's violin concerto"; "the Twenty-third Psalm"; a French lullaby; an encyclopedia index page) could hardly have more meaning than sets of nonsense syllables to adults. It is difficult to know for certain whether the stuffing as such has contributed essentially to the course of the psychopathologic condition. But it is also difficult to imagine that it did not cut deeply into the development of language as a tool for receiving and imparting meaningful messages.

As far as the communicative functions of speech are concerned, there is no fundamental difference between the eight speaking and the three mute children. Richard was once overheard by his boarding mother to say distinctly, "Good night." Justified skepticism about this observation was later dispelled when this "mute" child was seen in the office shaping his mouth in silent repetition of words when asked to say certain things. "Mute" Virginia—so her cottage mates insisted—was heard repeatedly to say, "Chocolate"; "Marshmallow"; "Mama"; "Baby."

When sentences are finally formed, they are for a long time mostly parrot-like repetitions of heard word combinations. They are sometimes echoed immediately, but they are just as often "stored" by the child and uttered at a later date. One may, if one wishes, speak of *delayed echolalia.* Affirmation is indicated by literal repetition of a question. "Yes" is a concept that it takes the children many years to acquire. They are incapable of using it as a general symbol of assent. Donald learned to say "Yes" when his father told him that he would put him on his shoulders if he said "Yes." This word then came to "mean" only the desire to be put on his father's shoulders. It took many months before he could detach the word "yes" from this specific situation, and it took much longer before he was able to use it as a general term of affirmation.

The same type of *literalness* exists also with regard to prepositions. Alfred, when asked, "what is this picture about?" replied: "People are moving *about.*"

John F. corrected his father's statement about pictures on the wall; the pictures were *"near* the wall." Donald T., requested to put something *down,* promptly put it on the floor. Apparently, the meaning of a word becomes inflexible and cannot be used with any but the originally acquired connotation.

There is no difficulty with plurals and tenses. But the absence of spontaneous sentence formation and the echolalia type reproduction has, in every one of the eight speaking children, given rise to a peculiar grammatical phenomenon. *Personal pronouns are repeated just as heard,* with no change to suit the altered situation. The child, once told by his mother, "Now I will give you your milk," expresses the desire for milk in exactly the same words. Consequently, he comes to speak of himself always as "you," and of the person addressed as "I." Not only the words, but even the intonation is retained. If the mother's original remark has been made in the form of a question, it is reproduced with the grammatical form and the inflection of a question. The repetition "Are you ready for your dessert?" means that the child is ready for his dessert. There is a set, not-to-be-changed phrase for every specific occasion. The pronominal fixation remains until about the sixth year of life, when the child gradually learns to speak of himself in the first person, and of the individual addressed in the second person. In the transitional period, he sometimes still reverts to the earlier form or at times refers to himself in the third person.

The fact that the children echo things heard does not signify that they "attend" when spoken to. It often takes numerous reiterations of a question or command before there is even so much as an echoed response. Not less than seven of the children were therefore considered as deaf or hard of hearing. There is an all-powerful need for being left undisturbed. Everything that is brought to the child from the outside, everything that changes his external or even internal environment, represents a dreaded intrusion.

Food is the earliest intrusion that is brought to the child from the outside. David Levy observed that affect-hungry children, when placed in foster homes where they are well treated, at first demand excessive quantities of food. Hilde Bruch, in her studies of obese children, found that overeating often resulted when affectionate offerings from the parents were lacking or considered unsatisfactory. Our patients, reversely, anxious to keep the outside world away, indicated this by the refusal of food. Donald, Paul ("vomited a great deal during the first year"), Barbara ("had to be tube-fed until 1 year of age"), Herbert, Alfred, and John presented severe feeding difficulty from the beginning of life. Most of them, after an unsuccessful struggle, constantly interfered with, finally gave up the struggle and of a sudden began eating satisfactorily.

Another intrusion comes from *loud noises and moving objects,* which are therefore reacted to with horror. Tricycles, swings, elevators, vacuum cleaners, running water, gas burners, mechanical toys, egg beaters, even the wind could on occasions bring about a major panic. One of the children was even afraid to go near the closet in which the vacuum cleaner was kept. Injections and examinations with stethoscope or otoscope created a grave emotional crisis. Yet, it is not the noise or motion itself that is dreaded. The disturbance comes from the noise or motion that intrudes itself, or threatens to intrude itself, upon the child's aloneness. The child himself can happily make as great a noise as any that he dreads and move objects about to his heart's desire.

But the child's noises and motions and all of his performances are as *monotonously repetitious* as are his verbal utterances. There is a marked limitation in the variety of his spontaneous activities. The child's behavior is governed by an *anxiously obsessive desire for the maintenance of sameness* that nobody but the child himself may disrupt on rare occasions. Changes of routine, of furniture arrangement, of a pattern, of the order in which everyday acts are carried out, can drive him to despair. When John's parents got ready to move to a new home, the child was frantic when he saw the moving men roll up the rug in his room. He was acutely upset until the moment when, in the new home, he saw his furniture arranged in the same manner as before. He looked pleased, all anxiety was suddenly gone, and he went around affectionately patting each piece. Once blocks, beads, sticks had been put together in a certain way, they were always regrouped in exactly the same way, even though there was no definite design. The children's memory was phenomenal in this respect. After the lapse of several days, a multitude of blocks could be rearranged in precisely the same unorganized pattern, with the same color of each block turned up, with each picture or letter on the upper surface of each block facing in the same direction as before. The absence of a block or the presence of a supernumerary block was noticed immediately, and there was an imperative demand for the restoration of the missing piece. If someone removed a block, the child struggled to get it back, going into a panic tantrum until he regained it, and then promptly and with sudden calm after the storm returned to the design and replaced the block.

This insistence on sameness led several of the children to become greatly disturbed upon the sight of anything broken or incomplete. A great part of the day was spent in demanding not only the sameness of the wording of a request but also the sameness of the sequence of events. Donald would not leave his bed after his nap until after he had said, "Boo, say 'Don, do you want to get down?'" and the mother had complied. But this was not all. The act was still not considered completed. Donald would continue, "Now say 'All right.'" Again the mother had to comply, or there was screaming until the performance was completed. All of this ritual was an indispensable part of the act of getting up after a nap. Every other activity had to be completed from beginning to end in the manner in which it had been started originally. It was impossible to return from a walk without having covered the same ground as had been covered before. The sight of a broken crossbar on a garage door on his regular daily tour so upset Charles that he kept talking and asking about it for weeks on end, even while spending a few days in a distant city. One of the children noticed a crack in the office ceiling and kept asking anxiously and repeatedly who had cracked the ceiling, not calmed by any answer given her. Another child, seeing one doll with a hat and another without a hat, could not be placated until the other hat was found and put on the doll's head. He then immediately lost interest in the two dolls; sameness and completeness had been restored, and all was well again.

The dread of change and incompleteness seems to be a major factor in the explanation of the monotonous repetitiousness and the resulting *limitation in the variety of spontaneous activity*. A situation, a performance, a sentence is not regarded as complete if it is not made up of exactly the same elements that were present at the time the child was first confronted with it. If the slightest ingredient is altered or removed, the total situation is no longer the same and therefore is not accepted as such, or it is resented with impatience or even with a reaction of profound frustration. The inability to experience wholes without full attention to the constituent parts is somewhat reminiscent of the plight of children with specific reading disability who do not respond to the modern system of configurational reading instruction but must be taught to build up words from their alphabetical elements. This is perhaps one of the reasons why those children of our group who were old enough to be instructed in reading immediately became excessively preoccupied with the "spelling" of words, or why Donald, for example, was so disturbed over the fact that "light" and "bite," having the same phonetic quality, should be spelled differently.

Objects that do not change their appearance and position, that retain their sameness and never threaten to interfere with the child's aloneness, are readily accepted by the autistic child. He has a good *relation to objects;* he is interested in them, can play with them happily for hours. He can be very fond of them, or get angry at them if, for instance, he cannot fit them into a certain space. When with them, he has a gratifying sense of undisputed power and control. Donald and Charles began in the second year of life to exercise this power by spinning everything that could be possibly spun and jumping up and down in ecstasy when they watched the objects whirl about. Frederick "jumped up and down in great glee" when he bowled and saw the pins go down. The children sensed and exercised the same power over their own bodies by rolling and other rhythmic movements. These actions and the accompanying ecstatic fervor strongly indicate the presence of *masturbatory orgastic gratification.*

The children's *relation to people* is altogether different. Every one of the children, upon entering the office, immediately went after blocks, toys, or other objects, without paying the least attention to the persons present. It would be wrong to say that they were not aware of the presence of persons. But the people, so long as they left the child alone, figured in about the same manner as did the desk, the bookshelf, or the filing cabinet. When the child was addressed, he was not bothered. He had the choice between not responding at all or, if a question was repeated too insistently, "getting it over with" and continuing with whatever he had been doing. Comings and goings, even of the mother, did not seem to register. Conversation going on in the room elicited no interest. If the adults did not try to enter the child's domain, he would at times, while moving between them, gently touch a hand or a knee as on other occasions he patted the desk or the couch. But he never looked into anyone's face. If an adult forcibly intruded himself by taking a block away or stepping on an object that the child needed, the child struggled and became angry with the hand or the foot, which was dealt with per se and not as a part of a person. He never addressed a word or a look to the owner of the hand or foot. When the object was retrieved, the child's mood changed abruptly to one of placidity. When pricked, he showed fear of the *pin* but not of the person who pricked him.

The relation to the members of the household or to other children did not differ from that to the people at the office. Profound aloneness dominates all behavior. The father or mother or both may have been away for an hour or a month; at their homecoming, there is no indication that the child has been even aware of their absence. After many outbursts of frustration, he gradually and reluctantly learns to compromise when he finds no way out, obeys certain orders, complies in matters of daily routine, but always strictly insists on the observance of his rituals. When there is company, he moves among the people "like a stranger" or, as one mother put it, "like a foal who had been let out of an enclosure." When with other children, he does not play with them. He plays alone while they are around, maintaining no bodily, physiognomic, or verbal contact with them. He does not take part in competitive games. He just is there, and if sometimes he happens to stroll as far as the periphery of a group, he soon removes himself and remains alone. At the same time, he quickly becomes familiar with the names of all the children of the group, may know the color of each child's hair, and other details about each child.

There is a far better relationship with pictures of people than with people them- selves. Pictures, after all, cannot interfere. Charles was affectionately interested in the picture of a child in a magazine advertisement. He remarked repeatedly about the child's sweetness and beauty. Elaine was fascinated by pictures of animals but would not go near a live animal. John made no distinction between real and depicted people. When he saw a group photograph, he asked seriously when the people would step out of the picture and come into the room.

Even though most of these children were at one time or another looked upon as feebleminded, they are all unquestionably endowed with good *cognitive potentiali- ties.* They all have strikingly intelligent physiognomies. Their faces at the same time give the impression of *serious-mindedness* and, in the presence of others, an anxious *tenseness,* probably because of the uneasy anticipation of possible interference. When alone with objects, there is often a placid smile and an expression of beatitude, sometimes accompanied by happy though monotonous humming and singing. The astounding vocabulary of the speaking children, the excellent memory for events of several years before, the phenomenal rote memory for poems and names, and the precise recollection of complex patterns and sequences, bespeak good intelligence in the sense in which this word is commonly used. Binet or similar testing could not be carried out because of limited accessibility. But all the children did well with the Seguin form board.

Physically, the children were essentially normal. Five had relatively large heads. Several of the children were somewhat clumsy in gait and gross motor performances, but all were very skillful in terms of finer muscle coordination. Electroencephalograms were normal in the case of all but John, whose anterior fontanelle did not close until he was 2½ years old, and who at 5¼ years had two series of predominantly right- sided convulsions. Frederick had a supernumerary nipple in the left axilla; there were no other instances of congenital anomalies.

There is one other very interesting common denominator in the backgrounds of these children. *They all come of highly intelligent families.* Four fathers are psychia- trists, one is a brilliant lawyer, one a chemist and law school graduate employed in the Government Patent Office, one a plant pathologist, one a professor of forestry, one an advertising copy writer who has a degree in law and has studied in three universitites, one a mining engineer, and one a successful business man. Nine of the eleven mothers are college graduates. Of the two who have only high-school educa- tion, one was secretary in a pathology laboratory, and the other ran a theatrical booking office in New York City before marriage. Among the others, there was a free-lance writer, a physician, a psychologist, a graduate nurse, and Frederick's mother was successively a purchasing agent, the director of secretarial studies in a girls' school, and a teacher of history. Among the grandparents and collaterals there are many physicians, scientists, writers, journalists, and students of art. All but three of the families are represented either in *Who's Who in America* or in *American Men of Science,* or in both.

Two of the children are Jewish, the others are all of Anglo-Saxon descent. Three are "only" children, five are the first-born of two children in their respective families, one is the oldest of three children, one is the younger of two, and one the youngest of three.

COMMENT

The combination of extreme autism, obsessiveness, sterotypy, and echolalia brings the total picture into relationship with some of the basic schizophrenic phenomena. Some of the children have indeed been diagnosed as of this type at one time or another. But in spite of the remarkable similarities, the condition differs in many respects from all other known instances of childhood schizophrenia.

First of all, even in cases with the earliest recorded onset of schizophrenia, including those of De Sanctis' dementia praecocissima and of Heller's dementia infantilis, the first observable manifestations were preceded by at least two years of essentially average development; the histories specifically emphasize a more or less gradual *change* in the patients' behavior. The children of our group have all shown their extreme aloneness from the very beginning of life, not responding to anything that comes to them from the outside world. This is most characteristically expressed in the recurrent report of failure of the child to assume an anticipatory posture upon being picked up, and of failure to adjust the body to that of the person holding him.

Second, our children are able to establish and maintain an excellent, purposeful, and "intelligent" relation to objects that do not threaten to interfere with their aloneness, but are from the start anxiously and tensely impervious to people, with whom for a long time they do not have any kind of direct affective contact. If dealing with another person becomes inevitable, then a temporary relationship is formed with the person's hand or foot as a definitely detached object, but not with the person himself.

All of the children's activities and utterances are governed rigidly and consistently by the powerful desire for aloneness and sameness. Their world must seem to them to be made up of elements that, once they have been experienced in a certain setting or sequence, cannot be tolerated in any other setting or sequence; nor can the setting or sequence be tolerated without all the original ingredients in the identical spatial or chronologic order. Hence the obsessive repetitousness. Hence the reproduction of sentences without altering the pronouns to suit the occasion. Hence, perhaps, also the development of a truly phenomenal memory that enables the child to recall and reproduce complex "nonsense" patterns, no matter how unorganized they are, in exactly the same form as originally construed.

Five of our children have by now reached ages between 9 and 11 years. Except for Vivian S., who has been dumped in a school for the feebleminded, they show a very interesting course. The basic desire for aloneness and sameness has remained essentially unchanged, but there has been a varying degree of emergence from solitude, an acceptance of at least some people as being within the child's sphere of consideration, and a sufficient increase in the number of experienced patterns to refute the earlier impression of extreme limitation of the child's ideational content. One might perhaps put it this way: While the schizophrenic tries to solve his problem by stepping out of a world of which he has been a part and with which he has been in touch, our children gradually *compromise* by extending cautious feelers into a world in which they have been total strangers from the beginning. Between the ages of 5 and 6 years, they gradually abandon the echolalia and learn spontaneously to use personal pronouns with adequate reference. Language becomes more communicative, at first in the sense of a question-and-answer exercise, and then in the sense of greater spontaneity of sentence formation. Food is accepted without difficulty. Noises and motions are tolerated more than previously. The panic tantrums subside. The repetitiousness assumes the form of obsessive preoccupations. Contact with a limited number of people is established in a twofold way: people are included in the child's world to the extent to which they satisfy his needs, answer his obsessive questions, teach him how to read and to do things. Second, though people are still regarded as nuisances, their questions are answered and their commands are obeyed reluctantly, with the implication that it would be best to get these interferences over with, the sooner to be able to return to the still much desired aloneness. Between the ages of 6 and 8 years, the children begin to play in a group, still never *with* the other members of the play group, but at least on the periphery *alongside* the group. Reading skill is acquired quickly, but the children read monotonously, and a story or a moving picture is experienced in unrelated portions rather than in its coherent totality. All of this makes the family feel that, in spite of recognized "difference" from other children, there is progress and improvement.

It is not easy to evaluate the fact that all of our patients have come of highly intelligent parents. This much is certain, that there is a great deal of obsessiveness in the family background. The very detailed diaries and reports and the frequent remembrance, after several years, that the children had learned to recite twenty-five questions and answers of the Presbyterian Catechism, to sing thirty-seven nursery songs, or to discriminate between eighteen symphonies, furnish a telling illustration of parental obsessiveness.

One other fact stands out prominently. In the whole group, there are very few really warmhearted fathers and mothers. For the most part, the parents, grandparents, and collaterals are persons strongly preoccupied with abstractions of a scientific, literary, or artistic nature, and limited in genuine interest in people. Even some of the happiest marriages are rather cold and formal affairs. Three of the marriages were dismal failures. The question arises whether or to what extent this fact has contributed to the condition of the children. The children's aloneness from the beginning of life makes it difficult to attribute the whole picture exclusively to the type of the early parental relations with our patients.

We must, then assume that these children have come into the world with innate inability to form the usual, biologically provided affective contact with people, just as other children come into the world with innate physical or intellectual handicaps. If this assumption is correct, a further study of our children may help to furnish concrete criteria regarding the still diffuse notions about the constitutional components of emotional reactivity. For here we seem to have pure-culture examples of *inborn autistic disturbances of affective contact.* *

---

*Since the completion of this paper, 2 more cases of inborn autistic disturbance of affective contact have come under our observation.

Childhood Aphasia—An Updated Concept Based On Recent Research

Jon Eisenson and David Ingram

Our concept of childhood or developmental aphasia is based on the assumption that the child's inability to process and produce language has its etiology in auditory perceptual dysfunction. As Myklebust indicates (1971, p. 1186), "Children having this disability demonstrate a discrepancy between expected and actual achievement in one or more of the following functions: auditory perception, auditory memory, integration, comprehension, expression." Further, as Myklebust observes, "The deficits referred to are not a result of sensory, motor, intellectual or emotional impairment, nor the lack of opportunity to learn. They are assumed to derive from dysfunctions in the brain . . . " Most aphasiologists would agree that often the evidence for the dysfunctioning is arrived at by behavioral observation and assessment rather than as a result of the findings ordinarily provided in the usual examination conducted by a neurologist. In practice, if we consider the findings of the psychologist relative to perceptual functioning to be an extension of the neurological, then we have considerably more evidence to support the impression that a developmentally aphasic child is impaired in the capacities necessary for the reception, integration and perception of the sequential auditory events that constitute spoken language.

Most of this paper will be devoted to considerations of the perceptual processes that we believe underlie normal language acquisition, and the evidence that indicates, directly or indirectly, what aspects of perception are impaired or deviant in the developmentally aphasic child. First, however, we shall present operational definitions of the terms *perception* and *developmental aphasia*.

Perception is a process by which a responding individual organizes sensory data on the basis of past experience. Perception implies corelated acts of discrimination, identification, categorization, and assignment of meaning. Overtly, perception results

From *Acta Symbolica, 3,* 108–116 (1972). Reprinted by permission of *Acta Symbolica* (J. Irwin, Ed.).
Research Report, National Institute of Neurological Diseases and Stroke, Grant No. NS 07514, Research Program of Aphasic Involvements.

in behavior appropriate to the assumed attributes and potentials of the events to which the individual is responding. As Richard Gregory indicated in a recent lecture at Stanford University (Lecture to Psychology Seminar, October, 1971), perception is a probability phenomenon. In the perceptual process, the mind assumes what an object or other stimulus event should or might be, and the individual acts according to his assumptions.

The congenitally aphasic child is one who is seriously retarded in language acquisition. These retardations are manifest in his delayed development of his phonemic, lexical, and syntactical systems. Basic to these retardations are perceptual dysfunctions in one or more modalities; the most obvious difficulties are for the auditory events that constitute spoken language.

PERCEPTUAL FUNCTIONS NECESSARY FOR NORMAL LANGUAGE ACQUISITION

In order for a child to acquire an oral language code, he must have the following capacities:

1. He must be able to receive stimuli that occur in a sequence or order.
2. He must be able to hold the sequence in mind, to hold the sequential impression, so that its components may be integrated in an identifiable, differential pattern. This may be achieved either by memory or by the application of a rule plus memory.
3. He must be able to scan the pattern from within so that it may be compared with other stored patterns or other remembered impressions.
4. He must be able to respond differentially, to assign meaning on some level, to the identified pattern or impression.
5. In order to speak, he must have an oral-articulatory system, or an equivalent manual system if he is deaf, to produce a flow or sequence of movements that constitute an utterance, audible and/or visible.

SENSORY AND MOTOR INVOLVEMENTS AND PERCEPTION

As a general observation, we believe that limitations for the reception of sensory stimuli do not in themselves interfere with perception, providing the stimuli are received. Thus, a peripheral hearing loss, or a visual refractory defect, does not impair perception once the stimuli have been received so that they can be processed by the central nervous system. To be sure, unless the limitations are corrected either by an adjustment to the loss—getting closer to the source of sound, or having an aid to amplify sounds, or making distance adjustments to the visual stimuli, or having properly fitted glasses—intake will be difficult and there may be problems related to such difficulty.

We believe that the combination of peripheral *and* central impairment certainly aggravates the problem. This we sometimes find in developmentally aphasic children who present evidence of mild to moderate peripheral hearing loss. We also suspect that this may be an underlying problem for non-verbal infantile (primary) autistic children.

PERCEPTUAL DISFUNCTIONS

In determining possible perceptual disfunctions in children who cannot report verbally whether or how they have received or organized stimuli presented for input (intake), we must resort either to conjecture or to the interpretation of experimental investigations. The first approach, conjecture, assumes that we know as "fact" what we accept in theory. What we know as "fact" in regard to the brain damaged comes for the most part from acquired impairments in adults. As a result of fairly recent investigations, we have gathered a considerable amount of information about breakdown in auditory perceptual functioning in adults. For the most part, the observed data are well reconciled with theory. We even know something about distorted perception in adult schizophrenics. By analogy we make assumptions for children. However, analogies may often be misleading. We need to be mindful of the differential effects of the time of onset of pathology on developmental processes. Thus, Eisenberg observes that injury before speech acquisition "is even more devastating than similar injury in the adult." An early injury to the brain, pre- or post-natal, might impair "an elementary psychological function, the lack of which could then distort subsequent development. Thus, complex functions, the anatomical equipment for which might otherwise be intact, could have failed to evolve. Whenever the injury is such as to impair the development of the capacity to symbolize (language) all subordinate functions which are ordered by language will develop less optimally and all patterns of social interaction will be grossly impaired" (Eisenberg, 1964, pp. 68–69).

If we resort to experimental investigations, we necessarily work on the assumption that the individual understands the task and the required response he is expected to make. We can, of course, train the child to make the responses, and so reduce the margin of error in our interpretation of what the child actually does. However, we can by no means be certain that the child does indeed understand, and so the possibility for error must always be entertained. Dyspraxic or dysarthric involvements may make it difficult for a child, or for an adult for that matter, to express his intake in the form expected for a normal, perceptual-motor activity. Thus, as Birch and Lefford (1964, p. 46) report, some brain damaged (cerebral palsied) children who make erroneous block design reproductions are able nevertheless to choose a correct reproduction over their own product when directed to identify the one which most closely resembles the model. We have made a similar observation on aphasic children in regard to Bender-Gestalt figures.

Despite all of these precautions, we believe that there are some perceptual disfunctions which underly the impairment for language acquisition in the developmentally aphasic child. For the present, let us consider the developmentally aphasic child as *brain different* and so *perceptually different*. As a general and introductory observation, we will state that perceptual disfunctions as far as language acquisition is concerned, may occur as a result of an impairment of any of the input processes considered in our summary statement above. Broadly stated, a perceptual disturbance for spoken language may be present because of the child's inability to organize sensory auditory events even though "received," to hold the events in mind, and to scan them and compare them with others stored by the central nervous system.

Perceptual disfunctions may also be a manifestation of categorical impairment. This may be on the basis of an absence or of an inadequate number of basic or innate categories from which further categories may be developed. Categorical development for phonemes (the sound system of a language) may also be impaired if the child does not modify his primary categories to permit the development of useful discriminations. If, for example, the primary category for sibilant sounds is so broad as to include all *s, sh, th,* and *f* sounds, he will be unable to make the necessary discriminations for what he hears to respond differentially to speech that includes these sounds. Similarly, if the stop sounds *t, p,* and *k* are perceived as one, or the nasals *n, m,* and *ng* perceived undifferentially, the child will not derive much meaning from a spoken utterance. At the other extreme is the possibility that the child's categories are too narrow, too restricted, and too rigidly set. Thus, the child may have too many categories for functional sound discrimination. The *s* in words such as *see, sue, its, pest* are somewhat different in duration and somewhat different in lip position, each determined by its context within the verbal utterance. Even more so are *t's* in *too, let Tom, get that,* and *letter.* However different allophonically, by the age of two almost all children "perceive" the /s/ sounds and the /t/ sounds as categories that encompass each of the varieties. If a child's categories are discrete, he necessarily has to overload his storage system with more individual sounds than he can readily recall and match as he is exposed to speech. If we bear in mind that no two persons articulate the same content in precisely the same manner, or that no person articulates precisely the same way twice even for the same content, we can appreciate the impairing implications of a precocious rigidity of sound categories. A child with such categorical involvement will be limited in his perceptual development for speech. He would, we conjecture, be considerably more impaired than would a child who can read only if the print type and size are the same as the first printed words to which he was exposed.

AUDITORY DISCRIMINATION FOR SEQUENTIAL CONTENT

Spoken utterance, as we indicated earlier, consists of sequences of sounds. The order in which they occur are in part determined by the phonemic "rules" of the given linguistic system. However unwittingly applied, unless we followed such "rules" which permit us to anticipate and to make correct guesses as to what we are hearing, it is extremely unlikely that any human being could literally hear (listen) and separately identify each sound in a flow of utterance. Nevertheless, it is necessary to be a fast listener to keep up even with a slow talker.*

---

* In an article by Liberman, A.M., Cooper, F.S., Shankweiler, D.P., and Studdert-Kennedy, M., "Perception of the Speech Code:, *Psychological Review,* 74, 6, 1967, 431–461, the authors point out that "Speech can be followed, though with difficulty, at rates as high as 400 words per minute. If we assume an average of four to five phonemes for each English word, this rate yields about 30 phonemes per second . . . Even 15 phonemes per second, which is not unusual in conversation, would seem more than the ear could cope with if phonemes were a string of discrete sounds" (p. 432).

In essence, what the Liberman, et al., article points out is that the ear can actually perceive more than it can possibly hear. This apparent inconsistency is related to the perceptual process-

How fast must a child be able to listen, to resolve what sounds he is hearing and to keep the order of sounds in mind in order to perceive the flow of sounds as speech? Unfortunately, we cannot answer this question directly. We can, however, present some evidence on aphasic adults, as well as on aphasic children, which indicates that auditory discrimination for sequential events is impaired, and that there may be a generalized impairment for dealing with sequential events. We can also present some experimental evidence of how little time it takes for a normal perceiver to determine whether he is listening to two like events, or two different events, and if it is the latter, the order of presentation (reception and perception) of the events.

A rather common subjective response on first exposure to foreign language speakers is that they seem to talk much more rapidly than we do. However, after increased opportunity for hearing the foreign speakers, even though we may not understand them, they seem to be speaking more slowly. This, of course, is not what takes place. It is much more likely that with added exposure, we begin to "tune in" and, in effect, become "faster" listeners. Recent experimental evidence supports our subjective impression about the effect of experience on our auditory perception. Broadbent and Ladefoged (1959) report an experiment in which they were themselves involved as subjects. They report that the time required for them to discriminate *pipp-hiss* from *hiss-pipp* was reduced from 150 millisecond (msec.) to 30 msec. after repeated trials of the task. Hirsh and Sherrick (1961) report that an experienced subject required an interval of 20 msec. to report correctly (75% of the time) the presented order when two events, a light and a sound signal, are presented repeatedly in the same order. In a later experiment, Hirsh and Fraisse (1965) report that naive subjects required about 60 msec. for the same percentage of accuracy of performance when the discriminating decision had to be made on the basis of a single exposure of a light and a sound signal.

We have relatively few investigations on the ability of persons with verified brain damage in discriminating-sequencing tasks. The evidence, however, clearly indicates that cerebral pathology markedly impairs this ability. Efron (1963) compared a group of aphasic adults who had incurred left temporal lobe lesions with neurologically normal adults in their ability to make correct judgments as to the order of two 10 msec. sound pulses which were markedly different in frequency. Efron found that the neurologically normal subjects required approximately 50-60 msec. to make correct judgments as to the presented order of the sound pulses. In marked contrast, most of the aphasic patients required significantly more time, a few as much as a full second interval between sound pulses, before they could make correct judgments.

Lowe and Campbell (1965) performed an experiment with children much along the lines of Efron. The subjects ranged in age from seven to fourteen years, eight with aphasic (aphasoid) involvements and eight normals. The experimental serial order task required that the subjects indicate the order of two 15 msec. pulses, one at 2200 cps and one at 400 cps. The time interval between pulses was varied in order for the investigator to determine the minimum time separation necessary for the

---

ing of speech sounds as part of a sound decoding system which, as we indicated earlier, permits us to anticipate what we should be hearing, and in effect responding as if we did. For an expanded explanation, we recommend reading the provocative article by Liberman and his associates.

subjects to indicate the correct order of the sound pulses. "Correctness" was assumed when the subjects reached a level of 75% accuracy. The range of interval time for the normal subjects was from 15 to 80 msec., with a mean of 36.1 msec. The range for the aphasoid children was from 55 to 700 msec., with a mean of 357 msec. The time interval difference between the groups was significant at the .005 level.

We need to be cautious about generalizing and applying the results of the studies we have just reported to aphasic children. On the face of it, signals such as discrete sound pulses and light flashes would seem to present a much simpler task for discrimination and sequencing (time-order determination) than would speech signals. However, signals of this sort do not permit anticipation of and "decoding" as spoken utterance might. The impairment for discrimination-sequencing, however, especially the appreciably longer time interval needed between signals for aphasic adults and children to make correct responses, is in keeping with clinical impressions. Aphasic children, as well as adults, seem to improve in comprehension of speech when the speaker reduces his rate of utterance. It is possible that this improvement is related to a reduction in quantity (bits of language to be processed) per unit of time. Investigations involving speech signals and spoken utterance are needed to give us the understanding we need about the perceptual functioning and impairments of the brain damaged for speech.

DISCRIMINATION OF SPEECH SOUNDS: ISOLATED SOUNDS VS. SOUNDS IN CONTEXT

McReynolds (1966) utilized operant conditioning to investigate the ability of aphasic and nonaphasic children for speech sound discrimination. She selected three pairs of sounds, /m/ and zh/ʒ/, /s/ and sh/ʃ/, and /v/ and /z/ on the basis of distinctive feature theory (Jakobson, Fant, and Halle), according to which differences between phonemes can be expressed by the number of units or features of difference between two sounds. Subjects were trained to the task and were given up to 300 trials to make ten consecutive correct discriminations. Only those subjects who succeeded were continued in the experiment proper. This required that the subject pull a lever to indicate which sound he was hearing. A correct choice was followed by a reinforcer, a bit of candy. An incorrect choice was left unrewarded. The experimental task was considered completed when the subject made a minimum of 16 correct responses out of 20 trials (80 percent correct), or completed 200 trials regardless of the number of correct responses.

In another phase of the McReynolds investigation, the subjects were limited to five presentations of the sound-lever association task for each sound, and provided with a total of 100 trials to reach criterion on each task. The results indicated that the aphasic children made 70 percent correct discrimination for sounds in isolation compared with 75 percent for the normal children. However, one aphasic child failed to reach criterion in 300 trials and was excluded from the experiment. The aphasic group as a whole required 1,640 trials compared with 1,040 for the normal children.

When the key sounds were embedded in context; e.g., hamak [hamak] vs. hashak [haʃak], or havak [havak] vs. hazak [hazak], the aphasic children had increased difficulty in their initial efforts compared with the normal children. However, with repeated trials, discrimination and association improved. Ultimately, the aphasic children made 61 percent correct responses based on 2,820 trials compared with 71 percent correct on 1,860 trials for the normal children. McReynolds notes that "Normal children not only perform more accurately within a fewer number of trials, but improve their performance more rapidly and more often than aphasic children." As a general observation, McReynolds notes " . . . the aphasic child requires more time (more trials) to respond reliably to a discrimination between speech sounds. Consequently, if he is given an insufficient amount of time, he will in all likelihood respond erroneously with the result that he would appear to be impaired in auditory discrimination ability."

Rosenthal (1970) investigated aphasic children and normal controls in experiments designed to study aspects of auditory temporal perception. Specifically, the experimental tasks required the subjects to make decisions on temporal order for speech and non-speech signals. The subjects were eight aphasic and eight normal children, ranging in age from six to ten years. They were directed, after training, to indicate which member of a pair of auditory stimuli came first when the order of occurrences was randomly varied. Six different stimulus pairs were used: pure tone—noise; high tone—low tone; vowel "ah"—affricative "ch"; vowel "ah"—vowel "ee"; fricative "s"—fricative "sh"; and fricative "sh"—affricate "ch." These stimuli were selected in order to contrast certain characteristics of auditory signals—speech versus non-speech and frequency versus temporal coding of information.

Rosenthal found significant differences in performance between normal and aphasic children as well as between different stimulus pairs. Under all stimulus conditions, the normal children exhibited superior performance as measured by the minimum stimulus interval needed to resolve temporal order; that is, to make correct decisions as to which member of a stimulus pair came first. The normal children also had a higher percentage of correct responses at various interstiumulus interval durations. In general, the pattern of response was similar for both groups, with errors increasing as the interstimulus interval decreased. The errors were not related with stimulus conditions based on a speech-non-speech dimension. Interestingly, the easiest pair for the aphasic children was the vowel-affricate sequence; the most difficult pair was the fricative-affricate sequence. The respective mean minimum interstimulus interval was 64 milliseconds for the vowel-affricate (ah-ch) and 650 milleseconds for the fricative-affricate (s-sh).

When analogous speech and non-speech pairs were compared (vowel-affricate versus pure tone—noise and vowel "ah"—vowel "ee" versus high tone—low tone), the temporal order of the speech pair members was more accurately determined than non-speech at shorter interstimulus intervals. Peak differences between these analogous pairs occurred at interstimulus intervals below 200 milliseconds for the aphasic group and below 100 milliseconds for the normal group. Comparisons of the frication "s"—fricative "sh" and fricative "s"—affricate "ch" conditions indicated that the former pair, the members of which are distinguished on the basis of spectral energy, was more easily processed by aphasic children. This trend was reversed for normal children, who more easily processed the fricative "s"—affricate "ch" pair, in which the members are identical in spectral or frequency composition but differ along a temporal dimension. This reversal was the only major difference in the pattern of responses between the groups.

The findings in Rosenthal's study indicate that aphasic children, even those who though linguistically retarded are not non-verbal, require more time than normal children to resolve temporal order for auditory stimuli. However, Rosenthal notes that "It is significant that seven of the eight aphasic subjects were able to resolve the temporal order of at least one stimulus pair when the interstimulus interval was less than 100 milliseconds. This suggests that in those children tested, the auditory system is capable of processing most of the acoustic segments which comprise the speech signal . . . It seems likely that the auditory temporal disorder which is presumed to underlie childhood or developmental aphasia serves to retard language development, but not to prevent its emergence completely. However, in older aphasic children, it is evident only under experimental conditions which test the limits of the auditory system."

Restated in non-laboratory terms, we may observe that aphasic children are less efficient in auditory processing than normal children and continue, even after functional language is established, to be somewhat slower and less efficient listeners than normal children.

PERCEPTION AND INTERSENSORY STIMULATION

Perceptual development of the infant changes from initial dependence on distance receptors. Birch and Lefford (1964, p. 48) observe along this line:

> In infants and young children, sensations deriving from the viscera and from stimuli applied to the skin surfaces appear to be predominant in directing behavior, whereas at these ages information presented visually or auditorily is relatively ineffective. As the child matures, the telo-receptive modalities assume an even more prominent position in the sensory hierarchy until, by school age, vision and audition appear to become the most important sensory modalities for directing behavior. Such hierarchial shifts are orderly and seem to be accompanied by increased intersensory liaison in normal children.

Our emphasis for the present part of our discussion is on the development of intersensory reactions and perception in brain damaged children. Birch and Lefford (1964, pp. 48–58) report the results of an intersensory study on a group of neurologically damaged (cerebral palsied) children. The sensory systems studied were vision, kinesthesis, and haptic (touch and active exploratory movement of the hand). The stimulus items were blocks cut out as geometric forms. The subjects were directed to judge whether simultaneously presented stimuli in pairs were the same or different. The same blocks were used as the visual and haptic stimuli. The findings for the brain damaged children were compared with those for normal children. Birch and Lefford note that for normal children, errors decrease with age for all conditions of intersensory interaction. For the brain damaged subjects, despite considerable variability, the overall finding was that "At the very least, the emergence of such relationships appears to be delayed in the 'brain-damaged' children, a factor which may seriously limit possibilities for the normal utilization and integration of environmental information."

We cannot assume that developmentally aphasic children who do not show the hard-sign evidence of the cerebral palsied are equally impaired in their sensory-integrative functioning. The clinical evidence we do have suggests that some aphasic children tend to ignore auditory signals, but respond relatively well to visual signals. Almost all aphasic children perform much better on visual association tasks of the Illinois Test of Psycholinguistic Abilities (ITPA), (Kirk and McCarthy, 1968), than they do on auditory association. This, of course, is not an unexpected finding. If a child can perform up to or close to age expectation on the auditory tasks of the ITPA, he would not be aphasic. In clinical training which emphasizes visual perception in the early stages, aphasic children at the Stanford University Institute for Childhood Aphasia seem better able to accept and integrate visual plus auditory input than training approaches which begin with auditory discrimination. May (1967) utilized nonsense word discrimination; e.g., *hathak* vs. *hatak,* and six-point random "nonsense" geometric forms, in an experimental investigation of auditory, visual, and combined discriminatory functioning. He found that auditory discrimination did not improve over 300 trials but remained approximately at 65% correct discrimination. In contrast, visual discrimination improved from initial chance discrimination (50%) to 80% after 300 trials. This improvement was found to be significant at the .10 level of confidence. Combined auditory plus visual discrimination (simultaneous presentation of forms and nonsense words) was at 78% after the first hundred trials and remained at this level after 200 trials. After 300 trials, the combined modality discrimination improved to 85% correct performance. The May study was an experimental investigation which involved paired associate learning for two sets of artificial stimuli. It is different therefore from a "natural" situation in which a stimulus event may be recognized by its form as well as by its sound; e.g., a bell.

Wilson, Doehring, and Hirsh (1960) compared the performance of a group of 14 aphasic children who were classified as sensory aphasics with a group of non-aphasic children in an associative learning task. Specifically, the children were taught to associate four auditory stimuli which differed in quality and duration (a long tone, a short tone, a long noise, and a short noise) with four visually presented letters of the alphabet. Eight of the aphasic children learned the task in about the same number of trials (fewer than 80) as the non-aphasic children. Six of the aphasic children failed to learn the task at the end of 80 trials. "The difference in learning ability within the aphasic group was unrelated to age, IQ, or amount of hearing loss." The investigator also notes that "Informal observation on further training of the children who had failed to learn the task indicated that they were able to make the required discriminations among auditory stimuli, and that their poor performance was the result of a specific difficulty in learning to associate four visual stimuli with four auditory stimuli."

Berry (1969, p. 124) presents a possible explanation for some of the experimental findings and for the clinical observation that some neurologically handicapped children show impaired rather than enhanced perceptual functioning with multi-modality stimulation. "We know that neural assemblies in several receptor systems may use the same routes; a child with CNS injury or deficit may be able to accommodate only impulses from one modality in a unit of time. In the normal child, on the other hand, the same neurones can participate in countless specific patterns of activity."

To summarize, aphasic children do not seem to show the severe degree of impairment for intersensory perception as do frankly cerebrally palsied children. Neither do they seem to do as well as normal children for integrating and perceiving multisensory events, and particularly for associating auditory and visual events. They seem to be more dependent and more proficient with visual input than with auditory input. Based on our clinical observation, aphasic children seem also to be able to accept auditory input when it is associated with the visual as the initially trained modality more readily than when training begins with the auditory.

LINGUISTIC PARAMETERS OF CHILDHOOD APHASIA

We have limited this paper so far to considerations of differences in perceptual processing which underlie and impair the acquisition of spoken language. We would like to turn now to an examination of the resulting linguistic systems of aphasic children. Specifically, we will discuss syntactic, morphological, and semantic aspects in the light of recent research.

The nature of the aphasic child's linguistic system has important theoretical implications. The question can be presented as follows: "Does the aphasic child follow the same development patterns in learning language as does the normal child?" If yes, we can say that the difference between the aphasic child and his normal counterpart is one of delay; i.e., that there is a *quantitative* difference. If, on the other hand, we claim that the aphasic child develops language in a different manner than does the normal child, then the difference is more than delay. Rather, it would be necessary to posit a different linguistic competence for the aphasic child, and argue for a *qualitative* difference.

There are several consequences in following one or the other of these positions. One concerns the preparation of materials for language training (therapy) with aphasic children. If it can be shown that the aphasic child follows a delayed version of normal language development, then language programs can be based by and large on what we know from normal language acquisition. If, however, the aphasic child uses unique linguistic formulations, our research will need to concentrate on these peculiarities and determine which route can be used so that ultimately he will arrive at the adult system.

Another important consequence concerns the issue of linguistic universals. Jakobson (1941) has emphasized the relationship between the dissolution of language in adult aphasia and the acquisition of language by children. The adult aphasic is assumed by Jakobson to lose features of his language in the reverse order that he acquired them as a child. Presumably, the universal aspects of language will be much more resistant to loss than the more idiosyncratic ones. This position extends itself without difficulty to childhood aphasia if we take the position that aphasia in children essentially represents a delay in language acquisition. It is not clear, however, what happens to the notion of linguistic universals when one assumes that there are qualitative differences. This position—the assumption of qualitative differences—implies that there are two kinds of language universals, those for normal people and adult aphasics, and those for aphasic children.

For the remainder of this paper, we will present research that has compared the linguistic systems of aphasic and normal children to answer the question "Do aphasic children develop language in the same stages as normal children?" Our position will be that present research indicates that the linguistic systems of aphasic children show linguistic delay rather than uniqueness, that the differences are quantitative rather than qualitative.

SYNTAX

The qualitative position can be contributed to Menyuk (1964) who was one of the first to compare the syntax of "linguistically deviant" children with normal children. Using 10 children in each population, she wrote transformational grammars for each child and compared the rules that each group used. From the comparison, she concluded that there was a qualitative difference:

> From the results obtained the term infantile seems to be a misnomer since at no age level did the grammatical production of a child with deviant speech match or closely match the grammatical production of a child with normal speech from two years on . . . Formally the grammatical usage of the two groups differed in that the children with normal speech used more transformations and the children with deviant speech used more restricted forms and used them much more frequently. (pp. 109–121)

She later updated her position (Menyuk, 1969) by using the Chomskyan distinction of competence (the internal rule system, the knowledge an individual has about his language), and performance (the use of the rules to speak, or understand what he hears). Menyuk argues that aphasic children manifest a different kind of linguistic competence than do normal speaking children.

Morehead and Ingram, in a paper which has not yet been published, are challenging Menyuk's position. In a similar study which they conducted, Morehead and Ingram compared the grammars written for 15 normal and 15 aphasic children. Rather than matching the groups on age, however, as Menyuk did, they matched the groups on the linguistic measure of *mean length of utterance* (MLU). The subjects were placed in five arbitrary levels of increasing MLU to approximate increasing levels of sophistication. Morehead and Ingram found that at each level the aphasics demonstrated the same linguistic rules as the normal subjects. They conclude:

> The major differences between normal and linguistically deviant children of comparable linguistic level were not in the organization or occurrence of specific subcomponents of their base syntactic systems. Rather, the significant differences were found in the onset and acquisition time necessary for learning base syntax and the utilization of an aspect of that system, once acquired, for producing major lexical items in a variety of utterances. (p. 60)

This finding, which seems to contradict Menyuk's earlier conclusion, becomes compatible with it once a closer look is taken at the results of both studies. In both cases, the aphasic children manifest the linguistic rules of the normal children; i.e., they are similar in linguistic competence. Both studies, however, also found that the aphasic children used their rules significantly less frequently than the normal children. Consequently, the groups differed in linguistic *performance,* or the implementation of their internalized rules.

MORPHOLOGY

Morehead and Ingram observed differences in morphological development when they matched the subjects on mean length of utterance. The first level that they used was one which is usually referred to as the two-word utterance stage. The speech of children at this point is characterized by predominantly one- and two-word sentences. There was no difficulty in finding both aphasic and normal children at this level. This was not the case, however, for the subsequent level, one which was set for an MLU of 2½ to 3 morphemes per utterance. The normal child, as is noted in various places in the literature, passes very quickly from the two-word utterance stage to three or more words per utterance. The two-word stage may last from two to six weeks but usually not much longer. Consequently, Level II was a transitory stage for the normal children. This was not the case for the aphasic population. For these children it was found to be a common and important level.

The linguistic analysis of both groups at this level revealed a difference in the use of morphological endings. The normal child at this period typically had two- and some three-word utterances with a virtual absence of grammatical inflection. The aphasic children, on the other hand, all used some grammatical inflections at this early level. Thus, while these children were delayed in their progress as measures by the length of their sentences in terms of using major categories, such as noun and verb, they nevertheless continued in their acquisition of inflectional endings on the words they were using.

SEMANTICS

The important ramifications of the difference found at Level II, however, go beyond the fact that aphasic children acquire inflections earlier than normals in relation to mean length of utterance. In recent years, child language investigators have noted that there are underlying semantic relations expressed in children's early speech. Bloom (1970), for example, has noted that the two-word utterance *mommy sock,* which consists of two nouns together, may represent two different semantic relationships. It may be "possessive + object" to mean "mommy's sock", and "agent + object" to mean "mommy puts on my sock". Consequently, there are important semantic relations that underlie children's early sentences.

Concerning the comparison between aphasic and normal children at Level II, it was found that both groups were using similar underlying semantic relationships. While the normal children very quickly passed from expressing two such relationships to three or more in an utterance, the aphasic children were limited by and large to only two semantic relations per utterance. This effect, based on a semantic rather than a syntactic phenomenon, led Morehead and Ingram to conclude that these children are probably not suffering from a syntactic deficit, but a more general dysfunction of those semantic-cognitive precursors that underlie language.

Ingram (1970) conducted a pilot study to compare normal and aphasic children on a cognitive feature of language to determine if the aphasic delay was the result of syntactic or semantic dysfunction. Specifically, he took the English question words *what, where, who, how, why, when,* and observed their occurrence in the spontaneous questions of 10 normal and 10 aphasic children. The normal children, between 2½ and 3 years of age, showed three stages of question word usage: 1) *what, where,* 2) *why, how,* and 3) *who, when.* These stages appeared to be cognitive ones, based on the child's age rather than his syntactic development.

The 10 aphasic children were all between 5 and 10 years of age and, consequently, far beyond the age of 3 when all of these question words typically first appear. It was hypothesized that if childhood aphasia was primarily a syntactic deficit, the aphasic children would use all of the possible questions, but with reduced syntax. This, however, was not the case. Instead, the aphasic children showed the same cognitive stages as did the normal children. As in the Morehead and Ingram study, the results suggested a deficit in those semantic aspects that underlie language.

SUMMARY: A PROFILE OF THE APHASIC CHILD

Our clinical observations and recent experimental findings support the impression that aphasic children are impaired in their perceptual abilities for the auditory events that constitute speech. The basic impairments are manifest initially in faulty discriminations and categorizations and in slow evolvement of rules that govern language. The congenitally aphasic child, as he acquires and improves in his ability for speech sound discrimination, and develops a vocabulary of fifty or more words, does not begin to combine words into two-word utterances as does a normal child. He seems to need a lexical inventory of almost 200 words before he produces two-word utterances. He is slow in developing syntax and remains at each syntactic level considerably longer than the normal child. We have some evidence to indicate that even when an aphasic child understands basic syntactical constructions, he does not employ them as readily and as often as does a normal child. As a general observation, we may state that up to age 9 or 10 there is a greater disparity between linguistic competence and performance for aphasic children than for normal children. A "typical" profile of a 9-year-old developmentally aphasic child who has received the benefit of two or more years of training would, on the basis of his productive language, reveal him to be at about the level of a 4-year-old child in his phonemic ability, at about the same level in lexical inventory, and perhaps at the level of a thirty-month-old child in his syntactical ability.

REFERENCES

Berry, M. F., *Language Disorders of Children.* New York, Appleton-Century-Crofts, 1969.

Birch, H. G., and Lefford, A., "Two Strategies for Studying Perception in Brain Damaged Children," in Birch, H. G., (Ed.), *Brain Damage in Children,* Baltimore, Williams and Wilkins, 1964.

Bloom, L., *Language Development.* Cambridge, Mass., The MIT Press, 1970.

Broadbent, D. E., and Ladefoged, P., "Auditory Perception in Temporal Order," *Journal of the Acoustical Society of America, 31,* 1959, 1539.

Bruner, J. S., "On Perceptual Readiness," *Psychological Review, 64,* 2, 1957, 123–152.

Efron, P., "Temporal Perception, Aphasia, and Deja Vu," *Brain, 86,* 1963, 403–424.

Eisenberg, L., "Behavioral Manifestations of Cerebral Damage in Childhood," in Birch, H. G., (Ed.), *Brain Damage in Children,* Baltimore, Williams and Wilkins, 1964.

Hebb, D. O., *A Textbook of Psychology.* 2nd ed., Philadelphia, Saunders, 1966.

Hirsh, I. J., and Sherrick, E. E., "Perceived Order in Different Sense Modalities," *Journal of Experimental Psychology, 62,* 1961, 423–432.

Hirsh, I. J., and Fraisse, P., (1965), cited in "Central Institute for the Deaf Periodic Progress Reports," *8,* 20 (July 1964-June 1965).

Ingram, D., "The Acquisition of Questions and Its Relation to Cognitive Development in Normal and Linguistically Deviant Children," paper presented to meeting of Western Psychological Association, 1971.

Jakobson, R., *Kindersprache, Aphasie und allgemeine Lautgesetze.* Uppsala, 1941.

Kirk, S., and McCarthy, J., The Illinois Test of Psycholinguistic Abilities, Urbana, Univ. of Illinois Press, 1968.

Liberman, A. M., Cooper, F. S., Shankweiler, D. P., and Studdert-Kennedy, M., "Perception of the Speech Code," *Psychological Review, 74,* 6, 1967, 431–471.

Lowe, A. D., and Campbell, R. A., "Temporal Discrimination in Aphasoid and Normal Children," *Journal of Speech and Hearing Research, 8,* 1965, 313–314.

May, M. Z., An Experimental Investigation of Multimodal Discrimination Learning by Aphasic Children Utilizing an Automated Apparatus, Ph.D. dissertation, Stanford University, 1967.

McReynolds, L. V., "Operant Conditioning for Investigating Speech Sound Discrimination in Aphasic Children," *Journal of Speech and Hearing Research, 9,* 1966, 519–528.

Menyuk, P., "Comparison of Grammar of Children with Functionally Deviant and Normal Speech," *Journal of Speech and Hearing Research, 7,* 1964, 109–121.

Menyuk, P., *Sentences Children Use,* Cambridge, Mass., The MIT Press, 1969.

Morehead, D., and Ingram, D., "The Development of Base Syntax in Normal and Linguistically Deviant Children," *Papers and Reports on Child Language Development,* Stanford University Committee on Linguistics, 1970.

Myklebust, H. R., "Childhood Aphasia: An Evolving Concept," in Travis, L. E. (Ed.), *Handbook of Speech Pathology and Audiology,* New York, Appleton-Century-Crofts, 1971.

Rosenthal, W. S., "Perception of Temporal Order in Aphasic and Normal Children as a Function of Certain Stimulus Parameters," Ph.D. dissertation, Stanford University, 1970.

Wilson, L. F., Doehring, D. G., and Hirsh, I. J., "Auditory Discrimination Learning by Aphasic and Nonaphasic Children," *Journal of Speech and Hearing Research, 3,* 2, 1960, 130–137.

Congenital Aphasia: A Clinicopathologic Study

William M. Landau, M.D., Robert Goldstein, Ph.D., and Frank R. Kleffner, Ph.D.

Congenital aphasia has been recognized sporadically in the neurologic literature for well over half a century.[1-5] Several authors have been especially concerned with the labeling of the phenomenon, for the term aphasia is uaually applied to a condition in which speech and language are affected after they develop normally. Since aphasia means absence of speech and since the child who loses normally acquired oral language and its understanding is often not behaviorally distinguishable from one with retarded language development,[6] we shall use the term congenital aphasia without apology.

These children are distinguished by a relatively isolated defect in the development of expressive and/or receptive aspects of oral language.[7,8] The lack of language is not primarily due to auditory insensitivity, emotional disturbances, or mental retardation.

The present case was examined during a neurologic survey of a school population of aphasic and deaf children.[9,10] No previous cases with pathologic study have been reported.

CLINICAL HISTORY

The white male subject was born in 1945, the product of an uneventful eight and one-half-month pregnancy and a five and one-half-hour labor. His only sibling, a female four years younger, has congenital maldevelopment of the musculotendinous structures in both legs. The mother also has had one spontaneous abortion after three months of gestation.

The boy was normal at birth but was subsequently noted to be cyanotic at the age of 10 days, when a cardiac murmur was also detected. He ate poorly and was always underweight. He had pneumonia at 3 months and again at 1, 2, and 3 years of age.

From *Neurology, 10,* 915–921 (1960). Copyright © 1960 by Harcourt Brace Jovanovich, Inc. Reprinted by permission.

From the Central Institute for the Deaf and from the Division of Neurology and Beaumont-May Institute of Neurology, Washington University School of Medicine, St. Louis.   Dr. Goldstein is now with the Audiology Section, Department of Otolaryngology, Jewish Hospital of St. Louis.

Dorsal scoliosis developed during the first year of life. He sat at 14 months and did not walk until 5 years. However, he was toilet trained at 18 months.

In 1952, at age 6, the patient was studied at the Johns Hopkins Hospital Cardiac Clinic. He was observed then to be poorly nourished and poorly developed, with marked right scoliosis. It was noted that he had no speech, although he seemed quite bright. He was cyanotic and polycythemic; red blood cell count was 7,600,000, hemoglobin 20 gm., and hemotacrit 53%. A precordial thrill and harsh systolic murmur were heard.

The cardiac tests were summarized: "All the cardiac studies indicated that there was a definite transposition of the great vessels. The facts that the pulmonary artery was catheterized from the apparent right ventricle, that the oxygen saturation of the pulmonary artery was higher than that of the femoral artery, and in turn, that the femoral artery was higher in saturation than the right ventricle, all were suggestive of a diagnosis of a Taussig-Bing syndrome, transposition complex. Supporting this diagnosis was the fact that cyanosis was present at birth, and in addition there was only mild cardiac enlargement with very large pulmonary arteries. That the child continues to do well so far as physical activity is concerned is also characteristic of the Taussig-Bing abnormality."

Early the same year, he was first seen at the Central Institute for the Deaf. Though he responded to a variety of sounds including speech, it was quite apparent that he did not comprehend spoken language. He obviously reacted to low intensity sounds. Attempts to communicate consisted of facial expressions and gestures accompanied by vocalizations that varied appropriately in pitch, inflection, and volume with the meanings he seemed to be trying to convey and occasionally included appropriate single words. This vocal pattern, "scribble speech,"[7] was usually devoid of actual words (compare with "indioglossia" of Worster-Drought and Allen[4]). He could imitate short words well enough to show that he heard them, but it was evident that he did not know their meanings. His attempts to imitate phrases and sentences resembled the original only in rhythm and inflection. The pattern of "scribble speech" remained constant as he repeated the same sentence.

He matched colors readily but did not say their names or identify colors named by the examiner. When shown a picture of a thermometer he said "house" and gestured to show that there was one in his home. When he saw a picture of a hammer, he hit his hand on the desk and said, "Ah dah dis too."

During the entire examination, the child was friendly and outgoing and was willing to attempt everything requested. He appeared socially and intellectually alert. His primary deficiency seemed to be a lack of ability to comprehend spoken language, a defect accompanied by lack of speech. He scored an IQ of 78 on the Advanced Performance Scale,[11,12] although the psychometrist thought that the child's general behavior indicated at least normal intelligence.

Individual instruction by techniques developed for aphasic children[7] was soon begun. He showed eager attention and concentration and demonstrated good ability to learn and retain new vocabulary. He began to use appropriately, though with poor articulation, occasional words and phrases heard in casual speech ("Let's see," "What's that?", "Mama wash"). However, the increase of language usage and comprehension in the next months was confined to the materials formally taught.

He entered full time classes for aphasic children in September 1952, and the first test by behavioral pure-tone audiometry was attempted in December (Figure 1). The right ear was tested first, and responses were fairly reliable. By the time the left ear was tested, the responses became more inconsistent. A repeat test on the right ear was entirely inconsistent. If these results are considered to be accurate, the subject's hearing was essentially normal, except for higher frequency tones in the left ear.

Speech audiometry with monitored live voice was also tried on the same day. The task was to identify familiar objects when their names were spoken (children, car, flower, baby, shoe, boat, and airplane). All of these words have previously been learned. His responses were quite consistent. With earphones, he showed a 5-db threshold hearing level (normal) in each ear and a 10-db level (normal) when the words came from the loudspeaker. He showed approximately the same threshold levels for white noise. Pure-tone audiometry attempted two days later was entirely unreliable. However, he again showed normal thresholds for noise.

On a repeat test of the Advanced Performance Scale in June 1953, he scored an IQ of 97. He had acquired a functional reading, writing, and speaking vocabulary of at least 175 words, which included nouns, adjectives of color, number, and size, gerunds, and a few verbs and prepositions. He knew numbers to 5, but his number concepts were poor. He had learned and could recite from memory simple 4- to 6-sentence descriptive stories and could use the learned sentences in answer to rote questions.

The next audiograms were made in January 1954 (Figure 1). Responses in pure-

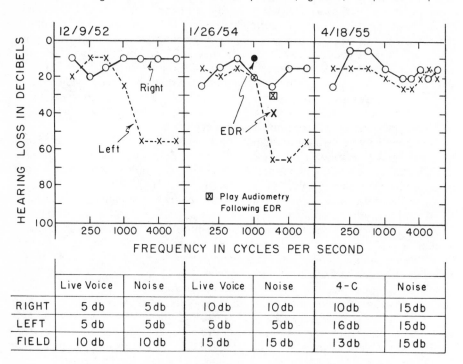

	Live Voice	Noise	Live Voice	Noise	4-C	Noise
RIGHT	5 db	5 db	10 db	10 db	10 db	15 db
LEFT	5 db	5 db	5 db	5 db	16 db	15 db
FIELD	10 db	10 db	15 db	15 db	13 db	15 db

Figure 1. Serial audiograms. See text for details.

tone audiometry were again inconsistent. With electrodermal audiometry, a 10-db threshold hearing level was obtained at 1,000 cps in the right ear and a 40-db threshold level for 2,000 cps in the left ear. Immediately after this test, the threshold level for 2,000 cps was found to be 30 db by play audiometry. Speech audiometry by monitored live voice again elicited the most reliable responses and indicated hearing levels within the normal range. Thresholds for white noise and speech were identical.

By the end of the second school year, he spoke in grammatically correct simple sentences. The quantity and flexibility of vocabulary and syntax that he used effectively were increased, and he could read and write both cursive script and printing. He could add and subtract accurately numbers up to 10. His capacity to learn from casual conversation was also increased.

In March 1955, the American School Achievement test showed an educational age of 7 years 3 months, with an educational quotient of 76 and a grade equivalent of 2.0. In April, his responses to pure-tone audiometry were again inconsistent (Figure 1), but the more reliably determined speech thresholds were practically normal. No bone conduction measurements were made.

A neurologic examination was performed in May 1955. The patient was misshapen, wizened, slightly cyanotic, and physically underdeveloped for his age. Marked right kyphoscolosis was noted, and the precordial systolic thrill and murmur were apparent. Both carotid arteries in the neck pulsated well, and there was no cervical or cephalic bruit. The child was bright and sentient, and no hearing deficit was evident. He was right-handed and left-eyed. The optic fundi were normal, and the visual fields were normal to confrontation with a small white light target. Both eyes tended to move upward upon medial gaze. The palate was asymmetric, with slightly less elevation on the left. Touch, pain, vibration, and position responses were intact. Figure writing on the hands was reported accurately about half of the time. Double simultaneous touch stimuli to both hands, both sides of the face, or face and hand on the same side were perceived accurately without training. The gait was mildly diplegic, with slight flexion of the left upper extremity and stiffness at the left knee. He could walk on his toes and on his heels. The Romberg sign was absent. General muscle strength was good. Finger-nose and heel-knee tests were well performed bilaterally, as were rhythmic movements. He performed fine rapid movements of the fingers and symmetrically. The plantar reflex was flexor on the left and extensor on the right.

The electroencephalogram showed slow dysrhythmia with left occipital focal trend (Figure 2A). Skull roentgenograms showed an asymmetric vault with right parietal flattening (Figure 2B).

A progress summary in June 1955 indicated successful comprehension and use of tenses, regular and irregular verbs, time phrases, partitives, and so forth, with a rapidly expanding vocabulary. His use of language was still best in the structured lessons, but spontaneous speech was effective even when less accurate. He comprehended oral language best when it was spoken slowly, with a definite pause after each word, and he failed to comprehend any but the most familiar expressions when spoken at a normal rate. (We believe that this is a feature characteristic of children we have classified as receptive aphasic.) He continued to be physically active in spite of his handicap and was socially happy, outgoing, and friendly.

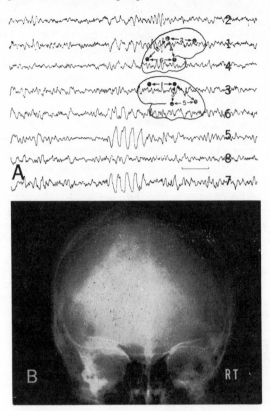

Figure 2.   Electroencephalogram, bipolar recording as indicated. B. Skull roentgenogram

In December 1955, at age 10, the child became ill with mumps and died suddenly,
presumably because of a cardiac complication.

PATHOLOGIC STUDY

The autopsy was supervised by Dr. Sarah Luse, who subsequently kindly supplied us
with all available tissue. The general pathologic diagnoses included:

- Congenital heart disease with [1] complete transposition of the great vessels, [2]
  interventricular septal defect (3 cm.) with overriding of the transposed
  pulmonary valve, [3] patent ductus arteriosus, [4] anterior noncoronary
  cusp of the aortic valve, [5] hypoplasia of the aorta, [6] hypertrophy
  of the pulmonary artery, [7] hypertrophy and dilation of the heart, [8]
  advanced pulmonary arteriosclerosis, and [9] clubbing of the digits of
  all extremities
- Scoliosis of the thoracic spine with prominence of the left anterior thoracic wall

●Congestion of the kidneys, left lobe of the liver, pancreas, spleen, small intestine, and
       bladder
●Focal atelectasis of the lungs
●Emphysema of the lungs, moderate
●Depigmented infarct of the middle lobe of the right lung
●Petechiae and ecchymoses of the thymus, small intestine, colon, and stomach
●Altered blood in the small intestine.

The brain weighed 1,150 gm., and external examination revealed no abnormality
of the vessels at the base. The anterior portion of the cerebrum was of normal size
and configuration. However, posteriorly, there was a bilateral loss of cortical sub-
stance starting from the inferior and posterior margin of the central sulci anteriorly
and extending backwards along the course of the insulae and sylvian fissures toward
the occipital lobes on each side. The area of loss on the right side was 6 cm. in length
and about 2 cm. in width, the gap bridged by slightly thickened meninges. The similar
area on the left had the same width but extended 8 cm., almost to the occipital pole.
The gyri of the posterior portion of the parietal, temporal, and occipital lobes bilaterally were reduced in size, and increased numbers of convolutions were present.
Multiple step sections through the brain failed to reveal any abnormalities anterior to
the central sulci, but, posterior to this region, there was atrophy of both white and
gray matter of the insulae, their opercula, and the tissue immediately behind extending into the occipital lobes. No thrombi or other vascular lesions were found to

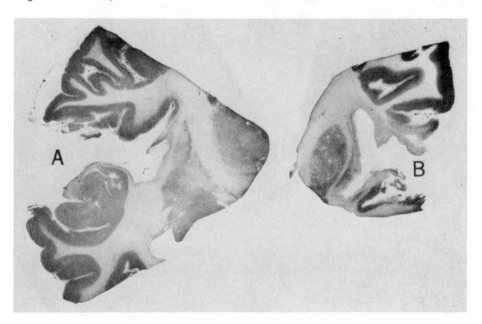

Figure 3.   Coronal sections through sylvian fissures showing gross degeneration
of insulae and opercula. Nissl stain. A. Left; B. Right, farther anterior plane

account for these infarcts, although the distribution was that of the middle cerebral arteries. On the left side, the terminal 2 cm. of the lateral ventricle just medial to the infarcted area was obliterated. Brain stem, cerebellum, and spinal cord were grossly normal.

Microscopic sections cut coronally through the sylvian fissures showed gross degeneration of the insulae and opercula bilaterally (Figure 3). In the brain stem, the normally distinct medial geniculate structures, closely related to the lateral geniculate nuclei and cerebral peduncles, were difficult to identify (Figure 4). Although it is not

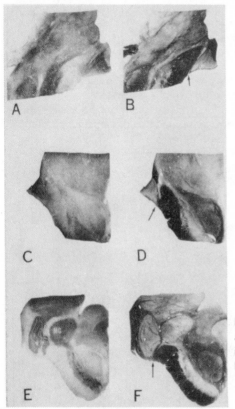

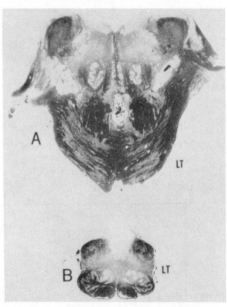

Figure 5.   A. Pons. Weil stain. Normal appearing eighth nerves. The right nerve is complete in adjacent sections. B. Medulla. Weil stain

Figure 4.   Brain stem cross sections. Nissl stain in left column, Weil stain in right. A and B: Level of posterior commissure, left side. C and D: Section farther posterior, right side. E and F: Normal brain stem from a 13-year-old child. Arrows indicate junction of cerebral peduncle and lateral geniculate nucleus, normally adjacent to medical geniculate nucleus (MG in E).

possible to say that there was complete atrophy of the medial geniculate nuclei, it was obvious that they were severely degenerated. Both pyramidal tracts were degenerated along their ventral margin in the medulla (Figure 5B). Both auditory nerves were histologically intact (Figure 5A). The inner ear structures were not examined.

COMMENT

Many authors have observed that a lesion of either the right or left cerebral hemisphere in the infant or young child does not lead to aphasia. Bilateral lesions were therefore to be expected in the present case.

Our pathologic data are sufficient to show severe damage to the primary auditory projection pathway bilaterally, with corresponding retrograde degeneration of the medial geniculate nuclei. We cannot say whether a possible small amount of residual functional tissue in this system may account for the subject's demonstrated capacity to develop speech and language. It seems more likely that the auditory, like other afferent systems,[13] has a functional sensory pathway in the brain stem and medial thalamus which is phylogenetically older than the laterally situated geniculate-cortical path; the old medial pathway may then be the essential neurologic substrate for language development in this child.

Against this hypothesis is the lack of evidence for conduction of auditory sensation by the medial pathway in the adult in whom bilateral hemispheral lesions have been reported to produce deafness,[14,15] but these reports lack modern audiometric tests and histologic study of the peripheral auditory apparatus. Further case studies may indicate only a quantitative difference in degree of compensatory function after equivalent lesions in infancy and in adult life.

The cerebral lesions in this case were not limited to the auditory system, and the clinical picture may be partially related to destruction of other structures in the sylvian region. Further, it would be gratuitous to infer that gross lesions of the geniculate-cortical system are likely to be found in most other cases of congenital aphasia, for a large portion of the congenital aphasic population shows no collateral clinical or laboratory evidence of such extensive lesions.[9,10]

The speech behavior of this boy was indistinguishable from that of other congenitally aphasic children; similar behavior also occurs in children who acquire and transiently lose language, presumably because of seizure states affecting the sylvian areas.[6] We would emphasize that residual function is due to residual tissue; the lesion may be less constant than the adaptive mechanism that remains undamaged.

SUMMARY

Congenital aphasia occurred in a child who also had cyanotic congenital heart disease, which led to his death. His hearing and intelligence were within normal limits, and, with special instruction, he had acquired considerable useful language. Autopsy revealed bilateral old infarctions in the sylvian regions and severe retrograde degeneration in the medial geniculate nuclei. Language function therefore appears to have been subserved by pathways other than the primary auditory thalamocortical projection system.

REFERENCES

1. Ewing, A.W.G.: Aphasia in Children. London, Oxford University Press, 1930.
2. Worster-Drought, C., and Allen, I. M.: Congenital auditory imperception (congenital word-deafness), with report of a case. J. Neurol. & Psychopath. 9:193, 1929.
3. Worster-Drought, C., and Allen, I. M.: Congenital auditory imperception (congenital word-deafness); investigation of a case by Head's method. J. Neurol. & Psychopath. 9:289, 1929.
4. Worster-Drought, C., and Allen, I. M.: Congenital auditory imperception (congenital word-deafness) and its relation to idioglossia and other speech defects. J. Neurol. & Psychopath. 10:193, 1930.
5. Morrison, A. G.: Congenital word-deafness, with some observations on the accompanying idioglossia. J. Neurol. & Psychopath, 11:28, 1930.
6. Landau, W. M., and Kleffner, F. R.: Syndrome of acquired aphasia with convulsive disorder in children. Neurology 7:523, 1957.
7. McGinnis, M. A., Kleffner, F. R., and Goldstein, R.: Teaching aphasic children. Volta Review 58:239, 1956.
8. Morley, M., Court, D., Miller, H., and Garside, R. F.: Delayed speech and developmental aphasia. Brit. M. J. 2:463, 1955.
9. Goldstein, R., Landau, W. M., and Kleffner, F. R.: Neurologic assessment of some deaf and aphasic children. Ann. Otol, Rhin. & Laryng. 67:468, 1958.
10. Goldstein, R., Landau, W. M., and Kleffner, F. R.: Ann. Otol. Rhin. & Laryng. 69: In press, 1960.
11. Lane, H. S., and Schneider, J. L.: Performance test for school-age deaf children. Am. Ann. Deaf 86:441, 1941.
12. Bilger, R. C.: Limitations on the use of intelligence scales to estimate the mental ages of children. Volta Review 60:321, 1958.
13. Bishop, G. H.: The relation between nerve fiber size and sensory modality; phylogenetic implications of the afferent innervation of cortex, J. Nerv. & Ment. Dis. 128:89, 1959.
14. Bramwell, E.: A case of cortical deafness. Brain 50:379, 1927.
15. Clark, W.E.L.G., and Russell, L.M.R.: Cortical deafness without aphasia. Brain 61:375, 1938.

A Comparison of the Language of Psychotic and Non-Psychotic Children Who Are Mentally Retarded

Morris A. Cunningham

INTRODUCTION

In this study we asked psychiatrists to submit to us children whom they considered definitely psychotic and also as exemplifying the "schizophrenic syndrome in childhood" as defined by Creak's 9 points (1961). The diagnostic terms used in this area are very confusing. Various labels have been used, such as autistic, schizophrenic, atypical, symbiotic. It has not been clear to what extent these terms cover identical, separate or overlapping sets of children. Rutter (1967a) has come nearest to producing order out of chaos. He states:

> Psychosis of the Kanner type, beginning in the first two years of life, is a quite different condition from the psychosis beginning in late childhood which appears to be related to the adult form of schizophrenia. Cases with an onset after three years, but before seven or eight years can often be shown to have brain disease. Children in whom the onset is between two and three years may be the most difficult to classify. Some appear indistinguishable from Kanner's syndrome, while others are found to have brain tissue pathology.

Schizophrenia beginning in late childhood was excluded from our sample. The latest onset was at 4½ years. But our group almost certainly included children who would not be regarded by Kanner as "autistic" since in only 6 out of the 13 cases was the onset reported to be in the first 2 years of life. Some of the children were described by the psychiatrists as autistic, some as schizophrenic (see Table 1), but they were all regarded as psychotic and as belonging to the group described by Creak et al. (1961) by the term "schizophrenic syndrome in childhood." Cases with gross neurological signs of brain damage were excluded, but less obvious kinds of brain damage could not be ruled out. Psychotic children whose scores on an intelligence test were average or above average were not included in the sample. Thus, the

From *Journal of Child Psychology and Psychiatry, 9,* 229–244 (1968). Reprinted by permission of Pergamon Press.

intention was to compare the language of retarded psychotic children with that of retarded non-psychotic children.

AIM OF RESEARCH

Various authors have commented on the language abnormalities to be found among psychotic children. Kanner (1956, 1958) in his descriptions of children suffering from infantile autism has mentioned absence of speech, late appearance of meaningful speech, and failure, even when speech is present, to use it for communicating meaning to others. He describes the parroting of words which the child does not understand, the repetition of stored phrases, and the failure to construct original sentences. He considers the reversal of personal pronouns (using "you" for "I," or "I" for "you") an important sign of autism, and he explains it as a product of the child's tendency to echo what is said to him, either immediately, or on a later occasion. The child frequently makes remarks which appear irrelevant or nonsensical, but Kanner (1946) regards these as private metaphors which have meaning for the child.

Wolff and Chess (1965) studied the language of 14 children, whom they described as suffering from "childhood schizophrenia." However they made it clear that their group in fact consisted of cases of infantile autism, who had been diagnosed according to the criteria of Kanner (1944) and Eisenberg (1956). They found that all the children were retarded in their language development as judged by average length of utterance. Most of them asked fewer questions than normals with the same average length of utterance, although 3 children who used relatively longer sentences did not show this dearth of questions. There was a great deal of repetitive speech. Immediate or delayed non-communicative repetition was found, and also communicative repetition, by which was meant using the exact words an adult had been heard to use in the past, to make a request or give information, e.g. "You want some ice cream, Thomas? Yes, you may," used as a request for ice cream. The ratio of repetitions to original speech was found to correlate highly with clinical estimates of the severity of the child's illness.

The results of the author's study of one autistic child (Cunningham, 1966) were in line with Kanner's findings and also with those of Wolff and Chess.

Rutter (1967b), in his careful follow-up study of 63 cases of "infantile psychosis," found that half of the psychotics were still without speech at 5 years compared with only 1 in 9 of his control group. Echolalia occurred in over three-quarters of the speaking psychotic children, a rate twice that in the control group. Pronominal reversal, usually forming part of a more general echoing tendency, was also significantly more common among the psychotics. Rutter also mentioned that echoing might be both immediate and delayed. In those whose speech improved, a monotonous, flat or mechanical delivery was often found, and obsessive questioning occurred.

Weiland and Legg (1964) compared 34 psychotic children with 60 non-psychotic and 11 brain-damaged children, using conversation taped from interview sessions. They found that the psychotics used a significantly greater number of imperative verbs, fewer conjunctions, and less often used the pronoun "we."

The observations of Kanner appear to have been based on clinical impressions. Rutter, who used a control group matched for age, sex and intelligence, only covered some aspects of speech as part of the wider research. Wolff and Chess used a systematic analysis of written records of speech but did not have a control group, while Weiland and Legg apparently did not match their controls for intelligence and language level. The aim of the present research was to study the possible abnormalities in the speech of psychotic children using a systematic analysis of taped speech records and a matched control group.

METHOD

THE SAMPLE

The psychiatrists in charge at Ladyfield, Dumfries and at High Wick, St. Albans, were asked to select all children in their units who could speak and who were regarded as definitely psychotic. One child from a school attached to an institution for the mentally defective (Gogarburn Hospital, Edinburgh) was included as she exhibited 8 of Creak's 9 points. Two psychotic children of average or above average intelligence were excluded. The sample thus obtained consisted of 13 children—5 from Ladyfield, 7 from High Wick and 1 from Gogarburn. The age range was from 5 to 13 years. Details of the psychotic children are given in Table 1. A group of non-psychotic children was collected to match the psychotics in age and mental age. The non-psychotic group was obtained from a day special school in Dumfries (6 children), from an occupation center in Dumfries (1 child) and from Gogarburn Hospital school (6 children). Children who showed gross neurological signs of brain damage (e.g., spastics) and also mongols were excluded from both groups.

MATCHING

Mental age was assessed on the basis of Terman Merrill tests in the case of the non-psychotic children. Because of the difficulties of cooperation, the Terman Merrill test could not be given to all the psychotic children. Seven children were assessed by the Terman Merrill. Five children of lower mental ages were assessed by the Merrill Palmer scale. With one child it was only possible to complete the formboard Matrices and the Peabody Picture Vocabulary test. In this case, an estimate was made of the child's mental age. Since different tests were used and the gaining of cooperation was somewhat difficult, the mental ages obtained for the psychotic children must be regarded as only approximate. Bearing in mind this limitation, 10 of the 13 pairs of children were matched to within a year for both age and mental age. In the case of 3 pairs there was a difference slightly greater than a year in either age or mental age. However, the means and standard deviations were very similar (Table 2). The two groups were not matched for sex, home versus institutional environment, or social class. Table 3 shows that relatively more of the psychotic children were in institutions, although they tended to come from higher social classes. Although the original matching was only in terms of age and mental age, the average length of sentence used by each child in four play sessions proved to be very similar in the two groups (Table 2). In fact, the members of the two groups could have been matched for mean number of words per sentence with no difference between pairs greater than 0.5 words. Thus, in spite of some defects in matching, the two groups were closely similar in language level as measured by the length of sentences they used.

Table 1   Clinical Details of the Psychotic Children

Ref. No. of child	Age at time of observation	Mental age (est.)	Mean sentence length	Age of onset (abnormality first noted)	Type of onset	Age of starting meaningful speech	Speech development	Indications of brain damage	Psychiatrist's diagnosis
1	12:2	6:6	1:91	3rd yr	Insidious	3-4 yr	Slow	—	Schizophrenic
2	8:11	5:0	2:17	1st yr	Insidious	5 yr	Slow	—	Autistic
3	8:7	4:0	2:31	4½ yr	Sudden	18 mth	Regression (at 2 yr and also at 4 yr)	Gas poisoning at 4½ yr	Psychotic (not austistic)
4	8:11	4:4	2:77	2 yr	Insidious	3 yr	Slow (abnormalities)	—	Autistic, with severe subnormality
5	8:11	5:0	2:80	3rd yr	Insidious	1-2 yr	Regression (at 3 yr stopped talking)	Abnormal E.E.G.	Psychotic (not autistic)
6	13:0	4:8	2:96	2nd yr	Insidious	2½-3 yr	Slow	—	Autistic

7	12:1	3:5	2:99	1 yr	Sudden	1 yr	Regression at 1 yr	Measles at 1 yr	Psychotic features (8 of 9 points)
8	8:7	7:0	3:32	1st yr	Insidious	2 yr	Slow (abnormalities)	Possible damage at birth	Schizophrenic
9	5:11	2:5	3:39	1st yr	Insidious	15 mth	Slow (abnormalities)	Possible damage at birth	Autistic
10	10:0	5:8	3:48	2 yr	Insidious	3½ yr	Slow	Difficult birth	Psychotic (not autistic)
11	7:11	6:0	3:95	3 yr	Sudden	2 yr	Slow	—	Psychotic (not autistic)
12	10:11	6:0	4:04	3½ yr	Sudden	3 yr	?Slow (abnormalities)	Long labor (36 hours) but normal birth	Schizophrenic
13	8:5	6:10	4:19	1st yr	Insidious	4 yr 3 mth	Normal speed (abnormalities)	—	Psychotic (not autistic)

Table 2   Comparison of Psychotic and Non-psychotic Groups

		Age	Mental age	Sentence length
Psychotic	M	9 yr 6.4 mth	5 yr 2.8 mth	3.10 words
	σ	1 yr 11 mth	1 yr 3.2 mth	0.63 words
Non-psychotic	M	9 yr 9.5 mth	5 yr 5.4 mth	3.03 words
	σ	1 yr 11.6 mth	1 yr 1.2 mth	0.91 words

THE 9 CRITERIA

The 9 criteria (Creak, 1961) were assessed for the psychotic children by the consultant psychiatrists in charge of the units of High Wick and Ladyfield. Both of them were very familiar with the 9 points, having been members of the working party which formulated them.

In the case of the mentally retarded children, the author had to ask teachers to complete the 9 points. He went over each point carefully with the teacher, asking him to give concrete descriptions of the child's behavior. All the psychotic children were marked positive on 3 or more of the 9 points, and the average number of points marked was 6.5. Eleven of the non-psychotics were not marked on any point, and the other 2 had one point positive. Every child in the psychotic group received a mark on point 1 ("Gross impairment of relationships with people"). This point is regarded by most clinicians as a *sine qua non* of childhood psychosis. In addition, they were all marked positive on point 7, which refers to abnormalities of speech. By contrast, none of the non-psychotic children was marked positively on either of these points. Point 6 ("acute, excessive and seemingly illogical anxiety") was marked for all but one of the psychotic group and for none of the non-psychotics.

Table 3   Sex, Residence and Social Class of Psychotic and Non-Psychotic Children

	Sex		Living in		Social class (by father's occupation)*					
	Boy	Girl	Own home	Institution	1	2	3	4	5	Not known†
Psychotic	9	4	1	12	3	4	4	1	0	1
Non-psychotic	7	6	10	3	0	0	5	5	1	2

*See Registrar-General (1960).
†Where father's occupation is "not known", this is because he no longer lives with the child.

Thus, the two groups were clearly distinguishable in terms of the 9 points, without overlapping.

METHOD OF OBSERVATION

A play session was used in which an adult sat with the child for a quarter of an hour, or until the child had made 50 remarks. Standard play material was used including toys, plasticine, paper and crayons, and two picture books. In many cases the child spoke spontaneously from the start, but if the child was silent the adult would try to interest him in the play material and sometimes asked him questions. The adult responded to the child's speech in a natural way. He was also ready to join in play with the child or to draw things for him if the child desired it. All speech was recorded on tape and the tape was played over and written out immediately after the session. Four play sessions were held with each child, these sessions being at weekly, or in some cases at rather shorter, intervals.

CLASSIFICATION OF REMARKS

An utterance was considered as a separate remark if it was marked off from preceding and succeeding utterances by pauses. However, if two or more sentences, which would be separated by full stops if written, were uttered without a pause, they were counted as separate remarks. For example:

"I must behave. I'm sorry. I'm sorry," was counted as three remarks.

Remarks were classified according to a scheme used by McCarthy (1930) in terms of comprehensibility, length, grammatical structure and function. In classifying function, we followed McCarthy and Piaget (1932) in contrasting egocentric and socialized speech. However, we also divided egocentric speech into the following subcategories:

1. Repetition of what the adult had just said (echolalia).
2. Repetition of what the child had just said (when such repetition was purposeless).
3. Inappropriate and purposeless remarks.
4. Thinking aloud.
5. Action accompaniments.

Socialized speech was divided into the categories of Information, Answers, Questions, and what McCarthy described as "Emotionally Toned" remarks, which included demands and requests.

Parts of speech were classified according to the scheme of Jones et al. (1963).

In the quantitative results, only the first 50 of the child's remarks in each of the four sessions were used. Thus, the number found for any category of remark was always a part of the same total. In counting parts of speech, a fairly small sample was considered sufficient and the first 100 words of one interview with each child were used. In counting personal pronouns, of which the numbers were very small, a larger sample was necessary and for this reason the first 100 words of all four interviews were used. Remarks were classified according to comprehensibility and function immediately after the play session. Length, structure, and parts of speech were

Table 4   Agreement Between Markers

| | Mean percent agreement* | | | | |
	Comprehensi-bility	Length	Function	Structure	Parts of speech
Non-psychotic	98.4	98.3	81.9	92.0	98.1
Psychotic	98.4	96.7	74.4	85.9	89.2
All	98.4	97.5	77.6	89.2	93.7

*There were three markers, the original marker and two later independent markers. Percent agreement was found between each pair of markers and the average of the three percentages taken.

scored from the written records by students according to careful instructions. As a check on reliability, a rescoring of a sample* of the records was carried out later by two independent scorers and the results compared.

STATISTICAL TECHNIQUES
Since there was no reason to expect our results to be normally distributed, the Mann-Whitney U-Test was used in finding the significance of differences between the groups (Siegel, 1956) and where correlations were calculated the Spearman Rank Coefficient was used.

RESULTS

RELIABILITY OF MARKING
The degree of agreement is shown in Table 4. It is satisfactory in the case of comprehensibility, length, structure, and parts of speech. The scorers agreed least well in this classification of the function of remarks. In this respect, they agreed better about the remarks of the non-psychotic children than about those of the psychotics. This might be expected in view of the "odd" nature of some of the psychotics' remarks which makes them difficult to classify.

COMPREHENSIBILITY
The psychotics made more remarks which consisted entirely or partially of incomprehensible words or sounds (Table 5). The reasons for the incomprehensibility of some of the remarks of the psychotics varied. Whispering or muttering occurred in the case of 5 psychotics, which made what they said difficult to understand. Neologisms were rare, but isolated instances were found in the speech of 4 psychotic children. For example,

---

* For rescoring sentences the first 10 responses of the fourth interview with each child were used and for parts of speech the first 20 words of the same interview.

Adult: "What's that?" (the windscreen of a plastic car).
B.P.:"An inkle," or
K.C. (looking closely at a watch-face): "There's a zeebar."

Two of the psychotic children distorted the vowel or consonant sounds to such a marked extent that what they said was often difficult to understand. Two others showed a variable degree of poor articulation.

EGOCENTRIC OR NON-COMMUNICATIVE REMARKS
The psychotics made significantly more remarks which were not used for ordinary communication (egocentric). These included repetition of the interviewer (echolalia), repetition of self, thinking aloud and inappropriate or purposeless remarks. They are dealt with separately below.

REPETITION OF INTERVIEWER'S REMARKS
The psychotic children echoed the interviewer significantly more often than the non-psychotics (Table 5). This occurred more frequently among those psychotics whose language was less developed, as judged by sentence length. For the psychotics the correlation between sentence length and number of repetitions of the adult was -0.61 ($p < 0.05$), whereas for the non-psychotics the correlation was $+0.20$ and not significant.

Sometimes a question was echoed, for example:

Adult: "What's he doing there?"
S: "What's he doing there?"

Or a request, for example:

Adult: "You make some chips."
S: "oo make some chips."

In some cases, it appeared that the child echoed something which he had not "taken in," e.g., the interviewer said "Set the table" and the child just echoed "Set the table," twice, without making any effort to do so. In other cases, the repetition of what had been said seemed to function as assent, e.g.:

Adult: "I'll put the man on the horse, shall I?"
S: "Put the man on the horse".

DELAYED REPETITION
"Repetition of interviewer" referred only to immediate repetition and did not include the repetition of a remark heard after some time had elapsed. The latter type of repetition appeared to occur in several cases, although it was difficult to establish whether what the child said was an exact repetition of something previously heard. For example, a child who wanted her dinner, said:

Table 5   Comprehensibility, Function and Structure
(Median number of remarks of each type for each interview and
significance of differences* between psychotic and non-psychotic
groups)

			Int. 1	Int. 2	Int. 3	Int. 4	Summed scores across 4 interviews
1.	Incomprehensible and	Psychotic	6.67	7.75	5.25	5.20	30.25
	semi-comprehensible	Non-psychotic	1.00	0.75	3.00	1.67	8.75
		$p <$	0.002	0.02	0.10	0.02	0.002
2.	Speech not used for	Psychotic	9.75	12.0	13.25	12.75	54.00
	ordinary communication	Non-psychotic	1.13	1.75	1.33	2.88	12.00
		$p <$	0.002	0.002	0.002	0.02	0.002
2a.	Repetition of	Psychotic	1.13	2.17	0.43	0.22	7.67
	interviewer	Non-psychotic	0.00	0.22	0.00	0.22	0.43
		$p <$	0.002	0.05	0.10	N.S.	0.002
2b.	Repetition of self	Psychotic	1.75	2.00	3.67	4.00	16.00
		Non-psychotic	0.43	0.31	0.80	0.60	2.75
		$p <$	0.05	0.05	0.05	0.02	0.02
2c.	Action accompaniments	Psychotic	0.32	0.31	0.31	0.88	2.33
		Non-psychotic	0.43	0.15	0.15	0.15	0.80
		$p <$	N.S	N.S	N.S.	N.S.	N.S.
2d.	Thinking aloud	Psychotic	0.67	2.25	1.33	2.25	9.00
		Non-psychotic	0.09	0.09	0.22	1.00	3.00
		$p <$	0.10	0.002	0.10	N.S.	0.05
2e.	Inappropriate or	Psychotic	0.92	1.75	1.25	1.00	7.00
	purposeless	Non-psychotic	0.04	0.00	0.04	0.04	0.09
		$p <$	0.02	0.002	0.05	0.05	0.002
3.	Emotionally toned	Psychotic	6.25	6.00	9.00	4.00	29.00
	remarks (demands and	Non-psychotic	0.63	0.43	0.88	1.25	4.00
	requests)	$p <$	0.02	0.02	0.05	0.10	0.002
4.	Answers	Psychotic	8.00	6.75	8.00	7.00	28.00
		Non-psychotic	12.33	10.00	6.00	12.25	44.00
		$p <$	N.S.	0.10	N.S.	0.10	N.S.
5.	Questions	Psychotic	1.75	3.00	1.75	2.00	13.75
		Non-psychotic	0.22	1.60	0.43	0.43	3.67
		$p <$	N.S.	N.S.	N.S.	N.S.	N.S.
6.	Volunteering information	Psychotic	10.00	8.38	8.00	7.75	34.00
		Non-psychotic	25.75	20.25	26.00	22.25	100.00
		$p <$	0.002	0.02	0.02	0.002	0.002
7.	Complete sentences	Psychotic	14.33	14.00	16.25	16.33	62.00
		Non-psychotic	17.00	13.00	16.75	20.75	76.00
		$p <$	N.S.	N.S.	N.S.	N.S.	N.S.
8.	Incorrect omissions	Psychotic	7.75	9.25	9.00	10.00	44.75
		Non-psychotic	4.25	7.25	5.00	7.25	24.00
		$p <$	0.10	N.S.	N.S.	N.S.	0.10(N.S.)
9.	Incomplete, but	Psychotic	15.00	17.33	16.00	15.75	62.00
	correct sentences	Non-psychotic	28.00	29.25	28.25	17.00	98.00
		$p <$	N.S.	N.S.	N.S.	N.S.	0.10(N.S.)

*The test of significance was the Mann-Whitney U-Test. 2-tailed tests have been used through-
out.

"Daresay she'd throw me out if I gave it you now."

This was apparently a repetition of what a house-mother had said when the child demanded dinner at the wrong time. Sometimes a child would repeat something previously heard, perhaps on television, without any relation to the context, e.g., "Nut milk chocolate cups," "You too Typhoo," "Oh what better flavor."

A phenomenon similar to delayed echolalia is that in which the child speaks as if someone else were speaking to him, e.g., a child who had felt impelled to smack the interviewer said "Be a good boy," or when eating plasticine chips against the interviewer's advice, he said "You mustn't eat the chip." If these were really instructions given to himself by the child, they had singularly little effect on his behavior.

REPETITION OF SELF

The psychotics repeated their own remarks significantly more often than the non-psychotics. The remarks were sometimes repeated in identical form and sometimes with slight variations, e.g.:

"It's going in the train"
"It's goes in the train"
"going in a t'ain"
"in the train."

ACTION ACCOMPANIMENTS

The differences between the psychotic and non-psychotic groups were not significant.

THINKING ALOUD

The psychotics made significantly more remarks which were classified as thinking aloud. The following is a clear example. A child seemed to be thinking while drawing and said:

"Do it dark"
"don't know why"
"so can't rub out."

This category was extended slightly to include remarks which were not such clear cases of thinking aloud, but which were non-communicative and did not fit any of the other categories. For example, one child whispered or muttered these remarks which did not seem addressed to anyone:

"Plastic one"
"what's a plastic one?"

Another poured out (quite regardless of her hearer) long, rambling and incoherent speeches apparently consisting to a large extent of snatches of conversation which she had heard at various times. For example:

"Sam is a clever boy"

"Sam is a clever boy, he said"
"He's a good boy"
"Who says 'too'?"
"What's dolly singing?"
"That's Margery and her doll, isn't it?," etc.

This type of speech was also included under thinking aloud.

INAPPROPRIATE OR PURPOSELESS REMARKS
The psychotics made significantly more remarks which were inappropriate or purposeless. In fact, all 13 of the psychotics made such remarks at times, but only two
of the non-psychotics. A remark was placed in this category if it made no sense at
all, for example:

"The master of balls"
"I'm the tennis ball,"

or if it was entirely inappropriate to the context and therefore conveyed no meaning,
e.g., a child was staring at a watch and said:

"There's the doors"
"Make the doors"
"There's the east."

EMOTIONALLY TONED REMARKS
The psychotics made significantly more "emotionally toned" responses than the
non-psychotics. These were nearly all demands or requests, often to the effect that
the interviewer should draw or model something for the child, but sometimes attempting to control other aspects of the interviewer's behavior, e.g., "Don't frown.
You make wrinkles," or "Use your 'ead. I told you."

VOLUNTEERING INFORMATION
The non-psychotics made a significantly larger number of remarks which volunteered
information than the psychotics. Such remarks usually consisted in telling the interviewer about the play material, what was happening in the child's play, or the pictures
in the books, e.g.:

"That's toys"
"That canna stand up"
"It's sitting down"
"The little girl is watching the TV."

At times also the non-psychotics would give information about their families and
other facts external to the interview situation. All the psychotics volunteered some
information, but the number of informative remarks made by the non-psychotics was
much greater.

ANSWERS
The difference between the groups in the number of answers was not significant.

QUESTIONS
There was no significant difference between the groups in the number of questions. Three of the psychotics and five of the non-psychotics asked no questions during the interviews. Two of the psychotics asked a great many questions, but so did one of the non-psychotics. The correlation between number of questions and mean sentence length was $0 \cdot 57$ ($p < 0 \cdot 05$) for the psychotics and $0 \cdot 53$ ($p < 0 \cdot 05$) for the non-psychotics. Thus, it seemed that children at a higher level of language development tended to ask more questions, whether they were psychotic or not. Two psychotics asked a great many questions. In one case, the questions were mostly connected with the child's obsessional interest in coins and money, e.g., "Where's it say Great Britain on the two shillings?." In the other case the questions of the psychotic child often seemed unrelated to his present situation, e.g. (out of the blue), "Do babies soil themselves?" or "What size is the handbasins in Crichton Hall?" (a ward with which he had nothing to do). Many of the questions asked by these psychotics were ones to which they already knew the answers. This, however, was also true of those non-psychotics who asked a great many questions.

INCOMPLETE SENTENCES
There was no significant difference between the groups in the number of complete grammatical sentences used. There was a slight tendency for the psychotics to use more incomplete and *incorrect* sentences, while the non-psychotics used more incomplete but *correct* sentences (Table 5).

There was no difference between the groups in the number of omissions of subject only, or verb and subject. The psychotics omitted verbs slightly more often and made miscellaneous omissions more often ($p < 0 \cdot 05$). "Miscellaneous omissions" included sentences in which there were several omissions (e.g., subject, auxiliary verb and preposition) and also sentences which were clearly incomplete, although it was difficult to decide what was omitted. The following are examples from psychotic children:

"Light it yellow"
"This is make it"
"Get some more watch"
"Change is six"
"That's Daddy got"
"Bear put."

Incorrect omissions by the non-psychotics were more often omissions of one word, leaving the rest of the sentences correctly constructed, e.g., "Shot the gun right out of his hands" (omission of subject). "There two more of them" (omission of verb, "are"), or the omission of a whole clause, for example, "So that you cannot get your meat on it". Thus it seemed that it was not grammatical incompleteness as such, which distinguished the psychotics, but the kind of incompleteness. Some of the psychotics used sentences which were abnormal in their whole structure, whereas the incomplete sentences of the non-psychotics were either quite legitimate to use or else merely involved the omission of a word or clause from a sentence which was otherwise correct.

PARTS OF SPEECH
The psychotics used a significantly greater proportion of verbs than the non-psychotics. No significant differences were found for any of the other parts of speech, namely, nouns, adjectives, pronouns, relative pronouns, articles, auxiliaries, quantifiers, prepositions, conjunctions, interjections and "unclassified."

PERSONAL PRONOUNS
In view of the reported difficulty of psychotic or autistic children with personal pronouns (Kanner, 1956, 1958, Creak, 1961, Bettelheim, 1967), special attention was paid to these. The first 100 words of each of the four interviews were studied in this connection. The results are given in Table 6. It will be seen that there was no difference between the numbers of psychotics and non-psychotics who used the first personal pronoun ("I" or "me"), no difference in the use of the second person ("you") and no significant difference in the number of uses of the third person ("he" or "him"). It cannot, therefore, be said that the psychotics avoided the use of the personal

Table 6   Use of Personal Pronouns*

	First person			Second person			Third person		
	No. of psychotics (N = 13)	No. of non-psychotics (N = 13)	Significance	No. of psychotics	No. of non-psychotics	Significance	No. of psychotics	No. of non-psychotics	Significance
Any use	12	12	N.S.	10	10	N.S.	10	13	N.S.
Correct use	9	12	N.S.	7	10	N.S.	10	13	N.S.
Incorrect use	1	0	N.S.	2	0	N.S.	1	0	N.S.
Doubtful use	10	1	$p < 0.01$ (2-tailed)	4	2	N.S.	6	1	N.S. $p < 0.10$ (2-tailed)
Use in repetition	1	0	N.S.	2	0	N.S.	2	1	N.S.

*The first 100 words of each of the four interviews were used.
Note: In the case of "any use" and "correct use" the Mann-Whitney U-Test was used to test significance, which took into account the *numbers of responses* of the given type used among the psychotics and the non-psychotics.
In the other rows the numbers of responses were too small to use the Mann-Whitney U-Test and the Fisher Yates Exact Test was used, comparing the number of psychotics who used a given type of response with the number of non-psychotics.

pronouns to any greater extent than the non-psychotics. In fact, 12 out of 13 psychotics used the first person, 10 the second person and 10 the third person. With regard to the *correct* use of the personal pronouns, there was no significant difference between the groups. Nine psychotics used the first person correctly at times, 7 psychotics correctly used the second person, and 10 psychotics the third person. The psychotics used the first person more often with doubtful correctness than did the non-psychotics. This arose from the fact that the psychotics used many sentences for purposes other than communicating information, and since their meaning was not clear one did not know to whom the personal pronoun referred. Incorrect uses of personal pronouns were confined to the psychotic group, although the differences were not significant. Only three of the psychotics clearly reversed personal pronouns. Of these one used the first and third personal pronouns incorrectly at times, while the other two used the second person incorrectly ("You" meaning "I"). But although they sometimes used these pronouns incorrectly, they were capable of using them correctly at other times. The use of "You" to mean "I" by two of the psychotics could not have been due to avoidance of or inability to use the word "I," since at times they used "I" correctly (Bettelheim, 1967). The following are examples of the misuse of personal pronouns:

S: "Smack me on" (as *S* punched the interviewer)
S: " 'e pull my tie (as *S* pulled the interviewer's tie)
Adult: "How did you do that?"
S: "You fall and hurt yourself."

DISCUSSION

GROUPING OF PSYCHOTIC CHILDREN ACCORDING TO LANGUAGE ABNORMALITIES SHOWN

It was considered of interest to investigate whether the psychotic children in this study could be divided into subgroups according to the cluster of language abnormalities shown.

This was done by drawing up Table 7 which shows various deviant features of language found in the psychotic children. Inspection of this table suggested provisionally that the psychotic children fell into two groups of 3 and 4 children, respectively, and that the remaining children did not fall into any obvious groupings. The first group consisted of children 2, 3 and 5, who used relatively short sentences, showed poor pronunciation of words, peculiar intonation, many incomplete and incorrect sentences and a good deal of echolalia and repetition of themselves. These children used personal pronouns rarely or incorrectly and scarcely ever asked questions. They gave the impression of having some language difficulty, similar to that of an aphasic child.

The other group, of four children (8, 10, 12, 13), used longer sentences, pronounced their words fairly well and were quite capable of forming complete and correct sentences. These children were able to ask questions and did not show excessive repetition of themselves or of the interviewer. They did not appear to have a severe language handicap. What they did show was a dearth of remarks giving spontaneous information. They showed either an excess of "thinking aloud" or of asking questions. The oddness of these children's speech appeared to lie less in its structure than in its content. In their conversation they showed odd or obsessional interests. Some of their remarks appeared strange or nonsensical, not because of incorrect structure but through the use of words in unusual combinations. Among these 4 children, muttered or whispered speech occurred in 3 cases.

Of the remaining children, child 9 had some resemblance to the first group, child 7 was more like the second group, while 4 children did not fit either group. We considered whether the two main groups might correspond to different diagnoses. However, no close correspondence was found with the diagnoses given by the psychiatrists. Of the 3 children in the first group, one was diagnosed as autistic and the other two as psychotic, but not autistic. Of the 4 children in the second group, two were diagnosed as schizophrenic and two as psychotic, but not autistic. It may be that the differences between the groups relate to the stage of language maturity and that a child of the first type might develop into one of the second type when he grows older.

Table 7   Relationship Between Sentence Length and Other Features of Language in the Psychotic Children

	Initials of child	Mean sentence length	Poor pronunciation and intonation*	Incomplete and incorrect sentences	Echolalia	Repetition of self	Information	Thinking aloud	Questions
1	B.D.	1.91		+					
2	D.M.	2.17	+	+	+	+			−
3	V.M.	2.31	+	+	+	+			−
4	A.Ga.	2.77							+
5	K.C.	2.80	+	+	+	+			
6	A.Ge.	2.96			+			+	
7	M.L.	2.99				+	−	+	
8	L.S.	3.32					−	+	+
9	S.B.	3.39		+		+	−		−
10	R.F.	3.48					−		+
11	D.S.	3.95	+			+			
12	R.S.	4.04					−		+
13	L.St.	4.19					−	+	

*Poor pronunciation and intonation was based on impressions.
+Indicates that the child is within the highest 6 of the combined groups.
−Indicates that the child is within the lowest 6.

GENERAL FEATURES OF LANGUAGE IN THE PSYCHOTIC GROUP

The study has shown that the language of retarded psychotic children is not merely retarded speech, but differs in several ways from that of mentally retarded children who are at a similar language level, as measured by sentence length.

Among the psychotics there was a dearth of speech giving information, and a more frequent use of non-communicative speech. Speech was often incomprehensible, either because of muttering, poor articulation or neologisms. Thinking aloud and snatches of speech not directed at the hearer were common, as also were inappropriate or purposeless remarks. The psychotics who were at a low language level often echoed the adult or repeated themselves. The psychotics made a greater number of demands and requests than the non-psychotics.

Although Wolff and Chess (1965) had found a shortage of questions among psychotics in comparison with normal children of corresponding sentence length, we did not find that our group of psychotics asked fewer questions than the mentally retarded children. Some of our psychotic children asked a great many questions. The psychotics of low sentence length asked very few questions, but this was also true of the mentally retarded children.

There was a slight tendency for the psychotics to make more remarks which were both incomplete and incorrect. A few of the psychotic children made many remarks of peculiar sentence structure, but others did not differ from retarded children in this respect. Difficulty in sentence construction appeared to be a characteristic of some, but not all of the psychotic children.

The comparison of parts of speech produced little of significance. The excess of verbs used by the psychotics might well be due to the greater number of demands and requests made, since these do not require the subject to be expressed (e.g., "come here"). This would accord with Weiland and Legg's (1964) finding of a greater number of imperative verbs.

With regard to personal pronouns, the results of this study do not give any support to the views of Bettelheim (1967), who considers that Kanner's idea of pronominal reversal is misleading. In his view, the basic fact is that autistic children *avoid* using personal pronouns, particularly "I." Apparent reversal arises because, in an effort to avoid using "I," the child sometimes uses "you" or "he" instead. The avoidance of the word "I" is regarded as a denial or an absence of awareness of selfhood. Our group of psychotics did not avoid using "I" or the other personal pronouns to any greater extent than the non-psychotics. Two of the psychotics used "you" to mean "I" at times, but on other occasions they used the word "I" correctly.

The main findings are that there is a dearth of informative speech in psychotic children, an excess of non-communicative speech, and also an excess of demanding or emotionally toned speech. Piaget (1932) found that egocentric or non-communicative speech was relatively common in young children, while McCarthy's results (1930) showed a greater frequency of emotionally toned or demanding remarks among the younger children. It seems, then, that the excess of demands and of non-communicative speech may represent a form of immaturity in the psychotic child. As Piaget (1932) has pointed out, the exchange of information requires the speaker to place himself at the point of view of his hearer. This, the psychotic child is unable to do. He shows a lack of empathy or ability to apprehend his hearer's state of mind and therefore falls back on non-communicative or demanding speech.

In terms of reinforcement theory (e.g., Lovaas, 1967), it may be suggested that the psychotic child is unable to discriminate between various social reinforcers (the smile of understanding, the frown of incomprehension, the nod of assent, the relevant answer). This would not be surprising in view of his well-known tendency to visual and auditory avoidance. If the psychotic's speech is more influenced by simpler reinforcers, for example, that of self-stimulation (hearing himself speak) or getting what he wants, one would expect a greater frequency of non-communicative or demanding speech.

SUMMARY

A group of 13 children diagnosed as psychotic and retarded was compared with a matched group of non-psychotic mentally retarded children. The psychotics showed an excess of incomprehensible remarks and non-communicative speech, including repetition of the adult, repetition of self and thinking aloud. The psychotic children showed deficiencies in sentence structure, but this was not so in all cases. Reversal of personal pronouns was only found in a small proportion of the group. Some of the group appeared to have a serious language handicap, while others did not. It is suggested that the excess of non-communicative and demanding speech may be due to lack of empathy or poor discrimination of social reinforcers.

ACKNOWLEDGEMENTS

I should like to thank Dr. W. J. Blachford Rogers for his advice and encouragement and for making this study possible.

I am also very grateful to Dr. George Stroh, Dr. R. Bailey, Dr. D. F. Robertson, Mrs. R. Doonan and Mr. W. J. Thomson for their helpfulness in arranging for me to study children under their care.

I am greatly indebted to Miss Dawn Manley and Mrs. Valerie Kear-Colwell for their assistance in making the observations and to those psychology students who helped to score the records.

REFERENCES

BETTELHEIM, B. (1967) *The Empty Fortress—Infantile Autism and the Birth of the Self.* The Free Press, Collier-Macmillan, New York.

CREAK, M. et al. (1961). Schizophrenic syndrome in childhood. Progress report of a working party. *Cerebral Palsy Bull.* **3**, 501–504.

CUNNINGHAM, M. A. (1966) A five-year study of the language of an autistic child. *F. Child Psychol. Psychiat.* **7**, 143–154.

JONES, L. V., GOODMAN, M. F. and WEPMAN, J. M. (1963) The classification of parts of speech for the characterisation of aphasia. *Language and Speech* **6**, 94–107.

KANNER, L. (1944) Early infantile autism. *J. Pediat.* **25**, 211–217.

KANNER, L. (1946) Irrelevant and metaphorical language in early infantile autism. *Am. J. Psychiat.* **103,** 242–246.

KANNER, L. and EISENBERG, L. (1956) Early infantile autism. *Am. J. Orthopsychiat* **26,** 556–564.

KANNER, L. and LESSER, L. I. (1958) Early infantile autism. *Pediatr. Clinics N. Am.* **5,** 711–730.

LOVAAS, O. I. (1967) A behaviour therapy approach to the treatment of childhood schizophrenia. In *Minnesota Symposium on Child Psychology* (Edited by HILL, J.) University of Minnesota Press, Minneapolis.

McCARTHY, D. A. (1930) *The Language Development of the Pre-School Child.* University of Minnesota Press, Minneapolis.

PIAGET, JEAN (1932) *The Language and Thought of the Child* (Translated by Gabain, M.). Kegan Paul, London.

REGISTRAR-GENERAL (1960) *Classification of Occupations.* H.M.S.O., London.

RUTTER, M. (1967a) Psychotic disorders in early childhood. In *Recent Developments in Schizophrenia,* (Edited by COPPEN, A. and WALK, A). The Royal Medical Psychological Association, London.

RUTTER, M. (1967b) A five to fifteen year follow-up study of infantile psychosis. *Br. J. Psychiat.* **113,** 1169–1182 and 1183–1199.

SIEGEL, S. (1956) *Nonparametric Statistics.* McGraw-Hill, New York.

WEILAND, H. and LEGG, D. R. (1964) Formal speech characteristics as a diagnostic aid in childhood psychosis. *Am. J. Orthopsychiat.* **34,** 91–94.

WOLFF, S. and CHESS, S. (1965) An analysis of the language of fourteen schizophrenic children. *J. Child Psychol. Psychiat.* **6,** 29–41.

Author's Comment Written for *Readings in Childhood Language Disorders:*

The group used in this study was rather mixed and included children who would be described as psychotic but not as pure cases of Kanner's infantile autism. Thus, it cannot be assumed that the results would apply to autistic children in this strict sense.

A difficulty in language comprehension has been found in autistic children by several authors (Rutter, 1968, Wing, 1966, Tubbs, 1966). The excess of non-communicative speech and deficiency of informative remarks in our psychotic group might have been due to a lower ability to comprehend more complex sentences. It is unfortunate that no test of language comprehension was used to check on this hypothesis.

Failure to use speech for communication is a well-known finding with autistic children and was also found in this study.

ADDITIONAL REFERENCES

Rutter, M. (1968) Concepts of Autism: A review of research. *J. Child Psychol. Psychiat.,* 9, 1–25.

Tubbs, V. K. (1966) Types of linguistic disability in psychotic children. *J. Ment. Def. Res. 10,* 230–240.

Wing, J. K. (1966) Diagnosis, Epidemiology, Aetiology. In *Early Childhood Autism* (Edited by Wing, J. K.) Pergamon Press, Oxford.

Differential Diagnosis Between Aphasic and Schizophrenic Language in Children

Katrina de Hirsch

The differential diagnosis between primary, specific communicative disorders—sometimes called "aphasic"—and those communicative difficulties which are secondary to psychopathology is rarely, if ever, straightforward.

In clinical practice one encounters a continuum of communicative deficits that range from severe defects in the codification of language at one end, to those which reflect a pathological orientation to the self, the love object, and the world, at the other. There exist, however, some more or less "pure" cases at either end of this continuum and it might be appropriate to discuss these first.

The consensus during the past few years has been to reserve the term "aphasic" for cases whose difficulties with the decoding and encoding of verbal symbols are related to demonstrable CNS impairment. However, not all children who, in the absence of significant sensory deficits or important limitations in intellectual potential, fail to interpret and use language have histories of brain damage or show positive signs on the classical neurological examination or the EEG. Jansky (1960) investigated 12 children with severe symbolic disorders—6 with histories of brain damage and 6 without—and found clear differences between these groups and normal controls in most of the 14 verbal and 14 nonverbal areas tested. No essential differences, on the other hand, were found between the children with verifiable histories of brain damage and those without such histories.

Children who partially or totally fail to interpret or use verbal symbols will be called "aphasoid" in this paper since, regardless of their histories, the overwhelming majority present a fairly typical constellation of dysfunctions, many of which have been discussed by such researchers as Worster-Drought (1943), Carrel and Bangs (1957), and others.

While aphasoid children's audiograms may fluctuate, their erratic auditory deficits do not account for their profound inattention to auditory and—more specifically—

From *Journal of Speech and Hearing Disorders, 32,* 3–10 (1967). Reprinted by permission of the American Speech and Hearing Association.

Katrina de Hirsch, F.C.S.T., is Director of the Pediatric Language Disorder Clinic, Columbia Presbyterian Medical Center, Columbia University, New York City; Lecturer in Pediatrics, College of Physicians and Surgeons, Columbia University; and Consultant in Language Pathology, New York State Psychiatric Institute.

to verbal stimuli. These children hear, but they do not necessarily understand. They have difficulties with "auding" (Hardy, 1965)—with perceiving, storing, and recalling the serial order of information received through auditory channels. Richard Masland (1965) says that the essential feature in verbal behavior is the sequencing of auditory events. Aphasoid children distort the temporal sequence of signals (Paine, 1965). Their auditory memory spans are extremely short, and they have difficulties in recalling both nonverbal and verbal configurations. They show limited ability to repeat patterns tapped out for them, and they have trouble reproducing digits, nonsense-syllables, and sentences in the correct order (Lowe and Campbell, 1965).

In these children, moreover, the perceptual field is poorly structured; words do not seem to stand out from the mass of unorganized stimuli impinging on the organism. In a recent experiment, Williams (1965) showed that her aphasic group's ability to separate the auditory figure from the background of noise was inferior. Words for such youngsters seem to be experienced in a diffuse, undifferentiated fashion as evidenced by their strikingly poor auditory discrimination. Above all, the configuration of the word, as well as its meaning, appears to be unstable (de Hirsch, 1965); the word never acquires a physiognomy, as it were, it never becomes familiar. As French (1953) puts it, such children are unable to maintain a linguistic Gestalt, thus they fail to assign consistent symbolic significance to input events.

These children's expressive language deficits are mostly secondary to their receptive disorders and mirror their poorly structured and diffuse intake and their inadequate feedback. The degree of expressive language impairment varies. Speech may be severely limited in quantity, crude, and undifferentiated in quality. Lenneberg (1964) comments on the primitiveness of these children's utterances. They simplify blends, telescope words, and their verbalizations are only crude approximations of the correct model. Masland and Case (1965) describe children's difficulties with the patterning of phonemic detail. Conceptual deficits and, in particular, difficulties with time and space concepts are pervasive and intimately related to symbolic deficits.

In these children, primitiveness and instability are not confined to verbal experiences; they are evident also in immature postural reflexes, global and undifferentiated motility, awkward fine motor control, fragmented human figure drawings, fluid Bender Gestalten. The children have difficulties on all levels of organization—perceptuo-motor and linguistic—in fact, they have trouble organizing and extracting meaning both from their external and internal worlds. As a result, they look—and often are—disoriented. This disorientation has an "organic" flavor; it differs from that of the psychotic youngster and appears to be part of the aphasoid child's specific constellation of dysfunctions.

These dysfunctions—and we avoid the term "minimal brain injury" since it constitutes an inferential diagnosis for which criteria vary from one clinical setting to another—may be related to encephalopathies, though there is as yet no way to correlate behavioral signs with specific neurological disease entities (Birch, 1964). These dysfunctions may rest on a familial basis as hypothesized by Orton (1937), who felt that "word deafness" and a tendency to motor awkwardness are prevalent in certain families. Finally, they may reflect a massive maturational lag which has interfered with the early establishment of basic sensori-motor schemata. That such a tendency to maturational lags may be genetically determined was postulated by Zangwill (1960).

Regardless of etiology, however, severe difficulties with expression and communication interfere with developing ego functions of mastery, impulse control, and ability to postpone gratifications. The child who lacks verbal tools, who cannot discharge tension and anxiety by way of words, who cannot verbalize anger and aggression, is forced to resort to action and remains tied to more archaic forms of coping. Emotional disturbance may be but one aspect of lack of neurological integrity—it is well known that "organic" children are profoundly anxious (Greenacre, 1963). Kurlander and Colodny (1965) speak of "primary" anxiety. Ego development is dependent on intactness of the CNS and any organic insult is bound to interfere with the epigenesis of the ego. The degree of disturbance varies not only with the pervasiveness and severity of the underlying condition, but also with the ability of the environment to support and tolerate this kind of child whose difficulties with control are severe and whose infantile and dependency needs are far greater than those of others. If one considers further that the speech-deprived child often fails to call forth communicative responses in the mother, it is not surprising to find that even under relatively favorable conditions a measure of emotional disturbance is the rule rather than the exception.

Some of the features which characterize aphasoid children—perceptuo-motor instability, figure-ground difficulties, and profound auditory inattention—are found also in a large number of schizophrenic youngsters. Their plastic motility, their tendency to melt into the background, their fluid perceptions, and the primitiveness of their organizational schemes, all reflect immature CNS patterning. Silver (1950) felt that plasticity is an attribute of the immature Gestalt. Bender (1953) discussed the persistence of primitive neural patterning in schizophrenic children; she conceived of childhood schizophrenia as a maturational lag on the embryonic level of development.

In aphasoid children, instability and fluidity are confined to the perceptuo-motor and linguistic realm; in schizophrenic children, this fluidity is pervasive and involves ego boundaries and the totality of the personality organization. The resulting radically different orientation to the world entails a fundamentally altered attitude toward the language function. Since in schizophrenic youngsters the boundaries between self and nonself are blurred, since there is little distance between the one who sends the message and the one who receives it, dialogue becomes precarious or impossible.

When one explores the various aspects of receptive and expressive language in the aphasoid and the schizophrenic groups, one finds both similarities and differences. However, even when the symptomatology is similar, underlying dynamics may vary.

Investigating the receptive language of schizophrenics is, of course, no easy task. These children are hard to reach, and they are sometimes more responsive to stimuli from within than from outside the organism—to wit, their occasional auditory hallucinations.

Both aphasoid and schizophrenic youngsters present limitations in comprehension of visual and auditory events. The failure of both psychotic and brain-injured children to make appropriate selection among stimuli from the environment has been discussed by Farnham-Diggory (1966). Aphasoid children, as a result of their symbolic deficits, have specific difficulties with the interpretation of spoken and printed language. In schizophrenic children as described by Goldfarb (1961), the avoidance of selected auditory and visual input signals must be interpreted in psychodynamic terms.

Hoberman and Goldfarb (1963) demonstrated that schizophrenic youngsters' auditory thresholds for speech—that is to say, for meaningful material—are higher than for pure tones, probably because their experiences are so fragmented that they cannot integrate meaningful information into an already existing framework. In aphasoid children, similar high speech thresholds are due to their difficulties with the decoding machinery.

The auditory memory span of aphasoid youngsters is usually extremely short, in striking contrast to that of schizophrenic children whose memory for meaningless material may be excellent and who, for instance, are able to reproduce long TV commercials. In fact, some schizophrenic children—in contrast to aphasic ones—may unexpectedly and spontaneously produce words and sentences of a highly complex structure, testifying to their good auditory memory span and their ability to incorporate sophisticated linguistic rules.

Feedback is distorted in both groups. Feedback in the very young organism, as shown by Wyatt (1958), is provided by the mother who playfully throws back the child's own sounds to him, elaborates on them, and clarifies them. It is only at a later stage that feedback becomes internalized. The schizophrenic child who is unseparated from the mother, or the one who is unable to "tune in," cannot use the mother as a model. The aphasoid youngster, on the other hand, may get the feeling tone of the message, but cannot use the mother as a model because his reception is diffuse and his ability to process and to organize auditory sequences is inferior.

The bizarre and idiosyncratic character of schizophrenic children's expressive language is usually unmistakable. There are at least three striking features in the communication of psychotic children.

The first is the often total absence of communicative intent. Communication requires a "complicity" (Ajurriaguerra, 1963), as it were, between partners, and schizophrenic children are not "in" on this arrangement. Their inability to establish stable object relationships is reflected in the absence of communicative intent. In these children, language is not consensually validated, to use Sullivan's (1959) expression; it is not an instrument of interpersonal behavior. Lack of communicative intent can be observed in their impoverished and sometimes wholly inappropriate gestures which do not—as gestures frequently do in aphasoid children—serve to reinforce communication. Verbal output is often severely limited. However, even when the quantity of verbalization is adequate or abundant, the wish or the ability to relate may be absent. The echolalic speech of schizophrenic children with its mechanical, high pitched, birdlike quality carries a feeling entirely different from that of the occasional echolalic utterances of children with severe and specific language deficits. The aphasoid children may repeat words or phrases for purposes of clarification—they may try words out for size, as it were. Although their voice quality may be somewhat monotonous and muffled, their pitch and inflection (which carry the emotional as against the conceptual load of communication) are largely normal. Goldfarb (1961) described the deviations in pitch, stress, and inflection of schizophrenic youngsters, their sometimes stilted and manneristic way of speaking, and the flat voice quality which reflects flatness of affect.

The second typical feature was described by Schilder (1942). He has pointed out that in schizophrenic language words are no longer referents, but are treated as if they were the things themselves. Words lose their symbolic status; they become concrete entities and as such acquire magic powers. Werner and Kaplan (1963) refer to the "thinglike" handling of linguistic forms. Since in schizophrenia speech is not an instrument of communication, specific words may be heavily emotionally invested, played with, juggled, telescoped, even truncated. As happens in dreams, words undergo condensation, a single word may represent a whole train of thought, sentences flow into each other, there is interpenetration of connotations, syntactical rules are disregarded. In a brilliant chapter, Werner and Kaplan discussed in detail what happens to morphophonological and lexical rules in the language of schizophrenics. Aphasoid children also show severe syntactical deficits. Masland and Case (1965) postulate that their inability to remember sequences interferes with the internalizing of syntactical rules. On the other hand aphasic speech, unlike schizophrenic language, does not show the looseness of associations and the kind of verbalizations which are only tangentially related to what is going on.

Language, with its potential for conceptualization, is normally, of course, a superb tool of the secondary process. Anna Freud (1965) says "verbalization is . . . the indispensable prerequisite for secondary process thinking." Freud (1957) has demonstrated that schizophrenic communication—and this is a third characteristic feature —is subject to "primary process distortion." Instead of being at the service of the ego, schizophrenic language is tied to early instinctual processes (Laffal, 1965). One schizophrenic youngster who came for help with his reading told me, "There is no point in learning to read the letter 'K', it is not nice, it has too many spikes!" For this boy, letters, like words, had no conventional objective significance; they did not serve reality or conscious purposes, but instead were experienced in terms of primary processes. In this case, "K" symbolized the child's archaic fears of aggression and retaliation. The fact that symbols are heavily invested with highly personalized meanings probably accounts for the fact that much of schizophrenic language is poorly conceptualized.

CONCLUDING REMARKS

The clinician who attempts to make a differential diagnosis between aphasoid and schizophrenic language finds that the two have many features in common: high auditory thresholds for speech, inferior auditory discrimination, feedback distortions, echolalia, limitations in verbal output, and conceptual deficits. Unlike schizophrenic youngsters, aphasic children have short auditory memory spans and they do not present the deviations in pitch, stress and inflection, the manneristic style, and the idiosyncratic use of words which are characteristic of those communicative disturbances that are clearly related to psychopathology.

Clinically, one finds innumerable admixtures along the communicative continuum discussed earlier. A great many youngsters are damaged on both the physiological and the psychological levels of integration. Classifying all language deficits as related either to organicity or to psychosis does not do justice to the complexity of the clinical phenomena. Many psychotic children present significant neurological dysfunctions, and a number of "organic" youngsters exhibit signs of withdrawal and are only tenuously related to the world around them. As Rappaport (1961) pointed out, organic dysfunctions and psychological disturbances may use identical mechanisms. Both involve ego functions and, thus, language.

In every case, therefore, the clinician has to evaluate neurophysiological, linguistic, and affective aspects of communication and the often enormously complex interaction between them. He must try, furthermore, to form an impression of the way the child deals with the original insult—be it psychological or physiological—and the effectiveness of the defenses he uses in order to cope. Defensive mechanisms in the two groups, however, may show certain superficial similarities and are thus not necessarily helpful in differential diagnosis. We find obsessive defenses not only in the primarily disturbed where they serve against the onslaught of internal threats from the unconscious, but we also observe obsession-like defenses in organic children. In the latter, such behavior may be used as a defense against severe difficulties with control and a tendency to primary disorganization.

The way a child copes with his handicap depends, of course, largely on the manner in which significant people in his environment respond to his deficit. A tentative assessment of the contribution of the environment is, therefore, an additional task of the clinician.

In many cases, only intensive work with the child will shed light on the nature of his deficit. No single aspect of it can be evaluated in isolation; every language dysfunction has to be viewed in terms of the organism as a whole.

REFERENCES

AJURIAGUERRA, J. DE, Les troubles du langage. *Confin. neurol.,* **23,** 91–107 (1963).

BENDER, LAURETTA, Childhood schizophrenia. *Psychiat. Quart.,* **27,** 663–681 (1953).

BIRCH, H. G., The problem of "brain damage" in children. In H. G. Birch (Ed.), *Brain Damage in Children.* Baltimore: Williams and Wilkins (1964).

CARREL, J., and BANGS, J., Disorders of speech comprehension associated with ideopathic language retardation. *Nerv. Child,* **9,** 64–76 (1957).

FARNHAM-DIGGORY, SYLVIA, Self, future, and time: a developmental study of the concepts of psychotic, brain-damaged and normal children. Monogr. Serial No. 103, *Soc. Res. Child Dev.,* **31** (1966).

FRENCH, E. L., Psychological factors in cases of reading difficulties. Paper read at 27th Ann. Conf. Second. Ed. Board, New York (1953).

FREUD, ANNA. *Normality and Pathology in Childhood.* New York: Internatl. Univ. Press (1965).

FREUD, S., *The Unconscious.* Stand. Ed., XIV. London: Hogarth (1957).

GOLDFARB, W., *Childhood Schizophrenia.* Cambridge: Harvard Univ. (1961).

GREENACRE, PHYLLIS, *Trauma, Growth and Personality.* London: Hogarth (1953).

HARDY, W. G., On language disorders in young children: a reorganization of thinking. *J. Speech Hearing Dis.,* **30,** 3–16 (1965).

HIRSCH, KATRINA DE, The concept of plasticity and language disabilities. *Speech Path. Ther.,* **8,** 12–17 (1965).

HIRSCH, KATRINA DE, and JANSKY, JEANNETTE, Word deafness. *J. S. Afr. Logoped. Soc.,* **4,** 13–15 (1957).

HOBERMAN, SHIRLEY E., and GOLDFARB, W., Speech reception thresholds in schizophrenic children. *J. Speech Hearing Res.,* **6,** 101–106 (1963).

JANSKY, JEANNETTE, Congenitally word deaf children. Master's thesis, College of City of New York (1960).

KURLANDER, L. F., and COLODNY, DOROTHY, "Pseudoneurosis" in the neurologically handicapped child. *Am. J. Orthopsychiat.,* **35,** 733–738 (1965).

LAFFAL, J., *Pathological and Normal Language.* New York: Atherton (1965).

LENNEBERG, E. H., A biological perspective of language. In E. H. Lenneberg (Ed.), *New Directions in the Study of Language.* Cambridge: M.I.T. (1964).

LOWE, AUDREY D., and CAMPBELL, R., Temporal discrimination in aphasoid and normal children. *J. Speech Hearing Res.,* **8,** 313–314 (1965).

MASLAND, MARY W., and CASE, LINDA, Limitation of auditory memory as a factor in delayed language development. Paper read at Meeting on Internatl. Assoc. Logopedics & Phoniatrics, Vienna, Aug. 1965. In print.

MASLAND, R., The neurologic substrata of communicative disorders. Paper read at Convention American Speech and Hearing Association, Chicago, Nov. 1965.

ORTON, S., *Reading, Writing and Speech Problems in Children.* New York: Norton (1937).

PAINE, R. S., Organic neurological factors related to learning disorders. In J. Hellmuth (Ed.), *Learning Disorders.* Seattle: Spec. Child Public. of Seattle Sequin School, **1,** 1–29 (1965).

RAPPAPORT, S. R., Behavior disorder and ego development in a brain injured child. *Psychoanal. Study Child,* **16,** 423–448 (1961).

SCHILDER, P., *Mind: Perception and Thought in their Constructive Aspects.* New York: Columbia Univ. 266 (1942).

SILVER, A., Diagnostic value of three drawing tests for children. *J. Pediat.,* **37,** 129–143 (1950).

SULLIVAN, H. S., *Clinical Studies in Psychiatry.* New York: Norton (1959).

WERNER, H., and KAPLAN, B., *Symbol Formation. New York: Wiley (1963).*

WILLIAMS, JULIA B., Auditory figure ground among dysphasic children. Paper read at Convention American Speech and Hearing Association, Chicago, Nov. 1965.

WORSTER-DROUGHT, C., Congenital auditory imperception (congenital word deafness) and its relation to idioglossia and allied speech defects. *Med. Pr.,* **210,** 411–417 (1943).

WYATT, GERTRUD L., Mother-child relationship and stuttering in children. Doctoral dissertation, Boston Univ. (1958).

ZANGWILL, O., *Cerebral Dominance and Its Relation to Psychological Functioning.* London: Oliver & Boyd (1960).

The Relation of Infantile Autism and Early Childhood Schizophrenia to Developmental Language Disorders of Childhood[1]

Don W. Churchill

Evidence and arguments are presented to support a thesis that central language deficits related to those found in children with developmental aphasia, but more severe, may be the necessary and sufficient cause of behavior which marks children as autistic and schizophrenic. Deficits which may cut across sensory modalities and differ between individuals, but remain stable within, can be identified in both groups. The two groups also share difficulties such as sequencing problems and deficiencies related to meaning of words that are more subtle than echolalia and pronominal reversal. Language deficits, however, are not said to be the only ones, as other handicaps may account for some variability in clinical cases. Also presented are two case reports illustrating results of an experimental nine-word language used in training and testing of psychotic children.

There are compelling reasons to consider that certain childhood psychoses, i.e., infantile autism and childhood schizophrenia, may be extreme examples of conditions recognized elsewhere in medicine and given such names as developmental aphasia or central language disorder. The thesis of this paper is that psychotic children with a psychiatric diagnosis of autism or schizophrenia may share with nonpsychotic brain-damaged children various perceptual and perceptual-motor deficits, but that the *sine qua non* of the psychotic condition (*distinguishing* the psychotic group) is a central language deficit which is closely related to but more severe than that found in children with various aphasic or central language disorders. At present, such a hypothesis is the most parsimonious way of explaining and relating the three most prominent and clinically significant features of childhood psychosis: impairment of communication, impairment of relationships, and impairment of appropriate object use. The purpose of this paper is to examine certain evidence and arguments which support this view.

From *Journal of Autism and Childhood, 2,* 182–197 (1972). Copyright © 1972 by Scripta Publishing Corporation. Reprinted by permission of Plenum Publishing Corporation.

[1] A part of this paper was presented at the Fifth World Congress of Psychiatry on November 30, 1971 in Mexico City. The study was supported in part by Public Health Service Grant No. MH 05154 and also by LaRue D. Carter Memorial Hospital, Indianapolis, Indiana.

It is recognized from the outset that diagnostic problems create formidable complications. Psychiatrists who diagnose infantile autism or childhood schizophrenia are vexed by problems of agreement on terms and diagnostic reliability. The same difficulties confront neurologists and language pathologists who diagnose developmental aphasia or central language disorders. Nevertheless, both fields recognize a cluster of disorders which are assigned such names or slightly modified ones. And in both fields there has been a marked surge of interest in these disorders over the past decade despite the continuing dissatisfaction with nosology.[2] Psychotic children are those diagnosed as autistic or schizophrenic, according to the DeMyer classification (DeMyer, Churchill, Pontius, & Gilkey, 1971; White, DeMyer, & DeMyer, 1964).[3] In all cases, such psychotic children are characterized at the time of diagnosis by severe impairment of speech for communication (mutism, echolalia, disorganized speech), severe affective withdrawal and impairment of interpersonal relationships (including avoidance of eye contact), and little or no appropriate object use. Often there is also bizarre ritualistic or stereotyped behavior, negativism, self-destructive behavior, or an abrupt emotional outburst which appeared excessive or not readily understandable. Psychotic children may also exhibit special abilities, such as striking memory feats, unusual manual dexterity or uncanny mechanical abilities, although these skills do not seem to serve their overall adaptation.

It has been suggested, particularly by investigators in England (Rutter, 1965a, 1968; Hermelin, 1968; Wing, 1969) that the most important factor in infantile autism and childhood schizophrenia may be an underlying language disorder. However, there has been a tendency to consider speech and language disturbances as merely one aspect of a broader and more complex disorder (Anthony, 1958; Cunningham, 1968; de Hirsch, 1967; Weiland & Legg, 1964). Pronovost (1961) was perhaps the first to point out clearly and in some detail the similarities in the speech of autistic and aphasic children, while Rutter (1965a) has gone furthest in stating the case explicitly and succinctly: "Speech abnormalities are perhaps the most characteristic of all the manifestations of child psychosis, and an aphasic-type disorder is probably a central element in the development of many cases of psychosis or autism." However, he goes on to say, " . . . it is also clear that developmental aphasia is not a sufficient explanation for the other behavioral abnormalities." In support of this reservation, Rutter notes that a good many aphasic children are not autistic and that, in contrast to autistic children, they often use gestures to communicate. He also notes that a family history of similar disorders is common only in aphasic children. Also, in contrast to the apparent developmental/maturational problem in aphasic children, most autistic children have clearer evidence of brain damage. Savage (1968), in

---

[2] In this paper the term "developmental aphasia" is discarded in favor of "central language disorder," and the corresponding clinical phenomena are in accord with those described by various authorities in the field of language pathology (Darley, 1964; Johnson, Darley, & Spriestersbach, 1963; Kleffner, 1958; McGinnis, Kleffner, & Goldstein, 1956; Morley, Court, Miller, & Garside, 1955; Myklebust, 1952, 1954; Russell, 1959; Schuell, 1966; Sheridan, 1961; Walker & Langueth, 1956; West, 1962; Wood, 1964; Worster-Drought, 1957).

[3] These children have also been diagnosed independently on the basis of several diagnostic checklists developed for these conditions (DeMyer et al., 1971).

describing the similarity between autistic children and those with developmental aphasia, also considered points which would presumably differentiate them. However, it seems likely that the phenomena which are used to differentiate psychotic children from those with central language disorders are actually either common to both groups or may best be seen as matters of *degree* of impairment. For instance, Rutter (1966) found that although similar speech retardation is present in IQ-matched controls, communication problems are "much more persistent" in psychotic children than in the control group; this suggests a difference in degree of impairment. Savage (1968) stated that the aphasic child is different in that his emotional disturbance is "reactive, and disappears with treatment of the language handicap." However, this is also true of autistic children (Churchill, 1969, 1971; Rutter, 1965b, 1968). Usually, the "autism" is cured but certain handicaps persist. Both Hauesserman (1962) and Myklebust (1954) remarked on the social withdrawal associated with receptive aphasia in children. And in still other respects the behavioral and emotional characteristics of autistic and schizophrenic children have been found not to differ significantly from those of other handicapped or even normal children (Churchill, 1969, 1970, 1971; Churchill & Bryson, 1972; Hermelin & O'Connor, 1963; O'Connor & Hermelin, 1967).

This is not to imply unitary etiology. Nor is it to say that a central language disability is the *only* deficit in psychotic children. Indeed, it is not. Many investigators have cited other abnormalities of sensory and perceptual function, most importantly perhaps visual perception (Bryson, 1970; Frith & Hermelin, 1969; Hermelin, 1966; Hermelin & O'Connor, 1964, 1965; Ottinger, Sweeney, & Loew, 1965; Schopler, 1966). The argument here is that a central language disorder may well be the necessary and sufficient cause of that behavior which marks children as autistic and schizophrenic, and not just one of many possible types of impairment which lead to the same condition. Most investigators are now in agreement that autistic and schizophrenic children present different patterns of disability. This variability may be accounted for by these additional sensory and perceptual handicaps. On the other hand, the so-called "classical" autistic child, as most rigorously defined in accordance with criteria delineated by Leo Kanner, may be one who has a central language disability which is profound but so circumscribed that he remains free of confounding disturbances in sensory, motor, and perceptual areas. In all cases of children diagnosed as autistic or schizophrenic, one finds such a defect of language integration regardless of any additional handicaps. There is also considerable agreement that language ability and/or improvement is one of the best indices of prognosis and is strongly related to social competence. Our own work with language training in such children, considering both the progress which can be made and the limit which is eventually reached, makes attractive the notion of linguistic structure advanced by Chomsky (1957, 1965) and others (Bellugi & Brown, 1964; Lenneberg, 1967; McNeill, 1966). Such children, it seems, can be taught language "performance" but not language "competence."

INDIRECT EVIDENCE

There are several intriguing congruities between psychotic and central language-disordered children. While none of them offers direct proof of the relatedness of the two types of conditions, taken together these congruities would cause surprise if we were to consider psychotic and central language-disordered children as belonging to unrelated groups. Five of these congruities are presented below:

(1) SEX RATIO: Virtually all kinds of language disorders in children occur more frequently in boys, with the sex ratio sometimes approaching 4:1. There is no satisfactory explanation for this differential. Nevertheless, empirically it is evident from a wide variety of sources that infantile autism and childhood schizophrenia occur much more often in boys than in girls and in some reports the sex ratio is again near 4:1 (Rutter, 1967).

(2) NEUROBIOLOGIC IMPAIRMENT: Underlying neurologic impairment is either demonstrated or comfortably inferred in cases of central language disorder. On the other hand, the symptoms of psychotic children have been attributed to problems with earliest interpersonal relationships, motivation, emotionality, drive and affect; by implication at least, and in many cases explicitly, psychotic children often have been considered free of significant neurobiological deficits. Thus, psychotic children have been considered separate from central language-disordered children: different cause, different condition. However, with more systematic and controlled studies of recent years, an increasing number of investigators have reached some agreement that psychotic children also suffer from neurobiologic impairment (Bryson, 1970; Gittleman & Birch, 1967; Hingtgen & Churchill, 1969; Ornitz, 1969; Rimland, 1964; Ritvo, Ornitz, Tanguay, & Lee, 1970; Rutter, 1965a, 1968; Walter, Aldridge, Cooper, O'Gorman, McCallum, & Winter, 1971; White et al., 1964; Whittam, Simon, & Mittler, 1966). At the same time, other controlled studies have failed to demonstrate significant differences in parental psychopathology and early mother-infant interaction between groups of psychotic and nonpsychotic brain-damaged children (Alpern & Yang, 1969; Pitfield & Oppenheim, 1964; DeMyer, Pontius, Norton, Barton, Allen, & Steele, 1972). Increasingly, as one compares the strength of evidence for neurobiologic impairment with evidence to the contrary, one must be more impressed with the similarity than with the distinctiveness of the two groups in question.

(3) PHENOMENOLOGICAL: Case histories and treatment records of psychotic children and of those with central language disorders often reveal remarkable overlap from the phenomenological standpoint alone. Echolalia and so-called pronominal reversal are only two of the more obvious examples (Fay, 1971). Clinicians representing different fields, between which there has been little or no intercourse, are dealing with remarkably similar children. Some state this explicitly (Strauss & Lehtinen, 1947); more often the likenesses seem unwittingly so described. This again suggests that the distinction between the two groups of children is specious, and our separating them may be more of a semantic artifact than an accurate and useful representation of nature.

(4) CLINICAL EXPERIENCE: An accumulation of personal clinical observations gained in the treatment of psychotic and central language-disordered children, though unsystematic, has also led to the impression that these children have much

more in common than is often supposed. These observations have been described in some detail elsewhere (Churchill, 1969). The general point to be made here is that we have observed repeatedly that sociability, cooperativeness, attentiveness, reliability of performance, and even the degree of engagement in ritualistic and bizarre behavior appear much more closely correlated with a child's level of mastery in a given situation than with other factors. Our overall experience is that the more colorful symptomatology of autism and schizophrenia decreases markedly during treatment while social and affective contact increases, and we are left with children who have a relatively hard and fast inability to learn particular precision skills, especially those prerequisite for language competence. These observations accord with those of others (Cunningham, 1966; Elgar, 1966; Rutter, 1968; Wing, 1969).

(5) PRIMA FACIE EVIDENCE: Finally, there is the *prima facie* evidence, obvious but unremarked, that the most salient and universal feature of autistic and schizophrenic children is simply a disturbance of communication with others. This is so regardless of what other symptomatology may be present. The child is "out of contact." But the communication problem with psychotic children does not reside only (or *even*) in impaired speech but rather in some disturbance of language—the representational or symbolic aspects of speech, including the referents of words, the manipulation of syntax, and the grasp of abstract meaning. Thus, in both groups of children we may see preserved speech but the absence of speech for communication. A profound language loss may simultaneously account for lack of substitute channels for communication (e.g., gestures or handsigns), lack of combinational uses of objects (Tilton & Ottinger, 1964; Weiner, Ottinger, & Tilton, 1969), and ultimately impairment of interpersonal relationships, whether this is conceived as a primary or secondary result of the language deficit.

DIRECT EVIDENCE

As for direct evidence to support the thesis of this paper, Rutter (1968) has noted systematic differences between performance and language subtest scores on standardized intelligence tests given to psychotic children. DeMyer (1971) has consistently observed the same, with language scores being much poorer than performance scores. Hermelin and O'Connor (1970), more than anyone else, have conducted systematic acute experiments comparing groups of psychotic and other types of children with respect to receptive, integrative, and expressive abilities. Though significant performance differentials are found in several areas, their data taken together provide significant support for an inference that disability in the area of language is critical.

While this evidence is derived from groups of children, an intense and systematic scrutiny of individuals reveals the same finding. Schuell (1966) has recommended a study of error patterns while testing across and between modalities in individual aphasic adults and children. In such persons the deficits are different between individuals but are stable within individuals. Over the past three years an experimental nine-word language, adapted from Mark (1969), has been used within an operant conditioning paradigm to systematically test processes which subserve the language function. Testing is across channel-specific sensory modalities as well as upward

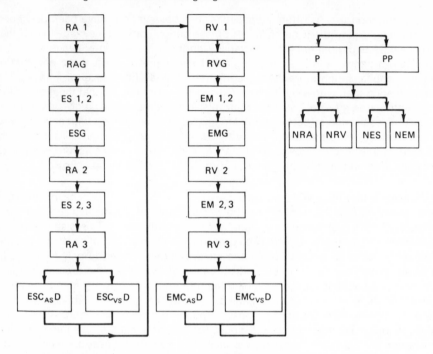

Note.—Numerals refer to number of words in task. R = receptive; E = expressive; A = auditory; V = visual; S = speech; M = motor; G = generalization (novel stimuli); C = cross-referencing; S^D = discriminative stimulus; P = pronouns; PP = prepositions; N = novel sentences (NRA– following directions; NRV–reading; NES–describing; NEM–writing).

Figure 1.   Sequence of tasks used in experimental nine-word language.

through integration systems of increasing complexity as shown in Figure 1. That reliable and consistent performance can be obtained from even the most negative and uncooperative autistic and schizophrenic children has been previously demonstrated (Hingtgen & Churchill, 1969; Churchill, 1971) and is extensively corroborated in work with the nine-word language. This is important to the limit-testing assumption which is implicit in our interpretation of the data.

Thorough testing of a single child may require 2 or 3 sessions a day for 3 or more months. Briefly, the procedure is to establish first a basal vocabulary consisting of three nouns, three adjectives, and three verbs.[4] Figure 2 displays these nine words as well as the nine objects used in experimental language. The nine words are assigned visual (hand signs) as well as auditory (spoken word) representation. Stimuli,

---

[4] A complete description of testing procedures and detailed analysis of the data will be presented elsewhere.

either auditory or visual, are initially presented one at a time so as to test the integrity of receptive auditory, receptive visual, expressive vocal, and expressive motor modalities for making simple associations within and across modalities. For each modality a generalization test is done in turn to test ability to abstract or generalize to novel stimuli. Stimuli are next presented in a series of two parts of speech, and finally three. At this point the basic components of a simple grammar should be attained: three nouns, three adjectives, and three verbs. The procedure then continues through cross-referencing tasks, which require using a discriminative stimulus to respond to the correct one of two overlapping properties of an object. Again, modalities can be checked independently. Finally, more abstract elements of linguistic structure, such as prepositions and pronouns, are introduced, and short novel sentences are presented.

All of the 16 tested autistic and schizophrenic children, ranging in age from 5 to 8 years, demonstrated a disability in processing auditory or visual information or in making those associations and/or groupings which would seem logically prerequisite to language competence. While each child showed a unique error pattern when examined in such detail, the pattern within each child was stable and could be reliably reproduced. Thus, one child might have difficulty in mastering one part but not other parts of speech. Another might show channel-specific or cross-modal problems. Others demonstrated intact modalities but did not learn at levels of integration higher than simple association. Even the most verbal children (who were not necessarily the highest functioning overall) showed marked difficulty in manipulating the grammati-

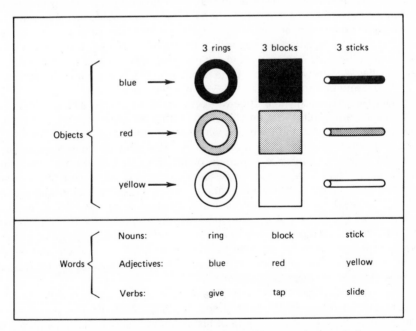

Figure 2.   Nine objects and nine words used in experimental nine-word language.

cal elements of a three- or four-word sentence even when the semantic significance or "meaning" of each word taken separately had been mastered. In such cases there seemed to be a severe limit imposed on their ability to respond appropriately to *novel* simple sentences using familiar words or to generate spontaneously new, comprehensible sentences of their own.

TWO CASE REPORTS

The argument must rest at present with two examples chosen for illustrative purposes:

CASE 1

George, diagnosed as autistic at age 3 years and 3 months, was not speaking or trying to communicate. Parents were treated as objects. Although he lived "in a world of his own" he showed unusual interest in and ability with mechanical things. Other behavior patterns were hand-posturing, rocking, head-banging, toe-walking, disregard for danger, negativism, and tantrums if intruded upon or denied his way. His father, an electronics engineer, was intellectual and aloof; the mother, who persistently infantilized George, was unable to express hostility directly.

Initial evaluation revealed no physical abnormalities, but during 3½ years of treatment two subsequent EEGs were abnormal, with pronounced spiking in the left central area during waking and sleep. During this time the child largely overcame his withdrawal and negativism, and most of his behavior problems subsided. He learned to feed and dress himself and was partially toilet-trained. Rocking and head-banging ceased, and he began to enjoy playing with normal children and to participate in family activities. A variety of objects were used appropriately, such as construction toys, and he continued to be fascinated with mechanical objects.

Eventually George was given a three-week period of intensive training in imitative behavior (Hingtgen, Coulter, & Churchill, 1967), after which it seemed clearer that he had some specific learning problems which were difficult to account for on the basis of negativism or emotional problems alone. We refer to what emerged as a cross-modal deficit; i.e., despite hundreds of hours of training George remained unable to make visual-vocal or auditory-visual associations. Because of his evident visual-motor proficiency, an effort was made to teach him a simple sign language as a kind of prosthetic device. Although he learned hundreds of associations quickly, there was never any evidence that he generalized from previously learned to novel stimuli. This result was repeated with the simpler and less ambiguous stimuli of the nine-word language. In minimum time he met criteria for visual-visual and visual-motor associations; however, he never responded above the chance level in making visual-vocal or auditory-visual associations.

Capitalizing on his visual-motor integrity, he was presented two hand signs at a time which represented two different parts of speech. In 6,370 trials over 91 sessions, George never met the criterion in spite of his ability to respond correctly to any of the signs singly. Of special interest is the pattern of his errors: 80% of the time he would miss the initial stimulus regardless of what part of speech it represented.

Reversing the sequence of parts of speech resulted in his responding correctly to the second (proximate) stimulus but missing the first. In addition, when he *would* respond correctly to the first stimulus, it was associated with an error on the second stimulus. After approximately 14,700 trials during the course of 210 sessions, a receptive visual generalization test was administered using novel stimuli which possessed some attributes of the colors or shapes of the nine-word language objects. The score was 49 out of 50 correct.

CASE 2

Larry had had several other evaluations before a referral to the Research Center at the age of 4 years and 8 months. His birth had been by Caesarian section after 36 hours of unsuccessful labor. He was considered a precocious child because he was able to sit upright at 4 ½ months and to walk at 8 months. At 8 months he also clearly said "ice" after which he slowly expanded a single word vocabulary. However, in his second year, during which time a sibling was born, he seemed to lose his speaking ability and became withdrawn. At the time of evaluation, Larry was a large, alert, attractive child who ignored people and engaged in many mannerisms, which included waving objects before his eyes and sucking them. He resisted any direction or intrusion and would abruptly pull away, shout, and swing things wildly. His only distinct word was "mine". There was little or no appropriate object use. An EEG disclosed generalized single and polyspike wave paroxysms during drowsiness and sleep, with greatest prominence on the left side anteriorly. He was considered autistic, with evidence of brain damage.

During 3½ years of residential treatment, which included language and special sensory training, there was general behavioral improvement, increased relating to others, higher levels of object use, and improvement in self-care skills. Following three weeks of intensive training (Hingtgen et al., 1967), some imitative speech was established as well as beginnings of writing skills. He developed a large receptive and expressive vocabulary for nouns. When presented with the nine-word language, the boy met in minimum time all criteria for both auditory and visual receptive functions and for vocal and motor expressive functions for single stimuli. He progressed in similar fashion through three-word combinations and scored high on each of the generalization tests. It was thought that Larry had all the elemental skills requisite for productive speech, yet, on cross-referencing tasks, although he met the criterion in only five sessions when the task was a visual-vocal one, the child was unable to cross-reference by auditory-vocal means in 213 sessions.

This task was then abandoned to concentrate on other parts of speech, notably prepositions. Using *in, on, under* and *beside* and a given set of objects, Larry learned to make motor responses appropriate to the relationships designated by the prepositions; however, when other objects were introduced, even though he knew them well by name, the boy could no longer apply the same prepositions to the "new" set of objects. We began working intensively with a four-word paradigm: verb—direct object—preposition—object of preposition, in which the verb was invariable (e.g., "Put shoe beside fork"). Ten months and over 200 hours of training intervened between the pre- and post-testing. In the results from the 100 randomized trials comprising the two tests, systematic errors were observed, together with a shift in types of errors from pre- to post-test. However Larry did not show overall improvement in responses to the four-word sentences. In the first test, most errors consisted of interchanging the direct object and the object of the preposition (object reversal). In some cases there were isolated errors in responding to either the direct object or the object of the preposition alone. In addition, there appeared certain "rigidities" in which a particular noun seemed to be preferentially associated with a particular preposition. For instance, any response to "beside" had a high probability of being beside-*cup*. The second test showed a narrowing of error patterns without any overall improvement. The object reversals and isolated object errors and rigidities had markedly declined or disappeared altogether. However, there were now many more preposition errors which occurred with or without associated object reversals. It was as though the main effect of the training was to improve one set of associations at the expense of the other, with no progress in integrating the two.

COMMENT

The systematic and detailed training-testing of psychotic children in precision language skills, with particular reference to the study of error patterns, provides some direct evidence of the similarity between the language handicaps of these children and others who are not psychotic but are identified as having a central language disorder. Deficits which may cut across sensory modalities and which differ between individuals but are stable within individuals are identified in *both* groups. The two groups also share not only the more obvious deviations of echolalia and pronominal reversal but also more subtle difficulties, such as sequencing problems and special problems with the meaning of words. Perhaps most devastating in terms of general language competence is the inability to handle the syntax or structure of language so as to be able to relate the word elements of a sentence independently to each other. For as other investigators have pointed out (Hebb, Lambert, & Tucker, 1971; McNeill, 1966; Osgood, 1957, 1963), it is this which gives language its power and permits an individual not just to learn separately a limited number of word combinations but to understand and generate an infinite variety of sentences. It is proposed that *psychotic children* share a *central language disorder* with other children who are given only the latter term as a diagnosis and that the fundamental difference between the two groups is severity of involvement.

REFERENCES

Alpern, G. D., & Yang, E. Objective personality differences between parents of brain damaged and non-brain damaged autistic children: Research report No. 9. Paper presented at the Clinical Research Center for Early Childhood Schizophrenia, Indianapolis, 1969.

Anthony, E. J. An experimental approach to the psychopathology of childhood autism. *British Journal of Medical Psychology,* 1958, **31,** 211–223.

Bellugi, V., & Brown, R. The acquisition of language. *Society for Research in Child Development Monographs,* 1964, **29** (92).

Bryson, C. Q. Systematic identification of perceptual disabilities in autistic children. *Perceptual and Motor Skills,* 1970, **31,** 239–246.

Chomsky, N. *Syntactic structures.* The Hague: Mouton, 1957.

Chomsky, N. *Aspects of the theory of syntax.* Cambridge, Mass.: The M.I.T. Press, 1965.

Churchill, D. W. Psychotic children and behavior modification. *American Journal of Psychiatry,* 1969, **125,** 1585–1590.

Churchill, D. W. The effects of success and failure on a heterogeneous group of untrained children: Research Report No. 7. Paper presented at the Clinical Research Center for Early Childhood Schizophrenia, Indianapolis, 1970.

Churchill, D. W. Effects of success and failure in psychotic children. *Archives of General Psychiatry,* 1971, **25,** 208–214.

Churchill, D. W., & Bryson, C. Q. Looking and approach behavior of psychotic and normal children as a function of adult attention or preoccupation. *Comprehensive Psychiatry,* 1972, **13,** 171–177.

Cunningham, M. A. A five-year study of the language of an autistic child. *Journal of Child Psychology and Psychiatry,* 1966, **7,** 143–154.

Cunningham, M. A. A comparison of the language of psychotic and non-psychotic children who are mentally retarded. *Journal of Child Psychology and Psychiatry,* 1968, **9,** 229–244.

Darley, F. L. *Diagnosis and appraisal of communication disorders.* Englewood Cliffs, N.J.: Prentice-Hall, 1964.

de Hirsch, K. Differential diagnosis between aphasic and schizophrenic language in children. *Journal of Speech and Hearing Disorders,* 1967, **32,** 3–10.

DeMyer, M. K. Perceptual limitations in autistic children and their relation to social and intellectual deficits. In M. Rutter (Ed.), *Infantile autism: Concepts, characteristics and treatment.* London: Churchill, 1971.

DeMyer, M. K., Churchill, D. W., Pontius, W., & Gilkey, K. M. A comparison of five diagnostic systems for childhood schizophrenia and infantile autism. *Journal of Autism and Childhood Schizophrenia,* 1971, **1,** 175–189.

DeMyer, M. K., Pontius, W., Norton, J. A., Barton, S., Allen, J., & Steele, R. Parental practices and innate activity in normal, autistic, and brain-damaged infants. *Journal of Autism and Childhood Schizophrenia,* 1972, **2,** 49–66.

Elgar, S. Teaching autistic children. In J. K. Wing (Ed.), *Early childhood autism.* Oxford: Pergamon, 1966.

Fay, W. H. On normal and autistic pronouns. *Journal of Speech and Hearing Disorders,* 1971, **36,** 242–249.

Frith, U., & Hermelin, B. The role of visual and motor cues for normal, subnormal and autistic children. *Journal of Child Psychology and Psychiatry,* 1969, **10,** 153–163.

Gittleman, M., & Birch, H. G. Childhood schizophrenia: Intellect, neurologic status, perinatal risk, prognosis, and family pathology. *Archives of General Psychiatry,* 1967, **17,** 16–25.

Hauesserman, E. In R. West (Ed.), *Proceeding of the Institute on Childhood Aphasia.* San Francisco: California Society of Crippled Children and Adults, 1962.

Hebb, D. O., Lambert, W. E., & Tucker, G. R. Language, thought and experience. *Modern Language Journal,* 1971, **55,** 212–222.

Hermelin, B. Recent psychological research. In J. K. Wing (Ed.), *Early childhood autism.* Oxford: Pergamon, 1966.

Hermelin, B. Recent experimental research. In P. J. Mittler (Ed.), *Aspects of autism.* London: British Psychological Society, 1968.

Hermelin, B., & O'Connor, N. The response and self-generated behavior of severely disturbed children and severely subnormal controls. *British Journal of Social and Clinical Psychology,* 1963, **2,** 37–43.

Hermelin, B., & O'Connor, N. Effects of sensory input and sensory dominance on severely disturbed, autistic children and on subnormal controls. *British Journal of Psychology,* 1964, **55,** 201–206.

Hermelin, B., & O'Connor, N. Visual imperception in psychotic children. *British Journal of Psychology*, 1965, **56**, 455–460.

Hermelin, B., & O'Connor, N. *Psychological experiments with autistic children.* Oxford: Pergamon, 1970.

Hingtgen, J. N., & Churchill, D. W. Identification of perceptual limitations in mute autistic children. *Archives of General Psychiatry*, 1969, **21**, 68–71.

Hingtgen, J. N., Coulter, S. K., & Churchill, D. W. Intensive reinforcement of imitative behavior in mute autistic children. *Archives of General Psychiatry*, 1967, **17**, 36–43.

Johnson, W., Darley, F., & Spriestersbach, D. *Diagnostic methods in speech pathology.* New York: Harper & Row, 1963.

Kleffner, F. The aphasic child. Paper presented at the 38th meeting of the Convention of the American Instructors of the Deaf, Washington, D.C., 1958.

Lenneberg, E. H. *Biological foundations of language.* New York: Wiley, 1967.

Mark, H. J. Psychodiagnostics in patients with suspected minimal brain dysfunction(s). (USPHS Publication No. 2015, *Minimal brain dysfunction in children*) Washington, D.C.: United States Government Printing Office, 1969.

McGinnis, M., Kleffner, F., & Goldstein, R. Teaching aphasic children. *Volta Review*, 1956, **58**, 239–244.

McNeill, D. Developmental psycholinguistics. In F. Smith & G. A. Miller (Eds.), *The genesis of language.* Cambridge, Mass.: The M.I.T. Press, 1966.

Morley, M., Court, D., Miller, H., & Garside, R. Delayed speech and developmental aphasia. *British Medical Journal*, 1955, **2**, 463–467.

Myklebust, H. Aphasia in children. *Exceptional Children*, 1952, **19**, 9–14.

Myklebust, H. *Auditory disorders in children.* New York: Grune & Stratton, 1954.

O'Connor, N., & Hermelin, B. The selective visual attention of psychotic children. *Journal of Child Psychology and Psychiatry*, 1967, **8**, 167–179.

Ornitz, E. M. Disorders of perception common to early infantile autism and schizophrenia. *Comprehensive Psychiatry*, 1969, **10**, 259–274.

Osgood, C. E. Motivational dynamics of language behavior. In M. R. Jones (Ed.), *Nebraska symposium on motivation.* Lincoln: University of Nebraska Press, 1957.

Osgood, C. E. On understanding and creating sentences. *American Psychologist*, 1963, **18**, 735–751.

Ottinger, D. R., Sweeney, N., & Loew, L. H. Visual discrimination learning in schizophrenic and normal children. *Journal of Clinical Psychology*, 1965, **21**, 251–253.

Pitfield, M., & Oppenheim, A. N. Child rearing attitudes of mothers of psychotic children. *Journal of Child Psychology and Psychiatry*, 1964, **5**, 51–57.

Pronovost, W. The speech behavior and language comprehension of autistic children. *Journal of Chronic Diseases*, 1961, **13**, 228–233.

Rimland, B. *Infantile autism.* New York: Appleton-Century-Crofts, 1964.

Ritvo, E. R., Ornitz, E. M., Tanguay, P., & Lee, J. C. M. Neurophysiological and biochemical abnormalities in infantile autism and childhood schizophrenia. Paper presented at the meeting of the American Orthopsychiatric Association, 1970.

Russell, W. R. *Brain, memory, learning.* Oxford: Clarendon Press, 1959.

Rutter, M. The influence of organic and emotional factors on the origins, nature and outcome of childhood psychosis. *Developmental Medicine and Child Neurology*, 1965, **7**, 518–528. (a)

Rutter, M. Speech disorders in a series of autistic children. In A. W. Franklin (Ed.), *Children with communication problems.* London: Pitman, 1965. (b)

Rutter, M. Behavioral and cognitive characteristics of a series of psychotic children. In J. K. Wing (Ed.), *Early childhood autism.* Oxford: Pergamon, 1966.

Rutter, M. Schooling and the autistic child. *Special Education*, 1967, **56**, 19–24.

Rutter, M. Concepts of autism: A review of research. *Journal of Child Psychology and Psychiatry,* 1968, **9,** 1–25.

Savage, V. A. Childhood autism: A review of the literature with particular reference to the speech and language structure of the autistic child. *British Journal of Disorders of Communication,* 1968, **3,** 75–88.

Schopler, E. Visual versus tactile receptor preference in normal and schizophrenic children. *Journal of Abnormal Psychology,* 1966, **71,** 108–114.

Schuell, H. Some dimensions of aphasic impairment in adults considered in relationship to investigation of language disturbances in children. *British Journal of Disorders of Communication,* 1966, **1,** 33–45.

Sheridan, M. D. Disorders of spoken language in young children. *Archives of Diseases of Childhood,* 1961, **36,** 11–16.

Strauss, A. A., & Lehtinen, L. E. *Psychopathology and education of the brain-injured child.* New York: Grune & Stratton, 1947.

Tilton, J. R., & Ottinger, D. R. Comparison of the toy-play behavior of autistic, retarded, and normal children. *Psychological Reports,* 1964, **15,** 967–975.

Walker, C., & Langueth, P. Developmental speech anomalies in apparently normal children. *British Medical Journal,* 1956, **2,** 1455–1458.

Walter, S. G., Aldridge, V. J., Cooper, R., O'Gorman, G., McCallum, C., & Winter, A. L. Neuro-physiological correlates of apparent defects of sensori-motor integration in autistic children. In D. W. Churchill, G. D. Alpern, & M. K. DeMyer (Eds.), *Infantile autism: Proceedings of Indiana University Colloquium.* Springfield, Ill.: Charles C Thomas, 1971.

Weiland, I. H., & Legg, D. R. Formal speech characteristics as a diagnostic aid in childhood psychosis. *American Journal of Orthopsychiatry,* 1964, **34,** 91–94.

Weiner, B. J., Ottinger, D. R., & Tilton, J. R. Comparison of the toy-play behavior of autistic, retarded, and normal children: A reanalysis. *Psychological Reports,* 1969, **25,** 223–227.

West, R. (Ed.) *Proceedings of the Institute on Childhood Aphasia, September, 1960.* San Francisco: California Society for Crippled Children and Adults, 1962.

White, P. T., DeMyer, W., & DeMyer, M. K. EEG abnormalities in early childhood schizophrenia: A double-blind study of psychiatrically disturbed and normal children during promazine sedation. *American Journal of Psychiatry,* 1964, **120,** 950–958.

Whittam, H., Simon, G. B., & Mittler, P. J. The early development of psychotic children and their sibs. *Developmental Medicine and Child Neurology,* 1966, **8,** 552–560.

Wing, L. The handicaps of autistic children—a comparative study. *Journal of Child Psychology and Psychiatry,* 1969, **10,** 1–40.

Wood, N. *Delayed speech and language development.* Englewood Cliffs, N.J.: Prentice-Hall, 1964.

Worster-Drought, C. Observations on speech disorders in children. *Postgraduate Medical Journal,* 1957, **33,** 486–493.

Part 4
CORRELATES OF CHILDHOOD LANGUAGE DISORDERS

There has been considerable interest in the nature of the processing skills of children with clinical syndromes associated with childhood language disorders—particularly the syndromes of autism, childhood schizophrenia, and congenital aphasia. The articles included here represent the type of research being done to identify the specific abilities required for processing information necessary for language learning and some views about the clinical application of such research.

Research into the specific abilities associated with language processing has focused on different levels or stages of processing such as attention to different types of stimuli, integration of input from different sensory modalities, and the discrimination, organization, and retention of input stimuli. The purpose of the research has been to discover differences in information processing skills, differences that might account for the deviant behaviors observed, including deviant language behaviors.

The study by Lovaas, Schreibman, Koegel, and Rehm (1971) is included here because it is one of the few that has examined children's differential attention to multisensory stimulation. The results for individual subjects are presented and intersubject variation in attending skills is explored and discussed. Attending to information from a number of different senses simultaneously, is, of course, only a part of the skill necessary for learning language. Such sensory information needs to be processed and integrated in order to induce the relationship between the auditory linguistic signal and ideas about the world which are derived from visual, tactile, and auditory experiences.

A number of studies have pointed out the difficulty some aphasic children have in processing rapidly presented auditory information. The study by Tallal and Piercy (1975) is one of a series of studies by these authors. The one presented here illustrates how the use of synthetic speech stimuli allowed the experimenters to manipulate components of the speech signal in order to observe their differential effects. Using meaningful natural speech stimuli, Hermelin and Frith (1971) reported a series of studies that investigated the organization and retention of linguistic stimuli. Their article is representative of numerous studies on the short-term memory of language-disordered children. It reports on the processing of non-linguistic patterned stimuli and discusses possible deficits in perceiving patterns, or rules, in any sensory input. The article by Churchill (1972) reprinted in the previous section, includes a discussion of the integration of stimuli from different sensory modalities. Each article illustrates some of the best research being done within this orientation. Each finds differences in the processing skills of certain language-disordered children as compared with normal children of equivalent chronological or mental age.

Are differences in such specific abilities the bases of the language disorder? Can deficits be remediated? Should intervention with the language-disordered child focus on remediating processing deficits rather than on teaching lauguage itself? These questions are dealt with in the accompanying textbook, *Language Development and Language Disorders* and by Rees (1973 not reprinted here). The last article in this section, Hammill and Larsen (1974), presents empirical evidence on the effectiveness of training in certain processing skills.

REFERENCES

Rees, N. Auditory processing factors in language disorders: The view from Procrustes' bed. *Journal of Speech and Hearing Disorders, 38,* 304–315 (1973).

Selective Responding by Autistic Children to Multiple Sensory Input[1]

O. Ivar Lovaas, Laura Schreibman, Robert Koegel, and Richard Rehm

Three groups of children (autistic, retarded, and normal) were reinforced for responding to a complex stimulus involving the simultaneous presentation of auditory, visual, and tactile cues. Once this discrimination was established, elements of the complex were presented separately to assess which aspects of the complex stimulus had acquired control over the child's behavior. We found that: (a) the autistics responded primarily to only one of the cues; the normals responded uniformly to all three cues; and the retardates functioned between these two extremes. (b) Conditions could be arranged such that a cue which had remained nonfunctional when presented in association with other cues could be established as functional when trained separately. The data failed to support notions that any one sense modality is impaired in autistic children. Rather, when presented with a stimulus complex, their attention was overselective. The findings were related to the literature on selective attention. Since much learning involves contiguous or near-contiguous pairing of two or more stimuli, failure to respond to one of the stimuli might be an important factor in the development of autism.

The unresponsivity of autistic children serves as one of the main criteria for their diagnosis. This unresponsiveness is typically apparent in a child during the first year of life when he behaves as if he were blind and deaf, causing his parents to seek professional opinion. Kanner (1944) describes such behavior in one of his patients as follows:

> When spoken to, he went on with what he was doing as

From, *Journal of Abnormal Psychology, 77,* 211–222 (1971). Copyright © 1971 by the American Psychological Association. Reprinted by permission.

[1] This investigation was supported by United States Public Health Service Research Grant 11440 from the National Institute of Mental Health. The authors express their appreciation for the help of: James Q. Simmons, Associate Program Director of Clinical Training for the Mental Retardation Center, Neuropsychiatric Institute, University of California, Los Angeles; Thomas Ball, of the Department of Psychology, Pacific State Hospital, Pomona, California; and Norbert Rieger, Superintendent of Children's Services, Camarillo State Hospital, Camarillo, California. They are grateful to B. Henker, W. E. Jeffrey, and I. Maltzman for their helpful comments on an earlier draft. They also wish to thank Bodil Sivertsen for her assistance in this research.

The essentials of this paper were presented at the Annual Meeting of the National Society for Autistic Children, San Francisco, California, June 24–27, 1970.

if nothing had been said. Yet one never had the feeling that he was willingly disobedient or contrary. He was obviously so remote that the remarks did not reach him. [p. 212].

Rimland (1964, cf, pp. 94–96) has presented several other illustrations of such unresponsivity. Description of the phenomenon points to a large variability which can be observed within a particular modality. For example, it may be impossible to observe a response in these children to a very loud (100-db.) sound, yet they may respond excessively to a barely audible siren. The child who behaves as if he does not see the person who greets him, or other objects in his environment, may spot a sugar-coated corn flake some 20 feet away. There also exists some speculation (Rimland, 1964) that the unresponsiveness may vary across modalities, such that visual, auditory, and pain stimulation are less likely to elicit a response than tactual, gustatory, or olfactory stimuli.

An example from our own laboratory serves to illustrate how such unresponsivity interferes with these children's treatment. We attempted to teach mute autistic children language by beginning with a program on the teaching of verbal imitation (Lovaas, Berberich, Perloff, & Schaeffer, 1966). We have tried to facilitate such imitations by providing the child with visual cues as well as auditory ones. Thus, the child can clearly see the teacher's face when she presents the various sounds, such as "mm," which has auditory and visual cues quite distinct from "ah." The child will learn under these conditions; that is, he comes to reliably emit the vocal response in apparent imitation of the teacher. Following this, the teacher presents the sounds while the child is looking away, or while she is purposely covering her face. Strikingly, the child remains mute. He only attended to the visual cues. It is as if he had never heard the sounds despite thousands of trial exposures.

Figure 1 presents an example from a large number of such instances in our speech training program. The figure is based on data from a patient, Johan, an 8-year-old mute boy diagnosed as a "textbook example of autism." He was trained to imitate the sound "ah" with full visual exposure to the teacher's face. Percentages of correct reproductions (S's "ah" to E's "ah") are given on the ordinate, and trials are given along the abscissa. The S had 1,180 trials preceding those which are plotted here, but his performance reflected no learning until after 1,400 trials. At this point he improved, and by Trial 1,740 he gave an onlooker the impression that he was listening to E and imitating what he had heard. However, when E removed the visual cues associated with the sound (Trials 1760–1780, 1800–1820, and 1840–1860), S's performance fell to zero. It is as if he had never heard E's voice.

The insert in the figure shows the same loss when visual cues are removed from the training of Johan's second sound, "mm." Eventually, as in the case of guttural sounds (e.g., "g," "k") without distinct visual components, the child learns to discriminate (imitate) the auditory cues. This acquisition is very slow. These observations raise several questions. Are the children particularly unresponsive to auditory cues? Are they unresponsive to auditory cues when these are presented together with visual cues? Do they have difficulty attending to any one cue in a multiple cue input, etc.?

The clinical observations that these children respond to cues in a particular modal-

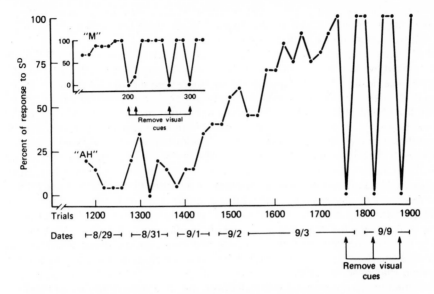

Figure 1. Acquisition of "Ah" and "Mm" trained with auditory and visual cues. (Percentages of correct reproductions of *E*'s presentations are plotted on the ordinate with trials plotted along the abscissa. Arrows indicate trials where visual cues were removed.)

ity on one occasion while not responding to these cues on another occasion have led to inferences regarding deficiencies in attentional, rather than sensory, mechanisms. These deficiencies in attentional mechanisms have been given a central, explanatory role in the child's failure of cognitive, social, or emotional development. For the reader who feels that there may be a similarity between attentional deficit in adult and childhood schizophrenia, excellent reviews of theories of attentional deficit in adult schizophrenia have been provided by Buss and Lang (1965), Lang and Buss (1965), and Feigenberg (1969).

Two main etiologies have been proposed to underlie the attentional deficiencies in autism. One of these is based on developmental models and draws heavily on Sherrington's work (1906). He postulated a transition from near-receptor dominance in lower organisms to far-receptor dominance in higher organisms. He considered, furthermore, that the far receptors are prerequisite for the development of complex psychological processes. This conceptualization has been employed by Goldfarb (1964) in his postulation of a distorted hierarchy of receptor dominance in autistic children, with motor-tactile orientation dominating auditory and visual inputs. Subsequent experimental studies (cf. Schopler, 1966) have failed to verify the propriety of this model in describing receptor orientation in autistic children.

The other proposed etiology of these attentional deficits is based on hypothesized deviations in their social history and draws heavily on psychodynamic formulations. The children's primary difficulty is seen to arise from inadequate early mother-child interactions, with a consequent failure in the development of perceptual activity, or it may be selective, largely restricted to social stimuli. As was the case with the developmental theories based on Sherrington's work, there has been a similar failure for research to confirm psychodynamic interpretations.

Much of the empirical work here has been carried out by Hermelin and O'Connor (summarized by Hermelin, 1966) and usually involved exposing the children to various stimulus displays, obtaining preferences for certain inputs as a function of the amount of their visual or tactual attending behavior. The conclusion which can be drawn from these studies is that, in contrast to normals, autistic children look less at the experimental stimuli, but do not selectively avoid social ones. Young (1969) found that they may attend proportionately less to complex, incongruous stimuli.

Although descriptions of visual attending behavior, which comprise the bulk of research in this area, may provide leads in understanding the psychopathology, such studies are quite inferential. That is, they require a model which relates visual attending to learning, or to some other behavior change. This is feasible since a person can visually attend to an environment without learning anything about it. Receptor orientation is necessary, but not sufficient, for learning. Viewed in that context, a discrimination learning situation may be a superior procedure for the study of attentional deficits, since it incorporates learning. We have employed such a procedure in the study we shall describe below.

The situation we constructed was as follows: the child was reinforced for responding in the presence of a stimulus display and was not reinforced for responding in the absence of that display. One can argue that the child attends to (is controlled by) certain stimuli when independent variation of these stimuli is associated with concurrent change in the child's behavior. We employed a multidimensional stimulus display, that is, a display which contained auditory, visual, tactual, and temporal cues. The study was designed such that, after the child's behavior was brought under the control of the display, separate components of that display could be presented singly so as to assess to which aspects the child was responding. One could then find out if certain components of the display were more functional than others, how many components had become functional, whether certain components had failed to acquire any function, etc.

METHOD

SUBJECTS

We ran three groups of Ss. The autistic group consisted of five boys and one girl, with mean CA of 7.2 years (range of 4 to 10 years). These children had been diagnosed by agencies not associated with the experiment. Four of the Ss were mute and would utter only unintelligible sounds without communicative intent. They gave sporadic response to the most elementary commands (e.g., "sit down," "close the door"). They were untestable on standard psychological tests. Two of the Ss were not toilet-trained, and other social and self-help skills were minimal. For example, they did not dress themselves; they did not play with toys; and they did not play with peers. Three had early histories of suspected deafness. They were inpatients, and in all likelihood faced permanent hospitalization. In short, they were extremely regressed and fell within the lower third of the psychotic continuum. The fifth child, Danny, differed from the rest in that he was echolalic, expressed simple demands, and was behaviorally more advanced so that he remained at home and made a marginal adjustment to a class for severely retarded children. Like the others, he would frequently act as if he did not see or hear adults. All Ss demonstrated bizarre self-stimulatory behavior (stereotyped motor acts).

The second group contained five mentally retarded children, four boys and one girl, with a mean CA of 8 years (range of 7 to 10 years) and a mean MA of 3.7 years (range of 3.5 to 4.0 years). Four of these Ss were institutionalized. Two had been diagnosed as Mongoloid, two as retarded due to birth trauma, and one as retarded from an unknown genetic origin. One of the retarded Ss had a history of suspected (but unconfirmed) deafness, while all other Ss had displayed normal responsiveness to external stimulation.

A normal control group consisted of five children with mean CA of 6.4 years (range of 6.0 to 7.5 years). These Ss, two boys and three girls, were obtained from parents working at the university.

APPARATUS

The S was seated in a 7 x 8 ft. experimental room in front of a 2½-ft.-high table holding a box with a 3-in. bar protruding from its front. The box also housed a Davis Model 310 universal feeder which delivered candy, potato chips, etc., to S through a chute at the left side of the box. Sound equipment and one-way vision screens connected the experimental room to an observation room from which E would present the various experimental manipulations. The experimental room was lighted by a 40-w. light, giving a dim illumination level of .50 ftc. The room was sound attenuated.

We employed four kinds of stimuli. (a) A visual stimulus, which consisted of a 150-w. red floodlight, was mounted on the ceiling behind S's back and out of his view. This light raised the room illumination level from .50 to 2.50 ftc. as measured by a Weston illumination meter, Model 756 (these readings were made on the front panel of the box which faced S). (b) An auditory stimulus, consisting of white noise, was fed from a tape recorder into a speaker located above S. The noise level generated was 63 db. (measured by a General Radio Co. sound-level meter, Type No. 1551-B, set at 20-kc. weighting). Since white noise consists of all frequencies, the possibility of Ss being differentially sensitive to particular frequencies was eliminated. (c) A tactile stimulus was applied by forcing air into a blood pressure cuff fastened around S's left calf. The cuff was attached by a rubber tube to an automobile tire pump operated by E. The arrangement allowed E to deliver a rather discrete tactile pressure (20 mm. of mercury), retain that pressure for the desired interval, and instantly remove (deflate) it. (d) A temporal cue was arranged by presenting all the stimuli for a 5-sec. interval every 20 sec. That is, S could obtain reinforcement simply by hitting the bar as a function of time elapsed since last reinforcement (a temporal cue) rather than on the basis of the three other cues.

The S was run in two kinds of sessions, training and testing. During training sessions, he was taught a discrimination where his bar presses were brought under the control of the stimulus complex. During the subsequent test sessions, he was presented with the various components of the stimulus complex to assess which one(s) had acquired functional control.

TRAINING

The S was seated before the bar and instructed that if he pressed it he would get candy. If S failed to respond to the instructions, E prompted the response manually. As soon as S had emitted two unassisted bar presses within 1 min., he was left alone in the experimental room and presented with the S^D (stimulus complex). The S^D was presented for 10 sec. or until it was terminated by a single bar press. When S had responded to the S^D on three successive presentations, the duration of the S^D period was gradually decreased in 1-sec. units to the ultimate 5-sec. S^D interval. At the same time, the reinforcement schedule was gradually changed from FR-1 to FR-4. In the final stages of training, S would eventually respond with a burst of four bar presses within the 5-sec. S^D period. The fourth bar press terminated the S^D. S^Δ was set to last for 20 sec. When S failed to give any evidence of decreased rate of response during the S^Δ interval after the first training session, E would deliver a loud "no" over the intercom contingent on such response. All steps, including the onset and timing of the S^D and S^Δ intervals, operation of the feeder, recording of the bar presses, etc., were carried out automatically through Davis relay programming equipment and a David Model CRRC 133 cumulative recorder. Session lengths, which varied between 20 and 50 min., were determined by the length of time it required S to obtain 36 reinforcements (which emptied the dispenser). The Ss received not more than two sessions per day, not more than 3 days apart. The discrimination training was considered complete, and test trials were begun, when S had completed two consecutive sessions in which at least 90% of his bar presses fell within the S^D interval.

TESTING

Upon completion of the training phase, each autistic and retarded S received 10 test sessions. Testing for the normal Ss was terminated after two successive tests showing 100% response to the auditory, visual, and tactile cues. The test sessions were of the same duration as the training sessions and were distributed such that S received no more than two tests a day nor less than one every third day. In the test trials, the single stimuli were randomly interspersed between training trials (trials with all the stimulus components present) except that: (a) each test trial was always preceded and followed by at least one training trial, and (b) E did not run more than three training trials in a row. The density of the training trials helped to maintain the discrimination. The S was reinforced if he responded correctly on a test trial. To test for temporal discriminations, the S^Δ interval was altered from 20 to 10, 15, 25, and 30 sec. The intervals with presentations occurring prior to 20 sec. potentially provided evidence for responses to individual stimuli in the absence of the normal temporal cue. The intervals greater than 20 sec., however, allowed S to respond on the basis of a temporal cue without the influence of the external stimuli. The S received, on the average, seven presentations of each individual stimulus in a test session. The temporal intervals were randomly selected among the 10, 15, 25, and 30 sec. Altogether, he received approximately 70 test trials on any one stimulus, distributed over 10 sessions.

RESULTS

There was a great deal of variability in the acquisition of the discrimination. The normal Ss learned to respond to the complex input within a matter of minutes. The retarded Ss required, on the average, less than five 30-min. training sessions, while the autistic group required approximately twice as many sessions as the retardates. One autistic child, Leslie, was run for a total of 3 mo., five sessions a week, and still could not maintain the discrimination (she responded less than 80% of the time to the S^D, and had large bursts of S^Δ responding). Her discrimination of the complex input was so poorly maintained that tests for component control were meaningless; hence her data are not included.

Once S had learned to discriminate the stimulus complex, the main question became centered on which stimuli within the complex were controlling his responding. The S's responding to the separate components will be presented as a percentage derived from the number of actual responses to a given stimulus over the total number of opportunities to respond to that stimulus. For example, if in a particular test session S gave eight bar presses to the tactile stimulus, and that stimulus was presented eight times during that session, which would allow for 32 possible responses (4 responses per presentation), his score would equal 25%. This value is used as an index of S's sensitivity to a particular stimulus element. There will be no discussion of the temporal cue since no evidence for a temporal discrimination was observed for any of the Ss.

The most general conclusion which can be made from the data is that autistic Ss respond primarily to one stimulus component, retardates to two, and normals to all three. We derived this conclusion from a statistical analysis which was carried out as follows: we divided the Ss' responses into three levels—high, medium, and low—on the basis of the amount of responding to the separate stimuli. High was the stimulus component to which S responded most (was most functional), medium was the next most functional, and low the least functional. The magnitude of these differences was tested as follows. If there was no significant difference in the amount of responding between these levels, then it could be inferred that S had not responded differently to the three stimuli. On the other hand, a significant difference between these levels would indicate differential control by the stimulus components. For example, a significant difference between high and medium and a lack of difference between medium and low would indicate that only one cue had acquired control.

The statistical analysis was performed on the first test session only. We limited the analysis to this test session because with additional sessions S received increasing reinforcement for responding to single cues.

Table 1   Analysis of Variance on Level of Responding to the Single Cues

Source	df	MS	F
Diagnosis (D)	2	1217	.548
Ss within groups	12	2218	
Level of responding (L)	2	9487	43.1*
D × L	4	1677	7.62*
L × Ss within groups	24	220	

*p <.005.

Table 2   Results of the Newman-Keuls Test on the Mean Levels of
Responding for Autistic, Retarded, and Normal Ss

Ss	Level of response	$p <$
Autistics	High vs. medium	.05
	Medium vs. low	ns
	High vs. low	.01
Retardates	High vs. medium	ns
	Medium vs. low	.01
	High vs. low	.01
Normals	High vs. medium	ns
	Medium vs. low	ns
	High vs. low	ns

Table 1 shows the analysis of variance. There was a significant ($p < .01$) interaction between diagnosis (autistic, retarded, and normal) and level of responding (high, medium, and low). There was no significant difference in regard to overall level of responding. A Newman-Keuls test on the means enabled a closer analysis of the individual populations. The result of that analysis has been presented in Table 2.

As Table 2 shows, there was no significant difference in the amount of responding to the separate stimuli for the normal Ss. The normals gave no evidence for a preference among the cues, or that they were selectively attending to some cues and not others. For the autistics, the significant difference between the high and medium cues and lack of significant difference between the medium and low cues show the dominance of one cue. The retardates differ from the autistics in that they responded to two of the cues. They did not show a significant difference between the two most functional cues (high versus medium), while the difference between these cues and the third cue (medium versus low) was significant.

The data from all the test sessions for the autistic Ss are presented in Figure 2. Percentages of correct responding are presented on the ordinate, while the test sessions are plotted along the abscissa. It is perhaps best to split these data into two parts. The first part can be limited to Test Session 1 and provides data on which cues had acquired control over S during training, when he was reinforced for responding to the stimulus complex. The second part of the data provides information about change in S's responding to the separate stimuli with continuation of testing conditions, when S was reinforced for responding to the separate presentations of these stimuli.

If we inspect the data from Test Session 1 in Figure 2, we observe that the performance on only one of the single cues lies close to the complex cue, and the response to the remaining two cues is very weak or absent altogether. This is clearly shown in regard to the tactile cue for all Ss. It is also apparent in Elmer and Kurt's minimal response to the visual cue, while Marty and Brian responded minimally to the auditory cue.

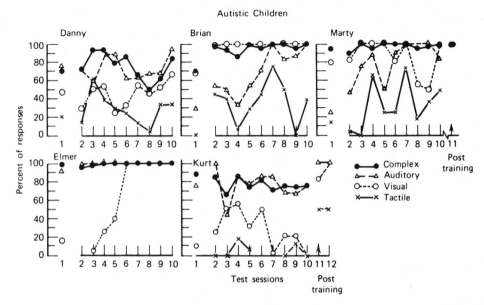

Figure 2. Test sessions for the autistic *S*s (Percentages of correct response to the stimuli are plotted on the ordinate and test sessions are plotted along the abscissa.)

If we now look at the data with continuation of testing (Session 2 on), we can observe much variability in *S*s' response to the separate stimuli. Elmer's record is the least variable. He was initially under auditory control only, but as he received reinforcement for responding to the separate presentation of the visual cue, that cue acquired control. Similar effects can be observed in Brian's and Marty's records. They were initially under visual control and later began responding to the auditory stimulus. This effect, however, is unpredictable. Thus, despite Kurt's reinforcement for responding to the visual cue, that cue eventually ceases to control him. Similar failures of separate elements to acquire control, despite reinforcement for responding in their presence, can be observed in Danny's response to the visual cue, and in Brian's, Marty's, and Danny's response to the tactile cue.

Since we were testing for the possible acquisition of temporal cues, we could not maintain the conditions for the suppression of S^Δ responding. One may therefore question whether response to the least functional cue(s) reflects control by that cue, or random responding. We attempted to answer this question by examining the correlation between S^Δ responding preceding an S^D trial and response during that trial. This analysis was performed on the data of three of the autistic *S*s. For each *S*, we correlated S^D and S^Δ to the two least functional stimuli and to the complex stimulus. This was done for five of the tests of each of the three *S*s. Of the 45 correlations, only 6 were significant. However, these 6 were based on few observations, thus increasing the possibility of the analysis reaching significance by chance.

We therefore concluded that S^Δ responding was not an important factor in determining S's level of responding to the least functional stimuli.

At the end of the test sessions, we took the cue which had not become functional in the earlier training (visual for Kurt, tactile for Marty) and attempted to establish it as functional by presenting it repeatedly with a variable S^Δ interval. Thus, in contrast to the test sessions, reinforcement could only be obtained by responding to the nonfunctional cue since none of the other cues were presented. Upon reaching criterion, S was reintroduced to the test sessions as before. The data from this training are presented as Post-training Trial 11 for Marty on the tactile cue and Post-training Trials 11 and 12 for Kurt on the visual cue. When the previously nonfunctional cues are trained separately, they do acquire control.

Data from the normal Ss are presented in Figure 3. The normal Ss differed from the autistics in three ways. First, they quickly acquired the discrimination and, second, their data show little variability. Third, while the autistic Ss responded differentially to certain components of the complex, the normals responded uniformly to all. Four of the normal Ss appeared to have formed a pattern discrimination, treating the separate components as different from the complex. With continuation of testing, this discrimination is broken, allowing for a demonstration of the equal control acquired by the separate cues.

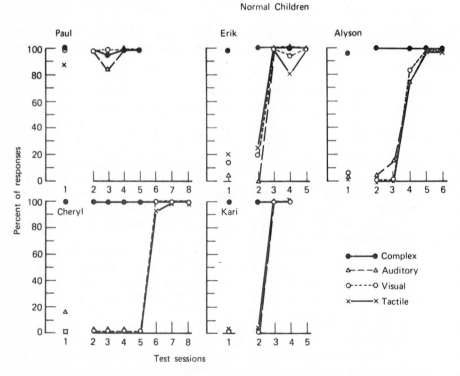

Figure 3. Test sessions for the normal Ss. (Percentages of correct response to the stimuli are plotted on the ordinate and test sessions are plotted along the abscissa.)

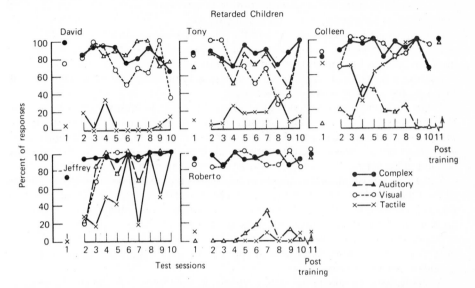

Figure 4. Test sessions for the retarded *S*s. (Percentages of correct response to the stimuli are plotted on the ordinate and test sessions are plotted along the abscissa.)

Individual responding of the retarded *S*s is presented in Figure 4. David's (Mongoloid), Tony's (genetic origin), and Colleen's (birth trauma) responding conform to the statistical analysis (Table 1) in that their response to two of the cues parallels their response to the complex. By the end of testing, Jeffrey's (only outpatient) record resembles a normal child, while Roberto's (Mongoloid) graph most closely resembles that of an autistic in that he responded to only one of the cues. These children, like most retardates, present heterogenous behavioral repertoires, and we have no way of accounting for the variability in their performance.

At the end of testing, we trained a nonfunctional stimulus separately (the auditory stimulus for Colleen and Roberto) in the same manner as we had for the autistic children. The data are presented in Session 11 for both children. The separate training established the cues as functional and allows us to rule out more easily understood problems in sensory deficiency.

DISCUSSION

Three groups of children were reinforced for responding to a complex stimulus involving the simultaneous presentation of auditory, visual, and tactile cues. Once this discrimination was established, elements of the complex were presented separately to assess which aspects of the complex stimulus had acquired control over the child's behavior. We found that (*a*) the autistics responded primarily to only one of the cues; the normals responded uniformly to all three cues; and the retardates functioned between these two extremes. (*b*) Conditions could be arranged such that a cue which had remained nonfunctional when presented in association with other cues could be established as functional when trained separately.

Our data failed to support notions that any one sense modality is impaired in autistic children, or that a particular sense modality is the "preferred" modality. Our data can perhaps best be understood as the autistics' problem of dealing with stimuli in context, a problem of quantity rather than quality of stimulus control. One can call this a problem of *stimulus overselectivity.*

There are some obvious qualifications which one has to impose upon these data. One pertains to the potentially unstable nature of *S*s responding with increased exposure to the training stimuli. This is left unclear in our experiment, since the stimuli were taken out of context and presented singly (from Test Session 1 on). But one may observe different results with different amounts of training prior to testing.

Perhaps the most important qualification centers on the choice of *S*s and the bases of their diagnoses. It is noteworthy that we have worked with the most regressed of autistic children, and that different results may have been obtained had we used children who were more advanced, having, for example, speech development. This problem may be even more pronounced with the retarded *S*s who show much heterogeneity. Roberto, for example, though he was diagnosed as retarded, responded like an autistic.

Similarly, we may qualify our data in regard to the *intensity* of the stimuli. Prior to the experiment we attempted to correct for unequal subjective intensities by choosing intensities which college students had rated as having "equal impact." It would have been more ideal to have autistic *S*s perform this task, but that would be extremely difficult to do. The results could also be a function of the particular *kind* of stimuli we employed. Perhaps it is the tactile cue which blocks response to other cues. One can also think of other qualifications, such as *S*s' motivational level, except that the retarded *S*s appeared motivated, yet showed parts of the deficiency. Training under more stress, however, as when the child is anxious or inhibiting self-stimulation, may wipe out the effect.

Although these results could be interpreted in several ways, the data conform closely to a selective attention, or stimulus selection, hypothesis. Selective attention refers to the process in which an organism, when presented with multiple cues, attends to, or comes under the control of, only a portion of the available stimuli. This fact has led to the distinction between "nominal" or perceived stimulus variables which consist of the total set of available elements and "functional" or effective stimuli which are those elements actually controlling behavior.

There has been a great deal of research on this differentiation, and excellent reviews of such research are available in recent texts by Fellows (1968) and Trabasso and Bower (1968). A comprehensive presentation will not be attempted here, but a short comment is appropriate.

Long ago, Pavlov (1927) found that the conditioned response to one element (the dominant) of a complex stimulus was as large as the response to the complex, leaving the response to the other elements negligible. Warren (1953) taught monkeys to discriminate between two objects differing in size, color, and form, using two, or all three of these dimensions. He found that although learning was facilitated by the inclusion of more relevant cues, the color cue alone was the most dominant. Similar results have been reported in other studies with animals (Harlow, 1945; Warren,

1954) and with children (Suchman & Trabasso, 1966). Studying nursery and kinder-garten children, Suchman and Trabasso found that when color, size, and form cues were simultaneously available for discrimination, younger children preferred the color cue while the older children preferred the form cue. Working within the operant training paradigm presented here, Reynolds (1961) trained two pigeons to discrimi-nate two white forms on differently colored backgrounds (red or green). In extinction test periods, it was found that one pigeon responded only to the white form and the other pigeon responded only to the colored background. Orlando (1961) reported similar instances of stimulus selection in the learning of retarded children. In a task in which a cue for S^D and S^Δ periods was employed, he found that one of these cues was not only sufficient, but exclusively functional in maintaining the discrimination.

There have been various mechanisms thought to underlie selective responding in normals. Sometimes the underlying mechanism is considered genetic, in that a par-ticular cue emerges as the dominant for the great majority of members within a species. One can also manipulate learning experiences in such a fashion as to render a cue dominant. Both Kamin (1968) in a classical conditioning paradigm and Tra-basso and Bower (1968) in a redundant relevant cue (RRC) paradigm have demon-strated blocking effects, finding that a first-learned cue blocks the learning of another relevant cue which was added during overtraining.

"Stimulus blocking" is said to occur when attention to one stimulus in a complex stimulus situation blocks or inhibits the attention to another cue also present. Tra-basso and Bower (1968) suggested that the observed dominance or selection in RRC tasks could be due to the blocking of a slower learned cue by a faster learned cue when both cues are present from the beginning of training. They see overshadowing as resulting when an S by chance responds to a particular cue and because he is reinforced does not broaden his learning to the other relevant cues.

One conclusion from all the work on normal children using RRC procedures is that normal children display stimulus selection and thus often come under the control of only a portion of the available stimuli. It is important, therefore, to use a control group of normal Ss to better assess selective responding in autistics. Our failure to observe selective responding in the normal children, which others so often report, was proba-bly based on the nature of the task. In most RRC tasks all the elements fall within one modality, rather than being distributed across modalities as was the case in our study. We also kept the number of stimuli small. Levine (1967) and Eimas (1969) have presented data which suggest that by the time normal children have reached the age of the Ss in this experiment, they will generally attend to about three or four simul-taneous cues during discrimination learning. In contrast to the normal children, the autistic children showed an extreme degree of stimulus selection, leaving large seg-ments of their environment essentially neutral.

Perhaps the first questions to be raised by this study regard a more accurate description of the stimulus overselectivity. For example, one may wonder whether the selectivity is a function of the kinds and number of cues in the complex stimulus; whether it is present also when all cues are presented in one modality; or whether it also presents itself when the cues are nonoverlapping but closely spaced in time. Studies are now in progress in our laboratory to investigate some of these questions.

The second line of questions deals with assessing some of the mechanisms which may underlie stimulus overselectivity. Perhaps the autistics tend to respond only to one cue because of a failure in "switching" behavior. Lindsay, Taylor, and Forbes (1968) and Treisman (1969) have suggested that normals seem to attend to only one stimulus component at a time and analyze complex cues by very rapidly switching attention to different aspects of the complex, going quickly through sets of "alternative analyzers." Autistics may not adequately sample stimuli, but settle on one stimulus which "blocks" the others. The problem with this line of reasoning can be easily seen when one considers the possibilities that inadequate switching may result in stimulus blocking, or, conversely, that stimulus blocking may result in inadequate switching. Either direction seems equally plausible.

A third line of questions may be directed toward a better description of stimulus selectivity among groups with different pathology. We included a retarded group to help isolate those peculiarities associated with autistic functioning. The retarded Ss showed less stimulus selectivity than the autistics. They also showed less behavioral deficiency (higher IQ scores, social adjustment, etc.). Perhaps future research will suggest that this kind of discrimination task differentiates between children with different degrees of behavioral deficiencies.

It may be of interest to speculate on how our findings may relate to the pathology in autistic children. Before we present this speculation, two considerations must be made. First, the pathology in autism is so profound and extensive that it is unlikely any one finding will provide insight into it all. Second, the speculations we make presuppose that our inference of stimulus overselectivity best describes the data. Additional studies will be needed to strengthen this inference.

IMPLICATIONS FOR UNDERSTANDING AUTISM

A necessary condition for much learning involves a contiguous or near-contiguous presentation of two stimuli. Such contiguous stimulus presentations are clearly present in classical conditioning when the CS is presented in close proximity to the UCS. In fact, this is a necessary condition for optimal learning. Contiguous presentations are also present in those aspects of operant conditioning where one seeks a shift in stimulus control. In these instances, the training stimulus is presented simultaneously with a prompt. Since this contiguous presentation of two stimuli involves presenting the child with a stimulus complex, it may be assumed that the autistics' response to one of these stimuli is blocked, overshadowed, or otherwise has failed to occur. Let us consider some of the implications of this assumption for certain kinds of learning.

1. One can consider that the acquisition of most human behavior, like language, interpersonal, and intellectual behavior, is based on the prior acquisition of conditioned reinforcers. A failure in this acquisition would lead to a failure in behavioral development (Ferster & DeMyer, 1962). If it is the case that conditioned reinforcers acquire strength by contiguous association with primary ones, then our finding should help to further describe the failure for such conditioning to take place in autistic children (Lovaas, Freitag, Kinder, Rubenstein, Schaeffer, & Simmons, 1966).

2. The autistic child's failure to give appropriate affect is well-known. The mechanisms for establishing appropriate affect may well be very similar to those involved in establishing conditioned reinforcers: contiguous presentation of two stimulus events which enables the affect, elicited by one of these events (the UCS), to be elicited by the other (the CS).

3. Many autistic children have topographically elaborate speech (echolalia), but it

appears without "meaning." One can argue that the speech exists without meaning to the extent it has an impoverished context. The acquisition of a context for speech probably involves a shift in stimulus control. To the extent that this involves simultaneous presentations of auditory with visual, tactile, or some other cue, one may expect that the autistic child would "overselect" and fail to learn.

4. From a consideration of the data in Figure 1, which illustrates the difficulties in the establishment of imitative behavior, it is also possible that such stimulus overselectivity as we have described might contribute importantly to the autistic child's failure in the acquisition of new behavioral topographies. In fact, the usual way we train new skills is to "aid" the child by adding large numbers of extra cues to the training situation. This, of course, may be exactly what makes it so difficult for the autistic child to learn what we want him to.

5. Whenever one postulates blocking of incoming stimuli, learning as well as performance should be impaired. Stimulus overselectivity may also be a factor which underlies the sporadic, highly variable nature of these children's responses to already functional stimuli. A number of other possibilities suggest themselves, which probably are best discussed in light of more extensive data.

REFERENCES

Buss, A., & Lang, P. Psychological deficit in schizophrenia. I. Affect, reinforcement, and concept attainment. *Journal of Abnormal Psychology,* 1965, **70,** 2–24.

Eimas, P. Multiple-cue discrimination learning in children. *Psychological Record,* 1969, **19,** 417–424.

Feigenberg, I. Probabilistic prognosis and its significance in normal and pathological subjects. In M. Cole & I. Maltzman (Eds.), *A handbook of contemporary Soviet psychology.* New York: Basic Books, 1969.

Fellows, B. J. *The discrimination process and development.* London: Pergamon Press, 1968.

Ferster, C. B., & DeMyer, M. A method for the experimental analysis of the behavior of autistic children. *American Journal of Orthopsychiatry,* 1962, **32,** 89–98.

Goldfarb, W. An investigation of childhood schizophrenia. *Archives of General Psychiatry,* 1964, **11,** 620–634.

Harlow, H. F. Studies in discrimination learning in monkeys. VI. Discriminations between stimuli differing in both color and form, only in color, and only in form. *Journal of General Psychology,* 1945, **33,** 225–235.

Hermelin, B. Recent psychological research. In J. K. Wing (Ed.), *Early childhood autism.* London: Pergamon Press, 1966.

Kamin, L. J. Attention-like processes in classical conditioning. In M. R. Jones (Ed.), *Miami Symposium on the Prediction of Behavior, 1967: Aversive stimulation.* Miami: University of Miami Press, 1968.

Kanner, L. Early infantile autism. *Journal of Pediatrics,* 1944, **25,** 211–217.

Lang, P. J., & Buss, A. H. Psychological deficit in schizophrenia. II. Interference and activation. *Journal of Abnormal Psychology,* 1965, **70,** 77–106.

Levine, M. The size of the hypothesis set during discrimination learning. *Psychological Review,* 1967, **74,** 428–430.

Lindsay, P. H., Taylor, M. M., & Forbes, S. M. Attention and multidimensional discrimination. *Perception and Psychophysics,* 1968, **4,** 113–117.

Lovaas, O. I., Berberich, J. P., Perloff, B. F., & Schaeffer, B. Acquisition of imitative speech in schizophrenic children. *Science,* 1966, **151,** 705–707.

Lovaas, O. I., Freitag, G., Kinder, M. I., Rubenstein, B. D., Schaeffer, B., & Simmons, J. Q. Establishment of social reinforcers in schizophrenic children using food. *Journal of Experimental Child Psychology,* 1966, **4,** 109–125.

Orlando, R. The functional role of discriminative stimuli in free operant performance of developmentally retarded children. *Psychological Record,* 1961, **11,** 153–161.

Pavlov, I. P. Lectures. In *Conditioned reflexes.* Oxford: University Press, 1927.

Reynolds, G. S. Attention in the pigeon. *Journal of the Experimental Analysis of Behavior,* 1961, **4,** 203–208.

Rimland, B. *Infantile autism.* New York: Appleton-Century-Crofts, 1964.

Schopler, E. Visual versus tactual receptor preference in normal and schizophrenic children. *Journal of Abnormal Psychology,* 1966, **71,** 108–114.

Sherrington, C. S. *The integrative action of the nervous system.* London: Cambridge University Press, 1906.

Suchman, R. G., & Trabasso, T. Color and form preference in young children. *Journal of Experimental Child Psychology,* 1966, **3,** 177–187.

Trabasso, T., & Bower, G. H. *Attention in learning.* New York: Wiley, 1968.

Treisman, A. Strategies and models of selective attention. *Psychological Review,* 1969, **76,** 282–299.

Warren, J. M. Additivity of cues in visual pattern discrimination by monkeys. *Journal of Comparative and Physiological Psychology,* 1953, **46,** 484–488.

Warren, J. M. Perceptual dominance in discrimination learning in monkeys. *Journal of Comparative and Physiological Psychology,* 1954, **47,** 290–292.

Young, S. Visual attention in autistic and normal children: Effects of stimulus novelty, human attributes, and complexity. Unpublished doctoral dissertation, University of California, Los Angeles, 1969.

Developmental Aphasia: the Perception of Brief Vowels and Extended Stop Consonants

Paula Tallal and Malcolm Piercy

Developmental dysphasics and matched controls were examined for their ability to discriminate (a) two synthesized vowel–vowel syllables and (b) two synthesized consonant–vowel syllables. For both vowels and consonants, dysphasics were impaired when the discriminable components of the two stimuli were brief (43 msec) but unimpaired when these components were 95 msec or longer. It is concluded that developmental dysphasics have no difficulty in discriminating transitional auditory information as such and that their impaired discrimination of synthesized stop consonants is attributable solely to the brief duration of the discriminable components.

INTRODUCTION

We are concerned with the possibility that developmental dysphasia may result from a defect of rapid auditory processing rather than specific verbal impairment.

We have previously tested the ability of developmental dysphasic and matched control children to perceive binary sequences of non-verbal stimuli and demonstrated that, unlike normals, dysphasics are incapable of discriminating two brief stimuli (75 msec) when these are separated by a brief interval (150 msec), but can discriminate the same stimuli normally when this interval is increased [1]. We have also shown that this defect occurs even when perception of sequence is not required (same–different discrimination), and that, on comparable tasks in the visual modality, dysphasics perform as well as controls [2].

We have also taken experimental advantage of evidence that vowels and certain consonants differ in the acoustic features which act as cues for perception [3, 4]. The major cue for vowels is the frequencies of the first three formants which remain constant throughout the stimulus and are of relatively long duration (approx. 250 msec). The essential cue for the stop consonants is the rapidly changing frequency spectrum of the second and third formant transitions. This is not only transitional in character but also of short duration (approx. 50 msec).

We predicted (i) that developmental dysphasics would show no impairment in discriminating two synthesized steady-state vowels (/E/ and /ae/) when these were of 250 msec duration, and (ii) that they would show significantly impaired discrimina-

From *Neuropsychologia, 13,* 69–74 (1975). Reprinted by permission of Pergamon Press.

tion of two synthesized stop consonant-vowel syllables (/ba/ and /da/) when these were of 250 msec duration, but with a discriminable transitional component of only 43 msec. Both of these predictions were sustained by experimental test, and it was suggested that it was the brief duration of the formant transitions which resulted in the dysphasics being unable to discriminate consonant stimuli [5].

However, an alternative explanation must be considered. It remains unclear whether the inability of dysphasics to discriminate consonants results from (i) the brief *duration* of the transitions or (ii) an inability to process transitional stimuli irrespective of their duration. The present experiments attempt to distinguish between these two possibilities. Experiment 1 is concerned with perception of vowel–vowel (v–v) syllables with no transitional component but with components of the same duration as the consonant–vowel (c–v) syllables used in our previous experiments. Experiment 2 is concerned with the perception of c–v syllables similar to those used previously, but containing a transitional component which is extended in time.

APPARATUS AND PROCEDURE

The apparatus for generating and presenting the synthesized auditory stimuli has been fully described elsewhere [2, 5]. The experimental procedure was identical to that described in a previous communication, except for the character of the stimuli used. In both Experiment 1 and Experiment 2 two methods were used. Briefly, in the Repetition Method, subjects were trained to respond on two identical depressible panels mounted side by side. Each panel corresponded to a particular sound and correct responses were rewarded on a variable ratio schedule. Subjects were first trained to respond on the correct panel to each sound separately and if, and only if, criterion ($P < 0.001$, Binomial Test) was reached within forty-eight trials, they were trained to respond to each of the four possible two-stimulus patterns by pushing the panels in the correct order. Four demonstrations by the experimenter were followed by eight training trials with knowledge of results and correction of errors, and then by twenty-four trials without knowledge of results. Throughout this training, an inter-stimulus interval (ISI) of 428 msec was employed. Subjects were then tested on two-stimulus patterns with ISIs of 8, 15, 30, 60, 150, and 305 msec. Each subject received a total of twenty-four two-stimulus patterns, four at each ISI, with a random order of presentation of the different intervals.

In the Same–Different Method, perception was examined without demanding a sequential motor response. The response panel was rotated 90 degrees to avoid confusion between the two methods and subjects were trained to press the top panel if two successive stimuli were the same and the bottom panel if they were different. The Paget sign system was known to all dysphasic children participating in these experiments and this, as well as visual examples, was used to ensure that all subjects fully understood the response required on the Same–Different task. The acoustic properties of the two stimuli were identical with those used in the corresponding test using the Repetition Method. With the ISI at 428 msec, training was continued for a maximum of 48 trials or until a criterion of 20 correct responses in a series of 24 consecutive trials was reached ($P < 0.001$, Binomial Test). If this criterion was reached, a total of 24 trials was given, 4 at each ISI, with ISIs of 8, 15, 30, 60, 150, and 305 msec occurring in random order.

STIMULI

EXPERIMENT 1   For the purposes of this experiment, it was necessary to use synthesized v–v syllables which were similar to the synthesized c–v syllables used in a
previously reported experiment [5], but which did not have the initial formant transitions. More specifically, the stimuli needed for comparison with the c–v syllables of
our previous experiment were v–v syllables which consisted of an initial 43 msec
steady-state vowel followed immediately by a different steady-state vowel of 207
msec duration. Figure 1 shows the acoustic properties of the two 250 msec v–v
stimuli /E + I/ and /ae + I/ which were synthesized for this experiment. Each syllable
commenced with a 43 msec steady-state vowel, which differed between the two
stimuli. These 43 msec steady-state vowels were immediately followed by the steady-
state vowel /I/ which continued in both stimuli for the remaining 207 msec. As in
the c–v syllables of our previous experiments, the discriminable acoustic information
in the v–v syllables occurred only within the first 43 msec of the stimuli. However,
unlike the c–v syllables, the information which occurred within this initial 43 msec
was of a steady-state as opposed to a transitional character.

EXPERIMENT 2   In this experiment the stimuli used were the synthesized stop c–v
syllables /ba/ and /da/ studied in our previous communication [5] but with the
modification that the initial transitional period of each stimulus was extended from
43 msec to 95 msec. During this initial 95 msec, the first three formant frequencies
of each consonant moved linearly towards the steady-state formant frequencies of
the vowel /a/, which then continued in both stimuli for the remaining 155 msec. In
order that the total duration of the stimuli should be the same in this as in previous
experiments (250 msec), the duration of the steady-state vowel was decreased from
207 msec to 155 msec. The discriminable acoustic information of the stimuli used

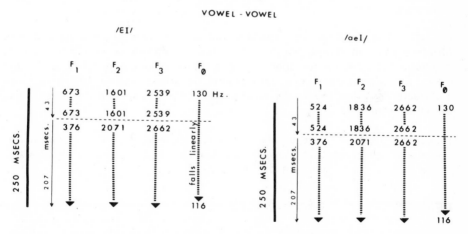

Figure 1.   The two vowel—vowel stimuli have the same fundamental frequency
but, during the first 43 msec, differ in their formant frequencies. F_1, F_2 and F_3
refer to the first, second and third formants respectively. $F\phi$ refers to the fundamental frequency.

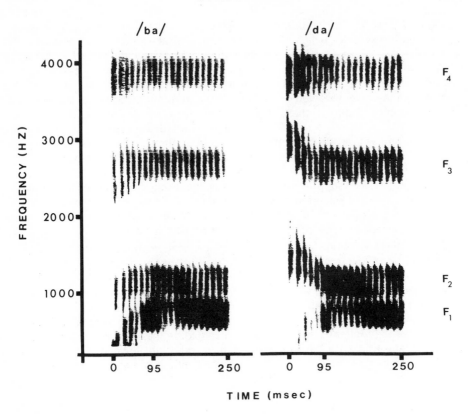

Figure 2. The two consonant-vowel stimuli differ only on the second and third formants and only during the first 95 msec. The difference in this transitional component is shown in the spectrographs. (In a previous paper [5] the frequencies of these same transitional components, occurring over only 43 msec, were incorrectly described.) F_1, F_2, F_3, and F_4 refer to the first, second, third, and fourth formants respectively.

in this experiment, like the c–v syllables reported earlier, is of a transitional nature. The duration of the transition however, has been more than doubled. The acoustic properties of these stimuli are shown in Figure 2.

RESULTS

EXPERIMENT 1

1. REPETITION METHOD. All twelve of the controls, but only five of the twelve dysphasics, reached criterion ($P < 0.001$, Binomial Test) on the initial discrimination between the two synthesized v–v syllables. Of the five dysphasics who reached

criterion on the v–v syllable discrimination, only two reached criterion on the repetition of two-syllable patterns with an ISI of 428 msec. These same two also reached criterion on the repetition of two-syllable patterns when the ISI was decreased. These were also the only two dysphasic subjects who reached criterion on the previously reported equivalent consonant tests. In contrast, all twelve of the control subjects reached criterion on two-syllable patterns at all ISIs studied. For all tests using the Repetition Method, the differences between the performance of the dysphasics and the controls was significant at the 0.1 per cent level of confidence (Likelihood Ratio Test) [6].

2. SAME–DIFFERENT METHOD.   Results for the Same-Different Method show a pattern of impairment closely similar to that demonstrated with the Repetition Method. All twelve of the controls, but only two of the twelve dysphasics (the same two who reached criterion on two-syllable stimulus patterns using the Repetition Method) reached criterion ($P < 0.001$, Binomial Test) on same-different judgments between the two synthesized v–v syllables separated by an ISI of 428 msec. These two also reached criterion when the ISI was decreased. For all tests using the Same–Different Method, the differences in performance between dysphasics and controls were significant at the 0.1 per cent level of confidence (Likelihood Ratio Test).

EXPERIMENT 2

1. REPETITION METHOD.   All twelve of the dysphasics and their matched controls reached criterion ($P < 0.001$, Binomial Test) on the initial discrimination between the two synthesized extended c–v syllables. Furthermore, the two groups did not differ significantly in their performance on the repetition of the two-consonant patterns with an ISI of 428 msec (Wilcoxon Matched Pairs Test, 1-tailed). When the interval between the two consonants was decreased, the dysphasics performed as well as the controls at all ISIs studies (8–305 msec); there was no significant difference between the performance of the two groups (Wilcoxon Matched Pairs Test, 1-tailed) at any of these ISIs. It should be mentioned that these results are not attributable to a ceiling effect because, at the shortest two ISIs, dysphasics' and controls' mean correct scores were 88 and 92 per cent respectively.

2. SAME–DIFFERENT METHOD.   Results for the same–different judgements were similar to those obtained for the Repetition Method. All of the dysphasics and all of the controls reached criterion ($P < 0.001$, Binomial Test) on the same–different judgement between the two synthesized extended consonants separated by an ISI of 428 msec. When the ISI was decreased (8–305 msec), all subjects in both groups continued to perform above criterion: there was no significant difference between the performance of the two groups (Wilcoxon Matched Pairs Tests, 1-tailed) at any of these ISIs.

These results may usefully be compared with the previously reported results in which the same subjects were tested in the same way except that the 250 msec consonants embodied a transitional period of only 43 msec [5]. Comparison between these two sets of results reveals highly significant differences in the performance of the dysphasics, but no difference in the performance of the controls. On both the Repetition and the Same–Different Methods, significantly fewer dysphasics reached criterion ($P < 0.001$, Binomial Test) when the synthesized c–v syllables contained formant transitions occupying a period of only 43 msec than when they contained formant transitions occupying the longer period of 95 msec ($P < 0.001$, Likelihood Ratio Test). Similarly, on the initial discrimination between the two stimuli and on all tests using two-element patterns, the dysphasics' performance differed significantly between the two stimulus conditions at the 0.1 per cent level of confidence (Likelihood Ratio Test).

DISCUSSION

The results of Experiment 1 using synthesized v–v syllables are identical to those reported previously using synthesized c–v syllables with 43 msec transitions. The same subjects who failed to reach criterion with the c–v syllables also failed to reach criterion with the v–v syllables. In other words, the discrimination ability of developmental dysphasics remained equally poor when the transitional components of the consonant stimuli were replaced by steady-state components of the same duration. It may therefore be concluded that one factor which limits the dysphasics' ability to discriminate verbal stimuli is the *duration* of the acoustically discriminable characteristics of the stimuli, regardless of whether these are steady-state or transitional in character.

However, the results of Experiment 1 using synthesized v–v syllables do not preclude a further possibility. In addition to a speed constraint on auditory processing, dysphasic children might also have selective difficulty in processing transitions as such, independently of their duration. The results of Experiment 2 would seem to resolve this issue. In this experiment using consonants with extended transitions, the results are identical with those obtained in previous experiments in which steady-state vowels or non-verbal stimuli of the same duration (250 msec) were used. In all of these cases, the developmental dysphasics performed as well as the controls. It appears therefore that our dysphasic subjects are not impaired in their ability to process transitional acoustic information provided that the transitions are of relatively long duration.

Our experiments with dysphasic children started with a study of their ability to discriminate non-verbal sounds and yielded the hypothesis that they are subject to a speed constraint in processing auditory (but not visual) information. Further experiments suggested that this speed constraint was unrelated to whether or not the auditory information was verbal and also demonstrated selective impairment of the perception of synthesized consonants whose discriminable components were both brief and transitional in their acoustic character. The two experiments reported here strongly suggest that it is the brevity and not the transitional character of this component of synthesized consonants which results in the impaired perception of our dysphasic children. Accordingly, our original hypothesis that the language defect of these children is not specifically linguistic but is secondary to an impaired rate of processing auditory information remains to be disconfirmed.

Finally, insofar as our hypothesis is correct, our results carry obvious implications for therapeutic training. "Extended" speech sounds of the type used in Experiment

2 were perceived by control subjects as normal speech, and might be used to train dysphasics to discriminate between speech sounds which were previously indiscriminable because they were too brief.

ACKNOWLEDGMENTS

Paula Tallal was supported in this work by the American Association of University Women (Ida Green Fellowship). This assistance is gratefully acknowledged. We also thank the staff and students of the John Horniman School for Aphasic Children and the staff and students of the Morley Memorial Primary School for their assistance and cooperation in our research.

REFERENCES

1. TALLAL, P. and PIERCY, M. Defects of non-verbal auditory perception in children with developmental aphasia. *Nature, Lond.* **241** (5390), 468–469, 1973.
2. TALLAL, P. and PIERCY, M. Developmental aphasia: impaired rate of non-verbal processing as a function of sensory modality. *Neuropsychologia* **11,** 389–398, 1973.
3. LIBERMAN, A. M., HARRIS, K. S., HOFFMAN, H. S. and GRIFFITH, B. C. The discrimination of speech sound within and across phoneme boundaries. *J. Exp. Psychol.* **54,** 358–367, 1957.
4. FRY, D. B., ABRAMSON, A. S., EIMAS, P. D. and LIBERMAN, A. M. The identification and discrimination of synthetic vowels, *Language and Speech* **5,** 171–188, 1962.
5. TALLAL, P. and PIERCY, M. Developmental aphasia: rate of auditory processing and selective impairment of consonant perception. *Neuropsychologia* **12,** 83–94, 1974.
6. WILKS, S. S. The likelihood test of independence in contingency tables. *Ann. Math. Stats.* **6,** 190–196, 1935.

Psychological Studies of Childhood Autism: Can Autistic Children Make Sense of What They See and Hear?

Beate Hermelin, Ph.D.

Uta Frith, Ph.D.

In 1943, the child psychiatrist Leo Kanner (1943) described a group of children he had encountered over the years who seemed to have certain unusual characteristics in common. The main symptoms he found were autistic aloneness, an obsessive desire for sameness, and severe disorder of language. He differentiated this group of children from the large, unspecified category of the childhood schizophrenias and named their condition "early infantile autism." The unusual pattern of symptoms captured the interest of many despite the rarity of the disorder; however, it took approximately 20 years to arrive at reasonably precise diagnostic criteria, taking into account prognosis and prevalence. Controversies still persist on the question of etiology.

Only 4 in 10,000 children and three times as many boys than girls are afflicted with early infantile autism (Lotter, 1966). There appears to be an association with high parental socioeconomic status, a finding which is not due to referral artifacts and which seems to be unique among the psychiatric childhood disorders (Lotter, 1967).

The illness first appears in early childhood, either at birth or before two and one-half years. The pattern of symptoms at this age may include a lack of response to sound or light, an apparent lack of recognition of the parents, and a lack of interest in the environment. Some children seem distressed for long periods and cry continuously, while others appear apathetic. Feeding and sleeping habits can be erratic and unpredictable. Subsequently the children show various obsessional features, aloofness and lack of interest in other people, abnormalities of language affecting speech as well as thought, and problems in the appropriate use of eyes and ears. The combination of symptoms may differ from child to child, and the symptoms may differ in severity and persistence. There are usually other handicaps, such as mental subnormality, which affect the majority of autistic children (Wing, 1970).

Though prognosis is not favorable, developmental changes do occur (Lockyer &

From *Journal of Special Education, 5,* 107–117 (1971). Reprinted by permission of Button-wood Farms Inc.

Rutter, 1969; Rutter, Greenfield, & Lockyer, 1967; Rutter & Lockyer, 1969), and various forms of treatment appear to lead to appreciable improvement (Rutter, 1967), particularly in the emotional and social spheres. Thus, the symptom of autistic aloneness, with its concomitants of social withdrawal, gaze avoidance, lack of interest in people, and inability to form close relationships, may subside and no longer be markedly present in older, improved autistic children.

The features associated with Kanner's symptom of insistence on sameness, i.e., resistance to change and obsessional ritualistic phenomena, are also subject to developmental changes. Thus, while this symptom in very young children may take the form of extreme attachment to a useless object such as a piece of cloth or a tin container, or become manifest in extreme food fads, it may later become a preoccupation with certain events or thoughts. Resistance to changes in the order of familiar surroundings, adherence to rituals and fixed routines, and stereotyped play are common at all stages. Probably related to these obsessional phenomena are the characteristic motor mannerisms found in almost all autistic children: compulsive finger flicking, spinning, and other odd and repetitive movements. These motor mannerisms and stereotyped behavior sequences seem self-reinforcing, circular, and automatic. They also seem to be unrelated to, and inappropriate for, environmental demands.

The third major symptom of childhood autism—the abnormalities associated with language and thought—comprises a large variety of clinical features (Hermelin & O'Connor, 1970), including complete failure or delay of speech development; echolalia, i.e., the tendency to repeat verbatim the last words of another person's utterances; inability to understand meaning; lack of spontaneous communication in either talk or gestures; and phenomena reminiscent of developmental aphasia. Language abnormalities persist even if behavioral improvements have occurred. Thus, even with good speech development, the language of autistic adolescents is recognizably odd, usually characterized by detachment, concreteness, and abundance of stereotyped utterances.

Apparent perceptual impairments without any detectable sensory defect are also often found in autistic children. In most cases this takes the form of an inability to interpret auditory or visual stimuli, frequently with a lack of orientation responses toward such stimulation (Hermelin & O'Connor, 1970). Occasionally young autistic children cover their eyes and ears with their hands. On the other hand, they often make extensive use of proximal receptor channels by licking or touching objects. Their movements are often described as graceful.

Not one of these symptoms is uniquely and exclusively associated with early infantile autism. Most of them can be found in other psychiatric disorders (Wing, 1969). However, the pattern of the combined symptoms and the course of the illness are very characteristic, and diagnosis is less problematic than it might appear.

There has been much speculation concerning the etiology of autism, especially about whether the cause is psychogenic or organic (Rutter, 1968). It is likely that the causes are manifold and varied, although they result in the same syndrome. No theory so far has factual substantiation; it seems unlikely that etiologic definition can be made before a more precise delineation of the symptoms. In this respect, childhood autism is no exception to the range of psychiatric disorders, since causes for most such disorders are as yet unknown. Our research (Hermelin & O'Connor, 1970) has concentrated on an analysis and delineation of the perception, memory, and language pathology. The approach was empirical rather than theoretical, as even a behavioral description of these phenomena is not yet complete.

PROCEDURE AND CONCLUSIONS

The autistic children who took part in our experiments were between 7 and 15 years old. They were diagnosed by experienced psychiatrists according to the described criteria. Two control groups were used, i.e.; normal and subnormal children of the same mental age (MA) as the autistic children. The MA was measured by standard IQ tests such as the Peabody Picture Vocabulary Test and the Wechsler scales. Owing to the MA criterion, the groups differed widely in chronological age (CA): the normal children were between 3 and 7 years old; the subnormal children were between 10 and 16 years old. The latter group included children presumably suffering from unspecified diffuse brain damage whose only common characteristic was severe mental retardation; they had no autistic symptoms. Because subnormality is also present in at least 75% of autistic children, it was important to control for this variable in investigations of cognitive processes. Since autistic children may be very difficult to test because of their various handicaps, experimental methods were chosen to take advantage of certain of their assets and to avoid elaborate verbal instructions. The intent was to present all tasks so as to spontaneously elicit the behavior to be analyzed.

In the first series of experiments, the tendency to echolalia in autistic children was utilized by selecting a recall task in which the subjects were required to repeat words spoken to them. In a first experiment, a comparison was made between memory for words that formed an orderly sequence (such as a sentence) with memory for words randomly arranged. The number and kind of words in both conditions were the same; they differed only in their arrangement. All words were familiar and are frequently used even by very retarded children. The word messages to be recalled were, for example, "We went to town" (sentence message) and "light what leaf we" (nonsentence message). It is well known that memory for sentences in normal people is superior to memory for random word strings (Miller & Selfridge, 1953). This phenomenon is usually explained by assuming that a special ability exists that enables people to make use of their knowledge of and familiarity with language and the redundancies therein. This means, for example, that if a sentence is to be recalled, such as "The bear climbed up the tree to get some honey," what actually need be remembered are only the key words "bear-tree-honey." All other words in such a simple sentence can be guessed on the basis of one's knowledge of syntax. The load which has to be carried by the memory system is thus much smaller than if every single word had to be remembered.

This experiment confirmed that both normal children and subnormal children with the same MA (4 years) remembered more words in sentences than in nonsentences, and that therefore some principle of making use of redundancy (that is, an economical remembering) can be assumed to operate even in very young children. The autistic children with a MA of 4 years also recalled sentences better than nonsentences; however, the difference between the two conditions was significantly less marked for the autistic than for the control groups. When repeating a random string of words, the autistic children were at least as good as, and often better than, the normal and

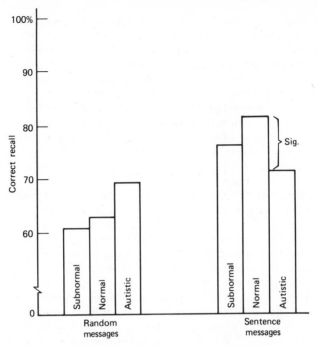

Figure 1. **Correct recall of word messages.**

subnormal children. When repeating a sentence, however, they were much less proficient.

The autistic children had a marked tendency to recall the last words of any message. To find out whether this tendency could be overcome, a second experiment was carried out for which we made up word strings partially out of sentences and partially out of nonsentences, e.g., "wall long cake send where is the ship" or "read them your book way spoon here like." Half the time the sentence was at the beginning of the message and half the time at the end. There were more words in all the messages than the children could recall after hearing them only once. Which words would be recalled: the sentences in preference to the randomly connected words, or the last words regardless of whether they were meaningfully connected or not? We found that normal children recalled sentences better than nonsentences, independent of their position in the word list. On the other hand, autistic children recalled the last words better than those in the first part of the message, even if the first words were the meaningful sentence portion. It has often been clinically observed that autistic children parrot speech without understanding its meaning. The experiments indicate that these children used their excellent memory like an echo rather than reorganizing inputs.

A further experiment was undertaken to test this hypothesis of relative lack of active reorganization in autistic children. Special word messages were constructed consisting of words denoting two separate categories, for example, "cup white glass pink plate blue." It is an established finding that normal subjects recalling messages of this type tend to cluster together words of the same category (Bousfield, 1953), this strategy appearing to facilitate recall. The results show that normal and subnormal children used the expected strategy of clustering. Thus, in the cited example they would recall all colors first, then the household objects, or vice versa. This was found to a much lesser extent in autistic children, who tended to repeat the exact order of the words as they were presented. Thus, the hypothesis was confirmed that autistic children do not actively reorganize material according to its meaning.

The results of all three experiments show that echo memory in autistic children is unimpaired. Even very young and very retarded children were able to process material by making use of structure and organization, whereas autistic children seemed to be much less efficient in this. Since very good immediate recall by autistic children can be obtained with unconnected words or digits, their main impairment may lie in those processes which categorize and organize material. Thus, suitable means of investigating these processes had to be found. If some processing defect is present, this could be limited to an inability to apply grammatical rules. Alternatively, the deficit could be more general, such as an inability to apply appropriate rules in various behavioral areas. The deficit might even consist in a failure to detect lawful sequential patterns in the environment.

To simplify the study of such deficit patterns it was opportune to restrict them to only one or two elements. Grammatical rules were considered far too complex for this study. The simplest sequential relationships of one word to another appeared to be repetitions, e.g., "one-one-one-one" and alternations, e.g., "one-two-one-two." Word lists of this type can be easily and immediately recognized by normal people as lawful and predictable. More complex patterns in binary sequences can be created

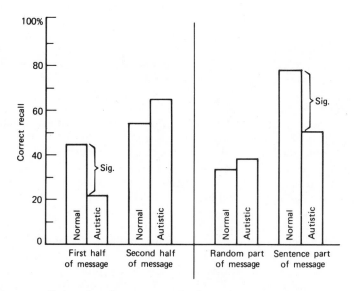

Figure 2. Correct recall of mixed messages.

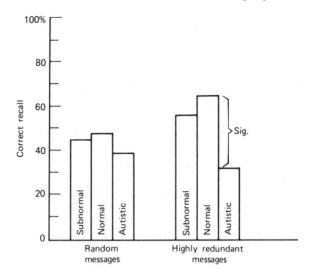

Figure 3.   Correct recall of binary messages.

simply by mixing repetitions and alternations together, such as "one-one-two-one" or "one-two-one-one-two." Sequences of this complex type cannot be so easily perceived as lawful. In order to quantify the structure of the mixed word sequences, the number of repetitions was counted within a repeating subunit of a message. The more often one is required to switch from one word to the other in the mixed sequences, the more difficult the sequence is to remember. The more repetitions there are in the sequence, the easier it is to remember.

In order to find out more about the processing mechanisms by which people make use of such redundancy, our subjects were asked to recall word sequences that varied in terms of repetitions and alternations. Normal, subnormal, and autistic children were selected and matched for their immediate memory capacity. As in the previous experiments, the children had to recall word lists that were longer than their immediate memory capacity. For example: "mouse-mouse-mouse-bag-bag-bag" or "spoon-horse-spoon-horse-horse-spoon." All children could remember the two words in each list, and they knew which one came first and which second. To obtain a high recall score, it was necessary to remember the arrangement of the words.

The analysis of recall was done in two stages. First, the number of correctly recalled words (that is, the right word in the right place) was examined (Figure 3). The figure shows that simple, highly redundant patterns like "mouse-mouse-mouse-bag-bag-bag" were recalled much better by the control groups than by the autistic children. However, with less redundant patterns of quasi-random arrangement, such as "spoon-horse-spoon-horse-horse-spoon," the autistic children did at least as well as the controls. The result is similar to the earlier findings in the comparison of sentences and random word strings. In both studies, the autistic children failed to make use of structure. Since this structure was syntactical in the first experiments, whereas in the second experiment it was not, it can be concluded that the deficit in extracting rules is not specific to the rules governing grammar.

The second stage of the analysis was concerned with the type of errors made. Just as key words alone, we observed, had to be stored in order to remember the sentence, possibly predominant features alone, in the sequences discussed above, needed to be stored in order to remember the sequence. Such predominant features would be the rules which govern the structure of the sequence. i.e., alternation or repetition. These rules could be used to reconstruct the original sequence with minimal loss. For example, the sequence "one-two-one-one" contains predominantly alternations. If this rule is used in recall, the sequence "one-two-one-two" is obtained, which is almost correct except for one error. Since it was found that the relative proportion of alternations and repetitions in a given sequence determined the difficulty of recall, it seemed most likely that this was the key feature. Thus, it was assumed that the children who succeeded with these sequences might have extracted the rule of whether a sequence contained predominantly repetitions or predominantly alternations.

The incorrectly recalled sequences were analyzed as follows: it was determined whether or not the dominant rule of the originally presented sequence was also the dominant rule of the recalled sequence. The results are illustrated in Figures 4 and 5. They show that the rules, "mainly repetitions" or "mainly alternations," were extracted and correctly retained by normal and by subnormal children even in otherwise incorrectly recalled messages. The results of the autistic children cannot be accounted for by the same strategy. It was found that errors made by normal children were in accordance with the dominant feature of the sequence. The rule which was correctly extracted was incorrectly applied, that is, applied in an exaggerated form. Instead of three repetitions besides one alternation ("one-two-two-two"), there would be, say, four repetitions besides no or one alternation ("two-two-two-two" or "one-two-two-two-two"). On the other hand, if a given sequence contained predominantly alternations, the recalled sequence tended to contain even more alternations. For example, "one-two-one-one" was often recalled as "one-two-one-two." The nondominant rule was hardly ever exaggerated by the normal and subnormal children and was sometimes even omitted, as in the previous example.

Autistic children performed quite differently. They also showed rule exaggeration. However, they tended to apply almost exclusively the repetition rule, whether or not

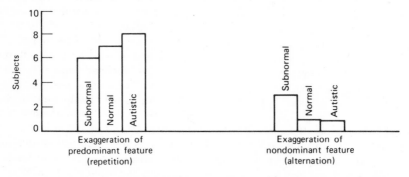

Figure 4.   Feature exaggeration in binary patterns: binary messages with predominant repetitions.

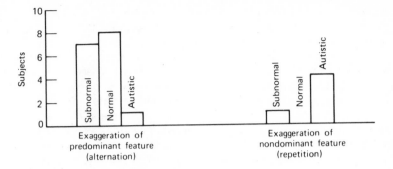

Figure 5. Feature exaggeration in binary patterns: binary messages with predominant alternations.

this was the dominant rule in the presented sequence. For example, the sequence "spoon-horse-spoon-horse-horse-spoon," containing four alternations and only one repetition, was recalled as "horse-horse-horse-spoon," containing only one alternation but two repetitions. In this case the nondominant rule was exaggerated.

Thus, one might hypothesize that normal children are able to extract either one of the two important rules present in the input and that autistic children have a bias towards applying only one rule, that of repetition, regardless of the input. Similar results were found when nonverbal material was used, i.e., sequences of green and yellow counters, which the children had to reproduce from memory. However, in this case, the autistic children showed no bias towards repetition exclusively; the bias was towards producing simple strings of either repetitions or alternations which were never present in the input. As in recall of binary word lists, the autistic children showed little evidence of feature extraction with color sequences. These findings suggest that errors in recall can be the result of incorrect feature extraction or the result of some independent imposition of rules by the subject. These two processes, i.e., the extraction and the imposition of rules, may be relatively independent of each other. The reality of the two processes can be illustrated by concrete examples. Feature extraction is, for instance, the ability to recognize and reproduce tunes even when they are transposed or when their tonal qualities are changed. An example of pattern imposition is the tendency to perceive various definite rhythms in the objectively monotonous noise of an engine.

Patterning and structuring are basic properties of the way in which human beings deal with information. This is seen particularly in studies dealing with quasi-spontaneous response sequences. When people are required to produce binary sequences, they respond not in a random but in a patterned series, although they may be quite unaware of it. On the whole, investigators have found that in children the complexity of the resulting patterns increases with increasing age (Gerjuoy & Winters, 1968).

The stereotyped, rigid, and ritualistic phenomena in the behavior of autistic children might be regarded as an exaggerated form of pattern imposition. On the other hand, the unpredictable, often inappropriate, and seemingly random responses to environmental stimuli typical of autistic children may indicate an impairment in the feature-extracting process.

In the next study, an attempt was made to investigate the nature of pattern-imposition tendencies on random input. Card guessing is a task where input is unstructured and where binary sequences can be elicited very naturally. The color, either red or black, is guessed for each card of an ordinary deck. The sequence of guesses can be analyzed in terms of response patterns. These response patterns might consist predominantly of repetitions or alternations or mixtures of the two. Such a guessing task was explained and carefully demonstrated to the children taking part in the experiment, i.e., autistic, subnormal, and normal children. Only those children who evidently understood the game were included as subjects. The age of the autistic and subnormal children ranged from 7 to 15 years. There were two groups of normal children, one group of 3-year-olds and one of 6-year-olds. Two hundred guesses were obtained from each child and were analyzed for significant response patterns.

The resulting sequence of guesses indicates highly significant pattern-imposition tendencies in all children tested. The rules governing the response sequences were either alternations or repetitions; only very rarely were they mixtures of the two. In line with other experiments of this type, a developmental progression appeared to be present: 90% of the 3-year-old normal children produced predominantly repetitions of color guesses (red-red-red . . . black-black-black . . .), and 80% of the 6-year-old normal children showed predominantly alternations of color guesses (red-black-red-black . . .). Autistic and subnormal children showed the same pattern-imposition tendencies as the normal children, the developmental change from repetitions to alternations being correlated with MA. Thus, approximately half of the autistic and subnormal children showed perseveration tendencies like younger normal children, while the other half showed alternation tendencies, like older normal children.

It was concluded that in the absence of structured input, all children, including autistic ones, imposed simple patterns of their own. The pattern shown was similar in all groups; thus, it seemed likely that autistic children did not function abnormally in this respect. Similar results were found when the children spontaneously constructed long rows of red- and green-colored counters.

The results of the experiments on spontaneous production of binary sequences show that all children of all groups imposed simple structures in situations where input was random or minimal. However, the groups differed in those experiments in which structured input was to be recalled or reconstructed. The normal and subnormal children reflected key input features even in otherwise incorrect reproductions. This was not true for the autistic children; they responded by producing the same simple patterns which they used when input was random or minimal. It thus seems that autistic children are largely insensitive to given sequential order and respond to such patterned input as if it were random. However, their responses themselves are not random, unlawful, and irregular; on the contrary, they are highly repetitive, predictable, and rigidly structured.

The experiments extended beyond the specific structure of language and it can therefore be assumed that the deficit found with autistic children may account for a wider area of cognitive dysfunctions. A lack of sensitivity to the inherent pattern of the input, combined with a tendency to impose simple patterns in different situations, might account for some of the stereotyped behavior of autistic children. A tendency towards pattern imposition may often be appropriate in apparently random situations, although it becomes inappropriate in situations governed by definite rules. The more complex and flexible those rules, as for instance in social interactions, symbolic play, and language, the more limiting and inappropriate stereotyped behavior becomes.

From this point of view, the behavior of the autistic child becomes less bizarre and mysterious and can be better understood in terms of a clearly delineated cognitive pathology.

REFERENCES

Bousfield, W. H. The occurrence of clustering in the recall of randomly arranged associates. *Journal of General Psychology,* 1953, **49,** 229–240.

Gerjuoy, I. R., & Winters, J. J. Development of later and choice-sequence preferences. In N. R. Ellis (Ed.), *International review of research in mental retardation.* Vol. 3. London: Academic Press, 1968.

Hermelin, B., & O'Connor, N. *Psychological experiments with autistic children.* London: Pergamon Press, 1970.

Kanner, L. Autistic disturbances of affective contact. *Nervous Child,* 1943, **2,** 217–250.

Lockyer, L., & Rutter, M. A five- to fifteen-year follow-up study of infantile psychosis. III. Psychological aspects. *British Journal of Psychiatry,* 1969, **115,** 865–882.

Lotter, V. Epidemiology of autistic conditions in young children. I. Prevalence. *Social Psychiatry,* 1966, **1,** 124–137.

Lotter, V. Epidemiology of autistic conditions in young children. II. Some characteristics of the parents and children. *Social Psychiatry,* 1967, **1,** 163–173.

Miller, G. A., & Selfridge, J. A. Verbal context and the recall of meaningful material. *American Journal of Psychology,* 1953, **63,** 176–185.

Rutter, M. Schooling and the "autistic" child. *Special Education,* 1967, **56,** 19–24.

Rutter, M. Concepts of autism: A review of research. *Journal of Child Psychology and Psychiatry,* 1968, **9,** 1–25.

Rutter, M., Greenfield, D., & Lockyer, L. A five- to fifteen-year follow-up study of infantile psychosis. II. Social and behavioural outcome. *British Journal of Psychiatry,* 1967, **113,** 1183–1199.

Rutter, M., & Lockyer, L. A five- to fifteen-year follow-up study of infantile psychosis. I. Description of sample. *British Journal of Psychiatry,* 1967, **113,** 1169–1182.

Wing, L. The handicaps of autistic children—a comparative study, *Journal of Child Psychology and Psychiatry,* 1969, **10,** 1–40.

Wing, L. The syndrome of early childhood autism. *British Journal of Hospital Medicine,* 1970, **4,** 381–392.

The Effectiveness of Psycholinguistic Training

Donald D. Hammill

Stephen C. Larsen

This article reviews the results of 38 studies which attempted to train children in psycholinguistic skills and which used the ITPA as the criterion of improvement. It was concluded that the effectiveness of such training has not been conclusively demonstrated and therefore that the rapid expansion of psycholinguistic training programs seems unwarranted.

Psycholinguistics is the study of language, as related to the general or individual characteristics of the users of language. It includes the processes by which a speaker or writer emits signals or symbols and the processes by which these signals are interpreted. In addition, attention is given to the way that the intentions of one individual are transmitted to another and, reciprocally, the way that the intentions of another person are received. In short, psycholinguistics deals with the psychological functions and interactions involved in communication.

While there are many theories of psycholinguistic functioning, the schemata presented by Osgood (1957) has had the greatest impact on education. The Osgood model encompasses two dimensions of language behavior: language processes and levels of organization. The process dimension includes decoding, association, and encoding. Decoding refers to the receiving and perceiving of stimuli, i.e., the recognition of what is seen or heard. Association implies the ability to manipulate linguistic symbols, i.e., the inference of relationships from what is seen or heard. Encoding is the expression of linguistic symbols, i.e., the use of skills necessary to express thoughts.

The processes just described are mediated at any one of three levels of neural organization. The most basic level is that of projection, which relates receptor and muscle events to the brain. The second organizational level is integration, which provides for the sequencing and organization of incoming and outgoing "messages." The most complex level of organization is the representational. At this level, the more

From *Exceptional Children,* 5–13 (September 1974). Reprinted by permission of the Council for Exceptional Children.

Donald D. Hammill is presently residing in Austin, Texas; and Stephen C. Larsen is Coordinator—Learning Disabilities, Department of Special Education, College of Education, The University of Texas at Austin.

sophisticated mediating operations necessary for meaningful symbolization are employed.

The educational applications of these particular psycholinguistic principles have generated both assessment techniques and remedial language programs. It was this model which Kirk, McCarthy, and Kirk (1968) adapted and used to construct the Illinois Test of Psycholinguistic Abilities (ITPA). This diagnostic instrument was designed to measure specific functions of psycholinguistic behavior and provides a framework for the amelioration of language disorders. The ITPA clinical model and the original Osgood schema have served as the basis for several remedial and developmental programs that are used extensively in schools (Karnes, 1968; Dunn & Smith, 1966; Bush & Giles, 1969; Minskoff, Wiseman, & Minskoff, 1972).

Psycholinguistic training is based upon the assumption that discrete elements of language behavior are identifiable and measurable, that they provide the underpinning for learning, and that if defective they can be remediated. When using this approach, an additional assumption is made that the cause of the child's learning failure is within himself and that strengthening weak areas will result in improved classroom learning. If this assumption is valid, then programs designed to alleviate psycholinguistic deficits would be appropriate and viable. However, if this assumption is not valid, much time, effort, and money is needlessly expended. Only through the accumulated results of carefully designed research may the efficacy of psycholinguistic training be proved to be of value. The purpose of this article is to report the results of studies that have attempted to develop psycholinguistic skills.

PROCEDURES

Only studies which used the ITPA or one or more of its subtests as the criterion for improvement of language behavior were reviewed. As the ITPA is based primarily upon the constructs of Osgood and as most of the training programs were generated either from the ITPA or from the original Osgood theory, it was felt that this stipulation would be the most efficient in determining the efficacy of psycholinguistic training. It was also assumed that the researchers who conducted these studies believed that there was some relationship between the ITPA and their intervention programs or they would not have selected this test to demonstrate the effects of their program.

The characteristics of the studies reviewed are presented in Table 1. The table includes (a) the names of the researchers; (b) the publication date of the research; (c) the number, (d) type, and (e) age of the experimental and control subjects; (f) the basic approach used with the experimental group, e.g., prescriptive (individualized) where a special program is designed for a child on the basis of diagnostic procedures or general (nonindividualized) where children are exposed to an overall language stimulation program; (g) the specific kind of experimental training, e.g., selected activities based on an ITPA psycholinguistic model (usually author designed but similar to the Kirk and Kirk, 1971, or Bush and Giles, 1969, activities), the Peabody Language Development Kits (PLDK), or other teaching systems; (h) the estimated duration of the treatment period; and (i) the number of hours devoted to training. The following example demonstrates how the table should be read. In 1967, Mueller and Dunn evaluated the effectiveness of the PLDK, a general, nonindividualized approach to teaching language. Their experimental and control subjects were elementary school

Table 1   Characteristics of Psycholinguistic Training Studies†

Authors	Date	Number E	C	Type	Age	Approach	Exp. Method	EHT	DOT
Blessing	1964	2	2	1	UTE	2	1	3	2
Blue	1970	2	2	2	UTE	2	1	1	2
Bradley et al.	1966	2	2	2	2+3	1	1	3	3
Carter	1966	3	3	3	2	2	2	2	3
Clasen et al.	1969	2	2	3	1	2	2	3	1
Crutchfield	1964	1	1	1+2	2+3	2	1	1	2
Dickie	1968	3	3	3	1	2	3	2	3
Dunn & Mueller	1966	3	3	3	2	2	2	3	3
Dunn & Mueller	1967	3	3	3	2	2	2	3	3
Ensminger	1966	3	3	3	2	2	2	3	3
Forgnone	1967	3	3	1	2	2	2	2	2
Gazdic	1971	3	2	4	2	2	2	3	3
Gibson	1966	2	2	1	2	2	2	2	3
Gray & Klaus	1965	3	3	3	1	2	3	3	3
Guess et al.	1969	3	3	2	3	2	2	3	3
Hart	1963	1	1	4	2	1	1	1	1
Hartman	1967	3	3	3	1	1	1	3	3
Hodges & Spicker	1967	2	2	3	1	2	3	UTE	3
Jones	1970	3	3	3	1	2	2	2	2
Karnes et al.	1970	3	3	3	1	2	1	3	3
Lavin	1971	3	3	3	1	2	3	3	3
Leiss	1974	3	3	2	2+3	2	1	3	3
McConnell et al.	1969 (a,b,c)	3	3	3	1	2	3	3	3
Minskoff	1967	1	1	1	3	1	1	1	3
Mitchell	1967	3	3	3	1	2	2	UTE	1
Morgan	1972	3	3	3	1	2	3	3	3
Morris	1967	*	*	*	*	2	2	3	3
Mueller & Dunn	1967	3	3	1	2	2	2	3	3
Painter	1966	1	1	3	1	2	3	2	1
Runyon	1970	2	2	1	2	2	1	2	3
Saudargas et al.	1970	2	1	1	2	1	2	1	2
Sapir	1971	2	1	4	2	2	3	UTE	3
Schifani	1972	1	1	1	3	2	2	3	3
Siders	1970	3	3	3	2	2	3	3	3
Smith	1962	2	2	1	2	2	2	1	2
Spollen & Ballif	1971	3	3	4	1	1	1	3	3
Stearns	1967	2	1	3	1	1	3	2	2
Strickland	1967	3	3	3	1	2	1	UTE	2
Wiseman	1965	1	1	1	2	1	1	2	1

*Information not obtained
†Note code on p. 255

Table 1   Characteristics of Psycholinguistic Training Studies

CODE:

Subjects:

Number

  E = Experimental

  C = Control

  1 = 5 to 10

  2 = 11 to 20

  3 = 20+

Type

  1 = EMR

  2 = TMR

  3 = Disadvantaged

  4 = Other

Age

 1 Preschool

 2 = 6 to 11 years

 3 = 11+ years

 UTE = unable to estimate

Approach:

1 = prescriptive/individualized

2 = general/nonindividualized

Exp. method:

1 = Selected activities, based on

    ITPA model

2 = PDLK

3 = Other

EHT (Estimated hours of

training):

1 = 30

2 = 30 to 50

3 = 50+

UTE = unable to estimate

DOT (Duration of training):

1 = 10 weeks

2 = 10 to 20 weeks

3 = 20+ weeks

aged, educable mentally retarded children. More than 20 subjects were in each group. The experimental subjects received in excess of 50 hours of training over a more than 20-week period.

While some of the researchers compared the experimental subjects with a variety of contrast subjects, e.g., those who received remedial reading instruction or speech therapy, we were interested only in the experimental-control group analyses. In all instances, the results discussed in this review refer to comparisons between children trained in language and those who received no formal instruction of any kind or those who were enrolled in "traditional" programs.

RESULTS

The findings of these studies are summarized in Table 2. A "+" indicates that the author reported that the trained subjects did considerably better than nontrained subjects on a particular ITPA subtest. A "0" indicates that the control subjects were equal to or better than the experimental subjects on a subtest analysis. In most of the cases "+" and "0" are the same as statistical significance (.05 level) or nonstatistical significance, respectively. Where this is not the case, the author's name is numbered and a description of the procedures used to designate the study's analyses as "+" or "0" are described in a footnote. The footnotes are also used to explain those occasions where our interpretations of a study's findings differed from its author's.

The reader will notice the many blank spaces in Table 2. This occurs because some authors used the 9 subtest 1961 ITPA and others used the 12 subtest 1968 version.

Table 2   Results of Studies Which Attempted to Train Psycholinguistic Processes

						ITPA Subtests							
Researcher	AR	VR	AA	VA	VE	ME	GC	VC	ASM	VSM	AC	SB	Total
Blessing	+												0
Blue					+								+
Bradley et al.[1]	+	+	0	+	+	+	+		0	0			+
Carter	0	+	+	+	+	+	+		+	+			0
Clasen et al.	+	+	0	+	0	0	0		0	0			0
Crutchfield[2]		0	0	0	0	0	0			+			+
Dickie			0		0								0
Dunn & Mueller[3]	0	0	+	+	+	0	0		0	0			0
Ensminger	0	0	+	0	+	0	0		0	0			0
Forgnone													0
Gazdic													+
Gibson	0	0	0	0	0	0	0		0	0			0
Gray & Klaus	+	+	+	+	+	0	+		+	+			+
Guess et al.[4]													0
Hart[5]	0	0	+	+	+	+	0		+	+			+
Hartman	0	0	0	0	0	0	0	0	0	0			0
Hodges & Spicker													0
Jones[6]	+	0	0	0	+	+	0	0	0	0			0
Karnes et al.	0	+	+	0	0	0	+		0	0			+
Lavin	0	0	0	0	0	0	0	0	0	0			0
Leiss	0	0			+	+	0						0
McConnell et al.	+			+	+	+	+		+	+			+
Minskoff[7]			0	0	0	0	0		0	0			0
Mitchell	0	0	+				0		+	0			0
Morgan	0	0	+				0	+		0			+
Morris			0			0	0			0			+
Mueller & Dunn	0												+

256

	AR	VR	AA	VA	VE	ME	GC	VC	ASM	AC	VSM	SB	Total
Painter	0	0	0	0	+	0	0	0	0	0	0	0	
Runyon													+
Saudargas et al.	0	0	0	0	0	0	+	0	0	0	0	0	+
Sapir	0	+	+	+	0	+	+	+	+	0	+	0	+
Schifani[8]	0	0	0	0	0	0	+	0	0	0	+	0	+
Siders	0	0	0	0	0	0	0	0	0				
Smith[9]	+	+	+	+	+	+	+	+	+	+	+		+
Spollen & Ballif	0	0	0	0	0	+							0
Stearns[10]	0	0	0	0	0	0	0	0	0	0			0
Strickland	+	+	+	+	+	+	+	+	+	+	+		0
Wiseman	0	0	0	0	+	0	0	0	0	0			+

CODE:

+ means experimental subjects did considerably better than control subjects

0 means control subjects were equal to or better than experimental subjects

ITPA Subtests: AR = Auditory Reception, VR = Visual Reception, AA = Auditory Association, VA = Visual Association, VE = Verbal Expression, ME = Manual Expression, GC = Grammatic Closure, VC = Visual Closure, ASM = Auditory Sequential Memory, AC = Auditory Closure, VSM = Visual Sequential Memory, SB = Sound Blending, Total = Total Language Age

FOOTNOTES

[1] Bradley et al. neglected to report the significance of difference in gain scores between experimental and control groups for the Auditory Sequential Memory subtest. Inspection of their Table 1 clearly indicates that the difference would be nonsignificant.

[2] Crutchfield did no tests of significance but did provide pretest and posttest subtest means. It was therefore possible to calculate pre-post gains for experimental and control subjects. His experimental subjects were subdivided into a younger (N=9) and older (N=8) group, but no such division was made of the control subjects (N=15). Because of the similarity in the N's of the two experimental groups, they were combined and their mean gains compared with those of the control group. Of the nine subtests, the gains of five favored the control subjects; in two instances, the differences were 2 months or less; and only two cases, where the differences exceeded seven months, could be taken as positive evidence of training.

[3] Dunn and Mueller undertook two studies, one dealt with the effects of training on the total ITPA score (1966) while the other dealt with the subtests (1967). No tests of significance were reported for the latter. Instead pre- and posttest means for the experimental and control groups and gain scores are provided. On four of the nine subtests gains favored the control subjects and these are recorded as "0." In each of these cases the difference between experimental and control groups on both the pretest and the posttest was less than two months. The results for Auditory Association, Visual Association, and Verbal Expression clearly demonstrated the positive effects of training and are recorded "+."

Table 2 Results of Studies Which Attempted to Train Psycholinguistic Processes

FOOTNOTES continued

[4] The Guess et al. sample was posttested twice—once at the end of the 9 month training period and again 9 months later. Differences between experimental and control groups were not significant at the first testing but were significant at the last testing. The nonsignificant value is used in Table 2 because "followup" research was not dealt with in this review.

[5] Hart does no tests of significance of difference on his subtest data. He did provide the pre- and posttest means for his experimental and control groups. It was then possible to estimate gain scores. On one subtest, Auditory Reception, the gains favored the control group; on two others, Visual Reception and Grammatic Closure, the gains of the experimental group exceeded those of the control groups by four or fewer months. These subtests were arbitrarily recorded as "0." The other differences all favored the experimental group and ranged from 6 to 24 months.

[6] Jones did no subtest analyses, though she did provide pre-post means for experimental and control groups (p. 119) which made it possible to compute gain scores for the groups. Experimental gains were subtracted from control gains for each subtest and the total score. On an additional four subtests and the total scores, the differences favored the experimental group by less than 2 points. These eight analyses are recorded as "0" in Table 2. The remaining three analyses favored the experimental group by differences ranging from 2.4 to 5.6 points and are recorded "+."

[7] Minskoff used the .10 level of confidence in his dissertation. As all other authors in this table employed the .05 level, we reinterpreted Minskoff's findings using the .05 level in order to be consistent.

[8] In his dissertation, Schifani tests only the significance of the differences relating to the ITPA total score. As he provided means and standard deviations for the subtests, it was possible to compute the significance of subtest differences.

[9] Smith reported no analyses regarding the significance of differences between experimental and control groups. It was possible, however, to compute the mean gain scores for the groups from data provided. The control subjects regressed or made no gain on five subtests and gains of less than 3 months on the four subtests, while the experimental subjects registered gains on all subtests ranging from 3 to 13 months. In Table 2 all the subtests with the exception of Auditory Sequential Memory are designated "+"; however, because of the small N, if analyses could have been run on these data, some of the results might have been nonsignificant.

[10] Stearns only tested the significance of the differences between experimental and control groups on the total ITPA score. Subtest means were provided but not the associated standard deviations. He concluded, from inspection, that training appeared to positively affect three of nine subtests.

Some researchers were concerned only with selected subtests while others were interested in the ITPA total score and not at all in the subtests. The effects of training on Auditory Closure and Sound Blending are almost nonexistent, which was likely due to the fact that these subtests only became available with the publication of the revised ITPA and are only supplemental tests in that version. Visual Closure is also a new subtest, but it is included in the ITPA proper and has therefore been studied more frequently.

For these analyses, no distinction is made between the 1961 and 1968 versions of the ITPA. To avoid confusion, the terminology of the more recent version is used throughout this review. It was our opinion that differences between the two tests were of a technical nature, e.g., some subtests were lengthened, instructions were altered slightly, names of the subtests were changed, etc.; but the basic constructs of the two remained essentially the same. This opinion is supported by the work of Waugh (1973) who compared the tests and concluded that for most purposes they could be used interchangeably.

Table 2 should be read as follows: Sapir reported that special psycholinguistic instruction was beneficial in developing the abilities measured by Auditory Association, Verbal Expression, Manual Expression, Auditory Sequential Memory, and the total ITPA Language Age. Such training was found to be no more beneficial than that in traditional classes regarding Visual Reception, Visual Association, or Visual Sequential Memory. No analyses were undertaken pertaining to the remaining ITPA subtests.

The authors of the 39 research studies reported (or provided the necessary information which allowed us to calculate and report) the results of 280 comparisons between the performance of experimental and control subjects on the subtest scores and the total scores of the ITPA. It was therefore possible to compute the percentage of analyses which indicated that special psycholinguistic training was beneficial.

VARIABLES ON INSTRUCTION EFFECTIVENESS

When integrating the information provided in Tables 1 and 2, one can evaluate the effectiveness of such instruction on differing types of children, e.g., retarded, disadvantaged, preschool, and elementary. The percentage of analyses, by subgroup, which found the intervention successful is found in Table 3. Where analyses were few, i.e., less than five, as was the case with Auditory Closure and Sound Blending, percentages were not computed.

Fifteen authors (103 analyses) studied the value of psycholinguistic training with retarded subjects with less than encouraging results. There was not a single subtest for which a majority of the researchers reported that training was beneficial. Therefore, the value of training retarded subjects in psycholinguistics has not been demonstrated to date.

The 18 authors (154 analyses) who used the instruction with disadvantaged children were apparently more successful, especially regarding improvement in associational and verbal expressive ability. However, as the positive percentages are only in the 50s and as most of the subtests of the ITPA did not respond to instruction, support for training disadvantaged children in psycholinguistic skills is at best limited.

The effects of age on training was probed at the preschool level by 15 authors (121 analyses) and at the elementary level by 19 authors (143 analyses). Apparently, the training programs used to date emphasize the development of Auditory Association abilities at the preschool level and expressive language abilities at the elementary level. Once again, the positive findings are limited to the representational level subtests.

Eight of the researchers (70 analyses) used a prescriptive approach, i.e., they diagnosed their subjects, usually with the ITPA, and designed programs specifically for each child. This approach was apparently successful in stimulating visual associational and expressive language abilities. The nonindividualized approach to instruction, i.e., the approach in which all children are exposed to a set program, was studied by 30 authors (208 analyses) and was evidently minimally effective in teaching auditory associational and verbal expressive abilities.

Two kinds of curricula were employed most often: the "selected activities" approach, used by 13 researchers (85 analyses), and the PLDK approach, used by 16 researchers (112 analyses). The selective activities approach was found to be useful in stimulating skills necessary to do well on the Manual Expression subtest. With the exception of Verbal Expression, the PLDK does not seem to be an efficient method for developing language processes.

The figures at the bottom of Table 3 associated with "Total" are of particular interest in that they reflect the overall situation relative to psycholinguistic training accomplished to date. It is apparent that for the most part, researchers have been unsuccessful in developing those skills which would enable their subjects to do well on the ITPA. The Verbal Expression subtest seems to be the most responsive to intervention, while Visual Closure, Grammatic Closure, Visual Reception, and Auditory Reception are the most resistant.

Each ITPA subtest relates to a particular psycholinguistic construct in the Osgood-Kirk model, i.e., level, process, and channel (modality). By assigning each subtest to its appropriate construct and by computing the percentages of "+'s" it is possible to estimate the success which researchers have had in stimulating the theoretical psycholinguistic dimensions underlying the ITPA. These constructs, the subtests which comprise them, and the percentages of positive analyses are presented in Table 4.

COLLECTIVE RESULTS

The collective results of the studies reviewed suggest that the idea that psycholinguistic constructs, as measured by the ITPA, can be trained by existing techniques remains nonvalidated. Comparatively speaking, the most encouraging findings pertained to training at the representational level, especially the expressive process. The most discouraging results were associated with training at the automatic level, the receptive and organizing processes, and both the auditory-vocal and visual-motor modalities.

There is one additional observation worth noting, i.e., the recent findings are considerably less encouraging regarding the benefits of training than were those of the earlier research. In the studies located, 110 experimental-control comparisons were made between 1962 and 1966; 73 comparisons were made between 1967 and 1969; and 98 between 1970 and 1973. The percentages supporting training were 52, 31, and 21, respectively. As we can generate no satisfactory explanation for this finding, we choose merely to report the observation without comment.

Table 3   The Percentage of Analyses, by Subgroup, Which Found Psycholinguistic Training to Be Successful

| Subgroups | ITPA Subtests[1] | | | | | | | | | | | | |
	AR	VR	AA	VA	VE	ME	GC	VC	ASM	VSM	AC	SB	Total
Retarded subjects	33	25	13	33	40	44	22	—	22	20	—	—	50
Disadvantaged subjects	27	29	59	50	50	29	27	—	33	21	—	—	40
Preschool subjects	27	27	54	45	42	27	27	—	33	18	—	—	31
Elementary subjects	31	25	43	46	57	54	23	—	31	29	—	—	56
Prescriptive approach	17	17	33	57	57	57	17	—	29	14	—	—	50
Nonindividualized approach	32	28	52	39	50	33	25	20	37	26	—	—	46
Selected activities	29	29	38	29	44	50	29	—	33	25	—	—	42
PLDK activities	27	30	42	40	55	30	17	—	30	18	—	—	47
TOTAL	28	24	48	44	52	40	23	20	35	23	—	—	47

[1] For ITPA subtest code, see Table 2.

Table 4   Psycholinguistic Constructs, the ITPA Subtests Which Comprise Them, and the Percentage of Positive Analyses

Language Dimensions	Constructs	ITPA Subtests[1]	Percentages of Positive Analyses
Levels	Representational	AR, VR, AA, VA, VE, ME	40
	Automatic	GC, VC, ASM, VSM, AC, SB	25
Processes	Reception	AR, VR	27
	Organization	AA, VA, GC, VC, ASM, VSM, AC, SB	33
	Expression	VE, ME	46
Modalities	Auditory-Vocal	AR, AA, VE, GC, ASM, AC, SB	37
	Visual-Motor	VR, VA, ME, VC, VSM	32

[1]For subtest code, see Table 2.

Additional analyses were undertaken to investigate the effects of hours of training and length of the training period on subject improvement. As the results indicated these were not significant variables, they are not reported.

DISCUSSION

It seems as though we are confronted with at least three possible explanations which could account for the findings of this review: (a) the ITPA is an invalid measure of psycholinguistic functioning; (b) the intervention programs and/or techniques are inadequate; and (c) most psycholinguistic dimensions are either untrainable or highly resistant to stimulation.

VALIDITY OF THE ITPA

Some researchers have reported that the subtests of the ITPA lack independence, and as a consequence the test measures only one or two psycholinguistic factors. These findings are usually based on factor analyses which used only the ITPA subtests or used the subtests with measures of achievement or intelligence. Such efforts may relate to the test's content validity but contribute little to estimating the test's construct validity, which is critical to this review. Sedlack and Weener (1973) have provided a particularly noteworthy review of the ITPA factor analytic research.

Only Hare, Hammill, and Bartel (1973) and Newcomer, Hare, Hammill, and McGettigan (1974) have factored the ITPA subtests with specifically designed psycholinguistic criterion tests. The findings suggest that only one subtest, Visual Sequential Memory, is clearly inadequate, and for the most part the subtests load independently and on factors which are easily recognizable in terms of the Osgood-Kirk constructs. Support was found for the concept of the levels, the processes, and the auditory-vocal modality. The visual-motor modality was not substantiated, however.

ADEQUACY OF THE TRAINING PROGRAMS

It seems likely that the instructional programs are uneven in that they seem to emphasize training associative and expressive abilities to the comparative exclusion of training receptive and automatic skills. This may be inherent in the programs, or teachers may avoid such activities and show preference for the associative and expressive activities. In any event, important variables are apparently not being taught using the presently available instructional systems.

It is suggested that teachers who attempt to train psycholinguistic processes pay particular attention to those skills, which have been slighted up to now. It is particularly important to do so if the teacher accepts the still questionable hypothesis of Kass (1966), Sabatino (1973), Wepman (1960), Bartin (1971), and Golden and Steiner (1969), among many others, that automatic level skills can be used to differentiate between good and poor readers and that deficits in these abilities may contribute to or even cause appreciable reading failure.

TRAINABILITY OF PSYCHOLINGUISTIC PROCESSES

The positive findings regarding Verbal Expression suggest that at least one of the skills tapped by the ITPA may be responsive to training. This leads one to speculate that under different situations, using improved techniques, others might also respond to instruction. Still, the results of the review strongly indicate that neither the ITPA subtests nor their theoretical constructs are particularly ameliorative. Approximately 70 percent or better of the analyses were unsuccessful in training Grammatic Closure, Visual Sequential Memory, Visual Closure, Visual and Auditory Reception, automatic level skills, receptive processes, or visual-motor modality skills.

Therefore, whether some of the subtests are unresponsive to instructional efforts because they are basically impossible or extremely difficult to teach, because the training programs do not provide sufficient attention to them, or because the ITPA subtests are not appropriate measures of these constructs, we cannot say. This is a matter for future research to clarify.

IMPLICATIONS

One of the major implications to be drawn from this review of research is that the efficacy of training psycholinguistic functionings has not been conclusively demonstrated. These findings are of importance when considering the amount of time, effort, and money that is currently being devoted to providing exceptional children with training programs designed to increase psycholinguistic skills. A concerted effort should be made to determine conclusively that the constructs are trainable by available programs and/or to identify the characteristics of the children for whom such training is beneficial.

Efforts should also be directed to establishing the effectiveness of training on educationally relevant variables. If this type of research indicated that psycholinguistic skills could be stimulated and that as a consequence academic abilities would improve, then educators could proceed with some assurance having evidence that training such skills is worthwhile. Until these results are available, however, programs designed to improve psycholinguistic functioning need to be viewed cautiously and monitored with care so that children experiencing difficulty in school will not be subjected to meaningless and irrelevant activities that will result only in a waste of valuable time.

REFERENCES

Bartin, N. The intellectual and psycholinguistic characteristics of three groups of differentiated third grade readers. Unpublished doctoral dissertation, State University of New York, Buffalo, 1971.

Blessing, K. R. An investigation of a psycholinguistic deficit in educable mentally retarded children: Detection, remediation and related variables. (Unpublished doctoral dissertation, University of Wisconsin, Madison) *International Dissertation Abstracts,* 1964, **25,** 2327.

Blue, C. The effectiveness of a group language program with trainable mentally retarded children. *Education and Training of the Mentally Retarded,* 1970, **5,** 109–112.

Bradley, B. H., Maurer, R., & Hundzial, M. A study of the effectiveness of milieu therapy and language training for the mentally retarded. *Exceptional Children,* 1966, **33,** 143–149.

Bush, W. J., & Giles, M. T. *Aids to psycholinguistic teaching.* Columbus, Ohio: Charles E. Merrill, 1969.

Çarter, J. L. The effect of a language stimulation program upon first grade educationally disadvantaged children. *Education and Training of the Mentally Retarded,* 1966, **1,** 169–174.

Clasen, R. E., Spear, J. E., & Tomaro, M. P. A comparison of the relative effectiveness of two types of preschool compensatory programming. *The Journal of Educational Research,* 1969, **62,** 401–405.

Crutchfield, V. M. E. The effects of language training on the language development of mentally retarded children in Abilene State School. (Unpublished doctoral dissertation, University of Denver) *International Dissertation Abstracts,* 1964, **25,** 4572.

Dickie, J. P. Effectivenss of structured and unstructured (traditional) methods of language training. In M. A. Brottman (Ed.), Language remediation for the disadvantaged pre-school child. *Monograph of the Society for Research in Child Development,* 1968, **33**(124), 62–79.

Dunn, L. M., & Mueller, M. W. The efficacy of the Initial Teaching Alphabet and the *Peabody Language Development Kit* with grade one disadvantaged children: After one year. IMRID papers and reports. Institute on Mental Retardation and Intellectual Development, George Peabody College, 1966.

Dunn, L. M., & Mueller, M. W. Differential effects on the ITPA profile of the experimental version of level # 1 of the *Peabody Language Development Kits* with disadvantaged first grade children. IMRID papers and reports. Institute on Mental Retardation and Intellectual Development, George Peabody College, 1967.

Dunn. L. M., & Smith, J. O. *The Peabody Language Kits.* Circle Pines, Minn.: American Guidance Service, 1966.

Ensminger, E. E. The effects of a classroom language development program on psycholinguistic abilities and intellectual functioning of slow learning and borderline retarded children. Unpublished doctoral dissertation, University of Kansas, 1966.

Forgnone, C. Effects of visual perception and language training upon certain abilities of retarded children. (Unpublished master's thesis, George Peabody College) *International Dissertation Abstracts,* 1967, **27,** 1197-A.

Gazdic, J. M. An evaluation of a program for those children ascertained to be not ready for regular first grade placement. Unpublished master's thesis, Northeastern Illinois State College, Chicago, 1971.

Gibson, R. C. Effectiveness of a supplemental language development program with educable mentally retarded children. (Unpublished doctoral dissertation, University of Iowa) *International Dissertation Abstracts,* 1967, **27,** 2726-A.

Golden, N. E., & Steiner, S. R. Auditory and visual functions in good and poor readers. *Journal of Learning Disabilities,* 1969, **2,** 476–481.

Gray, S. W., & Klaus, R. A. An experimental preschool program for culturally deprived children. *Child Development,* 1965, **30,** 887–898.

Guess, D., Ensminger, E. E., & Smith, J. O. A language development program for mentally retarded children. Final report. Project No. 7-0815, Grant No. OEG-0-8-070815-0216 (032), Bureau of Education for the Handicapped, August 1969.

Hare, B., Hammill, D. D., & Bartel, N. Construct validity of selected ITPA subtests. *Exceptional Children,* 1973, **40,** 13–20.

Hart, N. W. M. The differential diagnosis of the psycholinguistic abilities of the cerebral palsied child and effective remedial procedures. *Special Schools Bulletin,* No. 2, Brisbane, Australia, 1963.

Hartman, A. S. A long-range attack to reduce the educational disadvantage of children from poverty backgrounds. 1965–66, Progress Report to the Ford Foundation. Department of Public Instruction, Harrisburg, Pennsylvania, 1967.

Hodges, W. L., & Spicker, H. H. The effects of preschool experiences on culturally disadvantaged children. In W. W. Hartub & N. L. Smothergill (Eds.), *The young child: Review of research.* Washington, D.C.: National Association for the Education of Young Children, 1967.

Jones, E. L. H. The effects of a language development program on the psycholinguistic abilities and IQ of a group of preschool disadvantaged children. (Unpublished doctoral dissertation, University of Arkansas, Fayetteville) *International Dissertation Abstracts,* 1970, **31,** 2761-A.

Karnes, M. B. *Helping young children develop language skills: A book of activities.* Washington, D.C.: The Council for Exceptional Children, 1968.

Karnes, M. B., Teska, J. A., & Hodgins, A. S. The effects of four programs of classroom intervention on intellectual and language development of four-year-old disadvantaged children. *American Journal of Orthopsychiatry,* 1970, **40,** 58–76.

Kass, C. E. Psycholinguistic disabilities of children with reading problems. *Exceptional Children,* 1966, **32,** 533–539.

Kirk, S. A., & Kirk, W. D. *Psycholinguistic learning disabilities: Diagnosis and remediation.* Urbana: University of Illinois Press, 1971.

Kirk, S. A., McCarthy, J. J., & Kirk, W. D. *Illinois Test of Psycholinguistic Abilities.* Urbana: University of Illinois Press, 1968.

Lavin, C. M. The effects of a structured sensory-motor training program on selected cognitive and psycholinguistic abilities of preschool children. (Unpublished doctoral dissertation, Fordham University) *International Dissertation Abstracts,* 1971, **32,** 1984-A.

Leiss, R. H. The effect of intensity in a psycholinguistic stimulation program for trainable mentally retarded children. Unpublished doctoral dissertation, Temple University, 1974.

McConnell, F., Horton, K. B., & Smith, B. R. Effects of early language training for culturally disadvantaged preschool children. *The Journal of School Health,* 1969, **39,** 661–665. (a)

McConnell, F., Horton, K. B., & Smith, B. R. Language development and culturally disadvantaged. *Exceptional Children,* 1969, **35,** 597–606. (b)

McConnell, F., Horton, D. B., & Smith, B. R. Sensory-perceptual and language training to prevent school learning disabilities in culturally deprived preschool children. Final report, Project No. 5-0682, Grant No. OEG-32-52-7900-5025, USOE Bureau of Research. The Bill Wilkerson Hearing and Speech Center, Nashville, Tennessee, August 1972. (c)

Minskoff, E., Wiseman, D. E., & Minskoff, J. G. *The MWM program for developing language abilities.* Ridgefield, N.J.: Educational Performance Associates, 1972.

Minskoff, J. G. A psycholinguistic approach to remediation with retarded-disturbed children. (Unpublished doctoral dissertation, Yeshiva University, New York City) *International Dissertation Abstracts,* 1967, **28,** 1625-A.

Mitchell, R. S. A study of the effects of specific training in psycholinguistic scores of Head Start children. (Unpublished doctoral dissertation) *International Dissertation Abstracts,* 1968, **28,** 1709-A.

Morgan, D. L. A comparison of growth in language development in a structured and traditional preschool compensatory education program. (Unpublished doctoral dissertation, United States International University, San Diego) *International Dissertation Abstracts,* 1972, **32,** 4388-A.

Morris, S. K. Results of a study using the *Peabody Language Development Kit:* Level P. (Exper. ed.) Unpublished master's thesis, Vanderbilt University, 1967. Cited by L. M. Dunn & J. O. Smith, *The Peabody Language Kits.* Circle Pines, Minn.: American Guidance Service, 1966.

Mueller, M. W., & Dunn, L. M. Effects of level 1 of the *Peabody Language Development Kits* with educable mentally retarded children—An interim report after 4½ months. IMRID papers and reports. Institute on Mental Retardation and Intellectual Development, George Peabody College, 1967.

Newcomer, P., Hare, B., Hammill, D. D., & McGettigan, J. Construct validity of the ITPA subtests. *Exceptional Children,* 1974, **40,** 509–510.

Osgood, C. E. Motivational dynamics of language behavior. In M. R. Jones (Ed.), *Nebraska symposium on motivation.* Lincoln: University of Nebraska Press, 1957.

Painter, G. The effect of a rhythmic and sensory motor activity program on perceptual motor spatial abilities of kindergarten children. *Exceptional Children,* 1966, **33,** 113–116.

Runyon, M. J. L. The effects of a psycholinguistic development language program on language abilities of educable mentally retarded children. Unpublished master's thesis, Cardinal Stritch College, 1970.

Sabatino, D. Auditory perception: Development, assessment, and intervention. In L. Mann & D. A. Sabatino, *The first review of special education.* Philadelphia, Pa.: JSE Press, 1973.

Saudargas, R. A., Madsen, C. H., & Thompson, F. Prescriptive teaching in language arts remediation for Black rural elementary school children. *Journal of Learning Disabilities,* 1970, **3,** 364–370.

Sapir, S. G. Learning disability and deficit centered classroom training. In J. Hellmuth (Ed.), *Deficits in cognition.* Seattle: Special Child Publications, 1971.

Schifani, J. W. The relationship between the *Illinois Test of Psycholinguistic Abilities* and the *Peabody Language Development Kit* with a select group of intermediate educable mentally retarded children. (Unpublished doctoral dissertation, University of Alabama) *International Dissertation Abstracts*, 1972, **32,** 5076-A.

Sedlak, R. A., & Weener, P. Review of research on the *Illinois Test of Psycholinguistic Abilities*. In L. Mann & D. A. Sabatino, *The first review of special education*. Philadelphia, Pa.: JSE Press, 1973.

Siders, S. K. An analysis of the language growth of selected children in a first grade Title 1 project. (Unpublished doctoral dissertation, Kent State University) *International Dissertation Abstracts*, 1970, **30,** 4158-A.

Smith, J. O. Group language development for educable mental retardates. *Exceptional Children*, 1962, **29,** 95–101.

Spollen, J. C., & Ballif, B. L. Effectiveness of individualized instruction for kindergarten children with a developmental lag. *Exceptional Children*, 1971, **38,** 205–209.

Stearns, K. E. Experimental group language development for psycho-socially deprived preschool children. (Unpublished doctoral dissertation, Indiana University, Bloomington) *International Dissertation Abstracts*, 1967, **27,** 2078-A.

Strickland, J. H. The effect of a parent education program on the language development of underprivileged kindergarten children. (Unpublished doctoral dissertation, George Peabody College) *International Dissertation Abstracts*, 1967, **28,** 1633-A.

Waugh, R. Comparison of revised and experimental editions of the ITPA. *Journal of Learning Disabilities*, 1973, **6,** 236–238.

Wepman, N. N. Auditory discrimination, speech, and reading. *Elementary School Journal*, 1960, **60,** 325–333.

Wiseman, D. E. The effects of an individualized remedial program on mentally retarded children with psycholinguistic disabilities. (Unpublished doctoral dissertation, University of Illinois, Urbana) *International Dissertation Abstracts*, 1965, **26,** 5143-A.

Part 5
FACILITATING LANGUAGE LEARNING

The ultimate challenge for those working with language-disordered children is to help such children communicate through language. A number of issues relevant to this task are considered in the articles reprinted in this part 5 namely, who should be involved in facilitation; the non-linguistic context of facilitation; and techniques for eliciting and maintaining linguistic responses.

Is there an age beyond which language may not be learned? If a critical age for language learning exists, it has considerable importance for those concerned with selecting children who will take part in language intervention programs. The excerpt from Lenneberg (1967) included here deals with the relationship of physical maturation to language learning. Based on observations of language learning in mongoloid children and language recovery of children with acquired aphasia, Lenneberg proposed a critical age for language learning. In a more recent article, which is not reproduced here, Krashen (1973) has reexamined some of the same evidenced and suggested that the age may be even earlier than that hypothesized by Lenneberg. However, Fromkin, Krashen, Curtiss, Rigler, and Rigler (1974) present one exception to this concept: a case study of a child who has begun to learn a first language after the age of puberty. It is not yet clear how, or if, age should be used as a basis for selecting children who might benefit from intervention.

Language learning for most normal children takes place in the home environment. How does the home environment of the language-disordered child compare with that of the normal child, and can the parents of the language-disordered child be used to help in the facilitation of language learning? The article by Wulbert, Inglis, Kriegsmann, and Mills (1975) is one of the few, as well as one of the most complete, published studies of the interactions between mothers and children with language disorders. Both the procedures and the results of this study have possible clinical implications; it is necessary to understand how the child's home environment interacts with language development in order to successfully facilitate language learning. The article by MacDonald, Blott, Gordon, Spiegel, and Hartmann (1974) is an example of a program that has used parents as principal agents in facilitating language learning. It contains an outline of the parent training program and the measures used to evaluate its effectiveness.

The next two articles are concerned with the non-linguistic context of the language learning situation. The excerpt from Itard (1962) points to the necessity of a variety of contexts in facilitating the association between a word and the class of objects referred to by that word, and between these associations and the functions for which the word can be used. The article by Leonard (1975) demonstrates the importance of the non-linguistic contexts when facilitating the learning of early syntactic constructions. These articles illustrate the importance of planning the non-linguistic context that is presented with linguistic forms when attempting to facilitate the induction of language content, form, and use.

Operant conditioning has been widely used both in research with and in the education of language-disordered children. The article by Lovaas, Berberich, Perloff, and Schaeffer (1966) is a classic example of the use of operant conditioning. It specifies in detail the procedures used in such training, and is historically important because Lovaas and his colleagues were among the first to use these procedures for facilitating language in autistic children. The early use of these techniques was based on the premise that imitation and reinforcement were the building blocks of language learning. Although this premise is no longer an adequate account of normal language learning (see, for example, Bloom, Hood, and Lightbown, 1974), its usefulness in facilitating language learning in the language-disordered child has been supported by many individuals in addition to Lovaas, et al., (see, for example, Risley and Wolf, 1967 Whitehurst and Novak, 1973, or Gray and Ryan, 1973). Courtright and Courtright (1976), however, compared imitation training (without reinforcement) with modeling training (also without reinforcement), and found that modeling, where the children listened rather than produced the utterance, was a more effective technique for facilitating language learning (as measured by their ability to use the appropriate form when describing a picture).

With the exception of the selection from Itard, each of these articles is concerned with the auditory-vocal linguistic signal. Alternatives to the use of this modality are the subject of Part VI.

REFERENCES

*Bloom, L. Hood, L., and Lightbown, P. 1974 Imitation in language development: if, when, and why? *Cognitive Psychology, 6,* 380–420.

---

*Reprinted in Bloom, L. 1978 *Readings in language development* N.Y.: J. Wiley & Sons.

Gray, B. B., and Ryan, B. 1973 *A language training program for the non-language child.* Champaign, Ill.: Research Press.

Krashen, S. 1973 Lateralization, language learning and the critical period. *Language Learning, 23,* 63–74.

Risley, T. and Wolf, M. 1967 Establishing functional speech in echolalic children. *Behav. Res. and Therapy, 5,* 73–88.

Whitehurst, G. and Novak, G. 1973 Modeling, imitation training and the acquisition of sentence phrases. *Journal of Experimental Psychology, 16,* 332–345.

Age Limitations to Language Acquisition
Eric H. Lenneberg

AGE AND RECOVERY FROM TRAUMATIC APHASIA

The aphasic symptoms seen in the adult traumatized patient may also be observed in children with comparable lesions. The only possible exception is the so-called fluency aphasia or "logorrhea" in which the patient is either unable or unwilling to inhibit his flow of speech, producing a continuous train of semantically disconnected phrases or sentences. This symptom is rare or perhaps altogether absent among pediatric patients. Otherwise, the general characterization of aphasia as interference with existing verbal habits also applies to this group. However, there are other important differences between children and adult aphasics. If the aphasia occurs early in life, for example, at age four, two processes intermingle so intensely during the recovery period that a rather different clinical picture emerges. The two processes are the interference phenomena caused by the lesion and the extremely active language-learning process that may not be inhibited at all by the disease or may only very temporarily have come to an arrest, soon to be reinstated.

In patients between four and ten years of age, the symptoms are similar to adult symptomatology but there is an extraordinary difference in the prognosis in two ways: the overwhelming majority of these children recover fully and have no aphasic residue in later life (even though some individuals may always retain minor cognitive or perceptual deficits that may or may not be related to language, Teuber, 1950, 1960); and the period during which recovery from aphasia takes place may last much longer than in the adult. Instead of the adult trend toward a five-month period of improvement, children may show steady improvement over a period of several years, but usually not after puberty.

In Table 1 I have compiled 17 published case reports together with eight reports on children either examined personally in Children's Hospital Medical Center of Boston (CHMC) or whose record was made available to me. Only those published reports were included in which the exact age at injury and some information on the rate, progress, and residue of recovery was given and the pathology was lateralized. Apparently, aphasia runs a different course before the end of the first decade than after it. Neither in these cases nor in those published cases omitted here because of incomplete information on recovery is there any record of permanent residue from acquired unilateral, aphasia-producing lesions incurred during early childhood. If

From E. Lenneberg, *The Biological Foundations of Language*, New York: John Wiley & Sons, 1967, pp 145–157; 309–312. Reprinted by permission of John Wiley & Sons, Inc.

language had developed before the onset of the disease and if the lesion is confined to a single hemisphere, language will invariably return to a child if he is less than nine years old at the time of the catastrophe.

If aphasia strikes the very young during or immediately after the age at which language is acquired (between 20 and 36 months of age), the recovery is yet different. Cerebral trauma to the two or three year old will render the patient totally unresponsive, sometimes for weeks at a time; when he becomes cognizant of his environment again, it becomes clear that whatever beginning he had made in language before the disease is totally lost, but soon he will start again on the road toward language acquisition traversing all stages of infant vocalization, perhaps at a slightly faster pace, beginning with babbling, single words, primitive two-word phrases, etc., until perfect speech is achieved. In the very young, then, the primary process in recovery is *acquisition,* whereas the process of symptom-reduction is not in evidence.

Between the ages of three and four, language learning and language interference may compete for a few weeks, but within a short period of time, the aphasic handicap is overcome. In patients older than four and younger than ten, the clinical picture is that of a typical aphasia which gradually subsides. At the same time, the child appears to have no difficulty expanding his vocabulary and learning new and complex grammatical constructions.

By the time of puberty, a turning point is reached. Aphasias that develop from this age on or that have not had time to clear up completely by this stage, commonly leave some trace behind which the patient cannot overcome. These youngsters characteristically regain language and can carry on a conversation; but there will be odd hesitation pauses, searching for words, or the utterance of an inappropriate word or sound sequence that cannot be inhibited. Emotional tension magnifies the symptoms, making their aphasic nature very obvious. In the middle teens, the prognosis for recovery rapidly becomes the same as that for the adult patient.

Before we can accept these clinical findings as pertinent specifically to language (they may reflect merely a general facility to adjust to disease and handicaps during childhood), it is necessary to adduce evidence that the difference between childhood aphasia and adult aphasia is related to (1) speech-specific lateralized lesions in the brain, and (2) that it reflects a potential for speech-specific physiological readjustment which ceases to function after puberty.

AGE OF LATERALIZATION OF SPEECH FUNCTION IN THE BRAIN

We have previously referred to the phenomenon of cerebral dominance; ordinarily the left hemisphere is more directly involved in speech and language functions than the right, though the lesser hemisphere is not passive with respect to verbal communication. How obligatory is this lateralization with its shift of language function to the left hemisphere? Important clues to this problem are given by a study of massive lesions to either of the hemispheres incurred in early life.

Basser (1962) has contributed the most important study in this respect. His data are shown in Tables 2 and 3. Apparently, there is a period in infancy at which the hemispheres are still equipotential. In roughly half of the children with brain lesions sustained during the first two years of life, the onset of speech development is somewhat delayed; however, the other half of this population begins to speak at the

Table 1 Recovery from Aphasic Symptoms

Patients Age at Insult (Years)	Residual Deficit Remained After:			Etiology or Pathology	Comments	Source and Identification of Case
	3 months	1 year	2 or more years			
1 8/12	+	+	0	Trauma, L hemisphere worse than R	Complete speech loss; new onset 16 months later. L hemispherectomy at 12 followed by aphasia clearing within 9 months postoperative	Basser (1962) 28
2	+	+	0	Diphtheria with convulsions		Basser (1962) 1
2 4/12	+	0	—	Measles followed by right-sided spasm and hemiplegia		Bateman (1890)
3	+	+	0	Trauma followed by CVA. left		CHMC 63
4	+	0	0	Trauma, L forehead		Gutmann (1942) TP
4	?+	?0	—	Abscess, L temporal lobe with operative evacuation to internal capsule	Last follow-up 8 weeks postoperative. Child steadily improving but speech not yet normal	Brunner and Stengel (1932)
5	+	+	0	Sudden hemiplegia of unknown origin		Basser (1962) XII

				Cause	Comments	Reference
6	+	0	0	Ruptured aneurysm, left		CHMC 34
6	0	0	0	Sudden hemiplegia of unknown origin		Basser (1962) I
6	0	0	0	Trauma, left side		Gutmann (1942) AC
6	0	0	0	Trauma, left side		Gutmann (1942) JK
6	+	—	—	Meningo-encephalopathy	Satisfactory improvement reported but follow-up not clear	Branco-Lefevre (1950) MR
6	+	0	0	Trauma, left temporo-parietal		Andre-Thomas et al. (1935)
7	+	0	0	CVA R. hemisphere (confirmed by arteriogram)		CHMC 39
7	+	0	0	Unknown	Comprehension and expression deteriorating over 3-month period, followed by slow improvement over 9 months	Poetzl (1926)
8	+	0	0	Trauma, left temporal		CHMC 00
8	+	+	0	CVA, left		CHMC 51
9	+	+	+	?, Convulsions with hemiplegia	Permanent residue	Basser (1962) III
10	+	0	0	Trauma, left		Gutmann JJ
11	+	0	0	Trauma, left, probably followed by CVA		CHMC 63

Table 1   Recovery from Aphasic Symptoms   Continued

Patients Age at Insult (Years)	Residual Deficit Remained After:			Etiology or Pathology	Comments	Source and Identification of Case
	3 months	1 year	2 or more years			
11	+	+	+	Left otogenic abscess	Mild permanent residue: hesitation and grammatical mistakes	Gutmann (1942) JW
12	+	?0	?0	Trauma, left	No follow-up but substantial though slow improvement reported	Branco-Lefevre (1950) AJ
14	+	+	+	Trauma, left	Slight aphasic symptoms, permanent: marked agraphia and alexia, permanent	Branco-Lefevre (1950) MCS
15	+	+	+	Tumor, left parietal	Receptive aphasia preoperative; jargon aphasia postoperative, clearing within 9 months; other aphasic symptoms unchanged 2 years postoperative	CHMC 14
18	+	+	+	Trauma, left temporo-parietal	Marked aphasia, permanent	CHMC 70

+ = reported present
− = reported absent
? = report not clear

0 = no specific report but restoration of language is implied in article
CHMC = Children's Hospital Medical Center. Boston (unpublished case)

Table 2   Lesions Before Onset of Speech

	Onset of Speech		
	Normal	Delayed	Never
Left hemisphere	18	15	1
Right hemisphere	19	15	4

Based on Basser, 1962.

usual time. This distribution is the same for children with left hemisphere lesions as with right ones, indicating that during the first two years of life cerebral dominance is not yet well established. A lesion in the left hemisphere is apparently sufficient cause to confine the language function to the right side. At the beginning of language development both hemispheres seem to be equally involved; the dominance phenomenon seems to come about through a progressive decrease in involvement of the right hemisphere. If, however, the left hemisphere is not functioning properly, the physiological activities of the right hemisphere persist in their earlier function.

From Table 3 it is clear that by the time the child has matured into the stage at which language acquisition is possible and from that time on, left-sided cerebral dominance is manifest in a large proportion of children. Left-sided lesions result in speech disturbances in 85% of the cases, whereas right-sided lesions disturb speech only 45% of the time. All speech disturbances, as mentioned previously, are overcome in less than two years' time. In the adult, right-sided lesions cause aphasia only in about 3% of all patients; most of these patients are left-handed (further discussion and literature in Ajuriaguerra, 1957, and Zangwill, 1960).

HEMISPHERECTOMY (THE EFFECT OF REMOVAL OF AN ENTIRE HEMISPHERE):

At times it becomes necessary to remove an entire hemisphere surgically. This is most frequently done on patients with uncontrollable seizures originating from one hemisphere, but occasionally it is also performed in the surgical treatment of large, infiltrating tumors (Laine and Gros, 1956). Again we are indebted to Basser (1962) for a complete survey of the literature and a substantial contribution of case histories from his own practice. The material is summarized in Table 4. We see that the conse-

Table 3   Lesions After Onset of Speech and Before Age 10

	After Catastrophe Speech was:	
	Normal	Disturbed
Left hemisphere	2	13
Right hemisphere	8	7

Based on Basser, 1962.

quences of a left hemispherectomy depend upon the age at which the original insult was incurred. If the child had a lesion in infancy, regardless of side, speech function was eventually confined to the healthy hemisphere, so that when the diseased hemisphere had to be removed later in life, it caused no aphasia. In this group (lesions acquired in childhood), about 80% of the operations were performed sometime after age ten and the remainder in adult life.

However, patients who acquired their lesions in later life, and who had hemispherectomy subsequently, had permanent aphasic symptoms if the operation was done on the left side and no aphasia if it was on the right side.

There is only one case where the lesion was acquired during the early teens (Hillier, 1954), and a left hemispherectomy was performed at age fourteen. According to personal communication from Dr. Hillier, this patient had a global aphasia following the operation but within eight months could make himself understood fairly well, although gross speech deficits remained. He lived for another 19 months during which no further speech improvements were noted, and it became clear that a stable language deficit had been established. He died 27 months after his hemispherectomy due to recurrence of tumor (glioblastoma multiforme) which had invaded the brainstem.

PRELIMINARY SUMMARY

The outlook for recovery from aphasia varies with age. The chance for recovery has a natural history. This natural history is the same as the natural history of cerebral

Table 4   Hemispherectomy

Lesions Acquired	Hemisphere Operated On	Speech Not Affected or Improved Postoperatively	Permanent Aphasia
Before teens*	Left	49	3 (had aphasia before operation)
	Right	38	5 (had aphasia before operation)
During puberty† (single case)	Left	Slow improvement	Some residue to end of life (27 months postop.)
Adult*	Left	None	6 (1 had aphasia before operation)
	Right	25	None

*Based on Basser, 1962.
†Hillier, 1954 and personal communication.

lateralization of function. Aphasia is the result of direct, structural, and local interference with neurophysiological processes of language. In childhood such interference cannot be permanent because the two sides are not yet sufficiently specialized for function, even though the left hemisphere may already show signs of speech dominance. Damage to it will interfere with language; but the right hemisphere is *still* involved to some extent with language, and so there is a potential for language function that may be strengthened again. In the absence of pathology, a polarization of function between right and left takes place during childhood, displacing language entirely to the left and certain other functions predominantly to the right (Ajuriaguerra, 1957; Hécaen and Ajuriaguerra, 1963; Teuber, 1962). If, however, a lesion is placed in either hemisphere, this polarization cannot take place, and language function together with other functions persist in the unharmed hemisphere.

Notice that the earlier the lesion is incurred, the brighter is the outlook for language. Hence, we infer that *language learning* can take place, at least in the right hemisphere, only between the age of two to about thirteen. That this is probably also true of the left hemisphere follows from observations on language development in the retarded and in the congenitally deaf, discussed subsequently.

A unique pathological study of congenital aphasia was reported by Landau, Goldstein, and Kleffner (1960). This was a child who died of heart disease at age ten. This patient, in contrast to the cases discussed so far, had not begun to develop speech until age six or seven. At that time, he was enrolled in a class for congenitally aphasic children at the Central Institute for the Deaf. By age ten, the authors report, he had acquired considerable useful language. A postmortem examination of the brain revealed bilateral areas of cortical destruction around the sylvian fissure in the area of the central sulcus, together with severe retrograde degeneration in the medial geniculate nuclei deep in the brain. The authors conclude that "Language function therefore appears to have been subserved by pathways other than the primary auditory thalamocortical projection system." I am citing this case to illustrate the far-reaching plasticity of the human brain (or lack of cortical specialization) with respect to language during the *early* years of life. There is clinical evidence that similar lesions in a mature individual would have produced severe and irreversible defects in reception and production of speech and language.

The implication of this discussion is that the brain at birth and during the subsequent maturation process may be influenced in its normal course of organization which usually results in the specialization of areas. This is not a tabula rasa concept of the brain which would propose that any arbitrary reorganization is possible.

Postnatal cerebral organization has recently been demonstrated in cats (Scharlock, Tucker, and Strominger, 1963) who ablated auditory cortex in neonate kittens with control ablations on mature cats. When the kittens matured, they had no difficulty in learning to make auditory discriminations, which the older individuals after an identical postoperative waiting period could no longer perform. Comparable investigations on other sensory or motor functions and different cortical locations have been reported by Benjamin and Thompson (1959), Brooks and Peck (1940), Harlow, Akert, and Schiltz (1964), Doty (1953), and others. In short, various kinds of postnatal cortical ablations leave no or very minor deficit, whereas comparable ablations in later stages of development result in irreversible symptoms.

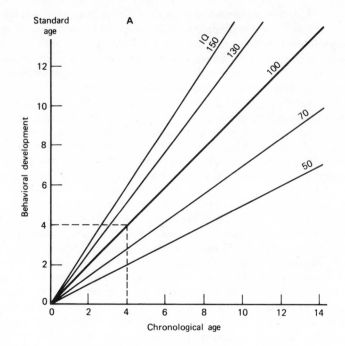

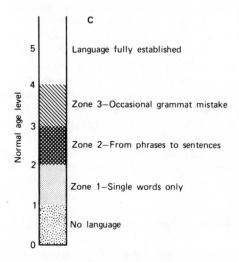

Figure 1.   Ideally, IQ-figures should remain constant through-out life as shown in *A;* in reality, however, they tend to fluctuate and the test-retest discrepancies are most marked in exception-ally high and low cases. In the mentally retarded, the IQ tends to decay fairly predictably as shown in *B*. The acquisition of

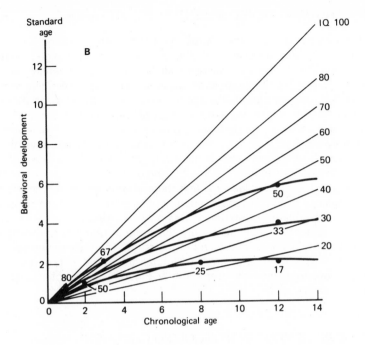

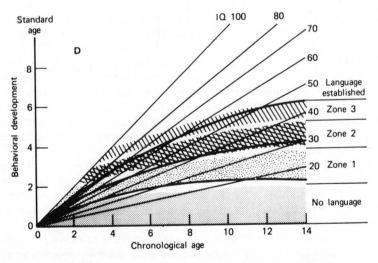

language proceeds through fixed developmental stages shown as zones in *C. D* shows the empirically determined relationship between nonverbal IQ and language development. After age twelve to thirteen, language development tends to "freeze." (Data based on a follow-up study of 61 mongoloid children and 23 children with other types of retarding disease.)

ARREST OF LANGUAGE DEVELOPMENT IN THE RETARDED

The material reviewed might give the impression that the age limitation is primarily due to better recovery from disease in childhood and that the language limitations are only a secondary effect. This is probably not so. In a study by Lenneberg, Nichols, and Rosenberger (1964), 54 Mongoloids (all raised at home) were seen two to three times a year over a three-year period. The age range was from 6 months to 22 years. The appearance of motor milestones and the onset of speech differed considerably from individual to individual, but all made some progress—although very slow in many cases—before they reached their early teens. This was true of motor development as well as of speech. In all children seen in this study, stance, gait, and fine coordination of hands and fingers was acquired before the end of the first decade. At the close of the study, 75% had reached at least the first stage of language development; they had a small vocabulary and could execute simple spoken commands. But interestingly enough, progress in language development was only recorded in children younger than fourteen. Cases in their later teens were the same in terms of their language development at the beginning as at the end of the study. The observation seems to indicate that even in the absence of gross structural brain lesions, progress in language learning comes to a standstill after maturity. Figure 1 is a graphic illustration of the empirical findings.

LANGUAGE DEVELOPMENT IN MONGOLOID CHILDREN

There are several different causes for mental retardation, and each disease has its typical manifestations. Nevertheless, the development of language, insofar as it occurs at all in these patients, follows some general laws of evolvement which may be traced among all of these conditions and which, indeed, are not different in nature from the unfolding of language in healthy children. Among the retarded the entire developmental process is merely slowed down or stretched out during childhood and is regularly arrested during the early teens. This affords the opportunity to study language development in slow motion, and the developmental arrest at puberty produces "frozen" primitive stages which are inalterable at that age by further training.

The study of children with Mongolism offers certain advantages for research. The condition may be spotted at birth. Victims have a relatively good chance of reaching middle age. The condition is common. The patient population is relatively homogeneous, and a large number of patients are taken care of at home and grow up in a normal social environment.

It is thought that Mongoloid stigmata are manifestations of slowed or incomplete embryological development, apparently due to a chromosomal, intracellular disorder. In the process of postnatal maturation, some but not all of the signs of immaturity gradually disappear. With increasing age, structure, physiology, and behavior tend toward the norm, but all developmental facets progress at markedly slowed rates. In some areas, development is arrested at a level corresponding to three- or four-year-old children in the normal population, whereas in other areas development continues to stages comparable to adolescence.

A large proportion of Mongoloids pass their motor milestones with only mild delay, and menarche and secondary sexual characteristics appear in the midteens. Yet these individuals may never learn to make any social discriminations, to write more than a few words, or to change money. The order in which developmental tasks are mastered is disarranged by differential slowing; those tasks which depend on common sense seem to suffer most.

Lenneberg, Nichols, and Rosenberger (1964) studied, over a three-year period, sixty-one Mongoloid children who were all raised by their own parents and were living at home. The children were examined periodically, the frequency of the visits differing in accordance with the patient's stage of development. Data consisted of medical history, neurological examination, psychological testing, tape recording of spontaneous utterances made while playing, performance on an articulation test and a sentence-repetition test; and assessments of vocabulary, understanding of commands, and nature of vocalization.

An interesting question concerns the role of intelligence in the acquisition of language. Is mastery of this, in a sense, highly abstract behavior dependent upon measurable intelligence? The problem is complicated (1) by the definition of intelligence and (2) by the changing intelligence quotients with chronological age among the feebleminded. An individual whose cognitive status remains constant on a level comparable to that of the normal three-year-old appears to have a steadily falling IQ

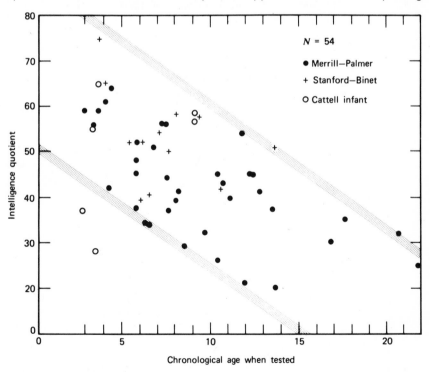

Figure 2.   **Relationship between chronological age and IQ in 54 Mongoloid children.**

throughout childhood due to the peculiar way in which this figure is computed. The situation is well-illustrated in the scattergram of Figure 2. (Compare also Zeaman and House, 1962.) The study of the mongoloid population, as well as that of additional cases of mental retardation, indicates that there is a certain "IQ threshold value" that varies with age and that must be attained for language to be acquired. Individuals below this threshold have varying degrees of language primitivity, as illustrated in Figure 1. It is noteworthy that this threshold is relatively low. If we take a population whose IQ is at or just above threshold, which is the case of Mongoloids, intelligence figures correlate quite poorly with language development. Only if we confine our observations to the low grades of feeblemindedness can a relationship between intelligence and language learning be established.

Among the Mongoloids, whose prognosis for mental development is not the worst, chronological age is a much better predictor for language development than computed IQs.

The relationship between physical maturation and language development has been treated earlier. Relevant to the same topic is Table 5. (The criteria for "language developing" was the predominance of words and phrases in all utterances and absence or at most a modicum of random babbling.) The relationship between development of gait and of language appears to be roughly similar to that of normal children;

Table 5   Relationship Between Stages of Language Development and Various Aspects of Motor Skill*

	Language Development		
	Mostly Babble	Language Developing	Total
Motor skill			
Walk and run	14	39	53
Toddle or less	7	1	8
Total	21	40	61
	$X^2 = 8.94$	$P < 0.01$	
Dress self	4	27	31
Need help dressing	17	13	30
Total	21	40	61
	$X^2 = 12.93$	$P < 0.001$	
Feed self well	11	35	46
Feed self poorly	10	5	15
Total	21	40	61
	$X^2 = 7.36$	$P < 0.01$	
Are right-handed	6	23	29
Are left-handed	3	3	6
Are ambidextrous	3	3	6
Have no determined handedness	9	11	20
Total	21	40	61

*Entries are number of subjects. Yate's correction was used.

there is greater likelihood for language acquisition after gait is established than before. The development of hand preference is particularly interesting. Right-handedness emerges at the time that language unfolds, even though this occurs at a considerably later time than in normal children.

REFERENCES

Ajuriaguerra, J. de (1957). Langage et dominance cérébrale. *J. Français d'Oto-Rhino-Laryngol.* **6:**489–499.

André-Thomas, Sorrel, E. and Sorrel-Dejerine, Mme., Un cas d'aphasie motrice par traumatisme craniocerebral chez l'enfant. *Rev. Neurol.* **63:**893–896.

Basser, L. S. (1962), Hemiplegia of early onset and the faculty of speech with special reference to the effects of hemispherectomy, *Brain* **85:**427–460.

Bateman, F. (1890), *On Aphasia, or Loss of Speech, and the Localisation of the Faculty of Articulate Language.* (2nd ed.) Churchill, London.

Benjamin, R. M. and Thompson, R. F. (1959), Differential effects of cortical lesions in infant and adult cats on roughness discrimination. *Exp. Neurol.* **1:**305–321.

Branco-LeFèvre, A. F. (1950), Contribuição para o estudo da psicopatologia da afasia em criança, *Arq. Neuropsiquiat.* (São Paulo) **8:**345–393.

Brooks, C. and Peek, M. E. (1940), Effect of various cortical lesions on development of placing and hopping reactions in rats, *J. Neurophysiol.* **3:**66–73.

Brunner, H. and Stengel, E. (1932), Zur Lehre von den Aphasien im Kindesalter, *Z. Neur. Psychiat.* **142:**430–450.

Doty, R. W. (1953), Effects of ablation of visual cortex in neonatal and adult cats, *Abstracts Comm. XIX Int. Physiol. Congr.,* p. 316.

Gutmann, E. (1942), Aphasia in children, *Brain* **65:**205–219.

Harlow, H. F., Akert, K., and Schiltz, K. A. (1964), The effects of bilateral prefrontal lesions on learned behavior of neonatal, infant, and preadolescent monkeys, in *The Frontal Granular Cortex and Behavior.* J. M. Warren and K. Akert (Eds.), McGraw-Hill, New York.

Hécaen. H. and Ajuriaguerra, J. de (1963), *Les Gauchers, Prévalence Manuelle et Dominance Cérébrale.* Presses Universitaires de France, Paris.

Hillier, W. F.. Jr. (1954), Total left cerebral hemispherectomy for malignant glioma, *Neurology* **4:**718–721.

Laine, E. and Gros, C. (1956), *L'Hémispherectomie,* Masson, Paris.

Landau, W. M., Goldstein, R., and Kleffner, F. R. (1960), Congenital aphasia; a clinicopathologic study, *Neurology* **10:**915–921.

Lenneberg, E. H., Nichols, I. A., and Rosenberger, E. F. (1964), Primitive stages of language development in mongolism, in *Disorders of Communication Vol. XLII: Research Publications,* A.R.N.M.D. Williams and Wilkins, Baltimore, Maryland.

Marks, M., Taylor M., and Rusk, H. A. (1957), Rehabilitation of the aphasic patient, *Neurology* **7:**837–843.

Poetzl, O. (1926), Ueber sensorische Aphasie im Kindesalter, *Z. Hals- N.-Ohrenhlk.* **14:**190–216.

Russell, W. R. and Espir, M. L. E. (1961), *Traumatic Aphasia,* Oxford University Press, Oxford, England.

Scharlock, D. P., Tucker, T. J., and Strominger, N. L. (1963), Auditory discrimination by the cat after neonatal ablation of temporal cortex, *Science* **141** (Sept. 20):1197–1198.

Teuber, H.-L. (1962), Effects of brain wounds implicating right or left hemisphere in man: hemisphere differences and hemisphere interaction in vision, audition, and somesthesis, in *Interhemispheric Relations and Cerebral Dominance*, pp. 131–157. V. B. Mountcastle (ed.), Johns Hopkins Press, Baltimore.

Woodward, F. R. (1945). Recovery from aphasia; report of two cases, *Bull. Los Angeles Neurol. Soc.* **10:** 73–75.

Zangwill, O. L. (1960), *Cerebral Dominance and its Relation to Psychological Function.* Oliver and Boyd, Edinburgh.

Zeaman, D. and House, B. J. (1962), Mongoloid MA is proportional to log CA. *Child Development* **33:** 481–488.

The Development of Language in Genie: A Case of Language Acquisition beyond the "Critical Period"[1,2]

Victoria Fromkin

Stephen Krashen

Susan Curtiss

David Rigler

Marilyn Rigler

The present paper reports on a case of a now 16-year-old girl who for most of her life suffered an extreme degree of social isolation and experiential deprivation. It summarizes her language acquisition which is occurring past the hypothesized "critical period" and the implications of this language development as related to hemispheric maturation and the development of lateralization. The results of a series of dichotic listening tests administered to her are included.

When Descartes observed that ". . . there are none so depraved and stupid, without even excepting idiots, that they cannot arrange different words together, forming of them a statement by which they make known their thoughts," he did not consider children who are denied, for a multiplicity of reasons, language input in their formative years. Despite the wide range of views on the subject of language acquisition, there is unanimity on one aspect. Neither the empiricist who believes with Locke that we are born with a mental "tabula rasa" with all language the result of "experience," nor the rationalist who supports the Descartian position of a complex, highly specific, innate language mechanism denies that certain environmental conditions are neces-

From *Brain and Language, 1,* 81–107 (1974). Reprinted by permission of Academic Press, Inc.

[1] The research reported on in this paper was supported in part by a grant from the National Institutes of Mental Health. U.S. Department of Health, Education and Welfare, No. MH-21191-03

[2] This is a combined and expanded version of a number of papers presented before the American Psychological Association, the Linguistic Society of America, the Acoustical Society of America, and the American Speech and Hearing Association, including S. Curtiss (1972); Curtiss et al. (1972, 1973); Krashen et al. (1972a, 1972b); Fromkin (1972); D. Rigler (1972).

sary for the acquisition of language. One need not attempt to replicate the apochryphal experiments conducted by Psammeticus or that of the Scottish King John to know that children will not learn any language when deprived of all linguistic input.[3] The cases of children reared in environments of extreme social isolation attest to this.

Ten such children are mentioned by Carl Linneaus in his *System of Nature* published in 1735, and are included by Linnaeus under his subdivision of Homo Sapiens which he called Homo Ferus (Wild Man). One of the defining characteristics of Homo Ferus, according to Linnaeus, was his inability to speak. All the cases of isolated children reported in the literature since his time show this to be a correct observation.

In the 18th century, the interest in such cases was stimulated by the struggle between the "geneticists" and the "environmentalists," and figured sharply in the debate over the theory of innate ideas. The different views continue to be debated today in somewhat different (perhaps more sophisticated) forms. [See, for example, Skinner (1957), Chomsky (1962), Katz and Bever, (1973), Bever (1970), Lenneberg, (1967); see also the *Synthese* Symposium on Innate Ideas, Vol. 17, No. 1, March 1967, pp. 1–28].

Despite the continuing interest, the study of children reared under conditions of social isolation and sensory deprivation represents a relatively inaccessible area of scientific research. Such children include those who are reported to have undergone a significant period of their development alone in the wilderness or to have been reared with wild animals (Itard, 1962; Singh and Zingg, 1966). The most celebrated of such cases is that of Victor, the "Wild Boy of Aveyron" (Itard, 1962). In addition, there have been studies of children reared within the confines of institutional life (e.g., Spitz, 1949; Dennis and Najarian, 1957; Clarke and Clarke, 1960), and of children whose isolation has been associated with congenital or acquired sensory loss (e.g., Howe and Hall, 1903; Dahl, 1965; Fraiberg and Freedman, 1964). Yet another category is that of children whose isolation resulted from deliberate effort to keep them from normal social intercourse (Von Feuerbach, 1833; Mason, 1942; Davis, 1940, 1947; Freedman and Brown 1968; Koluchova, 1972).

The case discussed in this paper is that of a child who falls into the last category. Genie, the subject of this study, is an adolescent girl who for most of her life underwent a degree of social isolation and experiential deprivation not previously reported in contemporary scientific history. It is a unique case because the other children reported on in contemporary literature were isolated for much shorter periods and emerged from their isolation at much younger ages than did Genie. The only studies

---

[3] In the 5th century B.C., the Greek historian Herodotus reported that the Egyptian Pharaoh Psammetichus (664–610 B.C.) sought to determine the most primitive "natural" language by placing two infants in an isolated mountain hut to be cared for by a servant who was cautioned not to speak in their presence on pain of death. According to the story, the first word uttered was "bekos," the Phrygian word for "bread," convincing the Pharaoh that this was the original language. James IV (1473–1513) of Scotland is reported to have attempted the same "experiment." The Scottish children, however, were said by John to "Spak very guid Ebrew." Two hundred years before James, the Holy Roman Emperor Frederick II of Hohenstaufen was said to have carried out a similar test but the children died before they spoke at all.

of children isolated for periods of time somewhat comparable to that of this case are those of Victor (Itard, 1962) and Kaspar Hauser (Singh and Zingg, 1966).

All cases of such children reveal that experiential deprivation results in a retarded state of development. An important question for scientists of many disciplines is whether a child so deprived can "catch up" wholly or in part. The answer to this question depends on many factors including the developmental state achieved prior to deprivation, the duration, quality, and intensity of the deprivation, and the early biological adequacy of the isolated child. In addition, the ability of such "recupera-tion" is closely tied to whether there is a "critical period" beyond which learning cannot take place. The concept of a "critical period" during which certain innately determined faculties can develop derived from experimental embryology. It is hypothesized that should the necessary internal or external conditions be absent during this period, certain developmental abilities will be impossible.

Lenneberg (1967) presents the most specific statement about critical periods in man as it concerns the acquisition of language. He starts with the assumption that language is innately determined, that its acquisition is dependent upon both neces-sary neurological events and some unspecified minimal exposure to language. He suggests that this critical period lasts from about age two to puberty: language acquisition is impossible before two due to maturational factors, and after puberty because of the loss of "cerebral plasticity" caused by the completion of the develop-ment of cerebral dominance, or lateralized specialization of the language function.

The case of Genie is directly related to this question, since Genie was already pubescent at the time of her discovery, and it is to this question that the discussion is primarily directed. The case also has relevance for other linguistic questions such as those concerning distinctions between the comprehension and production of language, between linguistic competence and performance, and between cognition and language.

There are many questions for which we still have no answers. Some we may never have. Others must await the future developments of this remarkable child. The case history as presented is therefore an interim report.

CASE HISTORY

Genie was first encountered when she was 13 years, 9 months. At the time of her discovery and hospitalization she was an unsocialized, primitive human being, emo-tionally disturbed, unlearned, and without language. She had been taken into protec-tive custody by the police and, on November 4, 1970, was admitted into the Childrens Hospital of Los Angeles for evaluation with a tentative diagnosis of severe malnutrition. She remained in the Rehabilitation Center of the hospital until August 13, 1971. At that time she entered a foster home where she has been living ever since as a member of the family.

When admitted to the hospital, Genie was a painfully thin child with a distended abdomen who appeared to be six or seven years younger that her age. She was 54.5 inches tall and weighed 62.25 pounds. She was unable to stand erect, could not chew solid or even semi-solid foods, had great difficulty in swallowing, was inconti-nent of feces and urine, and was mute.

The tragic and bizarre story which was uncovered revealed that for most of her life

Genie suffered physical and social restriction, nutritional neglect, and extreme experiential deprivation. There is evidence that from about the age of 20 months until shortly before admission to the hospital Genie had been isolated in a small closed room, tied into a potty chair where she remained most or all hours of the day, sometimes overnight. A cloth harness, constructed to keep her from handling her feces was her only apparel of wear. When not strapped into the chair she was kept in a covered infant crib, also confined from the waist down. The door to the room was kept closed, and the windows were curtained. She was hurriedly fed (only cereal and baby food) and minimally cared for by her mother, who was almost blind during most of the years of Genie's isolation. There was no radio or TV in the house, and the father's intolerance of noise of any kind kept any acoustic stimuli which she received behind the closed door to a minimum. (The first child born to this family died from peneumonia when three months old after being put in the garage because of noisy crying.) Genie was physically punished by the father if she made any sounds. According to the mother, the father and older brother never spoke to Genie, although they barked at her like dogs. The mother was forbidden to spend more than a few minutes with Genie during feeding.

It is not the purpose of this paper to attempt to explain the psychotic behavior of the parents which created this tragic life for Genie, nor to relate the circumstances which led to the discovery. [See Hansen (1972); D. Rigler (1972).] It is reported that Genie's father regarded her as a hopelessly retarded child who was destined to die at a young age and convinced the mother of this. His prediction was based at least in part on Genie's failure to walk at a normal age. Genie was born with a congenital dislocation of the hips which was treated in the first year by the application of a Frejka pillow splint to hold both legs in abduction, and the father placed the blame for her "retardation" on this device.

On the basis of what is known about the early history, and what has been observed so far, it appears that Genie was normal at the time of birth and that the retardation observed at the time of discovery was due principally to the extreme isolation to which she was subjected, with its accompanying social, perceptual, and sensory deprivation. Very little evidence exists to support a diagnosis of early brain damage, primary mental deficiency, or infantile autism. On the other hand, there is abundant evidence of gross environmental impoverishment and of psychopathological behavior on the part of the parents. This is revealed to some extent in Genie's history and equally by the dramatic changes that have occurred since her emergence. [See D. Rigler (1972); M. Rigler (1972).]

Genie's birth was relatively normal. She was born in April, 1957, delivered by Caesarian section. Her birth problems included an Rh negative incompatibility for which she was exchange transfused (no sequelae were noted), and the hip dislocation spoken of above. Genie's development was otherwise initially normal. At birth she weighed 7 pounds, 7.5 ounces. By three months she had gained 4.5 pounds. According to the pediatrician's report, at 6 months, she was doing well and taking food well. At 11 months she was still within normal limits. At 14 months Genie developed an acute illness and was seen by another pediatrician. The only other medical visit occurred when Genie was just over 3.5 years of age.

From the meager medical records at our disposal, then, there is no indication of early retardation. After admission to the hospital, Genie underwent a number of medical diagnostic tests. Radiology reported a "moderate coxa valga deformity of both hips and a narrow rib cage" but no abnormality of the skull. The bone age was reported as approximately 11 years. Simple metabolic disorders were ruled out. The neurologist found no evidence of neurological disease. The electroencephalographic records reported a "normal waking record." A chromosomal analysis was summarized as being "apparently normal."

During the first few months of her hospitalization, additional consultations were undertaken. The conclusion from among all of these evaluative efforts may be summarized briefly. Functionally Genie was an extremely retarded child, but her behavior was unlike that of other mentally defective children. Neither, apparently, was she autistic. Although emotionally disturbed behavior was evident, there was no discernible evidence of physical or mental disease that would otherwise account for her retarded behavior. It therefore seems plausible to explain her retardation as due to the intensity and duration of her psycho-social and physical deprivation.

The dramatic changes that have occurred since Genie's emergence reinforce this conclusion. Approximately four weeks after her admission to the hospital a consultant described a contrast between her admission status and what he later observed [Shurley (personal communication)]. He wrote that on admission Genie

> was pale, thin, ghost-like, apathetic, mute and socially unresponsive. But now she had become alert, bright-eyed, engaged readily in simple social play with balloons, flashlight, and toys, with familiar and unfamiliar adults . . . . She exhibits a lively curiosity, good eye-hand coordination, adequate hearing and vision, and emotional responsivity . . . . She reveals much stimulus hunger . . . . Despite her muteness . . . Genie does not otherwise use autistic defenses, but has ample latent affect and responses. There is no obvious evidence of cerebral damage or intellectual stenosis—only severe (extreme) and prolonged experiential, social and sensory isolation and deprivation during her infancy and childhood . . . . Genie may be regarded as one of the most extreme and prolonged cases of such deprivation to come to light in this century, and as such she is an "experiment in nature."

GENIE'S LINGUISTIC DEVELOPMENT

Important elements in Genie's history are still unknown and may never be known. We have no reliable information about early linguistic developments or even the extent of language input. One version has it that Genie began to speak words prior to her isolation and then ceased. Another is that she simply never acquired language at all beyond the level observed on hospital entry. One thing is definite; when Genie was discovered she did not speak. On the day after admission to the hospital she was seen by Dr. James Kent who reports (Kent, 1972):

> Throughout this period she retained saliva and fre-

quently spit it out into a paper towel or into her pajama top. *She made no other sounds except for a kind of throaty whimper* . . . . (Later in the session) . . . she imitated "back" several times, as well as "fall" when I said "The puppet will fall." . . . She could communicate (her) needs non-verbally, at least to a limited extent . . . . Apart from a peculiar laugh, frustration was the only other clear affective behavior we could discern . . . . When very angry she would scratch at her own face, blow her nose violently into her clothes and often void urine. During these tantrums *there was no vocalization* . . . . We felt that the eerie silence that accompanied these reactions was probably due to the fact that she had been whipped by her father when she made noise.

At the outset of our linguistic observations, it was not clear whether Genie's inability to talk was the result solely of physiological and/or emotional factors. We were unable to determine the extent of her language comprehension during the early periods. Within a few days she began to respond to the speech of others and also to imitate single words. Her responses did not, however, reveal how heavily she was dependent on nonverbal, extra-linguistic cues such as "tone of voice, gestures, hints, guidance, facial and bodily expressions" (Bellugi and Klima, 1971). To determine the extent of her language comprehension, it was necessary to devise tests in which all extra-linguistic cues were eliminated.[4] If the comprehension tests administered showed that Genie did comprehend what was said to her, using linguistic information alone, we could assume that she had some knowledge of English, or had acquired some linguistic "competence." In that case, the task facing Genie would not be one of language learning but of learning how to use that knowledge—adding a performance modality—to produce speech. If the tests, on the other hand, in addition to her inability to speak, showed that she had little ability to understand what was said to her when all extra-linguistic cues were eliminated, she would be faced with true first-language acquisition.

LINGUISTIC COMPREHENSION

The administration of the comprehension tests which we constructed had to wait until Genie was willing and able to cooperate. It was necessary to develop tests which would not require verbal responses since it was her comprehension, not her active production of speech, to be tested at this state. The first controlled test was administered in September, 1971, almost 11 months after Genie's emergence. Prior to these tests Genie revealed a growing ability to understand and produce individual words and names. This ability was a necessary precursor to an investigation of her comprehension of grammatical structure, but did not in itself reveal how much language she

---

[4] The tests were designed, administered and analyzed by S. Curtiss.

knew since the ability to relate the sounds and meanings of individual lexical items, while necessary, is not a sufficient criterion for language competence.

It was quite evident that at the beginning of the testing period Genie could understand individual words which she did not utter herself, but, except for such words, she had little if any comprehension of grammatical structures. Genie was thus faced with the complex task of primary language acquisition with a post-pubescent brain. There was no way that a prediction could be made as to whether she could or would accomplish this task. Furthermore, if she did not learn language it would be impossible to determine the reasons. One cannot draw conclusions about children of this kind who fail to develop. One can, however, draw at least some conclusions from the fact that Genie has been acquiring language at this late age. The evidence for this fact is revealed in the results of the 17 different comprehension tests which have been administered almost weekly over the last two years. A slow but steady development is taking place. We are still, of course, unable to predict how much of the adult grammar she will acquire.

Among the grammatical structures that Genie now comprehends are singular-plural contrasts of nouns, negative-affirmative sentence distinctions, possessive constructions, modifications, a number of prepositions (including *under, next to, beside, over,* and probably *on* and *in*), conjunction with *and,* and the comparative and superlative forms of adjectives. [For further details on the comprehension tests, see Curtiss et al. (1973).]

The comprehension tests which are now regularly administered were designed by Susan Curtiss who has been most directly involved in the research of Genie's linguistic development. (New tests are constantly being added.) The nouns, verbs, and adjectives used in all of the tests are used by Genie in her own utterances (see below for discussion on Genie's spontaneous speech production). The response required was primarily a "pointing" response. Genie was familiar with this gesture prior to the onset of testing. One example can illustrate the kinds of tests and the procedures used.

To test Genie's singular/plural distinction in nouns, pairs of pictures are used—a single object on one picture, three of the identical objects on the other. The test sentences differ only by absence or presence of plural markers on the nouns. Genie is asked to point to the appropriate picture. The words used are: balloon(s), pail(s), turtle(s), nose(s), horse(s), dish(es), pot(s), boat(s). Until July, 1972, the responses were no better than chance. Since July, 1972, Genie gives 100% correct responses. It is important to note that at the time when she was not responding correctly to the linguistically marked distinction, she could appropriately use and understand utterances including numbers ("one," "two," "three," etc.) and "many," "more," and "lots of."

SPEECH PRODUCTION AND PHONOLOGICAL DEVELOPMENT

Genie's ability to comprehend spoken language is a better indication of her linguistic competence than is her production of speech because of the physical difficulties Genie has in speaking. At the age when normal children are learning the necessary neuro-muscular controls over their vocal organs to enable them to produce the sounds of language, Genie was learning to repress any and all sounds because of the physical punishment which accompanied any sounds produced. This can explain why her earliest imitative and spontaneous utterances were often produced as silent articulations or whispered. Her inability to control the laryngeal mechanisms involved in speech resulted in monotonic speech. Her whole body tensed as she struggled to speak, revealing the difficulties she had in the control of air volume and air flow. The intensity of the acoustic signal produced was very low. The strange voice quality of her vocalized utterances is at least partially explainable in reference to these problems.

Because of her speech difficulties, one cannot assess her language competence by her productive utterances alone. But despite the problems which still remain, there has been dramatic improvement in Genie's speech production. Her supra glottal articulations have been more or less normal, and her phonological development does not deviate sharply from that observed in normal children. In addition, she is beginning, both in imitations and in spontaneous utterances, to show some intonation and her speech is now being produced with greater intensity.

Like normal children, Genie's first one-word utterances consisted of Consonant-Vowel (CV) monosyllables. These soon expanded into a more complex syllable structure which can be diagrammed as (C) (L/G) V (C), where L stands for liquid, G, glide, and the parenthesized elements optional.

Words of two and three syllables entered into her productive vocabulary, and in these words stress was correctly marked by intensity and/or duration of the vowel as well as vowel quality (with the unstressed vowel being ə). To date, all of the consonants of Standard American English are included in her utterances (with the inter-dental fricatives occurring only in imitations, and the affricates occurring inconsistently). She still deletes final consonants more often than not. Their correct sporadic presence, however, shows them to be part of her stored representation of the words in which they occur. Consonant clusters were first simplified by the deletion of the /s/ in initial /sp/ /sk/ /st/ clusters: at the present time, in addition to this method of preserving the CV syllable structure, she sometimes adds an epenthetic schwa between the two consonants.

Other changes in Genie's phonological system continue to be observed. At an earlier stage, a regular substitution of /t/ for /k/, /n/, and /s/ occurred in all word positions: this now occurs only word medially. /s/ plus nasal clusters are now being produced.

What is of particular interest is that in imitation Genie can produce any English sound and many sound sequences not found in her spontaneous speech. It has been noted by many researchers on child language that children have greater phonetic abilities than are revealed in their utterances. This is also true of Genie; her output reflects phonological constraints. rather than her inability to articulate sounds and sound sequences.

Neither Genie nor a normal child learns the sound system of a language totally independent from the syntactic and semantic systems. In fact, the analysis of the syntactic and semantic development of Genie's spontaneous utterances reveals that her performance on the expressive side is parallelling (although lagging behind) her comprehension.

As stated above, within a few weeks after admission to the hospital Genie began to imitate words used to her, and her comprehension of individual words and names increased dramatically. She began to produce single words spontaneously after about five months.

SENTENCE STRUCTURE

For normal children, perception or comprehension of syntactic structures exceeds production; this is even more true in Genie's case, possibly for the reasons given above. But even in production it is clear that Genie is acquiring language. Eight months after her emergence, Genie began to produce utterances, two words (or morphemes) in length. The structures of her earliest two-word "sentences" were Modifier + Noun and Noun + Noun genitive constructions. These included sentences like "more soup," "yellow car," "Genie purse" and "Mark mouth." After about two months, she began to produce strings with verbs—both Noun (subject) + Verb, and Verb + Noun (object), e.g., "Mark paint" (N + V), "Curtiss cough" (N + V), "want milk" (V + N) and "wash car" (V + N). Sentences with a noun followed by a predicate adjective soon followed, e.g., "Dave sick."

In November, 1971, Genie began to produce three and four word strings, including Subject + Verb + Object strings, like "Tori chew glove," modified noun phrases like "little white clear box," subject-object strings, like "big elephant long trunk," and four word predications like "Marilyn car red car." Some of these longer strings are of interest because the syntactic relations which were only assumed to be present in her two-word utterances were now overtly expressed. For example, many of Genie's two-word strings did not contain any expressed subject, but the three-word sentences included both the subject and object: "Love Marilyn" became "Genie love Marilyn." In addition, Modifier-noun Noun Phrases and possessive phrases which were complete utterances at the two-word sentence stage are now used as constituents of her longer strings, e.g., "more soup" occurred in "want more soup" and "Mark mouth" became a constituent in "Mark mouth hurt."

In February, 1972, Genie began to produce negative sentences. The comprehension test involving negative/affirmative distinctions showed that such a distinction was understood many months earlier. (In the tests she had no difficulty in pointing to the correct picture when asked to "show me 'The girl is wearing shoes'" or "Show me the bunny that has a carrot" vs. "Show me the bunny that does not/doesn't have a carrot.") The first negative morpheme used by Genie was "no more." Later she began to use "no" and "not." To date, Genie continues to negate a sentence by attaching the negative morpheme to the beginning of the string. She has not yet acquired the "Negative movement transformation" which inserts the Negative morpheme inside the sentence in English.

About the same time that the negative sentences were produced, Genie began to produce strings with locative-nouns, such as "Cereal kitchen" and "play gym." In recent months prepositions are occurring in her utterances. In answer to the question "Where is your toy radio?" she answered "On chair." She has also produced sentences such as "Like horse behind fence." "Like good Harry at hospital."

In July, 1972, Verb plus Verb-phrase strings were produced: "Want go shopping," "Like chew meat." Such complex VPs began to emerge in sentences that included both a complex Noun-phrase and a complex Verb-phrase, e.g., "Want buy toy refrigerator" and "Want go walk (to) Ralph." Genie has also begun to add the progressive aspect marker "ing" to verbs, always appropriately to denote ongoing action: "Genie laughing," "Tori eating bone "

Grammatical morphemes that are phonologically marked are now used, e.g., plurals as in "bears," "noses," "swings," and possessives such as "Joel's room," "I like Dave's car."

While no definite-indefinite distinction has appeared, Genie now produces the definite article in imitation, and uses the determiner "another" spontaneously, as in "Another house have dog."

At an earlier stage, possession was marked solely by word order; Genie now also expresses possession by the verb "have," as in "Bears have sharp claw," "bathroom have big mirror."

A most important syntactic development is revealed by Genie's use of compound NPs. Prior to December, 1971, she would only name one thing at a time, and would produce two sentences such as: "Cat hurt" followed by "dog hurt." More recently, she produced these two strings, and then said "Cat dog hurt." This use of a "recursive" element is also shown by the sentence "Curtiss, Genie, swimming pool" in describing a snapshot.

Genie's ability to combine a finite set of linguistic elements to form new combinations, and the ability to produce sentences consisting of conjoined sentences shows that she has acquired two essential elements of language that permit the generation of an infinite set of sentences.

This is of course an overly sketchy view of the syntactic development evidence in Genie's utterances. [For further details, see Curtiss et al. (1973).] It is clear even from this summary that Genie is learning language. Her speech is rule-governed—she has fixed word-order of basic sentence elements and constituents, and systematic ways of expressing syntactic and semantic relations.

LINGUISTIC DEVELOPMENT IN RELATION TO NORMALS

Furthermore, it is obvious that her development in many ways parallels that of normal first-language acquisition. There are, however, interesting differences between Genie's emerging language and that of normal children. Her vocabulary is much larger than that of normal children whose language exhibits syntactic complexity parallel to Genie's. She has less difficulty in storing lists than she does learning the rules of the grammar. This illustrates very sharply that language acquisition is not simply the ability to store a large number of items in memory.

Genie's performance on the active/passive comprehension test also appears to deviate from that of normal children. Bever (1970) reports on experiments aimed at testing the capacity in young children "to recognize explicitly the concept of predication as exemplified in the appreciation of the difference between subject-action and action-object relations." The children in these experiments were requested to act out, using toys, both simple active sentences and reversible passive sentences, such as "The cow kisses the horse" and simple passives such as "The horse is kissed by the cow." He reports that "children from 2.0 to 3.0 act out simple active sentences 95 percent correctly, (and) . . . do far better than 5 percent on simple passives. He concludes that "since they perform almost randomly on passives . . . they can at least distinguish sentences they can understand from sentences they cannot understand.

Thus, the basic linguistic capacity evidenced by the two-year-old child includes the notion of reference for objects and actions, the notion of basic functional internal relations, and at least a primitive notion of different sentence structures." Genie was similarly tested but with the "point to" response rather than the "acting out" response. That is, she was asked to point to "The boy pulls/is pulling the girl" or "The girl is pulled by the boy." For each such test sentence, she was presented with two pictures, one depicting the boy as agent, the other with the girl as agent. Unlike the children tested by Bever, Genie's responses to both active and passive sentences have been random, with no better than a chance level of correct responses for either the active or the passive sentences. This is particularly strange when compared with Genie's own utterances which show a consistent word order to indicate Subject-Verb-Object relations. While she never produces passive constructions, her active sentences always place the object after the verb and the subject before the verb (when they are expressed).

Another difference between Genie and normal children is in the area of linguistic performance. Genie's linguistic competence (her grammar, if we can speak of a grammar at such an early stage of development) is in many ways on a par with a two or two and a half year old child. Her performance—particularly as related to expressive speech—is much poorer than normal children at this level. Because of her particular difficulties in producing speech, however, a number of relatively successful efforts have been directed to teaching her written language. At this point she recognizes, names, and can print the letters of the alphabet, can read a large number of printed words, can assemble printed words into grammatically correct sentences, and can understand sentences (and questions) constructed of these printed words. On this level of performance, then, she seems to exceed normal children, at a similar stage of language development.

Genie's progress is much slower than that of normals. Few syntactic markers occur in her utterances; there are no question words, no demonstratives, no particles, no rejoinders. In addition, no movement transformations are revealed. Such rules exist in the adult grammar and in normal children's grammars as early as two years. Transformational rules are those which, for example, would move a negative element from the beginning of the sentence to the position after an auxiliary verb. Such a transformational rule would change *I can go* in its negative form from *Neg + I + can + go* to *I + can + neg* (can't) + *go*. As stated above, Genie continues to produce negative sentences only by the addition of the negative element to the beginning of the sentence. e.g., *No more ear hurt, No stay hospital, No can go.*

Cognitively, however, she seems to be in advance of what would be expected at this syntactic stage. Her earliest productive vocabulary included words cognitively more sophisticated than one usually finds in the descriptions of first vocabulary words. Color words and numbers, for example, were used which usually enter a child's vocabulary at a much later grammatical stage (Castner, 1940; Denckla, 1972).

At the time that Genie began to produce utterances of two-words (June, 1971), she had an active vocabulary of over 200 words, which far exceeds the size of the normal children's lexicon at this stage (about 50 words). This development seems to parallel that found in aphasic children (Eisenson and Ingram, 1972). She comprehends all the WH questions; normal children ordinarily learn HOW, WHY and

WHEN questions later than WHO, WHAT, and WHERE (Brown, 1968), although syntactically such questions are similar. Her comprehension of the comparative and superlative, and the differences between "more" and "less" also indicate cognitive sophistication not revealed by her syntax, suggesting at least a partial independence of cognition and language.

COGNITIVE DEVELOPMENT

The attempt to assess Genie's cognitive development is extremely difficult. All tests purporting to measure cognitive abilities, in fact, measure knowledge that has been acquired through experience. In addition, many tests are substantially dependent on verbal response and comprehension. The distinction between cognition and language development is therefore not always possible. A number of tests have, however, been utilized.

Genie could not easily be psychologically tested by standard instruments at the time of her admission. It is still difficult to administer many of the standard tests. On the Vineland Social Maturity Scale, however, she averaged about 15 months at the time of admission, and on a Gesell Developmental Evaluation, a month and a half later, scores ranged from about one to about three years of age. There was a very high degree of scatter when compared to normal developmental patterns. Consistently, language-related behavior was observed to occur at the lower end of the range of her performance and was judged (by the psychologists at the hospital) to be at about the 15 months level.

Her cognitive growth, however, seemed to be quite rapid. In a seven-month span, her score had increased from 15 to 42 months, and six months after admission, on the Leiter International Performance Scale (which depends relatively little on culturally based, specific knowledge, and requires no speech), she passed all the items at the four-year level, two at the five-year level, and two out of four at the seven-year level. In May 1973 her score on this test was on the six- to eight-year level. At the same time, the Stanford Binet Intelligence Scale elicited a mental age of 5–8. In all the tests, the subsets which involved language were considerably lower than those assessing other abilities.

From this brief summary of Genie's linguistic development, we can conclude the following: (1) When she first emerged from isolation, Genie, a child of 13 years, 9 months had not acquired language. (2) Since there is no evidence of any biological deficiencies, one may assume this was due to the social and linguistic isolation which occurred during 11 years of her life. (3) Since her emergence she has been acquiring her first language primarily by "exposure" alone. This is revealed both by her own speech and by her comprehension of spoken language. (4) Her cognitive development has exceeded her linguistic development.

THE "CRITICAL AGE" HYPOTHESIS AND LANGUAGE LATERALIZATION

As mentioned above. Genie's ongoing language acquisition is the most direct test of Lenneberg's critical age hypothesis seen thus far. Lenneberg (1967) has presented the view that the ability to acquire primary language (and the acquisition of second languages "by mere exposure") terminates with the completion of the development of cerebral dominance, or lateralization, an event which he argues occurs at around puberty. As we have demonstrated above, however, while Genie's language acquisition differs to some extent from that of normal children, she is in fact in the process of learning language, as shown by the results of tests and by the observations of her spontaneous and elicited speech. Thus, at least some degree of first language acquisition seems to be possible beyond the critical period.

Genie also affords us the opportunity to study the relationship of the development of lateralization and language acquisition.

Lateralization refers to the fact that each hemisphere appears to be specialized for different cognitive functions: that is, some functions seem to be "localized" primarily on one side of the brain. This assumption is based on operational criteria. The discovery, more than a century ago by Broca (1861, and Bonin, 1960) that lesions to the left hemisphere produce language problems whereas lesions to the right do not, and that therefore the left hemisphere is dominant for language, has been supported by other aphasia studies (Russell and Espir, 1961), by experiments with split-brains (Gazzaniga and Sperry, 1967), and by a variety of other experimental techniques. For example, temporary aphasia is more often the result of left hemisphere anesthetization (Wada, 1949). It has also been shown that the right visual field excels for verbal stimuli (Bryden, 1965). Evoked potential and EEG techniques have confirmed these findings (Wood, Goff, and Day, 1971: McAdam and Whitaker, 1971; Buchsbaum and Fedio, 1970). In addition, dichotic listening tests have consistently shown a right-ear preference when verbal stimuli are presented, which preference is not shown with non-verbal stimuli (Broadbent, 1954; Kimura, 1961; Curry, 1967; Borkowsky, Spreen and Stutz, 1965; Pettit and Noll, 1972; Studdert-Kennedy and Shankweiler, 1970; Berlin et al., 1972; Kimura and Folb, 1968; Zurif and Sait, 1969; Van Lancker and Fromkin, 1973).

There is ample evidence, in addition, to show that certain other cognitive functions are similarly lateralized. In addition to language, the left hemisphere is specialized for temporal order judgments (Carmon and Nachson, 1971) while the right hemisphere is dominant for spatial relations (Bogen, 1969), part to whole judgments (Nebes, 1971), "gestalt" perception (Kimura, 1966), the perception of musical chords (Gordon, 1970), and the perception of environmental sounds (Curry, 1967). Finally, for certain stimuli, no hemispheric specialization has been found, and hence it is concluded, no lateralization of function (Schulhoff and Goodglass, 1970; Milner, 1962).

That the two sides of the brain appear to show differential abilities seems clear. It is still a matter of debate as to what, if any, the role of the "minor" hemisphere is in carrying out functions associated with the "major" hemisphere. While Lenneberg has maintained that lateralization is complete by puberty and corresponds to the critical period. Krashen and Harshman (1972; see also Krashen, 1972 and 1973a) have argued that lateralization is complete at about five and that this process is not associated with a critical period limiting language acquisition. Instead, they argue that the lateralization and simultaneous maturation of certain mental abilities (e.g., temporal order judgments) underlying the language faculty must precede or at least be simultaneous with language acquisition (argued in greater detail in Krashen, 1972 and 1973b). Whether lateralization has already taken place in Genie is thus of interest. Was her left hemisphere "prepared" for language or would left hemisphere specialization occur along with language acquisition?

Dichotic listening procedures are simple and easy to administer, and for this reason such tests were used in our attempt to investigate lateralization development in Genie. In all these tests, a subject is presented with competing simultaneous stimulus pairs. For example, in the right ear he may hear /da/ or "big" and in the left ear /ga/ or "pig." When the stimuli are verbal, items presented to the right ear are generally reported more accurately by normal right handed subjects. This is assumed to be due to left hemisphere "dominance" for language. When the stimuli are non-verbal (musical chords, Gordon, 1970; environmental sounds, Curry, 1968) a left ear preference is revealed indicating right hemisphere dominance.

The dichotic listening tests administered to Genie were designed, administered, and analyzed by Stephen Krashen. The stimuli were prepared at the UCLA Phonetics laboratory using computer programs developed by Lloyd Rice. Two sets of stimuli were prepared; the "verbal" tape consisted of 15 pairs of "point to" words. Each pair of words was preceded by the binaural instructions "point to the————." Genie pointed to toys or pictures representing the words. [Knox and Kimura (1970) used a similar procedure and found a right ear advantage.] The words were familiar to Genie: baby, boy, car, picture, table, mirror.

The non-verbal tape, prepared by Sarah Spitz, consisted of pairs of environmental sounds recorded from Genie's actual environment (piano chords, car horn, water running, telephone ringing, squeal of toy chimp). She responded by pointing to snapshots of the sound source.

Genie was first tested monaurally; that is, the stimuli were presented to her one ear at a time. She had no difficulty whatsoever in either ear in responding appropriately. Monaural presentation was used as a "warm up" in subsequent sessions and in every case Genie scored 100%. This finding is consistent with her audiometry results of no obvious unilateral hearing loss.

Tables 1 and 2 present the results of the dichotic tests using verbal stimuli. The results show an extreme left ear advantage, suggesting right hemisphere dominance for language. This is an unusual finding since it is very rare to find a right-handed subject who is right dominant, and Genie is right handed. [EEG data that were obtained during studies of Genie's sleep are described as "typical of a left hemispheric dominance" (Shurley and Natani, 1972).] Approximately 1/3 of left handers are also right dominant for language. It is clear that the hypothesis that lateralization had not yet been complete because of the language acquisition taking place is not supported by these results.

Table 1   Genie's Dichotic Listening Results—Single Pairs of Words
             Presented Dichotically

Date	No. of pairs	No. correct right ear	No. correct left ear
3/27/72	29	6	29
5/10/72	15	1	15
8/16/72	30	5	30
overall%		16%	100%

Table 2   Genie's Dichotic Listening Results—Two Pairs of Words,
Presented Dichotically, Separated by ½ Second

Date	No. of pairs	No. correct right ear	No. correct left ear
6/3/73	28	0	28
Controls (N = 2) right handed adults with normal hearing): (p .025, one tail)			
	28	23.5	21.4

The degree as well as the direction of lateralization is also unusual. Dichotic listening in normals nearly always produces a slight, but statistically significant, right ear advantage for verbal stimuli. Genie's left ear was perfect while her right ear performed at a chance level.

The results of the tests using dichotically presented environmental sounds, given in Tables 3 and 4, show that Genie is not simply one of the rare but attested individuals with reversed dominance, with language on the right and certain non-verbal faculties on the left. These show a moderate left ear advantage with her overall accuracy only slightly lower than that of the controls run thus far. This indicates right hemisphere processing of environmental sounds and is a normal finding for right-handed subjects (Curry, 1968). It appears that Genie's right hemisphere is doing all the work.

A comparison with other subjects who show similar extreme ear differences, namely split-brain and (right) hemispherectomized patients, may provide some insight into these unusual results. This is presented in Table 5.

A brief examination of the mechanisms thought to underlie dichotic listening may be helpful in attempting to understand the parrallel between Genie's verbal results and those of the split-brain and hemispherectomized subjects.

Figure 1 is a model of dichotic listening for normal subjects.[5] It has been suggested

Table 3   Genie's Dichotic Listening Results—Single Pairs of
Environmental Sounds Presented Dichotically

Date	No. of pairs	No. correct right ear	No. correct left ear
8/2/72	20	12	18
8/16/72	20	14	19
6/3/73	20	14	20
		67%	95%

---

[5] Figures 1 and 2 are taken from Krashen (1972), and Krashen et al. (1972a, 1972b).

Table 4   Genie's Dichotic Listening Results—Two Pairs of Environmental Sounds, Presented Dichotically, Separated by ½ Second

Date	No. of pairs	No. correct right ear	No. correct left ear
6/3/73	28	15	27

(Kimura, 1961) that when stimuli are presented dichotically, the contralateral, or crossed auditory pathways suppress the ipsilateral pathways. Thus, in dichotic listening, the uncrossed pathways can be regarded as relatively non-functional. The left primary auditory receiving area then receives only stimuli presented to the right ear while the right primary auditory receiving area receives stimuli presented to the left ear. Since the left primary auditory receiving area is "closer" to the language areas in the left hemisphere, stimuli presented to the right ear have a perceptual advantage. In other words, left ear stimuli must first be routed to the right hemisphere and this gives them a slight disadvantage in competition with the right ear stimuli in the language processing areas. In both split-brain and (right) hemispherectomy, as shown in Figure 2, there is no input to the language areas from the right hemisphere; thus, any contribution from the left ear is due to the weak (suppressed) ipsilateral pathway.

In monotic listening, both split-brains and hemispherectomies perform quite well, at or near 100%. For dichotic listening suppression occurs and the ipsolateral pathway is occluded; because of suppression, the right ear does about four times as well as the left ear. The typical scores presented in Table 5 have been replicated in other studies (Sparks and Geschwind, 1968; Curry, 1968).

Genie similarly scores 100% in each ear when stimuli are presented monaurally; dichotically, she shows the extreme ear difference only parallelled by split-brains and hemispherectomies. In a recent study, however, Netley (1972) found that extreme ear differences were found only in hemispherectomized subjects who incurred lesions late (around 17 months), as opposed to those who were injured at birth. It is interesting to note that Genie's case history corresponds more closely to the late lesioned group both with respect to ear difference and onset of lesion.

Genie's results indicate that she is utilizing only her contralateral left ear and

Table 5   Comparison of Genie's Verbal Dichotic Listening Results with Normal, Split-Brain, and Hemispherectomized Subjects

	% Correct better ear	% Correct weaker ear
Normal subjects	60.3	51.9 (Curry, 1968)
Genie	100	16
Right hemispherectomized	99	24.3 (Berlin et al., 1972)
Split-brain	90.7	22.2 (Milner et al., 1968)

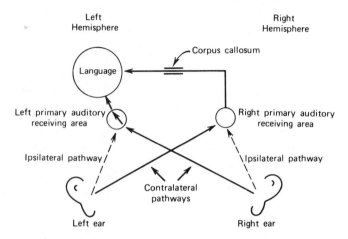

Figure 1. A model of auditory processing in "normal"
dichotic listening.

ipsilateral right ear pathways in language processing. This does not seem to be true
for her non-verbal auditory perception.

In trying to assess this unusual situation, it is important to note that Genie seems
very proficient in what are considered right hemisphere functions. It was pointed out
above that in psychological tests her development can be comprehended more meaningfully when performance on two kinds of test tasks are distinguished: those that
require analytic or sequential use of symbols, such as language and number; and
those that involve perception of spatial configurations or Gestalts. On the first group
of tasks Genie's performance is consistently in the low range, presently approximating an age of two and a half to three years, approximately the age level of her
linguistic performance using comparative linguistic criteria. On configurational tests,
however, her performance ranges upwards, lying somewhere between eight years
and the adult level, depending on the test (see above for Leiter results). The rate of
growth on these tests has been very rapid. One year after admission to the hospital,

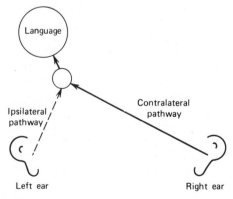

Figure 2. Dichotic listening for the
split-brain and (right) hemispherectomized subject—supression only.

and about two and a half months after she entered the foster home, Genie made mental age scores on the French Pictorial Test of intelligence that spanned the range from 4.5 to 9 years. About 3 months later, her performance on the Raven Matrices could not be scored in the usual manner but corresponded to the 50th percentile of children aged 8.5 to 9 years. Her performance on the Street Gestalt Test, administered by Dr. Joseph Bogen, also attests to the fact that her right hemisphere is mature. This test is known to be dependent on the ability to make part to whole judgments; patients with right hemisphere lesions perform worse on this test than other brain-damaged or normal subjects (De Renzi and Spinnler, 1966). Genie scored 7 and 9 out of 12 on two occasions, an unusual performance in view of the fact that the mean for adults is about 7 and the test is somewhat culture-bound. (For example, one of the items to be recognized on the test is a pot-bellied stove, an object never seen by Genie.) In addition, Genie is quite proficient at finding her way around, a skill that is impaired in cases of right lesions.

It would appear then that Genie is lateralized to the right for both language and non-language functions. This assumes that these non-linguistic abilities, which have been shown to be right-hemisphere lateralized, are indeed functions of Genie's right hemisphere. We are now in the process of designing tests involving other modalities which will hopefully provide more conclusive evidence on this question.

If this proves to be the case, one tentative hypothesis to explain how this developed is as follows: At the time of her isolation, Genie was a "normal" right-handed child with potential left hemisphere dominance. The inadequate language stimulation during her early life inhibited or interfered with language aspects of left hemisphere development. This would be tantamount to a kind of functional atrophy of the usual language centers, brought about by disuse or suppression. Apparently, what meager stimulation she did receive was sufficient for normal right hemisphere development. (One can imagine her sitting, day after day, week after week, year after year, absorbing every visual stimulus, every crack in the paint, every nuance of color and form.) This is consistent with the suggestion (Carmon et al., 1972) that the right hemisphere is the first to develop since it is more involved with the perception of the environment. Genie's current achievements in language acquisition, according to this reasoning, is occurring in that hemisphere which somehow did mature more normally.

The hypothesis that Genie is using a developed right hemisphere for language also predicts the dichotic listening results. The undeveloped language areas in the left hemisphere prevent the flow of (just language) impulses from the left primary auditory receiving areas to the right hemisphere. This explains why Genie's scores are so similar to split-brain and hemispherectomized subjects; the only auditory pathways that are functional for *verbal* stimuli are the right ipsilateral and left contralateral. The low right score is due to the suppression that occurs under the dichotic condition. Her perfect monotic scores are predicted, since suppression only takes place dichotically.

If this hypothesis is true, it modifies the theory of the critical period: while the normal development of lateralization may not play a role in the critical period, lateralization may be involved in a different way; the left hemisphere must perhaps be linguistically stimulated during a specific period of time for it to participate in normal language acquisition. If such stimulation does not take place during this time, normal language acquisition must depend on other cortical areas and will proceed less efficiently due to the previous specialization of these areas for other functions.

A comparison of Genie's case with other instances of right (minor) hemisphere speech in adults implies that Genie's capacity for language acquisition is limited and will cease at some time in the near future. Such cases are rare and not well described from a linguistic point of view. A. Smith's (1966) description of a left hemispherecto-mized man is the best of these. This man could not speak at all after his left hemi-sphere was removed but did begin to communicate in "propositional language" ten weeks later. The patient continued to make linguistic progress but remained severely aphasic 8 months after surgery (see also Bogen, 1969). Similarly, Hillier (1954) reported a left hemispherectomy performed on a 14-year-old boy for a tumor whose onset was one year previous to surgery. Again, there was early progress in language learning but after 19 months progress ceased and the deficit became stable.

It is unfortunate that there is no information concerning cerebral dominance for other cases of isolated children—those that acquired language as well as those that didn't. Itard suggests that Victor was about 12 years of age when he was found in the woods of Aveyron, and that "It is . . . almost proved that he had been abandoned at the age of four or five years" (Itard, 1962). If, in those first years he was not genetically deficient, lateralization should have been complete and language should have been acquired. Itard states further that "if, at this time, he already owed some ideas and some words to the beginning of an education, this would all have been effaced from his memory in consequence of his isolation." How, why, and if such "memory effacement" occurs, are questions open to speculation. Despite this "effacement," Victor "did acquire a very considerable reading vocabulary, learning, by means of printed phrases to execute such simple commands as to pick up a key" (Itard, 1962, p. xii), but he never learned to speak. The scar "which (was) visible on his throat" may have damaged his larynx. It is impossible to tell from Itard's reports the exact extent of Victor's comprehension of spoken language.

Another case, similar to some extent to that of Genie, is that of a child who was not exposed to language until she was six and a half years old because of her imprisonment with a mute and totally uneducated aphasic mother (Mason, 1942). Within twenty-two months, she progressed from her first spoken words ("ball," "car," "bye," "baby") to asking such questions as "Why does the paste come out if one upsets the jar?" The rapidity with which she acquired the complex grammar of English provides some support for the hypothesis that the language learning mech-anism is more specific than general.

This case is also consistent with a two-to-puberty critical period theory. The lan-guage learning capacity of the right hemisphere, then, may be limited either in time or amount of learning. Because we have no grammatical descriptions of right hemi-sphere speech, we cannot predict how far Genie will progress from comparisons with such cases. On the other hand, Genie's progress in language acquisition impressionis-tically seems to have far exceeded that of the other reported cases. We intend to continue administering dichotic listening tests to see if the left hemisphere begins to show increasing language function. If this occurs, one plausible conclusion would be that language acquisition and use is a precondition for such lateralization to occur. We note, of course, that this would be contrary to the Krashen and Harshman position that lateralization *precedes* language acquisition. There is also some evidence of laterality differences in neonates (Wada, quoted in Geschwind, 1970; Molfese, 1972).

It is clear from this report that we have more questions than answers. We are hopeful that Genie's development will provide some of these answers.

As humanists, we are hopeful that our tentative prognosis of a slowing down of language and permanent dysphasia will prove to be wrong. For despite the predictions of our hypothesis. Genie continues to make modest but steady progress in language acquisition and is providing us with data in an unexplored area, first language acquisition beyond the "critical period." After all, a discarded hypothesis is a small price to pay for confirmation of the astonishing capabilities and adaptability of the human mind.

REFERENCES

Bellugi, U., and Klima, E. 1971. Consultation Report. March.

Berlin, C. I., Lowe-Bell, S. S. Cullen, J. K. and Thompson, C. L. 1972. Dichotic speech perception: An interpretation of right ear advantage and temporal offset effects. *Journal of the Acoustical Society of America* (in press).

Bever, T. G. 1970. The cognitive basis for linguistic structures. In J. R. Hayes (Ed.) *Cognition and the Development of Language.* New York: John Wiley, Pp. 279–362.

Bogen, J. E. 1969. The other side of the brain 1: Dysgraphia and dyscopia following cerebral commissurotomy. *Bulletin of the Los Angeles Neurological Societies,* 34, July, 73–105.

Bonn, G. von 1960. *Some Papers on the Cerebral Cortex,* Springfield, Illinois: C. C. Thomas.

Borkowski, J., Spreen, O. and Stutz, J. 1965. Ear preference and abstractness in dichotic listening. *Psychonomic Science 3,* 547–548.

Broadbent, D. E. 1954. The role of auditory localization in attention and memory span. *Journal of Experimental Psychology 47,* 191–196.

Broca, P. 1861. Remarques sur le siege de la faculte du language articule, suivies d'une observation d'aphemie. *Bulletin de la Societe d'anatomie 5,* 330–357.

Brown, R. 1968. The development of WH questions in child speech. *Journal of Verbal Learning and Verbal Behavior 7,* 279–290.

Bryden, M. 1963. Ear preference in auditory perception. *Journal of Experimental Psychology 65,* 103–105.

Bushbaum, M. and Fedio, P. 1970. Hemispheric differences in evoked potentials to verbal and nonverbal stimuli in the left and right visual fields. *Physiology and Behavior 5,* 207–210.

Carmon, A., Harishanu, Y., Lowinger, R., and Levy, S. 1972. Assymmetries in hemispheric blood volume and cerebral dominance. *Behavioral Biology* (in press).

Carmon, A. and Nachson, I. 1971. The effect of unilateral brain damage on perception of temporal order. *Cortex 7,* 410–418.

Castner, B. M. 1940. Language development in the first five years of life. Ed. A. Gesell. N. Y.: Harper & Row.

Chomsky, N. 1962. Explanatory models in linguistics. In E. Nagel, P. Suppes, and A. Taiski, (Eds.) *Logic, Methodology, and the Philosophy of Science.* Stanford University Press.

Clarke, A. D. B. and Clarke, A. M. 1960. Some recent advances in the study of early deprivation. *Child Psychology and Psychiatry, 1.*

Curry, F. 1967. A comparison of left-handed and right-handed subjects on verbal and non-verbal dichotic listening tasks. *Cortex 3,* 343–352.

Curry, F. 1968. A comparison of the performance of a right hemispherectomized subject and twenty-five normals on four dichotic listening tasks. *Cortex 4,* 144–153.

Curtiss, S. 1972. The development of language in Genie. Paper presented to the 1972 Annual Convention of the American Speech and Hearing Association, San Francisco, Calif. Nov. 18–20.

Curtiss, S., Fromkin, V., and Krashen, S. 1972. The syntactic development of Genie. Paper presented to the Dec., 1972 Annual meeting of the Linguistic Society of America, Atlanta, Georgia.

Davis, K. 1940. Extreme social isolation of a child. *American Journal of Socialogy, 45,* 554–565.

Davis, K. 1947. Final note on a case of extreme isolation. *American Journal of Sociology, 52,* 432–437.

Denckla, M. B. 1972. Performance on color tasks in kindergarten children. *Cortex 8,* 177–190.

Dennis, W., and Najarian, P. 1957. Infant development under developmental handicap. *Psychological Monographs 71,* No. 7.

De Renzi, E., Scotti, G. and Spinnler, H. 1969. Perceptual and associative disorders of visual recognition. *Neurology, 19.*

Eisenson, J. and Ingram, D. 1972. Childhood aphasia—an updated concept based on recent research. *Papers and Reports on Child Language Development.* Stanford University, 103–120.

Fraiberg, S., and Freedman, D. A. 1964. Studies in the ego development of the congenitally blind child. *The Psychoanalytic Study of the Child, 19,* 113–169.

Freedman, D. A., and Brown, S. L. 1968. On the role of coenesthetic stimulation in the development of psychic structure.

Fromkin, V. 1972. The development of language in Genie. Paper presented at the 80th Annual Convention of the American Psychological Association, Honolulu, Hawaii, Sept. 1–8.

Gazzaniga, M. S. and Sperry, R. 1967. Language after section of the cerebral commissures. *Brain, 90,* 131–148.

Geschwind, N. 1970. The organization of language and the brain. *Science 170,* 940–944.

Gordon, H. W. 1970. Hemispheric asymmetries in the perception of musical cords. *Cortex, 6,* 387–398.

Haggard, M. and Parkinson, A. 1971. Stimulus and task factors as determinants of ear advantage. *Quarterly Journal of Experimental Psychology, 23,* 168–177.

Hansen, H. 1972. The first experiences and the emergence of "Genie." Paper presented at the 80th Annual Convention of the American Psychological Association, Honolulu, Hawaii, Sept. 1–8.

Hillier, F. 1954. Total left hemispherectomy for malignant glaucoma. *Neurology, 4,* 718–721.

Howe, M. and Hall, F. G. 1903. *Laura Bridgeman.* Little, Brown and Co.

Itard, J. 1962. *The Wild Boy of Aveyron.* New York: Appleton-Century-Crofts.

Katz, J. J., and Bever, T. G. 1973. The fall and rise of empiricism, or the truth about general semantics. (Forthcoming).

Kent, J. 1972. Eight months in the hospital. Paper presented at the 80th Annual Convention of the Americal Psychological Association, Honolulu, Hawaii, Sept. 1–8.

Kimura, D. 1961. Cerebral dominance and the perception of verbal stimuli. *Canadian Journal of Psychology, 15,* 166–171.

Kimura, D. 1966. Dual functional asymmetry of the brain in visual perception. *Neuropsychologia 4,* 275–285.

Kimura, D. and Folb, S. 1968. Neural processing of backwards speech sounds. *Science, 161,* 395–396.

Knox, C. and Kimura, D. 1970. Cerebral processing of non-verbal sounds in boys and girls. *Neuropsychologia, 8,* 227–237.

Koluchova, J. 1972. Severe deprivation in twins. *Child Psychology and Psychiatry, 13.*

Krashen, S. 1972. Language and the left hemisphere. *Working Papers in Phonetics, 24,* UCLA.

Krashen, S. 1973a. Lateralization, language learning, and the critical period: some new evidence, *Language Learning 23,* 63–74.

Krashen, S. 1973b. Mental abilities underlying linguistic and non-linguistic functions. *Linguistics* (in press).

Krashen, S., Fromkin, V., Curtiss, S., Rigler, D., and Spitz, S. (1972a). Language lateralization in a case of extreme psychological deprivation. Paper presented to the 84th meeting of the Acoustical Society of America.

Krashen, S., Fromkin, V. and Curtiss, S. 1972b. A neurolinguistic investigation of language acquisition in the case of an isolated child. Paper presented to the Linguistic Society of America, Winter meeting, Atlanta, Georgia, Dec. 27–29.

Krashen, S. and Harshman, R. 1972. Lateralization and the critical period. *Working Papers in Phonetics 23,* 13–21. UCLA (Abstract in *Journal of the Acoustical Society of America, 52,* 174.)

Lenneberg, E. H. 1967. *Biological Foundations of Language.* New York: Wiley.

McAdam, D and Whitaker, H. 1971. Language production: Electroencephalographic localization in the normal human brain. *Science, 172,* 499–502.

Mason, M. K. 1942. Learning to speak after six and one-half years. *Journal of Speech Disorders, 7,* 295–304.

Milner, B. 1962. Laterality effects in audition. In V. B. Mountcastle (Ed.) *Interhemispheric Relations and Cerebral Dominance.* Baltimore: Johns Hopkins Press.

Milner, B., Taylor, L., and Sperry, R. 1968. Lateralized suppression of dichotically presented digits after commissural section in man. *Science, 161,* 184–186.

Molfese, D. L. 1972. Cerebral asymmetry in infants, children and adults: auditory evoked responses to speech and musical stimuli. *Journal of the Acoustical Society of America 53,* 363 (A).

Nebes, R. 1971. Superiority of the minor hemisphere in commissurotomized man for the perception of part-whole relations. *Cortex 7,* 333–349.

Netley, C. 1972. Dichotic listening performance of hemispherectomized patients. *Neuropsychologia, 10,* 233–240.

Petit, J. M. and Noll, J. D. 1972. Cerebral dominance and the process of language recovery in aphasia. Paper presented to the 1972 Annual Convention of the American Speech and Hearing Association, San Francisco, Calif. Nov. 18–20.

Rigler, D. 1972. The Case of Genie. Paper presented to the 1972 Annual Convention of the American Speech and Hearing Association. San Francisco, Calif. Nov. 18–20.

Rigler, M. 1972. Adventure: At home with Genie. Paper presented at the 80th Annual Convention of the American Psychological Association, Honolulu, Hawaii, Sept. 1–8.

Russell, R. and Espir, M. 1961. *Traumatic Aphasia.* Oxford: Oxford University Press.

Schulhoff, C. and Goodglass, H. 1969. Dichotic listening, side of brain injury and cerebral dominance. *Neuropsychologia, 7,* 149–160.

Shurley, J. T. and Natani, K. 1972. Sleep EEG patterns in a fourteen-year old girl with severe developmental retardation. Paper presented at the 80th Annual Convention of the American Psychological Association, Honolulu, Hawaii, Sept. 1–8.

Singh, J. A. L., and Zingg, R. M. 1966. *Wolf-Children and Feral Man.* Archon Books.

Skinner, B. F. 1957. *Verbal Behavior.* New York: Appleton-Century-Crofts.

Smith, A. 1966. Speech and other functions after left (dominant) hemispherectomy. *Journal of Neurology Neurosurgery and Psychiatry, 29,* 467–471.

Sparks, R. and Geschwind, N. 1968. Dichotic listening in man after section of neocortical commissures. *Cortex, 4,* 3–16.

Spitz, R. A. 1949. The role of ecological factors in emotional development. *Child Development, 20,* 145–155.

Studdert-Kennedy, M. and Shankweiler, D. 1970. Hemispheric specialization for speech perception. *Journal of the Acoustical Society of America, 48,* 579–594.

Van Lancker, D. and Fromkin, B. 1973. Hemispheric specialization for pitch and "tone": Evidence from Thai. *Journal of Phonetics, 1,* 101–109.

Von Feverbach, A. 1833. *Casper Hauser.* (Translated from the German) London: Simpkin and Marshall.

Wada, J. 1949. A new method for the determination of the side of cerebral speech dominance: a preliminary report on the intracartoid injection of sodium amytal in man. *Medical Biology, 14,* 221–222.

Wood, C., Goff, W. and Day, R. 1971. Auditory evoked potentials during speech production. *Science, 173,* 1248–1251.

Zurif, E. B. and Mendelsohn, M. 1972. Hemispheric specialization for the perception of speech sounds: the influences of intonation and structure. *Perception and Psychophysics, 11,* 329–332.

Zurif, E. B. and Sait, P. E. 1970. The role of syntax in dichotic listening. *Neuropsychologia, 8,* 239–244.

Language Delay and Associated Mother-Child Interactions

Margaret Wulbert, Susan Inglis, Elinor Kriegsmann, and Barbara Mills

The home environments and mother-child interactions of a language-delayed group and a matched control group of normal preschool children were assessed using the Caldwell Inventory of Home Stimulation. Twenty language-delayed children were defined by a discrepancy between their Stanford-Binet, language-based, IQ score and their Leiter, non-language-based, IQ score, and by a language evaluation. Children in both groups were distributed across all socioeconomic strata. The language-delayed group had significantly lower scores in five of the six subcategories of the Caldwell. Greatest differences were found in the involvement and responsiveness of the mother and in her avoidance of restriction and punishment. Low Caldwell scores were found through the socioeconomic strata, indicating that language delay had a stronger influence on the mother-child relationship than did socioeconomic factors.

In the past decade, there has been increased recognition of a population of children with low verbal abilities and/or delayed language acquisition. Attempts have been made to differentiate these children from those with other types of learning disabilities, including problems resulting from mental retardation (Ackerman, Peters, & Dykman, 1971; Kirk & Kirk, 1971; Marge, 1972). Standard procedures used in assessing the "intelligence" of such children have often emphasized IQ scores rather than differentiating between patterns of language-related and non-language-related behavior. Consequently, there has been an increased emphasis on selection of appropriate diagnostic tools that will identify the child with specific language disabilities.

This group of children has been most discussed in the literature documenting a significant relationship between social class and IQ (Eells, Davis, Havighurst, Herrick, & Tyler, 1951; Kennedy, Van de Ritt, & White, 1963). These studies have shown that the highest prevalence of low verbal skills occurs within the "culturally deprived"

From *Developmental Psychology*, *11*, 61–70, (1975). Copyright© 1975 by the American Psychological Association. Reprinted by permission.

This research was supported by Maternal and Child Health Services, Health Services and Mental Health Administration, U.S. Department of Health, Education, and Welfare, Project 913, and by BCHS Grant 909. This research was also supported in part by Nursing Research Facilitation Grant NU 00369.

Margaret Wulbert is now at the San Diego County Mental Health Services, San Diego, California.

segment of the population. Thus, when culturally deprived children have been given strongly language-oriented IQ tests, such as the Stanford-Binet, they earn lower scores than middle-class children; but on non-language or perceptual-motor problem-solving skills, they appear to be commensurate with their middle-class counterparts (Cazden, 1966; Eells et al., 1951; Sandler, Van Campen, Rather, Stafford, & Weisman, 1970).

Low language-related IQ scores have also been studied in relation to maternal behavior occurring within a culturally deprived population. Hess and Shipman (1965, 1967), for instance, have focused upon the maternal variables which they feel account for depressed academic and intellectual performance in culturally deprived children. They have found that children with low Stanford-Binet IQ scores tend to have mothers who are more restricting and controlling of their children. It has been shown that in addition to being more disapproving and controlling, lower-class mothers tend to use more impoverished language models with their children (Bee, Van Egeren, Streissguth, Nyman, & Leckie, 1969). Children with normal intelligence but low verbal abilities have also been studied within the context of exploring mother-child interactions (Bing, 1963; Jones, 1972). Low verbal children received less maternal attention than normal control groups, especially in the area of stimulating verbal interchange.

Maternal variables within the home environment which may affect language development in children may not necessarily be tied to socioeconomic factors. In the present study, the home environments and mother-child interaction patterns of children from homes of all social classes who showed a significant delay in language development were investigated. It was hypothesized that the same tendency toward greater restriction and less positive involvement with these children might be found across all social strata. If this were true, the maternal-child relationship could be said to be a better predictor of depressed language skills than social class.

The home environments and parent-child interaction patterns in a population of 20 language-delayed children were investigated. A discussion of the specific means for identifying this language-delayed group is included. These interaction patterns were compared with those occurring in a matched group of 20 normal children and a group of 20 genetically handicapped children with Down's syndrome. Normal distribution of social class was respresented in all three sample populations.

METHOD

LANGUAGE-DELAYED SUBJECTS

Children between the ages of 2.5 and 6 years who were referred to the Child Development and Mental Retardation Center during a 1-year period, June 1972 to May 1973, formed the pool from which the sample was selected. Children were referred for one or more of the following reasons: (a) suspected mental retardation; (b) suspected language delay; and (c) unmanageable behavior, either in a home or school setting.

Children were selected for the sample on the basis of their performance during psychological testing. Each child was tested by a certified staff psychologist using the standard language-oriented Stanford-Binet Intelligence Scale (Terman & Merrill,

1960). They were also given the relatively language-independent Arthur Adaptation of the Leiter International Performance Scale, a highly useful test for determining nonverbal intellectual functioning of preschool language-delayed children (Weiner, 1971). Children included in this study were required to have a Leiter IQ score at least 15 points higher than their Stanford-Binet IQ score. The Leiter IQ score was required to fall within at least the normal range of functioning, an IQ greater than 85. There were no bounds placed upon the Stanford-Binet score.

Of the 93 referrals between the ages of 2.5 and 6 years made to the Early Childhood Team (a diagnostic team of the child development center) during the year, 20 children met these criteria. The children ranged in age from 2.83 years to 5.66 years, with a mean age of 4.33 years. Table 1 describes their demographic distribution. All resided in the Seattle metropolitan area.

Not included in the sample were children who had significant problems with hearing or who had major medical problems that could affect their development. Also not included were those children who did not reside with their natural mothers or who were placed in all-day child care facilities.

NORMAL CONTROL SUBJECTS

Each of the 20 children in the language-delayed group was matched to a normal child according to five variables: (a) age within a range of 4 months; (b) sex; (c) birth order (either first born or later born); (d) marital status of the mother; and (e) socioeconomic status. Socioeconomic status was determined according to the criteria of Hollingshead (Note 1) based on education and occupation of head of household. Race was not matched directly, but the control group contained 5 minority and 15 Caucasian children, while the language-delayed population contained 4 minority and 16 Caucasian subjects.

Children in the normal sample came primarily from well-child clinics operated by the facility. Each of these children was administered the Stanford-Binet and the Leiter International Performance Scale. All of the 20 children in the normal sample had scores within the normal range on the Stanford-Binet. None of the children showed a 15-point or greater discrepancy in their Leiter IQ score over their Stanford-Binet IQ score.

HANDICAPPED CONTROL SUBJECTS

There was some concern that the mother-child interaction pattern seen with the language-delayed group might be that generally seen between mothers and their handicapped children and might not be peculiar to language delay. Therefore, a population of preschool children with Down's syndrome from the center (see Table 1), who had also been assessed with the Caldwell Inventory of Home Stimulation, was chosen to be a handicapped comparison group (Lemmen, Note 2). Home visits to these children were made by a clinical nursing specialist who had established reliability on the Caldwell tool with one of the nurses making the visits to the language-delayed and normal children.

It is acknowledged that the group of Down's syndrome children does not match the language-delayed sample with the precision of the normal control. However, these handicapped children can be compared to the language-delayed group for

Table 1   Demographic Data

Item	Subjects		
	Language-delayed	Normal	Down's syndrome
Socioeconomic Status[a]			
Upper class	2	2	1
Upper middle class	5	5	4
Middle class	6	6	10
Working class	6	6	4
Lower class	1	1	1
Single parent home	3	3	1
Sex			
Male	16	16	10
Female	4	4	10
Race			
Chicano	0	0	2
Black	2	4	0
Native American	1	0	0
Oriental	1	1	1
Caucasian	16	15	17
Birth order			
First born	12	12	5
Later born	8	8	15

[a]Determined according to criteria of A. B. Hollingshead. Two-factor index of social position.

purposes of discussing mother-child interaction. Since Down's syndrome is a genetic handicap, differences from the normal mother-child relationship, if discovered, might reasonably be attributed to the influence of the abnormal development of the child upon the parent. On the other hand, if the Down's group resembled the normals, and differences were found in the language-delayed group, this would lend credence to the hypothesis that the mother-child interaction was, in some sense, contributory to the language delay.

ASSESSMENT OF LANGUAGE DEVELOPMENT
In addition to the psychological testing, each child in the language-delayed population was given a language evaluation by (or under the supervision of) a clinically certified speech pathologist from the American Speech and Hearing Association. Aspects of both comprehension and expression skills were assessed. Receptive skills included the ability to (a) understand the meaning of words; (b) discriminate between words; (c) understand directions of varying length, complexity, and grammatical structure; and (d) comprehend basic concepts such as color, texture, number, and shape. Expressive skills included the ability to (a) imitate sequences of words and sentences; (b) respond verbally to questions; (c) modify appropriate grammatical forms; (d) use

varying sentence structures; (e) be intelligible; and (f) use appropriate communicative behaviors.

Each child was given (a) the Sequenced Inventory of Language Development (SILD, Experimental Edition, Hedrick & Prather, Note 3),[1] and in some cases selected subtests of the Illinois Test of Psycholinguistic Abilities (ITPA; Kirk, McCarthy, & Kirk, 1968); (b) the Peabody Picture Vocabulary Test (PPVT); (c) an assessment of articulation difficulties; and (d) an audiological assessment. If the child had verbal expressive communication skills, a 50-utterance language sample was obtained through the use of toys and pictures. Structural complexity analysis and mean length of utterance ages were determined by normative data (McCarthy, 1930; Templin, 1957). Also used to determine approximate syntactical age ranges were descriptive references given in Brown and Fraser (1964), Menyuk (1969), and Bloom (1970).

ASSESSMENT OF HOME ENVIRONMENT
The Caldwell Inventory of Home Stimulation (Caldwell, Heider, & Kaplan, Note 4) was employed to evaluate the child's daily environment. This tool consists of 48 items which are checked as either present or absent in the home. Most items are a matter of direct observation, such as "mother spontaneously praises the child's qualities or behavior twice during the visit." Some items are taken from the mother's report, such as "someone takes the child to the grocery store at least once a week." A few items depend upon the observer's judgment, such as "child's environment appears safe and free of hazards." The schedule has been factor analyzed into six categories, listed in Table 2.

The score in each category represents the percentage of items scored as present in the home. Categories I, II, V, and VI include items primarily related to the quality of the mother-child interaction, while Categories III and IV are related more to the child's inanimate environment.

Because this tool was designed for children aged birth to 3 years, a few revisions were necessitated by the older age of the subject children. These changes were made, principally, in Category IV and involved inclusion of more age-appropriate play materials. Three items in Categories I, II, and V refer directly to mother-child interaction, the area of particular concern to the study. However, in the revised version (Caldwell et al., Note 5), 22 of the 25 items in these sections remained unchanged from the original tool.

RELIABILITY OF OBSERVERS
The majority (37 of the total of 40) of the home observations included at least one of the two nurses on the investigative team. Both nurses were clinical specialists in pediatrics on the staff of the child development center and had had previous experience with the Caldwell tool in their clinical practice. A reliability check between these nurses was made on three of the visits, and mean agreement reliability was calculated at .99. Three of the home visits were made by other staff members (one by a nurse and two by a psychologist). Reliability checks were then made between all four observers, and mean agreement reliability for 12 visits was .92.

---

[1] The revised 1973 edition (Hendrick & Prather, 1975) is now in print.

Table 2   Categories and Sample Items from Caldwell Inventory of Home Stimulation

---

I.   Emotional and verbal responsivity of mother

Offers direct praise to child at least once;
Spontaneously praises child's behavior at least twice
Caresses or kisses child at least once

II.   Avoidance of restriction and punishment

Does not shout at child during visit;
Does not express overt annoyance toward child;
Neither slaps nor spanks child during visit

III.   Organization of physical and temporal environment

Takes child to store at least once a week;
Takes child out of house at least 4 times a week;
Sees the environment is free of hazards

IV.   Provision of appropriate play materials

Provides muscle activity toys or equipment;
Provides eye-hand coordination toys;
Provides toys for literature and music

V.   Maternal involvement with child

Encourages developmental advance;
Structures child's play periods;
Introduces child to interviewer

VI.   Opportunities for variety in daily stimulation

Reads stories at least three times weekly;
Is taken care of by father some time each day;
Shares at least one meal with mother and father

Because of the readily detectable differences in language behavior and appearance of the normal, Down's syndrome, and language-delayed children, it was not possible for the observers to be blind as to the clinical status of the child. However, Caldwell ratings of the Down's syndrome children had been made as part of a diagnostic test battery prior to the decision to include them as a control group in this study. Hence, their Caldwell scores could not have been influenced by the expected outcomes of this study.

RESULTS

INTELLIGENCE TEST SCORES

The two-tailed *t* test for related measures was used to determine whether the normal and language-delayed groups had indeed been selected in such a manner that their Stanford-Binet IQ scores differed significantly from each other, while their Leiter or performance IQ scores did not. Table 3 confirms that such was the case.

The language-delayed group had a mean Binet IQ of 80.3, the normal group 115.7, t (19) = 8.05, p <.001. There was no significant difference in the intellectual performance of the two groups, however, as assessed through perceptual problem-solving modes using the Leiter International Performance Scale, t (19) = .20. While the language-delayed group showed a mean gain of 23.9 IQ points on the Leiter as compared to the Binet score, the normal group showed a mean loss of 10.65 IQ points. That the Leiter IQ is 5 to 10 points less than the Binet for the normal population corroborates a similar finding by Leiter (Leiter, 1969).

The range scatter of the two groups on the Leiter and the Binet was also analyzed using the two-tailed *t* test for related measures. The range of scatter on the Binet and on the Leiter was determined for each subject by subtracting his basal age from his ceiling age. Table 3 shows that the language-delayed group had considerably more scatter on the Leiter than did the normal group, t (19) = 3.56, p <.01; while the normal group showed greater scatter on the Binet than did the language-delayed group, t (19) = 4.63, p <.001.

LANGUAGE ASSESSMENT

The language performance of each child in the language-delayed group is presented in Figure 1 in order of chronological age. The profiles of these children reveal that, in 13 of 20 cases, expressive abilities were somewhat more delayed than were receptive abilities. However, with the exception of Subjects 2 and 4, there appears to be at least a year's delay in the receptive as well as the expressive abilities of these

Table 3   Mean IQ Scores and Range of Scatter

Test	Subjects Language delayed	Normal	Difference
Binet (1960)[r] IQ	80.33	115.70	35.40**
Leiter IQ	104.20	105.05	.85
Leiter IQ minus Binet IQ	23.90	−10.65	34.55**
Range of Scatter in Years on			
Binet IQ	2.58	3.45	.87**
Leiter IQ	3.65	2.85	.80*

[r] Note *p*s refer to significance of difference between language-delayed and normal subjects.
*p <.01.
**p <.001.

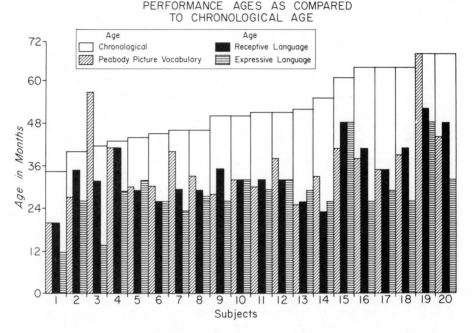

Figure 1.   **Performance ages as compared to chronological age for each subject in the language-delayed group in order of chronological age.**

children, as assessed by the Sequenced Inventory of Language Development (Hedrick & Prather, 1970). In 4 cases, receptive and expressive abilities were commensurate with each other, though at least a year delayed. And in 3 cases, expressive skills were actually at a higher level than were receptive skills. It needs to be clarified that the description "language delay" does not necessarily refer just to how the child "talks." Inspection of Figure 1 also indicates that even as chronological age increased, language functioning continued to hover at the 2.5 to 3.5 year level. There appears to be a tendency for language functioning to become more discrepant with chronological age expectations as the child approaches public school age. The mean and range of the intellectual and language functioning of the language-delayed children in comparison to their chronological age is depicted in Figure 2. Looking at this group as a whole, the mean performance of their visual processing skills (Leiter) is above their age expectation. The overall functioning when both verbal and performance items are considered (Stanford-Binet) is below age level, with a downward progression noted when looking at verbal comprehension skills and specific expressive linguistic behaviors (SILD).

HOME ENVIRONMENT DIFFERENCES
The results of the Caldwell Inventory of Home Stimulation were analyzed using an analysis of variance, two-factor mixed design. The Duncan multiple range test was

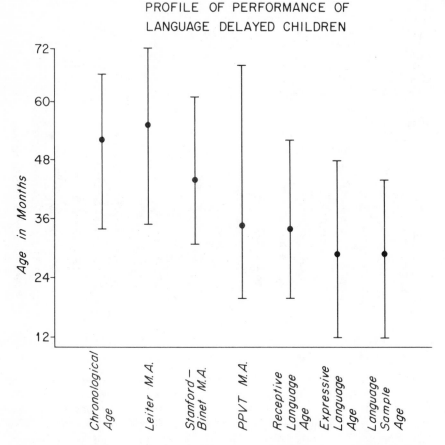

Figure 2. Profile of performance of language-delayed children showing the mean and range of: chronological age; Leiter International Performance Scale Mental Age; Stanford-Binet (1960) Mental Age; Peabody Picture Vocabulary Mental Age; Sequenced Inventory of Language Development Receptive Language Age and Expressive Language Age; Language Sample Age.

used for making multiple comparisons. The pattern of differences found in the homes of the language-delayed group, as compared to both the matched, normal control group and the group of Down's syndrome children, are delineated in Table 4 and Figure 3. The language-delayed, normal, and Down's syndrome groups differed statistically in their total Caldwell scores, $F (2, 57) = 73.23, P < .001$. And there was significant interaction effect, $F = 9.28, p < .001$. An analysis of variance of the interaction effect showed that although the language-delayed group was statistically different from both the normal, $F (10, 285) = 6.12, p < .001$, and the Down's syndrome group, $F(10, 285) = 6.17$, $p < .001$, in their pattern of Caldwell scores, the Down's syndrome group did not differ significantly from the normals.

As described in Table 4, this pattern held across all of the subscores of the Caldwell with the exception of Category III, organization of the physical and temporal environment, in which none of the three groups differed statistically. In all of the other categories, the language-delayed group scored significantly below both the Down's syndrome and the normal group, which did not differ from each other. It is notable that the greatest discrepancies occurred in the three categories which deal directly with the mother-child interaction: I. emotional and verbal responsiveness of mother; II. avoidance of punishment; and V. maternal involvement with child. There was less discrepancy in categories dealing with provision of play materials and opportunity for stimulation.

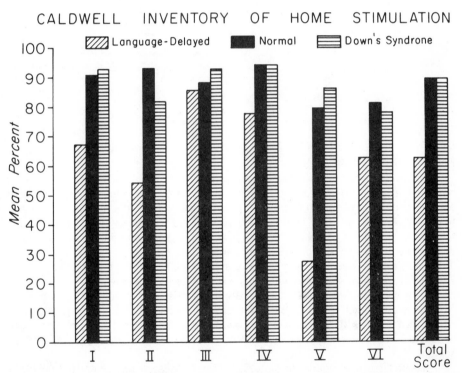

Figure 3.   Mean scores of the language-delayed, normal, and Down's syndrome groups on the six categories of the Caldwell Inventory of Home Stimulation. (I. Emotional and verbal responsiveness of mother; II. Avoidance of restriction and punishment; III. Organization of the physical and temporal environment; IV. Provision of appropriate play materials; V. Maternal involvement with child; VI. Opportunities for variety in daily stimulation.)

Table 4   Mean Caldwell Scores

	Subjects		
Caldwell inventory of home stimulation	Language-delayed	Normal	Down's syndrome
I. Emotional and verbal responsiveness of mother	.67	.91	.93
II. Avoidance of restriction and punishment	.54	.93	.82
III. Organization of physical and temporal environment	.84	.88	.92
IV. Provision of appropriate play materials	.77	.94	.94
V. Maternal involvement with child	.27	.79	.85
VI. Opportunities for variety in daily stimulation	.62	.81	.78
Total	.62	.88	.88

Note. Underlined scores differ statistically at $p < .01$

CORRELATIONS BETWEEN MATCHING, TESTING, AND HOME ENVIRONMENT VARIABLES

Pearson product-moment correlations were used to determine possible relationships between several of the matching, testing, and home environment assessment variables. With data pooled from both the language-delayed and the normal groups, the following was found. The Caldwell evaluation of the home environment was positively related to the Binet IQ of the child ($r = .76$, $p < .01$) and negatively related to the degree of discrepancy between the Leiter IQ and the Binet IQ ($r = -.51$, $p < .01$). The Caldwell was not significantly related to the Leiter IQ of the child ($r = .20$). Hence, the maternal and home variables were related to two measures of language performance but were not related to non-language-oriented intellectual performance. Notably, the Caldwell rating of the home proved statistically unrelated to socioeconomic status ($r = .13$). The correlation between the Caldwell and language performance did not prove statistically significant when examining the language-delayed sample.

It was felt that socioeconomic status might be related to several of the other parameters. For instance, one might conjecture that middle- and upper-class mothers would be more cognizant of delay in their children and hence might refer their child to the clinic at an earlier age. In fact, however, socioeconomic status was unrelated to the chronological referral age of the language-delayed child ($r = .14$). One might also hypothesize that mothers of lower socioeconomic status would be more likely to receive a low rating on the Caldwell category, avoidance of restriction and punishment. But again, this proved not to be the case ($r = .08$). Socioeconomic status was, however, significantly related to IQ in an interesting fashion. Socioeconomic status was positively correlated to Leiter non-language IQ ($r = .56, p <.01$) but not to Binet IQ ($r = .02$) for the language-delayed group. Just the reverse was true for the normal group. For the normals, socioeconomic status was significantly related ($r = .66, p <.01$) to Binet IQ but not to Leiter IQ ($r = .38$).

DISCUSSION

Naturalistic observations of the interaction between mother and child in the home have assumed increasing importance for the study of child development in recent years (Bell, 1964; Moss, 1965; Yarrow, 1963). To date, however, studies of pre-school age children have been conducted primarily in laboratory situations or in preschools (Lytton, 1971). Perhaps this is a result of the difficulties inherent in attempting to keep an active preschooler and mother together for an extended period of time while preserving the "natural flavor" of the observation. The Caldwell Inventory of Home Stimulation offers distinct advantages in this regard, since it is conducted within the framework of an interview about the child, though the mother's behavior is being observed. The mothers were told the purpose of the visit was to observe the child and his daily home routine—a procedure generally cited as reducing the possibility of "faked behavior" on the part of the mother (Lytton, 1971).

The Caldwell data show clearly that the most significant differences between the mothers of language-delayed children and mothers of normal children were in Categories I, II, and V of the tool (refer to Figure 3)—those sections related to direct mother-child interaction. Significant differences also occurred in the area of availability of play material (IV) and variety of stimulation (VI), which are not related to direct interaction. However, these sections are indirectly related in that the language-delayed children did not have mothers who as readily understood their developmental status and who provided ways to promote it.

Category I (see Table 2) of the Inventory of Home Stimulation contains items that are observed in relation to the mother's direct verbal interaction *with* the child. Also included are items that refer to the way she talks *about* her child. In general, mothers of the normal children tended to talk about the child in very positive terms, to speak to the child in a warm and accepting manner, and to openly caress the child. In fact, these mothers often structured the visit so that the child could "show off" for the observer. Mothers of the language-delayed children, on the other hand, showed few of these behaviors. They tended to talk about the children in critical tones and seldom praised or caressed.

Category II looks at ways in which the mother may or may not restrict and punish the child during the visit. Children from both groups were observed to behave in ways that displeased their mothers, but there were important differences in the way the mothers handled this. The mothers of normal children generally tried to reason with the child, and frequently this was effective. The mothers of the language-delayed children were much more quick to shout, threaten, and, in some cases, spank the child.

The biggest difference, however, occurred in Category V—maternal involvement with the child. In most of the homes of the language-delayed children, the mothers and children lived together in parallel fashion. The mothers were generally conscientious in meeting the physical needs of the child, but, aside from this, there was little interaction. The mothers of the normal children, on the other hand, were more likely to say that they spent time playing with the child and encouraged him to learn new things.

To summarize, it seemed that on the whole, the mothers of the normal children enjoyed them, actively encouraged their development, and took pride in their accomplishments. However, the language-delayed children were a source of great frustration to their mothers, and it was obvious that the mutual interaction was not pleasurable for either child or mother.

The data concerning mother-child interaction in the Down's syndrome group supports the hypothesis that mothers do not necessarily behave differently toward children who are developmentally deviant. Also supporting this conclusion is the fact that none of the language-delayed children was defined by their parents as abnormal until language was noticeably behind development in other areas which were within normal limits. Thus, mother-child interaction was well established before any deviancy was diagnosed.

Of question here is the importance of the mother-child interaction on development of language skills. There is little evidence to show that the linguistic aspect of the mother's verbal input is directly related to the child's language competency (Cazden, 1968; Dale, 1972). It might instead affect both the child's cognitive development and *how* he uses language. However, observations of the verbal environment of normal children (Adler, 1973; Broen, 1972; Wyatt, 1969) indicate that what is essential is a "dynamic verbal interchange" where the mother gives positive responses to the child's attempts to use verbal communication and also modifies her own verbal behavior to meet the child's ability to respond.

However, in view of the current emphasis on the ways in which children affect parents' behavior (Kogan & Winberger, 1966), it is important to state that most of the mothers had for some time viewed their language-delayed children as "different" and "difficult." Frequently, in discussing why they did not structure play or reading activities with the child, the mothers would state that their own attempts in this direction had been consistently rebuffed by the child. In essence, from an early age many of these children had shown a reluctance to interact with their mothers; at least this was the perception of the mothers. This perception is supported by observational data during the language assessment, where 16 out of 20 children had negative communicative behaviors. That is, in general, they did not attempt to respond to requests for imitation, did not consistently try to answer questions or follow directions; they had limited directed utterances and often displayed interfering, manipulative behaviors.

Therefore, it is important to emphasize that by the time these observations were made, the poor interaction was definitely reciprocal in nature. It should be emphasized that neither the parent nor the child should be "blamed" for the breakdown in the communication interaction.

It is interesting to note that the vast majority of the language-delayed children (80%) were males. Although in the normal population there is some indication that males aged 3–6 receive higher language scores than do females (Templin, 1957), in a clinic population, there is a prevalence of males with language difficulties. One might question whether a different mother-child relationship exists with male children which is more fragile than that with females and which can easily influence language development negatively.

Indeed, in the Fels and Berkeley longitudinal studies (Bayley & Schaefer, 1964; Honzik, 1967; Moss & Kagan, 1958), the relationship of early maternal behavior to IQ has been impressive for males. An early, loving, positive maternal relationship has proved predictive of Wechsler-Intelligence-Scale-for-Children IQ scores for males even at age 36 (Bayley & Schaefer, 1964). For females, however, the relationship of maternal affectional ties to IQ does not persist past the age of 3. This may indicate that intellectual, and especially language, development of male children is particularly vulnerable to the parameters of mother-child interaction, as measured by Caldwell.

Adler (1973) discredits the assumption that the verbal stimulation encountered in lower-class homes is necessarily inferior to that of middle-class homes. Within each class, there appears to be great variation in both type and quantity of such stimulation. The results of the present study corroborate this. Language-delayed children were found to occur in all social strata with the greatest preponderance in the upper-middle, middle, and working classes, rather than in the lower class. While this particular distribution may be argued to be an artifact of the type of helping agency involved in the referral process, rather than reflective of the actual distribution in the population, it is notable that the Caldwell ratings of the home were not related to the social class of the family for either the language-delayed or the normal groups. Rather, low Caldwell ratings were indicative of language delay irrespective of socioeconomic standing.

From the Caldwell profiles, particularly Categories I, II, and V, it would seem that intervention and prevention techniques need to emphasize the area of parent–child interaction rather than to necessarily change the physical environment or the child's routine. While most of the referral children from this study are currently enrolled in a special preschool classroom designed to ameliorate communication disorders (Experimental Education Unit, Child Development and Mental Retardation Center, University of Washington), the mothers of these children should be as much a part of the intervention program as are the children. These mothers need to know how to structure their interchanges so that both parent and child can mutually succeed and reinforce each other.

Further investigation is indicated in the area of identification of the specific variables that might be different in the environments of language-delayed children as compared to normally developing children. Changing the behavior of mother as well as the children can be more successful once these variables have been specified.

Longitudinal research on a similar population of language-delayed preschool children is needed in order to ferret out the possible predictive pattern for later social and communicative development. It may well be that these are the children who during the school age years show continued deficits in language-related academic skills. In addition, they may have difficulties later on in the development of normal social relationships.

REFERENCE NOTES

1. Hollingshead, A. B. *Two-factor index of social position.* Unpublished manuscript, 1957.

(Available from A. B. Hollingshead, Department of Sociology. Yale University, New Haven, Connecticut 06510.)

2. Lemmen, S. J. *Group education with mothers of children with Down's syndrome.* Paper presented at the meeting of the American Association on Mental Deficiency, Portland, Oregon, October 1973.

3. Hedrick, D., & Prather, E. *Sequenced Inventory of Language Development* (experimental edition). Unpublished manuscript, University of Washington, Child Development and Mental Retardation Center, 1970.

4. Caldwell, E. M., Heider, J., & Kaplan, B. *The Inventory of Home Stimulation.* Unpublished manuscript, Syracuse University, 1968.

5. Caldwell, E. M., Heider, J., & Kaplan, B. *The Inventory of Home Stimulation* (Preschool revision) Unpublished manuscript, 1973. (Available from Susan Inglis. Child Development and Mental Retardation Center. WJ-10, University of Washington, Seattle, Washington 98195.)

REFERENCES

Ackerman, P. T., Peters, J. E., & Dykman, R. A. Children with specific learning disabilities. *Journal of Learning Disabilities,* 1971, *4,* 33–49.

Adler, S. Social class bases of language: A reexamination of socioeconomic, sociopsychological and sociolinguistic factors. *American Speech and Hearing Association,* 1973, *15,* 3–9.

Bayley, N., & Schaefer, E. S. Correlations of maternal and child behaviors with the development of mental abilities: Data from the Berkeley Growth Study. *Monographs of the Society for Research in Child Development,* 1964, *29* (6, Whole No. 97).

Bee, H. L., Van Egeren, L. F., Streissguth, A. P., Nyman, B. A., & Leckie, M. S. Social class differences in maternal teaching strategies and speech patterns. *Developmental Psychology,* 1969, *1,* 726–734.

Bell, R. D. Structuring parent-child interaction situations for direct observation. *Child Development,* 1964, *35,* 1009–1020.

Bing, E. Effect of childrearing practices on development of differential cognitive abilities. *Child Development,* 1963, *34,* 631–648.

Bloom, L. *Language development—Form and function in emerging grammars.* Cambridge: The MIT Press, 1970.

Broen, P. The verbal environment of the language-learning child. *American Speech and Hearing Association Monographs,* 1972, No. 17.

Brown, R., & Fraser, C. The acquisition of syntax. In U. Bellugi & R. Brown (Eds). The acqusition of language. *Monographs of the Society for Research in Child Development,* 1964, *29* (1, Whole No. 92).

Cazden, C. B. Subcultural differences in child language: An interdisciplinary review. *Merrill-Palmer Quarterly,* 1966, *12,* 185–221.

Cazden, C. B. The acquisition of noun and verb inflections. *Child Development,* 1968, *39,* 433–448.

Dale, P. *Language development: Structure and function.* Hinsdale, Ill.: Dryden Press, 1972.

Eells, K., Davis, R., Havighurst, V., Herrick, E., & Tyler, R. (Eds.) *Intelligence and cultural differences.* Chicago: University of Chicago Press, 1951.

Hedrick, D., & Prather, E. *Sequenced Inventory of Communication Development.* Seattle: University of Washington, Press, 1975.

Hess, R. D., & Shipman, V. C. Early experience and the socialization of cognitive modes in children. *Child Development,* 1965, *36,* 869–886.

Hess, R. D., & Shipman, V. C. Early experience and the socialization of cognitive modes in children. *Symposia on Child Psychology,* 1967, *1,* 57–81.

Honzik, M. Environmental correlates of mental growth: Predictions from the family setting at 21 months. *Child Development,* 1967, *38,* 337–364.

Jones, P. Home environment and the development of verbal ability. *Child Development,* 1972, *43,* 1081–1086.

Kennedy, W. A., Van de Ritt, V., & White, J. C. A normative sample of intelligence and achievement of Negro elementary school children in the Southeastern United States. *Monographs of the Society for Research in Child Development,* 1963, *28* (6, Whole No. 90).

Kirk, S., & Kirk, W. *Psycholinguistic learning disabilities: Diagnosis and remediation.* Urbana: University of Illinois Press, 1971.

Kirk, S., McCarthy, J., & Kirk, W. *Illinois Test of Psycholinguistic Abilities.* Urbana: University of Illinois Press, 1968.

Kogan, K., & Winberger, H. C. An approach to defining mother-child interaction styles. *Perceptual and Motor Skills,* 1966, *23,* 1171–1177.

Leiter, R. G. *General instructions for the Leiter International Performance Scale.* Chicago: Stoelting, 1969.

Lytton, H. Observation studies of parent-child interaction: A methodological review. *Child Development,* 1971, *42,* 651–684.

Marge, M. The general problem of language disabilities. In J. Irwin & M. Marge (Eds.), *Principles of childhood language disabilities.* New York: Appleton-Century-Crofts, 1972.

McCarthy, D. The language development of the preschool child. *Child Welfare Monographs,* 1930, No. 4

Menyuk, P. *Sentences children use.* Cambridge, Mass: The MIT Press, 1969.

Moss, H. A. Methodological issues in studying mother-infant interaction. *American Journal of Orthopsychiatry,* 1965, *35,* 482–486.

Moss, H. A., & Kagan, J. Maternal influences on early IQ scores. *Psychological Reports,* 1958, *4,* 655–661.

Sandler, L., Van Campen, J., Rather, G., Stafford, C., & Weisman, R. Responses of urban preschool children to a developmental screening test. *Journal of Pediatrics.* 1970, *77,* 775–781.

Templin, M. Certain language skills in children: Their development and interrelationships. *Child Welfare Monographs,* 1957, No. 26.

Terman, L. M., & Merrill, M. A. *Stanford-Binet Intelligence Scale.* Boston: Houghton-Mifflin, 1960.

Weiner, P. Stability and validity of two measures of intelligence used with children whose language development is delayed. *Journal of Speech and Hearing Research,* 1971, *14,* 254–261.

Wyatt, G. *Language learning and communication disorders in children.* New York: Free Press, 1969.

Yarrow, M. R. Problems of methods in parent-child research. *Child Development,* 1963, *34,* 215–226.

An Experimental Parent-Assisted Treatment Program for Preschool Language-Delayed Children

James D. MacDonald, Judith P. Blott, Kathleen Gordon, Bernard Spiegel, and Marianna Hartmann

Six preschool children with Down's syndrome were subjects in an experimental program using parents as the primary language trainers. Three children served as experimental subjects and three as controls. The program applied the Environmental Language Intervention Strategy to effect a generalized functional language in children who primarily were capable of only single-word utterances. The major objective was to increase utterance length and grammatical complexity. The two essential procedures were to train immediate generalization of language changes from imitation to parallel conversation and play activities and to educate parents as language trainers to effect immediate transfer of training. The five-month program ran in two stages: two months with professionals and mothers as language trainers and three months in the home with parents as the sole language trainers. Results from the two-month stage indicated marked increases in utterance length and grammatical complexity in imitation and conversation for all experimental subjects but negligible changes for the controls. Follow-up assessment indicated continued language increments for the experimental subjects over three months of home programming with parents as the sole language trainers. The experimental language growth in the mean length of utterance over three months of home programming for the retarded children was comparable to growth for normally developing children. An epilogue reports successful replication of the program with the original control subjects.

Little familiarity with retarded and other developmentally-delayed children is needed to realize that one of the essential barriers to their educational and social development is the lack of an environmentally useful language. Some questions that arise in the development of a model for expressive language training of retarded children are (1) what language classes are to be the content for training, (2) how a program is to be designed to train spontaneous social use of new language behaviors, and (3) whether training will be carried out entirely by professionals or whether parents can be taught to conduct the language training to effect transfer into the home.

The most fruitful content for language training may come from our knowledge of

From *Journal of Speech and Hearing Disorders, 39*, 395–415 (1974). Reprinted by permission of the American Speech and Hearing Association.

the development of language classes in nondelayed children. Recent findings in the study of language development suggest that children develop expressive language in markedly uniform ways across languages (Brown, 1973a; Bloom, 1970; Schlesinger, 1971; Bowerman, 1974). This recent breakthrough is the result, in part, of the consideration that the environmental context suggests the semantic intent of children's utterances. Thus, Brown has compiled a finite set of semantic relations that seem universally to be the subject matter of the speech of children as it develops from the one- to two-word stage. These semantic relations may be said to be propositions concerning the sensory-motor world and seem to represent the linguistic expression of the sensory-motor intelligence, which Piaget (1952) has described as the principal acquisition of the first 18 months of life (Brown, 1973a, p. 101). The relevance of these recent findings is that they suggest possible content for early language training of language-delayed children. In fact, Brown (1973b) suggests that these rules are the basic building blocks for children's language development beyond the two-word stage:

The recently proposed Environmental Language Intervention Strategy (ELIS) (MacDonald and Blott, 1974) provides a design for both testing and training the rules underlying children's early sentences. The major therapeutic objective of the ELIS is to effect a generalized functional language in children whose expressive language consists of primarily single-word utterances. The specific content of the training strategy reported in this experiment included those eight semantic-grammatical rules that Schlesinger (1971) found to govern children's early two-word combinations. The eight rules account for all but one of the 12 first sentence types that Brown (1973a) has found in developmental studies of several languages.

The second issue in developing programs to effect functional use of language is the selection of ways to train generalization of novel language behaviors to spontaneous social use. Certain programs proposed in the literature train new language structures first in imitation and then report conversational use to occur through a system of fading imitative cues (in particular, Gray and Fygetakis, 1968). Other programs (for example, Bricker, 1972) train more naturalistic use of the new language structures by first training them in imitation and subsequently extending stimulus control of the new structures to discriminate stimuli such as questions, thus approximating conversation. Rather than train the new rules in more natural usage after establishing a broad imitative repertoire, the present experimental program involves simultaneous training in imitation, conversation, and play from the beginning. Thus, training the new language rules for functional use is the immediate as well as long-range objective of the strategy.

The third issue is the feasibility of using parents as language trainers for their children. The major assumption was that the inadequate language behaviors of language-delayed children do not result from constructs such as "mental retardation" or "brain damage," but rather from the lawful consequence of inadequate training or the lack of appropriate training. For these children, then, language learning has been viewed as an active process functionally related to the environmental contingencies accompanying their language performances. From such a viewpoint, intervention must establish contingencies in the child's environment that will stimulate him with appropriate language input and provide adequate consequences to his utterances to shape those utterances toward appropriate communicative form. Consequently, it was decided that the principal determiners of the child's natural training contingencies—his parents—would be primary language trainers to maximize the probability of integrating any language changes into the child's natural and functional communication system. Additionally, the availability of professional language trainers is strikingly inadequate, especially in light of the need for early preschool language intervention with a great proportion of children with suspected retardation and learning disabilities. Thus, the present study sought to investigate parents' performances in implementing a language program in the home after nonacademic, in-service training.

METHOD

SUBJECTS.   The subjects were six children, three to five years of age, with Down's syndrome. All satisfied the preprogram criteria of speaking primarily in single-word utterances and having parents willing to participate in language training at home. Three served as experimental subjects and three as controls. All the families were similarly "middle-class" and both parents lived at home. These somewhat ideal families were selected to test the feasibility of a novel set of conditions—an untested language training program and an initial attempt at teaching parents to be language trainers.

EXPERIMENTERS.   The professional language trainers were three graduate students in speech and hearing science at Ohio State University, who served as Maternal and Child Health trainees at The Nisonger Center, a university-affiliated center for interdisciplinary training in mental retardation. All trainers were involved in designing the program with the primary author. The mothers of the three experimental subjects also served as experimenters. The mothers were all housewives who had no professional training in speech, language, or child development. The highest formal education level of the mothers in the experimental and control groups was comparable; two in each group held high school degrees and one in each group had had nursing training. Fathers and siblings were reported to participate at least three times a week in the home training sessions. The number of siblings in the experimental subjects' homes was four, one, and none, and in the control subjects' homes, one, three, and four, respectively.

PROCEDURE.   The experimental program ran five months in two phases. Phase 1 consisted of a seven-week training period including sessions twice a week at The Nisonger Center (clinic) with mothers and professional language trainers, and daily at home with mothers as sole language trainers. Phase II involved six months of home sessions with parent language trainers alone and monthly follow-up meetings with the professional language trainers.

PHASE I—CLINIC
Phase I at the clinic included an orientation meeting with all parents, two pretest sessions, one training session for the mothers, 10 language training sessions with the child, two posttest sessions, and a final transfer-of-training session. A three-hour

evening orientation meeting was held with all parents and the language staff to introduce the objectives and design of the program. Fathers were involved in the orientation to encourage them to help implement the program at home, thus providing a stronger home support system.

Preprogram (baseline) language performance was assessed in two sessions separated by one week. Inasmuch as identical testing was conducted immediately before and after Phase I, a single description of the testing is offered. Pre- and postprogram language assessment was made with the Environmental Language Inventory (ELI) (MacDonald and Blott, 1974). The ELI is a strategy that assesses eight early developing semantic-grammatical rules that comprise the first two-word relations expressed by normally developing children in several languages (Brown, 1973a; Schlesinger, 1971; Bloom, 1970). The ELI assesses the child's production of the rules in both imitative and conversational production.

Because the training objective of the experimental program was to increase the children's utterance length and grammatical complexity, it is appropriate to present the rules assessed by the ELI. It was by these rules that grammatical complexity was defined and utterance length expanded. For clarification, the rules are presented within the following example. Imagine the two-word utterances a child might make as he is playing ball with his father. The child might express the agent + action rule by saying, "Daddy throw," or the action + object rule by saying, "Throw ball." In addition, the child might express location of an action or object by the $\times$ + locative rule, as in "ball chair" or "throw here." The child might also enter into descriptions by expressing the modifier + head rule in utterances such as "big ball" (attribution), "my ball" (possession), and "more ball" (recurrence). In expressing denial, rejection, or nonexistence with the negation + $\times$ rule, the child may say, "no ball" or "all-gone ball." Additionally, the child might use the unadultlike expression "daddy ball," reflecting the agent + object rule. In asking for the ball to be thrown, the child might express the $\times$ + dative rule by saying, "throw me." Finally, the child would express the eighth rule, introducer + $\times$, with utterances such as "see ball" or "hi daddy." In the ELI, each rule is assessed by means of four conversational cues and four imitative cues for production of two-, three-, four-, and five-word utterances.

In addition to the ELI, the experimental subjects' language was sampled in a "free" speech sample (according to a procedure described in Johnson, Darley, and Spriestersbach, 1963). No free sample was available in one subject's pretesting. The control subjects' language was assessed in procedures identical to those for the experimental subjects. For them, data from the ELI and free samples were obtained before and after a seven-week, no-training period and after a three-month period, paralleling the testing for experimental subjects.

BASELINE PERFORMANCE AND SELECTION OF RESPONSE CLASSES FOR TRAINING

On the basis of the experimental subjects' baseline performance on the ELI, the action + object and $\times$ + locative rules were selected as the major classes for training, for three reasons. First, they were the two most frequent rules in the subjects' baseline performance. Second, they are those rules reported by recent investigators to be the relations occurring most frequently in early normal langauge development (Brown,

1973a). Finally, action + object and × + locative appeared to be rules with sentence integrity and ones from which longer, more complex utterances could generate easily. The action + object grammatical rule specifies that the experience of perceiving an action on a direct object is expressed in a child's language generally with the action word preceding the object word, for example, "throw ball." The × + locative grammatical rule indicates that when a child verbally expresses the location of a thing or an action (notated as ×) the location word follows the word to be located, for example, "ball there," "throw here," "dolly bed," and "go car."

After the child's baseline performance was summarized in tabular form, each language trainer and mother met to interpret the child's baseline in practical terms of language behaviors and introduce the mothers to the training procedures.

EXPERIMENTAL TRAINING MODEL

A single session consisted of training the action + object and × + locative rules in imitation, conversation, and play. Each of these three training procedures was introduced individually in one of the first three training sessions. While the child played alone, the mothers were taught to record responses and administer the procedure in a role-playing situation with two professional language trainers. After they became comfortable and accurate with these procedures, the mothers recorded actual responses of the child during training and then administered the procedures to the child under supervision. Once the three procedures had been introduced in separate training sessions, they were combined into a single training model for the duration of the program. The stimuli were trained first in imitative production for 15 minutes. After being modeled imitatively, the same language classes were trained for 15 minutes in conversational use. In the third 15-minute segment, structured play, the child was required to use in play activities those rules and utterance lengths that occurred in the imitative and conversational productions of the first two training segments. Following the three 15-minute segments, the mother and professional language trainer reviewed home language records, discussed the child's progress, and made necessary adjustments in the home training and recording.

Since a behavioral contingency model was used, parents were trained in contingency management procedures as part of the program. Antecedent linguistic and nonlinguistic stimuli were designed, and their use was demonstrated. The professional language trainers used modeling, role-playing, and feedback discussion to train the parents in behavioral shaping procedures. Parents were then trained to distinguish among the properly consequent correct language responses, incorrect language responses, and approximations. Major consequences to language responses in Phase I were social praise, tokens, and repetition of the language cue for correct and approximate responses or timeout from attention for incorrect responses. Considerable portions of each session at the center involved training the parents to use the behavioral training and recording procedures with precision and reliability. Tables 1, 2, and 3 present schema for the three training models and examples. As the tables indicate, in training imitative and conversational production of a given rule, parallel linguistic and nonlinguistic cues served as the training stimuli. For example, for training the action + object rule, the language trainers (both mothers and professionals) designed several nonlinguistic cues to elicit the rule both imitatively and conversationally. The same nonlinguistic cue (for example, throwing a ball) was used for

Table 1 Training Model for the Imitation Phase of Program. The Objective Is to Train Imitative Productions of Particular Semantic-Grammatical Rules and Utterance Lengths for the Purpose of Establishing the Imitative Productions as Models for Conversational and Spontaneous Use

Antecedent Stimulus	Response	Consequences	Examples
A pair of parallel linguistic and nonlinguistic cues designed to elicit a verbal imitation reflecting a particular utterance length. The linguistic cue specifies the response to be given. The nonlinguistic cue specifies the semantic event represented by the linguistic cue. Example: Nonlinguistic cue: Throwing a ball into the air. Linguistic cue: "Say, throw ball."	Correct (that is, complete repetition of linguistic cue).	1. Repetition of linguistic cue as model for desired response. 2. Social praise. 3. Token. 4. Proceed to next trial.	1. "Throw ball." 2. "Good talking." 3. Plastic chip leading to tangible reward (any token).
	Approximation (that is, a response closer to linguistic cue than previous attempts or response including either correct grammatical rule of utterance length).	1. Repetition of linguistic cue as model for desired response. 2. Social praise. 3. Token.	1. "Throw ball." 2. "Good try." 3. Token.
	Incorrect (that is, shorter utterance length than in the linguistic cue, or a response with no obvious relation to the stimulus set).	1. Pause: no attention for three seconds. 2. Repetition of same stimulus set (that is, linguistic and nonlinguistic pair) up to twice.	Trainer says, "Say, throw ball," as he throws a ball into the air.
	No response (that is, no verbal response within five seconds).	1. Pause: no attention for three seconds. 2. Repetition of stimulus set up to twice.	Trainer says, "Say, throw ball," as he throws a ball into the air.

Table 2   Training Model for the Conversation Phase of Program. The Objective is to Train, in Conversation-like Production, Verbalizations Consisting of Those Grammatical Rules and Utterance Lengths Concurrently Being Trained in Imitative Production in the Same Session. This Training Model is Designed to Effect Immediate Carryover from Imitative to Conversational Production

Antecedent Stimulus	Response	Consequences	Examples
A parallel pair of nonlinguistic and linguistic cues designed to elicit a conversation-like production reflecting a given semantic-grammatical rule. The nonlinguistic cue is intended to stimulate the experience represented by a particular grammatical rule. The linguistic cue is a question or command-like stimulus designed to elicit a conversation-like response. Example: Nonlinguistic cue: Throwing a ball into the air. Linguistic cue: "What am I doing?"	Correct (that is, a response containing the rule and utterance length being trained).	1. Imitative cue (as feedback model). 2. Social praise. 3. Token. 4. Proceed to next trial.	1. "Say, throw ball." 2. "Good talking." 3. Token. 4. Next stimulus set.
	Approximation (that is, a response closer than the previous attempt or one correct in either the utterance length or grammatical rule being trained).	1. Imitative cue. 2. Social praise. 3. Token. 4. Repetition of conversation stimulus set once.	1. "Say, throw ball." 2. "Good try." 3. Token. 4. "What am I doing?" Concurrent with throwing ball
	Incorrect (that is, a response that is briefer than the utterance length being trained and not including the grammatical rule being trained).	1. Pause: no attention for three seconds. 2. Imitative cue. 3. Repetition of conversation stimulus set once.	1. "Say, throw ball." 2. "What am I doing?" Concurrent with throwing ball.
	No response (that is, no verbal response after five seconds).	1. Pause for three seconds of no attention. 2. Imitative cue. 3. Repetition of conversation stimulus set.	1. "Say, throw ball." 2. "What am I doing?" Concurrent with throwing ball.

Table 3   Training Model for the Structured Play Phase of Program. The Objective is to Train the Child to Use, In Play, Verbalizations that Consist of Those Grammatical Rules and Utterance Lengths Concurrently Being Trained in the Imitation and Conversation Stages of the Same Training Session

Antecedent Stimulus	Response	Consequences	Examples
Adult conversational response related to child's play activity (for example, in the "London Bridge" game, the adult may say, "What do you want me to do?" in response to the child's gesture for hands to be raised to form the bridge.)	Correct (that is, child's verbalization reflecting the grammatical rule and utterance length being trained in the previous imitation and conversation stages, for example, "Mommy hands up").	1. Compliance with the child's request or some behavior affirming the child's response. 2. Repetition of the response with expansion, if appropriate.	1. Mother puts hands up to play the game. 2. "Say, Mommy *put* hands up."
	Approximation (that is, a response closer than the previous attempt or one including either the correct grammatical rule or utterance length).	1. Social praise. 2. Expansion to correct production 3. Compliance with child and verbalization.	1. "Good try." 2. "Say, Mommy hands up." 3. Put hands up to play the game.
	Incorrect (that is, a response satisfying neither the grammatical rule nor utterance length criterion in training).	1. No compliance with child. 2. Pause followed by model response with desired rule or utterance length.	1. Do not raise hands. 2. After pause, "Say, Mommy hands up," concurrently with request if child approximates the desired response.

imitative and conversational training on a given trial, but the linguistic cues varied. That is, the linguistic cue for an imitative production was a direct verbal model of the desired response (for example, "Say, throw ball"), whereas the linguistic cue for a conversational production was a verbalization designed to elicit the rule in discourse (for example, "What am I doing?"). Thus, the training design provided both the linguistic and nonlinguistic environmental cues representing the full intention or meaning of the semantic-grammatical rule to be trained.

TRANSFER TRAINING

Following the 10 training sessions at the clinic, all mothers and professional language trainers participated in a transfer-of-training session, which involved writing examples of stimuli for training the remaining six rules in varying utterance lengths. Mothers were taught through modeling and feedback to develop training sets parallel to those in Phase I sessions but more representative of the child's interests and needs at home. The intention of transfer-of-training was to develop in the parents the ability to generate new training stimuli, not only for formal language sessions but also for more casual training in everyday ad hoc situations, such as travel activities and daily living routines.

PHASE I—HOME

Parents were instructed to conduct at-home daily language sessions paralleling those held concurrently at the clinic. The same training stimuli were used both at home and at the clinic. Recording of the home sessions were required a minimum of three times a week on record sheets identical to those used in clinic sessions. Sixteen to 18 home training records are available for each child in Phase I at home.

PHASE II

Phase II, which immediately followed Phase I, involved language training sessions in the home at least three times a week with parents as language trainers. The design of the training procedures at home followed the model of using behavioral contingencies to train certain rules and utterance lengths in imitation, conversation, and play in each single session. The content for training in Phase II included rules in addition to the two orginally trained. Mothers were trained to design stimuli for all eight semantic rules and selected training content on the basis of the child's progress in the home.

Monthly follow-up sessions with professional language trainers and parents were held individually for each child. The objectives of each session were to assess the child's language, review the procedures and data records, and develop rules and procedures for home sessions for the following month. During these sessions, parents were provided written instructions for writing new training stimuli and altering the program to meet progressively advanced training objectives.

RESULTS

This experimental program addressed two major issues. First, the program sought to determine the effectiveness of the ELIS (MacDonald and Blott, 1974) in establishing a generalized functional language in children with severe expressive language delay. The major changes sought were increased utterance length and increased use of semantic-grammatical rules. In keeping with the objective of an increase in "functional" or natural use of language, results are available for three language modes: imitation, conversation, and play.

The second major experimental issue was the feasibility of training parents to serve as successful language trainers with their children. This issue was evaluated by assessing language changes in both testing and training situations in Phase II, which involved parents as primary language trainers.

Primary results are available for changes in utterance length and grammatical complexity. Changes in utterance length are reported in two ways, mean length of utterance (MLU) and distribution of utterances by word length. Utterance length data in MLU and distributions of utterance lengths are available from performance on the ELI and in free play (pre-, post-, and follow-up testing). Additionally, data on MLUs are available from training sessions both at home and in the clinic in Phase I and at home in Phase II. Changes in grammatical complexity are reported in terms of the frequencies of eight semantic rules or meanings underlying the early sentence structures of children; these data are available from pre-, post-, and follow-up test sessions with the ELI.

LENGTH OF UTTERANCE

Figure 1 illustrates MLUs in conversation, imitation, and play from test sessions before and after Phase I training (with both professionals and mothers as language trainers), and at follow-up (three months into Phase II; home training with mothers as sole language trainers). The data are presented individually for experimental and control subjects. As the figure demonstrates, all children in the experimental group increased their MLUs in imitation and conversation over the seven-week Phase I. In contrast, the figure shows negligible changes over identical time for the control subjects. For the experimental subjects, the percentages of change in MLU across Phase I ranged from 16 to 71, with two of the three subjects demonstrating greater than 50% increase in both imitation and conversation over the seven-week period. In comparison, the greatest percentage of change across the seven weeks for the control subjects was 20% in two conversation cases, one an increase and the other a decrease. In the other conversation case and in all cases of imitation and play, the change was smaller than 10% of the MLU in baseline. The figure indicates that the speech of all three experimental subjects continued to progress in utterance length after three months of home language training without direct professional supervision. The gaps in the data for imitation and play reflect failure of the experimental situation to allow data collection. Two of the three control subjects demonstrated substantially less positive change in MLU than did the experimental subjects over a three-month period. One control subject, L, demonstrated greater MLU change in one mode, imitation, than did the experimental subjects.

The change in MLU across the entire experimental program ranged from an increase of 57 to 191% for the experimental subjects, whereas the changes in MLU for the control subjects over the identical time ranged from a decrease of 15% to an increase of 73%. To summarize, the experimental subjects made substantially

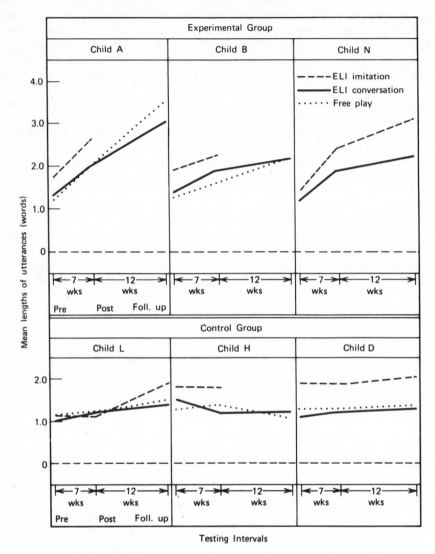

Figure 1. **Mean lengths of utterances in imitation, conversation, and play at pre-, post-, and follow-up testing of experimental and control subjects.**

greater change in MLU than did the control subjects in imitation, conversation, and play over the five months.

The language performance of the experimental subjects was also assessed in training sessions. Table 4 presents mean lengths of utterances across four training sessions each at the clinic Phase I, home Phase I, and home Phase II for the three training modes. In addition, the table presents the amount and percentage change in MLU from home training sessions in Phase I to the third month of Phase II. Increases in MLU for all subjects in all training modes from Phase I to Phase II in home training sessions also are demonstrated. The quantity of change reported in home training is comparable to the changes reported across Phase II in testing (see Figure 1). These changes reflect further evidence that the subjects' language performance continued to improve over time with mothers as sole language trainers. The question of accuracy of the mothers' recordings of utterance lengths can be assessed indirectly. Each mother was trained in Phase I to transcribe her child's verbalizations to agree with the professional language trainers. While accuracy of mothers' recordings was not assessed formally, comparison of the subjects' performance records made concurrently in home and clinic sessions offers informal validation of the mothers' home recordings of MLU. As Table 4 shows, the recordings of MLUs in concurrent home and clinic sessions are strikingly comparable; the MLU recorded by mothers in the home and by professionals in the clinic differed by no more than an average of two-tenths of a word, which at the most accounted for an 8% difference in the recordings. Thus, at least in terms of MLU, the mothers' recordings resulted in language data similar to professionals' recordings.

Table 4   Mean Lengths of Utterances (MLUs) in Concurrent Phase I Training Sessions in the Clinic and at Home and at Home During Phase II, Third Month. Data Are Based on Four Sessions Each for Imitation, Conversation, and Play. Amount and Percentage of Change in MLU Are Indicated for Home Training

Subject	Task	Phase I Clinic	Phase I Home	Phase II Home	Amount Change	Percentage Change
A	Imitation	2.7	2.8	4.0	1.2	43
	Conversation	2.6	2.8	3.8	1.0	36
	Play	2.1	2.3	3.0	0.7	30
B	Imitation	2.2	2.2	2.7	0.5	23
	Conversation	2.1	2.3	2.8	0.5	22
	Play	2.0	2.1	2.7	0.6	29
C	Imitation	2.3	2.4	—	—	—
	Conversation	2.3	2.4	3.3	0.9	38
	Play	1.8	1.9	3.1	1.2	63

A major objective of the study was to train children who used primarily single-word utterances to speak in multiple-word utterances. Figure 2 presents, for all experimental subjects combined, the percentages of total utterances that were one, two, three, four, and five words in length. Data are presented for pre- and post-Phase I for imitation and conversation, and for the third month into Phase II (follow-up) for conversation. The figure indicates, for both imitation and conversation, a sharp decline in single-word utterances over Phase I training with corresponding increases in both two- and three-word utterances. The figure further shows that the increases in utterance length continued to progress in Phase II with home training only. The follow-up points on the figure indicate that for conversation following 12 weeks of training at home without professional supervision, the children demonstrated further increases in three- and four-word utterances as single-word utterances continued to decrease and two-word utterances began to decrease. Parallel data for the control group indicate that in imitation the subjects increased their proportion of two-word utterances as they decreased their single-word responses to the test. However, the control subjects demonstrated negligible changes in conversation; at pre-, post-, and follow-up testing, over 75% of all utterances in conversation were single words. In summary, while the imitation performance demonstrated some control group changes in the direction of the experimental group, the data on conversation show stable brief utterances across the five-month period of no treatment for the control subjects.

GRAMMATICAL COMPLEXITY

In addition to the objective of increasing the children's utterance lengths, the experimental program sought to increase the grammatical complexity of their productions,

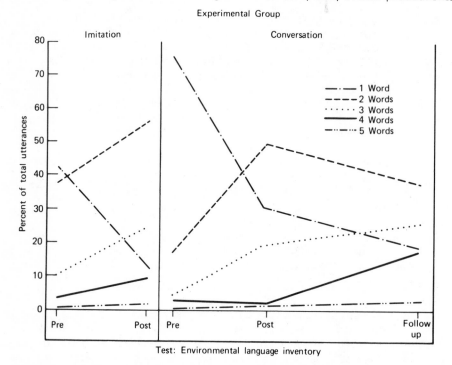

Figure 2.   Mean percentages of one-, two-, three-, four-, and five-word utterances in imitation and conversation at pre- and posttesting and in conversation at follow-up testing of experimental group.

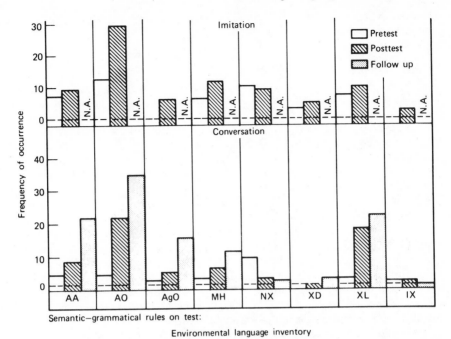

Figure 3.   Mean frequencies of semantic-grammatical rules in imitation and conversation at pre-, post-, and follow-up testing for experimental group.

as defined in terms of the range and frequencies of semantic-grammatical rules. Figure 3 illustrates, for all experimental subjects combined, the frequencies of each of the eight rules: *agent + action* (AA), *action + object* (AO), *agent + object* (AgO), *modifier + head* (MH), *negation + X* (NX), *X + dative* (XD), *X + locative* (XL), and *introducer + X* (IX). The data are presented for both imitation and conversation at pre- and posttesting and for conversation additionally at three-month follow-up testing. The figure indicates that the greatest increases occurred for the two rules trained directly, action + object (AO) and X + locative (XL). The figure also shows that for five of the eight rules, frequency of production increased from pre- to posttesting as well as from posttesting to follow-up testing. Negligible changes across the five months occurred for the control subjects. In summary, the figure suggests that the study succeeded in its objective of increasing grammatical complexity of language performance by increasing the frequency and range of semantic-grammatical rules in both imitation and conversation.

DISCUSSION

The findings from this experimental program speak to several issues: the effectiveness of a strategy to train functional language in children with severe expressive language delay, the feasibility of parents acting as primary language trainers, and the comparison of the experimental language gains with normal language growth over identical time periods.

EFFECTIVENESS OF THE ELIS

The results of the study provide experimental support for the effectiveness of the ELIS (MacDonald and Blott, 1974). The strategy is a clinical approach to training generalization of early sentence types (semantic relations) from imitation to conversation and play in a single program. The results indicate that the language increments occurred in all three training modes, thus suggesting that training for generalization to functional language need not wait for the establishment of a broad imitative repertoire. This conclusion may be made, however, only for the current subjects, who reflected adequate receptive language at the beginning of the program. Successful use of the generalization training mode with other classes of language-delayed children will have to be determined empirically.

A note on the comparability of all three subjects' performance patterns is in order. Figure 1 illustrates that the directions of change for all three subjects from pre- to post- to follow-up testing were identical for all three training modes. This commonality in growth patterns is interesting in light of the fact that the language trainers (both mothers and professionals) were different individuals for each child. All that can be said at this time is that the strategy yielded consistent results across subjects, professional trainers, and mothers who functioned as trainers.

The results indicate progressive increases not only in MLU but also in the children's use of semantic relations. While the program in Phase I included only two relations (action + object and X + locative) as formal training objectives, several other relations were necessarily included in the training sets. That is, to create training sets longer than two words, additional semantic relations were added. No specific design was arranged for the inclusion of other relations in the training sets. The stimuli for training were selected jointly by mothers and professional language trainers on the basis of each child's interests, and the current design resulted in marked language progress. Further study may reveal optimal combinations of semantic relations in a training design. It should be mentioned that each mother was trained to develop training sets for all eight semantic relations and was encouraged to use any training sets in Phase II at home that seemed appropriate to her child's progress.

While the graphic data illustrate language increases in all three modes—imitation, conversation, and play—information from parent interviews and anecdotal reports step beyond the testing data to suggest behavorial gains of a more global nature. On the basis of follow-up questionaires, we can conclude that, in the view of the parents, each child demonstrated marked increases in spontaneous social use of language. The parents offered several anecdotal reports (some verified by authors' observations) of the children responding with and initiating multiword sentences in situations in which they had been noncommunicative before the program.

PARENTS AS LANGUAGE TRAINERS

While the differential effects of the two classes of language trainers—mothers and professionals—cannot be determined from the design of the present study, certain statements can be made regarding the effectiveness of mothers as language trainers. Our personal impression was that the mothers did indeed learn the training procedures. The data from Phase II demonstrate that when the mothers were the sole language trainers in the home, the children continued to progress in language growth. Follow-up interviews with the mothers revealed that, while at times they found daily formal sessions difficult to carry out in the home setting, they felt that occasional formal training sessions in the home were essential to the child's progress. Additionally, mothers reported success in enlisting other family members both for recording the formal sessions and for integrating the language training into the daily family routine. An example reported by the mother of Subject B (Barbara) illustrates one of the ways the language objectives were extended to daily activities. Early in the program when Barbara was at the two-word training stage, she was playing with her eight-year-old brother and his friend. The friend was pushing Barbara on a swing but was not requiring a verbal request from the girl. When Barbara's brother noticed this, he told his friend to give Barbara a push only when she used at least two words to ask for a push. The mothers reported that informal language training became a natural and important part of the family's life style. The success of parents as language trainers appears to instill in them a new confidence in their ability to "teach" as well as "raise" their children. At the beginning, each mother showed reluctance to be her child's "teacher." As the program progressed, the mothers showed increasing confidence and, in many cases, real creativity in being language "teachers." In our view, a major task in parent training is to demonstrate to parents that, since they are their child's major language teachers, they can become more effective by incorporating language training principles into their natural interactions with their children.

COMPARISON OF EXPERIMENTAL LANGUAGE CHANGES WITH NORMAL DEVELOPMENT

The results discussed thus far have demonstrated that preschool language-delayed children (even "retarded" children, that is, children with Down's syndrome) can increase their functional language in a parent-assisted training program. At this point it might be reasonable to ask how these language changes compare to language development over identical time for nondelayed children. Figure 4 illustrates the comparison of changes in MLUs over three months for the experimental Down's syndrome children and for the three nondelayed children in the extensive longitudinal study conducted by Roger Brown and his associates at Harvard. The children were matched in MLUs in conversation; then utterance length was noted after three months. (Data on the normal children were taken from the graphic plot of monthly MLU changes in Brown, 1973a, p. 55). The figure demonstrates strikingly comparable changes for the three pairs of comparisons. The depicted period for the experimental children covered the three months of Phase II training. Thus, we can conclude that over three months of training with parents serving as sole language trainers, three preschool children with Down's syndrome increased their utterance lengths at the rate at which normally developing children (albeit younger in chronological age) advanced over three months from the same base MLUs.

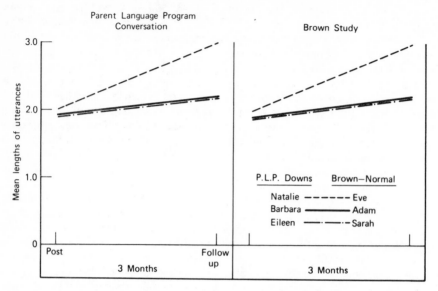

Figure 4.   Changes in mean lengths of utterances (MLUs) in conversation for the three experimental Down's syndrome children and three non-delayed children, plotted from matched MLU Baseline across three months.

EPILOGUE

The three control subjects for the initial language program reported here demonstrated, at the end of five months without training, negligible language change. The success of the program, manifest in the language growth of the children who participated in the experiment, suggested both a need to replicate the study for validation of the program and an opportunity to implement clinical assistance for the children who had served as control subjects.

A second program was therefore initiated, with the former control group as subjects and their mothers as recipients of training. Three changes were introduced into the procedure for this program: (1) Phase I, training of mothers and children at the clinic, was reduced from seven to four weeks; (2) two clinic sessions included direct behavior-management training to train the children to attend and respond to verbal cues and eliminate disruptive behavior; and (3) the training content (semantic-grammatical rules) was selected with a view to the naturally sequential expansion of utterance lengths (Brown, 1973a): two words—agent + action (for example, "Daddy throw"), action + object (for example, "Throw ball"), and action + locative (for example, "Throw here"); three words—agent + action + object (for example, "Daddy throw ball") and agent + action + locative (for example, "Daddy throw here"); four words—agent + action + object + locative (for example, "Daddy throw ball here").

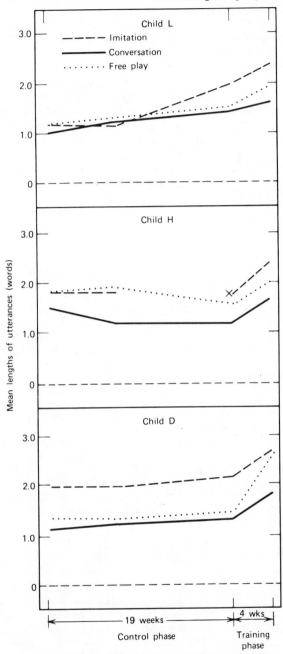

Figure 5. Mean lengths of utterances in imitation, conversation, and play for children serving as control subjects and for the same children under experimental treatment.

Results are available for the three subjects' changes in utterance lengths over the four-week period as evidenced in imitation, conversation, and play. Figure 5 reveals the contrast between the negligible growth in MLU across the 19-week period when the three children were the control group for the initial experiment and received no formal language intervention and the demonstrable growth during their own four-week training period. (The pretest MLU in imitation for Child H is estimated on the basis of his performance during the conversation and free play portions of the testing procedures, since the data for imitation at pretest are not available.)

Changes in MLUs were computed as composite values for all three children in terms of growth per week. It was found that the mean weekly rate of MLU expansion during the four-week Phase I of the second program was 7.8 times greater than that during the 19 weeks without intervention for ELI imitation, 30 times greater for ELI conversation, and 40 times greater for free play. These findings support the successful replication of the training strategy with the control subjects of the study.

REFERENCES

Bloom, L., *Language Development: Form and Function in Emerging Grammars.* Cambridge, Mass.: The MIT Press (1970).

Bowerman, M., *Early Syntactic Development: A Cross-Linguistic Study with Special Reference to Finnish.* Cambridge, Eng.: Cambridge Univ. Press (1974).

Bricker, W. A., A systematic approach to language training. In R. L. Schiefelbusch (Ed.), *Language of the Mentally Retarded.* Baltimore: University Park Press (1972).

Brown, R., *A First Language: The Early Stages.* Cambridge: Harvard Univ. Press (1973a).

Brown, R., Development of the first language in the human species. *Amer. Psychol.,* **28,** 97–106 (1973b).

Gray, B. B., and Fygetakis, L., Mediated language acquisition for dysphasic children. *Behav. Res. Ther.,* **6,** 263–280 (1968).

Johnson, W., Darley, F., and Spriestersbach, R., *Diagnostic Methods in Speech Pathology.* New York: Harper and Row (1963).

MacDonald, J. D., and Blott, J. P., Environmental language intervention: The rationale for a diagnostic and training strategy through rules, context, and generalization. *J. Speech Hearing Dis.,* 244–256 (1974).

Piaget, J., *The Origins of Intelligence in Children.* New York: International Universities (1952).

Schlesinger, I. M., Production of utterances and language acquisition. In D. I. Slobin (Ed.), *The Ontogenesis of Grammar.* New York: Academic (1971).

Authors' Comment Written for *Readings in Childhood Language Disorders:* April 1976

The program described in this article is part of a total programmatic approach to establishing the child's natural environment as his primary source of language training. The total program is described in a chapter by MacDonald in Withrow, F., and Nygren, C., *Language Materials and Curriculum Management for the Handicapped Learner,* Merrill: Columbus (1976). In addition, prescriptive programs for use in the home and school are available as *Ready, Set, Go: Talk To Me* by D. Horstmeier and J. MacDonald, published by The Nisonger Center, Ohio State University.

Development of the Intellectual Functions

Jean-Marc-Gaspard Itard

XVIII. Although presented separately, the facts which have just been related are connected in many ways with those which will form the subject matter of the following sections. For such, my Lord, is the intimate relation which unites physical with intellectual man that, although their respective provinces appear and are in fact very distinct; yet the borderline between the two different sorts of function is very confused.

Their development is simultaneous and their influence reciprocal. Thus while I was limiting my efforts to the exercise of the senses of our savage, the mind took its share of the attention given exclusively to the education of these organs and followed the same order of development. In fact it seemed that in instructing the senses to perceive and to distinguish new objects, I forced the attention to fix itself on them, the judgment to compare them, and the memory to retain them. Thus nothing was immaterial in these exercises. Everything penetrated to the mind. Everything put the faculties of the intelligence into play and prepared them for the great work of the communication of ideas. I was already sure that this would be possible by leading the pupil to the point where he would designate the thing he wanted by means of letters arranged in such a way as to spell the name of the thing he desired. In my pamphlet upon this child, I have given an account of the first step made in recognizing written signs, and I am not afraid to signalize it as an important epoch in his education, as the sweetest and most brilliant success that has ever been obtained upon a creature fallen as was this one, into the lowest extremity of brutishness. But subsequent observations, by throwing light upon the nature of this result, soon came to weaken the hopes that I had conceived from it. I noticed that Victor did not use words which I had taught him for the purpose of asking for the objects, or of making known a wish or a need, but employed them at certain moments only, and always at the sight of the desired things. Thus for example, much as he wanted his milk it was only at the moment when he was accustomed to take it and at the actual instant when he saw that it was going to be given him that the word for this favorite food was expressed or rather formed in the proper way. In order to clear up the suspicion that this restricted employment of the words awoke in me I tried delaying the hour of his

From Itard, Jean-Marc-Gaspard, *The wild boy of Aveyron,* New York: Appleton-Century-Crofts, 1962, pp. 67–86. Reprinted by permission of Prentice-Hall.

breakfast but waited in vain for the written expression of my pupil's needs although they had become very urgent. It was not until the cup appeared that the word *lait* (milk) was formed. I resorted to another test. In the middle of his lunch and without letting it appear in any way to be a punishment, I took away his cup of milk and shut it up in a cupboard. If the word *lait* had been for Victor the distinct sign of the thing and the expression of his want of it, there is no doubt that after this sudden privation, the need continuing to make itself felt, the word would have been immediately produced. It was not, and I concluded that the formation of this sign, instead of being for the pupil the expression of his desire, was merely a sort of preliminary exercise with which he mechanically preceded the satisfaction of his appetite. It was necessary then to retrace our steps and begin again. I resigned myself courageously to do this, believing that if I had not been understood by my pupil it was my fault rather than his. Indeed, in reflecting upon the causes which might give rise to this defective reception of the written signs, I recognized that in these first examples of the expression of ideas I had not employed the extreme simplicity which I had introduced at the beginning of my other methods of instruction and which had insured their success. Thus although the word *lait* is for us only a simple sign, for Victor it might be a confused expression for the drink, the vessel which contained it, and the desire of which it was the object.

XIX. Several other signs with which I had familiarized him showed the same lack of precision in application. An even more considerable defect was inherent in the method of expression we had adopted. As I have already said, this consisted in placing metal letters on a line and in the proper order, in such a way as to form the name of each object. But the connection which existed between the thing and the word was not immediate enough for his complete apprehension. In order to do away with this difficulty, it was necessary to establish between each object and its sign a more direct connection and a sort of identity which fixed them simultaneously in his memory. The objects first submitted to a trial of this new method of expression had therefore to be reduced to the greatest simplicity, so that their signs could not in any way bear upon their accessories. Consequently I arranged on the shelves of a library several simple objects such as a pen, a key, a knife, a box, etc., each one on a card upon which its name was written. These names were not new to the pupil. He already knew them and had learned to distinguish them from each other, according to the method of reading which I have already indicated.

XX. The problem then was merely to familiarize his eyes with the respective display of each of these names under the object which it represented. This arrangement was soon grasped as I had proof when, displacing all the things and instantly replacing all the labels in another order, I saw the pupil carefully replace each object upon its name. I varied my tests, and the variation gave me the opportunity to make several observations relative to the degree of the impression which these written signs made upon the sensory apparatus of our savage. Thus, leaving all the things in one corner of the room and taking all the labels to another, I wished by showing them successively to Victor to make him fetch each thing for which I showed him the written word. On these occasions, in order for him to bring the thing it was necessary that he should not lose from sight for a single instant the characters which indicated it. If he was too far away to be able to read the label, or if after showing it to him thoroughly I covered it with my hand, from the moment the sight of the word escaped him he assumed an air of uneasiness and anxiety and seized at random the first object which chanced to his hand.

XXI. The result of this experiment was not very reassuring and would in fact have discouraged me completely if I had not noticed that after frequent repetitions the duration of the impression upon the brain of my pupil became by imperceptible degrees much longer. Soon he merely needed to glance quickly at the word I showed him, in order to go without haste or mistake to fetch the thing I asked for. After some time I was able to extend the experiment by sending him from my apartment into his own room to look in the same way for anything the name of which I showed him. At first the duration of the perception did not last nearly so long as that of the journey, but by an act of intelligence worthy of record, Victor sought and found in the agility of his legs a sure means of making the impressions persist longer than the time required for the journey. As soon as he had thoroughly read the word he set out like an arrow, coming back an instant later with the thing in his hand. More than once, nevertheless, the name escaped him on the way. Then I heard him stop in his tracks and come again towards my apartment, where he arrived with a timid and confused air. Sometimes it was enough for him to glance at the complete collection of names in order to recognize and retain the one which had escaped him. At other times the image of the word was so effaced from his memory that I was obliged to show it to him afresh. This necessity he indicated by taking my hand and making me pass my index finger over the whole series of names until I had shown him the forgotten one.

XXII. This exercise was followed by another which by offering his memory more work contributed more powerfully to develop it. Until then I had limited myself to asking for only one thing at a time. Then I asked for two, then three, and then four by showing a similar number of the labels to the pupil. He, feeling the difficulty of retaining them all, did not stop running over them with eager attention until I had entirely screened them from his eyes. Then there was no more delay or uncertainty. He set off hurriedly on the way to his room whence he brought the things requested. On his return his first care before giving them to me was to look hastily over the list, comparing it with the things of which he was the bearer. These he gave me only after he had reassured himself in this way that he had neither forgotten anything nor made a mistake. This last experiment gave at first very variable results but finally the difficulties which it offered were in their turn surmounted. The pupil, now sure of his memory, disdained the advantage which the agility of his legs gave him and applied himself quietly to this exercise. He often stopped in the corridor, put his face to the window which is at one end of it, greeted with sharp cries the sight of the country which unfolds magnificently in the distance, and then set off again for his room, got his little cargo, renewed his homage to the ever-regretted beauties of nature, and returned to me quite sure of the correctness of his errand.

XXIII. In this way memory, reëstablished in all its functions, succeeded in retaining the symbols of thought while at the same time the intelligence fully grasped their importance. Such, at least, was the conclusion that I thought I could draw when I constantly saw Victor, wishing to ask for various things, either in our exercises or spontaneously, making use of the different words of which I had taught him the meaning by the device of showing or giving him the thing when we made him read the word, or by indicating the word when he was given the thing. Who could believe that this double proof was not more than sufficient to assure me that at last I had reached the point to gain which I had been obliged to retrace my steps and make so great a detour? But something happened at this juncture which made me believe for a moment that I was further from it than ever.

XXIV. One day when I had taken Victor with me and sent him as usual to fetch from his room several objects which I had indicated upon his list of words, it came into my head to double-lock the door and unseen by him to take out the key. That done I returned to my study, where he was, and, unrolling his list, I asked him for some of the things on it, taking care to indicate none which were not also to be found in my room. He set out immediately, but finding the door locked and having searched on all sides for the key, he came beside me, took my hand and led me to the outer door as if to make me see that it would not open. I feigned surprise and sought for the key everywhere and even pretended to open the door by force. At last, giving up the vain attempt, I took Victor back into my study and showing him the same words again, invited him by signs to look about and see if there were not similar objects to be found there. The words designated were stick, bellows, brush, glass, knife. All these things were to be found scattered about my study in places where they could easily be seen. Victor looked at them but touched none of them. I had no better success in making him recognize them when they were brought together on a table and it was quite useless to ask for them one after the other by showing him successively their names. I tried another method. With scissors I cut out the names of the objects, thus converting them into single labels which were put into Victor's hands. By thus bringing him back to our original procedure, I hoped that he would put upon each thing the name which represented it. In vain. I had the inexpressible grief of seeing my pupil unable to recognize any of these objects or rather the connection which joined them to their signs. With a stupefied air which cannot be described he let his heedless glance wander over all these characters which had again become unintelligible. I felt myself sinking under a weight of impatience and discouragement.

I went and sat at the end of the room and considered bitterly this unfortunate creature reduced by the strangeness of his lot to such sad alternatives. Either he must be relegated as an unmistakable idiot to one of our asylums, or he must, by unheard-of labor, procure a little education which would be just as little conducive to his happiness. "Unhappy creature," I cried as if he could hear me, and with real anguish of heart, "since my labors are wasted and your efforts fruitless, take again the road to your forests and the taste for your primitive life. Or if your new needs make you dependent on a society in which you have no place, go, expiate your misfortune, die of misery and boredom at Bicêtre."

Had I not known the range of my pupil's intelligence so well, I could have believed that I had been fully understood, for scarcely had I finished speaking when I saw his chest heave noisily, his eyes shut, and a stream of tears escape through his closed eyelids, with him the signs of bitter grief.

XXV. I had often noticed that when such emotions had reached the point of tears, they formed a kind of salutary crisis that suddenly developed the intelligence which immediately afterwards was often able to overcome a difficulty that had appeared insurmountable some moments before. I had also observed that if at the height of this emotion I suddenly left off reproaching him and substituted caresses and a few words of affection and encouragement, I obtained an increase of emotion which doubled the expected effect. The occasion was favorable and I hastened to profit by it. I drew near to Victor. I made him listen to a few kind words which I spoke in such terms as he could understand and which I accompanied by evidences of affection still more intelligible. His tears redoubled and were accompanied by gasps and sobs, while I myself redoubled the caresses, raising his emotion to the highest intensity and causing him, if I may thus express myself, to vibrate to the last sensitive fiber of his mentality. When all this excitement had entirely calmed down I placed the same objects again under his eyes, and induced him to indicate them one after the other as soon as I successively showed him the names. I began by asking him for the book. He first looked at it for rather a long time, made a movement towards it with his hand while trying to detect in my eyes some signs of approval or disapproval which would settle his uncertainty. I held myself on guard and my expression was blank. Reduced then to his own judgment he concluded that it was not the thing asked for, and his eyes wandered, looking on all sides of the room, pausing, however, only at the books which were scattered upon the table and mantelpiece.

This examination was like a flash of light to me. I immediately opened a cupboard which was full of books and took out a dozen among which I was careful to include one exactly like the one Victor had left in his room. To see it, quickly carry his hand to it and give it to me with a radiant air was for Victor only the affair of a moment.

XXVI. Here I stopped the experiment. The result was enough to revive the hopes which I had too easily abandoned and to make clear to me the difficulties which this experiment had brought to light. It was evident that my pupil, far from having conceived a wrong idea of the meaning of the symbols, had only made too rigorous an application of them. He had taken my lessons too literally and as I had limited myself to giving him the nomenclature of certain things in his room he was convinced that these were the only things to which it was applicable. Thus every book which was not the one he had in his room was not a book for Victor, and before he could decide to give it the same name it was necessary that an exact resemblance should establish a visible identity between the one and the other. This is a very different procedure in nomenclature from that of children, who, when beginning to speak, give to particular terms the value of general ones but keep the restricted meaning of the particular term.[21]

What could account for this strange difference? If I am not mistaken it grew out of an unusual acuteness of visual observation which was the inevitable result of the special education given to his sense of sight. By the method of analytical comparison I had trained this sense organ so thoroughly in the recognition of the visible qualities of objects and the differences of dimension, color and conformation, that he could always detect between two identical things such points of dissimilarity as would make him believe there was an essential difference between them. With the source of the error thus located, the remedy became easy. It was to establish the identity of the objects by demonstrating to the pupil the identity of their uses or their properties. It was to make him see common qualities which earned the same name for things apparently different. In a word, it was a question of teaching him to consider things no longer with reference to their differences but according to their similarities.

XXVII. This new study was a kind of introduction to the act of comparison. At first

---

[21] E.g., a child calling all men daddy (particular term) will really think of them all as father (tr.).

the pupil gave himself up to it so completely that he was inclined to go astray again by attaching the same idea and giving the same name to things which had no other connection than the conformity of their shapes or uses. Thus under the name of book he indicated indiscriminately a handful of paper, a note book, a newspaper, a register, a pamphlet. All straight and long pieces of wood were called sticks. At one time he gave the name of brush to the broom, and at another that of broom to the brush and soon, if I had not repressed this abuse of comparison, I should have seen Victor restricted to the use of a small number of signs which he would have applied indiscriminately to a large number of entirely different things which had only certain general qualities or properties in common.

XXVIII. In the midst of these mistakes, or rather fluctuations, of an intelligence tending ceaselessly to inaction but continually provoked by artificial means, there apparently developed one of those characteristic faculties of man, and especially thinking man, the faculty of invention. When considering things from the point of view of their similarity or of their common qualities, Victor concluded that since there was a resemblance of shape between certain objects, there ought in certain circumstances to be an identity of uses and functions. Without doubt this conclusion was somewhat risky. But it gave rise to judgments which, even though obviously found to be defective, became so many new means to instruction. I remember that one day when I asked him in writing for a knife, he looked for one for some time and contented himself with offering me a razor, which he fetched from a neighboring room. I pretended it would do and when his lesson was finished gave him something to eat as usual. I wanted him to cut his bread instead of dividing it with his fingers as was his custom. And to this end I held out to him the razor which he had given me under the name of knife. His behavior was consistent, he tried to use it as such, but the lack of stability of the blade prevented this. I did not consider the lesson complete. I took the razor and, in the actual presence of Victor, made it serve its proper use. From then on the instrument was no longer and could not be any longer in his eyes a knife. I longed to make certain. I again took his book and showed him the word *couteau* (knife) and the pupil immediately showed me the object he held in his hand and which I had given him a moment ago when he could not use the razor. To make the result convincing it was necessary to reverse the test. If the book were put in Victor's hands while I touched the razor, it was necessary that he should fail to pick out any word, as he did not yet know the name of this instrument. He passed this test also.

XXIX. At other times his substitutions were evidence of much more bizarre comparisons. One day when he was dining in town he wished to receive a spoonful of lentils offered him at a moment when there were no more plates and dishes on the table, I remember that he had the idea of going and taking from the mantelpiece and holding it out as if it were a plate, a little circular picture under glass, set in a frame, the smooth and projecting edge of which made it not at all unlike a plate.

XXX. But very often his expedients were happier, more successful and better deserving the name of invention. Quite worthy of such a name was the way by which he provided himself one day with a pencil case. Only once in my study had I made him use one to hold a small piece of chalk too short to take up with the end of his fingers. A few days afterwards the same difficulty occurred again but Victor was in his room and had no pencil-holder at hand to hold his chalk. I put it to the most industrious or the most inventive man to say, or rather do, what he did in order to procure one. He took an implement used in roasting, found in well-equipped kitchens but quite superfluous in one belonging to a poor creature such as he was, and which for that reason had remained forgotten and corroded with rust at the bottom of a little cupboard—namely a skewer. Such was the instrument which he took to replace the one he lacked and which by a further inspiration of really creative imagination he was clever enough to convert into a real pencil-holder by replacing the slide with a few turns of thread. Pardon, My Lord, the importance which I attach to this act. One must have experienced all the anguish of a course of instruction as painful as this had been; one must have followed and directed this man-plant in his laborious developments from the first act of attention up to this first spark of imagination before one can have any idea of the joy that I felt, and can pardon me for introducing at this moment, and with something of a flourish, so ordinary and so simple a fact. What also added to the importance of this result when considered as a proof of actual progress and as a guarantee of future improvement is that, instead of occurring as an isolated incident which might have made it appear accidental, it was one among many incidents, doubtless less striking, but which, coming at the same period and evidently emanating from the same source, appeared in the eyes of an attentive observer to be diverse results of a general impulse. It is, indeed, worthy of notice that from this moment many routine habits which the pupil had contracted when applying himself to the little occupations prescribed for him, spontaneously disappeared. While rigidly refraining from making forced comparisons or drawing remote conclusions, one may, I think, at least suspect that this new way of looking at familiar things which gave birth to the idea of making new applications of them, might be expected to have precisely the result of forcing the pupil out of the unvarying round of, so to speak, automatic habits.

XXXI. Thoroughly convinced at last that I had completely established in Victor's mind the connection of the objects with their signs, it only remained for me to increase the number gradually. If the procedure by which I established the meaning of the first signs has been thoroughly grasped it will be seen that it could be applied only to a limited number of objects and to things small in size, and that a bed, a room, a tree, or a person, as well as the constituent and inseparable parts of a whole, could not be labeled in the same way. I did not find any difficulty in making the sense of these new words understood, although I could not, as in the preceding experiments bind them visibly to the things they represented. In order to be understood it was sufficient for me to point to the new word with a finger and with the other hand to show the object to which the word belonged. I had little more trouble in making him understand the names of the parts which enter into the composition of the whole object. Thus for a long time the words fingers, hands, forearms could not offer any distinct meaning to the pupil. This confusion in attaching the signs was evidently due to the fact that he had not yet understood that the parts of a body considered separately formed in their turn distinct objects which had their particular names. In order to give him the idea I took a bound book, tore off its covers, and detached several of its leaves. As I gave Victor each of these separate parts I wrote its name upon the blackboard. Then taking from his hands the various pieces, I made him in turn indicate their names to me. When they were thoroughly engraved on his memory, I replaced the separated parts and when I again asked their names he indicated them as before; then showing him the whole book without indicating any part in particular, I asked him the name. He pointed to the word book.

XXXII. This is all that was necessary to render him familiar with the names of the various parts of compound bodies; and to avoid confusion between the names of the separate parts and the general name of the object, I was careful in my demonstrations to touch each part directly and, when applying the general name, to content myself with indicating the thing vaguely without touching it.

XXXIII. From this lesson I passed on to the qualities of the bodies. Here I entered into the field of abstractions and I entered it with the fear of not being able to penetrate or finding myself soon halted by insurmountable difficulties. None showed themselves, and my first lesson was grasped instantly although it bore upon one of the most abstract qualities, that of extension. I took two books of similar bindings but of different sizes, the one an octodecimo, the other an octavo. I touched the first. Victor opened his book and pointed to the word *book.* I touched the second. The pupil indicated the same word. I began again several times and always with the same result. Next I took the little book, and giving it to Victor, made him put his hand flat upon the cover which it hid almost entirely. I then made him do the same thing with the octavo volume; his hand covered scarcely half of it. So that he could not mistake my intention I showed him the part which remained uncovered, and induced him to stretch out his fingers towards this part which he could not do without uncovering a part equal to that which he covered. After this experiment which demonstrated in such a tangible manner to my pupil the difference in size of these two objects, I again asked him the name. Victor hesitated. He felt that the same name could no longer be applied indiscriminately to two things which he had just found so unequal. This was what I was waiting for. I wrote the word *book* upon two cards and placed one upon each book. I next wrote upon a third the word *big,* and the word *little* upon a fourth. I placed them beside the others, the one on the octavo and the other upon the small volume. Having made Victor notice this arrangement I took the labels again, mixed them several times, and then gave them to him to be replaced. This was done correctly.

XXXIV. Had I been understood? Had the respective sense of the words *big* and *little* been grasped? In order to be certain and to have complete proof, this is what I did. I got two nails of unequal length. I compared them in almost the same way as I had done with the books. Then having written upon two cards the word *nail* I gave them to him without adding the two adjectives big and little, hoping that if my preceding lesson had been thoroughly grasped he would apply to the nails the same signs of relative size as he had served to mark the difference of dimension of the two books. He did this with a promptness that rendered the proof still more conclusive. Such was the procedure by which I gave him the idea of size. I used it with the same success to render intelligible the signs which represent the other sensible qualities of bodies such as color, weight, resistance, etc.

XXXV. After the explanation of the adjective, came the verb. To make this understood by the pupil I had only to submit to several kinds of action an object of which he knew the name. These actions I designated as soon as executed, by the infinitive of the verb in question. For example I took a key and wrote its name upon the blackboard. Then *touching* it, *throwing* it, *picking* it up, *kissing* it, *putting* it back in its place, and so on, I simultaneously wrote in a column at the side of the word *key*, the verbs *to touch, to throw, to pick up, to kiss, to replace*, etc. For the word *key* I then substituted the name of another object which I submitted to the same functions, pointing at the same time to the verbs already written. It often happened that in thus replacing at random one object by another in order to have it governed by the same verbs, there was such an inconsistency between them and the nature of the object that the action asked for became odd or impossible. The embarrassment in which the pupil found himself generally turned out to his advantage as much as to my own satisfaction; for it gave him the chance to exercise his discernment and me the opportunity of gathering proofs of his intelligence. For example, when I found myself one day, after successive changes of the objects of the verbs, with such strange association of words as *to tear stone, to cut cup, to eat broom*, he evaded the difficulty very well by changing the two actions indicated by the first two verbs into others less incompatible with the nature of their objects. Thus he took a hammer to break the stone and dropped the cup to break it. Coming to the third verb (eat) and not being able to find any word to replace it, he looked for something else to serve as the object of the verb. He took a piece of bread and ate it.

In our study of these grammatical difficulties we were obliged to creep painfully and by endless detours, and so we simultaneously practised writing both as an auxiliary means of instruction and as a necessary diversion. As I had anticipated, the beginning of this work offered innumerable difficulties. Writing is an exercise in imitation, and imitation was yet to be born in our savage. Thus when for the first time I gave him a bit of chalk and arranged it conveniently in his fingers, I could obtain from him no line or stroke which might lead me to suspect any intention on the pupil's part to imitate what he had seen me do. Here then it was necessary once more to retrace our steps and to try and rouse from their inertia the imitative faculties by submitting them, as we had the others, to a kind of gradual education. I proceeded to the execution of this plan by practising Victor in the performance of acts when imitation is crude, such as lifting his arms, putting forward his foot, sitting down and getting up at the same time as myself; then opening his hand, shutting it, and repeating with his fingers many movements, first simple, then combined, that I performed in front of him. I next put into his hand, as in my own, a long rod sharpened to a point, and made him hold it as if it were a quill for writing, with the double intention of giving more strength and poise to his fingers through the difficulty of holding this imitation pen in equilibrium, and of making visible, and consequently capable of imitation, even the slightest movement of the rod.

XXXVII. Thus prepared by preliminary exercises we placed ourselves before the blackboard, each furnished with a piece of chalk, and placing our two hands at the same height I began by making a slow vertical movement towards the bottom of the board. The pupil did just the same, following exactly the same direction and dividing his attention between his line and mine, looking without intermission from the one to the other as if he wished to compare them successively at all points.

The result of our actions was two lines exactly parallel. My subsequent lessons were merely a development of the same procedure. I will not describe them. I will only say that the result was such that at the end of some months Victor could copy the words of which he already knew the meaning. Soon after he could reproduce them from memory, and finally make use of his writing, entirely unformed though it was and has remained, to express his wants, to solicit the means to satisfy them and to grasp by the same method of expression the needs or the will of others.

XXXVIII. In considering my experiments as a real course in imitation, I believed that the actions should not be limited to manual activity. I introduced several procedures which had no connection with the mechanism of writing but which were much more conducive to the exercise of intelligence. Such among others is the following. I drew upon a blackboard two circles almost equal, one opposite myself and the other in front of Victor. I arranged upon six or eight points of the circumference of these circles six or eight letters of the alphabet and wrote the same letters within the circles but disposed them differently. Next I drew several lines in one of the circles leading to the letters placed in the circumference. Victor did the same thing on the other circle. But because of the different arrangement of the letters, the most exact imitation nevertheless gave an entirely different figure from the one I had just offered as a model. Thence was to come the idea of a special kind of imitation which was not a matter of slavishly copying a given form but one of reproducing its spirit and manner without being held up by the apparent difference in the result. Here was no longer a routine repetition of what the pupil saw being done, such as can be obtained up to a certain point from certain imitative animals, but an intelligent and reasoned imitation, as variable in its method as in its applications, and in a word, such as one has a right to expect from a man endowed with the free use of all his intellectual faculties.

XXXIX. Of all the phenomena observable during the first developments of a child perhaps the most astonishing is the facility with which he learns to speak. When one thinks that speech, which is without question the most marvelous act of imitation, is also its first result, admiration is redoubled for that Supreme Intelligence whose masterpiece is man, and Who, wishing to make speech the principal promoter of education, could nōt let imitation, like the other faculties, develop progressively, and therefore necessarily made it fruitful as well as active from its beginning. But this imitative faculty, the influence of which extends throughout the whole of life, varies in its application according to age. It is used in learning to speak only during earliest childhood. Later other functions come under its influence and it abandons, so to speak, the vocal instrument, so that a young child, even an adolescent, after leaving his native country, promptly loses its manners, etiquette and language, but never loses those intonations of voice which constitute what is called accent. It follows from this physiological truth that in awakening the faculty of imitation in this young savage, now an adolescent. I ought not to have expected to find any disposition in the vocal organ to profit by this development of the imitative faculties, even supposing that I had not found a second obstacle in the obstinate lethargy of the sense of hearing. With respect to hearing, Victor could be considered as a deaf mute although he was certainly much inferior to this class of unfortunates since they are essentially observers and imitators.

XL. Nevertheless, I did not believe that I should allow this difference to bring me to a standstill or to let it deprive me of the hope of making him speak, with all the resulting advantages which I promised myself. I felt I should try a last resource, which was to lead him to the use of speech through the sense of sight, since it was out of the question to do so through the sense of hearing. Here the problem was to practise his eye in observing the mechanism of the articulation of sounds, and to practise his voice in the reproduction of the sounds by the use of a happy combination of attention and imitation. For more than a year all my work and all our exercises were directed towards this end. In order to follow the previous methods of insensible gradation, I preceded the study of the visible articulation of sounds by the slightly easier imitation of movements of the face muscles, beginning with those which were most easily seen. Thus we have instructor and pupil facing each other and grimacing their hardest; that is to say, putting the muscles of the eyes, forehead, mouth and jaw into all varieties of motion, little by little concentrating upon the muscles of the lips. Then after persisting for a long time with the movements of the fleshy part of the organ of speech, namely the tongue, we submitted it also to the same exercises, but varied them much more and continued them for a longer time.

XLI. Prepared in this way, it seemed to me that the organ of speech ought to lend itself without further trouble to the imitation of articulate sounds and I considered this result both near and inevitable. I was entirely mistaken. This long preparation resulted in nothing but the emission of unformed monosyllables sometimes shrill, sometimes deep and still far less clear than those which I had obtained in my first experiments. Nevertheless, I persisted, and still struggled for a long time against the obstinacy of the organ. Finally, however, seeing that the continuation of my efforts and the passing of time brought about no change, I resigned myself to the necessity of giving up any attempt to produce speech, and abandoned my pupil to incurable dumbness.

Relational Meaning and the Facilitation of Slow-Learning Children's Language

Laurence B. Leonard

Through a modeling procedure, 24 slow-learning children acquired the use of two-word subject-verb utterances. The children were assigned to conditions designed to examine the effects of two variables: (a) the number of different semantic relations theoretically underlying the subject-verb utterances on which the children were trained and (b) the extent to which these semantic relations were associated with nonlinguistic events. Stimuli in the form of situational events proved facilitative in the children's subject-verb usage. Apparently, situational evidence may provide the child with useful relational information about his environment. Implications for intervention were discussed.

During the last decade, a considerable amount of work has been devoted to the development of training procedures for facilitating the retarded child's use of syntactic features of language. Since the appearance of transformational grammar, proper attention has been paid to the structure of language, where such syntactic "rules" have been taught as the plural -z (Guess, Sailor, Rutherford, & Baer, 1968), past tense -ed (Schumaker & Sherman, 1970), and "pivot-open" constructions (Jeffree, Wheldall, & Mittler, 1973).

Unfortunately, the semantic component of language has not received adequate attention in the existing studies on language intervention. Thus far, this component has been treated as roughly synonomous with referential meaning (i.e., the meaning of specific words) and thus has been incorporated into language intervention studies primarily in the form of "vocabulary" training (cf. Gray & Ryan, 1973).

Recent work in normal language acquisition, however, has suggested that another aspect of semantics may be critical to the language-learning process: the *relational* meaning expressed in a child's utterances (Bloom, 1971; Schlesinger, 1971). Such semantic relations express something beyond referential meaning. The meaning of the child's utterance "mommy coat," for example, cannot be adequately conveyed by the meanings of the individual words "mommy" and "coat" (Bloom, 1970). These semantic relations do not appear to be entirely dependent upon grammatical constructions (Fillmore, 1968). For example, the dative relation, the notion that an animate is being affected by the action, can be expressed in forms such as "The *girl* is

From *American Journal of Mental Deficiency, 80,* 180–185 (1975). Reprinted by permission of the American Association on Mental Deficiency.

dying." "He pushed the *boy,*" and "The *woman* was tripped." Similarly, the same grammatical construction may be employed in the expression of different semantic relations. The auxiliary *is* construction, for example, may express an agentive relation where an animate is the instigator of an activity. ("The boy is watching"), an instrumental relation where an object is causally involved in the action ("The knife is cutting"), or a dative relation ("The girl is falling").

The semantic relations underlying children's utterances seem to play a central role in language learning (Bloom, 1970; Bowerman, 1973; Brown, 1973; Schlesinger, 1971). Apparently, the child's early language usage reflects in large part the knowledge he has acquired about nonlinguistic features in his environment. Some writers relate the child's language usage directly to specific stages of cognitive development during which the child develops hypotheses about the various relationships among features of his environment (Morehead & Morehead, 1974; Sinclair, 1971). In a longitudinal study of children from 12 through 26 months of age, Sinclair (1970) noted that her subjects progressed through three stages of cognitive development which served as bases for language usage. In the first stage, the children engaged in activities concerned with acquiring knowledge of objects themselves; in the second stage, the children engaged in activities introducing some organization into the objects; and in the third stage, the children acted on objects "as if" they were other objects. Sinclair (1970) interprets the appearance of utterances expressing semantic relations such as nomination as reflecting an object-knowledge level of thinking, whereas utterances expressing the possessive, objective, and other potentially "topic-comment" utterances may reflect the organizing activity of the child. Similarly, Morehead and Morehead (1974) have suggested that such utterances might derive from physical knowledge and logical-mathematical knowledge, respectively.

Since the expression of semantic relations may be quite related to cognitive factors, the role such relations might play in the slow-learning child's acquisition of language may be critical, particularly since the aspects of verbal behavior closest to the cognitive processes might be most affected by the condition of retardation. Since such relations are already being proposed as possible components in future language-intervention programs with retarded children (Miller & Yoder, 1974), the need for an examination of the role of semantic relations in language learning seems immediate. The present study was designed to investigate the role of this relational meaning in the slow-learning child's acquisition of early language.

METHOD

SUBJECTS
Subjects were 24 children, ages 3.1 to 4.8 years. Eighteen subjects were male, 6 were female. The subjects were selected from the clinic population of the Memphis Speech and Hearing Center according to several factors. On the basis of medical records and interviews with mothers, all subjects revealed delays in motor, social, and language development. As a result of psychological assessment, subjects were described as functioning in the mild range of retardation. No subject revealed a deficit clearly attributable to genetic origins. The test instrument varied from subject to subject, though the block building and form board tasks of the Stanford Binet were

generally presented. Due to apparent difficulties in following strict protocol in the administration of standardized test instruments with these children, test administrators rarely reported IQs or mental ages (MAs). Six of the subjects attended preschool programs.

All of the subjects were diagnosed as displaying language difficulties. The subjects' language usage was characterized by one-word utterances expressing names of people and objects (e.g., "mommy," "truck"), actions (e.g., "eat"), rejection (e.g., "no"), and recurrence (e.g., "more"). All subjects showed use of at least one standard word of both the traditional noun and verb classes.

MODEL

The experimenter was assisted in the experimental sessions by a speech pathologist who served as a model by providing the subject, in those phases of the experiment when modeling was designated, with demonstrations of how a particular utterance form should be produced.

TESTING PROCEDURE

Immediately before and after the experimental sessions, the subjects were tested for their use of two-word subject-verb utterances expressing underlying agentive (e.g., "man walk"), dative (e.g., "baby fall"), instrumental (e.g., "hammer hit"), and objective (e.g., "ball roll") semantic relations (cf. Fillmore, 1968). Persons, objects, and pictures of persons and objects were employed as stimuli during testing. Twelve pictures of ongoing activities were presented to the subject along with the request "Tell me what's happening here." Three pictures depicted activities with each of the four semantic relations as salient features. Twelve events were also staged, employing persons such as the model and experimenter and objects such as puppets, toy cars, spoons, and hammers; again, three events depicted each of the four semantic relations. The use of each was tested by recording the subject's response to the experimenter's request to "Tell me what's happening here."

In order to ensure that a subject's performance was not hindered because of unfamiliarity with the lexicon, each noun and verb, along with pictures and events representing the nouns and verbs, was presented as a single-word utterance prior to the presentation of the test stimuli.

DESIGN

After pretesting (which verified that no subject used the subject-verb form when expressing any of the semantic relations), the subjects were trained in the single-word use of nouns (subsequently, serving as sentence subjects) and verbs as a preliminary step to subject-verb training.

Sixteen subjects acquired the use of the appropriate utterance forms when describing actual ongoing (staged) events. Eight of these subjects were exposed to agentive events (situational A condition) and 8 to agentive, dative, instrumental, and objective events presented randomly (situational ADIO condition). For example, the subjects assigned to the situational A condition were required to describe events such as the examiner walking across the room or eating. The subjects in the situational ADIO condition were asked to describe events such as the examiner falling off a chair (dative), a hammer hitting a wooden peg (instrumental), or a ball rolling (objective), as well as agentive events. Finally, 8 subjects acquired the use of the appropriate utterance forms in a condition where the subject was merely presented a clue to a "likely" event, suggesting an appropriate utterance to use. For example, the experimenter might stand in the middle of the room pointing alternately to himself and a chair next to him, suggesting an utterance involving the act of sitting. The actual event which the utterance described was never carried out. The persons, objects, and clues presented to the subject suggested possible utterances involving agentive, dative, instrumental, and objective relations presented randomly and will hereafter be termed the nonsituational ADIO condition.

The subjects were randomly assigned to experimental conditions. Of the 6 subjects who attended preschool programs, 2 were assigned to each of the three conditions. The sex distribution was not as equal, however; 4 females were assigned to the situational A condition, and 1 was assigned to each of the remaining two conditions.

ONE-WORD TRAINING PROCEDURE

Subjects were seen twice weekly on an individual basis in sessions of 30 to 45 minutes in duration. A modeling procedure representing a modification of the Bandura and Harris (1966) procedure was employed. In this procedure, the experimenter, subject, and model were seated at a table. The subject was told to listen and pay close attention to the model, for the model was going to talk about the events/ clues in a "special way." Only when the model talked in this manner would he be reinforced. The reinforcers varied from child to child and were determined from conversations with those working closely with the child. Depending upon the condition to which the subject was assigned, the experimenter then enacted or presented a clue to an event. He then requested the model to talk about what was happening. The clues or events involved varying semantic relations; the relation(s) to which the subject was exposed was once again dependent upon the condition to which he was assigned. In order to assist the subject in identifying the characteristics shared by all reinforced utterances, the model intentionally failed to use the appropriate form in approximately 20 percent of his utterances. Only utterances of the noun (e.g., "boy") or verb (e.g., "eat") form were reinforced, depending upon the stage of training in which the subject was engaged.

After observing the model make up ten utterances (involving all ten of the nouns or all ten of the verbs which the child would be required to produce during training), the subject was encouraged to talk about events/clues in the same manner as that used by the model in order to earn reinforcers. At this point, the model and the subject alternated producing appropriate utterances to describe presented events/clues.

TWO-WORD TRAINING PROCEDURE

When the subject reached the criterion of ten consecutive correct responses on both noun and verb training, training in the use of two-word subject-verb (e.g., "mommy sit") utterances commenced. During this training, each subject remained in the same semantic (situational A, situational ADIO, or nonsituational ADIO) condition to which he was assigned during one-word training. The frequency and duration of the training sessions were not altered from one-word training. The modeling procedure was also employed throughout subject-verb training. That is, the subject was told to listen and pay close attention to the model, for the model was going to talk about the events/clues in a "special way." In this phase of training, only utterance forms conforming to the subject-verb form were reinforced. Once again, the model intentionally failed to produce an appropriate utterance form in approximately 20 percent of his utterances, in order to aid the subject in determining what the desirable response form was. The experimenter provided the model and subject with the event/clue and asked, "Tell me what's happening here." Criterion remained at ten consecutive correct (subject-verb) responses by the subject. Total training time varied from subject to subject and averaged approximately 5 hours.

After each subject reached criterion on subject-verb training, he was again tested for his use of this utterance form. The construction of the events/clues employed during training ensured that each subject was exposed during training to one-half of the nouns and verbs employed during testing. Again, however, each subject was exposed to each noun and verb (using pictures and events not employed during testing) as a single-word utterance immediately prior to testing.

A control condition was created in order to ensure that any lack of differences between the experimental groups during posttesting was not due to a general failure of the subjects to acquire the desired forms. This control condition was created by delaying the experimental sessions after pretesting for one-half of the subjects (4 from each of the three semantic relation conditions) until the remaining subjects reached criterion. At this point, all subjects were once again tested. The experimentally delayed subjects were then trained to criterion and again tested.

RESULTS

Results were analyzed employing the posttest scores as data. An examination of the children's posttest scores appeared crucial since this test included novel stimuli that could yield untrained utterances, thereby providing an estimate of the child's acquisition of the subject-verb *form*, over and beyond his acquisition of specific responses. Results of the trained subject/experimentally delayed subject comparison indicated that the subjects immediately assigned to the experimental conditions showed significantly greater gains in their overall posttest scores than the experimentally delayed subjects during this same period ($F = 7.21$, $1/22$ df, $p < .05$). The mean overall test score for the trained subjects was 6.33 (standard deviation $[SD] = 3.64$). During this same period, the experimentally delayed subjects remained at a one-word level and thus revealed a mean of 0.00 ($SD = 0.00$). It appeared, then, that the experimental procedure itself was effective.

A mixed-design analysis of variance was utilized in order to compare the subjects' use of the subject-verb form in expressing the various semantic relations included in the posttest. Results indicated a difference according to subject condition ($F = 15.96$, $2/21$ df, $p < .001$). Post-hoc comparisons indicated that the situational ADIO condition resulted in significantly higher overall posttest performance than the nonsituational ADIO condition ($p < .05$). Subjects also seemed to perform differently as a result of the semantic relation being expressed in the posttest ($F = 5.10$, $3/63$ df, $p < .005$). The results of post-hoc comparisons indicated that the agentive relation was appropriately expressed more frequently (p < .05) on the posttest than either the instrumental or objective relation. No subject condition by semantic relation interaction was observed. The posttest means and *SD*s according to subject condition and semantic relation are presented in Table 1.

DISCUSSION

The finding that the subjects in the situational ADIO condition produced a significantly greater number of relational utterances in the posttest than the subjects in the nonsituational ADIO condition suggests that the nonlinguistic factors surrounding a child's utterances during language learning are important factors. The influence of these factors, while intuitively reasonable, have perhaps been easy to overlook in light of the heavy influence that procedures emphasizing the surface features of language (e.g., imitation) have had on intervention programs with retarded children (cf. Guess, Sailor, & Baer, 1974). The subjects in the nonsituational ADIO condition were provided with clues to the appropriate lexicon and modeled demonstrations of the appropriate subject-verb word order, but the events were not carried out and therefore the relational meaning of the utterances may not have been made explicit. If the agentive relation was to be expressed in a child's subject-verb utterances, for example, more was needed than exposure to word order and lexicon; at some point the child needed to learn that the first word represented the instigator of an action, and the second word represented the action instigated. A child may have known who "Larry" was and what "wash" referred to, for instance, but exposure only to the utterance "Larry wash" with no situational evidence did not apparently tell the child whether Larry was washing something or someone was washing Larry.

Table 1   Means and Standard Deviations (*SD* s) for Posttest Performance for Each Subject Condition and Semantic Relation

	Semantic relation[a]									
	Agentive		Dative		Instrumental		Objective		Total test[b]	
Condition	Mean	SD	Mean	SD	Mean	SD	Mean	SD	Mean	SD
ADIO[c]										
Nonsituational	.88	.93	.75	.97	.63	.70	.50	.50	2.75	2.22
Situational	3.00	.79	2.63	1.11	2.38	1.11	2.63	1.32	10.63	3.60
Agentive relation[d]										
Situational	3.00	1.00	2.13	.93	1.25	.83	1.13	1.17	7.50	1.66

[a]Each relation was composed of six items.
[b]24 items.
[c]Agentive, dative, instrumental, and objective relations.
[d]Also referred to as situational A in text.

The finding that subjects in the situational A condition did not differ statistically in their posttest performance from subjects in the situational ADIO and nonsituational ADIO conditions is difficult to interpret. It is possible that the performance of the situational A subjects reflects the joint influence of the facilitative effects of receiving situational clues and the impeding effects of receiving exposure during training to only one semantic relation. It should be pointed out, however, that in a study utilizing less involved children as subjects, the author observed that situational agentive exposure resulted in the use of utterances expressing other semantic relations as well (Leonard, 1975). Future investigation of the nonretarded vs. retarded child's ability to make semantic generalizations seems warranted.

The observation that subjects produced more appropriate utterances expressing agentive relations than utterances expressing instrumental or objective relations follows expectations quite closely; all subjects were exposed to events portraying, or clues suggesting, the agentive relation. This was not the case for the other semantic relations. The failure to observe any subject condition by semantic relation interaction cannot be explained quite so easily. Though the subject groups differed in the total number of appropriate utterances during the posttest, the particular semantic relations with which they had the greatest (as well as least) amount of difficulty seemed quite similar. For example, one might have expected the situational A subjects to perform appropriately in their use of subject-verb utterances expressing the agentive relation and poorly in their use of utterances expressing other relations. The absence of such a finding raises some questions concerning the adequacy of certain semantic relation systems when describing the cognitive and linguistic development of a child. The relations employed in this study were proposed by Fillmore (1968) as reflecting some of the universal and presumably innate judgments humans are capable of making about their environment. Though the basic judgments such relations may represent may have some basis in the child's functioning, some recent work suggests that children's judgments about their world, and therefore the relations they express in their language, may not always fit into the adult system. Bowerman (Note 1), for example, observed one child expressing agentive relations in a manner suggesting that she subdivided this semantic class, apparently according to whether or not the instigated action would result in the relocation of an object. It would seem premature to dismiss the possibility of idiosyncratic cognitive operations in the retarded child as well.

Regardless of the specific judgments the child might make, it appears from this study that the judgments themselves may be dependent upon situational evidence that allows the child to develop hypotheses about the relationships among features in his environment. The inclusion of situational experiences during the intervention process, then, appears worthy of consideration.

REFERENCE NOTE

1. Bowerman, M. *Relationship of early cognitive development to a child's early rules for word combination and semantic knowledge.* Paper presented at the meeting of the American Speech and Hearing Association, Las Vegas, 1974.

REFERENCES

Bandura, A., & Harris, M. Modification of syntactic style. *Journal of Experimental Child Psychology,* 1966, 4, 341–352.

Bloom, L. *Language development: Form and function in emerging grammars.* Cambridge: The M.I.T. Press, 1970.

Bowerman, M. Structural relationships in children's utterances; Syntactic or semantic? In T. Moore (Ed.). *Cognitive development and the acquisition of language.* New York: Academic Press, 1973.

Brown, R. *A first language: The early stages.* Cambridge: Harvard University Press, 1973.

Fillmore, C. The case for case. In E. Bach & R. Harms (Eds.), *Universals in linguistic theory.* New York: Holt, Rinehart, & Winston, 1968.

Gray, B., & Ryan, B. *A language program for the nonlanguage child.* Champaign: Research Press, 1973.

Guess, D., Sailor, W., & Baer, D. To teach language to retarded children. In R. Schiefelbusch & L. Lloyd (Eds.), *Language perspectives: Acquisition, retardation, and intervention.* Baltimore: University Park Press, 1974.

Guess, D., Sailor, W., Rutherford, G., & Baer, D. An experimental analysis of linguistic development: The productive use of the plural morpheme. *Journal of Applied Behavior Analysis,* 1968, 1, 297–306.

Jeffree, D., Wheldall, K., & Mittler, P. Facilitating two-word utterances in two Down's syndrome boys. *American Journal of Mental Deficiency,* 1973, 78, 117–122.

Leonard L. The role of nonlinguistic events and semantic relations in children's acquisition of grammatical utterances. *Journal of Experimental Child Psychology,* 1975, 19, 346–357.

Miller, J., & Yoder, D. An ontogenetic language teaching strategy for retarded children. In R. Schiefelbusch & L. Lloyd (Eds.), *Language perspectives: Acquisition, retardation, and intervention.* Baltimore: University Park Press, 1974.

Morehead, D., & Morehead, A. From signal to sign: A Piagetian view of thought and language during the first two years. In R. Schiefelbusch & L. Loyd (Eds.), *Language perspectives: Acquisition, retardation, and intervention.* Baltimore: University Park Press, 1974.

Schlesinger, I. Production of utterances in language acquisition. In D. Slobin (Ed.), *The ontogenesis of grammar.* New York: Academic Press, 1971.

Schumaker, J., & Sherman, J. Training generative verb usage by imitation and reinforcement procedures. *Journal of Applied Behavior Analysis,* 1970, 3, 273–287.

Sinclair, H. The transition from sensory motor behavior to symbolic activity. *Interchange,* 1970, 1, 119–126.

Sinclair, H. Sensorimotor action patterns as a condition for the acquisition of syntax. In R. Huxley & E. Ingram (Eds.), *Language acquisition: Models and methods.* New York: Academic Press, 1971.

Acquisition of Imitative Speech by Schizophrenic Children

O. Ivar Lovaas, John P. Berberich, Bernard F. Perloff, Benson Schaeffer

Two mute schizophrenic children were taught imitative speech within an operant conditioning framework. The training procedure consisted of a series of increasingly fine verbal discriminations; the children were rewarded for closer and closer reproductions of the attending adults' speech. We found that reward delivered contingent upon imitation was necessary for development of imitation. Furthermore, the newly established imitation was shown to have acquired rewarding properties for the children.

With the great majority of children, the problem of teaching speech never arises. Speech develops within each child's particular environment without parents and teachers having to know a great deal about how it occurs. Yet, in some children, because of deviations in organic structure or prior experience, speech fails to develop. Children with the diagnosis of childhood schizophrenia, especially autistic children, often show little in the way of speech development (1). The literature on childhood schizophrenia suggests two conclusions regarding speech in such children: first, that the usual treatment setting (psychotherapy) in which these children are placed might not be conducive to speech development (2); and second, that a child failing to develop speech by the age of 5 years remains withdrawn and does not improve clinically (2). That is, the presence or absence of speech is an important prognostic indicator. It is perhaps obvious that a child who can speak can engage in a much more therapeutic interchange with his environment than the child who has no speech.

The failure of some children to develop speech as a "natural" consequence of growing up poses the need for an increased knowledge of how language is acquired. A procedure for the development of speech in previously mute children would not only be of practical importance but might also illuminate the development of speech in normal children. Although several theoretical attempts have been made to account for language development, the empirical basis for these theoretical formulations is probably inadequate. In fact, there are no published, systematic studies on how to go about developing speech in a person who has never spoken. We now outline a procedure by which speech can be made to occur. Undoubtedly, there are or will be other ways by which speech can be acquired. Furthermore, our procedure centers on the acquisition of only one aspect of speech, the acquisition of vocal responses. The development of speech also requires the acquisition of a context for the occurrence of such responses ("meaning").

Casual observations suggests that normal children acquire words by hearing speech; that is, children learn to speak by imitation. The mute schizophrenic children with whom we worked were not imitative. Thus, the establishment of imitation in these children appeared to be the most beneficial and practical starting point for building speech. The first step in creating speech, then, was to establish conditions in which imitation of vocal sounds would be learned.

The method that we eventually found most feasible for establishing verbal imitation involved a discrimination training procedure. Early in training the child was rewarded only if he emitted a sound within a certain time after an adult had emitted a sound. Next he was rewarded only if the sound he emitted within the prescribed interval resembled the adult's sound. Toward the end of training, he was rewarded only if his vocalization very closely matched the adult's vocalization—that is, if it was, in effect, imitative. Thus, verbal imitation was taught through the development of a series of increasingly fine discriminations.

The first two children exposed to this program are discussed here. Chuck and Billy were 6-year-old in-patients at the Neuropsychiatric Institute at UCLA. These children were selected for the program because they did not speak. At the onset of the program, vocal behavior in both children was restricted to occasional vowel productions with no discernible communicative intent. These vowel sounds occurred infrequently, except when the children were tantrumous, and did not resemble the pre-speech babbling of infants. In addition, the children evidenced no appropriate play (for example, they would spin toys or mouth them). They engaged in a considerable amount of self-stimulatory behavior such as rocking and twirling. They did not initiate social contacts and became tantrumous when such contact was initiated by others. They evidenced occasional self-destructive behavior (biting self, head-banging, and so forth). Symbolic rewards such as social approval were inoperative, so biological rewards such as food were substituted. In short, they were profoundly schizophrenic.

Training was conducted 6 days a week, 7 hours a day, with a 15-minute rest period accompanying each hour of training. During the training sessions, the child and the adult sat facing each other, their heads about 30 cm apart. The adult physically prevented the child from leaving the training situation by holding the child's legs between his own legs. Rewards, in the form of single spoonsful of the child's meal, were delivered immediately after correct responses. Punishment (spanking, shouting by the adult) was delivered for inattentive, self-destructive, and trantrumous behavior which interfered with the training, and most of these behaviors were thereby suppressed within 1 week. Incorrect vocal behavior was never punished.

Four distinct steps were required to establish verbal imitation. In step 1, the child was rewarded for all vocalizations. We frequently would fondle the children and we avoided aversive stimulation. This was done in order to increase the frequency of vocal responses. During this stage in training, the child was also rewarded for visually fixating on the adult's mouth. When the child reached an achievement level of about one verbal response every 5 seconds and was visually fixating on the adult's mouth more than 50 percent of the time, step 2 of training was introduced.

Step 2 marked our initial attempt to bring the child's verbal behavior under our verbal control in such a manner that our speech would ultimately stimulate speech in the child. Mastery of this second step involved acquisition of a temporal discrimination by the child. The adult emitted a vocal response—for example, "baby"—about once on the average of every 10th second. The child was rewarded only if he vocalized within 6 seconds after the adult's vocalization. However, any vocal response of the child would be rewarded in that time interval. Step 3 was introduced when the frequency of the child's vocal responses within the 6-second interval was three times what it had been initially.

Step 3 was structurally similar to the preceding step, but it included the additional requirement that the child actually match the adult's vocalization before receiving the reward. In this and in following steps, the adult selected the verbalization to be placed in imitative training from a pool of possible verbalizations that had met one or more of the following criteria. First, we selected vocal behaviors that could be prompted, that is, vocal behaviors that could be elicited by a cue prior to any experimental training, such as by manually moving the child through the behavior.

An example of training with the use of a prompt is afforded in teaching the sound "b." The training would proceed in three stages: (i) the adult emitted "b" and simultaneously prompted the child to emit "b" by holding the child's lips closed with his fingers and quickly removing them when the child exhaled; (ii) the prompt would be gradually faded, by the adult's moving his fingers away from the child's mouth, to his cheek, and finally gently touching the child's jaw; (iii) the adult emitted the vocalization "b" only, withholding all prompts. The rate of fading was determined by the child; the sooner the child's verbal behavior came under control of the adult's without the use of the prompt, the better. The second criterion for selection of words or sounds in the early stages of training centered on their concomitant visual components (which we exaggerated when we pronounced them), such as those of the labial consonant "m" and of open-mouthed vowels like "a." We selected such sounds after having previously found that the children could discriminate words with visual components more easily that those with only auditory components (the guttural consonants, "k" and "g," proved extremely difficult and, like "l" and "s," were mastered later than other sounds). Third, we selected for training sounds which the child emitted most frequently in step 1.

Step 4 was a recycling of step 3, with the addition of a new sound. We selected a sound that was very different from those presented in step 3, so that the child could discriminate between the new and old sounds more easily. To make certain that the child was in fact imitating, we randomly interspersed the sounds of step 3 with the sound of step 4, in a randomized ratio of about 1 to 3. This random presentation "forced" (or enabled) the child to discriminate the particular sounds involved, in order to be rewarded. There was no requirement placed upon the child in step 3 to discriminate specific aspects such as vowels, consonants, and order of the adult's speech; a child might master step 3 without attending to the specific properties of the adult's speech. Each new introduction of sounds and words required increasingly fine discrimination by the child and hence provided evidence that the child was in fact matching the adult's speech. All steps beyond step 4 consisted of replications of step

3, but new sounds, words, and phrases were used. In each new step, the previously mastered words and sounds were rehearsed on a randomized ratio of 1 to 3. The next step was introduced when the child had mastered the previous steps—that is, when he had made ten consecutive correct replications of the adult's utterances.

One hour of each day's training was tape-recorded. Two independent observers scored the child's correct vocal responses from these sessions. A correct response was defined as a recognizable reproduction of the adult's utterance. The observers showed better than 90 percent agreement over sessions. When the child's correct responses are plotted against days of training, and the resulting function is positively accelerated, it can be said that the child has learned to imitate.

The results of the first 26 days of imitation training, starting from introduction of step 3, have been plotted for Billy (Figure 1). The abscissa denotes training days. The words and sounds are printed in lower case letters on the days they were introduced

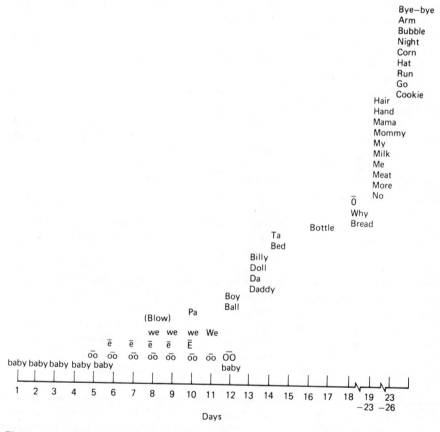

Figure 1. Acquisition of verbal imitation by Billy. The abscissa denotes training days. Words and sounds are printed in lower case letters on the days they were introduced, and in capital letters on the days they were mastered.

and in capital letters on the days they were mastered. It can be seen that as training progressed the rate of mastery increased. Billy took several days to learn a single word during the first 2 weeks of the program, but a single day to master several words during the last 2 weeks. Chuck's performance was very similar to Billy's.

After 26 days of training both children had learned to imitate new words with such ease and rapidity that merely adding verbal responses to their imitative repertoire seemed pointless. Hence, the children were then introduced to the second part of the language training program, wherein they were taught to use language appropriately.

The imitation training took place in a rather complex environment, with many events happening concurrently. We hypothesized that it was the reward, given for imitative behavior, which was crucial to the learning. To test this hypothesis, the adult uttered the sounds as during the training and the children received the same number of rewards as before. However, the rewards were contingent upon time elapsed since the last reward, regardless of the child's behavior.

The data show a deterioration in imitation behavior whenever rewards are shifted from response-contingent to time-contingent delivery. It is concluded, therefore, that reward immediately following correct, imitative behavior (and withholding of reward following incorrect responding) is a crucial variable in maintaining imitative behavior in these children. The same finding has been reported by Baer and Sherman (*3*) who worked with imitative behavior in normal children.

Since the child was rewarded whenever he responded like the adult, *similarity* was consistently associated with food. Because of such association, similarity should become symbolic of reward. In other words, imitative behavior, being symbolic of reward, should eventually provide its own reward (Baer and Sherman, *3*). To test this hypothesis, both children were exposed to Norwegian words which they were unable to reproduce perfectly when first presented. The adult simply stated the Norwegian word and the child always attempted to repeat it; no extrinsic rewards were delivered. However, occasionally the child was presented with English words which the adult rewarded when correctly imitated. This procedure was necessary to maintain the hypothesized symbolic (learned) reward function of imitation.

The children improved in the imitation of the Norwegian words over time. It is as if they were rewarded for correct behavior. In view of the data pointing to the need for rewards in maintaining imitative behavior, and in the absence of extrinsic rewards, we would argue that the reward was intrinsic and a function of the prior imitation training. There is one implication of this finding which is of particular interest for therapeutic reasons: children may be able to acquire new behaviors on their own. (This finding contrasts with the frequent stereotype of a conditioning product, namely, that of an automaton unable to function independently.)

Currently, three new schizophrenic children are undergoing the same speech training program as Billy and Chuck. After 3 days of training, one of these children achieved a level of imitative behavior similar to that shown by Billy and Chuck after 26 days. It should be pointed out that schizophrenic children are a very heterogeneous group with respect to their speech histories and symptomatology in general, and that Billy and Chuck had failed in development to a profound degree. Insofar as one works with such a diverse population, it is likely that numerous procedures could be helpful in establishing speech.

REFERENCES AND NOTES

1. B. Rimland, *Infantile Autism* (Appleton-Century-Crofts, New York, 1964).
2. J. Brown, *Amer. J. Orthopsychiat.* **30,** 382 (1960).
3. D. Baer and J. Sherman, *J. Exp. Child Psychol.* **1,** 37 (1964).
4. Study supported by grants from Margaret Sabl of Los Angeles. We express appreciation to James Q. Simmons and the staff at the Children's Unit, Neuropsychiatric Institute, University of California, Los Angeles.

Imitative Modeling As A Theoretical Base For Instructing Language-Disordered Children

John A. Courtright

Illene C. Courtright

A modification of Bandura's social learning theory (imitative modeling) was employed as a theoretical base for language instruction. This approach was experimentally compared to an alternative technique which required the subject to literally match each stimulus statement made by the clinician (mimicry). The results support the prediction that modeling is more effective in teaching the subject the appropriate grammatical rule, which he or she initially lacked. Moreover, subjects in the modeling condition exhibited both greater retention of the rule and a more successful generalization of it to novel contexts. The results are explained in terms of an "interference hypothesis," which suggests that a client's overt verbalization may interfere with the cognitive processing necessary to learn an abstract language rule.

Recent developments in the fields of psychology and psycholinguistics have suggested that children can acquire novel linguistic rules through a process of "imitative modeling" (Hartup and Coates, 1972; Zimmerman and Rosenthal, 1974). This stream of research, which is grounded in the "social learning theory" proposed by Albert Bandura (1971a, b), provides evidence that children are capable of learning and generalizing abstract language rules which they have acquired by modeling the language behavior of an adult.

The term *modeling* is not synonymous with the often-used concept of *mimicry* (Rees, 1975; Zimmerman and Rosenthal, 1974). On the contrary, the hypothesis that children mimic (that is, literally match) the individual utterances of adult speakers has been both theoretically and empirically dismissed as a viable explanation of language acquisition (Chomsky, 1964; Ervin-Tripp, 1964; Hopper and Naremore, 1973; Slobin, 1968). Social learning theory, however, does not propose this one-to-one process of literal matching. Rather, it assumes that "modeling influences operate principally through their informative function and that observers acquire mainly symbolic representations of modeled events rather than specific stimulus response associations" (Bandura, 1971b, p. 16). That is, Bandura has theorized that abstract rules of behavior are internalized and retained by one of two means of coding—

From *Journal of Speech and Hearing Research, 19*, 655–663 (1976). Reprinted by permission of the American Speech and Hearing Association.

imaginal or verbal, both of which require the cognitive use of symbols (Rees, 1975). As we shall suggest later, requiring an immediate response to a stimulus can disrupt the retention process by not allowing sufficient time for coding to take place.

It is this emphasis on "symbolic representations" that makes this theory both attractive and useful for explaining how children might acquire the syntactic rules of language. More important, however, is that Bandura's theoretical conceptions have received widespread and consistent validation from numerous empirical investigations.

Bandura and Harris (1966), for example, found that exposure to an adult model increased the frequency with which children employed both prepositional phrases and passive constructions. Moreover, they discovered that the addition of "attentional and reinforcement variables" further increased the use of the desired grammatical constructions.

Subsequent research (Liebert et al., 1969) replicated the Bandura and Harris study and found both modeling and reinforcement to be effective in increasing the use of the desired constructions. In addition, this research was able to elicit increased usage of an ungrammatical construction (for example, "the house to" instead of "to the house"). Clearly, these were novel phrases—ones to which the children would not have been exposed in their natural environment. In their discussion the authors of this research maintain, "unlike previous studies conducted within a social learning framework, the present study provides direct information about the *acquisition* of novel language rules and suggests that these can be imparted by a combination of modeling and reward variables" (Bandura and Harris, 1966, p. 111).

Several researchers have investigated the effects of modeling when it is employed without an accompanying reinforcement variable. Carroll, Rosenthal, and Brysh (1973), for example, introduced no reinforcement variable in their study and found that modeling alone led to the adoption and transfer (that is, generalization to novel contexts) of both sentence structure and three verb tenses. Similarly, Harris and Hassemer (1972) found that modeling alone was sufficient to elicit increased sentence length and complexity for both monolingual and bilingual children. Although Rosenthal and Whitebook (1970) did introduce a reinforcement variable, they found that money incentives did not significantly increase the usage of similar sentence structures and verb tenses. Also, Rosenthal and Carroll (1972) found that high rewards ($20) did not significantly increase the production of elaborate, complex sentences, while the main effect for modeling alone was significant.

These findings are suggestive of the ways in which children might naturally acquire the rules of language. More important, however, are the hypotheses these findings suggest about the most appropriate method of "teaching" linguistic rules to those children who have not acquired them through the natural acquisition process (Leonard, 1975).

This entire line of research would seem to have direct implications for speech clinicians, especially those who are concerned with the management of language disorders. In fact, the hypothesis which is generated by these findings is relatively straightforward; namely, methods of instruction which employ modeling techniques will be more effective in managing language disorders than those which employ mimicry as their framework. Mimicry was selected as the instructional method for comparison, because it has been observed that some form of it is widely used by speech clinicians. That is, many clinicians attempt to provide models which act as stimuli for language-disordered children, but actually, by requiring a one-to-one literal matching response for each stimulus statement, the clinician has established a mimicry and not a modeling context.

The purpose of the present study, therefore, was to empirically investigate the previously stated hypothesis. Accordingly, two methods of instruction (modeling and mimicry) were employed in teaching the correct usage of the personal pronoun *they* to eight grade-school children. The study was conducted across three instructional sessions and included a postexperimental "generalization" task. Throughout the study, both baseline and postinstruction measures of the frequency of the desired pronoun were kept, so that a direct index of the increase in production could be maintained.

METHOD

SUBJECTS
Subjects were eight grade-school children, six males and two females, ranging in age from five to 10 years. Prior to the study, all of the children were judged to be disordered in their use of the personal pronoun *they* by their school speech clinician. These judgments were confirmed by anecdotal reports from their classroom teachers. In all instances, the subjects appeared to comprehend the pronoun *they*, but were observed to consistently substitute the accusative form *them* in spontaneous speech.

The reasons for selecting the pronoun *they* were twofold. First, it was necessary to find a grammatical form absent in enough children to allow for an adequate test of the proposed hypothesis. More importantly, because of the seminal nature of this research, it was believed that a grammatical form was needed that, when produced, could easily be classified as correct or incorrect. The pronoun *they* fulfilled both of these requirements.

PROCEDURE
The study was conducted longitudinally across three separate, instructional sessions, which correspond to the children's regularly scheduled, 20-minute therapy session. Because of this scheduling, three to four days of noncontact intervened between each session. The experimenter was the children's regular school speech clinician, who had been specially trained for this task. Although the clinician administered both therapy techniques, she was not aware of the specific hypothesis of this study.

At the beginning of each session, the experimenter took a baseline measure of the subject's frequency of usage of the pronoun *they*. To obtain baseline scores, each subject was shown a series of 20 pictures, each of which required him to respond with a single sentence involving the pronoun *they*. The only verbal prompt the experimenter used was "Tell me about them."

At the outset of this study, it was anticipated that several grammatically correct patterns of response could be generated (for example, "The boys are running" instead of "They are running"). To counteract this tendency, the prompt "Tell me about them" was employed. This prompt had the effect of channeling the subjects' response patterns toward the desired construction and away from alternative, yet correct, responses. As a result, error responses assumed one of two forms, either *them* or no response.

Once the baseline scores were obtained in each session, the experimenter administered the designated method of instruction. The same series of 20 pictures was used for this procedure. In the mimicry condition, the experimenter would hold up one of the pictures, perform the appropriate and correct grammatical utterance (for example, "They are playing"), and ask the subject to immediately repeat the utterance. No form of reinforcement was offered to the subjects between trials. This procedure was repeated for the entire series of pictures.

In the modeling condition, the experimenter again held up a single picture and performed the grammatical description of its contents using the pronoun *they*. Unlike the mimicry condition, however, this procedure was repeated 20 times before the subject was asked to respond. At that time, the subject was required, without additional modeling, to respond to all 20 of the pictures that had just been modeled by the experimenter. Again, no form of reinforcement was offered between trials.

The final task produced the postinstruction measure of frequency, that is, the generalization or transfer task. During this stage, a new and totally different set of pictures was employed. The subject was again asked to "Tell me about them." As in the baseline task, the total number of correct utterances out of a possible 20 was recorded.

One week after all three instruction sessions were completed, a final, postexperimental generalization task was performed. The subjects were simply asked to re-

Table 1   Display of Data for the Eight Subjects. Scores Represent the Number of Correct Utterances out of a Possible 20

	Session						
	1		2		3		
Subject	Base	Gen	Base	Gen	Base	Gen	Post
Mimicry							
1	6	13	12	18	10	15	13
2	2	13	4	9	0	14	3
3	13	15	10	15	12	15	15
4	7	16	10	12	9	14	14
Modeling							
5	0	17	8	20	4	20	20
6	0	18	7	19	13	20	14
7	0	11	1	20	2	20	20
8	0	13	7	20	15	20	20

spond with a single sentence to each of a new series of 20 pictures. Again, the total number of correct utterances was the criterion measure.

RESULTS

The experimental design used in this study was a $2 \times 2 \times 3$ factorial design, with method (mimicry versus modeling) being a between-subjects variable, and baseline to generalization (BG) and sessions (S) being analyzed as repeated measures (Bruning and Kintz, 1968). Table 1 presents the data obtained in this study.

The analysis revealed an overall increase in performance from the baseline condition to the generalization ($f = 74.42$; $df = 1,6$; $p < 0.001$). This finding suggested that subjects in both experimental conditions significantly increased their number of correct utterances after having received instruction. Similarly, the data revealed that subjects in both experimental conditions increased their overall performance across the three instructional sessions ($F = 10.32$; $df = 2,12$; $p < 0.005$).

Given these findings for the performance of the combined experimental conditions, this initial analysis showed that there was not a significant difference between the instructional methods ($F < 1$). Although this initial finding did not provide support for the hypothesis under investigation, the significant interaction between method $\times$ sessions ($F = 7.36$; $df = 2,12$; $p < 0.025$) should serve to clarify this nonsignificant

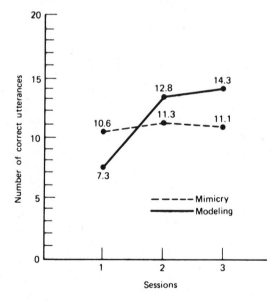

Figure 1.   Method $\times$ sessions interaction. The scores represent the means in each of the three clinical conditions. These were obtained by summing the scores across the baseline to generalization condition.

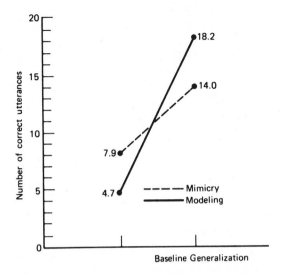

Figure 2. Method × baseline to generalization interaction. The scores represent the
means in the baseline to generalization condition. The scores were obtained by summing across the three clinical sessions.

result. Figure 1 aids in the interpretation of this interaction. Obviously, the two
experimental groups performed differently across the three instruction sessions. Figure 1 suggests that in the modeling condition the subjects consistently increased
their performance across the three trials. In contrast, the subjects in the mimicry
condition did not exhibit such an overall increase, and, in fact, exhibited a decrease
in performance from session 2 to session 3.

The significant method × baseline to generalization interaction ($F = 8.40$; $df =$
$1,6$; $p < 0.05$) also helps to explain the nonsignificant main effect for method. Figure
2 shows that subjects in the modeling condition exhibited an overall lower frequency
of correct responses in the baseline measure ($t = 2.31$; $df = 22$; $p < 0.025$;
one-tailed), but demonstrably increased their performance in the generalization task.
The mimicry subjects also increased, but they began with a higher frequency of
correct responses and ended with a lower frequency than their modeling counterparts ($t = 5.24$; $df = 22$; $p < 0.0005$; one-tailed).

These significant interactions, then, strongly suggest that any "true" differences
between the experimental conditions are hidden by the obvious disparity in performance on the baseline task. Hence, in order to investigate the generalization measures
without the influence of the baseline scores, an analysis of covariance was conducted
on the data (Kerlinger and Pedhazur, 1973). This provided a statistically precise
adjustment of the generalization scores (Carlson, 1967).

The results of the analysis on these adjusted data indicated a highly significant
difference between the mimicry and modeling conditions ($F = 52.97$; $df = 1,5$; p
< 0.001). This analysis confirms our previous suspicions that the between-methods

differences were being influenced by the baseline scores, that is, influenced in a manner which negated the true difference in our sample population. More importantly, the adjusted data provide support for our primary hypothesis that modeling is a more effective method of language instruction. Additional evidence which confirms this hypothesis is provided by the analysis of the postexperimental generalization task. These results not only suggest that modeling is more effective as an instructional technique, but also that subjects in the modeling condition tend to better generalize and transfer their knowledge to novel situations ($t = 2.29$; $df = 6$; $p < 0.05$; one-tailed).

DISCUSSION

The results of the present research offer evidence that modeling is superior to mimicry in the teaching of the personal pronoun *they*. Similarly, this research indicates that subjects who were in the modeling condition retained and transferred their knowledge of the language rule to a greater extent than did subjects in the mimicry condition.

Using social learning theory as our conceptual framework, we believe that these results can best be explained in terms of what Zimmerman and Bell (1972) have termed the "interference hypothesis." Basically, this approach maintains that an abstract rule (for example, a language rule) is best learned by passive observation of the imitative model. Moreover, it asserts that overt verbalizations by the observer during the learning process serve only to disrupt the cognitive processing necessary to acquire the rule and, hence, inhibit both learning and transfer. This is similar to a suggestion made by Winitz (1973). In discussing the experimental results on this question, Zimmerman and Bell (1972, p. 230) write:

> Regardless of the . . . type of rule being learned, passive observation proved the most effective method of vicarious learning because verbalization by the observer during vicarious learning interfered with rule induction. . . . From a pedagogical point of view, teachers should be more discerning about requiring overt verbalization during observational learning since it could potentially interfere with acquisition. They should direct more attention to the presence of subvocal speech in children as one important cue.

Obviously, the data from the present study are not extensive enough to provide more than tangential support for this hypothesis. This is especially true in the light of the significant main effects for sessions and baseline to generalization, which suggest that subjects in both experimental conditions improved their performance from the baseline measure. Moreover, previous studies (Whitehurst and Novak, 1973) have obtained results that would challenge those obtained in this study. The case for one instructional technique being superior to the other, then, is not clear-cut.

We believe, nevertheless, that the interference hypothesis deserves rigorous empirical investigation. The need for research into this area becomes even more pressing when one considers that many contemporary methods of speech and language instruction involve some form of overt client verbalization. In fact, several authors have explicitly claimed that the amount of client verbalization is positively related to increases in the learning of language structures (Mowrer, 1970). In contrast to these claims, it is possible that modeling could be proven to be a relatively easy, uncomplicated method of instruction—a method that is significantly more effective than others proposed or used for teaching specific types of grammatical rules or overcoming certain language disorders.

Additional research, we believe, should focus on the effects of other variables on the modeling process. As was indicated earlier, a better understanding of the role of reinforcement is clearly requisite before imitative modeling would be suitable for widespread use as an instructional technique (Kent et al., 1972; Miller and Yoder, 1972). Similarly, questions concerning the type of stimuli which could be most efficaciously employed, for example, pictures, verbal stimuli, and so on (Asher, 1972; Mann and Baer, 1971), and whether they should be administered by the clinician or by a separate model (Leonard, 1975) must be investigated and answered.

In conclusion, this study has supplied initial findings about the potential for imitative modeling as a theoretical base for speech and language instruction. Subsequent studies, then, must attempt to determine the exact nature of this potential and the scope of its usefulness with regard to a wide variety of speech and language deficiencies.

REFERENCES

ASHER, J. J., Children's first language as a model for second language learning. *Mod. Lang. J.,* **56,** 133–138 (1972).

BANDURA, A., *Social Learning Theory.* New York: General Learning (1971a).

BANDURA, A., Analysis of Modeling Processes. In A. Bandura (Ed.), *Psychological Modeling: Conflicting Theories.* New York: Aldine-Atherton, 1–62 (1971b).

BANDURA, A., and HARRIS, M. A., Modification of syntactic style. *J. Exp. Child Psychol.,* **4,** 341–352 (1966).

BRUNING, J. L., and KINTZ, B. L., *Computational Handbook of Statistics.* Glenview, Ill.: Scott, Foresman (1968).

CARLSON, N. T., The appropriateness of the analysis of covariance to the simple randomized design in physical education research. Doctoral dissertation, Univ. of Iowa (1967).

CARROLL, W. R., ROSENTHAL, T. L., and BRYSH, C. G., Social transmission of grammatical parameters. *J. Ed. Psychol.,* **63,** 589–596 (1973).

CHOMSKY, N., Formal discussion. In U. Bellugi, and R. Brown (Eds.), *The Acquisition of Language. Monogr. Soc. Res. Child Dev.,* **29,** 37 (1964).

ERVIN-TRIPP, S., Imitation in children's language. In E. H. Lenneberg (Ed.), *New Directions in the Study of Language.* Cambridge, Mass.: The MIT Press, 172 (1964).

HARRIS, M. B., and HASSEMER, W. G., Some factors affecting the complexity of children's sentences: The effects of modeling, age, sex, and bilingualism. *J. Exp. Child Psychol.,* **13,** 447–455 (1972).

HARTUP, W. W., and COATES, B., Imitation: Argument for a developmental approach. In R. D. Parke (Ed.), *Recent Trends in Social Learning Theory.* New York: Academic (1972).

HOPPER, R., and NAREMORE, R. C., *Children's Speech: A Practical Introduction to Communication Development.* New York: Harper and Row (1973).

KENT, L. R., KLEIN, D., FALK, A., and GUENTHER, H., A language acquisition program for the retarded. In J. E. McLean, D. E. Yoder, and R. L. Schiefelbusch (Eds.), *Language Intervention with the Retarded*. Baltimore: University Park (1972).

KERLINGER, F. N., and PEDHAZUR, E. J., *Multiple Regression in Behavioral Research*. New York: Holt, Rinehart and Winston (1973).

LIEBERT, R. M., ODOM, R. D., HILL, J. A., and HUFF, R. L., Effects of age and rule familiarity on the production of modeled language constructions. *Dev. Psychol.*, **1**, 108–112 (1969).

LEONARD, L. B., Modeling as a clinical procedure in language training. *Lang. Speech Hearing Serv. Schools*, **6**, 72–85 (1975).

MANN, R. A., and BAER, D. M., The effects of receptive language training on articulation. *J. Appl. Behav. Anal.*, **4**, 291–298 (1971).

MILLER, J. F., and YODER, D. E., A syntax teaching program. In J. E. McLean, D. E. Yoder, and R. L. Schiefelbusch (Eds.), *Language Intervention with the Retarded*. Baltimore: University Park (1972).

MOWRER, D. E., An analysis of motivational techniques used in speech therapy. *Asha*, **12**, 491–493 (1970).

REES, N. S., Imitation and language development. *J. Speech Hearing Dis.*, **40**, 339–350 (1975).

ROSENTHAL, T. L., and CARROLL, W. R., Factors in vicarious modification of complex grammatical parameters. *J. Educ. Psychol.*, **63**, 174–178 (1972).

ROSENTHAL, T. L., and WHITEBOOK, J. S., Incentives versus instruction in transmitting grammatical parameters with experimenter as model. *Behav. Res. Ther.*, **8**, 189–196 (1970).

SLOBIN, D. I., Imitation and grammatical development in children. In N. S. Endler, L. R. Boulter, and H. Osser (Eds.), *Contemporary Issues in Developmental Psychology*. New York: Holt, Rinehart and Winston (1968).

WHITEHURST, G. J., and NOVAK, G., Modeling imitation training, and the acquisition of sentence phrases. *J. Exp. Child Psychol.*, **16**, 332–345 (1973).

WINITZ, H., Problem solving and the delaying of speech as strategies in the teaching of language. *Asha*, **15**, 583–586 (1973).

ZIMMERMAN, B. J., and BELL, J. A., Observer verbalization and abstraction in vicarious rule learning, generalization, and retention. *Dev. Psychol.*, **7**, 227–231 (1972).

ZIMMERMAN, B. J., and ROSENTHAL, T. L., Observational learning of rule-governed behavior by children. *Psychol. Bull.*, **81**, 29–42 (1974).

Part 6
ALTERNATIVE MODALITIES IN LANGUAGE FACILITATION

This section is concerned with alternatives to the use of the auditory modality for language learning—generally by supplementing or replacing the auditory-vocal linguistic signal with a visual-motor linguistic signal. Spurred by the reported success with which researchers have been teaching certain language behaviors to chimpanzees by using visual symbols in place of speech (for example, Gardner and Gardner, 1969, and Premack, 1971), a number of clinicians and researchers have been using these same symbols with language-disordered children. A rationale for the use of the visual modality is that some children may be having difficulty with language learning because of processing problems which are specific to the auditory modality or to the integration of auditory information with visual information. While a visual linguistic system has long been used with deaf children, its use with normal hearing children has only recently received much attention. This is not to say that such methods have not been used in the past. Itard, for example, used written language with Victor, the wild boy of Aveyron, in the 1700s when it seemed Victor could not learn the auditory-vocal language. (See the excerpt from Itard, 1962, reprinted in Part V.)

The four articles reprinted here illustrate the successful use of visual-motor linguistic systems to facilitate language learning. Bricker (1972) trained the imitation of motor signs (signs that represented the objects, or actions associated with the objects presented) as a means of facilitating the association of the spoken label with the object. Miller and Miller

(1973) taught both expressive and receptive use of manual signs in meaningful contexts and reported on the transition from the visual-motor system to the auditory-vocal system for two of the children. The article by Bonvillian and Nelson (1976) presents a description of the development of sign language in an autistic child. Rather than signs, McLean and McLean (1974) used abstract wooden symbols and taught a limited visual-motor linguistic system to two autistic children. (A similar approach, not reprinted here, has also been used by Carrier, 1974 with retarded children.)

The reported research has included both autistic and retarded children as candidates for alternative modalities. It is not yet clear which children will most benefit from the use of alternative modalities in learning language, nor is it clear why certain children benefit from this approach. It may be that, for some, the processing or integration of the auditory signal had been the barrier to language learning; for others, it may be that hand signs seem more representative of the objects and events symbolized and serve as a transition to more abstract coding. But these articles do suggest that the use of alternative modalities is an approach worthy of consideration by the researcher and clinician when efforts to teach the auditory-vocal language system have repeatedly failed.

REFERENCES

Carrier, J. 1974 Application of functional analysis and a nonspeech response mode to teaching. In L. McReynolds (Ed.) *ASHA Monographs* #18, 47–95

Gardner, A. and Gardner, B. 1969 Teaching sign language to a chimpanzee, *Science,* 165, 664–672.

Premack, D. 1971 Language in chimpanzee? *Science,* 172, 808–822.

Imitative Sign Training as a Facilitator of Word-Object Association with Low-Functioning Children[1,2]

Diane D. Bricker[3]

A 90-item two-choice discrimination test was given to 26 institutionalized mentally retarded children. The experimental group was given a sequence of training in which imitative-sign movements were taught and subsequently were paired with appropriate words followed by pairing with appropriate objects. Periodic word-object association probe tests were administered to both groups. The control subjects were exposed to no other training. Following training, a posttest was administered. The posttest was a replication of the 90-item word-object discrimination test using the object's name to indicate the correct choice. The results indicated that reliable differences were found between the experimental and control groups on the criterion measure, suggesting that the imitative-sign training facilitated word-object association.

The focus of this investigation was on the development of initial word meaning by young low-functioning children. An initial step in the development of meaning is the ability to appropriately name or respond to the names of objects in the environment. Bricker and Bricker (1970) attempted to teach responses to names using a word-object association paradigm with a group of young low-functioning children. The subjects were presented two-choice discrimination problems with an auditory stimulus (object name) to indicate the correct object. Although the experimental groups performed significantly better on the criterion task than the controls, a number of the experimental subjects did not learn from the training procedures which consisted of repeatedly having the subject select one of the two stimuli and having all correct choices reinforced. Since object names did not become consistent discriminative

From *American Journal of Mental Deficiency, 76,* 509–516 (1972). Reprinted by permission of the American Association on Mental Deficiency.

[1] This study was done while the investigator was at Parsons State Hospital and Training Center and was supported by USOE Grant No. 2–3–070218–1639 and NICHHD Grant No. HD 00870.

[2] This paper is based upon a doctoral dissertation submitted to George Peabody College for Teachers, Nashville, Tennessee.

[3] The author gratefully acknowledges the assistance given by Charles Galloway, Robert Mattos, Samuel Ashcroft, and William Bricker.

stimuli (S^Ds) for choice for the nonlearners, these investigators questioned the relevance of this training for this population of children.

In a subsequent study (Bricker & Bricker, 1971), again with severely retarded children, name and no-name training conditions were compared with a control procedure. In the name training, the correct object was labeled on each trial while in the no-name training subsequent reinforcement or nonreinforcement following choice was the only indication of the correct object. Although both experimental groups performed significantly better on the criterion and generalization tasks than did the controls, the name training group was not significantly different from the no-name training group. These results were contrary to previous investigations which had demonstrated that verbal labeling facilitated discrimination learning in young nonretarded (Weir & Stevenson, 1959) and retarded children (Dickerson, Girardeau, & Spradlin, 1964). It is possible that severely retarded children are generally unable to use verbal labels as cues for appropriate discriminations without some prior alternative discrimination training. For example, a manual sign paired with an object and its name might increase the discriminability between various objects and between various words. The ability to distinguish between objects and between names should increase the chances of the object's name becoming a discriminative stimulus for choice. The recent success of the Gardners (1969) in teaching two-way communication to an infant chimpanzee through the use of manual signs suggests the feasibility of attempting certain forms of initial language training by using gestural signs rather than words.

PURPOSE

Although there have been numerous attempts to facilitate visual discrimination tasks, there have been few studies reported in the literature in which the association between an auditory signal and its corresponding referent was facilitated in a population of low-functioning children (Bricker & Bricker, 1970; Bricker & Bricker, 1971). The purpose in the present study was to determine the effect of a sequence of imitative-sign, sign-word, and sign-object training on the development of labels as discriminative stimuli for choice between objects. The subject's task in this study was to select the correct stimulus across two-choice discrimination problems. On each trial the correct object was indicated by the experimenter verbalizing the name of the correct object subsequent to the subject's choice.

METHOD

SUBJECTS

The subjects used in the present investigation were residents of the Parsons State Hospital and Training Center, Parsons, Kansas. Only 32 children were located who met the studies' criteria (severely limited language skills, CAs under 15 years, no severely disruptive behavior, and hearing within specified limits) and who were not engaged in other competing programs. Of these 32 subjects, the 26 having the lowest pretest scores were selected. The mean chronological age (CA) for the experimental and control groups was 12.70 (SD = 1.85) and 11.62 (SD = 1.54), respectively. The social quotients (SQ) were taken from the Vineland Social Maturity Scale and the mean SQ for the experimental group was 32.09 (*SD* = 11.18) and 30.23 (*SD* = 7.31) for the control group. All children had been given audiometric assessments by the institution's Speech Department. According to the audiometric records, 19 of the children had hearing within normal limits while the remaining 7 children had mild losses. Three of the children with losses were in the experimental and the other four were in the control group. A 2 $\times$ 2 chi-square analysis using normal versus mild loss and high versus low pretest scores was not statistically significant ($p > .20$). The 7 females and 19 males were matched on the basis of CA, SQ, and pretest scores, with one member of each pair assigned randomly to the experimental and the other to the control group.

APPARATUS AND STIMULI

The training and testing were done in a sound-treated experimental room located in the research building on the institution grounds. A Wisconsin General Test Apparatus (WGTA) was used to present the stimulus objects for the testing and probing phases of the investigation. The WGTA is a large box-like structure with a movable door in the front and an open back. Located on the floor of the WGTA is a movable tray with two food wells cut into the top 15.2 cm apart. The subjects were seated in front of the WGTA while the experimenter sat behind the apparatus. The door was closed between trials so the subject was not able to observe the placement of the reinforcer or the stimuli over the wells. At the beginning of each trial, the door was opened and the tray moved toward the subject. The duration of each trial was automatically recorded by a timer which was activated by a switch located on the door of the WGTA. When the door was opened, the timer began running and continued until the door was closed.

Small three-dimensional toy-like objects mounted on wooden squares 7.6 $\times$ 7.6 cm were selected as follows: (*a*) objects which were easily associated with distinctive motor movements or signs, (*b*) objects which had phonetically different names, and (*c*) objects with which low-functioning children would probably not be familiar.

The auditory stimuli (object names) used during the testing portion of this study were recorded using an Ampex Model 602 tape recorder with a volume-units meter to monitor the recording intensity level. The auditory cues were then presented on a Magnecord 1022 tape recorder through a Grason-Stadler Model 162 Speech Audiometer which permitted presentation of the auditory signal at the desired sound pressure level (SPL) intensities. The auditory stimuli were presented at 68 dB (SPL) which is considered normal conversational level and is approximately 46 dB above speech threshold (1953, ASA) which compensated for the signal reduction of the seven subjects with mild losses. The auditory cues were presented through TDH-39 headphones worn by all the children during all pretesting and posttesting.

Edibles such as ice cream, pop, and candy were provided for each correct response or successive approximation throughout the study. The experimenter remained alert to a child's responsiveness and changed the type of consequence whenever necessary to maintain appropriate behavior.

GENERAL PROCEDURE

The subjects were brought to the experimental room individually for testing and training. Sessions lasted approximately 20 minutes, and the children participated on consecutive week days until all training was completed.

Figure 1 presents a procedural lattice of the sequence of testing and training steps administered to the experimental subjects for each of the six object groups. The control subjects were given the pretest, 18 probe tests, and the posttest.

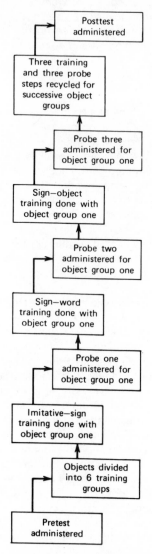

Figure 1.   A procedural lattice presenting the sequence of testing and training steps given to the experimental subjects.

PRETEST

The pretest consisted of 30 items (see Table 1). Each item appeared as the labeled object three times for a total of 90 trials. To construct this instrument, items were randomly paired with each other with the restriction that each stimulus object appeared as the labeled or named item three times and as the distractor or non-labeled object three times. Following the pairings, the items were divided into three groups in which each one of the 30 items appeared once as the named object. Then in each of the three groups the items were randomly sequenced from 1 to 30. The left-right position of the named objects were randomly generated with the restriction that the correct object would not appear on the same side more than two consecutive trials. The sequence of pairs and presentation were the same for all subjects. During the pretest, a tape recorder was used to deliver the auditory cue through ear phones worn by the subject. Each trial followed a standard procedure: (a) the door on the WGTA was closed; (b) the experimenter filled one of the two wells with a small edible and placed the stimuli over the wells; (c) the door was opened and the tape recorder activated; (d) the name of the correct object was presented via the tape recorder; (e) the experimenter pushed the tray forward; (f) the child was allowed to select one of the objects; (g) the door was lowered; and (h) the experimenter recorded the child's selection, the trial time, and reset the timer.

Table 1   A Schematic of the Study's Experimental Design and a list of the Training Objects for Each Group

	Imitative Sign	Probe	Sign Word	Probe	Sign Object	Probe
Training block one Objects: rake, eraser, cross, five, detergent	X	X,C	X	X,C	X	X,C
Training block two Objects: handle, stroller, heart, pliers, axe	X	X,C	X	X,C	X	X,C
Training block three Objects: triangle, hook, stork, utensil, bow	X	X,C	X	X,C	X	X,C
Training block four Objects: two, commode, ladder, T, candle	X	X,C	X	X,C	X	X,C
Training block five Objects: banjo, helmet, switch, vest, ten	X	X,C	X	X,C	X	X,C
Training block six Objects: pitcher, tulip, harp, bristles, binoculars	X	X,C	X	X,C	X	X,C

Note.—X=experimental group; C=control group.

TRAINING

Following the administration of the pretest, the subjects were equally divided into an experimental and a control group. The experimental group was given three phases of training with probe tests administered between each phase. The control group received the probe tests with no intervening training. Table 1 contains a schematic of the study's design and the objects assigned to each training group. Order presentation of the object groups was counterbalanced across subjects.

IMITATIVE-SIGN TRAINING.   The training in this phase was as follows: (a) the child was seated at a small table across from the experimenter; (b) the experimenter made eye contact with the child; (c) the experimenter performed a motor movement or sign while saying, "Do this"; and (d) if spontaneous imitation did not occur, the experimenter shaped the child to imitate the motor movement using physical prompts and fading. Each object had a specific representational movement such as a chopping motion for axe or a pouring motion for pitcher that the experimental subjects were to learn during this phase of training. Once the child was imitating the first movement, the experimenter introduced the next movement. Five motor movements or signs composed each training segment. Criterion for introduction of probe 1 was the production of seven appropriate imitations out of 10 trials in which each movement was modeled twice. If criterion was not reached within five training sessions for the first object group, the child was dropped from the study. However, if the subject failed to reach criterion on the second through sixth groups, he moved on to the next training phase.

SIGN-WORD TRAINING.   The experimenter obtained the subject's attention, repeated the name (auditory cue) of one of the training objects (i.e., rake), followed by the movement for rake previously learned in the imitative-sign training phase. If the subject did not spontaneously produce the *rake* sign-movement following the second emission of the auditory cue—*rake*—the experimenter physically prompted the motor behavior after saying, *"Do rake."* The experimenter reinforced all appropriate motor responses as well as approximations to appropriate responses. Gradually the physical prompts were faded across trials until the subject produced the appropriate motor response following the presentation of the auditory cue without prompting. All five stimuli in each training group were trained using the same procedure. Criterion for terminating training and moving to probe 2 was the same as for the imitative-sign phase.

SIGN-OBJECT TRAINING.   The final phase of training consisted of presenting the three-dimensional objects such as *rake* to the subject while saying, "Do rake," followed immediately by modeling the appropriate previously learned sign for the object. Again, shaping procedures were employed if the child did not spontaneously produce the sign or produced the wrong sign. This final phase assured that the child at least had the opportunity to associate the imitative-sign with its name and referent. Criterion for moving to probe 3 was the same as in the previous phases.

PROBE TESTING. After each training phase, a 10-item test probe was administered. For each of the six training blocks, 30 probe trials were given to both the experimental and control groups. For example, after completion of imitative-sign training with the experimental group, a probe test covering the trained items was administered to the experimental subjects and their matched control who had received no training. After sign-word training, the second training phase for the experimental subjects, the probe test was readministered to the experimental subjects and their matched controls. Following the third phase of training, sign-object, a third probe was administered to both the experimental and control subjects. This sequence was replicated six times using different groups of objects.

Each probe test consisted of 10 trials with the five training objects appearing twice as the named object and twice as the distractor. The 10 trials were presented using the WGTA. The food well was filled and the objects positioned while the door was closed. When the door was opened, the experimenter named the correct objects twice before the tray was pushed forward so the child could make his selection.

POSTTEST

The posttest was a replication of the pretest and was administered following the completion of training for each subject.

RESULTS

PRETEST

The pretest was administered to 32 children and a split-half correlation between the first and second half of the test for these subjects was .88, which was increased to .94 when the Spearman-Brown correction formula for length was applied.

For the experimental group, pretest scores ranged from 35 to 58 with a mean of 46.0 and an SD of 5.74. The control pretest scores ranged from 38 to 61 with a mean of 45.07 and an SD of 6.63. The mean latency per trial was 7.52 seconds (SD = 1.89) for the experimental group and 8.60 seconds (SD = 1.34) for the control group.

TRAINING

Two experimental subjects failed to reach criterion during training on the first object group, and these subjects plus their matched controls were eliminated from the remainder of the investigation. The elimination of these two matched pairs produced shifts of one or two points in the mean SQ and pretest scores.

Total training time for the six object groups for the remaining 11 experimental subjects ranged from 84 to 488 minutes with a mean training time of 251.55 minutes. The Pearson product-moment correlation for the combined groups between training time and change scores derived from pretest-posttest comparisons was − .88.

Following each training phase, a 10-item probe test was administered to the experimental and control subjects. The mean-performance of the control and experimental groups on the 18 probe tests are shown in Figure 2.

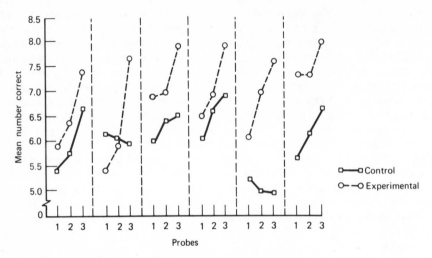

Figure 2.   Mean number correct on the 18 probe tests for the experimental and control groups across object groups.

The mean performances across probes plotted in Figure 2 show differences between the control and experimental groups. Further analyses were indicated in order to determine whether these differences were reliable, and if so, which aspects of training were responsible for the differences.

The first step in the analysis of the training data was to determine if object groups produced a differential effect between the experimental and control conditions or within these conditions. Presentation order of object groups was counterbalanced across subject pairs. A two-way analysis of variance with Conditions and Object Groups as the dimensions revealed no reliable effects for Conditions, or Object Groups, nor a significant Condition × Object Group interaction. Consequently, Object Group as a dimension was eliminated from further analyses.

The next step in the analysis of the training data was to determine the effects of the Experimental Conditions, Probes, and Presentation Order. Presentation Order refers to the sequence in which object groups were presented to subjects for training. This analysis revealed a reliable difference in Presentation Order ($F = 2.56$, 5/100 df, $p < .05$). Probes were also reliably different ($F = 14.77$, 2/40 df, $p < .001$). All other effects and interactions were statistically unreliable. However, probes by Experimental Conditions approached significance ($F = 2.98$, 2/40 df, $.05 < p < .10$).

POSTTEST
A split-half correlation between the first and second half of the posttest was .85, which was increased to .92 when the Spearman-Brown correction formula for length was applied.

Scores on this test ranged from 45 to 81 for the experimental group with a mean of 63.18 and an SD of 13.13. The control group scores ranged from 40 to 75 with a mean of 54.00 and an SD of 12.43.

The mean latencies per trial for the experimental and control groups were 7.75

(*SD* = 2.51) and 7.16 (*SD* = .69) seconds, respectively. The mean response latencies shifted .23 seconds for the experimental subjects, indicating the speed of responding changed very little for these subjects.

Figure 3 presents a graph of the mean number of correct responses on the pretest and posttest for the experimental and control groups. An inspection of this figure shows the comparability of the control and experimental groups on the pretest and the divergent performances of these groups on the posttest.

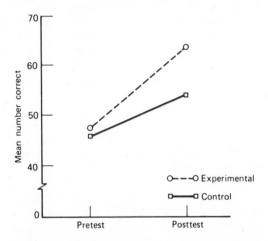

Figure 3. Mean number correct on the pretest and posttest for the experimental and control groups.

A two-way analysis of variance using Tests and Conditions as the dimensions resulted in a statistically unreliable difference between treatment Condition, but a highly reliable Tests effect ($F = 25.56$, $1/20$ *df*, $p < .001$) was found. The interaction between Tests and Conditions was also statistically reliable ($F = 4.72$, $1/20$ *df*, $p < .05$). An examination of the raw data suggested that much of the average gains of the control group could be accounted for by two subjects, while the gains were more evenly distributed in the experimental group.

DISCUSSION

The purpose in the present investigation was to determine the effect of a sequence of imitative-sign, sign-word, and sign-object training on word-object association in low-functioning children. An analysis of the change scores from the pretest to the posttest revealed a reliable difference in favor of the experimental group, suggesting that the experimental training procedure operated as a facilitator for the development of word-object association with this particular group of children. Although the differences between the experimental and control groups could be attributed to the additional training time given the experimental subjects, this explanation would seem improbable in the light of the results of the Bricker and Bricker (1970) study discussed previously. This investigation using a similar population and procedure indicated that a Hawthorne control group receiving equal time with an experimenter and training stimuli as well as an equal amount of tangible reinforcement as the experimental did not differ from a do-nothing control but did differ significantly from the two experimental training procedures.

An analysis of the training data revealed some interesting effects which allow some tentative conclusions to be drawn about the training procedure. First, the composition of the object groups made no statistically reliable difference for either the experimental or the control groups; however, presentation order of the object groups was shown to produce a reliable difference within subjects. The primary index of training progress was the 10-item probe tests administered following each phase of training for the experimental subjects and simultaneously for the experimentals' matched controls. An analysis of these measures revealed no statistically reliable effect for probes by experimental conditions.

Training time ranged from approximately 1 ½ hours to over 8 hours. The variations in training time, as well as the differential gains on the posttest by the experimental group, demonstrated the marked heterogeneity of low-functioning children. The range of scores across probes and tests also reveals the heterogeneity of this population. Although the experimental procedure produced superior median scores and more scores in the upper quartile range, the range of scores for the experimental group was generally more extensive, suggesting the training technique had a differential effect across children. This heterogeneity is an important factor when evaluating the efficacy of the training procedure with low-functioning children. For those children who gained slightly on the posttest after several hours of training, a more economical and efficient approach needs to be developed. However, for those children who made large gains after only a few hours of training, the procedure was effective and should be at least considered for use in the education of low-functioning children.

Since two previous investigations (Bricker & Bricker, 1970, 1971) indicated that many subjects with severe language deficits failed to acquire word-object associations after extensive training, it might be worthwhile to hypothesize why the procedure in this study was more successful in establishing labels as discriminative stimuli for choice among objects. In the present study, the subjects were required to produce a manual sign following the presentation of a word and/or object. To produce the appropriate sign the subject had to discriminate between the words and objects. It may be that this forced discrimination resulted in facilitating development of the labels as discriminative stimuli for object choice.

In conclusion, it would seem that the results of this investigation would justify expanded examination of the use of motor movements or manual signing as an educational technique for children with severe language handicaps.

REFERENCES

Bricker, W. A., & Bricker, D. D. Development of receptive vocabulary in severely retarded children. *American Journal of Mental Deficiency*, 1970, 74, 599–607.

Bricker, W. A., & Bricker, D. D. Receptive vocabulary as a factor in the discrimination performance of low-functioning children. *American Journal of Mental Deficiency*, 1971, 75, 599–605.

Dickerson, D., Girardeau, F. L., & Spradlin, J. E. Verbal pretraining and discrimination learning by retardates. *American Journal of Mental Deficiency,* 1964, 68, 476–484.

Gardner, R., & Gardner, B. Teaching sign language to a chimpanzee. *Science,* 1969, 165, 664–672.

Weir, M. W., & Stevenson, H. W. The effect of verbalization in children's learning as a function of chronological age. *Child Development,* 1959, 30, 143–149.

Cognitive-Developmental Training with Elevated Boards and Sign Language[1]

Arnold Miller and Eileen Eller Miller

A study is presented to describe cognitive-developmental training involving use of connected boards elevated 3 to 6 feet above the ground together with special language signs. The subjects, 12 boys and 7 girls, were mute autistic children. Thirteen were in residential treatment and 6 attended day school. Signs were systematically paired with appropriate spoken words which all children learned to understand. Also, all learned to initiate signs to achieve desired objects or goals. The day school children, a younger group, achieved significantly greater expressive use of signs and words than residential school children. Two children, whose case histories are summarized, made the transition from signs to expressive spoken language. The training program is discussed in some detail.

Cognitive-developmental training refers to the systematic use of selected procedures to ameliorate the massive language and cognitive deficits which recent investigators (Rutter, 1965, 1968; Rutter & Bartak, 1971; Hermelin, 1968; Wing, 1969; Churchill, 1972) regard as central in childhood psychoses. These procedures are used judiciously depending on the level of deficit manifested by the child. Thus, training of mute autistic children, the focus of the present report, emphasizes both communication and improved contact with the immediate environment, while training of children with some spoken language endeavors to expand their capacity to speak while developing abilities to read and write.

   The developmental assumptions on which such training procedures are based merit an introductory mention. To begin with, it is assumed that the development of language and cognition follows a regular progression (Piaget, 1954; Werner, 1948), and that during such progression children *first* learn to direct their body actions, *then* their distal senses (vision, audition), and *finally* their language and thought toward

From *Journal of Autism and Childhood Schizophrenia 3*, 65–85 (1973). Copyright © 1973 by V. H. Winston & Sons, Inc. Reprinted by permission of Plenum Publishing Corporation.

[1] The authors wish to express their appreciation to Dr. and Mrs. Jacques M. May, Directors of the May Institute for Autistic Children, Mrs. Kay Morgenthau, Director of the League School of Boston, and Dr. John F. Scott, Director of the Worcester Youth Guidance Center, for the cooperation which made this study possible. Special thanks are also due to Mr. Roland E. Vandal and Dr. John Murphy, officers of AMIC, Region 2, for their help and enterprise in establishing a pilot Cognitive-Developmental Training Program at the Day Care Unit for Autistic Children at the Worcester Youth Guidance Center.

objects and events beyond their immediate reach. A second assumption is that directed body action, the earliest to develop, provides the foundation on which subsequently developing intentional activity builds. Thus, a child unable to voluntarily direct his body toward his immediate environment or to make transition from his large body activity to more sense-dependent contact with his surroundings should be unable to achieve more symbolic modes of experience.

Autistic children seem to have serious difficulty with both intentional body activity and transition from body action to more symbolic functioning. These difficulties seem closely related to the way in which they are dominated by impressive aspects of their immediate experience. Unlike normal children who act toward and connect one event with another, autistic children become "captured" by their total body response to one event. Once "captured," each sequence of response, whether twiddling or complicated ritual, appears to harden into a circumscribed sphere of reality (Uexküll, 1957; Werner, 1948) detached from every other sphere. Each sphere of reality seems to have its own integrity and engages the child in a "single-track" manner so that he is quite oblivious to any ongoing event outside that sphere. For example, an autistic child on a hike might initially adapt his body to broken terrain as he climbs a hill. However, in the process, he becomes so involved with this particular action (hill-climbing) that he loses contact with the reason for climbing the hill (the hike). Then, unless the child is urged forward, he may begin, endlessly, to repeat his hill-climbing.

We suggest that it is the autistic child's "single-track" involvement within each of a series of such disconnected spheres which seems to preclude his deliberate disengagement from the preoccupying object or ritual, so that he might relate his body in a more functional manner to the larger situation or to new situations. This form of encapsulation is distinctly different from the conditions that must exist before intentional activity is possible. Schilder (1950) characterized such conditions as follows:

> There must always be the knowledge that I am acting with my body, that I have to start the movement with my body, that I have to use a particular part of my body. But in the plan there must also be the aim of my action. There is always an object toward which the action is directed . . . . In order to act we must know something about the quality of the object of our intention. And finally, we must also know in what way we want to approach the object. The formula contains, therefore, the image of the limb or part of the body which is performing the movement.

Unfortunately, the awareness of body and body part in relation to the object, which Schilder considers necessary for intentional action, seems largely absent among autistic children immersed in their rituals. And, without awareness of the body as a separate entity *in relation to* external goals, there can be no self-directed activity. In a world without awareness that the body is a separate entity which moves among and acts upon objects and events, the autistic child cannot distinguish stimulation from his own body from impinging stimulation deriving from objects and events external to his body. Unable to distinguish where his body ends and the world begins, the autistic child has no foundation from which to launch purposeful action.

Our observations of autistic children suggest that they themselves may be aware of the lack of definition between their bodies and the world. Such children may periodically try to compensate for this by seeking "edge" experiences which dramatize the relationship between their bodies and the immediate environment. Behavior at the beach by one of our subjects, a 10-year-old autistic boy named Philip, appeared to demonstrate such awareness and attempt to compensate. Philip would run back and forth across the line which divided water from sand. In addition, although unable to swim, he would bob up and down at the greatest depth he could stand with only his mouth and nose above water. During the course of such bobbing, he would at times breathe water instead of air, and then bob higher. In another example, 4-year-old Nancy, an autistic girl quite aware of height, had on several occasions hung by her hands outside her third-story window until her unsuspecting mother, reacting to the alarm of people below, discovered the danger and pulled her in.

While such "edge" experiences may momentarily provide the child with a more accented experience of his body, they cannot, by themselves, solve the problem of his encapsulation. For this to happen, some means of guiding him from his detached sphere of reality to more functional contact with the world appears to be required. It is interesting to note in this regard that Donald T., one of Kanner's (1943) original 11 cases who achieved a satisfactory adjustment, did so, at least in part, because the couple who cared for him guided the boy from his autistic preoccupation to more functional behavior. Kanner (1971) described this transformation as follows:

> They made him use his preoccupation with measurements by having him dig a well and report on its depth. When he kept collecting dead birds and bugs, they gave him a spot for a "graveyard" and had him put up markers . . . . When he kept counting rows of corn over and over, they had him count the rows of corn while plowing them. On my visit, he plowed six long rows; it was remarkable how well he handled the horses and plow and turned the horses around . . . .

Kanner's case, of course, involved a child who could talk and count. Consequently, the couple who worked with him could draw on this cognitive ability to guide the boy from his autistic preoccupations. However, in order to guide a mute autistic child from *his* circumscribed reality, the worker has only the child's ritualized body activity with which to work. This he must guide and transform into a more directed contact with his surroundings. Then, for the achievement of spoken language, the worker must find some means of helping the child relate his newly directed body activity to his utterances. But here, the child's difficulty lies not only in his encapsulation but also in the remoteness of spoken words from their referents. Typically, there is nothing in the form of our spoken words which hints at their inner meanings. Thus, to understand the intent of a spoken word, e.g., "stop," "come," the autistic child must first understand that it is possible for utterances to convey meanings, i.e., that they are not merely noises but noises which intend meanings relevant to what he sees and does. Accordingly, we suggest that before mute autistic children can begin to develop language, they must first free themselves from their autistic preoccupations. They must then achieve awareness of their own bodies in relation to objects and events in order to deliberately initiate directed action. Finally, they must achieve a means of relating the directedness of their body actions to spoken language.

In order to create conditions that might enable mute autistic children to resolve these problems, we have established "edge" situations for them at elevations 3 to 6 feet above the ground. These "edges," comprising a variety of connected boards, obstacles, tunnels, and drawbridges to cope with, were designed to both enhance body awareness and guide children from autistic maneuvers to more directed and functional activity. To link directed actions to spoken language, we then introduced manual signs adapted from the American Sign Language (ASL) for the deaf both on the boards and in other relevant contexts. This report describes these procedures in some detail and considers their effect with a sample of 19 mute autistic children from residential and day school settings.

SUBJECTS

The 19 mute autistic subjects who participated in our cognitive-developmental training represented a population of the most severely disturbed and unresponsive children from four therapeutic centers. All had little or no ability to understand or use spoken words when they began the program, and all but two (Teresa and Sidney) had been diagnosed prior to admission as shown in Table 1.

The median chronological age of the 12 boys and 7 girls was 11 years. The median Creak score, assigned to each child by the authors after some observation and consultation with appropriate teachers, was 48.[2]

Residential ($N = 13$) and day school ($N = 6$) children differed markedly only in age. Those in day school who lived at home were significantly ($p < .05$) younger than the 13 children in residence at the May Institute for Autistic Children (MIAC); the median chronological age of the day school group was between 7 and 8 years. The two groups did not differ significantly with respect to sex distribution, Creak scores, or time in program.

Three of the day school children (Donald, Larry, and Philip) participated in the program at the League School of Boston (LSB) and, during the summer, at the Language and Cognitive Development Center (LCDC). Nancy was trained solely at LCDC. All residential children were trained at MIAC. The median time in the training program was 13 months.

The Spearman rank order correlation (ρ) was used to investigate the relationship between the children's responses to signs and to spoken words as well as that between their diagnostic and training characteristics and achievement of signs and words. In addition, the Fisher test (Siegel, 1956) was used to test the significance of differences between residential and day school children on both diagnostic and achievement measures.

---

[2] On the Creak Scale (Creak, 1964) a score of 56 (14 ratings of 4) reflects the most severe autistic state, while scores of 42 or less reflect relatively less severe states.

Table 1   Characteristics of 19 Mute Autistic Children

Name	Sex	CA at commencement of training program (months)	Months in training program	Creak score	Source and Timing of diagnosis	
					Prior to admission to training program	At commencement of program
			Residential School Children			
Mona	F	144	14	48	MIAC	
Hank	M	108	11	50	MIAC	
Nina	F	132	14	46	PCC	
Thomas	M	180	14	51	PCC	
Carl	M	192	11	56	MIAC	
Margaret	F	144	12	56	MIAC	
Teresa	F	108	7	42		MIAC
Kirk	M	276	14	50	PCC	
Barry	M	240	4	54	PCC	
Sidney	M	72	10	48		MIAC
Neal	M	132	14	52	MIAC	
Elliot	M	180	4	52	PCC	
Bella	F	120	14	46	PCC	
			Day School Children			
Karen	F	114	12	54	WYCG	
Tod	M	144	12	54	WYGC	
Donald	M	84	18	52	LSB/LCDC	
Larry	M	72	18	50	LSB/LCDC	
Philip	M	96	36	48	LSB/LCDC	
Nancy	F	60	14	46	PCC/LCDC	

Note.-MIAC = May Institute for Autistic Children; PCC = Putman Children's Center; WYGC = Worcester Youth Guidance Center; LSB = League School of Boston; LCDC = Language and Cognitive Development Center.

METHOD AND MATERIALS

ENHANCING BODY AWARENESS WITH BOARDS

The use of boards described in this study was based on preliminary work with several mute autistic children on 10-inch wide boards elevated 3 to 6 feet above the ground. These boards constituted "edges" highlighting the children's body experience in relation to their immediate surroundings. Autistic children who were unresponsive on

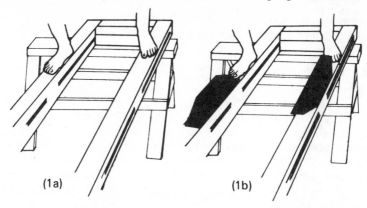

Figure 1.   Parallel board used to help differentiate sides of the body (1a). Obstacles added to accent awareness of feet (1b).

the ground became more aware of their surroundings as soon as they stepped on such boards. This was apparent in the sudden cessation of autistic mannerisms, the steadiness of eye-contact, and the alternating of searching looks at the worker with careful checking of foot placement and the direction in which the board led. We speculated that this heightened awareness of surroundings stemmed from the proximity of the body boundaries to the edges of the boards. As the child looked down the sides of his body and perceived them in direct relationship to the edges of the plank, he simultaneously experienced his sides and feet in relation to board edge and distance above ground. In such a situation, there was no need to conceptualize the body's relationship to the immediate environment since it was given in a glance. Thus, the immediate impact of the experience was to establish a more polar experience of the body and a greater outward orientation than had previously existed.

As children crossed different kinds of board structures, we noted that their outward orientation varied in accord with the kinds of structures they confronted. For example, as long as the boards ahead of them were solid they continued without hesitation. However, if the next connected board was constructed of parallel 2 by 3 inch boards fastened 6 inches apart,[3] they hesitated and did not move forward until they learned to place one foot, then the other, on each 2-inch board and to alternately shuffle each foot forward. When a further complication involving small blocks was introduced on each board, as shown in outline 1b of Figure 1, the children did not move forward until they could shift their weight to one foot so that they could pull back and lift the other foot over the obstacle. In still another kind of board situation, as shown in Figure 2, children had to coordinate both hands and feet to find appropriate space for the footing they needed to move along the board. It seems clear that autistic children could not solve such board problems unless they gained at least momentary awareness (as they shifted weight) of how one side of their bodies differed from the other,

---

[3] See outline 1a in Figure 1.

of the relationship each foot had to its obstacle, and the way in which hands and feet could work together to make progress on the boards possible.

ESTABLISHING INTENTIONAL ACTS

Earlier, we suggested that "edge" experiences by themselves could not solve the autistic child's encapsulation. For this to occur, he had to be aware of his moving body as he was guided into more functional activity. We found that the boards helped achieve both goals. They not only induced heightened body awareness, but also enabled us to guide the child into more functional activity. The boards helped achieve this, in Lewinian (1935) terms, by exerting a "pull" (positive valence) on the child's body to move in accord with the manner in which they were organized. For example, an autistic child's presence on a 10-inch board, situated 4 feet above the ground, which went from point A to point B 8 feet away, helped induce him to *walk* from A to B. If an obstacle (a foot-high box) were placed in the middle of the board, the child would walk from A to the obstacle, *stop,* step *on* or *over* the obstacle, and continue to B. Thus, in order to induce the child to perform various intentional acts, it was necessary to construct board situations that he must solve in order to go from one point on the boards to another. Situations constructed on the boards included doors that had to be *opened,* bridges that had to be *crossed,* drawbridges *lowered,* and positions from which he had to *slide down, push-pull,* or *pick-up* something and *jump.* At first the children required assistance and support from staff or parents who worked with them under supervision. Later, they would go through the course with little or no assistance.

In each instance, the boards contributed toward the intentional act because they prevented the child from avoiding the directly confronting problem while at the same time making it difficult to lapse into one of the autistic maneuvers readily available on the ground. Nevertheless, as the children repeated the same act several times, it would tend to lose its intentional quality and become a ritual. To prevent this from happening, we constantly changed both the configuration of the boards and the tasks

Figure 2.   Child picking his way by coordinating hands and feet on a parallel board with varied block obstacles.

built within them. With each such change we found that the child's activity again became purposeful.

SIGN LANGUAGE

The body awareness course which the boards evolved into demonstrated that it was possible to encourage an unsuspected range of intentional behavior among autistic children. Our task now was to transform this intentional activity into meaningful language. We chose sign language to link action to spoken language after preliminary research (Miller, 1959, 1963; Miller, 1968) indicated that body gesture could facilitate spoken language. We reasoned that children who could not understand spoken language but could perform intentional actions on the boards might be able to transfer the meanings of such actions first to signs (which resembled them) and then to the spoken word which accompanied the manual signs. Until signs transferred their meanings and function to spoken language, they could provide them with a means of understanding and communicating with us.

To facilitate the transfer of meaning and function from action to sign, we selected 50 functional signs closely related to everyday activities of the children. Then, to make the signs relevant, we introduced them in three different contexts. The first context involved the use of signs on the boards. The second taught signs with training films, and the third sought to generalize the learned signs to everyday contexts.

SIGNS ON BOARDS

We found that autistic children could learn signs more readily on the boards because many such signs closely resembled or could be related to the intentional acts that they performed on the boards. Thus, the sign *open* (hands parting) was taught by the worker saying "Open" and interposing his parting hands in front of the door the child was opening. In similar fashion, he would say "Walk," and walk his hands (sign for *walk*) in step with the child as he walked from place to place on the boards, or say "Push," and "Pull," with the appropriate *push* or *pull* signs as the child performed these actions. Signs for *come* (beckoning fingers), *stop* (the edge of one palm meets the other and simulates a barrier), *up* and *down* (index finger pointing in the appropriate direction) were taught somewhat differently because they related closely to board vectors. To teach the sign *come,* the worker would say the word while beckoning to the child from the end of the board's length. In this way the utterance, sign, and board vector mutually supported each other in the common "pull" they exerted on the child to move toward the worker. The sign *stop* required a similar strategy; just as the child met an obstacle in the middle of the board the worker would say "Stop!" and interpose the manual sign so that real barrier, sign barrier, and utterance again shared the same vector. We suggest that it is the sharing of common vectors that made it possible for the spoken word to assume, by itself, the significance initially shared by all three factors (board vector, sign, and utterance).

After establishing receptive understanding of a certain group of signs, the varied problem situations built into the course were used to encourage the children to initiate signs. Then, a child poised 5 feet above the ground and wishing to get through a box enclosure with doors on each end had to make the sign for *open* (hands parting) before the teacher would open the door and let the child through. In the same fashion, he had to perform a *down* sign before a drawbridge would be lowered, or a *pick-up* sign before an obstacle would be removed from his path. Once children could respond to and use signs effectively above ground, they were trained to generalize this understanding to everyday situations on the ground.

TRAINING FILMS

In alternation with the awareness course, signs were also taught with the help of carefully prepared training films. In using films, we drew upon strategies described elsewhere (Miller & Miller, 1968, 1971) designed to accent the relationship between many signs and the objects or events to which they related. The utility of motion picture films becomes evident when one notes how directly many of the manual signs may be related to their referents through careful film editing. For example, the hand sign for *jump* (two fingers of the right hand jump off the left palm) blends readily with and thus assumes the meaning of a child jumping off a stool, just as the hand sign for *break* (two hands simulate breaking something) readily blends on film with two hands actually breaking a stick. Similarly, manual signs for *eat, drink, fork, knife, spoon, pour, plate,* and many others are juxtaposed on film with their objects in such a way that the sign and its meaning become intimately related. Other clusters of signs relate to toileting (*wash, toothbrush, comb*) and to actions directed toward objects (*push, pull, pick-up, drop, open-close*). These films first presented signs from the child's subjective view and then gradually shifted the sign orientation to a fully objective angle so that the child could see the signs as they would be presented by a person opposite him.

PROCEDURE

Although the intensive work with boards and signs averaged about an hour a day (5 days a week) at both residential and day school settings, the hour was integrated differently within the two settings. For example, within the residential setting a teacher and an aide would work intensively with two or three children at a time in a classroom, first with boards (20 to 30 minutes), and for the remaining time, with sign films, 2-concept phrases, etc. Then, to facilitate generalization of learning, kitchen staff as well as day and night workers were instructed in sign-word procedures to enable them to respond to and also encourage the children's use of signs and words at meal times, bed times, and in the course of dressing, toileting, or washing. However, because the residential school operated on a 24-hour basis, teachers would not directly observe nor supervise the institution staff during this phase of the program.

In the day school setting, on the other hand, teachers' work with boards and signs was carefully integrated within the child's school day. This permitted them to directly control the important generalization of signs from training to real life situations. A typical school day began with a few minutes of orienting and body play and continued with 10 to 15 minutes of board work concerned with body awareness. This was followed by another 10 to 15 minutes of board work during which concepts like *come, go, stop, up,* or *down* were developed. During the outside walk which followed, teachers actively generalized these board-developed concepts in a more natural setting. On their return, children had a 10- to 15-minute intensive training session with sign films concerned with eating and drinking. Then, during the immediately following snack period, these food-related signs (*eat, drink, pour, glass,* etc.) were used and elicited by teachers. After snack time, the children participated in small group games which encourage interaction. They then toileted themselves and washed in preparation for lunch. During the lunch period, each of the children helped set table, prepared food (usually with assistance), moved chairs to table, dined, and then cleared the table. Each of these activities was guided and accompanied by the appropriate sign-word combinations. Following a brief rest period, the children experienced another 10- to 15-minute training period with another group of sign films (e.g., *push-pull, pick-up,* and *drop*), after which the teachers systematically provided opportunities for generalizing these concepts. Thus, teachers were able to work intensively with the children and control generalization of concepts during much of the school day.

In both residential and day school settings, the relevant adults were taught to understand, elicit, and use the 50 signs designed for the children. They were taught to speak economically and directly (waiting for eye contact) to the children as well as to *pair each sign with the appropriate spoken word* so that the meaning inherent in the sign might transfer to the spoken word. To facilitate this transfer, both staff and parents were also taught to vary their utterances both rhythmically and in intensity. Thus, as a worker beckoned to a child she might say "Come" in a loud, urgent manner and then abruptly shift both gesture and utterance to a soft, gentle pattern. Wherever possible, the rhythmic pattern of the gestures was closely related to the relevant spoken words and to the child's total body involvement. For example, as a child went *up* a ladder or went *up* on a seesaw, the worker would, in the course of performing the relevant sign (upward gesture), utter the word "Up" with a rising vocal inflection timed to coincide with the child's upward movement. Conversely, a downward gesture and vocal inflection were paired with the child's downward body movement. When a sign was paired with a hyphenated phrase like "Get up" or "Sit down," the worker would "hyphenate" the sign (palms moving upward or downward) to correspond to both parts of the phrase.

Conventional speech therapy procedures (mouth manipulation, etc.) were not used initially because of our impression that the children became so preoccupied with the therapist's manipulation of their mouths that they lost referential contact with the objects or events to which their articulations were supposed to relate. However, when a child produced a relevant utterance *in context* of the appropriate situation, workers would mimic this utterance *with* the relevant sign and express delight with the child's new achievement.

Once a child had grasped 20 or 30 signs, he and the adults who cared for him were taught 2-sign 2-word combinations, e.g., pick up ball, bring hat (or spoon), etc. As part of the training, children would bring desired objects from one end of a board to the worker waiting at the other end. After the child in response to a signed and spoken request could bring an object to one person, he was taught to bring the same object to another person, etc. Then, relative positions were reversed so that the child could learn that his response to signs and words was completely independent of his starting position. As soon as these cognitive tasks could be performed at both higher and lower levels on the boards, the child was trained to perform them on the ground, in different rooms, or outside.

RESULTS

RECEPTIVE LANGUAGE

Table 2 indicates that all children could respond appropriately, first to signs paired with spoken words, and later, to spoken words without signs. The median number of receptive signs achieved was 27 while that of receptively understood spoken words was 26. The rank order correlation (p .66) between signs and words achieved is consistent with the view that pairing signs with spoken words in the manner described enabled the spoken words to assume significance for the children. The children seemed somewhat less able to understand and respond appropriately to 2-sign (paired with 2-word) combinations (e.g., *pick up fork, bring hat,* etc.) since only 12 of the 19 could respond correctly to these combinations. These 12, however, demonstrated their understanding of the 2-concept combinations by responding appropriately to interchanged verb-noun pairs.

EXPRESSIVE LANGUAGE

The children used significantly fewer signs expressively than they did receptively. The median expressive use of signs was 8. Nevertheless, even the most profoundly autistic children (Carl, Margaret, and Barry) could initiate a few signs (usually for *eat, drink, open*). It is of note that signs learned and used were not restricted to the context in which they were learned. For example, children would use their *eat, drink* signs not only in conventional eating situations at dining hall or dinner table, but at picnics and restaurants as well. This was also true for signs *open, come,* etc. when these were mastered. Only 7 of the 19 children produced some spoken words related to the signs they learned. And, thus far, only one of the 19 (Philip) has learned to both understand and use appropriate syntactical spoken language.

INTERCORRELATIONS

Table 3 indicates that the duration of a child's participation in the program, his Creak score, and chronological age were highly correlated with his language achievement. Thus, the number of months in the program was significantly (p < .01) correlated with 3 of the 4 language scores. The longer the child participated in the program, the more likely was his achievement of higher levels of receptive and expressive use of signs and increased receptive understanding (although not expressive use) of spoken words. Creak scores, on the other hand, were negatively correlated with language achievement. Thus, the more profoundly disturbed children with high Creak scores did significantly worse (p < .05) on 2 of the 4 measures (expressive signs and receptive words) while the less disturbed children with lower Creak scores did significantly better on those measures. The chronological age of the children, another important

Table 2   **Achievement of Signs and Spoken Words by 19 Mute Autistic Children**

Name	Signs paired with spoken words		Spoken words without signs		Two-sign *plus* two-word combinations			
					Receptive		Expressive	
	Receptive	Expressive	Receptive	Expressive	yes	no	yes	no
Residential School Children								
Mona	44	12	40	1	x			x
Hank	27	6	28	0	x			x
Nina	39	19	39	0	x			x
Thomas	24	6	25	0	x			x
Carl	7	3	9	0		x		x
Margaret	11	4	12	0		x		x
Teresa	27	4	26	3	x			x
Kirk	33	12	29	0	x			x
Barry	6	1	17	0		x		x
Sidney	13	7	14	2		x		x
Neal	22	2	23	0	x			x
Elliot	15	7	21	0		x		x
Bella	28	11	31	0	x			x
Day School Children								
Karen	36	10	40	3		x		x
Tod	40	12	40	0		x		x
Donald	20	8	20	0	x			x
Larry	37	25	40	4	x			x
Philip	50	50	50	50	x		x	
Nancy	40	25	45	7	x			x

factor, was negatively correlated ($p < .05$) with the expressive use of signs and spoken words. Thus, the younger the child at the start of the program, the *more likely* his achievement of both the expressive signs and words.

COMPARING RESIDENTIAL AND DAY SCHOOL CHILDREN

A comparison of the residential with day school children reveals a more vigorous response to the program among the latter. This difference was most striking in the expressive use of language. The day school children's median expressive use of signs (about 18) was significantly greater ($p < .05$) than the median of 8 expressive signs for residential children. Similarly, in appropriate use of spoken words only 3 of the 13 residential children uttered words, while this was true for 4 of the 6 day school

Table 3   Intercorrelations Between Chronological Age, Duration of Training, Creak Score, and Achievement of Signs and Words

Signs and words	CA		Creak score		Duration of training*	
	ρ	$\rho†$	ρ	$\rho†$	ρ	$\rho†$
Receptive signs	−.15		−.36		.57	<.01
Expressive signs	−.41	<.05	−.47	<.05	66	<.01
Receptive words	−.36		−.46	<.05	.55	<.01
Expressive words	−.45	<.05	−.26		.36	

*Months in program; †one-tailed test.

children. Further, the group of day school children included the boy (Philip) who achieved syntactical language and the girl (Nancy) who is currently adding about a word a week to her vocabulary; the two children are briefly described below.

CASE ILLUSTRATIONS

CASE 1

Philip, a handsome, sturdy-looking boy, began the program 3 years ago at the age of 8. At that time, he was completely mute except for periodic staccato emissions of strings of vowel sounds. The child was also given to bursts of activity during which he would hurl himself back and forth against the walls of his room. At other times, he would spend hours humming, lining up blocks, sniffing and piling them in rows of two and three before he would break them up and start all over. Philip would not respond to verbal commands, screaming piercingly when required to interrupt an activity.

The boy's parents reported normal development until 12 months of age, when, on the occasion of a viral infection, he suffered a grand mal seizure. At 18 months, following a vaccination, Philip experienced a prolonged series of convulsions which were subsequently controlled with Dilantin. Since then, no further seizures were in evidence. EEG examinations have shown no abnormalities during the past 5 years and Philip was taken off medication at the age of 6.

During the 3 years we have worked with Philip, he has moved from a comprehension and use of manual signs to an understanding and use of spoken language. As words became meaningful and useful, he has gradually given up the use of signs. Currently, he can understand and use sentences 6 to 8 words in length with proper use of pronouns, *I, you, he, she, we, they.* The boy is oriented in space and time. He can read at early second grade level,[4] and perform arithmetic at late first grade level.

---

[4] Philip learned to read with the help of Symbol Accentuation (Miller, 1968), a reading program which systematically helps children to link body gestures as well as speech to printed language.

Philip's parents report that most of his bizarre mannerisms have disappeared (as language developed) and that his increasing interest in people during the last 6 months is evidenced by play contact which he initiates. Special class placement in a public school within a year is a realistic possibility.

CASE 2

Nancy is a delicate, blonde little girl who began our program 14 months ago, 2 months before her fifth birthday. Before this she had been at a therapeutic nursery school which, at the end of two years, recommended Nancy's institutionalization. A teacher describing her first contact with Nancy at the school reported that

> She rocked almost constantly, screamed when brought into the playroom, banged her head, ground her teeth, . . . stared at lights, showed bizarre finger movements and arm-flapping, had no eye contact, wandered aimlessly . . . toe-walked, went into a panic if touched by other children, had no speech, wasn't weaned or toilet-trained . . . had no conception of walking downstairs, and was so withdrawn that formal testing was impossible.

Nancy's mother reported that there was no unusual illness during the girl's first 2 years of life. Neurological and EEG examinations revealed no abnormalities. Developmental milestones followed normal progression (walking at 15 months) and her mother was unaware of any problem until the child, a very quiet baby, never crying and not at all demanding, had reached the age of 1½ and did not talk. Great concern was expressed about Nancy's persistent efforts to climb out of a third story apartment window; on several occasions she was found hanging by her fingertips from the window's outer ledge.

Although somewhat improved when we first saw her (some eye contact was evident as well as fragments of organized behavior as she responded slightly to peek-a-boo games), the essential features of her behavior were the same. After 2 months of training, Nancy could respond to receptive signs for *come, stop,* and *jump* (first on the boards and then on the floor), and within 3 months she could appropriately initiate her first expressive signs (*open, eat*). Currently, she understands 40 signs and can initiate 25 in appropriate situations. Her understanding and use of signs is not limited to one situation, and she has spontaneously begun to generalize them to related situations. For example, the sign *open* no longer applies only to a door, but is used by her to get someone to open a jar of peanut butter, etc. The integration of signs within cognition is evident in the girl's signing to herself before she performs a particular act. Thus, Nancy will make a covert *jump* sign to herself before she jumps off the boards or a quick *run* sign before she begins to run. Most encouraging are her recent utterance of spoken words "Up," "Down," "Eat," (she no longer requires the sign with "Eat,") "A-ke" (for jacket), "Ma," "Ball," "Baby," and the fact that for the past few weeks she has been adding about a word a week to her vocabulary.

Autistic rituals and mannerisms both at our Center and at home have dramatically decreased while her awareness of surroundings and people (particularly for games of "chase-me") have steadily increased. The mother reports that Nancy now seeks out and plays simple games with children. The girl also "panhandles" candy by standing in front of a child with candy and, while gazing at him steadily, performing the *eat* sign toward her mouth. She also helps set table and is beginning to assist her mother with house chores. She has not attempted to climb out the window for the past 6 months, a report which correlates well with our observation that Nancy has become quite cautious, even fearful, as she walks the boards at our Center. Presumably, having become more aware of her body in relation to her immediate environment, she no longer requires "edge" experiences of such desperate nature.

DISCUSSION

Since none of the children could respond to and use signs when they began the program and all could respond and use some signs when retested, it appears that even severely autistic children can benefit from the present approach. The results also indicate that the ability to respond to signs can contribute to the understanding of spoken language. The procedure of pairing signs and spoken words both on the boards and in other relevant situations seems to have facilitated the transfer of meaning to spoken words so that mute autistic children can understand them even without the accompanying signs. Further, the results with several children suggest that training with signs may, at least for some, stimulate the development of expressive spoken language.

These findings, however, leave several important questions unanswered. For example, how important are the elevated boards in accounting for these results? Might not the presentation of manual signs and spoken words without the boards have been sufficient to teach the children? We cannot answer these questions decisively because we have not conducted a controlled study in which all factors but the use of boards are held constant. Our clinical observations, however, support the importance of elevated boards. We found that some children could not begin to learn signs until they were first presented within a board context. Other children could learn certain signs without the boards (e.g., *eat, drink*), but could not grasp action signs (*come, stop,* etc.) until they were first taught with boards. Some demonstrated the importance of the boards quite concretely by transferring certain aspects of their board experience to the ground. Nancy, for example, had to use a wide stance as she shuffled on a parallel board (as shown in outline 1a of Figure 1) toward her mother in her initial response to mother's "Come." When the procedure was repeated on the ground (without the board), Nancy could at first respond to her mother's "Come" only by assuming the same wide stance and shuffling feet movement that she had used on the boards. Several days later, she could respond to her mother's call without having to use this board gait. These and similar observations with other children are consistent with the view that the boards facilitate a directed body response to signs and words.

The program's overall effectiveness seems implicit in the findings that the longer a child participated the greater his achievement of receptive and expressive signs and receptive understanding of spoken words. The fact that duration of training in the program did not correlate significantly with expressive use of spoken words suggests either that the children were not in the program long enough, or that they had passed a critical period during which expressive spoken language could develop. Support for the latter view is inherent in the finding that the younger children were more likely to achieve some capacity for expressive use of both signs *and* spoken words.

If this is correct, the greater achievement of expressive signs and spoken words by day school children (in contrast to residential school children) may be largely due to their relative youth. The median age of 7 to 8 years of the day school children is significantly below that of the residential school children. It seems likely that younger children with less entrenched autistic patterns may be more responsive to cognitive-developmental training than their older counterparts. An additional factor which may have helped generate more expressive language among day school children is the greater involvement of parents in the school program. Parents of the day school children worked directly with their children under supervision in a manner similar to that described by Schopler and Reichler (1971), while parents of residential school children did not have this opportunity. We found that the more parents are involved with their children's training the more likely is the children's functioning to generalize to home and other settings.

One further issue concerns the desirability of teaching manual signs to autistic children. It has been argued that if these children are unable to use signs as a transition to expressive spoken language, then the manual signs may merely add another set of mannerisms to their bizarre behavior. We suggest that the inability of a mute autistic child to attain meaningful speech via signs does not invalidate their use. The signs offer such children the means of understanding both signs *and* spoken language as well as the possibility of communicating with other people. Without such human contact, most mute autistic children tend to lapse into states in which they pass their days rocking back and forth and twiddling objects.

REFERENCES

Churchill, D. W. The relation of infantile autism and early childhood schizophrenia to developmental language disorders of childhood. *Journal of Autism and Childhood Schizophrenia,* 1972, **2,** 182–197.

Creak, M. Schizophrenia syndrome in childhood: Further progress report of a working party. *Developmental Medicine and Child Neurology,* 1964, **6,** 530–535.

Hermelin, B. Recent experimental research. In P. J. Mittler (Ed.), *Aspects of autism.* London: British Psychological Society, 1968.

Kanner, L. Autistic disturbances of affective contact. *Nervous Child,* 1943, **2,** 217–250.

Kanner, L. Follow-up study of eleven autistic children originally reported in 1943. *Journal of Autism and Childhood Schizophrenia,* 1971, **1,** 119–145.

Lewin, K. *A dynamic theory of personality.* New York: McGraw-Hill. 1935.

Miller, A. *An experimental study of the role of sensorimotor activity in the maintenance of verbal meaning of action words.* (Doctoral dissertation, Clark University), Worcester, Mass.: 1959.

Miller, A. Verbal satiation and the role of concurrent activity. *Journal of Abnormal and Social Psychology,* 1963, **66,** 206–212.

Miller, A. *Symbol accentuation—A new approach to reading.* New York: Doubleday Multimedia, 1968.

Miller, A., & Miller, E. E. Symbol accentuation: The perceptual transfer of meaning from spoken to written words. *American Journal of Mental Deficiency,* 1968, **73,** 200–208.

Miller, A., & Miller, E. E. Symbol accentuation, single track functioning and early reading. *American Journal of Mental Deficiency,* 1971, **76,** 110–117.

Miller, E. E. Symbol accentuation: Application to special language problems. In E. Meshorer (Ed.), *Symbol accentuation: A new approach to language development with retardates.* Montpellier, France: First International Congress for the Scientific Study of Mental Deficiency, 1968.

Piaget, J. *The construction of reality in the child.* New York: Basic Books, 1954.

Rutter, M. The influence of organic and emotional factors on the origins, nature and outcome of childhood psychosis. *Developmental Medicine and Child Neurology,* 1965, **7,** 518–528.

Rutter, M. Concepts of autism: A review of research. *Journal of Child Psychology and Psychiatry,* 1968, **9,** 1–25.

Rutter, M., & Bartak, L. Causes of infantile autism: Some considerations from recent research. *Journal of Autism and Childhood Schizophrenia,* 1971, **1,** 20–32.

Schilder, P. *The image and appearance of the human body.* New York: International Universities Press, 1950.

Schopler, E., & Reichler, R. J. Parents as cotherapists in the treatment of psychotic children. *Journal of Autism and Childhood Schizophrenia,* 1971, **1,** 87–102.

Siegel, S. *Non-parametric statistics for the behavioral sciences.* New York: McGraw-Hill, 1956.

Uexküll, J. von. A stroll through the worlds of animals and men. In C. H. Schiller (Ed.), *Instinctive behavior.* New York: International Universities Press, 1957.

Werner, H. *A comparative study of mental development.* Chicago: Follett, 1948.

Wing, L. The handicaps of autistic children—A comparative study. *Journal of Child Psychology and Psychiatry,* 1969, **10,** 1–40.

Sign Language Acquisition In A Mute Autistic Boy

John D. Bonvillian

Keith E. Nelson

A mute autistic boy learned to communicate extensively through American Sign Language. Over a six-month period he produced many spontaneous signs and sign combinations, and analyses of the child's sign combinations indicated the presence of a full range of semantic relations. Further evidence of conceptual progress was provided by the child's increased score on the Peabody Picture Vocabulary Test. In addition, parents' and teacher's reports indicated that the child's social behavior improved. The extent of the boy's linguistic progress and associated improvement in social behavior markedly exceeds that usually reported for mute autistic children.

A nine-year-old autistic boy was given a special instructional program in sign language communication. The child showed considerable and increasing facility in the appropriate use of individual signs and of signs in combination, in contrast to a well-documented previous history of no productive language and of highly limited receptive language skills. As the child's sign communication developed, no concomitant development of speech was observed. These findings have implications for the education of autistic children and for theories of cognitive and linguistic development.

One of the most salient characteristics of infantile autism is a severe disturbance of speech—for example, echolalia, delayed speech, or mutism. Indeed, disturbance in language function has been considered by certain investigators to be the primary handicap of autism, from which the severe social and behavioral abnormalities of this variety of childhood psychopathology arise (Churchill, 1972; Rutter and Bartak, 1971). Furthermore, Eisenberg (1956) has shown that the absence of useful speech at the age of five years generally carries a poor prognosis for the child's later adjustment (for exceptions see Rutter, Greenfield, and Lockyer, 1967).

In working with mute autistic children, most clinicians or educators have used techniques designed to encourage speech. Some success in eliciting speech in previously mute autistic children using an operant conditioning training procedure has been reported (Lovaas et al., 1966). However, most children given such training did

From *Journal of Speech and Hearing Disorders, 41,* 339–347 (1976). Reprinted by permission of the American Speech and Hearing Association.

not go beyond specifically trained utterances to spontaneously generate new sentences.

In the present study, we used the sign language predominant in the deaf community, American Sign Language (ASL). The decision to use a sign language, instead of speech, was based on a number of reasons. One reason lies in the distinction between language and its various manifestations—the production and the comprehension of speech, written language, and sign language. Thus, a child's difficulty in learning to produce speech could rest upon rather specific deficits in producing or processing speech, while leaving visual and motor processing skills sufficient for mastering other forms of language relatively unimpaired. Sign language, in comparison with speech, has two other apparent advantages. First, teachers can readily mold the subject's hands into the appropriate signs, and second, for many signs there is an observable relationship between the sign and its referent. A further reason for staying with our initial choice of sign language rested in several recent reports indicating some acquisition of individual signs by autistic children (Creedon, 1973; Miller and Miller, 1973) and in nonverbal retarded children (Berger, 1972; Wilson, 1974). However, with the relatively little detail that is included in these reports on the process of sign language acquisition, it is difficult to determine either the pattern of acquisition or level of mastery of sign language in these children.

Signs in ASL represent ideas or concepts and are largely analogous to words in spoken languages. Each sign consists of a particular configuration of the hand or hands, movement, and the place on or near the body where the movement begins and ends. Recent analyses of ASL syntax and semantics indicate structural consistency, which in turn suggests a rule-based syntactic system (Stokoe, 1972). Further evidence of speech-sign similarity is seen in studies of the young deaf child's learning of sign language, which have indicated that the stages in the acquisition of sign language closely parallel the stages in the language acquisition of hearing children (Bonvillian, Charrow, and Nelson, 1973; Schlesinger and Meadow, 1972). With the preceding observations on sign language in mind, we hoped in this investigation to describe in detail one autistic child's progress in acquiring sign language and to compare such progress with prior evidence on children's language development.

PATIENT HISTORY

At the time of his introduction to sign language, Ted was nine years one month old and had never produced speech. He uttered a limited number of apparently meaningless vocalizations, the most frequent was "etta" (etʌ). His parents recalled that he responded abnormally from early infancy in that he failed to cuddle and appeared insensitive to pain. At the age of two years 10 months, he was diagnosed as aphasic or dysphasic with severe emotional disturbance. An EEG recording was within normal limits. The examiner reported a session of incessant screaming and resistance to unfamiliar surroundings, as well as failure to respond to language or to react socially. At that time an auditory examination revealed hearing within normal limits (ISO): a 10 dB HL, pure-tone threshold at 500 and 1000 Hz, a 15 dB HL pure-tone threshold at 2000 and 4000 Hz. Continued observation of Ted's responses to sound has indicated that hearing loss does not account for his marked difficulties in speaking. He turns his head and otherwise shows attention not only to normal speaking levels but also to whispers. At three, Ted entered a "computer-interaction language program" for nonspeaking children, in which he participated for about 18 months. This program utilized computer-accessed games designed to engage the child in visual, tactile, and auditory language interaction with the computer. The games focused on the combination of English sounds and letters into words and expressions. Ted was the most unresponsive child to all experimental stimuli in the program and was one of two subjects (out of 10) who were rated as unimproved (Colby, 1968). Ted's resistance to other people and his extreme hyperactivity and negativistic behavior were also emphasized in this report. In addition, it was observed that Ted seemed to understand words, but "simply shut them out" (Colby, 1968, p. 649). This computer-aided language program was supplemented by individual language training and group play therapy, but this combined program also was ineffective in stimulating Ted's speech or social development. At five, he tested at the two-year four-month level (IQ 46) on the Merrill-Palmer Scale of Mental Tests.

In light of his failure to respond successfully to any of the therapeutic interventions, Ted was extensively reevaluated at six and one-half by the Diagnostic School for Neurologically Handicapped in San Francisco and classified as childhood autistic. At this time Ted showed, as he had earlier, bizarre stereotyped gestures, tantrums, and absence of speech. Ted was then placed in a residential setting where he made some progress toward acquiring a few personal care skills, such as the ability to get dressed with only minimal assistance. At seven and one-half he was admitted to the day treatment and educational center he currently attends for approximately six hours each weekday. Here he was first introduced to a language (speech) program based on operant conditioning methods. In this system, different foods and tokens were used as rewards for attempts at verbalization, for vocalizations, and for paying attention to the teacher-clinician or his mother. Still he failed to use words or even to imitate sounds at age nine; his few vocalizations were produced with difficulty and appeared to lack meaning. However, his teacher reported that his receptive language skills appeared to have very slightly improved, and that he would sometimes point to objects or pull on people in order to make himself understood. Nevertheless, Ted at age nine was generally uncommunicative, negativistic, and markedly disturbed in his social interactions. Given this background, it was evident at the present study's initiation that if Ted could learn sign language, he would be mastering productive language for the first time and would also be moving beyond severely limited receptive language. The study was begun with these goals in mind, with Ted as the only subject.

TREATMENT PROGRAM

Across the six months of the present study, Ted was systematically exposed to new signs and drilled on previously introduced signs in a daily half-hour language period. Two different techniques were employed to teach him signs: molding and imitation. Molding required the teacher to shape Ted's hands into the appropriate configuration and to guide them through the proper motion. Imitation required Ted to form the sign after observing its use by the teacher. Both of these techniques were used in the initial stages of teaching a vocabulary item. In addition, when teaching vocabulary, Ted's teacher usually paired each sign with its spoken English equivalent. Once Ted learned to produce a specific sign, he was asked to identify appropriate objects and pictures. And to further encourage Ted's use of signs in the language period, an additional method was employed—a token reward system. In this system, once he reached a predetermined criterion of success he could exchange accumulated tokens for the opportunity to play with a favorite toy or to play outside. The criteria of success were increased gradually in order to keep pace with Ted's sign productivity. In the opening sessions we were satisfied with approximations to signs, but after several months we required correct production of about a dozen previously learned signs along with approximations to newly introduced signs. By the end of the six-month period, in each session we expected Ted to produce spontaneously sign combinations to describe appropriately a series of about 10 different pictures (containing objects and actions with which he was familiar), as well as to produce correctly the most recently introduced signs.

The language period instruction was supplemented by his family and by additional members of the center staff, all of whom used signs to communicate with him in everyday interaction. But only Ted's mother and his teacher-clinician received formal training in ASL—at least an hour of instruction and practice each week. We included Ted's mother because she had been involved in previous therapeutic efforts with Ted, so that his use of ASL would generalize to his home, and because previous studies had shown that parental involvement often facilitated autistic children's development (Schopler and Reichler, 1971). Records of Ted's signing during his language period were obtained twice weekly by a trained observer. Ted's spontaneous sign combinations and their contexts were recorded by his mother, his teacher, or the observer, whether these sign combinations occurred during or outside his regular half-hour language periods.

RESULTS AND DISCUSSION

Ted made marked progress in acquiring individual signs during the six months of training. Table 1 lists all signs recorded by the trained observer across 51 sessions. Ted used a total of 56 different signs correctly and spontaneously without immediately preceding imitation or molding. Even more impressively, if Ted has used a sign correctly at least once, he was very likely (in 96% of cases) to produce the sign accurately on two or more additional occasions. Ted's acquisition data indicated a gradual but steady growth in his sign lexicon: he acquired an average of slightly more than two new signs each week.

Ted's spontaneous sign combinations were interpreted in terms of possible underlying semantic relations. The interpretive schema used to analyze the sign combinations is adopted from Fillmore's (1968) and Chafe's (1970) attempts to specify a limited set of basic semantic relationships embodied in sentences. For example, basic semantic aspects of an event include *agent* (who did it), *experiencer* (who it happened to), *instrument* (what it was done with), *location* (where it happened), *possession* (whose it was), *object* (what it was done to), and *time* (when it happened). This structural semantic approach has proved valuable in analyses of word combinations and their contexts in children's early speech (Brown, 1973).

Ted produced his first sign combination (go town dump car: verb + location + instrument) after about three months of training in the production of single signs.

Evidence of the presence of all the above postulated semantic relationships became apparent soon after this initial combination, as he began to combine signs frequently. Most of his sign utterances were two-sign combinations, and predominantly (68.2% of all two-sign combinations) of one type—an animate agent or experiencer combined with a verb. Other examples of Ted's two-sign combinations and their semantic interpretations include: "boy drink" (agent + verb), "swim school" (verb + location), "father haircut" (experiencer + verb), "Ted ball" (possessor + object), and "tomorrow play" (time + verb).

In terms of grammatical structure and meaning, Ted's range of two-sign combinations closely resembles the range of two-word sentences which normal young children produce (Brown, 1973). Additional examples of similarities between Ted's sentences and normal children's sentences include his use of the sign "more" (for example, "more milk," "more cookie") to request or signal recurrence, and his use of negation preceding other signs (for example, "no food," "no go") to indicate nonexistence or refusal. Ted also was occasionally observed signing to himself, a phenomenon that resembles children's early world play. Unlike the first short utterances of the normal child learning speech (Bloom, 1970), however, some of Ted's earliest sign combinations included coherent combinations of some length—up to five signs. Two examples of such complex sign utterances were: "No mother car play

Table 1   Ted's Acquisition of Individual Signs

| Signs | Twice-Weekly Sessions | | | | |
	1-10	11-20	21-30	31-40	41-51
Number of new signs introduced	14	12	13	19	19
Number of new signs learned	9	9	11	12	15
New signs learned	yes	drink	boy	toilet	cry
	no	come	bicycle	baby	apple
	ball	good-bye	school	on	break
	Ted	hello	shoe	me	month
	eat	haircut	telephone	off	Ruth
	daddy	swim	work	bird	turkey
	book	town dump	play	tomorrow	today
	sleep	car	cookie	tree	kitty
	mother	go	more	golf	sick
			pants	coat	candy
			light	water	bath
				milk	chocolate
					love
					fix
					hat

school" (negation: agent + instrument + verb + location; Ted's mother was not coming to pick him up in the car because he was going to play at school), and "Man work water school" (agent + verb + object + location; the repairman had fixed the water pipes at the school). Another kind of complexity is indicated by the presence of some accurate time elements in Ted's early signing (for example, "Eat turkey tomorrow," verb + object + time). Such time elements are usually absent or inaccurate in children's early speech (Bloom, 1970).

Besides his acquisition of many components of a sign language communicative system, Ted was reported by his parents and teacher to have made major improvement on a number of other dimensions. His incidence of bladder incontinence declined dramatically, from an average of over twice a day to about once a week; further, for the first time in his life his bowel movements were completely controlled, and Ted often signed "toilet" to indicate his need appropriately. The frequency of his tantrums at school gradually lessened to one-quarter their initial rate of occurrence. And there was a gradual lessening as well of his bizarre, stereotyped movements or gestures, together with an improved ability to focus on and attend to the different people and actions in his environment. Finally, Ted's score on the Peabody Picture Vocabulary Test (often used with nonverbal children, its scores correlate highly with Stanford-Binet IQ scores; Dunn and Hottel, 1961) rose from the three-year six-month level to the four-year 11-month level (less than the first percentile) during the six months of this study. This change in performance on a set of vocabulary test items may, in part, have been stimulated by more general semantic progress; through advances in sign language Ted may have found new ways of organizing and categorizing his experience. In addition, it seems likely that a component of the change in tested vocabulary was a change in the level of communication with the person conducting the test. At the beginning of the study, test questions could only be posed in speech, but by the end of the study, comprehension was much improved and appeared equal whether statements were given in ASL alone or simultaneously in ASL and English speech. All these changes help to open up new possibilities for further educational advance. In addition, the changes sharply contrast with Ted's previously limited progress in these areas.

Since the completion of this six-month study, Ted has continued to acquire new signs and to generate new combinations of signs. Like a young child using spoken words, Ted can remember a large number of signs and employ these signs appropriately in different situations. Also, by spontaneously combining signs, he is effective in conveying to adults a wide range of information. Finally, we have seen above that there are close similarities in the kinds of semantic relationships Ted used in early signed sentences and those used by normal young children in spoken sentences. Overall, then, Ted's first steps toward language acquisition resemble in many ways the early steps taken by young children acquiring speech. This may seem a bit less surprising when it is noted that the sign language he has begun to acquire is a language which appears to match spoken language in efficiency of communication (Bellugi, 1972) and in semantic and syntactic complexity (Bonvillian, Nelson, and Charrow, in press).

Although Ted has yet to acquire significant expressive oral language skills, it remains possible that with further work he, and the other autistic children like him who are now receiving programs of sign language communication, may make some progress towards speech. Among the 19 autistic subjects observed in the sign program of Miller and Miller (1973), two were reported to have made progress toward speech. Though it is conceivable that training in sign might hinder a child's progress in speech mastery, the evidence so far suggests that for autistic and retarded children speech may be either unaffected or stimulated by sign language progress—a conclusion also noted by Schlesinger and Meadow (1972) in regards to speech and sign acquisition in deaf children. A more extensive review of language learning (Bonvillian, Nelson, and Charrow, in press) indicates that progress toward language can take place not only in speech and sign, but also in other visual communication systems. The abilities of the child clearly need to be matched as closely as possible with the demands of an educational communication system.

From the present observations on a single boy, it is impossible to determine what elements of his treatment program or background were essential to his considerable advances in social skills and in language production (signs) and comprehension (signs and speech). But Ted's success in both producing and comprehending sign language suggests that his cognitive and linguistic abilities had been relatively untapped by previous speech-oriented family and therapeutic settings. This success, in turn, carries implications for developmental theories and educational practice. A child may have the cognitive capacities necessary for communication despite the presence of receptive or productive speech disorders. And at least a few other autistic children who have failed to acquire speech may be capable of mastering an effective means of communication through sign language or, as in the present study, through a combination of listening and signing. Again, however, we would urge caution in the sense that there is great difficulty in matching the characteristics of a communication system with any child's available levels of skills.

ACKNOWLEDGMENT

The authors thank Kelly Flanagan, Rachel Vasiliev, and the child's parents for their many hours of assistance during the study. Gloria Leiderman, E. David Burk, and the staff of the Peninsula Children's Center in Palo Alto, California, provided support in all phases of the study. Thanks are also due Veda R. Charrow and William George McKee for their helpful comments on the manuscript.

REFERENCES

Bellugi, U., Studies in sign language. In T. J. O'Rourke (Ed.), *Psycholinguistics and Total Communication: The State of the Art*. Washington, D.C.: American Annals of the Deaf, 68–84 (1972).

Berger, S. L., A clinical program for developing multi-modal language responses with atypical deaf children. In J. E. McLean, D. E. Yoder, and R. L. Schiefelbusch (Eds.), *Language Intervention with the Retarded*. Baltimore: University Park, 212–235 (1972).

Bloom, L., *Language Development: Form and Function in Emerging Grammars*. Cambridge, Mass.: The MIT Press (1970).

Bonvillian, J. D., Charrow, V.R., and Nelson, K. E., Psycholinguistic and educational implications of deafness. *Hum. Dev.*, **16**, 321–345 (1973).

BONVILLIAN, J. D., NELSON, K. E., and CHARROW, V. R., Languages and language-related skills in deaf and hearing children. In S. Ghosh (Ed.), *Biology & Language*. Baltimore: University Park (in press).

BROWN, R., *A First Language*. Cambridge, Mass.: Harvard Univ. Press (1973).

CHAFE, W. L., *Meaning and the Structure of Language*. Chicago: Univ. of Chicago Press, (1970).

CHURCHILL, D. W., The relation of infantile autism and early childhood schizophrenia to developmental language disorders of childhood. *J. Autism Child. Schizo., 2*, 182–197 (1972).

COLBY, K. M., Computer-aided language development in nonspeaking children. *Archs Gen. Psychiat., 19*, 641–651 (1968).

CREEDON, M. P., Language development in nonverbal autistic children using a simultaneous communication system. Paper presented at the biennial meeting of the Society for Research in Child Development, Philadelphia (1973).

DUNN, L. M., and HOTTEL, J. V., Peabody Picture Vocabulary Test performance of trainable mentally retarded children. *Am. J. Ment. Defic, 65*, 448–452 (1961).

EISENBERG, L., The autistic child in adolescence. *Am. J. Psychiat., 112*, 607–612 (1956).

FILLMORE, C. J., The case for case. In E. Bach and R. T. Harms (Eds.), *Universals in Linguistic Theory*. New York: Holt, Rinehart and Winston, 1–88 (1968).

LOVAAS, O. I., BERBERICH, J. P., PERLOFF, B. F., and SCHAEFFER, B., Acquisition of imitative speech in schizophrenic children. *Science, N.Y., 151*, 705–707 (1966).

MILLER, A., and MILLER, E. E., Cognitive developmental training with elevated boards and sign language. *J. Autism Child. Schizo., 3*, 65–85 (1973).

RUTTER, M., and BARTAK, L., Causes of infantile autism: Some considerations from recent research. *J. Autism Child. Schizo., 1*, 20–32 (1971).

RUTTER, M., GREENFIELD, D., and LOCKYER, L., A five to fifteen year follow-up study of infantile psychosis: II. Social and behavioural outcome. *Br. J. Psychiat., 113*, 1183–1199 (1967).

SCHLESINGER, H. S., and MEADOW, K. P., *Sound and Sign: Childhood Deafness and Mental Health*. Berkeley: Univ. of California (1972).

SCHOPLER, E., and REICHLER, R. J., Parents as cotherapists in the treatment of preschool autistic children. *J. Autism Child Schizo., 1*, 87–102 (1971).

STOKOE, W. C., JR., *Semiotics and Human Sign Languages*. Hague: Mouton (1972).

WILSON, P. S., Sign language as a means of communication for the mentally retarded. Paper presented at the annual meeting of the Eastern Psychological Association, Philadelphia (1974).

Author's Comment Written for *Readings in Childhood Language Disorders*:

Ted has continued to make progress both in terms of his language and social development over the three years since preparation of the report covering the initial six-month period. His vocabulary has grown considerably, and current estimates of his total vocabulary indicate about 400 different individual signs. Ted also much more frequently engages other individuals in sign language conversations than he did at the beginning of the study. At the same time, the lengths of his sign language utterances remain much reduced in comparison with normal children's productions; most of Ted's sentences are two or three signs in length. His parents and teacher report that his social behavior has also improved, as he interacts more frequently with others, and his stereotypic movements and toilet difficulties now occur only very rarely.

More recent discussions of Ted's progress in particular, and of the effectiveness of sign language training programs for nonspeaking children in general, can be found in the following two articles:

Bonvillian, J.D., and Nelson, K.E. Development of sign language in autistic children and other language-handicapped individuals. In P. Siple (Ed.), *Understanding language through sign language research*. New York: Academic Press, in press.
Bonvillian, J.D., Nelson, K.E., and Charrow, V.R. Languages and language-related skills in deaf and hearing children. *Sign Language Studies*, 1976, *12*, 211–250.

A Language Training Program For Nonverbal Autistic Children

Linda P. McLean*

James E. McLean

This paper describes a nonspeech language training program for nonverbal autistic children. The two children who completed the program were able to respond differentially to a limited number of social transactions by placing the appropriate plywood word symbols to describe the events on a slate tray. Interexperimenter and intersetting generalization were demonstrated, as was retention of the trained responses.

Recent studies from several disciplines suggest that the process of language acquisition may rest more heavily on cognition (the language user's knowledge of the world) than on knowledge of linguistic structure or imitation. Olson (1970), in an extremely provocative paper, advances the theory that the language user's choice of words in an utterance is a function of neither syntactic nor semantic selection restrictions, narrowly defined, but rather of the speaker's knowledge of the perceived and intended referent. He argues that perceptual knowledge rather than linguistic markers is the basis of semantic meaning and that meaning rather than linguistic structure is the speaker's primary goal.

Premack (1970, 1971a, b, c) describes language as "mapping" of existing knowledge. Premack's mapping construct appears to negate the assumption that language capacities necessarily lie only in the areas that are specific to linguistic structures produced in the oral (speech) mode. Premack's work in the functional analysis of acquisition of a synthetic language by a chimpanzee emphasizes two particularly productive thrusts for applied language research and programming. The first is the obvious one of simply more rigorous and systematic investigation of the conditions of language acquisition per se. The second thrust is the methodology of investigating language acquisition by training it in a mode other than the vocal-verbal mode which seems to be so compelling to most teachers and researchers working on language acquisition.

Premack makes an assumption that symbolic responses that use a set of plastic

From *Journal of Speech and Hearing Disorders, 39,* 186–193 (1974). Reprinted by permission of the American Speech and Hearing Association.
    * Now Linda McCormick

forms as "words" might be considered analogous to language responses in other forms. In arriving at this assumption, Premack has sought quantifications of the properties of language that are free of form or mode bias. Hockett (1959, 1960) provides some basic criteria regarding the properties of language per se and, from these, Premack's work suggests the following "characteristics" of language which can be demonstrated in a response mode other than speech: interchangeability (functional for both speaker and listener), semanticity, arbitrariness, displacement, and productivity.

Premack's use of a nonspeech language system and his treatment of language from the perspective of its functional properties rather than its abstracted linguistic structure appear to provide highly pertinent information for the development of language intervention procedures for children who have demonstrated a low propensity for acquiring language in training programs that concentrate on the oral production mode. Premack's work offers an adjunct or alternative method for training an expressive response in something other than the vocal-verbal language form. Because speech production requires a constant matching and monitoring from both the motor and the auditory learning systems, it is extremely complex. A nonvocal, synthetic language system that does not require speech production may also be complex, but the relatively less demanding response forms seem to allow the expresser to attend more to the essential cognitive discriminations that govern the relevancy of the language content.

LANGUAGE THERAPY FOR AUTISTIC CHILDREN

The disappointing results from most forms of language remediation programs for nonverbal autistic children are not surprising, in view of the strong evidence of impaired intellectual and perceptual functioning in autistic children (Bryson, 1970; O'Conner and Hermelin, 1965). Visual-motor, visual-discrimination, and auditory-discrimination skills all tend to be below age level. Autistic children show evidence of particularly severe deficits in short-term memory and cross-modal information processing (Bryson, 1972). The use of a synthetic system such as the one used by Premack attenuates the need for either short-term memory or the standard cross-modal (auditory-vocal) information processing required for speech.

The study reported here was prompted by the desire to investigate further the language acquisition potential of nonverbal autistic children who, because of the severity of their learning deficits, had not benefited from several years of speech and language training. The expressive language system trained in this program requires a visual-motor modality switch, thereby avoiding the visual-vocal transfer which is presumably problematic for autistic children. This system further eliminates the need for the language producer to remember his previous responses in the expressive sequence.

The procedures used in this study were adapted from Premack's work with a chimpanzee and Carrier's (1973) work with retarded children. They were systematically applied to the problem of attaining the acquisition of a limited symbol repertoire from three nonverbal autistic children. Three of the generalization transfer properties of the responses acquired in the teaching program were also investigated.

SUBJECTS

Two of the children (Subjects A and C) were eight years of age. The third (Subject B) was 10. They were in a private inpatient facility for severely disturbed children in Nashville, Tennessee. These children shared, with varying degrees of severity, the common features of preferred isolation and primitive social interactions. They demonstrated limited and stereotyped response to objects, and their communicative behavior was severely deficient. All three were untestable by any standard psychological methods, but their hearing had been assessed and found to be within the normal range.

Each of the children met the following selection criteria: (1) no functional speech —a determination based on reports and anecdotal records of the child's teachers, absence of intelligible verbal responses to object and picture-naming tasks, and absence of intelligible imitative responses to the presentation of five short declarative sentences; and (2) the ability to imitate correctly one or more motor behaviors after it had been presented as a stimulus model for no more than five trials.

Each child was seen individually for training sessions which lasted approximately 30 minutes a day. After the study began, a decision was made (based on pilot study evidence) to terminate the training of a child who did not reach criterion on the first stimulus condition of the program by the end of the first 10 training sessions.

TRAINING PROGRAM

The goal of the program was to train the children to produce six three-element sentences. The word symbols were small plywood forms of ambiguous but discrete shapes. Through training, the symbols were embued with discriminative properties which allowed them to function as words in the specified tacting operations. The transactions to be tacted (Skinner, 1957) by the children were:

Linda give ball.	Jim give ball.
Linda give glass.	Jim give glass.
Linda give car.	Jim give car.

By intent, there were no systematic relationships between properties of the plywood words and their meanings. For example, the word for the green glass was a rectangular orange symbol and the word for the white toy car was an irregular shaped red symbol. Sentences were produced by placing the symbols horizontally on a slanted wooden tray. The child was seated at a table with the "slant" tray directly in front of him and the word symbol or symbols designated by the appropriate program steps within easy reach on the table.

Because most functions of language serve to represent and distinguish the elements of experience (Premack, 1970), the first step in the program was the pretraining condition of establishing a simple social transaction between the trainer and child. The transaction of giving the child the objects (ball, car, and glass) was established, with the child being reinforced for appropriate acceptance of each object. Throughout the training program, each correct response was followed by verbal praise paired with a preferred food.

The first training condition was designed to generate correct discriminative responses to each of the three object-class stimuli, that is, *ball, glass, car*. The first step began with the trainer offering a ball to the child and reinforcing him for placement of the symbol for *ball* on the slant tray after the words *Linda give,* which were already in place on the slant tray. Prompts (physical placement of the child's hand on the correct symbol) were provided throughout the program when they seemed indicated. Prompted responses were reinforced but scored as incorrect. Distracter (nonrelevant) symbols were introduced throughout the training program. Initially, the child had only the correct symbol (no distracters) before him for placement. As the training progressed, the child was required to choose the correct symbol from among an increasing number of distracter symbols.

When criterion (80% in two successive five trial blocks) was reached on the first step, one distracter symbol was added to the response display (Step 2), and then a third distracter symbol was added in Step 3. When criterion was met on all three

Table 1   **Summary of Training Conditions. The Number in Parentheses Represents the Number of Distracter Symbols Introduced in Each Training Phase**

	I. Object Class	II. Action Class	III. Donor Class
1.	*ball* (3 steps)	*give* ball (3 steps)	first donor
a.	ball (0)	give ball (0)	*Linda* give ball (0)
b.	ball (1)	give ball (1)	*Linda* give car (0)
c.	ball (2)	give ball (2)	*Linda* give glass (0)
2.	*car* (3 steps)	*give* glass (3 steps)	second donor
a.	car (0)	give glass (0)	*Jim* give car (0)
b.	car (1)	give glass (1)	*Jim* give ball (0)
c.	car (2)	give glass (2)	*Jim* give glass (0)
3.	*glass* (3 steps)	*give* car (3 steps)	
a.	glass (0)	give car (0)	*Linda* give (randomized objects) (2)
b.	glass (1)	give car (1)	*Jim* give (randomized objects) (2)
c.	glass (2)	give car (2)	
4.	randomized presentation of *ball, car, glass*)	randomined presentation of *give* ball, *give* car, *give* glass (2)	*Linda/Jim* alternate randomized objects

steps for use of the symbol for *ball,* the same procedures were followed for *car* and *glass.* In the fourth and final step of object class training, presentation of the three objects was randomized and the subject had to choose the correct object symbol from the three symbols available to him. Table 1 shows the training series.

Condition II was designed to evoke a two-word response to the act of giving the object to the child. As shown in Table 1, the correct response was placement of the referent symbols for both the action and the object in correct sequence on the slant tray. The child had only the two word symbols for *give ball* before him in the first step. First one and then two distracters were added, with the stimulus remaining the same. When criterion was reached for all steps of this subcondition, similar procedures were implemented to train placement of the action symbol with the symbols for *glass* and *car.* The fourth step of action class training was similar to the fourth step of the previous condition except that the child was required to use both the action symbol and the appropriate object symbol. Throughout Condition II only the donor symbol was in place on the slant tray.

Donor class training, shown as Condition III in Table 1, was designed to train the child to respond differentially to the presentation of the objects by one or the other of two donors. The terminal objective of this last training condition was for the child to correctly "map" the six discrete transactions. They were to use three object words, one action word, and two donor words to form six descriptive sentences. As an additional cue during the early sessions, the trainers wore their donor symbols (duplicate plywood forms) prominently displayed as necklaces. The stimulus objects were presented in the same manner as the previous conditions. Initially, the child had only the three correct symbols available to him for placement on the slant tray. When criterion was reached on the first sentence distracters were added, but the same stimulus event maintained. The same procedure used to train *Linda give ball* was replicated with *Linda give car* and *Linda give glass.* Then a second trainer was introduced. He followed the same training sequence to train the child to appropriately use the symbol for *Jim* with the action and object symbols. The third step trained the child to appropriately respond to randomized object presentation with the donors alternating randomly.

GENERALIZATION TESTS

In Condition IV, a second action class symbol, *insert,* was introduced to offer a test of the transfer of training properties of the previous action word training. This new action word was used to tact the transaction of inserting the car, glass, or ball into a transparent plastic box. The training procedures implemented in Condition II were duplicated in the first three steps of Condition IV except that the use of a symbol for *insert* was trained. The fourth step assessed the differential use of both action words (*give* and *insert*) with each of the three object symbols. Table 2 shows this training condition.

Experimental Condition V was designed to assess the availability of the previously trained responses in the presence of a new experimenter. Table 2 gives the elements of this condition. A third adult, in whose presence the child had never emitted the trained responses, was recruited to act as donor. This new trainer presented the object stimuli, using the same procedure described for the last subcondition of

Table 2   Summary of Generalization Tests

IV. Transfer of Training (New Action Word)	V. Generalization to a New Experimenter	VI. Generalization to a New Setting	VII. Retention
1. *insert* ball	Randomized presentation of *give ball, give glass,* and *give car* by a new experimenter (identical to Condition II, Subcondition 4, except for new experimenter)	Linda/Jim (two donors) alternate presentation of objects: *Linda give ball* *Jim give ball* *Linda give glass* *Jim give glass* *Linda give car* *Jim give car* (identical to Condition III, Subcontion 4, except for different setting)	Scheduling of Condition VI for one week after termination of Condition V
2. *insert* car			
3. *insert* glass			
4. randomized presentation of *give* ball *insert* ball *give* glass *insert* glass *give* car *insert* car			

Condition II. A third donor symbol was placed on the slant tray to represent the name of this new donor.

Condition VI, as shown in Table 2, was implemented to probe intersituational generalization of the trained responses. The children were required to demonstrate their entire six-sentence repertoire in a setting which was physically very different from the training room.

Condition VI (generalization to a new setting) was scheduled for one week after termination of Condition V so as to serve as a test of the children's retention of the original six-sentence repertoire. It is summarized in Table 2.

RESULTS AND DISCUSSION

Two of the three children selected for the study acquired the criterion language repertoire of six three-element sentences. In addition, both children generalized the use of the action and object words, to a new experimenter and produced the entire sentence repertoire in a new setting one week later. At no time did either of the subjects confuse symbols across classes. For example, they might incorrectly use the symbol for ball rather than car, but they never substituted an action symbol for an object symbol or an object symbol for a donor symbol. All errors were within class members.

The perseverative pattern of response of one of the children prevented his attaining terminal criterion on the first training condition within the specified 10 sessions. His training and, thus, his participation in the study was terminated at the end of the tenth session (after 800 trials).

Table 3   Trials to Criteria

Training Conditions	Subject A	Subject C
Object Class Training (Condition I)	180	700
Action Class Training (Condition II)	250	70
Donor Class Training (Condition III)	175	230
Transfer of Training (Condition IV)	110	320
New Experimenter (Condition V)	10	10
New Setting and Retention (VI and VII)	15	15

The number of trials to criteria in all seven conditions for each of the remaining two children is presented in Table 3.

Autistic children appear to be extremely limited in the number of learning systems available to them for either receiving, organizing, or encoding information. As suggested by Premack (1970a), Schmidt, Carrier, and Parsons (1971), and Carrier (1973), it may indeed be productive to approach the language acquisition process in a response-topography less complex than speech. The expressive language training program proposed in this paper reduces the response demands on the child by eliminating the requirement of vocal speech production. Because this symbol system does not require that the child actually construct each response unit and retain each part of the sentence sequence in his memory, it is considerably less complex than even a manual signing or finger spelling system.

With children who show a particularly low propensity for verbal language acquisition, the use of a simple nonvocal language system may be the only means of attaining an initial expressive repertoire. For other children who may be progressing satisfactorily in speech imitation training programs, this system may serve as an adjunct device for teaching grammatical constructions which can be further developed as the child acquires higher-level speech response forms. An additional use would be as a means of assessing the cognitive or prelinguistic readiness of language-deficient children for symbolic representation and syntactic constructions. When readiness had been demonstrated, the symbols might be used as prompts to teach either a manual or a vocal language.

The training procedures developed in this study, while they resulted in the desired limited symbolic repertoire for two of the three children, still need considerable refinement and expansion. Carrier (1973) is carrying out extensive research with retarded children, using a similar language system. Premack[1] is also assessing its

---

[1] D. Premack, personal communication (1973).

value with an autistic child. Its ultimate value, of course, can only be determined on the basis of the data from the system's use with many language-deficient children in a variety of experimental and training settings.

In summary, this program was theoretically and pragmatically productive in that it demonstrated, at least in a limited fashion, that two nonverbal autistic children who had made no progress in a number of years of traditional speech-oriented training could be trained to use symbols in a manner closely analogous to standard expressive language performance.

ACKNOWLEDGMENT

The research reported in this article was completed as part of the senior author's doctoral dissertation under the direction of Ronald Wiegerink, with financial support from a Tennessee Department of Mental Health training stipend. Linda McLean is director of Regional Outpatient Programs, Children and Youth Services, Central State Psychiatric Hospital, Tennessee Department of Mental Health. James McLean is an associate professor and the chairman of the Department of Special Education, George Peabody College for Teachers, Nashville, Tennessee.

REFERENCES

BRYSON, D. Q., Systematic identification of perceptual disabilities in autistic children. *Percept. Mot. Skills,* **31,** 239–246 (1970).

BRYSON, C. Q., Short-term memory and cross-modal information processing in autistic children. *J. Learn. Disabil.,* **5,** 25–35 (1972).

CARRIER, J. K., Application of functional analysis and a non-speech response mode to teaching language. Rep. No. 7, Kansas Center for Research in Mental Retardation and Human Development, Parsons, Kansas (1973).

HOCKETT, C. F., Animal "languages" and human language. In J. N. Spuhler (Ed.), *The Evolution of Man's Capacity for Culture.* Detroit: Wayne State Univ. (1959).

HOCKETT, C. F., The origin of speech. *Sci. Amer.,* **3,** 88–96 (1960).

O'CONNER, N., and HERMELIN, B., Visual analogies of verbal operations. *Lang. Speech,* **8,** 197–207 (1965).

OLSON, D. R., Language and thought: Aspects of a cognitive theory of semantics. *Psychol. Rev.,* **77:4,** 257–273 (1970).

PREMACK, D., A functional analysis of language. *J. Exp. Anal. Behav.,* **14,** 107–125 (1970).

PREMACK, D., On the assessment of language competence in the chimpanzee. *Behavior of Non-Human Primates,* **4,** 185–228 (1971a).

PREMACK, D., Language in chimpanzee? *Science,* **172,** 808–822 (1971b).

PREMACK, D., A functional analysis of language. Short course presented at the Annual Convention of the American Speech and Hearing Association, Chicago (1971c).

SCHMIDT, M. F., CARRIER, J. K., and PARSONS, S. D., Use of a non-speech response mode for teaching language. Paper presented at the Annual Convention of the American Speech and Hearing Association, Chicago (1971).

SKINNER, B. F., *Verbal Behavior.* New York: Appleton (1957).

Comment by Linda McCormick for *Readings in Childhood Language Disorders:*

A manual sign training program was implemented with the three children immediately subsequent to completion of this program. Of interest is the fact that the two children who demonstrated their ability to use the "Premack-Symbols" efficiently acquired a basic signing repertoire while the child who did not complete the symbol program similarly made no progress in acquisition of manual language.